MASTERPLOTS

BRITISH FICTION
SERIES

MASTERPLOTS

Revised Category Edition

BRITISH FICTION SERIES

1

A-Hor

Edited by

FRANK N. MAGILL

SALEM PRESS
Englewood Cliffs, N.J.

23665

Library of Congress Cataloging in Publication Data
Main entry under title:

Masterplots: revised category edition, British
  fiction series.

  Includes index.
  1. English fiction—Stories, plots, etc. 2. English fiction
—Commonwealth of Nations authors—Stories, plots, etc.
3. Fiction—Stories, plots, etc. 4. English fiction—History
and criticism. 5. English fiction—Commonwealth of Nations
authors—History and criticism. I. Magill, Frank Northen,
1907–   .
PR825.M37 1985   823'.009   85-2165
ISBN 0-89356-504-0 (set)
ISBN 0-89356-505-9 (volume 1)

The material in this three-volume set includes all digests and critical evaluations dealing with British fiction that appear in MASTERPLOTS, *Revised edition. The 383 titles included herein are reprinted exactly as they appear in the revised* MASTER-PLOTS *volumes, except for updated research, minor editorial alterations, and format changes.*

THE PUBLISHER

LIST OF TITLES IN VOLUME 1

MASTERPLOTS

MASTERPLOTS

BRITISH FICTION
SERIES

THE ABSENTEE

Type of work: Novel
Author: Maria Edgeworth (1767–1849)
Type of plot: Social criticism
Time of plot: Early nineteenth century
Locale: England and Ireland
First published: 1812

Principal characters:

LORD CLONBRONY, an absentee landlord
LADY CLONBRONY, his affected, ambitious wife
LORD COLAMBRE, their son
GRACE NUGENT, a cousin
MISS BROADHURST, an heiress
ARTHUR BERRYL, Lord Colambre's friend
COUNT O'HALLORAN, an Irish gentleman
SIR TERENCE O'FAY, an impecunious nobleman
LADY DASHFORT, a designing noblewoman
LADY ISABEL, her daughter
MR. MORDICAI, one of Lord Clonbrony's creditors
MR. BURKE, an honest estate agent
NICHOLAS GARRAGHTY, a dishonest estate agent

The Story:

Lord Clonbrony was an absentee landlord. The owner of large but encumbered Irish estates, he lived in England because Lady Clonbrony, an extravagant, ambitious woman, would have nothing to do with Ireland or the Irish. People of wealth and position laughed at her and the silly determination with which she aped English manners and speech. They ignored Lord Clonbrony. A respected peer in Dublin and a good landlord when he had lived on his own estates, he was a nobody in his wife's fashionable world, and so he associated with questionable and dissipated companions like Sir Terence O'Fay. Little was known about Lord Colambre, the Clonbrony heir, except that he was a student at Cambridge and a young man of considerable expectations from a distant relative. A cousin, Grace Nugent, was well thought of because of her beauty and good manners.

Lady Clonbrony was anxious to have her son marry Miss Broadhurst, a young woman of much sense and large fortune. Although Lady Clonbrony and Mrs. Broadhurst did their best to promote the match, the young people, while friendly, were not drawn to each other. Lord Colambre was too much attracted by Grace's amiability and charm, and Miss Broadhurst respected his feelings for his cousin.

In execution of a commission for Arthur Berryl, a Cambridge friend,

Lord Colambre went to the establishment of Mr. Mordicai, a coachmaker and moneylender. There he overheard some talk which revealed that his father's financial affairs were not in good order. When questioned, Lord Clonbrony admitted that his situation was grave but that he relied on Sir Terence, often his intermediary with his creditors, to prevent legal action against him. The father reflected with some bitterness that there would be no need for such expediency if landowners would live on their own estates and kill their own mutton.

Lord Colambre saw for himself the results of reckless borrowing when Sir John Berryl, the father of his friend, was taken suddenly ill. Mordicai, demanding immediate payment of a large debt, attempted to have the sick man arrested and thrown into prison. Only Lord Colambre's presence and firm words of rebuff kept the moneylender from carrying out his intention. Mordicai left with threats that Lord Colambre would someday regret his insults. Sir John Berryl died that night, leaving his family almost penniless.

Deeply concerned for his own family's welfare, Lord Colambre decided to visit Ireland to see for himself the state of his father's affairs. Lady Clonbrony used every possible argument to dissuade her son, and Sir Terence suggested that the young man could best help his father by marrying a woman as wealthy as Miss Broadhurst. When Lord Colambre left suddenly for Ireland, his mother, refusing to give up her matrimonial plans for her son, allowed her friends to believe that he had gone to attend to private business in connection with his marriage settlement. Since many people expected him to marry Miss Broadhurst, that story satisfied the Clonbrony creditors for the time being.

Arriving in Dublin, Lord Colambre met Sir James Brooke, a British official well-informed on Irish affairs, and the two men became good friends. The young nobleman, pleased with everything he heard and saw, was unable to understand his mother's detestation of the Irish. He tried to meet Nicholas Garraghty, his father's agent, but the man was away on business. Instead, he was entertained by the agent's sister, a silly, affected woman named Mrs. Raffarty.

He also met Lady Dashfort, who saw in him a possible husband for her widowed daughter, Lady Isabel. Although he heard no favorable reports of Lady Dashfort or her daughter, he became a frequent visitor in their home. At last, interested in securing an alliance for her daughter, Lady Dashfort proposed that he accompany her to Killpatrickstown, where she was going to visit Lord and Lady Killpatrick. It was her intention to show him Irish life at its worst so that he would have no desire to live on the Clonbrony estates after his marriage to Lady Isabel. Aware of his affection for Grace, Lady Dashfort arranged matters so that Lady Killpatrick asked her to exhibit her genealogical table, which had been prepared as evidence in a lawsuit. She did so with seeming reluctance, on the grounds that she was ashamed of her remote connection with the scandalous St. Omars. She then revealed that Grace's mother had been a St. Omar.

Lord Colambre wrote to his mother to ask the truth. She replied that the girl's mother had been a St. Omar but that she had taken the name Reynolds after an affair with a gentleman of that name. When the Reynolds family refused to acknowledge her child, she had married Mr. Nugent, who had generously given the daughter his own name. The young man realized that this disclosure put a barrier between Grace and himself.

Through the Killpatricks, Lord Colambre met Count O'Halloran, regarded by his neighbors as an oddity because of his learning, his fondness for animals, and his liking for the Irish. When the Count returned the visit, Lady Dashfort took issue with him because he criticized the improper conduct of an English officer with whom both were acquainted. Lady Dashfort's lack of good manners and moral sense and the further revelation of Lady Isabel as a malicious flirt showed the two women to Lord Colambre in their true light. He decided to leave the Dashforts and continue his tour alone.

Count O'Halloran prevailed upon Lord Colambre, however, to accompany him to Oranmore. There Lord Colambre found a family of taste and breeding, interested in affairs of the day and the welfare of their tenants. Stimulated by the example of Lord and Lady Oranmore, he planned to go immediately to his father's estate, but incognito, so that he could observe more accurately the conditions of the tenantry and the conduct of the estate agents.

He found the village of Colambre neat and prosperous, well looked after by Mr. Burke, the agent. After a dinner with the Burkes, the agent showed him around the estate with evident pride in all he had accomplished. He regretted, however, that the absentee owner took no interest in the land or the tenants, aside from the revenues derived from them. Burke's fears that Lord Clonbrony was displeased with his management were confirmed by the arrival of a letter in which his lordship dismissed the agent and directed him to turn over his accounts to Nicholas Garraghty.

Lord Colambre went next to Clonbrony. He learned from a driver that the tenants hated and feared Nicholas Garraghty, the factor, and Dennis Garraghty, his brother and assistant. Since his carriage had broken down, Lord Colambre spent the night with Mrs. O'Neill, a widow whose niece had been named after Grace Nugent. The next day the young nobleman was present when Dennis Garraghty refused to renew a lease promised to Mrs. O'Neill's son Brian. The arrival of Mrs. Raffarty and her identification of Lord Colambre caused Garraghty to change his mind quickly. Disgusted by the man's methods of doing business and by the unkempt, poverty stricken appearance of the village, Lord Colambre wrote to his father and asked him to have no further dealings with the Garraghtys.

During the voyage back to England, Lord Colambre's ship was delayed by a storm, so that the Garraghtys arrived in London ahead of him. He returned, however, in time to confront the agent and his brother with a report on their transactions. Hearing his son's story, Lord Clonbrony would have dismissed them on the spot if he had possessed the cash necessary to settle their entangled accounts. Lord Colambre then asked his father and Sir Terence for a full accounting of the distressed nobleman's obligations. In return, he proposed to settle the debt with the inheritance he would receive when he came of age, a date only a few days off, if his father would end all business relations with the Garraghtys and go to Ireland to live. Lord Clonbrony welcomed the proposal, but his wife, when she heard of it, treated the idea with scorn. She was already displeased with her son because he had not pressed his suit upon Miss Broadhurst, and the heiress was to marry his friend, Sir Arthur Berryl. When Lord Colambre expressed pleasure over his friend's good fortune, Lady Clonbrony retired in disgust.

Under persuasion by every member of her family, Lady Clonbrony at last ungraciously agreed to return to Ireland. Meanwhile Lord Colambre, busy with his father's accounts, discovered that many of the London bills had been deliberately overcharged and that Nicholas Garraghty was, in reality, his lordship's debtor, not his creditor, as the agent had claimed. With some ready money sent by Lady Berryl, the former Miss Broadhurst, through her husband, Lord Colambre was able to settle his father's most pressing debts, and Sir Terence was able to reclaim Mordicai's bond at a discount. After Garraghty had been dismissed in disgrace, Mr. Burke was appointed agent of the Colambre and Clonbrony estates.

On the day he came of age, Lord Colambre's first duty was to execute a bond for five thousand pounds in Grace's name, the amount of her own inheritance having been lent to her guardian years before. The young man's secret regret was that he could not offer his heart with his cousin's restored property.

Arriving in London, Count O'Halloran called on Lord Colambre. When the young nobleman confided his true feelings for Grace and told his friend something of her story, the count recalled Captain Reynolds whom he had known in Austria. Dying, the officer had told of his secret marriage with Miss St. Omar and had entrusted to the count a packet of private papers, among them a marriage certificate. The count had given the papers to the English ambassador, and they had passed in turn into the keeping of Sir James Brooke, the executor of the ambassador's estate. Acting on this information, Lord Colambre went to Sir James and obtained the papers, which had never been carefully examined. When he presented them to the dead officer's father, old Mr. Reynolds accepted the proof of his granddaughter's legitimacy with delight and declared his intention to make her his heiress. Because Grace had never known of the shadow cast on her birth, Lady Berryl was delegated to tell her the whole story, a task which the friendly young woman performed with great delicacy and tact.

Acquainted with the true state of affairs, Lady Clonbrony offered no objections to her son's marriage to Grace. Lord Clonbrony and his wife returned to Ireland and there, in due time, Grace became Viscountess Colambre, much to the satisfaction of Lady Clonbrony, who saw so happily fulfilled her hopes that her son would marry an heiress.

Critical Evaluation:

The Absentee, published in the second series of Maria Edgeworth's "Tales of Fashionable Life," is a novel of protest against the system of landlordism under which the owners of Irish estates disported themselves in fashionable London society while their tenants lived in misery and squalor, at the mercy of agents who were often unscrupulous and concerned only with their own interests. The Irish scenes of this novel are as fresh and vivid as those in the earlier *Castle Rackrent*, and the picture of London society, a world of thriftless absentees, wealthy snobs, fortune hunters, and matchmaking mothers, is excellent in critical and satirical detail. In this work, the writer displayed a talent for caricature as well as deep regional feeling. Her vulgar Lady Clonbrony, Nicholas Garraghty, the dishonest agent, and Sir Terence O'Fay, an impecunious sponger, suggest later figures in the work of Surtees and Dickens.

If the romantic plot of *The Absentee* ends happily in marriage and the restoration of the Clonbrony estates, it also delineates a tragic social phenomenon, which formed a prelude to Britain's development of a modern economy. During the last half of the eighteenth century, agriculture in England and Ireland was slowly being changed into a factory system. The realization that huge plots of land under single ownership could be run more profitably than scattered farms brought about incorporation and the enclosure of commons. At the end of the century, the process was speeded by the increased demand for food during the Napoleonic Wars and the invention of numerous labor-saving devices. Incorporation and mechanization transformed rural society from a populous and self-sustaining one to one that was gradually depleted in people and controlled from London. Agriculture was being prepared as a subordinate to and supplier of the new urban, industrial complex.

Maria Edgeworth dramatizes the moral impact of this revolution on rural society and the new cosmopolitan gentry. The Clonbrony estates, left in the hands of Nicholas Garraghty, a manager whose only motive is profit, no longer provide a moral or economic stability for the countryside. The Clonbronys themselves, cut off from the land, deteriorate in a London of fortune hunting and marriage markets where wealth is no longer measured

in land but in money. Fortunately, Lord Colambre, their son, perceives the
corruption that has set in and through a marvelous series of good fortunes
is able to return his family to the land and the estates to economic and social harmony. Edgeworth's conclusion, however, is a romantic dream rather
than a realistic account of social developments: For better or worse,
Britain's future lay in industrialism. The great agricultural past, together
with the eighteenth century, was over.

ADAM BEDE

Type of work: Novel
Author: George Eliot (Mary Ann Evans, 1819–1880)
Type of plot: Domestic romance
Time of plot: 1799
Locale: England
First published: 1859

Principal characters:
ADAM BEDE, a carpenter
SETH BEDE, his brother
MARTIN POYSER, the proprietor of Hall Farm
MRS. POYSER, his wife
DINAH MORRIS, her niece and a Methodist preacher
HETTY SORREL, another niece
CAPTAIN ARTHUR DONNITHORNE, the young squire

The Story:

In the village of Hayslope at the close of the eighteenth century, there lived a young carpenter named Adam Bede. Tall and muscular, Adam was respected by everyone as a good workman and an honest and upright man. Even the young squire, Captain Arthur Donnithorne, knew Adam and liked him, and Adam in turn regarded the squire as his best friend.

Adam was, in fact, so good a workman that his employer, Mr. Jonathan Burge, the builder, would have welcomed him as his son-in-law and partner. Adam, however, had no eyes for Mary Burge; his only thoughts were of distractingly pretty Hetty Sorrell, niece of Mrs. Poyser, whose husband, Martin, ran the Hall Farm. Hetty, however, cared nothing for Adam. She was interested only in Captain Donnithorne, whom she had met one day in her aunt's dairy.

No one in Hayslope thought Hetty would make a good wife for Adam, least of all Adam's mother, Lisbeth, who would have disapproved of any girl who threatened to take her favorite son away from her. Her feelings of dependence upon Adam were intensified after her husband, Matthias Bede, drowned in Willow Brook while on his way home from the village inn.

Adam's brother Seth had fallen in love with the young Methodist preacher, Dinah Morris. Dinah was another niece of Mrs. Poyser, as unlike her cousin Hetty as Adam was unlike Seth. Hetty was as soft and helpless as a kitten, but Dinah was firm and serious in all things. One evening, while she and Seth were walking home together from the village green, he had proposed marriage. Dinah sadly declined, saying she had dedicated her life to preaching the gospel.

When funeral services for Matthias Bede were held in Hayslope Church on the following Sunday, the thoughts of the congregation were on many events other than the solemn occasion they were attending. Adam's thoughts of Hetty blended with memories of his father. Hetty's thoughts were all of Captain Donnithorne, who had promised to make his appearance. She was disappointed, however, for Donnithorne had already departed with his regiment. When he returned on leave, the young squire celebrated his twenty-first birthday with a great feast to which nearly all of Hayslope was invited. Adam was singled out as a special guest to sit at Donnithorne's table. Adam's mother was both proud and jealous, since her son seemed to be getting more and more out of her reach.

One August night, exactly three weeks after the Donnithorne party, Adam was returning home from his work on the Donnithorne estate when he saw two figures in close embrace. They were Donnithorne and Hetty Sorrel. When Adam's dog barked, Hetty hurried away. Donnithorne, embarrassed, tried to explain that he had met the girl by chance and had stolen a kiss. Adam called his friend a scoundrel and a coward. They came to blows, and Donnithorne was knocked senseless. Adam, frightened that he might have killed the young squire in his rage, revived him and helped him to a nearby summerhouse. There he demanded that Donnithorne write a letter to Hetty telling her that he would not see her again.

The next day, Donnithorne sent the letter to Hetty in Adam's care, thus placing the responsibility for its possible effect upon Adam himself. Adam gave her the letter while they were walking the following Sunday. When she read the letter, in the privacy of her bedchamber, Hetty was in despair. Her dreams shattered, she thought only of finding some way out of her misery. Then in November, Adam was offered a partnership in Mr. Burge's business, and he proposed to Hetty. Mr. and Mrs. Poyser were delighted to find that their niece was to marry the man they so much admired.

The wedding, however, had to be delayed until two new rooms could be added to the Bede house. In February, Hetty told her aunt that she was going to visit Dinah Morris at Snowfield. Actually, however, she was determined to find Donnithorne. When she arrived at Windsor, where he was supposed to be stationed, she found that his regiment had been transferred to Ireland. Now in complete despair, Hetty roamed about until in a strange village, and in the house of a widow named Sarah Stone, her child by Donnithorne was born. Frightened, Hetty wandered on, leaving her baby to die in the woods. Later, tortured by her conscience, she returned to find the child gone.

When his grandfather died, Donnithorne returned to Hayslope to discover that Hetty was in prison, charged with the murder of her child. He did everything in his power to free her, and Dinah Morris came to her prison cell and prayed with her to open up her heart and tell the truth.

Finally, poor Hetty broke down and confessed everything that had happened since she left Hayslope. She had not intended to kill her baby; in fact, she had not actually killed the child. She had considered taking her own life. Two days later, Donnithorne, filled with shame and remorse, brought a reprieve. Hetty's sentence was commuted to deportation. A few years later, she died on her way home. Donnithorne went to Spain.

Dinah Morris stayed with the Poysers often now. Gradually she and Adam were drawn to each other, but Dinah's heart was still set on her preaching. She left Hall Farm and went back to Snowfield. Adam Bede found his only satisfaction toiling at his workbench. Then one day, his mother spoke again of Dinah and her gentle ways. Adam could wait no longer. He went to find her.

Critical Evaluation:

This novel of English pastoral life probably shows George Eliot's quality as a novelist better than any other of her works, with the possible exception of *Middlemarch*. When Eliot was writing of the peasants, the artisans, the yeomen, the clergy, and the squires of Warwickshire, she was writing out of memories of her own childhood; and her characters come to life as people she had known. Moreover, she superimposes upon them an awareness of fate, not as majestic as in Hardy, but growing out of her convictions that there is a cause and effect relationship in human behavior, just as there is in the rest of nature.

In *Adam Bede*, Eliot makes three important contributions to the development of the modern novel in her use of narrative technique and in her handling of both physical realism and psychological realism.

In her overall narrative, Eliot uses the third-person, omniscient-author voice; but she frequently sets aside this basic form to address the reader directly. Eliot uses these first-person comments to establish an intimacy with the reader—such as in the first paragraph of the novel—or to heighten the verisimilitude of the plot. In addition, she experiments quite successfully with stream-of-consciousness narration in chapters fifteen and sixteen. A few critics have faulted Eliot for what they see as inconsistency and choppiness, resulting from shifts in narrative voice, but the only genuine disruption of narrative continuity occurs in chapter seventeen where Eliot digresses from the story to explain her theory of art. Aside from this digression, most critics praise her ingenuity and her willingness to experiment with what were then avant-garde narrative techniques.

Physical realism deals with outward appearance; it attempts to represent scene, atmosphere, and characters exactly as they are observed in real life. Eliot is more successful with scene and atmosphere than with characters. Certainly she presents some vivid portraits, such as her description of the physical contrast between Adam and Seth or her memorable introduction of Dinah Morris. Other character descriptions, however, are not as effective. Hetty, for example, is repeatedly compared to a kitten, and she is so frequently described with words such as "dimpled," "round," "soft," "pink," and "white," that the effect is monotonous. By contrast, Eliot's treatment of scene and atmosphere is guided by a landscapist's eye for detail and a peasant's intuitive understanding of the relationship between weather and crops, producing what has been called the most natural setting in any English novel.

Psychological realism, focusing on the inner being of a character, derives from details about the thoughts and the emotions of characters: their personalities, their motives, their feelings about themselves, each other, and their surroundings. In this regard, Eliot's work is superb. She carefully plots the actions and motivations of her characters, never oversimplifying. Her forte is the "soul struggle" to which both Adam and Arthur Donnithorne fall victim—in which a character is torn in conscience between something he knows is morally and ethically right and something that is tempting and attractive. Eliot's penetrating insights into Hetty's motives are another example of her grasp of psychological realism. In fact, Eliot has been hailed as one of the first psychological novelists, while *Adam Bede* is recognized as one of the earliest novels in the psychological tradition.

THE AFFAIR

Type of work: Novel
Author: C. P. Snow (1905–1980)
Type of plot: Social realism
Time of plot: 1953–1954
Locale: London and Cambridge
First published: 1960

Principal characters:

LEWIS ELIOT, a lawyer representing the aggrieved parties, a
former Fellow of the College, and the narrator
MARGARET, his wife
DONALD HOWARD, a young physicist, dismissed by a Cam-
bridge College on a charge of faking scientific evidence,
seeking redress
LAURA HOWARD, his wife
MARTIN ELIOT, Lewis' brother and a Junior Tutor of the
College
RONALD EDMUND NIGHTINGALE (ALEC), the College Bursar, a
physicist, and the long-standing enemy of Lewis
TOM ORBELL, a young political scientist and historian
JULIAN SKEFFINGTON, a physicist and the leader of the faction
demanding Howard's reinstatement
MAURICE HARVEY LAWRENCE GAY, Professor Emeritus of Ice-
landic, who tries to employ Lewis to sue the College
FRANCIS ERNEST GETLIFFE, a distinguished physicist who
presents crucial evidence in Howard's favor
ARTHUR BROWN, the Senior Tutor who hopes to become the
next Master of the College
REDVERS THOMAS ARBUTHNOT CRAWFORD, the present Master
PAUL JAGO, a retired professor who helps convince Brown of
Howard's possible innocence
G. S. CLARKE, a crippled modern language don who opposes
Howard on religious and moral grounds
G. H. WINSLOW, the former College Bursar, who sits on the
Court of Seniors

C. P. Snow's *Strangers and Brothers* sequence tells the traditional story
of a young man's rise in the world and his concurrent education in the ways
of that world. Snow follows Lewis Eliot, the hero and narrator of the
series, from working class origins to a place in the Establishment. In *The
Affair*, Eliot has gained this position, and his special status as narrator of
the novel and the fact that he came into the Establishment from the out-

side give the reader a special perspective on the workings of the men of power with whom Eliot associates. This perspective is important, for the novel is less concerned with Donald Howard, the rather foolish young man on trial, than with those who are judging him; the Establishment, its way of running things, and its morality are themselves on trial. Specifically, Snow examines the somewhat ponderous way in which officialdom struggles with its conscience, tries to avoid deciding how to reconcile its own best interest with the demands of justice, and finally strikes a balance.

The Establishment is not, of course, an institution, and it is not a group of men of unanimously shared values and goals. Rather, it is composed of men of many types, brought together primarily by their desire to possess power and by their sense of responsibility, grasped in a variety of ways and to varying degrees, for using their power wisely. The obstacles to this task, both internal and external, are numerous; they are also a major object of Snow's attention. Power, the reader would imagine Snow to say, may well corrupt, but it does so many other interesting things and brings out such strange latencies in those who possess it, that any blanket statement about its possessors and effects would be ridiculous. A minute study of its agents and their actions, however, can be enlightening.

As he did in *The Masters*, Snow studies power microcosmically, focusing on the closed society of a Cambridge College. Lewis Eliot, once a Fellow of the College, but now a high-ranking civil servant and established lawyer, is approached in London by Tom Orbell, a young political scientist, and Laura Howard, whose husband, a physicist and a Communist, has been dismissed by the college for using a fake photograph in a research publication. They appeal to Eliot as having influence with older Fellows, particularly with his brother Martin and Sir Francis Getliffe, both physicists, the latter a probable choice as next Master of the College. After Lewis asks some questions of his friends in the college and, at Mrs. Howard's insistence, confers with Donald Howard, he is completely convinced that Howard has been dealt with fairly.

Several weeks later, when Lewis is at Cambridge to spend Christmas with his brother, Julian Skeffington, a young physics Fellow, tells Martin and Lewis that he has evidence that Howard is innocent. Skeffington, a Conservative, strict, and absolutely correct, is co-executor of the estate of his wife's late uncle, Cecil Palairet, under whom Howard did his doctoral work. Going through Palairet's notebooks as they arrive at the college bursary, Skeffington discovers that a photograph is missing from one of them: the accompanying notation suggests that it was probably a copy of the photograph Howard had used in his research. From this discovery, Skeffington infers that old Palairet, for some unknown reason, gave Howard the photograph as a bona fide piece of scientific evidence on which Howard, then in all good faith if not in good judgment, based his subsequent work.

Skeffington is now absolutely convinced of Howard's innocence, but Lewis and Martin are much less so, though they ultimately come around to the view that Howard's case should be reopened.

Skeffington and Martin try to form a majority of the Fellows to demand the reopening of the case. This attempt allows Snow to explore the power structure of the college and the changes in it, since Lewis was personally involved in its politics. As Snow is fond of pointing out, politics obeys strange rules. Martin and Getliffe are liberals, Orbell and Skeffington conservatives, but all are for reopening the case. Most of the younger Fellows are either conservatives or apolitical, the exact opposite of the case at the time of the election described in *The Masters*, published in 1937. Martin is a natural politician, but, as described in *The New Men*, he once threw away an opportune chance to wield great power in the scientific-administrative establishment by publicly condemning the bombing of Nagasaki. Getliffe is politically naïve, was a major power in scientific research during World War II, and is already a scientist of extreme distinction, something Martin Eliot will never be. Martin and Francis Getliffe, however, both want the Mastership (about to be vacant), and both are willing to sacrifice important influence to help Howard, whom they both find stupid, ungrateful, and obnoxious. Skeffington seems to have everything: He was a war hero and could have succeeded in almost any field; instead, he has chosen a career in physics and is engaged in study of the ionosphere, a field in which he has little natural ability. Orbell is a student of politics but has even less political sense than Getliffe or Skeffington.

The decision-making body in this case is the Court of Seniors, composed of Crawford (the Master), Winslow (the former Bursar), Arthur Brown (the Senior Tutor), and Nightingale (the Bursar and a bitter rival of Eliot since the days of Crawford's election). Two other Fellows have seniority, but one, M. L. H. Gay, now somewhat senile at age ninety-two, has been excluded, and Paul Jago, a virtual recluse since losing the last Mastership election, excludes himself. Gay, in fact, tries to engage Lewis to sue the College for excluding him; Snow develops this comic subplot extensively, presumably to show what men of great distinction—as Palairet was—can do in their dotage. Brown, Crawford, and Winslow reexamine the evidence and still find Howard guilty. At this point, however, Skeffington threatens to make a *cause célèbre* of the case, and to avoid publicity, the Seniors agree to conduct a quasi-trial with Lewis Eliot representing Howard and Dawson-Hill, a former student of some legal fame, representing the Seniors. Almost half the novel is devoted to the trial.

The trial goes badly for Howard. A weak self-advocate, he seems almost uninterested in establishing his innocence. Palairet had been respected as an important scientist; if the issue boils down to which of the two was more likely to have faked evidence, anyone—Martin, Lewis, and Getliffe included—would say Howard. It soon becomes clear, in fact, that the only way to save Howard is to suggest how the missing photograph disappeared. To do so, however, means covertly accusing Nightingale, the first to receive the books, of tampering with them. The Howard party finally decides to act. Getliffe insists on making the suggestion to the Board, though he, as the favorite for the next Mastership, has the most to lose and is not well-suited by temperament for such a task. He does so, and Nightingale makes the mistake of countering with the suggestions that the missing photograph was not the one used by Howard and that Skeffington could have removed the photograph from the Palairet notebooks in order to reopen the case.

This tactic convinces Winslow of the possibility of Howard's innocence and leaves Brown with the deciding vote; Nightingale, of course, votes against acquittal, and Crawford is still undecided. That night, Paul Jago comes to see Brown; the two had been close friends before Jago lost the election to Crawford. Though it causes him great anguish, Jago tells Brown that, after Nightingale had made a personal attack on Mrs. Jago during the 1937 election, she had tried to kill herself. By divulging this information, he hopes to convince Brown, who is realistic and shrewd yet stubborn, that Nightingale might be guilty and that Howard might be innocent. He succeeds, paving the way for a compromise by which Howard is reinstated with full pay but has the period of his suspension counted against his contract so that he can soon be dismissed. This finding is considered a victory for Howard. Although Skeffington and Orbell want to ask for complete exoneration, Howard, apparently tired of the whole affair, decides to accept it.

In *The Affair*, a group of reasonable, good-natured, intelligent men commit, or appear to commit, a serious injustice. Only the determined efforts of another group correct the injustice—if, indeed, Howard is innocent; the novel leaves the question open. Snow's primary interest, however, is not the question of innocence and guilt or that of justice and injustice. Rather, he examines the ways in which the individuals working in various groups make decisions on moral questions: what peculiar combinations of ideology, self-interest, ethical principle, and insight activate these men; how their decisions can be challenged and changed.

This focus is not merely a perspective; it also represents a value. By returning Lewis Eliot to the milieu of his young adulthood, Snow invites comparison of the various generations. He finds the young men of the college poor politicians—in the sense that Arthur Brown has been a superb politician—and the older men less flexible, the system working less well than it was even in the late 1930's. Justice, his story implies, is best served by those who know its limitations and its dependence on imperfect human beings; it is often damaged by moral absolutists. Readers are reminded that Snow is primarily a novelist—a storyteller and observer of human nature in action—and not a moralist. He leaves no clear-cut answers, not even with a final judgment of who is innocent and who is guilty. Readers are left with a clear picture of how men work with and against each other to achieve what they consider to be worthy goals, the ironic knowledge that, more often than not, these men miscalculate and misunderstand, and the prediction that the ability of men to work well together is decreasing.

AGNES GREY

Type of work: Novel
Author: Anne Brontë (1820–1849)
Type of plot: Sentimental romance
Time of plot: Mid-nineteenth century
Locale: England
First published: 1847

Principal characters:
AGNES GREY, a young governess
EDWARD WESTON, a curate and later Agnes' husband
MARY GREY, Agnes' sister
RICHARD GREY, Agnes' father
MRS. GREY, Agnes' mother
MRS. MURRAY, the owner of Horton Lodge and Agnes' second employer
ROSALIE MURRAY, her older daughter
MATILDA MURRAY, her younger daughter
MR. HATFIELD, the Rector at Horton and Rosalie's suitor
SIR THOMAS ASHBY, later Rosalie's husband
HARRY MELTHAM and
MR. GREEN, Rosalie's other suitors
NANCY BROWN, an old widow at Horton
MRS. BLOOMFIELD, the owner of Wellwood and Agnes' first employer
TOM BLOOMFIELD, her oldest child
MARY ANN BLOOMFIELD, her older daughter
FANNY BLOOMFIELD, her younger daughter
UNCLE ROBSON, Mrs. Bloomfield's brother

The Story:

Mrs. Grey, a squire's daughter, had offended her family by marrying for love a poor parson in the north of England. She bore him six children, but only two, Mary and Agnes, survived. Nevertheless, the Greys were happy with their humble, educated, pious life in their small house and garden.

Mr. Grey, never wholly at his ease because his wife had been forced to give up carriages and fine clothes in order to marry him, attempted to improve their fortunes by speculating and investing his patrimony in a merchant's sea voyage; but the vessel was wrecked, everything was lost, and the Greys were soon left penniless. In addition, Mr. Grey's health, never robust, began to fail more perceptibly under the strain of his guilt for bringing his family close to ruin. Mary and Agnes, reared in the sheltered atmosphere of a clergyman's household, had spent their time reading, studying, and working in the garden. When the family situation became desperate, however, Mary began to try to sell her drawings to help with the household expenses, and Agnes, the younger daughter, decided to become a governess.

Overcoming the qualms her family felt at the idea of her leaving home, Agnes found employment and, on a bleak and windy autumn day, arrived at Wellwood, the home of the Bloomfield family. She was received coldly by Mrs. Bloomfield and told that her charges, especially Tom, a seven-year-old boy, were noble and splendid children. She soon found that the reverse was true. Tom was an arrogant and disobedient little monster whose particular delight was to pull the legs and wings off young sparrows. Mary Ann, his six-year-old sister, was given to temper tantrums and refused to do her lessons. The children were frightened of their father, a peevish and stern disciplinarian, and the father, in turn, blamed Agnes when the children frequently got out of control.

Agnes found it impossible to teach the children anything because all her efforts to discipline them were undermined by Mrs. Bloomfield, who felt that her angels must always be right. Even four-year-old Fanny lied consistently and was fond of spitting in people's faces. For a time, Agnes was heartened by Mr. Bloomfield's mother's visit, but the pious old lady turned out to be a hypocrite who sympathized with Agnes verbally and then turned on her behind her back.

Matters became a great deal worse with the visit of Uncle Robson, Mrs. Bloomfield's brother, who encouraged young Tom to torture small animals. One day, after he had collected a whole brood of young birds for Tom to torture, Agnes crushed them with a large stone, choosing to kill them quickly rather than to see them suffer a slow, cruel death. The family felt she had deprived Tom of his normal, spirited pleasure. Shortly after this incident, she was told that her services would no longer be required; the Bloomfields felt that she had not disciplined the children properly or taught them very much.

Agnes spent a few months with her family at home before taking up her next post. She found the Murrays, the owners of Horton Lodge, more sophisticated, wealthier, and less bleak and cruel than the owners of Wellwood; but they were still hardly the happy, pious, warm family that Agnes had hoped to encounter. Her older charge, Rosalie, was sixteen years old, very pretty, and interested only in flirting and in eventually making the most suitable marriage possible; her younger charge, Matilda, fourteen years old, was interested only in horses and stables. Although they treated her with politeness, neither girl had any respect for the learning and piety that Agnes had to offer. If Agnes' work was less unpleasant than it had been at Wellwood, it was equally futile.

After living at Horton Lodge for nearly a year, Agnes returned home for a month for her sister's wedding. During this time, the Murrays had given Rosalie a coming-out ball, after which she began to exercise her charms on the young men at Horton. When she returned, Agnes was shocked to find Rosalie flirting with all the men and summarizing the marital possibilities of each with a hardened and materialistic eye. In the meantime, a new curate had come to Horton. Edward Weston was a sober and sincere churchman, neither climbing nor pompous like the rector, Mr. Hatfield. Weston and Agnes, attracted to each other, found many opportunities to meet in their sympathetic visits to Nancy Brown, an old widow who was almost blind. At first, Rosalie found Weston both dogmatic and dull, but Agnes found him representative of the true piety and goodness that she believed were the qualities of a clergyman. Rosalie, continuing to play the coquette, first conquered the unctuous rector, Mr. Hatfield, and then after he had proposed and been quickly rejected, she turned her charms on Mr. Weston. Although Agnes was fiercely jealous of Rosalie's flirtation, she never really acknowledged her own growing love. Finally, Rosalie accepted Sir Thomas Ashby; his home, Ashby Park, and his fortune were the largest in the vicinity of Horton.

Shortly after Rosalie's marriage, before Agnes had the opportunity to see much of Edward Weston, she was called home by the death of her father. She and her mother decided to start a school for young ladies in the fashionable watering place of A———. Although Agnes returned to Horton Lodge for another month, she did not see Weston before she resignedly left to rejoin her mother. Although the school began to prosper after a few months, Agnes still seemed weary and depressed, and she welcomed an invitation from Rosalie, now Lady Ashby, to visit Ashby Park. She found Rosalie disappointed in her marriage to a grumbling, boorish man who ignored her and who, after a honeymoon on the Continent, had forbidden her the frivolous pleasures of London and European society. Agnes also learned from Rosalie that Weston had left Horton a short time before.

A few days after Agnes returned to her mother and the school, she was walking along the waterfront one morning when she was surprised by Weston. He had secured a living in a nearby village. He promptly began calling on Agnes and her mother and as time passed gained Agnes' love and her mother's esteem. One day, while walking with Agnes to the top of a high hill, he proposed. As husband, father, clergyman, and manager of a limited income, he was in later years the perfect mate for virtuous and worthy Agnes.

Critical Evaluation:
The youngest child of the Reverend Patrick Brontë, Anne Brontë is the most shadowy figure among the Brontës. Gentle and timid, she stands behind her more famous sisters and notorious brother, yet her two novels

have an interest of their own, on their own merits. Although *Agnes Grey* does not possess the vigorous writing of *The Tenant of Wildfell Hall* or its depth of characterization, in its quiet way it is a more solid novel and presents a fuller picture of the life that Brontë knew so well. *Agnes Grey* is a minor book by a minor writer, but it will continue to be read for its gentle humor and the integrity of its realism.

This novel, written in the first person, is the account of the tribulations of a poor governess trying to achieve respectability and independence in nineteenth century England. Agnes Grey, a governess because of economic necessity, finds the people among whom she works either bleak or frivolous representatives of the upper classes. They are neither understanding nor helpful, and Agnes, saddled with impossibly arrogant charges, is not a great success as a governess. Fortified by a loving though poor family and by an irreproachable character, she eventually marries a sterling and attractive clergyman. Agnes is a sentimental heroine, and the plot is not to be distinguished from that of the conventional sentimental romance. The good and the true ultimately triumph; the evil and the frivolous are ultimately unhappy. In spite of Agnes' pious sentiments, however, the novel is marked by sharp observations of contemporary life and a gentle and penetrating sarcasm in some of Agnes' comments on her employers. Brontë never became an important novelist, but this novel suggests her ability lay more in the direction of Jane Austen than in that of her sister Emily.

Brontë was twice a governess in private houses, so she was all too familiar with the humiliations and difficulties inherent in such a position. The story of Agnes, the governess, is told in the first person in short, straightforward chapters. The ending of the novel is sentimental, but the narrative along the way is at times sharp and always well-observed. When Agnes and Rosalie discuss the engagement of a sister to a neighboring vicar, Rosalie wonders if he is rich or handsome or young, but Agnes replies "... only middling." Every aspect of the life facing Agnes and the other characters is only middling; the author does not glamorize her heroine's existence. The characters, for the most part, are described without Romanticism, sometimes almost mercilessly; their lives are dragged out day by day, duty by duty. Perhaps Agnes is saved at the end by her clergyman husband but only in a very limited sense. After her difficulties, Agnes is content with a very modest existence; in fact, from the beginning, she is a young woman of slight expectations and no pretensions. Rather like its heroine, this novel is modest and without pretensions but is pleasantly satisfying.

THE ALEXANDRIA QUARTET

Type of work: Novel
Author: Lawrence Durrell (1911–   )
Type of plot: Psychological realism
Time of plot: Just before and during World War II
Locale: Alexandria, Egypt
First published: Justine, 1957; *Balthazar,* 1958; *Mountolive,* 1958; *Clea,* 1961;
  The Alexandria Quartet, 1962

Principal characters:

L. G. DARLEY, an Anglo-Irish schoolteacher and would-be
  writer
PERCY PURSEWARDEN, an erudite, ironical English writer
LIZA PURSEWARDEN, the writer's blind sister
DAVID MOUNTOLIVE, a British diplomat
JOSHUA SCOBIE, an English pederast employed by Egyptian
  police
JOHN KEATS, an English journalist
MASKELYNE, a British intelligence officer
LORD ERROL, Head of Chancery in the British Embassy in
  Egypt
NESSIM HOSNANI, a Coptic banker and conspirator
JUSTINE HOSNANI, his Jewish wife
FALTHAUS HOSNANI, his father and a fervid Copt
LEILA HOSNANI, his intellectual and beautiful mother, who
  loves Mountolive
NAROUZ HOSNANI, his younger, hairlipped brother and a
  religious fanatic
S. BALTHAZAR, a Jewish doctor and mystic
AMARIL, a gynecologist and Romantic
PAUL CAPODISTRA, an ugly, rich lecher and a conspirator
GEORGES GASTON POMBAL, a French Foreign Service official
MELISSA ARTEMIS, a pale, sick Greek dancer and prostitute
CLEA MONTIS, a golden blonde painter
MNEMJIAN, a dwarf barber
COHEN, a furrier and conspirator in league with Nessim
MEMLIK PASHA, the Egyptian Minister of Interior
HAMID, Darley's one-eyed houseboy
TOTO DE BRUNEL, a gigolo and homosexual serving as a
  French agent
SELIM, Nessim's servant
NIMROD, an Egyptian magistrate
CAPODISTRIA

Lawrence Durrell's four-volume novel, for a work of such size and difficulty, was a surprisingly popular success from the moment the first volume of it was published in 1957. Perhaps it was so enthusiastically received because it is a love story, a ubiquitous romantic adventure done up in a somewhat flamboyant manner. This love story, however, is narrated in a fragmented, involuted, obscure manner and refracted through complex ideas and experimental techniques. As a plethora of interpretative studies already published by scholar-critics testify, the work is as intellectually subtle and demanding as fiction can be and certainly is too formidably so to be pleasurable casual reading for a general audience. Whatever the reasons for its popular success, *The Alexandria Quartet* violates the first prejudice of modern criticism by uniting intelligence with feeling in a way that engages and entertains all the human faculties without compromising the loftiest aesthetic aims. In doing so, it confutes established clichés about alienation, dissociation of sensibility, and dehumanization as the inescapable predicament both of the artist and man in the twentieth century.

There is nothing secret about the ideas that provide the intellectual scaffolding for *The Alexandria Quartet*; Durrell states them quite explicitly in the novel itself and then reiterates them in appended notes and comments elsewhere on the work. Conscious of himself as a modern writer with immediate predecessors who gave great weight in their work to the chaos and disorder of contemporary experience, Durrell regards his purpose in writing this work as a search for a morphological form appropriate to modern time. This statement, taken from a note appended by Durrell to *Balthazar*, is accompanied by the further explanation that the form must be taken from science—Einstein's relativity physics, to be exact—because contemporary literature lacks classic unity. The scientific concept of a space-time continuum, an infinitely ramifying and exfoliating process-reality without fixable boundaries or exhaustible possibilities, serves as the structural foundation for a realistic narrative intended to mirror the qualities of such a universe, and so is "a word continuum," Durrell's suggested descriptive subtitle for *The Alexandria Quartet*, supplied in a note to *Clea*; but all novels, this one no exception, must have finite boundaries, no matter how arbitrary they may be. So Durrell, though he concludes *Clea* with "work points" for further possible expansion of the word *continuum*, limits himself to four volumes, three, as he says, of space and one of time. Einsteinian space-time theories are as much theories of knowing as they are theories of natural reality.

Correspondingly, the first three volumes, covering roughly the same time span and serving as reconstructions of the past, "interlap" and "interweave" perspectives and evidence on events that occurred among a coterie of people with diverse national backgrounds living in Alexandria, Egypt, just prior to World War II. Moreover, the first two, in the subjective mode, are narrated by L. G. Darley, the "subject" and protagonist of the quartet, and the third, *Mountolive*, is a Naturalistic novel in the third person in which Darley participates as a character and becomes, as Durrell points out, an "object." The last novel, though in the past tense, covers the present, a later time period than the first three, providing a sequel to them. Described in this manner, the ideas do not present much difficulty, but they imply and issue into entanglements foreign to the reader's customary thought habits.

All of this relativity scaffolding, as Durrell admits, might seem rather pretentious, a dillettantish display of scientific mumbo-jumbo, and if it were nothing more than superficial learning pawned off as profundity, then it would be. In *The Alexandria Quartet*, however, a thought-out work, a typically self-conscious performance for modern literature, ideas are an integral part of its theme and form. It is a novel about writing a novel (it ends at its beginning, with Darley prepared to assume his artisthood and writing down that age-old opening for a story, "Once upon a time . . ."), but its self-consciousness is functional. All the major characters, especially Pursewarden, a novelist himself, take the advanced ideas of relativity as commonplaces in their world and pass them on to Darley in such a way that they outline for him the novel that he and Durrell eventually write. Active powers in the plot of the novel, the ideas, produced by the imagination reflecting upon its own position and impulsions, are a shaping force in the novel's generation, so much so that their role in Darley's maturation is as great as love, the book's subject and the ultimate energy source. Love and intellect, or the counterpoles of energy and form, mutually abet each other in the upward course of the life of the imagination. This role of ideas in the novel is perhaps most evident in Darley's progress, or the novel's movement, from subjective Impressionism in *Justine* to objectivity in *Mountolive*, whereby Darley matures as he becomes better acquainted with the truth, and the novel frees itself from extreme subjectivism. The relativity scaffolding, therefore, equips Durrell with the instrument whereby he and his characters can come into touch with an external order of time and space, the inner and outer realities thereby confirming one another, the head complementing and reinforcing the heart.

On another level, this happy marriage of opposites amounts to a marriage of reason and imagination, the offspring of which is "science-fiction," Durrell's suggested classification for *The Alexandria Quartet*; the author's meaning of this term represents a blending of scientific truth and the fictive imagination rather than the science fantasy of the popular arts. Love, the subject of this novel, is, after all, a passion to unite, whether it be bodies in sex, minds in truth, or souls in spiritual oneness. In Whitman's phrase, when love is the keelson of creation, everything that exists does so in a mysterious tension with its opposite to which it is simultaneously drawn to complete itself, from which it is repelled for self-survival, and through which, regardless of whether attraction or repulsion is uppermost, interdependence makes the existence of both possible. In this respect, space and time are "married," simultaneously separate yet interrelated, and their union, a field with change occurring within it, is a prerequisite to events. So are subject and object, thought and love, science and fiction "married." A pair of such terms, in fact, points to polarities in tension characteristic of whatever exists, including the psyche, which has a "bisexual nature." Darley, an egoist, hates being alone and a bachelor; Balthazar, a Jewish doctor, says of Cavafy, a poet, that he subscribed to the proposition that if one imagines, he therefore belongs and is free. These are instances of polarities in tension in human behavior.

Durrell calls this phenomenon dimorphism, and it is one of the three most important principles in the novel. The second is cyclism, the rhythmic swing from one pole to the other, then back again. This dynamic process is most obvious in Darley's three love affairs, where the first and third women are essentially the same, but Darley cannot love the first, Melissa, a Greek whose identifying trait is "charity," because he has not passed through the dark lady. When he has, he can love Clea, a Frenchwoman, and like the Greek a fair lady, whose identifying traits are "innocence and generosity." Mysteriously, the poles in tension generate the power which begets change or growth, as in organic life and fortunate human psychic development. The sea, appropriately, is Darley's clock: it keeps the time, symbolically and literally, of the diastolic-systolic process by which change or growth proceed in their inexorable course.

The Alexandria Quartet is a book of changes, a charting of numerous transformations. The largest, unobtrusively in the background, is the culturewide one represented by World War II. The work is a novel of the city, of urban man's historically unique human environment. (Although romantic, nature plays a minimal role in it; structurally the novel is a gallery of people, what is exchanged between man and man, or in love, being the matrix from which growth issues; for this and other reasons, *The Alexandria Quartet* is a strange hybrid that can be labeled "romantic humanism.") One important pair of terms is "country-city," embodied in the Hosnani brothers Narouz-Nessim and associated with "ancient ways—the new culture," and the transformation from the former to the latter is made through the cultural crisis and agony manifested in war. The fact that the initial events for the individuals occur just prior to the war in the period of gathering gloom, that Darley goes through his night of self-examination and purification, and that the novel ends as the war is drawing to a close is not accidental: this sequence of events allows the personal life and the public world to evolve simultaneously into a new synthesis. A new era is announced at the end of the cycle for individual and society.

The dimorphic features in this work are far too numerous and inter-related to do justice to here; in addition to those already mentioned, these features range from overall motifs such as politics-love and life-art through the commonplace sexual ones to character pairings. Since the book is about Alexandria, however, little sense can be made out of what is happening in the novel unless the role of the city, its opposition to the individual, is kept clearly in mind. Durrell originally intended to use Athens as his setting, but finally he decided on Alexandria, he said, because it is the historical gateway through which civilization has passed. When laying down his purpose in writing early in *Justine*, Darley states his intention to "rebuild" the city in his imagination, and he comments further that the city should be judged, for here people have suffered its conflicts, which they mistook for their own; but the city is the people who comprise it. When Justine claims that people are caught by a projected will too strong and deliberate to be human, she is saying something about herself, being, as she must, an incarnation of the city's spirit. Justine departs from Alexandria once but then returns and remains there; Darley and several other major characters depart twice, the second time for good. (They move on to Paris, another city of love, a maturer and more human one.) The novel, consequently, is not a Naturalistic one based on the tyranny of environment over the person. Alexandria does not have a death grip on its inhabitants; rather, it is a juncture through which they must pass. During the time they are there, they are subject to its necessities; but they can, given a talent for it, pass beyond its determinism to freedom. Environment and individual can be in or out of phase, but only when they are in phase is the environment, Alexandria in this case, experienced as a projection of one's self-enslavement.

Though simple in its outlines and rigorously governed by dimorphism and cyclism, this novel is exceedingly complex in its details. One reason for this complexity is the fact that, within the shifting perspectives of time and personality, nothing specific ever comes, or can come, into clear focus. First, since three of the volumes are in the first person, the structure of the novel is based on the narrator's associations rather than on temporal or logical sequence; second, in a world of relativity, chance or random events are as important as predictable causality. Finally, and most importantly, this world is governed by the principle of indeterminacy, the third principle along with dimorphism and cyclism. No ultimate or absolute certainty about a fact is possible. It wears infinite masks and changes guises with the eye of the beholder, a kaleidoscope undergoing perpetual rearrangement. Temporal sequence in the novel, therefore, is extremely vague (Durrell gives no calendar dates by which to guide), and events that seem to be coming into clear focus suddenly blur again or, after a moment's comparison of present with past accounts of them, become interminable.

Quite aware that this vagueness exists, Durrell insists that the novel be regarded as a "relativity poem," a tale on one level, a poetic parable on another, that its characters are not only people but also symbols. Suggestiveness, not literalness, stimulation of the imagination, not conceptual certitude, are its intended effect. For this reason, Durrell has compared the novel to a pack of Tarot cards; like the Tarot pack, it reveals the truth, from the most gross to the rarest, which its reader is prepared to receive. Durrell would engage his reader in his novel in the same relative way that he is engaged in life and the scientist in nature. The honest reader of true fiction, Durrell implies, is necessarily in that fix anyway; like that of the universe he inhabits, his being is dimorphic, and he can perceive that range of wavelengths in the spectrum between the poles that his consciousness, owing to his temperament, culture, and stage of development, is capable of receiving and recording. The novel, indeed, the world, is a mirror reflecting not the times or nature but one's inner self, which paradoxically is also the external universe or a facet of it. As in Wallace Stevens' phrase, it is experienced as "a pressure pushing back," and so it is out there at the same time that it is within. The subjective and objective are no longer dichotomized and open to the chicken-egg question but are inseparable, unfathomable functions of each other.

The poetic quality of *The Alexandria Quartet* makes it difficult to follow in detail and almost impossible to summarize, but the general narrative framework, the overall pattern in which all the parts must fit to make sense, is as clear as the structural framework. Darley, an Anglo-Irish schoolteacher living in Alexandria, Egypt, undergoes an education in love and time. Durrell has explained in interviews what Darley's education consists of by stating that men are not born human, but life makes them so. Thus, sex-love-truth (or body-soul-mind), the facets in man of that power which the physicist calls energy, impels Darley toward self-realization. Since all external change is meaningless, Darley's humanization must come from forces awakened within, which will bring him to a state of poetic illumination. Darley, as man and artist, is in pursuit of an awakening or illumination, whereby love-truth will make him free. The creative principle of man, his imagination, is capable of love at its highest, most moral level and is equipped with the wisdom that follows from self-knowledge. When liberated, man's imagination will be able to act as God reputedly did in creating the world, and in that act it will have returned to the pristine source of all being—it will have performed the aboriginal act.

The various people and events in the novel make sense insofar as they contribute, narratively and thematically, via contrast, relevant orchestration, or dramatic progression, to elucidating Darley's education. If the preceding description of what happens in the novel is accurate, then Darley must be ignorant at the beginning of his story; he must be suffering from an erotic-knowledge deficiency, and indeed he is. Situated on an island in the

Cyclades, to which he has withdrawn after the collapse of his love affair with Justine Hosnani, Darley speaks of himself at the time he begins writing as a sick man needing to heal himself by understanding all that has happened to him in Alexandria. He meditates upon Alexandria and the people he had known intimately there. With his memories, Justine's diaries, and *Moeurs*, a diary-novel by Arnauti, Justine's first husband, he intends to review that era in his immediate past in order to find the meaning in the pattern of events. Though at one point he proclaims to have no pretensions to art, he wants the people, especially Melissa Artemis and Justine Hosnani, two women in his life in Alexandria, to reveal the truth that art can uncover. To cure himself of the sickness with which erotic love has infected him, Darley must learn the truth about the ordeal to which he has been subjected; through understanding the powers of darkness and by transforming suffering into life, he will grow and love again.

Like Stendhal in *The Life of Henri Brulard*, Darley measures his life in love affairs. Strangely for the conventions of fiction, he has no past—no birthplace, family, educational, or vocational background—prior to meeting Melissa, who also is without a history. At the time they became lovers, both had reached a point of existential nullity, but love becomes, for Darley, a suddenly opened door. Three loves serve as the landmarks in his progress and together constitute a self-enclosed psychological episode. The first and last, Melissa Artemis and Clea Montis, are remarkably alike beneath superficial differences, but Melissa, who dies, is a victim of Darley's ignorance because he is not prepared at the time of their affair to value and return her kind of love. Though eventually her face disappears from his memory, that is, drops from the life of his imagination, Darley's guilty feelings over abandoning her for Justine are powerful psychic forces in preparing him to love Clea. An originally virginal fellow artist, Clea, whose voice in the form of letters concludes all three of the volumes narrated by Darley (so is the terminal toward which he is blindly, unconsciously moving throughout his ruminations), undergoes the same education (including a secret love affair with Amaril) in order to be prepared for and finally joined with Darley. To get to Clea, however, Darley must pass through Justine, the black goddess, who captures and holds him in thrall during the important phase of his life in Alexandria.

As a juncture through which civilization and the people in the novel pass, Alexandria represents a hub where the tensions between the flesh and the spirit are at their most pronounced. Justine, as an incarnation of the city's sensuality, is correspondingly possessed by its contradictory demons of self-indulgence and self-revulsion. Hounded by her egoistic self-absorption, she desperately seeks escape from herself through fantasies, political causes, and sex but succeeds only in devouring others. Balthazar, another point of revelation, a doctor at a venereal disease clinic, and a devotee of the mystical Cabbala, has no deep interest in obsessive love but tries to cultivate a philosophical detachment. He is the opposite extreme from Justine, and together the two exemplify Alexandria's schizophrenia, a madness revealed in symptoms of exhaustion and world-weariness, a sense of deracination and failure, and an inability to respond to personal, individual assessments. Darley, though for a time the city's drugged prisoner, a failure with people, and an increasingly deficient lover, is saved from its demons ultimately because he is both a part of the city's life and the observer who sits apart to watch it all.

The remedy for the seizure by passion or the furies of the self with which Justine afflicts him, Darley feels, is to understand her. That way he can free himself. He never succeeds, however, because in the world of relativity, personality as a thing of absolutes is an illusion; yet he does free himself of her simply by abandoning his desire to penetrate and really know, so that when he returns to Alexandria at the beginning of *Clea*, she is passive and unbearable. The three preceding novels trace Darley's evolution to this point by submitting some crucial events to repeated and, as previously indicated, increasingly objective interpretations. In the first volume, *Justine*, which is written by Darley while in the mood of a melancholy lover, all events get a romantic reading. In the second volume, *Balthazar*, which consists essentially of Balthazar's comments on Darley's interpretation of the crucial events in *Justine*, all events get a philosophical reading, that is, one that favors intellectual motives and values. In the third volume, *Mountolive*, a third-person narrative, all events get a straight political reading. Love and politics have been fundamental antitheses in the novel from the beginning, opposite forms of power associated with man's private and public lives; and Mountolive also undergoes the same education Darley does, though he starts with a diplomat's severe self-denial as compared with Darley's self-concern as an artist, and Egypt replaces Alexandria as his abetting environment. Mountolive moves primarily on a political plane, Darley on an erotic or imaginative one. For example, in the first novel, Justine loves Darley for reasons of passion; in the second, she loves Balthazar, jolting Darley out of his romantic illusions, she claims she loved Pursewarden, who makes her laugh at herself, and used Darley as a decoy to distract her husband; in the third, it is revealed that she loved her husband, Nessim, and was carrying on affairs with Darley and Pursewarden to assist his political intrigues. It is hard to determine what role, if any, *Mountolive* has in Darley's progressive rehabilitation, but regardless of its role, though he never reaches final understanding of Justine, Darley does get self-perspective and so is purged through objectivity of his romantic affliction.

The major event in the novel is Darley's act of imagination by which, through reconstructing what has happened to him, he liberates himself to the freedom of art. In performing his act of imagination, however, he weaves an intricate web of personal relations and political intrigue. The former occupy the foreground most of the time and are hopelessly entangled; the latter entails elaborate espionage and counterespionage centering around a plot by the Copts to protect their interests against the Moslems through giving aid to the establishment of an Israeli state in Palestine. (Darley serves as a British and Justine as a Coptic agent.)

Only two people besides Justine, however, have a major constructive influence on Darley. The first is Clea, his unobtrusive instructress in love. Calm, patient, and generous, she quietly entices him toward mature, selfless love by precept and presence. The second is Pursewarden, an English writer of pronounced intellectual bent, a man given to irony, laughter, and cynicism. Pursewarden, who commits suicide, is, in fact, Darley's alter ego, his polar opposite in a dimorphic pair. He is the master in the training of Darley's imagination. Too much aware, Pursewarden cannot act upon what he knows; he must pass it on to Darley, whose innocence, goodness, and readiness to love make his life wide open, while the others' lives, including Pursewarden's, are enclosed. The intellect must thrive for the awareness necessary to art and truth to be possible, but then it must yield to naïve faith, hope, and passion so that the will to live can prevail. Before he serves his function and dies, Pursewarden describes the kind of novel he would like to write, the book that Darley and Durrell actually do write. Since Durrell and his characters are so articulate, and this articulateness is an integral element in the life of the imagination as *The Alexandria Quartet* defines it, it is appropriate to conclude on Durrell's unsurpassably accurate characterization of the novel's aims and dominant qualities.

No greater evidence of Durrell's success in this endeavor could be found than the enthusiastic reception of *The Alexandria Quartet* both popularly and critically. As an exploration into modern love, organized on the proposition of relativity, this work is a happy fusion of a simple passion with the most advanced understanding of reality. In effect, like all advanced contemporary thought and art, it is an answer to the "dissociation of sensibility" in Western culture during the past three centuries; it yokes thought and feeling, in classical terminology, reason and passion, in a brilliantly illuminating synthesis through a new form accurately reflecting the new world of the post-World War II period. Durrell has both thought and felt out his subject.

The place of *The Alexandria Quartet* in modern fiction can be best appreciated if it is kept in mind that Einsteinian physics, emerging around the turn of the century, produced a revolution not only in science but in the general understanding of life. The initial reaction by European writers to its overthrow of boxed space and clock time was despair. By eliminating absolutes, Einstein destroyed the grounds of established European social order, thought, and art. The despair resulted in an extreme subjectivity, if not solipsism. As George Orwell said about Henry Miller, the artist was "inside the whale"; his predicament was such that he could not seize hold of or affect the external world but could only record its violent impact upon his otherwise impotent spirit. The novel of sensibility, or the psychological novel, dedicated to rendering a state of mind, replaced the Realistic novel, the literary mode that evolved out of Newtonian physics, as a consequence; its great exemplars were James Joyce and Marcel Proust. In the post-World War II period, however, after living in Einstein's world long enough to become accustomed to its novelties, the Western writer has adopted a new tone of confidence, and with that new tone has come an acceptance of man's position and powers in a creative universe.

The Alexandria Quartet, a loving book about love (all the characters are allowed just to be; they are not judged: even Justine has revived and started a new life at the end), exemplifies the new sense of man's being at home in the world, a new sense of a confirmation of the interior man by the exterior reality, which allows man to exercise vital powers along lines of excellence in a world affording them scope. To the state of awareness staked out as the province belonging to the novel of sensibility, *The Alexandria Quartet* adds time, the dimension in which action occurs. Durrell has succeeded, therefore, in his desire to incorporate imagination in and thereby bring back to the novel the force and meaning of action. His novel, open-ended like Darley, affirms a new era of hope like Camus' *The Plague*. It is a consummate statement, the broadest in scope and profoundest in depth, for the present stage in the exploration of the territory discovered by Einstein. An engaging story on the most popular of subjects and at the same time a monument in the life of the mind in the twentieth century, Darley's "relativity poem" demands and is worthy of the reader's most careful attention; it consists of the very stuff of which life is made today.

ALICE'S ADVENTURES IN WONDERLAND

Type of work: Imaginative tale
Author: Lewis Carroll (Charles Lutwidge Dodgson, 1832–1898)
Type of plot: Fantasy
Time of plot: Victorian England
Locale: The dream world of an imaginative child
First published: 1865

Principal characters:
ALICE
THE WHITE RABBIT
THE DUCHESS
THE QUEEN OF HEARTS

The Story:

Alice was quietly reading over her sister's shoulder when she saw a White Rabbit dash across the lawn and disappear into its hole. She jumped up to rush after him and found herself falling down the rabbit hole. At the bottom, she saw the White Rabbit hurrying along a corridor ahead of her and murmuring that he would be late. He disappeared around a corner, leaving Alice standing in front of several locked doors.

On a glass table, she found a tiny golden key that unlocked a little door hidden behind a curtain. The door opened upon a lovely miniature garden, but she could not get through the doorway because it was too small. She sadly replaced the key on the table. A little bottle mysteriously appeared. Alice drank the contents and immediately began to grow smaller, so much so that she could no longer reach the key on the table. Next, she ate a piece of cake she found nearby, and soon she began to grow to such enormous size that she could only squint through the door. In despair, she began to weep tears as big as raindrops. As she sat crying, the White Rabbit appeared, bewailing the fact that the Duchess would be angry if he kept her waiting.

The White Rabbit dropped his fan and gloves. Alice picked them up, and as she did so, she began to grow smaller. Again she rushed to the garden door, but she found it shut and the golden key once more on the table out of reach.

Then she fell into a pool of her own tears. Splashing along, she encountered a mouse who had stumbled into the pool. Alice tactlessly began a conversation about her cat Dinah, and the mouse became speechless with terror. Soon the pool of tears was filled with living creatures—birds and animals of all kinds. An old Dodo suggested that they run a Caucus Race to get dry. Having asked what a Caucus Race was, Alice was told that the best way to explain it was to do it, whereupon the animals ran themselves quite breathless and finally became dry.

Afterward, the mouse told a "Tail" to match its own appendage. Alice was asked to tell something, but the only thing she could think of was her cat Dinah. Frightened, the other creatures went away, and Alice was left alone.

The White Rabbit appeared once more, this time hunting for his gloves and fan. Catching sight of Alice, he sent her to his home to get him a fresh pair of gloves and another fan. In the Rabbit's house, she found the fan and gloves and also took a drink from a bottle. Instantly, she grew to be a giant size and was forced to put her leg up the chimney and her elbow out of the window in order to keep from being squeezed to death.

She managed to eat a little cake and shrink herself again. As soon as she was small enough to get through the door, she ran into a nearby wood where she found a caterpillar sitting on a mushroom. The caterpillar was very rude to Alice, and he scornfully asked her to prove her worth by reciting "You Are Old, Father William." Alice did so, but the words sounded very strange. Disgusted, he left her after giving her some valuable information about increasing or decreasing her size. She broke off pieces of the mushroom and found to her delight that by eating from the piece in her left hand she could become taller, and from the piece in her right hand, smaller.

She came to a little house among the trees. There a footman, who looked very much like a fish, presented to another footman, who closely resembled a frog, an invitation for the Duchess to play croquet with the Queen. The two amphibians bowed to each other with great formality, tangling their wigs together. Alice opened the door and found herself in the chaotic house of the Duchess. The cook was stirring a large pot of soup and pouring plenty of pepper into the mixture. Everyone was sneezing except the cook and a Cheshire cat, which sat on the hearth grinning. The Duchess herself held a sneezing, squalling baby and sang a blaring lullaby to it. Alice, in sympathy with the poor child, picked it up and carried it out into the fresh air, whereupon the baby turned slowly into a pig, squirmed out of her arms, and waddled into the forest.

Standing in bewilderment, Alice saw the grinning Cheshire cat sitting in a tree. He was able to appear and disappear at will, and after exercising his talents, he advised Alice to go to a tea party given by the Mad Hatter. The cat vanished, all but the grin. Finally, that, too, disappeared, and Alice left for the party.

There, Alice found she had to deal with the strangest people she had ever seen—a March Hare, a Mad Hatter, and a sleepy Dormouse. All were too lazy to set the table properly; dirty dishes were everywhere. The Dormouse fell asleep in its teacup; the Mad Hatter told Alice her hair needed cutting; the March Hare offered her wine and then told her there was none. They asked her foolish riddles that had no answers. Then, worse, they ignored her completely and carried on a ridiculous conversation among themselves. She escaped after the Dormouse fell asleep in the middle of a story he was telling.

Next, she found herself in a garden of talking flowers. Just as the conversation was beginning, some gardeners appeared with paintbrushes and began to splash red paint on a rosebush. Alice learned that the Queen had ordered a red bush to be placed in that spot, and the gardeners had made a mistake and planted a white one. Now they were busily and fearfully trying to cover their error before the Queen arrived. The poor gardeners, however, were not swift enough. The Queen caught them in the act, and the wretched gardeners were led off to be decapitated. Alice saved them by shoving them down into a large flowerpot, out of sight of the dreadful Queen.

A croquet game began. The mallets were live flamingoes, and the balls were hedgehogs which thought nothing of uncurling themselves and running rapidly over the field. The Duchess cornered Alice and led her away to the seaside to introduce her to the Mock Turtle and the Gryphon.

While engaged in a Lobster Quadrille, they heard the news of a trial. A thief had stolen some tarts. Rushing to the courtroom where a trial by jury was already in session, Alice was called upon to act as a witness before the King and Queen of Hearts, but the excited child upset the jury box and spilled out all of its occupants. After replacing all the animals in the box, Alice said she knew nothing of the matter. Her speech infuriated the Queen, who ordered that Alice's head be cut off. The whole court rushed at her, and Alice defiantly called them nothing but a pack of cards. She awoke from her dream as her sister brushed away some dead leaves blowing over her face.

Critical Evaluation:

One summer afternoon in 1862, the Reverend Charles Lutwidge Dodgson, an Oxford friend, and three little girls set out on a boat trip. Somewhere along the way, *Alice's Adventures in Wonderland* was born. Although it was not the first story that Dodgson had told the girls, children of Henry George Liddell, dean of Christ Church, Oxford, it was one that immediately captured Alice Liddell, the prototype for the fictional seven-year-old heroine. Her later requests for Dodgson to "write it down" were to turn him into one of the world's favorite authors, with his work translated into more than forty-five languages and part of the heritage of most literate people.

Dodgson, who transposed his first two names into the pen name Lewis Carroll, was on the surface a shy but seemingly conventional Oxford mathematician. Today, however, his outwardly harmless affinity for little girls is viewed as the sign of a serious neurosis, an inability to grow up, which also revealed itself in his writings. Alice was only one of many young girls who would provide Carroll with the only love—innocent and sexless as it seemed—to which he could respond. As she matured, each child was replaced in Carroll's affections by another young lady who shared the secret world of childhood in which he spent much of his adult life.

Expressing itself in many ways, this attraction to fantasy gave rise to Carroll's love of whimsical letters, gadgets, theatricals, toys, and, of course, to the Alice stories. First prepared in a handwritten manuscript book for Alice Liddell (then called *Alice's Adventures Under Ground*), the book was published in its present form in 1865 and was almost immediately popular. Adding to its originality were the famous illustrations by Sir John Tenniel who did not use the real Alice for his model. She, unlike the pictured child, had short dark hair and bangs.

Followed in 1871 by the even more brilliant sequel, *Through the Looking-Glass and What Alice Found There*, the book has always been enjoyed on several levels. Initially, it is a very special children's story, but it is also a book teeming with fascination for certain specialists—mathematicians, linguists, logicians, Freudians, and even those who envision the book as an example of a drug trip. Yet, perhaps its philosophical suggestions give the work most of its never-ending appeal for adults.

If readers examine the book as children's literature, readers see that it offered its young audience a charming new outlook, dispensing with the moralistic viewpoint then prevalent in almost all tales for youngsters. Alice is neither continuously nice nor thoroughly naughty, for she is simply a curious child whose queries lead her into strange situations, and in the end, she is neither punished nor rewarded. A moral, proposing that she do this or that, is absent. Departing even further from the saccharine stories praising standard virtues, Carroll pokes fun at many of the ideas with which Alice, a well-bred English child, has been imbued. The Mock Turtle, for example, chides the sacred subject of learning by terming the branches of arithmetic Ambition, Distraction, Uglification, and Derision. Children who read the book are permitted to see adults quite unlike the perfect beings usually portrayed. It is the story's adults rather than Alice who are rude, demanding, and ridiculous.

As a work for the specialist, *Alice's Adventures in Wonderland* touches on many puzzles more thoroughly presented in *Through the Looking-Glass and What Alice Found There*. Its playfulness with language, for example, involves puns, parodies, and clever phrasing, but it does not deal as fully with the basic nature of language as does its sequel. Even in *Alice's Adventures in Wonderland*, however, Carroll's casual amusement with words often has deeper meaning. When he parodies the well-known poems and songs of his day, he is again questioning their supercilious platitudes. When he makes a pun (the Gryphon tells the reader that boots and shoes under the sea are "done" with whiting rather than blacking and are, of course, made of soles and eels), Carroll is asserting the total logic of illogic. When he designs a Cheshire cat, he is taking a common but unclear phrase of his time ("Grin like a Cheshire cat" referred either to inn signs in the county of Cheshire depicting a grinning lion or to Cheshire cheeses modeled in the shape of a smiling cat) and turning it into a concrete reality. Logicians also find a multitude of tidbits. The Cheshire cat "proves" it is not mad by adopting the premise that if a dog is not mad, anyone who reacts in ways opposite to a dog must be. The March Hare offers a nice exercise in logic and language with his discussion of taking "more" versus taking "less" and his challenge as to whether "I mean what I say" is the same as "I say what I mean."

For mathematicians, Carroll presents the Mad Hatter's watch, which tells the day of the month rather than the hour. The watch does not bother with the hour, since from the center of the earth, the sun would always look the same, whereas the moon's phases would be visible. For the Freudians, the book is also a mass of complicated mysteries. Freudians see significance in most of the characters and incidents, but the fall down the rabbit hole, the changes in size, the great interest in eating and drinking, the obnoxious mature females, and Alice's continual anxiety are some of the most revealing topics, all of them suggesting Carroll's neuroses about women and sex.

The larger philosophical questions raised by Alice center on the order of life as readers know it. Set in the context of the dream vision, a journey different from a conscious quest, the book asks whether there is indeed any pattern or meaning to life. Alice is the curious innocent who compares so favorably with the jaded and even wicked grown-ups. Always sensible and open to experience, she would seem the ideal messenger to bring readers a true concept, yet her adventures hint that all readers may know is the ridiculousness of logic and what readers imagine to be reality and the logic of nonsense. Readers see that Wonderland is no more incomprehensible than Victorian England, that the Mad Duchess lives next door, that as the Cheshire cat says, "We're all mad here."

Alice brings to Wonderland a strong belief in order and certain concepts, and she must continually refuse to accept the chaos that she finds there. When Wonderland turns her views askew, she can withstand the strain for only so long. Then she must rebel. The trial, which is the last refuge of justice in man's world, is the key factor in Alice's rejection of Wonderland, for it is a trial of Wonderland itself, with many of the earlier encountered creatures reassembled to assert forcefully, once more, that expectations and rules are meaningless. Like the child of the world that she is, Alice (and Carroll) must deny the truth that there is no truth. She must shout "Nonsense" to it all. As one critic has pointed out, she rejects "mad sanity in favor of the sane madness of the ordinary existence." Facing the same confusion and frightened by what it hints, the reader also rebels, laughing and turning to more serious considerations.

ALL HALLOWS' EVE

Type of work: Novel
Author: Charles Williams (1886–1945)
Type of plot: Supernatural thriller
Time of plot: October, 1945
Locale: London
First published: 1945

Principal characters:

LESTER FURNIVAL, a dead young wife
RICHARD FURNIVAL, her husband
EVELYN MERCER, her dead friend
BETTY WALLINGFORD, another friend
LADY SARA WALLINGFORD, Betty's mother
JONATHAN DRAYTON, Betty's artist fiancé
SIMON THE CLERK, the leader of a religious group

Charles Williams' last novel is set in the locale he knew best, central London, but in a time which he did not live to appreciate: the first autumn of the peace after World War II. To Lester Furnival, standing on Westminster Bridge at twilight, the lights of the city and the drone of a friendly plane overhead are symbols of the peace, a return to the natural order of life, yet Lester becomes conscious of a silence that is unnatural. Through Lester's gradual awareness of the fact that she is dead, Williams crosses and removes the barrier between the natural and the supernatural worlds. Lester is the central character in a spiritual drama that illustrates Williams' mystical and imaginative interpretation of Christian doctrine.

Fundamentally, the plot traces the triumph of love over evil during Lester's period of purgatory. A vital and passionate young wife killed in a completely fortuitous plane crash, she is a modern version of the figure of Beatrice, who was Williams' focus in his interpretation of Dante. Her love for her husband, which has survived her death, leads to his conversion, the defeat of evil, and her own salvation. When she first finds herself alone in the city with Evelyn, the friend who was killed with her, she realizes that theirs was never a true friendship. As the two dead women try to establish a genuine relationship in their new existence, they become involved in the affairs of the living. Lester's husband Richard has an artist friend, Jonathan, who is in love with Betty, a school friend whom Lester and Evelyn had never liked. Betty is completely dominated by her mother, Lady Wallingford, who is a disciple of a mysterious faith healer who calls himself Simon the Clerk.

The action of the novel begins when Lady Wallingford and Betty call to see a portrait of Father Simon commissioned from Jonathan. Because

Jonathan is a Christian, he has, without realizing it, revealed in the portrait the essence of evil, which Simon represents. Lady Wallingford, infuriated, calls off Betty's engagement to Jonathan, takes Betty away, and Jonathan calls on Richard for help. On the supernatural level, the conflict between mother and lover for possession of Betty becomes the conflict between the God of love and the power of darkness for the human soul.

The character of Simon is developed with all the resources of Williams' interest in magic and witchcraft. Surrounded by a band of zealous converts whom he has healed, preaching to a mesmerized audience in his shabby backstreet headquarters, Simon is the re-embodiment of Simon the Magus, of the Jew who rejected Christ; he is, in fact, the Antichrist. Exploiting the devotion of Lady Wallingford, he had conceived Betty to be his agent and fears that his power over his daughter is now threatened by the human love of Jonathan. He decides that the time has come for the final magical operation that will separate her human soul from her physical body and substitute his will in its place, but he is thwarted by love in action. At each crisis, he makes a mistake, because his magic powers cannot perceive what love will do.

The sequence of events combines natural and supernatural elements with a Realism that is not merely a matter of literary technique but an expression of Williams' belief that the material and the spiritual, the temporal and the eternal, are equally real. This tenet of faith was a basic fact of the creative imagination for Williams. There is no question of fantasy, allegory, or symbol; the novel form is used simply for its traditional purpose of revealing some phase of life's reality. Underlying the events is a pattern that Williams considered fundamental in human life: the power of substitution. He believed that a person who loves can bear another's burdens in a way which he considered physical as well as spiritual. This power means not simply praying for the burdened but loving so deeply that the burden of suffering is transferred from one to the other. As the human form of Christ on the cross suffered for all mankind, so the central character of this story, as of other of Williams' novels, saves a victim by substituting herself.

When Simon goes to Betty's bedroom to perform the final operation of magic, Lester is already there, having gone to ask Betty's forgiveness for rejecting her friendship. As Betty's forgiveness of Lester releases Lester's spirit, so Lester's love sustains Betty and becomes her substitute to receive Simon's curse. Because Lester is already dead, Simon has no effect on her, and Betty is released from his spell to rebel against her mother and rejoin Jonathan. The defeated Simon then turns his attention to the wretched soul of Evelyn, who has sought his aid to regain her power of persecuting Betty as she had done at school. Lester tries to rescue Evelyn, as she has rescued Betty, by joining her within the miserably deformed physical body, which Simon creates for her with his magic powers. Simon attempts to control this body and use it to trap Betty, Jonathan, and Richard; but Lester exercises a greater control through the power of love and warns them in time for them to expose Simon and bring his work and his house to ruins.

The climax of the action takes place on a gray, rainy Halloween, All Hallows' Eve, when the deformed body containing the souls of Lester and Evelyn moves through the streets of London and keeps a rendezvous at Jonathan's flat, where the engaged couple have invited the bereaved Richard to join them for dinner. The circumstances of this final encounter between the living and the dead are typical of the relationship between the material and the spiritual worlds throughout the novel. When Lester wants to warn Richard of the approach of the magical body, she thinks of the telephone. Having begged two pennies from a passerby, she goes into a telephone box opposite the Charing Cross Tube Station, a natural enough sight on the streets of London. When Richard comes to the phone, however, he hears Lester's voice as clearly as he has seen her form several times in the last few days. She gives him the message that they must wait at the flat until the old woman comes. Instead of going out to dinner, they spread a meal of bread, cheese, cold scraps, and wine and thus prepare themselves for the crisis of All Hallows' Eve. After they have met, the three living friends take the deformed body with them in a taxi through the rainy midnight streets of London to the darkened house where Simon and Lady Wallingford are forestalled in their last desperate act of magic.

From the moment when Lester finds herself alone on Westminster to the climax of her final disappearance from Simon's house, there is always a strong sense of London as the background to the action. At first, Lester can see only the city, but as her spirit develops, she hears all the familiar noises of people and traffic, feels the pavement under her feet, and smells the river and the October rain. Betty and Jonathan go together to call on her old nurse at 59 Upper Clapham Lane. There, they discover that she had taken it upon herself to baptize Betty as a baby, secretly and in defiance of Lady Wallingford. The literalness of London sights, sounds, and addresses is not merely a device to root the supernatural story in the natural world. For Williams, London is an image of the Civitas Dei, the Holy City, the community or communion of the saints. When the city is first mentioned, the term indicates the ancient borough of London, site of St. Paul's and the Bank of England as well as Jonathan's flat, as distinguished from Holborn where Simon's headquarters are, or Westminster where Richard's flat is, or Highgate where the Wallingfords live. Through Lester's developing spiritual perception, however, the spiritual reality of the eternal city is revealed. Its identity is hinted to mortal eyes on the fateful afternoon when Lady Wallingford and Betty call to look at Jonathan's portrait of Simon. Lady Wallingford is equally antagonized by another picture which Jonathan and Richard consider the best he has done, a painting of a part of London after a raid, a scene of desolation ironically bathed in living light from the still unrisen sun.

This city, emerging from war and night, is the setting in which Richard meets his wife again with deeper understanding of their love. At the end of the novel, Jonathan and Betty give Richard the picture, and Lester disappears into light. Although the action of the novel centers around the conflict over Betty, the major interest is focused on the dead Lester and the living Richard as they move through the city, at first absolutely separated, then gradually reunited as each comes to understand the reality of love, and finally separated when the understanding is complete. These two characters are developed with a psychological depth, dramatic sensitivity, and humor that make them as fully credible as the protagonists of the traditional nineteenth century novel. Jonathan and Betty are less fully delineated and are seen more from the outside, through the eyes of their friends, than from the inside. The dead Evelyn is no longer a human personality but merely the epitome of egocentric peevishness, which was her dominant trait. In descending scale, Simon and Lady Wallingford are agents of evil, as much puppets as the bodies which Simon can create. This apparent lack of consistency in characterization depends not on literary technique or point of view but on Williams' theory of personality, his belief that only love can make a human being whole. Jonathan and Betty, in their initial stages of love before physical consummation, cannot be as fully developed as Lester and Richard. In characterization, as in every aspect of the novel, Williams' story is perfectly integrated with his doctrine. Final assessment of his achievement requires the resolution of a basic ambiguity: whether the credibility of the story makes the doctrine convincing or whether the credibility of the story in fact depends on conviction about the doctrine.

ALMAYER'S FOLLY
A Story of an Eastern River

Type of work: Novel
Author: Joseph Conrad (Józef Teodor Konrad Korzeniowski, 1857–1924)
Type of plot: Romantic realism
Time of plot: Late nineteenth century
Locale: Dutch East Indies
First published: 1895

Principal characters:

ALMAYER, an unsuccessful trader of Dutch ancestry
MRS. ALMAYER, his Malay wife
NINA, his half-caste daughter
DAIN MAROOLA, Nina's Malay lover
LAKAMBA, Rajah of Sambir and Almayer's enemy

The Story:

By marrying Lingard's adopted Malay daughter, Almayer had inherited the prosperous merchant's business and his plans for amassing a huge fortune in gold from rich mines up the Pantai River. Almayer and his wife had one daughter, Nina, a beautiful girl, who had been sent to Singapore, where for ten years she was educated as a European. She returned home to Sambir unexpectedly at the end of that time, for she could not bear to be treated as a half-caste in a white community. Unsuccessful in business, Almayer nursed dim hopes that he could find a gold mine and, his fortune made, take Nina to Amsterdam to spend his last days in prosperous retirement.

News that the English were to seize control of the Pantai River caused Almayer to begin building a new house in his compound, not far removed from the one in which he was living. He wanted a house fine enough to receive the British. When the project was abandoned and the Dutch were left in nominal power, Almayer stopped work on his new house. A company of Dutch seamen christened the structure "Almayer's Folly."

Lakamba, the native rajah, had a compound across the river from Almayer's home. There he lived with his women, his slaves, and his principal aide, Babalatchi. Lakamba kept close watch on Almayer when he would leave for several days at a time with a few of his men. After a time, Almayer gave up his trips and settled down to empty daydreams on his rotten wharf. His native wife despised him.

Nina's presence in Sambir offered another problem for Almayer, for the young men of the settlement were eyeing her with interest.

One day, the handsome son of a Malayan rajah came sailing up the river in a brig and wanted to trade with Almayer. His name was Dain Maroola.

At length, after conversations with Lakamba and long conferences with Almayer, Dain got the gunpowder he had been seeking. Meanwhile, he had fallen passionately in love with Nina. One night she came into the women's room in her father's house and discovered her mother counting out the money Dain had been giving her in payment for Nina. Mrs. Almayer had been arranging meetings between Nina and Dain and giving them warning at the approach of Almayer. Mrs. Almayer wished her daughter to remain native. She had a deep distrust of white men and their ways.

Dain went away, promising that he would return to help Almayer in locating the hidden gold mine. When he did return, he saw Almayer for just a moment and then hurried to see Lakamba. He told the rajah that his brig had fallen into the hands of the Dutch and that he had narrowly escaped with one slave. Most of his men had been killed, and in a day or two, the Dutch would be up the Pantai looking for him.

After this interview, Lakamba told Babalatchi he must poison Almayer before the arrival of the Dutch. Now that Dain knew where the gold treasure was located, Almayer was no longer needed. If allowed to live, he might reveal his secret to the white men.

Next morning, the body of a Malay was found floating in the river. The head was smashed beyond recognition, but it wore an anklet and a ring that had belonged to Dain. Almayer was overcome with grief, for Dain was his last hope of finding the gold. The Dutch officers who came looking for Dain told how he had escaped. As the Dutch approached his brig, the gunpowder it carried ignited and blew up the boat, killing two of the Dutch. Almayer promised his visitors that after they had dined he would deliver Dain into their hands.

Meanwhile, Babalatchi was telling Lakamba the true story of Dain. Nina had been waiting for the young Malay on the night of his conference with Lakamba, and she had taken him to a secluded clearing farther up the river. He was now hiding there. The corpse that had floated down the river was that of his slave, who had died when the canoe overturned. Mrs. Almayer had suggested that Dain put his anklet and ring on the body and let it float down the river. Lakamba and Babalatchi planned Dain's escape from his Dutch enemies. Knowing that Dain would not leave without Nina, Babalatchi and Mrs. Almayer plotted to get her away from Almayer, who was drinking with the Dutch. After some persuasion, Almayer did lead his guests to the grave of the man recovered from the river. The Dutch took the anklet and ring as proof that Dain was dead. Then they left for the night.

Nina, willing to go with Dain, felt an urge to see her father once more before she left, but her mother would not let her go into the house where her father lay in a drunken sleep. Nina went to the clearing where Dain

was hiding. Soon afterward, a slave girl awakened Almayer and told him of
Nina's whereabouts. Almayer was panic-stricken. He traced Nina to Dain's
enclosure and begged her to come back to him, but she would not. She did
not want to run the risk of insults from white people. With Dain she would
be a ranee, and she would be married to a Malay, a brave warrior, not a
lying, cowardly white man. Almayer threatened to send his servant to tell
the Dutch of Dain's hiding place.

While they argued, Babalatchi approached and cried out that the slave
girl had revealed Dain's hiding place to the Dutch, who were now on their
way to capture the young Malay. Babalatchi, astounded when Dain
announced that he would stay with Nina, left them to their fate. After he
had gone, Almayer said he would never forgive Nina, but he offered to
take the two to the mouth of the river. In heavy darkness, the fugitive
lovers escaped their pursuers.

On an island at the mouth of the river Dain, Nina, and Almayer
awaited the canoe that would take the lovers to Lakamba's hidden boat.
After the two had gone, Almayer covered up Nina's footprints and returned to his house up the river. His compound was deserted. Mrs.
Almayer and her women had gone to Lakamba for protection, taking
Dain's gift of money with her. Almayer found the old rusty key to his
unused office. He went inside, broke up the furniture, and piled it in the
middle of the room. When he came out, he threw the key into the river
and sat on his porch until the flames began to billow from his office. He
was burning down his old house.

He lived out the rest of his days in "Almayer's Folly." Finally, he began
the practice of smoking opium in an effort to forget his daughter Nina.
When he died, the opium had given his eyes the look of one who indeed
had succeeded in forgetting.

Critical Evaluation:

Almayer's new house stands as the palpable symbol of "the undying folly
of his heart"; Joseph Conrad calls it "that new ruin," meaning both the
house, built in unrealistic expectation of commercial prosperity, and the
edifice of his imagination, that castle of air reared up out of his invincible
and seemingly willful misunderstanding of the motives of everyone about
him. His is the folly of Europeans who, taking for granted a natural superiority in respect of civilization and inferring from it the right of command
in native affairs, ignore the very nature of the people they expect to control. This is a favorite theme of Conrad, this despairing bafflement in the
face of the unyielding complexity of native life; such meddling leads eventually to paralysis of the spirit.

Almayer's feverish preparations for the gold-seeking expedition, after
years of virtual immobility, are the last gasp of his will. When that hope is

shattered, he sinks into mortal fixity, accusing Nina in his heart. It is not Nina, however, who has betrayed him; it is rather his own reliance on people who despise him, a blind belief in what is due him as a European. Captain Lingard's role brings another change on this motif, for his assumption of power over the life of a Malay orphan (whom he does not at all understand) fires Almayer's at once exalted and trivial ambitions to wealth and social standing.

The novel is also profoundly misogynist, linking the immobilizing moil of sexuality to the enormous, indifferent, and soul-battering wilderness where "the very air seemed dead . . . poisoned with the corruption of countless ages." Mrs. Almayer's passionate hatred and contempt for her husband that cause her to cuckold him with Lakamba; Nina's love for Dain so intimately mixed with policy; Taminah's passion that instigates the most craven revenge—all find their judgment in Dain's words: " 'The sea, O Nina, is like a woman's heart.' "

AMELIA

Type of work: Novel
Author: Henry Fielding (1707–1754)
Type of plot: Domestic realism
Time of plot: 1740's
Locale: England
First published: 1751

Principal characters:
CAPTAIN BOOTH, a soldier
AMELIA, his wife
ELIZABETH HARRIS, her sister
SERGEANT ATKINSON, her foster brother
DR. HARRISON, Booth's benefactor
MISS MATTHEWS, a woman of the town
COLONEL JAMES, Booth's former officer

The Story:
One night, the watchmen of Westminster arrested Captain William Booth, seizing him during his attempt to rescue a stranger who was being attacked by two ruffians. The footpads secured their own liberty by bribing the constables, but Booth, in spite of his protests, was hailed before an unjust magistrate. The story he told was a straightforward one, but because he was penniless and shabbily dressed, the judge dismissed his tale and sentenced him to prison. Booth was desperate; there was no one he knew in London to whom he could turn for aid. His plight was made worse by his reception at the prison. His fellow prisoners stripped him of his coat, and a pickpocket stole his snuffbox.

While he was smarting from these indignities, a fashionably dressed young woman was brought through the gates. Flourishing a bag of gold in the face of her keepers, she demanded a private room in the prison. Her appearance and manner reminded Booth of Miss Matthews, an old friend of questionable background whom he had not seen for several years; but when the woman passed him without a sign of recognition, he believed himself mistaken.

Shortly afterward, a guard brought him a guinea in a small parcel, and with the money, Booth was able to redeem his coat and snuffbox. He lost the rest of the windfall in a card game. Booth was penniless once more when a keeper came to lead him to Miss Matthews, for the woman was indeed she. Seeing his wretched condition as he stood by the prison gate, she had sent him the mysterious guinea.

Reunited under these distressing circumstances, they proceeded to relate the stories of their experiences. Miss Matthews told how she had been

committed to await sentence for a penknife attack on a soldier who had seduced her under false promises of marriage.

Booth, in turn, told this story. He had met Miss Amelia Harris, a beautiful girl whose mother at first opposed her daughter's marriage to a penniless soldier. The young couple eloped but were later reconciled with
Amelia's mother through the efforts of Dr. Harrison, a wise and kindly curate. Shortly before a child was to be born to Amelia, Booth's regiment
was ordered to Gibraltar. He left reluctantly, leaving Amelia in the care of
her mother and her older sister Elizabeth. At Gibraltar, Booth earned the
good opinion of his officers by his bravery. Wounded in one of the battles
of the campaign, he was very ill. Amelia, learning of his condition, left her
child with her mother and sister and went to Gibraltar to nurse her sick
husband. Then Amelia, in her turn, fell sick. Wishing to take her to a
milder climate, Booth wrote to Mrs. Harris for money, but in reply he
received only a rude note from Elizabeth. He hoped to get the money from
his army friend, Major James, but that gentleman was away at the time.
Finally, he borrowed the money from Sergeant Atkinson, his friend and
Amelia's foster brother, and went with his wife to Montpelier. There the
couple made friends with an amusing English officer named Colonel Bath
and his sister.

Joy at the birth of a second child, a girl, was dampened by a letter from
Dr. Harrison, who wrote to tell them that old Mrs. Harris was dead and
that she had left her property to Amelia's sister. The Booths returned
home, to be greeted so rudely by Elizabeth that they withdrew from the
house. Without the help of Dr. Harrison, they would have been destitute.
Harrison set Booth up as a gentleman farmer and tried to help him make
the best of his half-pay from the Army. Booth, however, made enemies
among the surrounding farmers because of several small mistakes. Dr. Harrison was traveling on the Continent at the time, and in his absence, Booth
was reduced almost to bankruptcy. He came to London to try his fortunes
anew. He preceded Amelia, found modest lodgings, and wrote her of his
location. At this point, another misfortune landed him in prison. At the
end of Booth's story, Miss Matthews sympathized with his unfortunate situation, congratulated him on his wife and children, and paid the jailer to let
Booth spend the next few nights with her in her cell.

Booth and Miss Matthews were shortly released from prison. The soldier wounded by Miss Matthews had completely recovered and dropped his
charges against her. Miss Matthews also secured the release of Booth, and
the two were preparing to leave prison when Amelia arrived. She had come
up from the country to save him, and his release was a welcome surprise.
The Booths established themselves in London. Shortly afterward, Booth
met his former officer, now Colonel James, who in the meanwhile had
married Miss Bath and grown quickly tired of her. Mrs. James and Amelia

resumed their old friendship. Booth, afraid that Miss Matthews would inform Amelia of their affair in prison, told Colonel James of his difficulties and fears. The colonel gave him a loan and told him not to worry. Colonel James was also interested in Miss Matthews, but he was unable to help Booth by his intercession. Miss Matthews continued to send Booth reproachful and revealing letters, which might at any time have been intercepted by Amelia.

While walking in the park one day, the Booths met Sergeant Atkinson. He joined their household to help care for the children, and soon he started a mild flirtation with Mrs. Ellison, Booth's landlady.

Mrs. Ellison proved useful to the Booths; a lord who came also to visit her advanced money to pay some of Booth's debts. Meanwhile, Miss Matthews had spitefully turned Colonel James against Booth. Colonel Bath, hearing his brother-in-law's poor opinion of Booth, decided that Booth was neither an officer nor a gentleman and challenged him to a duel. Colonel Bath strongly believed in a code of honor, and when Booth had run him through in the duel without serious injury, the colonel was so impressed by Booth's gallantry that he forgave him and brought about a reconciliation between James and Booth.

During this time, Mrs. Ellison had been trying to arrange an assignation between Amelia and the nobleman who had given Booth money to pay his gambling debts. Amelia was innocently misled by her false friends. The nobleman's plan to meet Amelia secretly at a masquerade, however, was thwarted by another neighbor, Mrs. Bennet. This woman, who had been a boarder in Mrs. Ellison's house, had also met the noble lord, had encountered him at a masquerade, and had drunk the drugged wine he provided. To prevent Amelia's ruin in the same manner, Mrs. Bennet came to warn her friend. Then she informed Amelia that she had recently married Sergeant Atkinson, whom Amelia had thought in love with Mrs. Ellison; but Amelia's joy at learning of both the plot, which she now planned to escape, and of the marriage, was marred by the news that Booth had again been put into prison for debt, this time on a warrant of their old friend Dr. Harrison.

Amelia soon discovered that Dr. Harrison had been misled by false rumors of Booth's extravagance and had put him in jail in order to stop his rash spending of money. Learning the truth, Dr. Harrison had Booth released from prison.

On the night of the masquerade, Amelia remained at home but sent Mrs. Atkinson dressed in her costume. At the dance, Mrs. Atkinson was able to fool not only the lord but also Colonel James. There were many complications of the affair, and almost every relationship was misunderstood. Booth fell in with an old friend and lost a large sum of money to him. Again, he became worried about being put in jail. Then he became involved in a duel with Colonel James over Miss Matthews, whom Booth had visited only at her insistence. Before the duel could take place, Booth was again imprisoned for debt, and Dr. Harrison was forced to clear his name with Colonel James. Finally James forgave Booth, and Miss Matthews promised never to bother him again.

Called by chance into a strange house to hear the deathbed confession of a man named Robinson, Dr. Harrison learned that Robinson had at one time been a clerk to a lawyer named Murphy who had made Mrs. Harris' will. He learned also that the will, which had left Amelia penniless, was a false one prepared by Elizabeth and Murphy. Dr. Harrison had Robinson write a confession so that Amelia could get the money that was rightfully hers. Murphy was quickly brought to trial and convicted of forgery.

Booth's troubles were now almost over. He and Amelia returned home with Dr. Harrison to confront Elizabeth with their knowledge of her scheme. Elizabeth fled to France, where Amelia, relenting, sent her an annual allowance. Booth's adventures had finally taught him not to gamble, and he settled down with his faithful Amelia to a quiet and prosperous life blessed with many children and the invaluable friendship of Dr. Harrison and the Atkinsons.

Critical Evaluation:

As Henry Fielding stated in his introduction to *The History of Amelia*, he satirized nobody in the novel. Amelia, the long-suffering wife of every generation, is charming and attractive. The foibles of her husband still ring true. Dr. Harrison is a man each reader would like to know. Some of the interest of the novel lies in Fielding's accurate presentation of prison life and the courts. Having been a magistrate for many years, he was able to present these scenes in a most modern and realistic way, for aside from presenting the virtuous character of Amelia, Fielding wanted his novel to interest people in prison and legal reform. Although the novel lacks the extravagant humor of his earlier novels, the plot presents many amusing characters and complex situations.

Amelia was intended to appeal to a psychological and social awareness rather than to an intellectual consciousness. Between the publication of *Tom Jones* and *Amelia*, the nature of Fielding's moral feelings deepened and with it the means and techniques by which he expressed his thoughts concerning his intensified ethical purposes. Impressed by the social problems he encountered daily in the world around him, he adopted a reformist spirit and felt an immediate necessity to promote virtue and to expose the evils that infected England. He abandoned his satirical comic mode and all of its traits such as impartiality, restraint, mockery, irony, and aesthetic distance. He adopted a serious, sentimental, and almost consciously middle-class tone.

The characters in *Amelia* give strong indications of Fielding's intensified moral purposes. They are more fiery, vehement, and immediate embodiments of his beliefs and concern than the figures of his earlier works. Abandoning the aesthetic distance between himself and his characters, he seems, in *Amelia*, to live and act directly in them. This results in a new kind of immediacy and closeness between the novel's characters and the writer's psychological concerns. The cost of this immediacy is the rejection of almost all formal conventions of characterization. The description of the heroine is typical. On a number of occasions, she is described by the emotions which are reflected in her face or by her physical reactions to situations which bring pain or joy; but in contrast to Fielding's elaborate descriptions of the beauty of the heroines of his earlier works, the beauty of Amelia is never delineated. Amelia's beauty in Fielding's eyes and in those of the reader is embodied in the qualities she represents. The same might be said for the other characters in the novel. Fielding is more concerned with the moral makeup of each one than in their physical appearance.

In *Amelia*, the author does not segregate the reader and the characters. Each character reveals himself to the reader through his own words and deeds. This technique causes the characters to appear as individuals rather than types.

The central theme of Fielding's portrait of a marriage concerns not so much the issue of adultery as it does the tragic irony of the marital distrust that accompanies it. Although Booth's infidelity with Miss Matthews strains the marriage and seems disgusting when contrasted with Amelia's steadfast loyalty, that is not what almost wrecks the marriage. Amelia, of course, knew about it before Booth made his confession and had forgiven him for it. The marriage is almost undone because Booth, throughout most of the novel, cannot bring himself to confess his adultery because of fear and pride. He does not trust in his wife's understanding and love for him. Amelia, who is beset almost from the beginning of her marriage by amorous advances, fails to confide to her husband the real motive behind James's pretense of friendship, because she fears Booth will lose his temper and attack James. Man and wife, therefore, work unconsciously to the detriment of their marriage because they will not trust in each other totally.

In *Amelia*, the reader cares more about the heroine, but the action turns on Booth. It is on the adequacy or inadequacy of Booth that the novel succeeds or fails for the reader. Amelia is the stable character. Booth constantly poses the problems of marriage, while she endures and solves them.

Booth's ordeal reflects Fielding's own increasing despair with social conditions. The grim social picture of this novel is Fielding's solemn warning that society may destroy itself on the larger plane, as it very nearly destroys the Booths on the smaller plane. The placement of a woman of Amelia's moral character within a society that preys upon her, effectively points up the evils of that society in relation to the constant moral Christianity of the heroine. It is Fielding's most emphatic statement of Christian morality through the treatment of the subject within marriage. The loss of faith in individual morality, as portrayed in this novel through the assaults on Amelia's virtue and the setbacks suffered by Booth, is easily transferred from the plane of individuals to reflect criticism of society as a whole.

Amelia was published to much rancor and ridicule on the part of the majority of the critics. This book unfortunately lent itself to ridicule more readily than any other Fielding wrote. The characters were reviled as being low and the situations as being too sordid. Enemies gleefully pounced on Fielding's oversight in failing to mend his heroine's broken nose. Earlier victims of Fielding's satire, notably Samuel Richardson, author of *Pamela*, were gleeful over the adverse reception of this novel and joined in denouncing it.

In spite of the early critical reaction, the success of the novel with the modern reader depends on a willingness to take it for what it is, a serious denunciation, as Fielding himself said, "of glaring evils of the age."

ANNA OF THE FIVE TOWNS

Type of work: Novel
Author: Arnold Bennett (1867–1931)
Type of plot: Domestic realism
Time of plot: Late nineteenth century
Locale: Rural England
First published: 1902

Principal characters:
EPHRAIM TELLWRIGHT, a miser
ANNA, his older daughter
AGNES, his younger daughter
HENRY MYNORS, Anna's suitor
WILLIE PRICE, a man in love with Anna
BEATRICE SUTTON, Anna's friend

The Story:

Ephraim Tellwright was a miser, one of the wealthiest men in any of the Five Towns, a group of separate villages joined by a single road. He was a former preacher, concerned more with getting congregations in sound financial shape than with the souls of his parishioners. Although he had made money from rentals and foreclosures in addition to marrying money, he lived in the most frugal way possible and gave his two daughters nothing but the barest essentials. Both of his wives had died, the first giving him his daughter Anna and the second producing Agnes before her death. Mr. Tellwright was usually amiable. As long as his meals were on time, no money was wasted, and the house was never left alone and unguarded, he paid little attention to his daughters.

Anna loved her father even though she could never feel close to him. Agnes, much younger, followed her sister's lead. The two girls were especially close, since their father ignored them most of the time.

On Anna's twenty-first birthday, her father called her into his office and told her that she would that day inherit almost fifty thousand pounds from her mother's estate. He had invested the original sum wisely until it had grown to a fortune. Anna, who had never owned one pound to call her own, could not comprehend an amount so large. Accustomed to letting her father handle all business affairs, she willingly gave him control of her fortune. The income from the stocks and rentals was deposited in the bank in her name, but she gave her father her checkbook and signed only when she was instructed to do so. The money made little difference in Anna's life; it simply lay in the bank until her father told her to invest it.

One result of the money, however, created unhappiness for Anna. Among her properties was a run-down factory owned by Titus Price. Because Price was continually behind in his rent, Mr. Tellwright forced Anna to keep demanding something on account. Knowing that the property would never rent to anyone else, the old miser never put Price out but kept hounding him for as much as the man could pay. Anna usually had to deal with Willie Price, the son, and she always left the interview with a feeling of guilt. Although the sight of Willie's embarrassment left her unhappy, she always demanded his money, because she was afraid to face her father without it.

A teacher in the Sunday school in which Anna taught was Henry Mynors, a pillar in the church and a successful man in the community. Anna, attracted to him, tried to join in his religious fervor, but she could not quite bring herself to repent and to accept God publicly. She felt repentance to be a private matter, not one to be dragged out in meetings. Henry was patient with her, however. When the townspeople said that he was interested mainly in her money, Anna refused to believe the gossip. Henry began to call on her occasionally, combining his courtship with business with Mr. Tellwright. The miser persuaded Anna to invest some of her money in Henry's business after first arranging for a large share of the profits and a high interest. Anna, caring little for the money, liked to be associated with Henry and spent much time with him.

After Anna had received her fortune, she was invited for the first time to the house of Mrs. Sutton, the town's social leader. Mrs. Sutton's daughter Beatrice and Anna became friends. Rumors spread that Beatrice and Henry Mynors had once been engaged. The Suttons took Anna and Henry to the Isle of Man on a vacation, and Anna thought there could never again be such luxurious living. It had been necessary for her to take ten pounds of her own money without her father's knowledge in order to get clothes for the trip, and the miser had berated her viciously when she told him what she had done. Her time spent with Henry and the Suttons, however, helped her forget his anger. When the vacation was marred by Beatrice's serious illness, Anna won a permanent place in the Suttons' affection by her unselfish and competent nursing.

After Beatrice had recovered, Anna and Henry returned home. Before they left the island, Henry proposed to Anna, and she accepted. Later her father gave his consent, because Henry knew the value of money. Young Agnes was enchanted by the romantic aspects of the courtship, and Anna was happy in her quiet love for Henry. The joy of her engagement, however, was soon clouded by the news that old Mr. Price, Willie's father, had hanged himself. Anna felt that she and her father were to blame, because they had hounded him for his rent. Henry assured her that Mr. Price was in debt to many people and that she need not feel guilty. Nevertheless, Anna worried a great deal about the suicide and about Willie.

Later, Willie confessed to her that a bank note he had given in payment had been forged. The confession seemed to reduce Willie to nothing. Anna, realizing that he and his father had been driven to desperation, tried to protect Willie and his father's reputation by taking the forged note from her father's office. When she told Mr. Tellwright that she had burned the note, he was so furious with her that he never forgave her.

Because Willie was planning to make a fresh start in Australia, Henry arranged to buy the Price house for them to live in after he and Anna were married. Although Anna was sure she could never be happy in a house the miserable Prices had owned, she was docile and let Henry make all the arrangements.

When Anna told her father that she needed one hundred pounds to pay for her linens and her wedding clothes, Mr. Tellwright denounced her for a spendthrift. Handing over the checkbook, he told her not to bother him again about her money. Henry, pleased at the turn of events, was full of plans for the use of Anna's fortune. Then there was more bad news about Mr. Price. Before his death, he had defrauded the church of fifty pounds. Anna tried to cover up for him so that Willie would never know, but someone told the secret. Willie, ready to leave for Australia, heard of the theft. When he told Anna good-bye, he was like a whipped child. As Anna looked into his eyes for the last time, she knew suddenly that he loved her and that she loved him. She let him go, however, because she felt bound by her promise to Henry. She had been dutiful all her life; it was too late for her to change.

Willie was never heard from again. Had anyone in Five Towns happened to look into an abandoned pitshaft, the mystery of Willie would have been solved. The meek lad had found his only way to peace.

Critical Evaluation:

Anna of the Five Towns was the first of Arnold Bennett's novels dealing with the pottery region of the Five Towns. It is primarily a novel of character, but Anna changes so slightly that the reader is hardly aware of any development in her attitudes or actions. In fact, her tragedy occurs because she cannot change her original nature. In spite of certain weaknesses, however, the story has touches of Bennett's great writing skill and human insight and is worth the time of all Bennett lovers. The novel is also Bennett's most detailed study of the repressive effects of Wesleyanism, which affects all his characters in one degree or another.

The story of Anna Tellwright is different from the novels dealing with the Five Towns following it. *The Old Wives' Tale* and *The Clayhanger Tril-*

ogy are epic in nature, panoramic studies of life crammed with social and natural detail. It became Bennett's forte to continue in the vein of Trollope and provide the plenitude of the real English world. He advanced on Trollope's easygoing Realism by introducing his own brand of Naturalism. Life was brought into sharp focus by the "scientific eye."

Anna's pliability and deference to her miser-father are treated with conpassion rather than detached judgment. In Bennett's later work, his compassion for his characters tends to give way to the often belittling revelations of the "scientific eye." Even at her weakest moment, however, Anna is ennobled by the tragic dimension of her situation; although she realizes that she loves Willie Price, she remains true to her promise to marry Mynors. Always a child of duty, Anna cannot suddenly become a reckless and passionate girl. She cannot run away with Willie and remain herself. Hers is a tested identity, fired in the realization that renunciation is her truth.

Bennett persuades the reader to believe in the moral strength of Anna by balancing her innocence and humility with powerful examples of her honesty and courage. Despite her commitment to Mynors and her loyalty to her father, she cannot deny her deepest convictions and is unable to accept public salvation at the Methodist revival. Her most tender feelings for Willie and his father give her the fortitude to stand up to her enraged father in the matter of the forged note. Anna, finally, is *of* the Five Towns, but she is not *with* them in soul.

ANNALS OF THE PARISH
Or, The Chronicle of Dalmailing

Type of work: Novel
Author: John Galt (1779–1839)
Type of plot: Social chronicle
Time of plot: 1760–1810
Locale: Scotland
First published: 1821

Principal characters:
> THE REVEREND MICAH BALWHIDDER, the minister at
> Dalmailing
> LORD EAGLESHAM, the minister's friend and patron
> BETTY LANSHAW, the first Mrs. Balwhidder
> LIZY KIBBOCK, the second Mrs. Balwhidder
> MRS. NUGENT, a widow and the third Mrs. Balwhidder
> MR. CAYENNE, an industrialist
> LADY MACADAM, a high-spirited old lady in the parish

The Story:

As a young man just out of divinity school at the University of Glasgow and recently accepted for the ministry, the Reverend Micah Balwhidder was appointed to the charge of the established Presbyterian Church in the village of Dalmailing in western Scotland. Because he had been appointed by a great landowner, without their approval, the people of Dalmailing tried to prevent Mr. Balwhidder from taking his post. On the Sunday Mr. Balwhidder was installed, the officiating ministers had to enter the church through a window, because the door had been nailed fast. Nor did they try to go to the church without a guard of soldiers.

Immediately after being installed, Mr. Balwhidder began a series of visits to his parishioners, as he believed a good Calvinistic clergyman should do. He was rebuffed at door after door, until Thomas Thorl, the minister's most outspoken opponent, relented and accepted him. The rest of the parish followed within a matter of weeks. Soon after the excitement died down, Mr. Balwhidder married his first wife Betty Lanshaw, a cousin with whom he had grown up; he believed strongly that a minister should be married to accomplish his best work.

During the first few years of his ministry in the 1760's, Mr. Balwhidder fought earnestly against two habits among his parishioners, smuggling and drinking. He felt that both were sinful. In the end, however, he became reconciled to tea as a beverage, for he thought it better for his people to drink that instead of spirituous liquors. His main objection to smuggling was that it encouraged lawlessness among his people and resulted in the appearance of illegitimate children.

One of the chief problems in Dalmailing, so far as the minister was concerned, was the Malcolm family, composed of Mrs. Malcolm, a widow, and her five children. The minister always tried to help them succeed, for they were hardworking folk who had known better days. The first ray of success for them came when Charles Malcolm was made an officer in the merchant marine, an event which gladdened Mr. Balwhidder's heart. In that same year, the first Mrs. Balwhidder died. Her death saddened the whole parish, for everyone had come to love her.

In the following year, 1764, Mr. Balwhidder tried to write a doctrinal book. He found, however, that he had too much to do to keep his house and servants in order and decided to look about for another wife; this decision was none too soon, for one of his maidservants was pregnant. Some of the village gossips blamed the minister, although the actual father admitted his part in the affair. As soon as a year and a day had passed after his first wife's death, Mr. Balwhidder married Lizy Kibbock, the daughter of a very successful farmer in the parish.

The second Mrs. Balwhidder immediately set out to augment her husband's stipend. She purchased cattle and hogs and set up a regular dairy. Within a year, she had sufficient income from her projects so that the minister's pay could be put into the bank. Her husband approved heartily of her industry, not only because he himself was made comfortable but because the industry of his wife encouraged greater efforts on the part of other women in the parish. In that year, three coal mines were opened in the parish, bringing new prosperity to the people.

In 1767, a great event occurred in the village's history. Lord Eaglesham, after being thrown in a muddy road that ran through the village, resolved to have a fine highway built to prevent a second occurrence. The new road made transportation much easier for the villagers. The event also caused the lord and Mr. Balwhidder to become friends, for at the time of the accident the clergyman had lent Lord Eaglesham some dry clothes. Through the nobleman's influence, Mr. Balwhidder was on many occasions able to help the people of his village.

Scandal threatened the pulpit in 1772, when a visitor from another parish, Mr. Heckletext, was invited to speak. Shortly after his sermon, the church session learned that he was the father of an illegitimate child by one of the village girls. It was a bitter lesson for Mr. Balwhidder, who resolved never again to permit a man to speak from his pulpit until he had thoroughly investigated the stranger's habits and character.

The 1770's were disturbing times for the minister of Dalmailing. Mr. Balwhidder was a peace-loving man who hated to see his young parishioners enlist to fight against the rebellious colonists in America. He especially hated to hear of the battles in which some of them were killed. The greatest blow given him by the war was the death of the widow Malcolm's son, who died a hero in a naval battle with the French. Mr. Balwhidder, who looked upon the fatherless Malcolm family as his charge, grieved as much as if the boy had been his own son.

He was also in difficulties with Lady MacAdam, an older woman who had been at court in England and France in her youth. A spirited woman who wanted to have a good time in life and to dictate to other people, she was distraught when she learned that her son, an officer in the Royal Scots regiment, was in love with the oldest Malcolm girl. She mistreated the girl shamefully, refusing even to listen to the minister's remonstrations. Using his own judgment, he finally had to marry the young people against her wishes. She soon became reconciled, however, after the marriage had taken place.

After the close of the American Revolution, a loyal American who had returned to Britain settled in Dalmailing. This man, Mr. Cayenne, had a temper as fiery as his name. The weaving mill he set up near the village brought prosperity to the parish, but it also brought troubles. During the 1790's, the weavers who settled there were in favor of the French Revolution, while Mr. Balwhidder and his more conservative parishioners were all opposed to it. Aside from their political differences, the weavers also belonged to different faiths, a fact which gave the minister grave concern, for he disliked any other church to set itself up as long as the Presbyterian Church was the official church of the land. He fought a lengthy but losing battle against churches which preached other doctrines than his own. It was the one problem which he felt he could not solve, for the tide of history was against him.

In 1796, Mr. Balwhidder again became a widower. Still of the opinion that to serve his people best he ought to be a married man, he took another wife a year later. His third wife was Mrs. Nugent, a widow of good reputation.

As the years passed, the minister's two children, a son and a daughter, grew up and were married. Finally, in 1810, the church authorities decided that Mr. Balwhidder, who had served his parish for fifty years, should have some help; but he had become so deaf and so forgetful that he himself decided to retire. He preached a farewell sermon to his crowded church and then began to write into a book the annals of the parish he had served so long.

Critical Evaluation:

John Galt was important to his own time both as a settler in Canada and as a novelist who presented Scottish life in fiction. As both a novelist and a leader in the Canada Company, he has, however, been largely forgotten. In the field of fiction Galt was so far overshadowed by Sir Walter

Scott in his own time that he never became widely known outside of Great Britain. A Scot himself, Galt wrote in the *Annals of the Parish: Or, The Chronicle of Dalmailing* about the Scotland he and his parents had known, and he wrote lovingly. His humane feeling and the love he gave to his own country can be marked on almost every page he wrote. In this novel, the strongest and most sympathetically portrayed character is of the Scottish Presbyterian clergyman of strict Calvinist persuasion. Hardly less important are the descriptions of the new class of industrialists.

In the tradition of Daniel Defoe's *Moll Flanders*, Galt's *Annals of the Parish* is a fictional autobiography, chronological in form. It is successful in conveying a diarist's immediate experience of the kind of daily living that has a way of becoming social and cultural history. Some critics think it blasphemous to juxtapose Defoe's story of a thief and bawd with Galt's account of a pious clergyman, but both works share a common psychological impulse: the need of the central protagonist to combine factual objectivity, confessional in spirit, with self-justification.

Galt noted that his desire to write *Annals of the Parish* was sparked by Goldsmith's *The Vicar of Wakefield*. He wanted to do for Scotland what that book had done for England: to record the life of a rural. In the early planning stages of his book, Galt almost switched from minister to schoolmaster because the latter promised to be a better vehicle for transmitting rural values but finally stuck to his original concept and began writing in the summer of 1813. However, publishers discouraged him from continuing with the project, and he did not actually finish the book until 1820 when there was renewed interest in Scottish themes.

With the appearance of Micah Balwhidder, the English literary public finally had the Scottish answer to Dr. Primrose—not to mention Pastor Balwhidder's similarity to other memorable English fictional characters like Parson Adams, Uncle Toby, and Sir Roger de Coverley. Like them, Balwhidder combined naïveté, ingenuousness, and occasional absurdity with common sense, tact, and kindness.

In addition to the memorable creation of Balwhidder, Galt's book is known as a rich repository of Scottish historical data: agricultural reform, industrialization, domestic economy, rural education, church affairs, and theological fashions. Modern critics find it a fault that Galt filters all the data through Balwhidder's limited intellect in such a way that readers are not always sure how reliable the information is.

THE ANTIQUARY

Type of work: Novel
Author: Sir Walter Scott (1771–1832)
Type of plot: Domestic romance
Time of plot: Late eighteenth century
Locale: Scotland
First published: 1816

Principal characters:
JONATHAN OLDBUCK OF MONKBARNS, the antiquary
LOVEL, an illegitimate son of unknown parents
SIR ARTHUR WARDOUR, a baronet and Oldbuck's friend
MISS ISABELLA WARDOUR, his daughter
EDIE OCHILTREE, a beggar
HECTOR M'INTYRE, Oldbuck's nephew
THE EARL OF GLENALLAN, the present head of a powerful
    family
DOUSTERSWIVEL, a magician

The Story:

When old Jonathan Oldbuck of Monkbarns first met young Lovel, he was impressed by the young man's good manners and conduct; but he was also mystified by the little he could learn of Lovel's past. It was obvious that Lovel was not the boy's real name and that there was something in his history of which he was ashamed.

From his good friend Sir Arthur Wardour, Oldbuck at last learned something of Lovel's history. The young man was the illegitimate son of unknown parents. Although a benefactor had settled a large estate on him, he lived in solitude and disgrace because of his questionable ancestry. To make matters worse, he was in love with Sir Arthur's daughter, Isabella. Although the girl loved him, she would not accept him because she knew her father would not permit an alliance with a man of unknown and illegitimate origins. Even after Lovel had saved her life and that of her father when they were trapped by the tides, she gave him no more than the thanks due him for his bravery.

Sir Arthur was in serious financial straits, in debt to dozens of tradesmen and friends, among them Oldbuck. In order to restore his fortune, he had fallen into a plot prepared by Dousterswivel, an evil magician who had promised his aid in finding valuable minerals on Sir Arthur's property. Sir Arthur, forced to put up money before Dousterswivel would work his magic, had already borrowed one hundred pounds from Oldbuck, who accurately suspected that Dousterswivel was a crook.

Before the magician could attempt to work his magic, Oldbuck's nephew, Captain Hector M'Intyre, came home for a visit. A hotheaded young man, he accused Lovel of lying about the little he told of his past. Hector challenged Lovel to a duel, and although Lovel did everything he could to prevent it, the duel was fought. Lovel wounded Hector fatally, or so it appeared, and was forced to flee the country on a boat provided by a friend. Hector did recover, but Lovel did not hear the news until much later. He had been aided in his flight by Edie Ochiltree, a beggar who knew all the secrets of the countryside. While Edie hid Lovel in a cave, they overheard Dousterswivel trying to convince Sir Arthur that he could find buried treasure there if Sir Arthur would put up the necessary money. Edie used that knowledge to good account.

When Sir Arthur asked Oldbuck for another hundred pounds to give to Dousterswivel so that he would get the treasure from the cave, Oldbuck insisted that they go to the cave and dig for the treasure. Although the magician tried to prevent the excursion, Oldbuck would not be denied. Everyone present was completely surprised when, after much digging, old Edie the beggar stuck a pick into the ground and hit a chest. When the chest was opened, the bewildered spectators found a fortune in coin; Sir Arthur was saved from disaster. Edie, in an attempt to pay back Dousterswivel, tricked him into digging for hours for more treasure that Edie said was also buried in the cave. He also arranged with a friend to have a specter appear and frighten the magician.

About the same time there occurred another event which was to have great influence upon Oldbuck, Sir Arthur, and their friends. An old woman in the neighborhood sent for the Earl of Glenallan, head of a wealthy and powerful family. Before she died, the old woman wanted to clear her conscience of a terrible wrong she had done the earl when he was a young man. The earl had been in love with a girl whom his mother hated, primarily because of her family. The earl had secretly married the girl before his mother, in a spiteful attempt to break up the romance, told her son that the girl was his own sister. Because of certain letters and the perjured testimony of servants, including the old woman telling the story, the earl had believed his mother's story. His wife had taken her own life, but before she died, she had given birth to a male child. A servant had whisked the child away, and the old woman did not know whether he had lived or died. The earl, who had lived a life of misery because of the horrible crime he thought he had committed in marrying his own sister, was joyful at the news given him by the old crone, even though he grieved at the useless death of the girl he loved. He told the story to Oldbuck and asked his help in determining whether the child had lived.

While Oldbuck and the Earl of Glenallan were conducting their investigation, news came that the French were about to raid the Scottish coast. Hector, who was now fully recovered from the wound suffered at Lovel's hands, prepared to gather troops and meet Major Neville, an officer in charge of local defense. Lovel had not been heard from since the duel, and there were rumors that he had died at sea. Then old Edie brought the joyful news that the ship carrying Lovel had put in to shore and that all aboard were safe. From his remarks to Oldbuck, the old gentleman learned that the money found in the cave on Sir Arthur's land had been buried there by Lovel and Edie after they had overheard the conversation between Dousterswivel and Sir Arthur. Lovel, hearing of Sir Arthur's financial difficulties, had chosen that way of helping Isabella's father without embarrassing the old gentleman by offering him money outright.

When Major Neville appeared to take charge of the garrison, everyone was amazed to see that he was in reality Lovel. Lovel, or rather Major Neville, brought word that there would be no battle. A watchman had mistaken a bonfire for a signal that the French were coming. As they all stood talking, the Earl of Glenallan noted the young man's marked resemblance to his dead wife. Then the mystery was solved. Through old papers and the words of old servants of the Glenallan family, the earl learned that, without doubt, Lovel was his son. While a baby, the boy had been cared for by the earl's brother and, unknown to the earl, had inherited his uncle's fortune.

Lovel was restored to his rightful place, and within a month, he and Isabella Wardour were married. From that time on, all the friends lived in peace, prosperity, and joy.

Critical Evaluation:

Not one of the most popular of Sir Walter Scott's novels, *The Antiquary* is nevertheless a respected member of the Waverley group and the novel most nearly contemporary to Scott's own time. Although it is a romance, it is also a novel of manners. Scott admitted that, when necessary, he sacrificed the plot in order to describe more clearly the manners of the characters, particularly those of the lower social classes. His characterizations of the Scottish peasants are much more vivid than are those of the upper classes. Scott's touch of magic is evident everywhere in this novel.

This third novel in the Waverley series, published in 1816, met with unprecedented sales. Scott himself remarked that "it has been more fortunate than any of them . . . for six thousand went off in the first six days." It reached a fifth edition in 1818 and was translated during ensuing years into at least seven languages.

In spite of its being a potpourri of Gothic, supernatural escapades among abbey ruins at night, scheming tricks of a charlatan magician, romantic rescues up sheer cliffs from a wild and sudden high tide, the usual genteel and static hero and heroine falling at the end into marriage as well as vast inherited wealth, the novel succeeded for other, more significant reasons.

Its true value is based upon the scenes of village life, the real lower-class people of Scotland, and their colorful dialogue. These scenes embody the wit and pathos of the novel, a sane balance to unreal elements in which the upper-class characters are involved. The links between the two levels of the tale are the antiquary, Jonathan Oldbuck of Monkbarns (who has much of Scott's interests and learning), and the wandering beggar Edie Ochiltree. These two characters move from fishing village and country people back and forth to the nobility and their estates, keeping the book from splitting literally into two different novels.

Scott drew the background of *The Antiquary* from history: religious opposition of Catholics and Covenanters and political conflict between England and France. These issues, however, form only a backdrop and do not enter seriously into the suspense and tension of the novel.

Lively scenes, like that in the Fairport post office when the village gossips speculate about the newly arrived mail, or truly pathetic ones, such as the Mucklebackit family's gathering in their cottage after their son Steenie's drowning, are remarkable because of their vividness. These scenes are the core of the novel: its color and poetry. Perhaps these lower-class characters in their milieu are more alive because Scott apparently drew them from individuals he had known from boyhood and sketched the topography from areas with which he had long been familiar.

The humor of *The Antiquary* ranges from sardonic comment to open slapstick. Although they aid the suspense, even the highly improbable events taking place among the lackluster protagonists cannot dim the prevailing comic atmosphere. In this penetrating and good-humored study of manners, Scott is at his best; he handles the Scots' dialogue with accuracy and spice. His common characters come alive and express themselves simply but with moving emotion.

The reader can ignore the usual contrived plot; action and meaning belong to old Elspeth crooning her eerie ballads, Edie Ochiltree maintaining his pride and religious feeling though merely an "auld" beggar, Maggie haggling with Monkbarns over the price of fish, and Mucklebackit Senior trying to cope with his grief. This is a novel of lower-class manners as Scott declared it to be; as such, it succeeds.

ARCADIA

Type of work: Novel
Author: Sir Philip Sidney (1554–1586)
Type of plot: Pastoral romance
Time of plot: Classical antiquity
Locale: Arcadia, Greece
First published: 1590

Principal characters:

PRINCE PYROCLES (ZELMANE), the son of Evarchus, King of
    Macedon
PRINCE MUSIDORUS (DORUS), Duke of Thessalia, Pyrocles'
    friend, and Evarchus' nephew
BASILIUS, Duke of Arcadia
GYNECIA, his wife
PAMELA, his older daughter
PHILOCLEA, his younger daughter
PHILANAX, an Arcadian general and Basilius' friend
DAMETAS, Basilius' chief herdsman
MISO, his wife
MOPSA, his daughter
EVARCHUS, King of Macedon

The Story:

Basilius was the powerful Duke of Arcadia, a quiet and peaceful province of Greece. He ruled his faithful subjects happily and well. Overcome by an ungovernable curiosity to learn what the future held for him, his wife Gynecia, and his beautiful daughters Pamela and Philoclea, he went to consult the Oracle at Delphos. There he was told that his older daughter, Pamela, would be stolen from him; his younger daughter would engage in an unsuitable love affair; his wife would commit adultery; and a foreign ruler would sit upon his throne—all within a year.

Basilius repeated the prophecy to his friend Philanax, whom he left in charge of the country while he, in an effort to escape the destiny foretold by the Oracle, took his wife and daughters into a secluded part of the country to live for the year. Basilius lived in one of two lodges with his wife and Philoclea; in the other, he put Pamela under the care of Dametas, a rude shepherd of whose honesty Basilius had a high opinion.

Shortly after the duke's retirement, two young princes, Pyrocles and Musidorus, arrived in Arcadia. Reared together in close friendship, these young men of great courage, personal beauty, and integrity had been swept ashore at Lydia after experiencing a shipwreck and many strange adventures as well as performing many daring and honorable acts.

Pyrocles saw a picture of Philoclea, learned of her enforced retirement, and fell in love with her. Determined to see the princess face-to-face, he told Musidorus of his love and of his plan to disguise himself as a chivalric Amazon and to approach Philoclea in woman's guise. For a name, he took that of his lost lady Zelmane.

After a lengthy debate, in which Musidorus attempted to convince his friend of the folly of love, Pyrocles still remained firm in his intention; and the two princes traveled to the place of the duke's retirement with Pyrocles in his disguise as an Amazon. While Musidorus waited in a nearby wood, Pyrocles, now Zelmane, sat down and sang a melancholy song that awakened Dametas, who hastened to the duke's lodge to tell him of a strange woman who had arrived in the vicinity.

Basilius, upon seeing Pyrocles in his disguise, fell in love with the supposed Amazon. His true identity still unsuspected, Basilius was introduced to the duke's family and invited to remain with them for a while. Soon, a young shepherd appeared. He was Musidorus, who had fallen in love with Pamela on sight and assumed a disguise of his own. Musidorus, under the name Dorus, was taken by the chief herdsman as a servant after telling his contrived tale of being sent by a friend to serve Dametas.

Zelmane saved Philoclea from a savage lion, but in doing so, he was discovered to be a man by Gynecia, the duke's wife. She immediately fell in love with him. Dorus, meanwhile, saved Pamela from a bear. Before long, both princesses began to become enamored of the disguised princes.

The Arcadian shepherds, as was their custom, met and exchanged poetic songs for their own entertainment and that of the duke's family and his guests. The songs, often accompanied by dancing, chiefly concerned the gods and the human passions. This occasion only increased the intensity of the tangle of love relationships that had so rapidly developed.

After the pastoral festival, Gynecia and Basilius both declared their love for Zelmane, and Philoclea was puzzled greatly by the strange passion she felt for the person she thought a woman. In the meantime, Dorus pretended to be in love with Mopsa in order to be near Pamela, who in this manner became aware of his affection for her. He also managed to reveal his true station to her by means of subtle stories and poems.

Pyrocles, distressed by the advances of Basilius, revealed his true identity to Philoclea, who at first embraced him joyously but then became ashamed of her sudden show of affection. Gynecia, suspecting this attachment, was overcome with jealousy.

While Gynecia, having sent Philoclea home from a meeting with Pyrocles, was starting to tell the disguised prince of the depth of her love, they were attacked by some roving ruffians. With the aid of some shepherds, Pyrocles, Basilius, and then Dorus drove off the attackers. This was only the prelude to an uprising by the citizens of a nearby Arcadian village, who had become enraged by the duke's seeming unconcern about his country. In an impassioned speech, however, Pyrocles convinced them of their error and stirred in them a renewed loyalty to Basilius. This triumph was celebrated by another pastoral entertainment, largely taken up with a poetic debate between Reason and Passion. Once more, the poems, dances, and stories served to increase the depth of the emotions felt by the royal party.

Dorus then told his friend of his moderate success with Pamela, whom he had urged to flee with him to Thessalia. Pyrocles, sharing Dorus' sorrow over their separation, decided to press his suit of Philoclea and to rid himself of the importunate demands of Basilius and Gynecia. When they renewed their entreaties, Pyrocles, still in his disguise and fearing to deny them outright, gave them hopeful but obscure answers.

Meanwhile, Dorus, having tricked Dametas and his family into leaving the lodge, had escaped with Pamela to a forest on the way to Thessalia. There they were set upon by a band of ruffians.

The false Zelmane, hard pressed by Gynecia's declarations, was forced to pretend a deep passion for her, a situation which so distressed Philoclea that she kept to her room in the lodge in profound sorrow. In order to be free to execute a plan to be alone with Philoclea, Pyrocles moved from the lodge to a dark cave not far away. He then took the duke and his wife aside separately and made an assignation with each at the same time in the cave.

Gynecia, who had dressed like Zelmane, met Basilius in the cave; she was not recognized by her husband. Ashamed of her actions, she embraced him lovingly. Back at the lodge, Pyrocles, now in his own person, crept into Philoclea's room and, after a brief time, won her over and stayed the night.

Dametas, realizing that he had been tricked, began a search for Pamela. Entering the duke's lodge by a secret entrance, he discovered Philoclea and Pyrocles asleep. He left hastily to inform the local citizens of the treachery.

Gynecia, angered at her husband's praise of Zelmane, revealed her identity in the cave. Basilius, ashamed, repented his weakness, pledged renewed love to his wife, and drank a long draught from a cup of a mysterious beverage standing close by. The liquid was a potion, believed by Gynecia to be a love philter, which the duchess had brought to give to Zelmane. After drinking it, Basilius fell to the ground and appeared to die.

After the duke's death was discovered, Philanax and his troop of soldiers imprisoned Gynecia, Pyrocles, and Philoclea.

The rogues who had attacked Dorus and Pamela, the remnant of the rebellious band which had earlier caused much trouble, overwhelmed the lovers and captured them. While in captivity, Musidorus revealed his actual name and rank. A short time later, some of Philanax's soldiers were sent to

search for Pamela and came upon the band and their prisoners. Recognizing the princess, the soldiers returned the entire group to Philanax, who
put the lovers under restraint.

There was now a great turmoil, and many opinions and beliefs were
exchanged as to the real guilt in the death of the duke and the disgrace of
the princesses.

Hearing that Evarchus, King of Macedon, had arrived in Arcadia to visit
the duke, Philanax persuaded him to be the judge in the trial of the five
people involved. Gynecia admitted her guilt and begged to be executed.
Then Evarchus, not recognizing his son and his nephew because they had
been away for such a long time, condemned the two princes to death and
the princesses to milder punishments. Even after learning the true identity
of the young men, Evarchus refused, from a deep sense of justice, to alter
his verdict.

At that point Basilius, who had swallowed only a powerful sleeping potion, awoke. The young lovers and the duchess were promptly forgiven.
Basilius pondered on how accurately the Oracle's prophecy had been fulfilled and how happily events had turned out. The princes and their loves
soon wed and assumed the high stations for which their rank fitted them.

Critical Evaluation:

The study of Sir Philip Sidney's *Arcadia* leads to the consideration of a
number of important biographical, literary, historical, and critical issues. A
difficult work—in all its variants—for the contemporary reader, it nevertheless raises important psychological and moral questions.

A serious man who thought deeply about serious matters, Sidney led a
short, complicated life. He was godson of a king, nephew to four earls,
brother of an earl, uncle to three earls, grandson of a duke, and a special
favorite of the queen and other powerful figures. He was endowed with a
pleasing personality and a fine intellect. He received schooling at Oxford
and on the Continent and was tutored by the remarkable scholar Hubert
Languet. He died, however, in his early thirties with much promise unful-
filled and was mourned by the most influential men and women of his
time.

The connection between Sidney's life and his work, as between the life
and work of any important writer, must remain speculative to a degree, but
some important links can be discerned. Sidney's connections and status
allowed him the freedom to develop his talents. He was influenced by the
medieval courtly love tradition, and this led him to consider, while in the
enviable environment of the court itself, the morality of human emotions,
especially that of love, as a prime human concern. At the same time, his
education permitted him access to the romances of later Greek civilization.
Consequently, he was neither too burdened with official duties to take up

the pen, nor so absorbed in the life of the court as to lose himself in its endless, petty intrigues. In short, the depth of his interests, the breadth of his literary background, the range of his activities as poet, soldier, and statesman, and the vigor of his expression mark him as a sort of exemplary figure of the English literary Renaissance.

Sidney became involved in two literary circles. One that included Edmund Spenser and Edward Dyer met at Leicester House in London during 1579 and 1580. The other group gathered at the home of his sister Mary, the Countess of Pembroke. If the Leicester group were more inclined to the romantic, that which collected at his sister's country estate was neoclassic in orientation, more concerned with the rules of literature than its reach, and more taken with the laws governing its dimensions than with love scenes in faraway lands; but it was at his sister's house (where he retreated after losing favor with the court) and in a climate rather uncongenial for literary romance that Sidney composed *Arcadia*. He wrote it, he said, for the entertainment of his sister. Arcadia, however, is more than mere entertainment.

Before evaluating the worth of *Arcadia*, however, there is a choice of texts to be made. Much scholarly debate over many years has centered on the textual problems of *Arcadia*, but the discussion can be organized around two points: the establishment of the various texts and the value that can be attributed to each.

There are actually three versions of *Arcadia*: the original, called "old" *Arcadia*, probably written in 1580; the "new" *Arcadia*, which is Sidney's incomplete revision of the "old" *Arcadia*; and finally, the last three books of the original "old" *Arcadia* combined with the revised, "new" *Arcadia*. The old *Arcadia*, which Sidney said he intended mainly for his sister and close friends, originally circulated in numerous manuscript copies. One of these copies of the old *Arcadia* was obtained by a London bookseller who wanted to print it. Fulke Greville, later Lord Brooke, Sidney's friend from school days and his biographer, objected to this printing. Greville stated that he had a revised edition—which he did have; but the revision only covered half of *Arcadia*, or two and one half of the five books. So another printer, Ponsanby, published the new *Arcadia* and, a few years later, this new *Arcadia* was joined to the old *Arcadia* and published to form the composite. This composite, which is the best known version of Sidney's *Arcadia*, is the one that was read by Shakespeare, Milton, and Lamb.

It was not until the twentieth century that the old *Arcadia* (known as *The Countess of Pembroke's Arcadia*) emerged from manuscript form to publication. Since then, however, there has been considerable controversy about which is more authentic, which reflects more clearly Sidney's "real" intent. Generally speaking, the old *Arcadia* is a relatively simple and straightforward story of prophecy, turmoil, love, disguise, reversal, and ingenious resolution. The five books of the old *Arcadia* correspond to five acts. There is rising action, complication, and seeming resolution by the end of book 3. Book 4 contains the reversal of fortunes, and book 5 resolves these final and potentially deadly problems to yield a happy ending.

In many ways, the new *Arcadia* (and the composite) are different and more complex versions of the same double-stranded love story. At the same time, however, book 3 has been altered and enlarged almost beyond recognition: new characters have been introduced, characters who play a new and decisive role in the action; new speeches, arguments, debates, and incidents have been carefully inserted into the narrative, so that their effect, and the cumulative effect of all the changes, is more a transformation of the old *Arcadia* than an expansion of it.

There is a great variety of sources in Greek, Roman, Italian, and English literature from which Sidney drew his scenes, plot, ideas, and style. He has also woven together two traditions, the pastoral and the romantic/chivalric. The latter, derived partly from adventures related in later Greek literature and full of intrigues, disguises, and mysteries, appealed greatly to writers of the English Renaissance. Scenes and incidents were taken directly from *Ethiopica* by Heliodorus. There are also characters and incidents from Malory's *Le Morte d'Arthur*, a work filled with tales of chivalrous knights, which no doubt suggested scenes and actions for *Arcadia*.

The contribution of earlier pastoral romances seems to have been largely, though not entirely, structural and organizational. The shape of the romance, its direction and main divisions, were determined by pastoral conventions.

The world of *Arcadia* and of the pastoral is based on the creation of an artificial, rural setting populated by shepherds and shepherdesses. In this setting, it is possible for men and women to establish relationships and to discuss questions that would be impossible in the turmoil of the world as it now exists. The postclassical pastoral writers were especially interested in having characters pursue the topic of love and having them establish more harmonious relations with the other sex and with nature, thus allowing them to move closer to God.

Sidney's *Arcadia* elaborates this pastoral convention and uses that elaboration to discuss ethics, politics, and theology. First, there is the tumultuous world outside Arcadia proper. This external world, including Asia Minor, and the homes of Pyrocles and Musidorus, stands in contrast to Arcadia itself. The second world, contained within the first, is the setting in which the two heroes fall in love. It is a transition between the outside chaos and the retreat within Arcadia that Basilius has chosen. This last and "purest" setting enables the process of love and its development toward perfection to occur.

Though modeled on an elaboration of the pastoral structure, Sidney's intention goes beyond the pastoral. First, there is a great variety of incidents, scenes, imagery, and concrete description ordinarily absent from the pastoral (these images provide the basis for more extensive discussions than are usually found in pastoral works). Second, although the thematic content of *Arcadia* is centered in the Neoplatonic searching for love and the purification of romantic feelings, there are many political, ethical, and philosophical questions considered that are outside the customary range of the pastoral.

Despite Sidney's description of his work as mere entertainment, it clearly has rather large ambitions. As Greville wrote in *The Life of the Renowned Sir Philip Sidney*, the goal of *Arcadia* "was not vanishing pleasure alone, but morall Images and Examples, (as directing threds) to guide every man through the confused *Labyrinth* of his own desires, and life."

ARGENIS

Type of work: Prose romance
Author: John Barclay (1582–1621)
Type of plot: Pseudoclassical heroic allegory
Time of plot: The Hellenistic era
Locale: Sicily and the Western Mediterranean
First published: 1621

Principal characters:

POLIARCHUS, the name assumed by Astioristes, Prince of France

ARGENIS, Princess of Sicily

MELEANDER, King of Sicily and the father of Argenis

ARCHOMBROTUS, the name assumed by Hyempsal, Prince of Mauritania, during his sojourn in Sicily

HYANISBE, Queen of Mauritania

RADIROBANES, King of Sardinia

LYCOGENES, a Sicilian noble and leader of the rebellion against Meleander

ARSIDAS, a Sicilian noble, Governor of Messana, and a friend to Poliarchus

GELANORUS, a French noble sojourning in Sicily in the guise of Poliarchus' servant

SELENISSA, a Sicilian matron and Argenis' nurse and companion

TIMOCLEA, a Sicilian matron, a friend to Poliarchus and, later, Argenis' companion

NICOPOMPUS, a Sicilian courtier-poet of pro-monarchical sentiments

The Story:

Before the Mediterranean world had ever come under the dominance of Rome, a young adventurer from Africa landed on the shores of Sicily and was met by a distraught lady who begged him to assist her friend, who was being attacked by thieves. The young man, who gave his name as Archombrotus, sped to the rescue only to find that his help was not needed: the lady's friend had dispatched the thieves single-handed. The three returned to the lady's house where Archombrotus learned that the lady was Timoclea, a respected Sicilian matron, and that her friend was young Poliarchus, also a stranger to Sicily, who had distinguished himself in the service of King Meleander against a rebel army led by the traitorous noble Lycogenes. Poliarchus, having urged more forceful resistance to the rebellion, had been banished when the overcautious King declared a truce.

Archombrotus learned that Meleander had a beautiful daughter, Argenis; Archombrotus concluded immediately that Poliarchus was in love with her.

While engaged in their discussion, they noticed signal fires blazing on the surrounding hilltops. Timoclea explained that these beacons were fired to warn the people that a traitor was at large. Presently, a servant entered with word that Poliarchus was the one accused of treachery; the "thieves" had been Lycogenes' ambassadors, and the King had interpreted his defense as an attempt to break the truce. Timoclea, loyal to her guest, hid him immediately in a cave on her estate and then sent for his friend Arsidas, the Governor of Messana. Arsidas arrived promptly, and he and Poliarchus' servant, Gelanorus, devised a plan whereby the rumor was spread that Poliarchus had been drowned after a fall from his horse. Arsidas pleaded with Argenis to tell her secretly the truth so that she would not be distracted by false news of Poliarchus' death.

Meanwhile, rustics on Timoclea's estate mistook Archombrotus for Poliarchus, seized him, and carried him off to the King. Meleander, realizing their mistake, took Archombrotus into his council but praised the peasants for their loyalty. At the same time, Arsidas arranged to have Argenis see Poliarchus. As a priestess of Pallas, presiding over the sacrifice to celebrate the truce, she was to insist that the common people be allowed to worship the goddess beforehand, and Poliarchus was to come before her in the dress of a peasant; thus, the lovers were briefly united. Poliarchus then fled with Arsidas to Italy. Argenis, throwing herself into a frenzy, claimed that the goddess would not honor the sacrifice or the truce.

Enraged, Lycogenes resumed the war, and Meleander fled with his train to the fortified seaport of Epercte. On the way, he was almost drowned when his coach, driven by a rebel spy, plunged into the river, but he was saved by Archombrotus, who was thus made secure in his favor.

The war was going badly for the King; Archombrotus convinced him that their only hope lay in the return of the champion Poliarchus. The King sent a precious brooch to Poliarchus as a peace offering; however, spies of Lycogenes poisoned the brooch, and the rebel sent his own messenger with a letter warning Poliarchus that the brooch was fatal. If the King's messenger arrived first, Poliarchus would be dead; if Lycogenes', he would become an enemy of the King—either way, Lycogenes would no longer have to fear him.

Poliarchus and his servant Gelanorus, however, had already left for Sicily. Shipwrecked off the coast, they were rudely hauled aboard a pirate craft. The two routed the pirates and turned the ship over to its rightful owner.

Discovering jewels and letters belonging to Queen Hyanisbe of Mauritania among the pirate treasure, Poliarchus immediately ordered the ship to Mauritania so that he could return the royal property. The Queen was delighted, for the letters concerned the whereabouts of her knight-errant son. She ordered a celebration that would have continued indefinitely had not Poliarchus been anxious to return to his beloved. In spite of his anxiety, however, he was forced to stay when smitten by an attack of the ague. Gelanorus was dispatched with letters in his stead.

Meanwhile, Meleander's situation was becoming untenable at Epercte. When matters seemed hopeless, the tremendous fleet of Radirobanes, King of Sardinia, arrived to help defend the rights of the monarch against rebel upstarts. The combined forces of Meleander and Radirobanes routed the army of Lycogenes, and Archombrotus slew the rebel leader in single combat.

Archombrotus became the King's favorite after the rebellion ended. Having fallen in love with Argenis during the siege and with Poliarchus gone, he thought himself the foremost claimant for her hand, but Radirobanes also announced his claim to the hand of the Princess. Meleander was in a quandary. Archombrotus was his favorite, but both gratitude and the armed fleet in the harbor lent weight to Radirobanes' cause. Meleander solved the problem by leaving the decision up to Argenis. The Sardinian ruler advanced his plea; the Sicilian Princess rebuffed him. Radirobanes then gained the confidence of Argenis' nurse and companion, Selenissa, who in nightly installments told him a story.

This story begins with Lycogenes, who had also demanded Argenis and who had threatened to abduct her after being refused. To forestall his design, Meleander had his daughter, along with Selenissa and certain young ladies of her court, placed in an inaccessible and heavily guarded castle. While they were secluded, a beautiful stranger who gave her name as Theocrine came to Selenissa and begged sanctuary. Admitted to the castle, she shared the chamber of the Princess. When Lycogenes' men stormed the castle, Theocrine seized a sword, and the attackers fled. The supposed Theocrine was in reality Poliarchus, who, having heard of the beauty of Argenis, had used that disguise to be near her. When he begged forgiveness, Argenis immediately fell in love with him. He had then disappeared to return later in Meleander's service. The King, convinced that Theocrine was warlike Pallas, had dedicated his daughter to the service of that beautiful, austere goddess.

Despairing of winning the Princess by fair means, Radirobanes planned to blackmail her into acceptance of his proposal, but Selenissa persuaded him that abduction would be the better course. Argenis, having overheard part of Selenissa's betrayal, feigned an illness that kept her inaccessible, thereby frustrating Radirobanes' plans. Thwarted, Radirobanes returned with his fleet to Sardinia, leaving a letter with Meleander, informing him of the true identity of Theocrine and demanding payment of three hundred talents for his aid. When Meleander confronted his daughter with the information he had received, she denied any improper dealings in the affair. Meleander, only half believing her, demanded that she marry Archombrotus. Seeing the damage she had done, Selenissa killed herself, and Timoclea succeeded her as chief lady of the household.

Meanwhile, Poliarchus, having recovered from his illness, had returned in disguise to Sicily. Seeing no chance of amicable dealings with Meleander, he asked Argenis to delay her marriage to Archombrotus while he found some means to settle the matter. Then he sailed away. Weeks passed and he failed to return. Finally, Argenis sent Arsidas to find him with letters pleading for his return.

Arsidas' ship was wrecked, however, and he was rescued and taken aboard the leading ship of a great war fleet. Gobrias, the captain, received Arsidas hospitably and informed him that the fleet belonged to the King of France, who was preparing to attack Sicily. The King himself was commanding the flagship, which was leading the second half of the fleet.

To entertain his guest, Gobrias told him the strange history of the French ruler, King Astioristes—how his mother had kept his birth a secret so that he would not be murdered in a rebellion that was going on at the time, how he had been reared by foster parents, had proved himself a hero in battle, and had finally been revealed as the true Prince; how he had heard of the beauty of the Sicilian Princess, Argenis, and had sojourned in Sicily under the name of Poliarchus to win her, and how now—as King, the old king having died in his absence—he was sailing to claim her.

Arsidas immediately identified himself as Poliarchus' friend and offered his assistance. Gobrias was delighted, but before the two halves of the fleet could establish a rendezvous, a terrible storm came up, driving each part to a different point on the African coast. The flotilla commanded by the French king found safety in the harbor of Mauritania, and once again Astioristes, the one-time Poliarchus, was entertained by Hyanisbe. His arrival was most fortunate, for Radirobanes was threatening Mauritania. Hyanisbe had sent for her son, Hyempsal, who was at the court of King Meleander in Sicily, but he had not yet returned. When the Sardinian troops arrived, they were repulsed by the French. Poliarchus and Radirobanes met in single combat, and the Sardinian ruler was slain. Disheartened, his followers were routed, but Poliarchus was injured and again confined in Mauritania.

Returning belatedly to his mother's defense, Hyempsal turned out to be Archombrotus. Hyanisbe was dismayed when she found that her son and her protector were enemies; but when she learned the cause of their quarrel, she was relieved and wrote a letter to Meleander that, she promised, would end their difficulties.

While Astioristes was recovering from his wounds, Hyempsal led a successful expedition to Sardinia. The two men then returned to Sicily and presented Hyanisbe's sealed letter to Meleander. The message proved as effective as Hyanisbe had promised. Hyempsal, it was revealed, was the son of Meleander and the King's secret first wife, Hyanisbe's sister. Thus he was both the heir to the Sicilian throne and Argenis' half brother. Since there was now no obstacle to the marriage of Argenis and Astioristes, Meleander gave them his blessing, the wedding took place at once, and an epithalamium was written by the courtier-poet Nicopompus.

Critical Evaluation:

John Barclay, the son of a Scot, was born in France, died in Italy, and wrote in Latin. His last work, *Argenis*, finished only a month before his death, became immediately popular and remained so for two centuries. Seven years after its publication, it had been honored by three translations into English (the first, by Ben Jonson, in 1623, is, unfortunately, not extant), and as late as the nineteenth century it received the high praise of Samuel Taylor Coleridge. Its original popularity was not entirely the result of its artistic merits, however, for it was as satire that it first caught the fancy of readers on both sides of the Channel.

Barclay had already a reputation as a satirist, but in *Argenis* the objects of his attacks are generalized behind a screen of allegory. The story of the love of Poliarchus and Argenis is supposed to represent the wars and intrigues in France before the Concordat under Henry IV. As revealed by the *Clovis*, published in the edition of 1623, Sicily, the scene of the action, stands for France, with Argenis a personified symbol of the throne contested during the religious wars, and Poliarchus and Archombrotus representing different aspects of Henry of Navarre (later Henry IV). Meleander is Henry III; Mauritania is England; Hyanisbe, Elizabeth; and Radirobanes, the rapacious and deceitful Philip of Spain. The whole work is aimed at opponents of the monarchical system.

Although interest in the work as satire lasted only as long as the controversy over the divine right of kings remained a vital issue, *Argenis* was long praised for the grandeur of its expression, the nobility of its theme, the heroic stature of its characters. Only its historical interest remains; it stands with Honoré d'Urfé's *L'Astrée* as an interesting transitional work between the Greek-influenced prose romances of the sixteenth century, on the one hand, and the interminable French romances of La Calprenède and Mademoiselle de Scudéry, on the other.

A literary curiosity, *Argenis* is not truly a novel; Thomas Deloney in *Jack of Newberry* and other works contributed more to the development of prose fiction as a popular art form. Where Deloney looked forward, Barclay looked backward, even to the point of composing his work in the "universal language"—Latin. The 1629 translation by Sir Robert le Grys is graceful and accurate but is now very difficult to obtain. Written in long, carefully constructed sentences, *Argenis* produces an effect of grandeur and majesty seldom, if ever, encountered in modern literature. The story, despite all of the embroidery, is at times exciting, filled with violent action and passions.

Argenis is probably the Scottish satirist's most famous work, although he was known in his day for his *Satyricon*, a severe satire on the Jesuits and modeled on Petronius. The reader of *Argenis* and Barclay's other writings should not look for realistic characterization or plot development. The characters are impetuous and the action often implausible; both are used freely by Barclay to help make his satirical point. The characters dance around one another in elaborate patterns, suggesting at times a baroque opera rather than a piece of realistic fiction. When the tale is romantic, it is *very* romantic; and when it is violent, the violence is extreme. The reader can almost visualize the story as a stage spectacle—the sets, costumes, and elaborate machinery all by Inigo Jones; but this very extravagance makes the work surprisingly enjoyable, providing the reader possesses the patience to persevere with the obscure allusions and the now forgotten political and social satire.

The work is crowded with incident, including storms and shipwrecks, violent battles, and pirate treasure; but the motivation of the characters is not always clear. Fierce anger, friendship, and several varieties of passion all play a part in the complicated, fairy-tale-like plot. Extravagant and amazing, *Argenis* is almost unique in British literature, interesting but possessing only the charm of a museum piece.

THE BACHELORS

Type of work: Novel
Author: Muriel Spark (1918–   )
Type of plot: Social satire
Time of plot: Mid-twentieth century
Locale: London
First published: 1960

Principal characters:

RONALD BRIDGES, the assistant curator at a London museum of graphology and an epileptic

MARTIN BOWLES, a barrister

PATRICK SETON, a spiritualistic medium charged with fraudulent conversion

ALICE DAWES, his pregnant mistress and a diabetic waitress

ELSIE FORREST, her friend

MRS. FREDA FLOWER, a wealthy widow interested in spiritualism

MRS. MARLENE COOPER, the patroness of a spiritualistic group

TIM RAYMOND, her nephew

EWART THORTON, a teacher

WALTER PRETT, an art critic

MATTHEW FINCH, the London correspondent of the *Irish Echo*

DR. MIKE GARLAND, a clairvoyant

FATHER T. W. SOCKETT, a spiritualistic clergyman ordained by Fire and the Holy Ghost

THE HONORABLE FRANCIS ECCLES, a British Council lecturer

MR. FERGUSON, a detective inspector of police

There are times when the novels of Muriel Spark suggest a mildly hallucinated card game in which the dealer declares the trump suit only after the last card has been played and then proceeds to take in all the tricks. This is not to say that she cheats or ignores the rules of the fictional game she is playing; however, she does add to her picture of the world some element of unearthly surprise or presents her people from an odd angle of vision in order to throw an oblique light on the troubled condition of man and, since she is a Christian writer, on his relation to God or to the devil. All of her novels deal in one degree or another with the problem of faith: the grace with which men accept it or the ways by which they try to evade it. The result is an original body of work by Spark which cannot be mistaken for that of anyone else writing today.

Satire is the literary climate in which her lively art appears to flourish best; but satire, touched with fantasy or the supernatural, is always a risky business. It demands, among other things, a sharp wit and a spirited style. The reader must also be sufficiently involved in order to go along with the game of pretense, and the story must make its point if the reader is to accept the satire as an insighted comment on the absurdities of the material world or the mysteries of the soul.

Spark takes her risks deliberately. Her first novel, *The Comforters*, relied for much of its effect on ghostly presences and double identities; in one scene, a character heard the clatter of the author's typewriter at work on the book. *Robinson* brought into congruous relationship such disparate elements as a desert island, a murder, and a spiritual dilemma resolved in a rather bizarre fashion. *Memento Mori*, however, was the novel in which Spark revealed to the fullest the audacity, altogether her own, which promises to become the guiding principle of her fiction. In this book, Death is a disembodied voice on the telephone, calling a group of old people and reminding them that they must die; what this chilling fable offers is a contrast between the selfish, trivial concerns of these people's lives and the inescapable fact of their mortality. *The Ballad of Peckham Rye* brings to the pubs and rooming houses of a London suburb a devil incarnate, if not the devil in person, who provides the people of Peckham with opportunities to display mankind's natural capacity for error and evil. By means of devices such as these, Spark shows a critical and moral imagination at work among observations of the clutter and waste of the contemporary scene.

The Bachelors is more restrained. It contains no open struggle with other-worldly forces, whether of God or of the devil. The only touch of the supernatural comes when a quack spiritualistic medium does, apparently, establish communication with the dead in an episode so briefly presented that it gives little weight to Spark's swiftly paced and crowded narrative. In this novel, her *deus ex machina* is bachelordom, the noncommunity of the unattached, uncommitted male. Here the bachelor's state is viewed as damnation, and for the ten examples she presents, the writer provides an atmosphere of fearful reality. The lodgings in which they live, the pubs they frequent, the stores where they shop, their problems with meals, mothers, and girls—all are images of the private hells of loneliness and trivial self-preoccupation in which each revolves. This vision is one that the more discerning of her bachelors share with their creator. Matthew Finch, who is Irish, Catholic, and plagued by sex, says that one's duty is to marry, to choose between Holy Orders and Holy Matrimony. Anything else, and he speaks from experience, is an unnatural life for a Christian. Ronald Bridges is a graphologist, who is unable to fulfill his desire to become a priest because he is an epileptic. Bridges claims that he is a confirmed bachelor, but at the end of the novel, he experiences a vision of the bachelor's selfish and uneasy life on the fringes of society: 17.1 bachelors to each of London's 38,500 streets, restless, awake, active with their bed partners, or asleep, all over the city.

In this noncommunity, the solitaries try to find substitutes for solidarity and faith. Some, like Ronald Bridges, find another vocation. Others, like Martin Bowles, become social and moral hypocrites. Still others, like Walter Prett, revile the world out of drunken self-pity. A few, like Patrick Seton, prey on human credulity. Most, like Matthew Finch, simply struggle. His predicament is amusing but nonetheless real, because he is trapped between spirit and flesh.

The uses to which Spark puts her social outsiders are crafty and entertaining. Patrick Seton, the fraudulent medium, is charged with converting to his own needs two thousand pounds that Mrs. Freda Flower, a rich widow, had given him for the work of The Wider Community, a spiritualistic group. Mrs. Flower and another patroness of the circle, Mrs. Marlene Cooper, are already rivals for the place of leadership within the group, and the charge against Seton further widens the split. Mrs. Cooper sees in the division an opportunity to direct the Inner Spiral, a secret group within The Wider Community; Mrs. Flower hopes to bring the members under the influence of Dr. Mike Garland, a clairvoyant of notorious reputation, and his friend Father Sockett, another medium. Ronald Bridges becomes involved because he is the friend of Tim Raymond, Mrs. Cooper's nephew, and because as a handwriting expert, he has been asked to testify to the authenticity of a letter forged by Seton. Other complications arise because Martin Bowles, who is also Bridges' friend, is the prosecuting counsel against Seton, and Matthew Finch has fallen deeply in love with Alice Dawes, Seton's pregnant mistress. Through information innocently supplied by Matthew, Elsie Forrest, Alice's friend, is able to steal the letter from Bridges' lodgings. Meanwhile, Garland and Father Sockett are also after the letter for reasons of their own.

Spark handles this complicated material with customary skill and dash. Patrick Seton is convicted of forgery and sentenced to five years. Matthew will marry Alice. Ronald Bridges will continue to suffer the demoniac nightmares of his epileptic seizures. They are his cross, but because of them, he has achieved a kind of wisdom and insight into the need of faith and the grace of compassion. This, the reader senses, is the meaning of Spark's concluding paragraphs, but she is too much an artist to flog a thesis or to point a moral. Her characters are good, foolish, sinister, and kind. They exist larger than life, and are illuminative of life, because they are self-contained in a world where sin and salvation coexist in precarious balance. It is a world where a man must earn the right to share commitment to his fellows or to God. This writer handles serious matters with a light but sure touch.

All Spark's novels create an effect of wild improvisation. Actually, the

opposite is true. They have been carefully planned, cleanly structured, and
lucidly styled. Few writers of the present time have a surer hold on the
comic convention of the English novel, which brings the fantastic and the
real together in a coherent whole.

BARCHESTER TOWERS

Type of work: Novel
Author: Anthony Trollope (1815–1882)
Type of plot: Social satire
Time of plot: Mid-nineteenth century
Locale: "Barchester," an English cathedral town
First published: 1857

Principal characters:

BISHOP PROUDIE, Bishop of Barchester
MRS. PROUDIE, his wife
THE REVEREND OBADIAH SLOPE, his chaplain
THE REVEREND SEPTIMUS HARDING, a member of the
    cathedral chapter
MRS. ELEANOR BOLD, his daughter
DR. GRANTLY, Archdeacon of Barchester
CHARLOTTE STANHOPE, Mrs. Bold's friend
LA SIGNORA MADELINE VESEY NERONI, née STANHOPE,
    Charlotte's sister
ETHELBERT STANHOPE (BERTIE), Charlotte's brother
MR. QUIVERFUL, Mrs. Proudie's candidate for warden of
    Hiram's Hospital
THE REVEREND FRANCIS ARABIN, the vicar of St. Ewold's

The Story:

After the death of Bishop Grantly of Barchester, there was much conjecture as to his successor. Bishop Grantly's son, the Archdeacon, was ambitious for the position, but his hopes were deflated when Dr. Proudie was appointed to the diocese. Bishop Proudie's wife was of Low Church propensities. She was also a woman of extremely aggressive nature, who kept the bishop's chaplain, Obadiah Slope, in constant tow.

On the first Sunday of the new bishop's regime, Mr. Slope was the preacher in the cathedral. His sermon was concerned with the importance of simplicity in the church service and the consequent omission of chanting, intoning, and formal ritual. The cathedral chapter was aghast. For generations, the services in the cathedral had been chanted; the chapter could see no reason for discontinuing the practice. In counsel, it was decreed that Mr. Slope never be permitted to preach from the cathedral pulpit again.

The Reverend Septimus Harding, who had resigned because of conscientious scruples from his position as warden of Hiram's Hospital, now had several reasons to believe that he would be returned to his post, although at a smaller salary than that he had drawn before. Mr. Harding, however, was perturbed when Mr. Slope, actually Mrs. Proudie's mouthpiece, told him that he would be expected to conduct several services a week and also manage some Sunday schools in connection with the asylum. Such duties would make arduous a preferment heretofore very pleasant and leisurely.

Another change of policy was effected in the diocese when the bishop announced, through Mr. Slope, that absentee clergymen should return and help in the administration of the diocese. For years, Dr. Vesey Stanhope had left his duties to his curates while he remained in Italy. Now he was forced to return, bringing with him an ailing wife and three grown children, spinster Charlotte, exotic Signora Madeline Vesey Stanhope Neroni, and ne'er-do-well Ethelbert. Signora Neroni, separated from her husband, was an invalid who passed her days lying on a couch. Bertie had studied art and had been at varying times a Christian, a Mohammedan, and a Jew. He had amassed some sizable debts.

The Proudies held a reception in the bishop's palace soon after their arrival. Signora Neroni, carried in with great ceremony, captured the group's attention. She had a fascinating way with men and succeeded in almost devastating Mr. Slope. Mrs. Proudie disapproved and did her best to keep Mr. Slope and others away from the invalid.

When the living of St. Ewold's became vacant, Dr. Grantly made a trip to Oxford and saw to it that the Reverend Francis Arabin, a High Churchman, received the appointment. With Mrs. Proudie and Mr. Slope advocating Low Church practices, it was necessary to build up the strength of the High Church forces. Mr. Arabin was a bachelor about forty years old. The question arose as to what he would do with the parsonage at St. Ewold's.

Mr. Harding's widowed daughter, Mrs. Eleanor Bold, had a good income and was the mother of a baby boy. Mr. Slope had his eye on her and attempted to interest Mrs. Bold in the work of the Sunday schools. At the same time, he asked Mr. Quiverful of Puddingdale to take over the duties of the hospital. Mr. Quiverful's fourteen children were reasons enough for his being grateful for the opportunity. Mrs. Bold, however, learned how her father felt about the extra duties imposed upon him, and she grew cold toward Mr. Slope. In the end, Mr. Harding decided that he simply could not undertake the new duties at his age, so Mr. Quiverful, a Low Churchman, was granted the preferment, much to Mrs. Proudie's satisfaction.

Mr. Slope was not the only man interested in Mrs. Bold. The Stanhope sisters, realizing that Bertie could never make a living for himself, decided that he should ask Mrs. Bold to be his wife.

Meanwhile, Mr. Slope was losing favor with Mrs. Proudie. She was repulsed that he would throw himself at the feet of Signora Neroni, and his interest in Mr. Harding's daughter, who refused to comply with her wishes, was disgraceful.

The Thornes of Ullathorne were an old and affluent family. One day, they gave a great party. Mrs. Bold, driving to Ullathorne with the

Stanhopes, found herself in the same carriage with Mr. Slope, whom by this time she greatly disliked. Later that day, as she was walking with Mr. Slope, he suddenly put his arm around her and declared his love. She rushed away and told Charlotte Stanhope, who suggested that Bertie should speak to Mr. Slope about his irregularity; but the occasion for this discussion never arose. Bertie himself told Mrs. Bold that his sister Charlotte had urged him to marry Mrs. Bold for her money. Naturally insulted, Mrs. Bold was angered at the entire Stanhope family. That evening, when Dr. Stanhope learned what had happened, he insisted that Bertie go away and earn his own living or starve. Bertie left several days later.

The Dean of Barchester was beyond recovery after a stroke of apoplexy. It was understood that Dr. Grantly would not accept the deanship. Mr. Slope wanted the position, but Mrs. Proudie would not consider him as a candidate. When the dean died, speculation ran high. Mr. Slope felt encouraged by the newspapers, which said that younger men should be admitted to places of influence in the church.

After Bertie had gone, Signora Neroni wrote a note asking Mrs. Bold to come to see her. When Mrs. Bold entered the Stanhope drawing room, Signora Neroni told her that she should marry Mr. Arabin. With calculating generosity, she had decided that he would make a good husband for Mrs. Bold.

Meanwhile, Mr. Slope had been sent off to another diocese, for Mrs. Proudie could no longer bear having him in Barchester. Mr. Arabin, through Oxford influences, was appointed to the deanship—a victory for the High Churchmen. With Mr. Slope gone, the Stanhopes felt safe in returning to Italy.

Miss Thorne asked Mrs. Bold to spend some time at Ullathorne. She also contrived to have Mr. Arabin there. It was inevitable that Mr. Arabin should ask Mrs. Bold to be his wife. Dr. Grantly was satisfied. He had threatened to forbid the hospitality of Plumstead Episcopi to Mrs. Bold if she had become the wife of a Low Churchman. In fact, Dr. Grantly was moved to such generosity that he furnished the deanery and gave wonderful gifts to the entire family, including a cello to his father-in-law, Mr. Harding.

Critical Evaluation:

As a young man, Anthony Trollope, son of a ne'er-do-well barrister of good family, seemed destined to further the decline of the family. An undistinguished student in two distinguished public schools, he had no hopes for university or career. His mother persuaded a family friend to find work for him in the London Post Office where his performance as a clerk was to be rated as "worthless." Indeed, the burdens of the family fell upon his indefatigable mother, who had converted a family business failure in Cincinnati, Ohio, into a literary career with her satiric study *Domestic*

Manners of Americans (1832). Like his mother, the son found his way after a change of scenery. When the Post Office sent him to the south of Ireland to assist in a postal survey, his career in the postal service began to advance, he married happily, and he began to write.

Success as a novelist came when the Post Office sent Trollope to survey southwest England. A midsummer visit to the beautiful cathedral town of Salisbury produced the idea for *The Warden* (1855) and, more importantly, furnished the outlines for a fictional county, Barsetshire, which is as impressive as Hardy's Wessex or Faulkner's Yoknapatawpha. When he returned in *Barchester Towers* to the milieu of *The Warden*, which had been a modest success, he achieved resounding acclaim. Later he was to write four more novels in the series known as the Barsetshire Novels. This series was set in the chiefly agricultural county with its seat of Barchester, a quiet town in the West of England, and was noted for its beautiful cathedral and fine monuments but hardly for its commercial prosperity. Thus at middle age began the career of one of the most prolific of the Victorians and, until his last years, one of the most popular.

In his day, Trollope was admired as a realist. He was delighted with Hawthorne's appraisal that his novels were "just as real as if some giant had hewn a great lump out of the earth and put it under a glass case, with all its inhabitants going about their daily business, and not suspecting that they were being made a show of." Today, Trollope's novels are generally viewed as comic works. Instead of merely being people going about their daily affairs, Trollope's characters are in the grip of a firmly controlled irony.

The irony that Trollope perceives in the affairs of the men of Barchester arises from discrepancies between the ideals they uphold and the means by which they uphold their ideals. A layman with no special knowledge of the Church of England, Trollope vividly depicts the internecine war that breaks out between the party of the new Bishop of Barchester and that of the former bishop's son, Archdeacon Grantly. Both parties intend to preserve the integrity of the Church. However, the Church is vested in buildings, furnishings, livings; and these clergymen fight for power over the appurtenances, the worldly forms of the Church spiritual.

Barchester Towers consists of a number of subplots, all of which are related to the ecclesiastical power struggle. Since buildings, furnishings, and livings are occupied by human beings, the clerics who guard the Church must also dispose of the lives of men. The subplots involve characters who become mere objects in a dispute over power—for example, Mr. Harding and the Quiverfuls in the competition for wardenship of Hiram's Hospital or Eleanor Bold in the rivalry of two clergymen for her hand in marriage. Episodes not directly related to the ecclesiastical battles serve to underscore them—as in the parallel between the rivalry of Mrs. Lookaloft and

Mrs. Greenacre and the absurd ploys of the higher orders that abound in the novel.

The main conflicts of the novel are those that engage the high and the mighty of Barchester. The strength of Trollope's satire lies in his refusal to oversimplify the motives of these worldlings of the Church or to deny them sincerity in their defense of the Church. Even as Slope genuinely believes Grantly and his type to be the enemies of religion, so also does the Archdeacon honestly believe that Slope is the kind who could well ruin the Church of England.

One of Trollope's devices for deflating these militant clerics is to treat their wars in the mock heroic vein. After the first meeting between the Archdeacon and the Proudies, the author declares, "And now, had I the pen of a mighty poet, would I sing in epic verse the noble wrath of the Archdeacon." In time, Mrs. Proudie is ironically likened unto Juno, Medea, even Achilles, while the archdeacon's extravagance in celebrating Eleanor Bold's marriage to his champion, Arabin, is suggestive of the glorious warrior returning from the fields with his spoils.

The reduction of marital glory is furthered by a recurrent analogy with games, underscoring the truth that Barchester's leadership is really concerned with social rather than spiritual or moral issues. Slope's major defeats arise from his indecorous behavior with Madeline Neroni, who is alert to every possible move. Worse, he underestimates his other opponent, Mrs. Proudie, and at the end, he discovers that "Mrs. Proudie had checkmated him."

Human strife is incongruous with the idealized setting of peaceful Barchester, its venerable church and close, its rural villages round about, all endowed with a loveliness suggestive of the age-old pastoral tradition. The cathedral itself seems to judge the folly of its worldly champions. As the battles commence, Archdeacon Grantly looks up to the cathedral towers as if evoking a blessing for his efforts. However genial the comedy played out beneath the Barchester towers, the outcome is not without serious significance; for the ultimate result is the further separation of man from his ideals. In the end, the bishop's wife finds that her "sphere is more extended, more noble, and more suited to her ambition than that of a cathedral city," while the bishop himself "had learnt that his proper sphere of action lay in close contiguity with Mrs. Proudie's wardrobe." As Mr. Slope makes his ignominious final departure from the city, "he gave no longing lingering look after the cathedral towers." As for the Archdeacon, it is sufficient for him to "walk down the High Street of Barchester without feeling that those who see him are comparing his claims with those of Mr. Slope."

Despite the futility of its human strivings, *Barchester Towers* is a cheerful novel, not merely because the satire provokes laughter, but also because occasionally, briefly, the real and the ideal meet. Mr. Harding, for example, is too peaceable, too naïve, too reticent to be effective in the world. Nonetheless, when prompted by his dedication to simple justice, Mr. Harding personally introduces Mr. Quiverful to his own former charges at Hiram Hospital. This act, representing the union of his profession and practice, creates a consequence greater than the act would suggest, for it causes the Barchester world to treat Mr. Quiverful with more respect as he assumes his duties.

Quite appropriately, then, Trollope brings the novel to its close with pastoral serenity by offering a word of Mr. Harding, who functions not as a hero and not as a perfect divine but as a good, humble man without guile.

BARNABY RUDGE
A Tale of the Riots of 'Eighty

Type of work: Novel
Author: Charles Dickens (1812–1870)
Type of plot: Historical romance
Time of plot: 1775–1780
Locale: England
First published: 1841

> *Principal characters:*
> EMMA HAREDALE, an heiress
> GEOFFREY HAREDALE, a man in love with Emma
> EDWARD CHESTER, a man in love with Emma
> JOHN CHESTER, his father
> JOHN WILLET, the landlord of the Maypole Inn
> JOE WILLET, his son
> GABRIEL VARDEN, a London locksmith
> DOLLY VARDEN, his daughter
> SIMON TAPPERTIT, Varden's apprentice
> RUDGE, a fugitive from justice
> MRS. RUDGE, his wife
> BARNABY RUDGE, their half-witted son
> LORD GEORGE GORDON, a fanatic
> GASHFORD, his secretary
> HUGH, a hosteler at the Maypole Inn
> DENNIS, the hangman

The Story:

At twilight of a wild, windy day in March, 1775, a small group of men sat in the bar parlor of the Maypole Inn, an ancient hostelry situated in Chigwell parish on the borders of Epping Forest. Two guests in particular engaged the attention of John Willet, the proprietor. One was a well-dressed young gentleman, preoccupied in manner. The other was a traveler who sat huddled in an old riding coat, his hat pulled forward to hide his face from the landlord's curious gaze.

After the young gentleman had left the inn, Joe Willet, the landlord's son, announced that Mr. Edward Chester was walking the twelve miles to London, since his horse had gone lame. He added that Miss Emma Haredale was attending a masquerade in town, and Edward, hoping to see her there, was willing to foot it in spite of the stormy weather.

The name Haredale seemed to interest the stranger as Solomon Daisy, the parish clerk, told the story of a murder, which had shocked the neighborhood twenty-two years before to the day. Mr. Reuben Haredale,

Emma's father, was at that time owner of The Warren, a great house near
the village. One morning, he was found murdered in his bedroom. His
steward, a man named Rudge, and a gardener were missing. Several
months later, Rudge's body, identified by the clothing he had been wearing, was recovered from a pond on the estate. There had been no trace of
the gardener, and the mystery was still unsolved. Since her father's violent
death, Emma Haredale had lived at The Warren with Mr. Geoffrey
Haredale, her bachelor uncle.

The stranger called abruptly for his horse and galloped away, almost
crashing into a chaise driven by Gabriel Varden, the Clerkenwell locksmith. By the light of a lantern, Varden saw the traveler's scarred, scowling
face. The rider warned the locksmith against interfering in his affairs.

On his way back to London that same night, Varden was alarmed by
cries for help. He found Edward Chester lying wounded on the highway.
About the fallen man capered the grotesque figure of Barnaby Rudge, son
of the Rudge who had been Reuben Haredale's steward. The boy had
been born half-witted on the day the murder was discovered. Helpless,
loved, and pitied, he lived on a shabby street nearby with his mother and
his tame, talking raven, Grip. Aided by Barnaby, Varden took the
wounded man to the Rudge house and put him to bed.

The next morning, Varden told the story of his night's adventures to
Dolly, his daughter, and thin-shanked Simon Tappertit, his apprentice.
Dolly, who knew of Emma's affection for Edward Chester, was deeply
concerned.

That night, Varden went to the Rudge house to inquire about Edward,
whom he found greatly improved. While he sat talking with Mrs. Rudge,
whose face clearly revealed the troubles and sorrows of her life, a soft
knocking sounded at the closed shutter. When she opened the door,
Varden saw over her shoulder the livid face and fierce eyes of the horseman he had encountered the night before. The man fled, leaving the locksmith convinced that he was also the highwayman who had attacked young
Chester. Mrs. Rudge, visibly upset by the man's appearance on her doorstep, begged Varden to say nothing about the strange visitor.

John Chester, Edward's father, was a vain, selfish man with great ambitions for his son. Shortly after the mysterious attack, he and Geoffrey
Haredale met by appointment in a private room at the Maypole. Although
the two families had been enemies for years, Chester felt that at last they
had a common interest: both should oppose a match between Emma and
Edward. Chester confessed frankly that he wished his son to marry a Protestant heiress, not the niece of a Catholic country squire. Haredale, resenting Chester's superior airs, promised that he would do his best to change
his niece's feelings toward Edward. The meeting of the two men caused
great interest among the villagers gathered in the bar parlor of the inn.

Haredale, true to his promise, refused to admit Edward to The Warren. When the young man confronted his father to demand an explanation for the agreement between him and Haredale, the older Chester sneered at his son for his sentimental folly and advised him not to let his heart rule his head.

The mysterious stranger came again to Mrs. Rudge's house. When permitted to enter, he demanded food and money. Frightened by the threats of the sinister blackmailer, she and her son moved secretly to a remote country village.

Edward, refusing to obey his father's commands, asked Dolly Varden to carry a letter to Emma, her foster sister. In turn, Emma gave her a message intended for Edward. Hugh, the brutish hosteler at the Maypole, took the letter from her and delivered it to John Chester, who was using every means to keep the lovers apart. Before long, he had involved Mrs. Varden, Simon Tappertit, and John Willet in his schemes.

Joe Willet became resentful when his father, trying to keep Joe from acting as a go-between for the lover's, began to interfere with his son's liberties. Meanwhile, Joe had troubles of his own. He had apprenticed himself to the locksmith in order to be near Dolly, but Mrs. Varden favored Tappertit's suit. Joe, annoyed by what he considered Dolly's fickleness, trounced his rival and declared that he would go off to fight the rebels in America. Dolly forgot that she was a coquette and wept bitterly when she heart of his enlistment.

Five years later, John Willet again presided over his bar parlor on the tempestuous nineteenth of March, the anniversary of Reuben Haredale's murder. Only Solomon Daisy was needed to make the gathering of cronies complete. When he appeared, he had a strange story to tell. In the village churchyard, he had seen a man believed murdered years before. Willet, disturbed by the clerk's story, carried it that same night to Geoffrey Haredale, who asked that the report be kept from his niece.

On the way home, Willet and the hosteler who had accompanied him on his errand were stopped by three horsemen. The travelers were Lord George Gordon, leader of an anti-Catholic crusade; Gashford, his secretary, and John Grueby, a servant. They stayed overnight at the Maypole.

Lord Gordon was a fanatic, his mind a muddle of Queen Besses and Bloody Marys. Gashford, his sly, malevolent helper, was the true organizer of the No-Popery rioters, a rabble of the disaffected and lawless from the London slums. Haredale gained the enmity of Gashford when he publicly revealed the past of Lord Gordon's hypocritical secretary. Sir John Chester, now a baronet, was interested in the Gordon cause. Among Gashford's followers were Tappertit, Hugh from the Maypole, and Dennis, the public hangman.

Barnaby Rudge and his mother journeyed by chance to London on the day the Gordon riots began. Separated from her by a yelling, roaming horde, Barnaby found himself pushed along in a mob led by Hugh and Tappertit. Catholic churches, public buildings, and the homes of prominent Papists were sacked and burned. Later, Barnaby was among those arrested and thrown into Newgate prison.

Gashford, wishing to be revenged on Haredale, sent part of the mob to destroy The Warren. On the way, the rioters, led by Tappertit, Dennis, and Hugh, plundered the Maypole and left the landlord bound and gagged. Haredale was not at home; he had gone to London in an attempt to learn the whereabouts of Barnaby and his mother. Fearing the destination of the mob headed toward Chigwell and alarmed for the safety of his niece and Dolly, her companion, he rode home as fast as he could. Solomon Daisy joined him on the way. Upon their arrival at the Maypole, they unbound Willet and heard his account of a strange face, which had peered through the window a short time before. Haredale and Daisy rode on to The Warren, a heap of smoking ruins. While they stirred among the ashes, they spied a man lurking in the old watchtower. Haredale threw himself upon the skulking figure. His prisoner was Rudge, the double murderer.

Haredale had Rudge locked in Newgate. A few hours later, rioters fired the prison and released the inmates. The mob was led by Hugh, who had learned of Barnaby's imprisonment from a one-armed stranger. The same armless man saved Varden from injury after the locksmith had refused to open the door of the prison. Tappertit and Dennis, meanwhile, had taken Emma and Dolly to a wretched cottage in a London suburb.

In an attempt to take refuge from the mob, Haredale went to the home of a vintner whom he knew, but rioters attacked the house. Escaping through a secret passage, they encountered Edward Chester, just returned from abroad. With him was Joe Willet, who had lost an arm in the American war. Edward and Joe succeeded in taking Haredale and the vintner to a place of safety.

Barnaby, his father, and Hugh, betrayed by Dennis, were captured and sentenced to death. Having learned where the girls were being held, Edward and Joe led a party to rescue them. The riots had been quelled in the city, and Gashford, hoping to save himself, had betrayed Lord Gordon. Dennis was also under arrest. Tappertit, wounded and with his legs crushed, was discovered in the house where Emma and Dolly had been held.

Mrs. Rudge vainly tried to get her husband to repent before he and Dennis died on the scaffold. Hugh, who was Sir John Chester's natural son, met the same end. After much effort, Varden was able to secure the release of innocent, feebleminded Barnaby.

Haredale withdrew all objections to a match between Edward and Emma. He planned to leave England. Before his departure, however, he revisited the ruins of The Warren. There he met Sir John Chester and killed his old enemy in a duel. That night, he fled abroad, and several years later, he died in a religious institution. Gashford survived Lord Gordon and died at last by his own hand.

These grimmer matters, however, were of little concern to Dolly, mistress of the Maypole, or to Joe, the beaming landlord; nor did they disturb the simple happiness of Barnaby Rudge, who lived many years on Maypole Farm, in company with his mother and Grip, his talking raven.

Critical Evaluation:

Barnaby Rudge: A Tale of the Riots of 'Eighty was Charles Dickens' first venture into the field of historical fiction. A novel filled with violence and melodrama, it undoubtedly owes much to Scott's *The Heart of Midlothian*, particularly in those scenes dealing with the historic Gordon riots and the burning of Newgate prison by the infuriated mob. Barnaby Rudge and his talking raven forecast at the beginning of the book the development of a nightmarish plot in which Dickens tried to combine two themes of interest and suspense: private crime and public disorder. As in many of his novels, the book lives chiefly in the lively and original minor characters whom he created. Lord George Gordon, drawn from history, is presented in a more sympathetic light than that in which he was viewed by Parliament and responsible citizens of that nobleman's own day.

Written when the author was already famous and financially successful, *Barnaby Rudge* heralds the period of his greater socially conscious novels, culminating with *Dombey and Son* (1846) and *David Copperfield* (1849). *Barnaby Rudge* treats the same theme of the evil effects of social institutions on children dealt with in *Oliver Twist* and *Nicholas Nickleby* but expands it considerably, concentrating on society's atrocities against the poor and implying that this phenomenon makes crime virtually inevitable. The madness spreading across all levels of society in this novel is reminiscent of Sir Walter Scott's depiction of the Porteous riots in *The Heart of Midlothian*.

The binding force of the novel, both thematically and structurally, is crime. Dickens' own unfortunate experiences from his youth emerge in themes repeated in most of his works: Barnaby's unhappy childhood; an irresponsible father; prisons in need of reform; a child improperly nurtured. Barnaby is not a half-wit by chance; rather, he merely pays the consequences of both his father's and society's malign neglect. These notions are combined with Barnaby's contribution to the riots in which he innocently participates solely for the pleasure of carrying a flag and wearing a bow. Romantic and Gothic views of society are also structurally interwoven by crime.

Many of Dickens' novels, including *Barnaby Rudge*, have been criticized for their melodrama. As Dickens' later attraction to theatrics suggests, melodrama was not a careless result of his plots. Rather, because he was a satirist, Dickens sought to involve his audience emotionally with his characters as a surer way of convincingly exposing social ills. As an example of this satirical technique, *Barnaby Rudge* is both pathetic and successful.

BARRY LYNDON

Type of work: Novel
Author: William Makepeace Thackeray (1811–1863)
Type of plot: Picaresque romance
Time of plot: Eighteenth century
Locale: England, Ireland, and Europe
First published: 1844 (serial), 1852 (book)

Principal characters:
REDMOND BARRY, a braggart and a bully
LADY HONORIA LYNDON, his wife
LORD BULLINGDON, her son

The Story:

Deprived of wealth and estates by relatives, Widow Barry devoted herself to the careful rearing of her son Redmond. Uncle Brady took a liking to the lad and asked the widow for permission to take the child to his ancestral home, Brady Castle. While there, Barry was treated kindly by his uncle. One of his cousins, Mick, persecuted him, however, and Mrs. Brady hated him.

Aggressive by nature, Barry invited animosity; his landless pride in his ancestral heritage led him into repeated neighborhood brawls until he had fought every lad in the area and acquired the reputation of a bully. At age fifteen, he fell in love with twenty-four-year-old Nora Brady, who was in love with Captain John Quinn, an Englishman. Deeply in debt, Uncle Brady hoped that Nora would marry the captain, who had promised to pay some of the old man's debts. Thoroughly unscrupulous and lacking in appreciation for his uncle's kindness, Barry insulted Quinn in a fit of jealousy and wounded him in a duel.

Believing the captain dead, Barry hurriedly set out on the road to Dublin. On the way, he befriended a Mrs. Fitzsimons, the victim of a highway robbery. She took him to her castle where Barry spent some of his own money in a lavish attempt to create a good impression. When he had lost all his money through high living and gambling, Mrs. Fitzsimons and her husband were glad to see him leave.

Barry next took King George's shilling and enlisted for a military expedition in Europe. Boarding the crowded and filthy ship, he learned that Captain Quinn had not died after all but had married Nora Brady; the pistols had been loaded only with tow.

Detesting service in the British army, Barry deserted to the Prussians. At the end of the Seven Years' War, he was garrisoned in Berlin. By that time, he was known as a thorough scoundrel and a quarrelsome bully. Sent by Frederick the Great to spy on the Chevalier Balibari, suspected of being

an Austrian agent, Barry learned that the officer was his own father's
brother, Barry of Ballybarry. This elderly gentleman actually made his way
by gambling, rising and falling in wealth as his luck ran. When the gambler
decided to leave Berlin, Barry, eager to escape from Prussian service, disguised himself and fled to Dresden. There he joined his uncle, who was
high in favor at the Saxon court.

Barry, living like a highborn gentleman, supported himself by operating
a gambling table. At the court of the Duke of X—, he pursued Countess
Ida, one of the wealthiest heiresses in the duchy. Disliking the countess
personally but greatly admiring her fortune, he ruthlessly set about to win
her from her fiancé, the Chevalier De Magny. Gambling with the hapless
man, Barry won from him all he possessed. At last, De Magny agreed to
play for the hand of Countess Ida and lost. Barry's scheme might have succeeded if he had not become involved in a court intrigue. He was forced to
leave the duchy.

Roaming through all the famous cities of Europe, Barry acquired a wide
reputation as a skillful gambler. At Spa, he met Lord Charles and Lady
Honoria Lyndon who held the former Barry lands, and he decided to
marry Lady Lyndon following the death of her sick husband. A year later,
hearing that Lord Charles had died at Castle Lyndon in Ireland, he set out
to woo Lady Honoria. Employing numerous underhanded devices, which
included blackmail, bribery, dueling, and intimidation, Barry forced himself
upon Lady Lyndon, who at first resisted his suit. Barry, however, pursued
the lady relentlessly, bribing her servants, spying on her every move, paying
her homage, and stealing her correspondence. When she fled to London to
escape his persistent attentions, he followed her. At last, he overcame her
aversion and objections, and she agreed to become his wife. Adding her
name to his own, he became Barry Lyndon, Esq.

Although she was haughty and overbearing by nature, Lady Lyndon
soon yielded to the harsh dominance of her husband, who treated her brutally and thwarted her attempts to control her own fortune. After a few
days of marriage, the Lyndons went to Ireland, where he immediately assumed management of the Lyndon estates. Living in high fashion, he spent
money freely in order to establish himself as a gentleman in the community. When Lady Lyndon attempted to protest, he complained of her ill
temper; if she pleaded for affection, he called her a nag. The abuse he
showered upon her was reflected in the way he used her son, Lord
Bullingdon, who, unlike his mother, did not submit meekly to Barry's
malice.

The birth of Bryan Lyndon added to Barry's problems. Since the estate
was entailed upon Lord Bullingdon, young Bryan would have no rights of
inheritance to Lady Lyndon's property. To provide for his son, Barry sold
some of the timber on the estates over the protests of Lord Bullingdon's

guardian. Barry gave the money obtained to his mother who used it to repurchase the old Barry lands, which Barry intended to bequeath to his son. Barry was actively despised in the community, but through foul means and cajolery, he won a seat in Parliament and used his victory to triumph over his enemies.

Barry made no attempt to disguise his contempt and disgust for his wife, who under his profligacy had become petulant. When she rebelled against his conduct, he threatened to remove Bryan from her; she was subdued many times in this manner. Little Bryan was completely spoiled by his father's indulgence. Barry also contrived to rid himself of his stepson, who finally obliged by running off to America to fight against the rebels. Barry's enemies used Lord Bullingdon's flight to slander the Irish upstart, and the young man's legal guardians continued their efforts to curb the wasteful dissipation of Lady Lyndon's wealth, which was dwindling under Barry's administration. In the end, Barry's unpopularity caused him to lose his seat in Parliament.

Heavily in debt, he retired to Castle Lyndon. When Lord Bullingdon was reported killed in America, young Bryan became heir to the estates. Soon afterward, the boy died when thrown from his horse. His death caused Lady Lyndon such anguish that a report spread that she was mad. Barry and his mother, now the mistress of Castle Lyndon, treated Lady Lyndon shabbily. Keeping her virtually a prisoner, spying on her every move, and denying her intercourse with her friends, they almost drove her mad. Under the necessity of signing some papers, she tricked Barry into taking her to London. There her indignant relatives and Lord George Poynings, Lady Lyndon's former suitor, gathered to free the unhappy woman from his custody; Barry was trapped.

Offered the alternative of going to jail as a swindler or of leaving the country with an annuity of three hundred pounds, he chose the latter. Later, he returned secretly to England and nearly succeeded in winning back his weak-willed wife. His attempt was foiled, however, by Lord Bullingdon, who reappeared suddenly after he had been reported dead. Barry was thrown into the Fleet Prison, where he died suffering from delirium tremens.

Critical Evaluation:

Published three years before *Vanity Fair*, *The Luck of Barry Lyndon: A Romance of the Last Century*, as it was titled in serial presentation, is a minor masterpiece of classic comedy, embodying many of the same concerns with sham, materialistic values, and egoism found in William Makepeace Thackeray's later major novel. The twentieth century reader will recognize the antihero type as many of Thackeray's contemporaries did not; for Barry, the appealing rogue, is true to his own code and values, reprehensible as they might seem. Thackeray's autobiography, cast in the vehicle of adult remembrance of some forty years of his life, shows skillful handling of time and imaginative creation of picaresque episodes so that Barry may ingenuously, naïvely, and yet arrogantly reveal his own vices and ambiguous virtues.

Readers who admit to an ambivalent delight in *Vanity Fair*'s picara, Becky Sharp, will recognize the psychology of Barry, a man whose vigor, daring, and self-concern vividly emerge far beyond mere revelations of eighteenth century life. Thackeray is much more than a social historian. · The three-part arrangement of the novel permits the reader to view Barry in adolescence and first love in Ireland, then abroad in English and Prussian military service, gambling in Europe, and the return to England in a marital conquest after his martial and monetary luck. In the tradition of Defoe, Smollett, and Fielding, Thackeray provides a picaro who can reveal the tawdriness of empire and gaming as well as reflect on the kinds of truths by which all people deceive themselves. Readers of Hardy's *Tess of the d'Urbervilles* recognize Barry's longing for place and position—for his rightful aristocratic heritage—distorted though such longing may be, along with his ruthless manipulation of others, especially women, to gain his goal.

In *Barry Lyndon*, Thackeray provides a deftly compressed, imaginative recreation of a past age. Ultimately, however, the "romance" is given far more substance than that offered by the usual historical novel through the skillfully sustained self-revelation of a man true to false values.

THE BEACH OF FALESÁ

Type of work: Novella
Author: Robert Louis Stevenson (1850–1894)
Type of plot: Adventure romance
Time of plot: Nineteenth century
Locale: An island in the South Seas
First published: 1892

> *Principal characters:*
> WILTSHIRE, a trader
> UMA, his wife
> CASE, another trader
> TARLETON, a missionary
> BLACK JACK, Case's confederate
> CAPTAIN RANDALL, Case's friend

The Story:

Wiltshire welcomed his transfer to the trading station at Falesá after spending four years on a Pacific island where he had no white neighbors. Case and old Captain Randall lived in Falesá. Even though they operated a competing store, Wiltshire was grateful for their presence. At first, he was not disturbed by the fates of his two predecessors. One of them, John Adams, had become ill and died after a period of insanity. The other, Vigours, had left suddenly because of his intense fear of Case and Black Jack.

When Wiltshire first met Case and his black colleague, Black Jack, he was pleased with the clean appearance of both and with the educated speech of the white man. Case was very obliging. He had suggested that Wiltshire get a native wife and had pointed out Uma, a shy, slender girl whom Wiltshire agreed to take. Because Wiltshire did not know the native tongue, Case made all the arrangements with the girl and her mother.

The wedding took place in the store operated by Randall, Case, and Black Jack. This store, a small and filthy place with few supplies other than firearms and liquor, was nominally owned by Randall, a sottish old derelict; but Case was obviously in charge. The marriage service was conducted by Black Jack, who pretended to read the service from a novel and said a few obscene words in English, which Uma could not understand. Case prepared a document, which stated that they were illegally married. At first sight, Wiltshire had been favorably impressed by Uma, and this impression was deepened by her modest and serious demeanor during the ceremony. His long-standing resolve to avoid serious involvement with a native woman was weakening.

A series of mysterious happenings began on the next day. In the morning, Wiltshire discovered a group of natives who were sitting quietly and staring with sorrowful expressions at his house. The crowd increased during the day and did not disperse until evening. On his first day of business, he had no customers; more surprising, not one curious spectator entered his store. On Sunday, attracted by the singing, he stuck his head in the window of a church. The native pastor, staggering from amazement and fear, pointed his finger at the white man. After a second business day had passed without a single visitor to the store, Wiltshire concluded that he had been tabooed by the natives.

Ostensibly to help his fellow Englishman, Case accompanied Wiltshire to a meeting with five of the chiefs of Falesá. Because Wiltshire was ignorant of the language, Case acted as his spokesman. Afterward, Case alleged that he had not succeeded in getting the chiefs to change their attitude toward Wiltshire. He said that the natives feared Wiltshire because of some unknown superstition, much the same as they had feared Vigours, and would not go near him.

That same day, Wiltshire gained his first insight into the plot that Case was working against him. Uma disclosed that the taboo had been placed on her originally and that it was now put on him because of his marriage. Case had told her that Wiltshire had married with full knowledge of the situation.

Wiltshire also learned that Case, when Uma and her widowed mother had come to Falesá a year before, had shown interest in the two women and had given them assistance. A native chief had proposed marriage to Uma, but quite unaccountably, he had deserted her. Just as unaccountably, the two women found themselves ostracized. Case, who continued to see the women in the evening, had proposed to Uma, but she had rejected his offer.

More information on the situation in Falesá came from Tarleton, a missionary. The missionary, who was on his regular tour of the island, performed a proper marriage service for Uma and Wiltshire at the latter's request. Then he acquainted the trader with some of Case's activities. One of Tarleton's native pastors had fallen under Case's influence and had encouraged the natives to use the sign of the cross to avoid the supposed evil eye of Vigours. To end this practice, Tarleton had hurried to Falesá. He had discovered that many of the villagers were under the subjugation of Case; by working on their superstitions, he had led them to perform diabolic acts, including the burying alive of a white trader. Tarleton had failed in his effort to nullify the influence of Case. An expert at legerdemain, Case had by sleight of hand pretended to snatch a dollar bill from Tarleton's head and had claimed that the missionary was interested only in increasing native contributions.

For about a month after the missionary left, all was quiet in Falesá. Unable to trade with the natives, Wiltshire worked on the copra that Uma's mother owned. Often he went hunting, and he found that in the woods the natives were not reluctant to talk with him. He learned that the eastern end of the island, which was uninhabited and seldom entered, was believed to be occupied by devils. Among many superstitions connected with this area was the belief that Case could travel freely in it because he was under the protection of a powerful devil.

One day, Wiltshire explored this wilderness. Fighting his way through the jungle growth and up a steep hill, he became aware of a weird, moaning sound. Fearfully he advanced and discovered the source of the noise, an aeolian harp suspended from a tree. Finding a well-beaten path, he followed it until he reached an old, tumbledown wall on the top of which was a line of queer, ugly figures, carved and painted, wearing hair and dressed in bright clothes. Noticing that they were newly made, he recalled that Case was a good forger of island curiosities. Nearby, he discovered a cellar. Entering it, he saw the face of a devil in luminous paint on the wall.

Returning from his expedition, he met Case, and unthinkingly mentioned the luminous paint. Case would now want to promptly dispose of Wiltshire, since his secret was now known. When Wiltshire arrived home, Maea, the richest and most powerful chief of Falesá, was there. He and Case were rivals for a girl, and he had decided to hurt Case by turning over his business to Wiltshire. Although he had not believed the stories about Uma that had led to her ostracism, he had, up to this time, played along with Case to further his own ends. Wiltshire explained to Maea the hoax that Case had perpetrated on the natives and told him that if he went into the wilderness the next morning, he would find the devils destroyed.

Wiltshire, equipped with dynamite fishing bombs, returned to the devils' den after dark. He pulled down the idols, placed them on the cellar roof, and prepared his charge. As he was walking toward the harp, he was startled by Uma, who had come to warn him that Case was coming. Hurriedly, he lit the fuse. The explosion scattered the woods with red coals, and one burning image fell close to the place where he and Uma sought to hide themselves. As he rushed to extinguish this light, two shots were fired, the second hitting the mark. His leg smashed, and in severe pain, he yelled out. As Uma ran to help him, she too was hit.

Having lost his gun, Wiltshire grasped his knife and pretended to be dead. After an interval, Case moved toward him and fired another shot, which barely missed. When Case came within reach, Wiltshire grabbed his ankle, threw him down, and stabbed him. After fainting twice, Wiltshire managed to get to Uma, who was badly frightened but not seriously hurt. Shortly after sunrise, Tarleton and a group of natives led by Maea appeared on the scene; they first buried Case and then helped the wounded couple home.

Tarleton set matters straight between the natives and Wiltshire. With

Case dead, Randall and Black Jack left Falesá, and Wiltshire settled down to a profitable business.

Critical Evaluation:

A suspenseful tale of intrigue in the South Seas, *The Beach of Falesá* is distinguished, among Robert Louis Stevenson's works of fiction, for its realism. It pictures unregenerate human nature—the natives with their superstition and gullibility; the traders with their crudeness, treachery, and degradation; the missionaries with their misguided zeal. A memorable feature of the story is the characterization of Wiltshire, a rough, uneducated man, something of a braggart, but withal a man of courage and rudimentary decency.

The apparently casual first-person narrative of *The Beach of Falesá* is written in the flawless, graceful prose of which Stevenson was a master. The colloquialisms that Wiltshire uses are just enough to suggest his character and degree of education (or lack of education), but the descriptions and action are the artful work of one of the finest prose craftsmen in the English language.

The story presents the hypocrisy of Europeans opposed to the simplicity and honesty of the islanders. From the tale's beginning with the fake "marriages," Stevenson establishes this conflict. At the same time, the question of morality and religion (in the person of the missionaries) is raised. The story is compact but dense and rich, suggesting much more than appears on the surface.

Wiltshire's reaction to Uma's story dramatically illustrates the kind of man he is; perhaps even he does not realize how extraordinary a gesture he is making when he destroys the fake marriage certificate and has the traveling missionary perform a legitimate ceremony. Although uncertain about the significance of the situation and the eventual outcome, the reader understands now that Wiltshire is a man of genuine—if rough and ready—integrity.

One of Stevenson's last completed long stories, *The Beach of Falesá* suggests that he was moving into a new realm of serious and symbolic fiction before he died. Not much longer than *The Strange Case of Dr. Jekyll and Mr. Hyde*, the tale penetrates more directly and perhaps more accurately the depths of the human personality. The scenes of the discovery and destruction of the fake devils are both terrifying and rich with meaning. As Wiltshire implies, all men internally nurse these irrational fears, a carryover possibly from childhood, and if men are to be free, they must destroy these devils. *The Beach of Falesá* is far more than an adventure yarn of the South Seas; it suggests some of the same concerns that Joseph Conrad was to investigate in such stories as *Heart of Darkness*.

BEAUCHAMP'S CAREER

Type of work: Novel
Author: George Meredith (1828–1909)
Type of plot: Political romance
Time of plot: Nineteenth century
Locale: England
First published: 1874–1875 (serial), 1876 (book)
> *Principal characters:*
> NEVIL BEAUCHAMP, a young naval officer
> EVERARD ROMFREY, his uncle
> MRS. ROSAMUND CULLING, the Romfrey housekeeper
> RENÉE ROUAILLOUT, née DE CROISNEL, Nevil's beloved
> COLONEL HALKETT, a staunch Tory
> CECELIA HALKETT, his daughter
> DR. SHRAPNEL, a radical
> JENNY DENHAM, his ward

The Story:

There was a diplomatic dispute between England and France with much rattling of swords on both sides. The affair, loudly taken up by the press, so stirred Nevil Beauchamp's national pride that he decided to post a challenge to the French Guard. Uncle Everard Romfrey's housekeeper, Mrs. Rosamund Culling, mailed the letter for Nevil. No reply ever came, and Nevil went off to fight the Russians in the Crimea. Uncle Everard expected his nephew to behave like a true Beauchamp.

Wounded in service, Nevil went to Venice with Roland de Croisnel, a French officer whose life he had saved at the risk of his own. Mrs. Culling also went to Italy. In Venice, Nevil drifted in a gondola with Roland de Croisnel's sister Renée, who was grateful to her brother's rescuer. The flirtation was interrupted by the arrival of the middle-aged Marquis de Rouaillout, intended as a husband for Renée. Nevil asked Renée to marry him, but she refused to disappoint her father by betraying Rouaillout. When Nevil persisted, Roland assured him that Renée did not love him.

The marquis arrived just as Nevil, Roland, Renée, and Mrs. Culling set out for an overnight jaunt in a boat. During the trip, Nevil secured Renée's promise to break her pledge to the marquis. They headed for Trieste, but Renée's phlegmatic consent and Roland's dismal viewpoint dissuaded Nevil from the elopement. They returned to Venice with nothing settled. The next day, Renée married the marquis. Nevil went to sea once more.

Later, in the famous port of Bevisham, Nevil began his campaign as a Liberal candidate for a seat in Parliament. Mrs. Culling followed the young man there and met Miss Denham, ward of Dr. Shrapnel, who seemed to be helping Nevil in his campaign. Mrs. Culling wished that she could influence Nevil to drop his foolish scheme. Uncle Everard scoffed at Nevil's political ambitions, especially because he despised Dr. Shrapnel.

While campaigning for votes, Nevil paid calls on his acquaintances and attended dinners. Colonel and Cecelia Halkett were steadfast Tories. Prompted by Uncle Everard, they tried to talk the young Liberal candidate out of his set course. They were strongly opposed to his views, but when the opposition wrote a rhyme comically depicting Nevil's romantic relationship with Renée, the colonel thought the thrust unfair.

Meeting Lord Palmet, who was secretly in the rival camp, Nevil invited the gentleman to accompany him on his campaign tour. While entangled in political plots from which Cecelia was trying to extricate him, Nevil received a note from Renée, bidding him to come to her at once.

Twice since her marriage Nevil had met Renée, both times in the company of her husband, and Roland had written to him occasionally. In France, Renée told Nevil that she had sent for him only to fulfill a wish to see him once again, a mere caprice. She was in the company of a Count Henri d'Henriel, who wore her glove. The marquis was traveling, and only his sister, Madame d'Auffrey, was staying with Renée. Later, Madame d'Auffrey told Nevil that Renée had wagered her glove to d'Henriel that Nevil would come immediately at her request. A storm had delayed Nevil; the Frenchman had kept the glove.

When Nevil returned from France with a lame leg, his enemies gossiped that he had fought a duel with the marquis. The report was not true, but Nevil did not win the election.

During the campaign, Cecelia Halkett, admiring courage, had fallen in love with him. Uncle Everard pressed his nephew's cause by proposing to Colonel Halkett an alliance between Nevil and Cecelia. Nevil, after promising to meet Colonel Halkett and his daughter, paid a call on Dr. Shrapnel to bid farewell to Jenny Denham, who was leaving for Switzerland. The young girl begged Nevil to look after the doctor.

A letter written by Dr. Shrapnel and filled with advice for the young man fell into Uncle Everard's hands. Indignant at the contents, he went to Dr. Shrapnel and horsewhipped the man who was attempting to undermine Nevil's future with radical theories. Cecelia, fearing that a break between Nevil and his uncle would end the marriage negotiations, tried to convince her father that Nevil was worthy of her. The more Colonel Halkett derided Nevil's political views and disdained the Shrapnel influence, the more Cecelia insisted that Nevil was a man of high honor. She added, however, that she would give him up if she ever learned that his honor was sullied.

Nevil challenged his uncle to give Dr. Shrapnel a personal apology. Trying to assist the injured man in earning his livelihood, Nevil next asked Uncle Everard for money. His request was refused. Penniless, Nevil left his uncle's house, but a short time later, an unexpected inheritance saved him from actual need.

One night, Renée appeared at Nevil's house. Having left her husband and believing in Nevil's courtesy and constancy, she had come to him. Since she had married the marquis to please her father, now dead, she had no other bonds to keep her chained to a cold and sullen husband. Nevil sent immediately for Mrs. Culling and pleaded with Renée that Roland be summoned. Close on Renée's heels came Madame d'Auffrey, who announced that the marquis was in London. When Renée became ill, it was necessary for her family to occupy Nevil's home until her recovery. Nevil, who no longer loved Renée, patched the shattered marriage, and the unhappy wife returned to France.

Cecelia still loved Nevil. In spite of all attempts to dissuade her, she had remained loyal to him; but the new scandal about the marquis shook her faith. She went to Italy with her father. When she returned, she yielded to her father's wishes and became engaged to a young man of stable notions, Mr. Blackburn Tuckham. Nevil's proposal of marriage came too late, and when she refused him, he became ill.

Some time before, Uncle Everard had married Mrs. Culling, who was soon to bear a child. When Nevil became ill, his uncle, in an effort to ease his wife's anxiety, begged Colonel Halkett to let Cecelia marry Nevil in order to hasten the sick man's recovery. Meanwhile, Jenny Denham was Nevil's nurse in Dr. Shrapnel's house.

Nevil's illness brought all of his friends to his bedside as well as his political enemies. In the end, a reconciliation between uncle and nephew was effected when Everard apologized to Dr. Shrapnel. Nevil was persuaded to sail to Italy to recuperate. He insisted that Jenny and the doctor accompany him.

Jenny had nursed Nevil back to health. More than that, she had been steadfast throughout all his difficulties. In love with Jenny, Nevil wanted her to marry him before they set out on their voyage. Until the last moment she refused, hoping that he and Cecelia would become reconciled.

The three went on their cruise. Jenny bore a child along the way. Shortly after their return to England, Nevil, trying to rescue a drowning child, was himself drowned. His career to reform the world was over.

Critical Evaluation:

George Meredith's novels have never attracted as wide an audience as the fiction of his contemporaries—Charles Dickens, William Makepeace Thackeray, and George Eliot—critics in his own day generally ignored Meredith's work. Not until the publication of *The Egoist* in 1879 did the author gain much critical attention or public popularity. Meredith's lack of popularity among the general public has been partially due to his difficult prose style and partially to the inaccessibility of his abstract and philosophical comic vision. His style is an odd mixture of the intellectual and emotional, the analytical and lyrical; his famous epigrams, for example, are often so compact and riddlelike as to elude easy understanding, while his descriptive passages and love scenes are frequently laden with rich images and inspired with great sensitivity. Meredith was primarily a philosopher who pleaded for the classical ideal of the golden mean; his witty comedy was aimed at restoring sanity and balance, at bringing men to their senses by making them laugh at the spectacle of their follies.

Beauchamp's Career appeared only a short time before Meredith published his famous *Essay on Comedy.* The novel, in consequence, bears the stamp of his theorizing, and in it comedy becomes a subtle and complex tool for character portrayal and social criticism, especially in the field of contemporary politics. Frederick Augustus Maxse, political reformer and Meredith's friend, was the original of Beauchamp. Other characteristics of the novel are typical of Meredith's work. There are delicately treated emotional conflicts and skillfully rendered personality differences. The dialogue is good, probably less discursive than in other Meredith novels. The plot is simple, and the satire follows the same pattern. The hero, Beauchamp, is an admirable character, as is Cecelia Halkett. Both are targets for ironic but poetic comedy.

In *Beauchamp's Career*, Meredith brings his rational comic vision to bear in his examination of politics; this novel is political, both on the surface and on the deeper thematic level. On the surface, the plot concerns the political career of Nevil Beauchamp and follows first his experiences in the Crimean War, and later, his campaign as candidate for Bevisham (based on Maxse's campaign in an election at Southampton). On a deeper level, however, *Beauchamp's Career* traces the hero's growth to political awareness through the events in his personal life; Meredith brilliantly dramatizes the inseparable nature of the political and personal in real life.

Nevil begins as a foolish young man, infatuated with hazy romantic notions, who rushes forth to defend English honor against French insolence, and then goes to fight in the Crimea. His first love affair with the French aristocrat Renée results from his naïve and idealistic Romanticism, which retains its hold on him for some time afterwards as seen in his chivalric answer to his old lover's summons during the height of his campaign in Bevisham. In his second love relationship with rich, beautiful, Tory Cecelia Halkett, Nevil becomes much more complexly and realistically involved; both he and Cecelia are forced to deal with the problem of their conflicting ideologies and backgrounds. His last involvement is with Jenny Denham, Dr. Shrapnel's niece. Although Meredith himself was a Radical, he uses the rather absurd figure of the doctor to illustrate the follies to which such a stance, untempered by good sense, can descend. Dr. Shrapnel's niece, however, is both sensitive and sensible, an intellectual woman who, unlike her uncle, blends emotional depth with rational intelligence. Ironically, it is Jenny—not an active person politically—who at last becomes Nevil's permanent partner; and, also ironically, it is shortly after their union and the birth of their child that Nevil dies as a result of an act of humanity, an act at once apolitical and the most intensely political of his career.

THE BELL

Type of work: Novel
Author: Iris Murdoch (1919–   )
Type of plot: Philosophical comedy
Time of plot: Mid-twentieth century
Locale: Imber Court, England
First published: 1958

Principal characters:

> MICHAEL MEADE, the owner of Imber Court and leader of the
> lay religious community
> JAMES TAYPER PACE, an energetic settlement worker
> CATHERINE FAWLEY, a girl about to enter a nunnery
> NICK FAWLEY, her drunken, malicious brother
> PAUL GREENFIELD, an art historian
> DORA GREENFIELD, his restless, unhappy wife
> TOBY GASHE, a young student
> MOTHER CLARE, the abbess of Imber Abbey

Iris Murdoch has the habit of seizing upon her material with a grasp so vigorous and complete that she is capable of an amazing variety of effects—joy, farce, grotesquerie, wit, violence, tenderness—always with shrewd insight into the oddities and frailties of the human animal. The result is that her novels exhibit a kind of thoroughgoingness rare in contemporary fiction, where most writers are satisfied to present only a fragmented view of experience or to achieve a picture of life in one of its familiar but flattish aspects such as social criticism, character painting, psychological analysis, symbolic context, or another of the well-charted courses that the novel has followed in the two-hundred-odd years of its history.

Because she is able to surround a subject rather than approach it, it is safe to say that Murdoch is the only writer among her English contemporaries who could have written a novel as richly detailed, as complex in theme and symbolism, and, in the final analysis, as completely satisfying as *The Bell*. First, the book is remarkable for its weaving in of fourteenth century legend, which brings medievalistic overtones of faith, damnation, and doom to the modern situation. Second, it is a novel of brilliant wit, a work in which the spirit of comedy presides, aloof and impartial, over the efforts of some earnest but misguided souls to find their way to the good life in a world where escape into a William Morris Utopia is no longer possible. Third, *The Bell* is an excellent example of the planned novel; themes and motifs appear early in the story, only to be dropped and later resumed, like the motifs of a fugue, with each development of the plot related by some recurring emotion or observation. Fourth, the novel is a work in which secondary and multiple meanings, reflected in imagery and symbolism, give the story its depth and weight of philosophical and moral seriousness.

If the real qualities of Murdoch's art were not apparent in her earlier novels, the reason was that they seemed, on a superficial level, a form of academic entertainment—in other words, the kind of novel that one might expect from a young woman of intellect and wit who lectured in philosophy at Oxford University. Also, in *Under the Net*, there was a suggestion of Kingsley Amis and John Wain in her picture of a romantic-minded young man who finally comes to commonsense, if rather irreverent, terms with his cultural environment; the end result suggested a blend of English-bred existentialism and social satire. *The Flight from the Enchanter* fared little better. It was read and praised without real appreciation of the paradox it presented in the writer's handling of the problem of evil and the subtlety of her defense of God's ways to man. *The Sandcastle* was the novel that won critical acclaim and public response for Murdoch. A gentler book than its predecessors with fewer effects of the symbolic and the bizarre, it was no less rigorous as a study of the romantic idealist confronted by truth and forced to accept the responsibility it imposes. It is now apparent that through these novels Murdoch was developing her command of humor, symbolism, character insights, and philosophical concept, qualities which in *The Bell* bring her into the front rank of her literary contemporaries.

The central situation of this novel reveals a mixture of the touching and the ridiculous. At Imber Court, a Palladian mansion located across the lake from Imber Abbey, which houses a group of Anglican Benedictine nuns, a group of social and spiritual misfits have set up a community of their own. Their reasons for withdrawal from the world are at least valid, a fact recognized by Mother Clare, abbess of the cloister of Anglican nuns, who says that there are many people in the world today who can neither live in it nor out of it. Soul-sick, they find no real home for their disturbed souls. The trouble is that the members of the Imber Court community represent the spiritual ruling caste that can neither take the world nor leave it alone, so that their withdrawal in search of happiness and peace ends in trivial gestures: a belief that to have flowers in one's room would be frivolous and debates on whether to sow seed by hand or to use a mechanical cultivator.

The leader of the ill-assorted group is Michael Meade, an unhappy, desperate man who had studied for the priesthood but whose sense of vocation failed when he discovered in himself a drive toward homosexuality. Other members include James Tayper Pace, a muscular idealist and a believer in the church militant, who had discovered his career and creed while founding boys' settlement houses in the East End slums; Catherine

Fawley, a quiet, brooding girl who is about to become a novitiate in the nunnery; her brother Nick, a middle-aged, neurotic drunk whose emotional background is as ambiguous and disturbed as Meade's; Toby Gashe, an eighteen-year-old innocent whom Pace has brought to Imber Court for a few weeks of rest and meditation before he enters Oxford; a commonplace couple trying to salvage their marriage by contemplation and prayer; Paul Greenfield, a brutal antiquarian and art historian staying at Imber Court while working on the old Abbey records, and his wife Dora, who has joined her husband, whom she fears and hates, after becoming bored with the fun and games of marital infidelity in London.

The moral and physical dissolution of this community becomes involved with the plan to install a new bell at the Abbey. According to legend, in the fourteenth century one of the Imber nuns had taken a lover who one night broke his neck in a fall. Unable to discover the guilty nun through confession, the bishop charged with cloister discipline cursed the Abbey, and its bell had flown from its tower and fallen into the lake. The Imber community believe that the new bell will give spiritual significance to their communal testing. Then the old bell is accidentally discovered by Toby Gashe, and he and Dora plan to substitute it for the new bell that has been ordered, a design that has ridiculous and startling results when the two, in a passionate embrace within the old bell, cause the clapper to give off a clang that arouses the whole community. Their plan to effect a fake miracle, however, is not the act that destroys the community. The true villain is Nick Fawley, who manages to distort Meade's sincere liking for Toby into a more sinister feeling; Meade finds himself once more involved in the same torment that he had suffered years before in his relations with Nick.

Once the process of disintegration begins, it rapidly gains momentum as the characters explode in fits of anger, mystery, and melancholy among themselves. Nick, hoping to bring the community to ridicule, weakens the causeway, and the bell again falls into the lake. His plan to frighten his sister out of her intention to enter the nunnery ends in her attempted suicide and later madness, a state brought on by her inherent neuroticism and her secret love for Meade. The community is dissolved but not before Nick himself has committed suicide. As both destroyer and destroyed, Nick points to the underlying themes of this novel, the corruption of innocence and the burden of ancient guilt symbolized by the bell. The situation, however, has its survivors on the plane of moral perception: Michael Meade, because the experience has taught him how one may best use his moral strength; Dora, because she realizes that her earlier efforts to escape her pompous, sadistic husband were no escape at all and that she must now face up to the failure of her marriage.

The Bell is beautifully organized, dramatic in story, rich in symbolism, absorbing in ideas. There is no chilling intellectualism in Murdoch's skillful handling of her moral theme, no difficulties in her use of image and symbol. Her book is firmly grounded in the realities of time and place, not in finely drawn abstractions. It is a work of physical and imaginative reality by a writer who views life with passionate concern for man's mortality and humorous appreciation of his illusions.

BETWEEN THE ACTS

Type of work: Novel
Author: Virginia Woolf (1882–1941)
Type of plot: Symbolic allegory
Time of plot: June, 1939
Locale: England
First published: 1941

> *Principal characters:*
> BARTHOLOMEW OLIVER, the owner of Pointz Hall
> GILES, his son
> ISA, his daughter-in-law
> MRS. LUCY SWITHIN, his widowed sister
> MRS. MANRESA and
> WILLIAM DODGE, the guests at the pageant
> MISS LA TROBE, the writer and director of the pageants

The Story:

Pointz Hall was not one of the great English houses mentioned in the guidebooks, but it was old and comfortable and pleasantly situated in a tree-fringed meadow. The house was older than the name of its owners in the county. Although they had hung the portrait of an ancestress in brocade and pearls beside the staircase and kept a watch under glass that had stopped a bullet at Waterloo, the Olivers had lived only a little more than a century in a district where the names of the villagers went back to Domesday Book. The countryside still showed traces of the ancient Britons, the Roman road, the Elizabethan manor house, and the marks of the plow on a hill sown in wheat during Napoleon's time.

The owner of the house was Bartholomew Oliver, retired from the Indian Civil Service. With him lived his son Giles, his daughter-in-law Isa, two small grandchildren, and his widowed sister, Mrs. Lucy Swithin. Bartholomew, a disgruntled old man who lived more and more in the past, was constantly snubbing his sister as he had done when they were children. Mrs. Swithin was a woman of careless dress, good manners, quiet faith, and great intelligence. Her favorite book was an *Outline of History*; she dreamed of a time when Piccadilly was a rhododendron forest in which the mastodon roamed. Giles Oliver was a London stockbroker who had wanted to be a farmer until circumstances decided otherwise. A misunderstanding had lately developed between him and his wife Isa, who wrote poetry in secret. She suspected that Giles had been unfaithful and fancied herself in love with Rupert Haines, a married gentleman farmer of the neighborhood. Isa thought that Mrs. Haines had the eyes of a gobbling goose.

On a June morning in 1939, Pointz Hall awoke. Mrs. Swithin, aroused by the birds, read again in the *Outline of History* until the maid brought her tea. She wondered if the afternoon would be rainy or fine, for this was the day of the pageant to raise funds for installing electric lights in the village church. Later, she went to early service. Old Bartholomew walked with his Afghan hound on the terrace where his grandson George was bent over a cluster of flowers. When the old man folded his newspaper into a cone to cover his nose and jumped suddenly at the boy, George began to cry. Bartholomew grumbled that his grandson was a crybaby and went back to his paper. From her window, Isa looked out at her son and the baby, Caro, in her perambulator that a nurse was pushing. Then she went off to order the fish for lunch. She read in Bartholomew's discarded newspaper the story of an attempted assault on a girl in the barracks at Whitehall. Returning from church, Mrs. Swithin tacked another placard on the barn where the pageant would be given if the day turned out rainy; regardless of the weather, tea would also be served there during the intermission. Mocked again by her brother, she went off to make sandwiches for the young men and women who were decorating the barn.

Giles was expected back from London in time for the pageant. The family had just decided not to wait lunch for him when Mrs. Manresa and a young man named William Dodge arrived unexpectedly and uninvited. They had intended, Mrs. Manresa explained, to picnic in the country, but when she saw the Olivers' name on the signpost, she had suddenly decided to visit her old friends. Mrs. Manresa, loud, cheerful, and vulgar, was a woman of uncertain background married to a wealthy Jew. William Dodge, she said, was an artist. He was, he declared, a clerk. Giles, arriving in the middle of lunch and finding Mrs. Manresa's showy car at the door, was furious; he and Mrs. Manresa had been having an affair. After lunch, on the terrace, he sat hating William Dodge. Finally, Mrs. Swithin took pity on the young man's discomfort and took him off to see her brother's collection of pictures. William wanted to tell her that he was married but his child was not his child, that he was a pervert, that her kindness had healed his wretched day; but he could not speak.

The guests, arriving for the pageant, began to fill the chairs set on the lawn, for the afternoon was sunny and clear. Behind the thick bushes that served as a dressing room, Miss La Trobe, the author and director of the pageant, was giving the last instructions to her cast. She was something of a mystery in the village, for no one knew where she came from. There were rumors that she had kept a tea shop and had been an actress. Abrupt and restless, she walked about the fields, used strong language, and drank too much at the local pub. She was a frustrated artist. Now she was wondering if her audience would realize that she had tried to give unity to English history in her pageant and to give something of herself as well.

The pageant began. The first scene showed the age of Chaucer, with pilgrims on their way to Canterbury. Eliza Clark, who sold tobacco in the village, appeared in another scene as Queen Elizabeth. Albert, the village idiot, played her court fool. The audience hoped he would not do anything dreadful. In a play performed before Gloriana, Mrs. Otter of the End House played the old crone who had saved the true prince, the supposed beggar who fell in love with the duke's daughter. Then Miss La Trobe's vision of the Elizabethan age ended, and it was time for tea during the intermission.

Mrs. Manresa applauded; she had seen herself as Queen Elizabeth and Giles as the hero. Giles glowered. Walking toward the barn, he came on a coiled snake swallowing a toad, and he stamped on them until his tennis shoes were splattered with blood. Isa tried to catch a glimpse of Rupert Haines. Failing, she offered to show William Dodge the greenhouses. They discovered that they could talk frankly, like two strangers drawn together by unhappiness and understanding.

The pageant began again. This time the scene showed the Age of Reason. Once more, Miss La Trobe had written a play within a play; the characters had names like Lady Harpy Harraden, Sir Spaniel Lilyliver, Florinda, Valentine, and Sir Smirking Peace-be-with-you-all, a clergyman. After another brief interval, the cast reassembled for a scene from the Victorian Age. Mr. Budge, the publican, was made up as a policeman. Albert was in the hindquarters of a donkey, while the rest of the cast pretended to be on a picnic in 1860. Then Mr. Budge announced that the time had come to pack and be gone. When Isa asked Mrs. Swithin what the Victorians were like, the old woman said that they had been like Isa, William Dodge, and herself, only dressed differently.

The terrace stage had been left bare. Suddenly, the cast came running from behind the bushes, each holding a mirror in which the men and women in the audience saw themselves reflected in self-conscious poses. The time was the present of June, 1939. Swallows were sweeping homeward in the late light. Above them twelve airplanes flying in formation cut across the sky, drowning out all other sounds. The pageant was over; the audience dispersed. Mrs. Manresa and William Dodge drove away in her car. Miss La Trobe went on to the inn. There she drank and saw a vision and tried to find words in which to express it—to make people see once more, as she had tried to do that afternoon.

Darkness fell across the village and the fields. At Pointz Hall, the visitors had gone, and the family was alone. Bartholomew read the evening paper and drowsed in his chair. Mrs. Swithin took up her *Outline of His-*

tory and turned the pages while she thought of mastodons and prehistoric birds. At last, she and her brother went off to bed.

Now the true drama of the day was about to begin, ancient as the hills, secret and primitive as the black night outside. Giles and Isa would quarrel, embrace, and sleep. The curtain rose on another scene in the long human drama of enmity, love, and peace.

Critical Evaluation:

Between the Acts was completed without final revision before Virginia Woolf's suicide in 1941; in it, she returns to the tightly controlled structure, the classical unities of time and place, used before in *Mrs. Dalloway. Between the Acts* takes place all in a single day, the day of the annual village pageant, and in the house or on the grounds of Pointz Hall.

The title suggests the book's three levels of meaning. *Between the Acts* refers first to events, relationships, and conversation taking place between the acts of the village pageant. Second, it refers to that precarious time between World War I and World War II. Third, the story occurs between the times when Giles and Isa truly communicate. Significantly, the novel's last lines are: "Then the curtain rose. They spoke."

Miss La Trobe, director of the pageant and probably a lesbian, is the one character who has contact with all others; she, with her pageant of English history, provides another unity to the work. She is also a representative of Woolf's ideal of the androgynous artist, a creator who is "womanmanly."

The impending war, although seldom spoken of directly, is always in the background in the novel and is briefly referred to in spectators' conversation and more directly in the sound of airplanes at the end. British civilization, celebrated in the pageant, is what may be lost in the coming battles. The last war had fragmented mankind both socially and psychologically; now the spectators see themselves in the mirrors held by the actors as somewhat fragmented. For a moment, however, Miss La Trobe creates a unity in the audience by means of music; a state of harmony is reached wherein male and female, the one and the many, the silent and the speaking, are joined. Woolf was always searching for such a unity in her art, a way to reconcile opposites.

The novel is filled with cryptic and portentous symbols. Written during the early years of World War II, it presents with poetic and fragmentary vision an outline of stark human drama against the vast backdrop of history. In Woolf's handling of background there is always an awareness of the primitive or historical past, conveyed in images of the flint arrowhead, the Roman road, or the manor house, which is the scene of the novel. England, rather than time, gives the novel its underlying theme. But the pageant which presents a picture of English history from the Middle Ages to

1939 is only an interlude between the acts. The true drama is found in the lives of the trivial, selfish, stupid, frustrated, idealistic people who watch the pageant and in the end are brought face-to-face with themselves, actors in an older drama than Miss La Trobe's pictures out of the past or the threat of the war to come in the planes droning overhead. The novel represents Woolf's final affirmation of the artist's vision, the ability to distinguish between the false and the true and to catch a glimpse of truth in the mirror of reality.

THE BLACK ARROW
A Tale of the Two Roses

Type of work: Novel
Author: Robert Louis Stevenson (1850–1894)
Type of plot: Historical romance
Time of plot: Fifteenth century
Locale: England
First published: 1888

Principal characters:

SIR DANIEL BRACKLEY, a political turncoat
RICHARD SHELTON (DICK), his ward
JOANNA SEDLEY, Lord Foxham's ward
SIR OLIVER OATES, Sir Daniel's clerk
ELLIS DUCKWORTH, an outlaw
LAWLESS, another outlaw and Dick's friend
RICHARD, Duke of Gloucester

The Story:

One afternoon in the late springtime, the Moat House bell began to ring. A messenger had arrived with a message from Sir Daniel Brackley for Sir Oliver Oates, his clerk. When the peasants gathered at the summons of the bell, they were told that as many armed men as could be spared from the defense of Moat House were to join Sir Daniel at Kettley, where a battle was to be fought between the armies of Lancaster and York.

There was some grumbling at this order, for Sir Daniel was a faithless man who fought first on one side and then on the other. He had added to his own lands by securing the wardships of children left orphans in those troubled times, and it was whispered that he had murdered good Sir Harry Shelton to make himself the guardian of young Dick Shelton and the lord of the Moat House estates.

As guardian, Sir Daniel planned to marry Dick Shelton to the orphaned heiress of Kettley, Joanna Sedley. He had ridden there to take charge of the girl. Dick, knowing nothing of these plans, remained behind as one of the garrison of the manor. Old Nick Appleyard, a veteran of Agincourt, grumbled at the weakness of the defense in a country overrun by stragglers from warring armies and insisted that Moat House lay open to attack. His prophecy came true. While he stood talking to Dick and Bennet Hatch, Sir Daniel's bailiff, a black arrow whirred out of the woods and struck Nick between the shoulder blades. A message on the shaft indicated that John Amend-All, a mysterious outlaw, had killed old Nick.

Sir Oliver Oates trembled when he read the message on the arrow. Shortly afterward, he was further disturbed by a message pinned on the church door, announcing that John Amend-All would kill Sir Daniel, Sir Oliver, and Bennet Hatch. Dick learned from the message that the outlaw accused Sir Oliver of killing Sir Harry Shelton, his father; but Sir Oliver swore that he had had no part in the knight's death. Dick decided to remain quiet until he learned more about the matter and in the meantime to act in all fairness to Sir Daniel.

It was decided that Hatch should remain to guard Moat House while the outlaws were in the neighborhood. Dick rode off with ten men-at-arms to find Sir Daniel. He carried a letter from Sir Oliver telling of John Amend-All's threats.

At Kettley, Sir Daniel was awaiting the outcome of a battle already in progress, for he intended to join the winning side at the last minute. Sir Daniel was also upset by the outlaw's threats, and he ordered Dick to return to Moat House with a letter for Sir Oliver. He and his men left to join the fighting; but not before he roundly cursed his luck because Joanna Sedley, whom he held hostage, had escaped in boy's clothing. He ordered a party of men-at-arms to search for the girl and then to proceed to Moat House and strengthen the defenses there.

On his return journey, Dick met Joanna, still dressed as a boy, who told him that her name was John Matcham. Dick, unaware that she was Sir Daniel's prisoner, promised to help her reach the abbey at Holywood. As they hurried on, they came upon a camp of the outlaws led by Ellis Duckworth, another man ruined by Sir Daniel. Running from the outlaws, they saw the party of Sir Daniel's retainers shot down one by one. The cannonading Dick heard in the distance convinced him that the soldiers of Lancaster were faring badly in the day's battle. Not knowing on which side Sir Daniel had declared himself, he wondered whether his guardian were among the victors or the vanquished.

Dick and his companion slept in the forest that night. The next morning, a detachment of Sir Daniel's men swept by in disorderly rout. Soon afterward, they saw a hooded leper in the woods. The man was Sir Daniel, attempting to make his way back to Moat House in disguise. He was dismayed when he heard that the outlaws had killed a party of his men-at-arms.

When the three arrived at Moat House, Sir Daniel accused Dick of distrust. He claimed innocence in the death of Dick's father and forced Sir Oliver to do the same. Another black arrow was shot through a window into a room in which the three were talking. Sir Daniel gave orders to defend Moat House against attack. Dick was placed under close watch in a room over the chapel, and he was not allowed to see his friend John Matcham.

That night, when John Matcham came secretly to the room over the chapel, Dick learned that the companion of his adventures in the forest was really Joanna Sedley, the girl to whom Sir Daniel had betrothed him. Warned that he was now in danger of his life, Dick escaped into the forest. There, he found Ellis Duckworth, who promised him that Sir Daniel would be destroyed.

Meanwhile, the war went in favor of Lancaster, and Sir Daniel's fortunes rose with those of the house he followed. The town of Shoreby was full of Lancastrians all of that summer and fall, and there Sir Daniel had his own house for his family and followers. Joanna Sedley was not with him; she was kept in a lonely house by the sea under the care of the wife of Bennet Hatch. Dick and an outlaw companion, Lawless, went to the town, and while reconnoitering Joanna's hiding place, Dick encountered Lord Foxham, enemy of Sir Daniel and Joanna's legal guardian. Lord Foxham promised that if Joanna could be rescued she would become Dick's bride. The two men attempted a rescue by sea in a stolen boat; but a storm almost sank their boat, and Lord Foxham was injured when the party attempted to land.

That winter, Dick and his faithful companion, Lawless, returned to Shoreby. Disguised as priests, they entered Sir Daniel's house and were there protected by Alicia Risingham, Joanna's friend and the niece of a powerful Lancastrian lord. When Dick and Joanna met, she told him that the following day she was to marry Lord Shoreby against her will. An alarm was given when Dick was forced to kill one of Lord Shoreby's spies. Still in the disguise of a priest, he was taken to Sir Oliver Oates, who promised not to betray Dick if he would remain quietly in the church until after the wedding of Joanna and Lord Shoreby. During the night, Lawless found Dick and gave him the message that Ellis Duckworth had returned and would prevent the marriage.

As the wedding procession entered the church, three archers discharged their black arrows from a gallery. Lord Shoreby fell, two of the arrows in his body. Sir Daniel was wounded in the arm. Sir Oliver Oates denounced Dick and Lawless, and they were taken before the Earl of Risingham. Aided by Joanna and Alicia, Dick argued his cause with such vigor, however, that the earl agreed to protect him from Sir Daniel's anger. Later, learning from Dick that Sir Daniel was secretly plotting with the Yorkist leaders, the earl set him and Lawless free.

Dick made his escape from Sir Daniel's men only to be captured by the old seaman whose skiff he had stolen on the night he and Lord Foxham had attempted to rescue Joanna from Sir Daniel. It took him half the night to elude the angry seaman and his friends. In the morning he was in time to meet, at Lord Foxham's request, young Richard of York, Duke of Gloucester. On his arrival at the meeting place, he found the duke attacked by bandits. He saved Richard's life and later fought with the duke in the battle of Shoreby, where the army of Lancaster was defeated. He was knighted for his bravery in the fight. Afterward, when Richard was giving out honors, Dick claimed as his portion only the freedom of the old seaman whose boat he had stolen.

Pursuing Sir Daniel, Dick rescued Joanna and took her to Holywood. The next morning, he encountered Sir Daniel in the forest near the abbey. Dick was willing to let his enemy escape, but Ellis Duckworth, lurking nearby, killed the faithless knight. Dick asked the outlaw to spare the life of Sir Oliver Oates.

Dick and Joanna were married with great honor. They lived quietly at Moat House, withdrawn from the bloody disputes of the houses of Lancaster and York. Both the old seaman and Lawless were cared for in their old age, and Lawless finally took orders and died a friar.

Critical Evaluation:
The Black Arrow: A Tale of the Two Roses is a historical romance intended primarily for younger readers. Set in the fifteenth century, the historical background of the plot deals with a minor battle fought in the Wars of the Roses and the appearance of the infamous Richard, Duke of Gloucester, as a young soldier. More interesting are the swift-paced adventures of Dick Shelton in his attempts to outwit his scheming guardian, Sir Daniel Brackley. Children have been fortunate that one of the gifted writers of the last century lent his talents to their pleasure.

It is reported that Robert Louis Stevenson never liked *The Black Arrow* and for that reason would never read it. Certainly, it is a passable adventure yarn with enough action and vivid characterization to satisfy most readers, but Stevenson's dislike of it is in many ways understandable. The incidents cohere poorly at times; often they seem to be selected gratuitously. None of the characters except Richard Shelton is sustained long enough in the novel to be very interesting, and even Richard is not a fully satisfying fictional character. The narrative reads aimlessly for chapters at a stretch and then seems to thrash out a conclusion rather than arrive at it naturally. In addition—and this is critical—the novel promises adventures and characterizations that it never fulfills. For example, the fellowship of The Black Arrow (it is the book's title, after all) has a Robin Hood appeal that strangely goes begging in the tale.

Where the novel succeeds best is in contrasting a youthful Richard Shelton with a cunning, sin-worn world. Beset on every side by duplicity and selfishness, he maintains at least an elementary sense of forthright honesty. His errors, then, result from youthful indiscretion, not calculated hypocrisy. He loves well, fights well, and succeeds well in a world where love, battle, and success are as whimsical as the daily change from Lancaster to York.

The Black Arrow is not without other redeeming features. Richard,

Duke of Gloucester, is a character who seems to have pleased Stevenson. Admittedly, he enters the novel almost at the last moment and is a rather one-dimensionally cruel figure, but his diabolical energy, akin to that of James Durie, Master of Ballantrae, makes for interesting reading. Lawless, whose very name suggests manifold possibilities, gets misplaced by the author during the book but flourishes throughout his brief stay. Alicia Risingham, companion to Joanna Sedley, is by far the more engaging female character with her bold, risqué manner. Finally, there are a few exciting episodes to spice up the action—one, the floundering of a rescue ship; another, the fierce battle of Shoreby.

Still, *The Black Arrow* is not a successful novel. It lies somewhere between *Treasure Island* and *Kidnapped*, on the one hand—both much better tales—and *The Master of Ballantrae*, on the other, a more artful study of man's dark, ambivalent nature. As a result, it is neither a child's tale nor an adult's novel but an odd mixture of both.

BLEAK HOUSE

Type of work: Novel
Author: Charles Dickens (1812–1870)
Type of plot: Social criticism
Time of plot: Mid-nineteenth century
Locale: London, Lincolnshire, and Hertfordshire, England
First published: 1852–1853

Principal characters:

JOHN JARNDYCE, the owner of Bleak House
RICHARD CARSTONE, his cousin
ADA CLARE, also his cousin
ESTHER SUMMERSON, his ward and companion to Ada
ALLAN WOODCOURT, a young physician
LADY DEDLOCK, Sir Leicester Dedlock's wife
TULKINGHORN, a solicitor
WILLIAM GUPPY, Tulkinghorn's clerk

The Story:

The suit of Jarndyce vs. Jarndyce was a standing joke in the Court of Chancery. Beginning with a dispute as to how the trusts under a Jarndyce will were to be administered, the suit had dragged on, year after year, generation after generation, without settlement. The heirs, or would-be heirs, spent their lives waiting. Some, like Tom Jarndyce, blew out their brains. Others, like tiny Miss Flite, visited the Court in daily expectation of some judgment that would settle the disputed state and bring her the wealth of which she dreamed.

Among those involved in the suit were John Jarndyce, grandnephew of the Tom Jarndyce who had shot himself in a coffeehouse, and his two cousins, Richard Carstone and Ada Clare. Jarndyce was the owner of Bleak House in Hertfordshire, a country place that was not as dreary as its name. His two young cousins lived with him. He had provided Esther Summerson as a companion for Ada. Esther had suffered an unhappy childhood under the care of Miss Barbary, her stern godmother, and a servant, Mrs. Rachel. The two had told the girl that her mother was a wicked woman who had deserted her. Miss Barbary was now dead, and Mr. Jarndyce had become Esther's benefactor.

Two others who took a strange interest in the Jarndyce estate were Sir Leicester and Lady Dedlock of Chesney Wold in Lincolnshire. Lord Dedlock had a solicitor named Tulkinghorn, who, like every other reputable lawyer in London, was involved in the Jarndyce suit. One day when Tulkinghorn was in the Dedlocks' home, the lawyer presented Lady Dedlock with a document. She swooned at the sight of the handwriting on the paper. Immediately suspicious, Tulkinghorn resolved to trace the hand-writing to its source. His search led him to Mr. Snagsby, a stationer, but the best that Snagsby could tell him was that the paper had been copied by a man named Nemo, a lodger in the house of Mr. Krook, a junk dealer. Mr. Tulkinghorn went to the house with Snagsby, only to find Nemo dead of an overdose of opium. Convinced that Nemo was not the dead man's real name, the lawyer could learn nothing of the man's identity or connections.

Esther Summerson soon found an ardent friend and admirer in William Guppy, a clerk in the office of Kenge and Carboy, Jarndyce's solicitors. It was Guppy who first noticed Esther's resemblance to Lady Dedlock. Allan Woodcourt, a young surgeon who had been called to administer to the dead Nemo, requested an inquest. One of the witnesses called was Jo, a crossing sweeper whom Nemo had often befriended. A short time later, Jo was found with two half crowns on his person. He explained that they had been given to him by a lady he had guided to the gate of the churchyard where Nemo was buried. Jo was arrested, and in the cross-examination which followed, Mr. Guppy questioned the wife of an oily preacher named Chadband and found that the firm of Kenge and Carboy had once had charge of a young lady with whose aunt Mrs. Chadband had lived. Mrs. Chadband was, of course, the Mrs. Rachel of Esther Summerson's childhood. She revealed that Esther's real name was not Summerson, but Hawdon.

The mystery surrounding Esther Summerson began to clear. A French maid who had left Lady Dedlock's service identified her late mistress as the lady who had given two half crowns to the crossing sweeper. The dead Nemo was promptly proved to have been Captain Hawdon. Years before, he and the present Lady Dedlock had fallen in love. Esther was their child, but Miss Barbary, angry at her sister's disgrace, had taken the child and moved to another part of the country. The mother later married Lord Dedlock. She was now overjoyed that the child her unforgiving sister had led her to believe dead was still alive, and she resolved to reveal herself to the child.

Mr. Guppy informed Lady Dedlock that a packet of Captain Hawdon's letters was in the possession of the junk dealer, Krook. Fearing that the revelation of these letters would ruin her position, Lady Dedlock asked Guppy to bring them to her, and the wily law clerk agreed; but on the night the letters were to be obtained, the drunken Krook exploded of spontaneous combustion, and presumably the letters burned with him.

In the meantime, Richard Carstone, completely obsessed by the Jarndyce case, had abandoned all efforts to establish his career. He lived in a false hope that the Chancery suit would soon be settled, spending the lit-tle money he had on an unscrupulous lawyer named Vholes. When Jarndyce remonstrated, Richard thought that his cousin's advice was prompted by selfish interests. Ada Clare also worried over Richard's behavior and secretly married him so that her own small fortune might stand between Richard and his folly.

Esther Summerson fell desperately ill of a fever, and when Lady Dedlock heard of the girl's illness, she went to her at once and revealed herself. Mother and daughter were finally reunited. As a result of her illness, Esther's beauty was completely destroyed. John Jarndyce, feeling free for the first time to declare his love for a woman so much younger than himself, asked her to marry him, and she accepted.

Tulkinghorn was murdered, and several nights later when she knew her secret was about to be revealed to her husband, Lady Dedlock left home. It was discovered that Tulkinghorn had been murdered by the French maid through whom he had learned of Lady Dedlock's connection with the crossing sweeper. The maid had attempted to blackmail the lawyer, and when he threatened her with imprisonment, she killed him. Inspector Bucket, who solved the mystery of the murder, also informed Lord Dedlock of his wife's past. The baronet told the detective to employ every means to bring about her return. It was Esther Summerson, however, who found her mother dead at the gate of the churchyard where Captain Hawdon was buried.

Among Krook's effects was a Jarndyce will made at a later date than the one that had been disputed in Chancery for so many years. It settled the question of the Jarndyce inheritance forever. Richard and Ada were declared the heirs; but unfortunately, the entire fortune had been eaten up in court costs, and the two young people were left to face a life of genteel poverty. Richard did not long survive this final blow. He died, leaving his wife and infant son in the care of John Jarndyce.

Esther became the mistress of her own Bleak House. John Jarndyce, discovering that her true love was young Doctor Woodcourt, released her from her promise to marry him and in his generosity brought the two lovers together. Before her wedding to Doctor Woodcourt, Jarndyce took her to see a country house he had bought at Yorkshire. He had named it Bleak House, and it was his wedding present to the bride and groom. There Esther lived, happy in the love of her husband and her two daughters and in the lasting affection of John Jarndyce, the proprietor of that other Bleak House, which would always be her second home.

Critical Evaluation:
Bleak House, after publication as a serial, first appeared in book form in 1853 at the height of Charles Dickens' career. Preceded by *Martin Chuzzlewit* and followed by *Hard Times*, it comes early in the group of Dickens' great novels of social analysis and protest. A major critical anatomy of mid-nineteenth century England, the novel nevertheless shows

some unfortunate signs of serial publication and of the author's concessions to his audience. Pathos, melodrama, and a somewhat strident moralism all reflect weaknesses in the public taste, yet Dickens manages to weave out of these a controlled assessment of the corruption at the heart of his society.

At the center of the novel's intricate plot is the lawsuit of Jarndyce and Jarndyce. To this meager frame, Dickens piles subplot upon subplot, all ultimately interrelated. In one sense, the plot is a series of thin detective stories woven together in such a way as to involve all strata of society. As character after fascinating character appears, each episode is interesting in its own right and, in the masterly resolution, no action or detail remains extraneous.

The third-person narrator of most of *Bleak House* is a sharply ironic commentator on the political, social, and moral evils that abound in the book. There is never any question of the narrator's attitude toward the selfishness and irresponsibility he recounts, but he is not quite so sardonic or homiletic as the narrator of *Hard Times*. The stern attitude of this narrator is both relieved and reinforced by the introduction of a second, first-person narrator, Esther Summerson. Many critics have seen the dual narration as an aesthetic flaw, but each narrator does contribute a different perspective. Although Esther is a bit simpering and saccharine, she does represent a sympathetic and morally responsible attitude that is rare in the world of *Bleak House*. She is a compassionate insider who adds both a perspective and a model which, if sometimes sentimental, are a corrective to her foul environment.

As the lawsuit of Jarndyce and Jarndyce lumbers to a close after years of litigation, a gallery of characters emerges, and each reveals how the moral contagion has spread to his sector. With his talent for caricature, Dickens has created memorable minor characters to flesh out the corrupt world. There is Mr. Chadband, the preacher enamored of his own voice; Mrs. Pardiggle, who would feed the poor Puseyite tracts rather than bacon; Mr. Turveydrop, who is the Model of Deportment and little else; Mrs. Jellyby, who supports noble "causes" while neglecting her own children; Mr. Skimpole, the model of unproductivity. Many of these characters betray the varieties of egoism and irresponsibility that have left society stagnant and infected. Perhaps the most striking is Krook, the law stationer and small-scale surrogate of the Lord Chancellor, who dies of "spontaneous combustion." Krook is a microcosm of the self-destructive tendency of a diseased society.

Despite Dickens' talent for plot and character, *Bleak House* is primarily a novel of image and symbol. The first chapter insistently sets the moral tone as it repeats its images of fog and mud, which surround the Court of Chancery and, by extension, all of English life. As the fog, which surrounds all in a miasma from which there seems no escape, is a symbol of

Chancery, the court itself, with its inert, irresponsible, and self-destructive wranglings, is a symbol of the calcified social and economic system strangling English life. The case of Jarndyce vs. Jarndyce is the perfect model of the social canker. Characters sacrifice their lives to its endless wrangling and forfeit the opportunity to accept individual responsibility and make something of themselves because of the illusory hope of instant riches. When the suit is finally settled, the fortune has been eaten up in court costs—an ironic commentary on the futility of such vain hopes.

People and places, too, in *Bleak House* so consistently have symbolic value that the novel occasionally verges on allegory. The cloudiness and rain that surround Chesney Wold symbolize the hopelessness of the nobility. Even the name of its inhabitants, Dedlock, is a sign of the moral deadlock and immobility of the ruling class. At the other end of the social spectrum, Tom-all-alone's, dirty and disease-ridden, is a symbol of the vulnerability and victimhood of the lowest classes. In gloom of one sort or another, many characters act as detectives searching out the guilty secrets and hypocrisies that permeate this world.

On the more positive side is Bleak House itself where the kindly John Jarndyce, aloof from involvement in the lawsuit, presides over a more orderly and benevolent demesne; but the contagion cannot even be kept from there. Occasionally, even the admirable John Jarndyce suffers when the East Wind, a symbol of the agony and frustration outside, blows across the estate. More strikingly, Ada and Richard Carstone bring the effects of the lawsuit into their uncle's house as Richard destroys himself and injures those around him in his obsession with the Chancery case. Richard is another victim of the anachronistic system that destroys those who participate in it, a system that is a symbol of the inertia, complacency, and hypocrisy of the whole society. Finally, that Esther, the housekeeper, contracts smallpox from Jo is a symbol of the interrelatedness of all levels of society. Jo is at the bottom, but his misfortune becomes the misfortune of many as his contagion spreads through the social organism. The implication is that an unfeeling society can create Jo and Tom-all-alone's, but it cannot protect itself from its victims.

Dickens offers no programmatic, revolutionary solution. If there is a solution, it is to be found in people like John Jarndyce, Esther Summerson, and Allan Woodcourt. Jarndyce is a figure of the selflessness that is necessary if injustice is to be rectified. Esther Summerson, as her name implies, is a bright antidote to the fog and rain. Her keys, which she shakes regularly, are a sign of her commitment to domestic duties and an acceptance of responsibility. Dr. Woodcourt is the kind of active man society needs. The marriage of Esther and Woodcourt is a vindication of what they have to offer, as is Jarndyce's generous acceptance of their love. The new Bleak House in which they live is ironically full of the joy and goodness that can reform society. The novel does not offer the easy optimism of radical political solutions, because it is only this revolution in the heart of man that Dickens believes can cure society.

THE BRACKNELS
A Family Chronicle

Type of work: Novel
Author: Forrest Reid (1875–1947)
Type of plot: Domestic chronicle
Time of plot: Early twentieth century
Locale: Ireland
First published: 1911

Principal characters:

MR. BRACKNEL, a self-made wealthy businessman
MRS. BRACKNEL, his sickly wife
ALFRED, the sport-loving son of the Bracknels
DENIS, the neurotic younger son
MAY, the charming older daughter
AMY, the sensual younger daughter
HUBERT RUSK, Denis Bracknel's tutor

The Story:

Mr. Bracknel, an Irish businessman, was disgusted with his family, for he felt that they all tried to oppose his wishes merely for the sake of displeasing him. The members of his family felt, however, that he was unduly tyrannical. Alfred Bracknel, the oldest child, had a place in his father's business, but he paid little attention to his work. Instead, he preferred to spend his time and thought on gambling, drinking, and women, much to his father's disgust. Seventeen-year-old Denis, the youngest child, displeased his father with his interest in everything mystical. Mr. Bracknel prided himself upon being a very practical person.

May, the oldest daughter, gave her father the least trouble, but Amy, a very sensual girl, constantly fell in love with undesirable young men whom her father had to discourage. Mrs. Bracknel annoyed her husband because she was sickly. Although only forty-six years old, she seemed much older, while her husband was still a lusty man.

The entire family thought that Denis was a little mad because of his interest in the occult. He had been sent away to school in England. After his career there had ended in failure, a series of tutors had not been able to cope with him. At last, a physician who specialized in mental cases recommended to Mr. Bracknel that he hire Hubert Rusk, a young Englishman, as a tutor for the boy. The doctor knew Rusk and felt that he could depend on the young man to be careful of the boy's mental condition.

The girls in the family, particularly Amy, looked forward to the arrival of the young tutor, for their father tried to keep them from social contacts with young men. Even before his arrival, Amy expressed a real interest in Hubert Rusk.

Rusk, a deferential and easygoing man, made himself quickly at home with the Bracknels, all of whom seemed anxious to have him as a confidant. Upon his arrival, he found that Denis had a wide knowledge of occult subjects but knew virtually nothing in other fields. He also found that his charge was an extremely odd young man who had been driven inward by the failure of the family to understand him.

On his first night at the Bracknel home, Rusk observed that Denis went out for a walk late at night. Later, he discovered that Denis, obsessed with moon worship, had discovered an ancient pagan altar in a wood near the house. At the ancient altar, Denis performed ceremonies in honor of the moon, including the sacrifice on occasion of small animals.

Before long, the two daughters of the house became rivals for Rusk's attentions. Amy, the more sensual of the two, intimidated her sister into letting her have what attentions the oblivious tutor gave. He, on his part, was unaware of the attraction he had for the girls, except that he did not like to have Amy constantly interrupting the lessons he was giving her younger brother.

During Rusk's stay with the Bracknels, Alfred gave his father a great deal of trouble. Once, Mr. Bracknel shipped Alfred off to an office of the business in Switzerland, but he had to bring him back because of the young man's incompetence. Later, he discovered that Alfred was stealing from the firm to pay his gambling debts. Finally, Alfred married a typist from the office, at which point Mr. Bracknel turned him out, but not without a scene in which Alfred accused his father of being partial to his illegitimate son, who was also in the business. Alfred even thought of publicly revealing the fact that his father had an illegitimate son, for no one except the mother of the young man, Alfred, and his father knew the fact.

In the meantime, Rusk was investigating Denis' behavior. One night he found the lad actually worshiping the moon, but the boy did not tell his tutor that he had visions, both at night and in the daytime, of the goddess of the moon, who appeared to him and even kissed him. As it was, healthy minded Rusk tried to convince the lad that such behavior was peculiar and not good for his own mental health. Despite his friendship with the doctor, who had requested him as a tutor, Rusk did not tell the medical man of Denis' visions. Learning that the boy believed the house to be haunted and that he lived in fear, he did decide to enlist the doctor's aid in getting Mr. Bracknel's permission to take Denis abroad for a year or two, as an aid to improving the young man's state of mind. The boy was so frightened by his illusions that he moved his bed from his own room to that occupied by his tutor.

Amy Bracknel, still infatuated with the young tutor, seized every opportunity to throw herself at him; she even had an old woman make up a love potion for her to administer to him. Almost pathologically obsessed, she found him alone in the library one evening and enticed him into kissing her. She then told her sister and her mother that Rusk and she were engaged to be married. Rusk prepared to leave, not knowing what Amy had said but thinking that her sister and Denis had been aware of the embrace. Rusk assumed that Mr. Bracknel would discharge him for making love to Amy.

As it was, Mr. Bracknel heard from Amy herself that she was in love with Rusk and wished to marry him. She also related to her father that she had gone to Rusk's room the night he had kissed her but that she had been deterred in carrying out her plans by the presence of Denis in the tutor's room. Mr. Bracknel sent Amy at once to an aunt's house and made arrangements to have Denis and the tutor leave within two days for a trip to the Continent.

Before the two could leave, however, Mr. Bracknel died of a heart attack, brought on by a heated interview with Alfred in the father's office. Alfred was glad rather than sorry to come into his own as the heir to the business. Mr. Bracknel's death was a great shock to Denis, who believed that he had seen a vision of his father's death. In spite of the young man's strange behavior, Rusk left him alone at tea time one day. When the lad failed to appear after nightfall, Rusk and the doctor went to look for him. They found him hanging from a tree limb beside the old pagan altar he had discovered.

His pupil dead and preparations for his departure already made, Rusk left the house after Mr. Bracknel's funeral. Two years later, he had an opportunity to emigrate to Australia. Before leaving, he decided to make a short trip to Ireland to see the Bracknels. He found them engaged in a great deal of social activity. Amy Bracknel was infatuated with a new beau. Alfred had turned the business over to a capable manager. No one paid any attention to Rusk. He realized that he no longer mattered to anyone in that strange family.

Critical Evaluation:

Forrest Reid was a novelist little known in the United States. Like Walter de la Mare, his friend, he found the supernatural inseparable from his conception of reality. Denis Bracknel, in this novel, reflects somewhat the author's personal experience, for in his imagination, at least, Reid himself lived in a pagan dreamworld not unlike that of his hero; and his interest in such imaginary existence, another reality quite different from the ordinary world, is apparent in most of his fiction. As a beginning novelist, he was influenced by Henry James, but their correspondence ended when James failed to comprehend fully Reid's first novel. As a novelist and as a person, Reid was poetical and mystical, qualities that are easily discernible in *The Bracknels*, especially in the character of young Denis, who finds the evil of the everyday world unbearable. In this book, as in most of Reid's fiction, there is reflected as well the author's strong interest in the psychology of the abnormal person.

Originally a lyrical tale titled *The Moon Story*, *The Bracknels* was expanded and reworked into a Realistic novel, keeping the moon story as a subsidiary theme but treating the overall work as a family chronicle. To counteract a tendency to the fantastic and bizarre, Reid rooted his stories in solid realistic surroundings; the setting of this novel, the valley and river, the houses and woods, were all founded on Reid's own childhood world and are described with poetic intensity.

The Bracknels was the real start of Reid's career as a writer; it was the first book in which he presented his personal vision of life. It is the story of the development of an unusually sensitive boy, but it is also the story of a family. The complicated plot, greater action, and broader canvas mark it as an important advance over its predecessors. Perhaps the book hovers between fantasy and realism without completely achieving either; later, Reid mastered the difficult task of successfully handling the commonplace and the marvelous in a single narrative; but the first experiment produced an unusual and interesting book.

Denis Bracknel stands out as the sensitive son of a self-made man—an unscrupulous Belfast merchant—and a pathetic and weak mother. Alfred, Denis' brother, is a coarse philistine, and his sisters are foolish and flirtatious. Denis' new tutor, Rusk, becomes the most important person in his life, the only one with a sense of the boy's secret inner life. Perhaps the central scene in the novel is the one in which Rusk sees Denis dancing in the moonlight naked as if performing some sacred rite. The relationship between the two is ambiguous and in a less innocent time might have been questioned. A nightmare quality reminiscent of James's *The Turn of the Screw* pervades the book until its natural ending in Denis' death. Reid's publisher insisted on a tacked-on ending in which Rusk returned to Ireland on a farewell visit before setting out for Australia, but in the revised version, published in 1947, this scene was omitted.

BRAVE NEW WORLD

Type of work: Novel
Author: Aldous Huxley (1894–1963)
Type of plot: Social satire
Time of plot: 632 years After Ford
Locale: London and New Mexico
First published: 1932

> *Principal characters:*
> BERNARD MARX, a citizen of the future
> LENINA CROWNE, an Alpha worker
> JOHN, the Savage
> MUSTAPHA MOND, a World Controller

The Story:

One day in the year 632 After Ford (A.F.), as time was reckoned in the brave new world, the Director of the Central London Hatchery and Conditioning Center took a group of new students on a tour of the plant where human beings were turned out by mass production. The entire process, from the fertilization of the egg to the birth of the baby, was carried out by trained workers and machines. Each fertilized egg was placed in solution in a large bottle for scientific development into whatever class in society the human was intended. The students were told that scientists of the period had developed a Bokanovsky Process by means of which a fertilized egg was arrested in its growth. The egg responded by budding, and instead of one human being resulting, there would be from eight to ninety-six identical humans.

These Bokanovsky Groups were employed whenever large numbers of people were needed to perform identical tasks. Individuality was a thing of the past; the new society bent every effort to make completely true its motto—Community, Identity, Stability. After birth, the babies were further conditioned during their childhood for their predestined class in society. Alpha Plus Intellectuals and Epsilon Minus Morons were the two extremes of the scientific utopia.

Mustapha Mond, one of the World Controllers, joined the inspection party and lectured to the new students on the horrors and disgusting features of old-fashioned family life. To the great embarrassment of the students, he, in his position of authority, dared use the forbidden words *mother* and *father*; he reminded the students that in 632 A.F., everyone belonged to everyone else.

Lenina Crowne, one of the Alpha workers in the Hatchery, took an interest in Bernard Marx. Bernard was different—too much alcohol had been put into his blood surrogate during his period in the prenatal bottle, and he had sensibilities similar to those possessed by people in the time of Henry Ford.

Lenina and Bernard went by rocket ship to New Mexico and visited the Savage Reservation, a wild tract where primitive forms of human life had been preserved for scientific study. At the pueblo of Malpais, the couple saw an Indian ceremonial dance in which a young man was whipped to propitiate the gods. Lenina was shocked and disgusted by the filth of the place and by the primitive aspects of all she saw.

The pair met a white youth named John. The young man disclosed to them that his mother, Linda, had come to the reservation many years before on vacation with a man called Thomakin. The vacationers had separated, and Thomakin had returned alone to the brave new world. Linda, marooned in New Mexico, gave birth to a son and was slowly assimilated into the primitive society of the reservation. The boy educated himself with an old copy of Shakespeare's plays that he had found. Bernard was convinced that the boy was the son of the Director of Hatcheries, who in his youth had taken a companion to New Mexico on vacation and had returned without her. Bernard had enough human curiosity to wonder how this young savage would react to the scientific world. He invited John and his mother to return to London with him. John, attracted to Lenina and anxious to see the outside world, went eagerly.

Upon Bernard's return, the Director of Hatcheries publicly proposed to dismiss him from the Hatchery because of his unorthodoxy. Bernard produced Linda and John, the director's son. At the family reunion, during which such words as *mother* and *father* were used more than once, the director was shamed out of the plant. He later resigned his position.

Linda went on a *soma* holiday, *soma* being a drug which induced forgetfulness. John became the curiosity of London. He was appalled by all he saw—by the utter lack of any humanistic culture and by the scientific mass production of everything, including humans. Lenina tried to seduce him, but he was held back by his primitive morality.

John was called to attend the death of Linda, who had taken too much *soma* drug. Maddened by the callousness of people conditioned toward death, he instigated a mutiny of workers as they were being given their *soma* ration. He was arrested and taken by the police to Mustapha Mond, with whom he had a long talk on the new civilization. Mond explained that beauty caused unhappiness and thus instability; therefore, humanistic endeavor was checked. Science was dominant. Art was stifled completely; science, even, was stifled at a certain point, and religion was restrained so that it could not cause instability. With a genial sort of cynicism, Mond explained the reasons underlying all of the features of the brave new world. Despite Mond's persuasiveness, the Savage continued to champion tears, inconvenience, God, and poetry.

John moved into the country outside London to take up his old way of life. Sightseers came by the thousands to see him; he was pestered by reporters and television men. At the thought of Lenina, whom he still desired, John mortified his flesh by whipping himself. Lenina visited John and was whipped by him in a frenzy of passion produced by his dual nature. When he realized that he, too, had been caught up in the "orgy-porgy," he hanged himself. Bernard's experiment had failed. Human emotions could end only in tragedy in the brave new world.

Critical Evaluation:

The best Utopian—or anti-Utopian—fiction is not really about the future; it is an indirect view of the present. The authors of such works begin with aspects of their own society that they like, dislike, desire, or fear, and by extrapolating them into a possible future, they demonstrate the likely consequences of such tendencies or pressures developed to extremes. If the reader does not see his own society reflected in an exaggerated, distinctive, but recognizable form, it is unlikely that the projected world will offer more than amused distraction. *Brave New World* has endured as a classic of the genre because Aldous Huxley's vision was not only frighteningly believable when first presented but has become more immediate since its initial appearance. Indeed, in *Brave New World Revisited* (1958), an extended expository gloss on the original, Huxley suggested that his only important prophetic error was the assumption that it would take six centuries to implement fully the brave new world; a scant twenty-six years after the novel's publication, Huxley revised his estimate of the time needed to less than a century.

The most disturbing aspect of *Brave New World* is the suspicion that many, perhaps most, people would like to live in such a society. After examining the modern Western world in general and America in the 1920's in particular, with its assembly-line techniques, its consumerism, its hedonistic tendencies, its emphasis on social conformity, and its worship of childhood and youth, Huxley projected his observations to their logical conclusions and then asked himself how a "sane" man would react to such an environment: the result was *Brave New World*.

Given modern industrial and scientific "progress," Huxley saw that the time would soon arrive when mankind would possess the knowledge and equipment to "solve" all of its material and social problems and achieve universal "happiness," but at a very high price—the sacrifice of freedom, individuality, truth, beauty, a sense of purpose, and the concept of God. The central question is this: How many people would really miss these things? Do they constitute enough of an intellectual, emotional, and moral force to alter the direction of modern society, and do they possess the requisite will, conviction, and energy to do so?

Compared to such earlier efforts as *Antic Hay* (1923), *Those Barren Leaves* (1925), and especially *Point Counter Point* (1928), *Brave New World* is a model of structural simplicity. The dynamics of a brave new world are presented in a long introductory tour of Huxley's futuristic society that takes up almost the first half of the book. Then a catalytic character, John the Savage, is introduced, who directly challenges the social system that has been described. This conflict leads directly to a confrontation between John, the representative of "sanity," and Mustapha Mond, who speaks for the brave new world. Their extended debate serves as the novel's ideological climax. The book ends as the Savage experiences the inevitable personal consequences of that debate.

The long opening sequence begins with assembly-line bottle births, in which the individual's potential is carefully regulated by a combination of genetic selection and chemical treatments and then follows the life cycle to show how all tastes, attitudes, and behavior patterns are adroitly controlled by incessant conditioning. The net result of the conditioning is a society that is totally and deliberately infantile. All activities are transitory, trivial, and mindless—promiscuity replaces passion, immediate sensory stimulation replaces art ("feelies"), hallucinatory escape replaces personal growth ("Soma").

At this point John, the Savage, enters the narrative. Reared among primitives by a mother who loved him in spite of her conditioning, John has known the beauty of great art, because of his reading of Shakespeare, and the pain of loneliness, having been ostracized by the natives because of his light skin and his mother's loose morals. Primed by Linda's nostalgic memories of her former life, the Savage is ready for contact with the outside world when Bernard Marx discovers him on the Reservation and connives to use him in a revenge scheme against the Director of the Hatcheries (John's natural father). At first, John is feted as an interesting freak, but, given his "primitive" moralism, a clash is inevitable. Reacting emotionally to the events surrounding Linda's death, John provokes a violent social disruption—the most serious crime in the brave new world—which leads to the discussion with Mustapha Mond, a World Controller.

In a bitterly funny way, this extended debate between John and Mond resembles the Grand Inquisitor scene in Fyodor Dostoyevski's *The Brothers Karamazov* (1879–1880) and is the rhetorical center of the book. Like Dostoyevski's Inquisitor, Mond justifies his social vision as the only one compatible with human happiness and, like his literary predecessor, he indicates that he, along with the other World Controllers, has taken the pain of life's ambiguities and indecisions upon his own shoulders in order to spare those less capable from having to endure such emotional and psychological pressures. The major difference between the Inquisitor's society and the brave new world is that Dostoyevski's hero-villain had only a vision, but, with the aid of modern science and industry, the World Controllers have succeeded in making the vision a permanent reality—providing all distractions such as beauty, truth, art, purpose, God, and, ironically, science itself, are suppressed. Savage rejects Mond's world out of hand, for he demands the right to be unhappy, among other things.

Unfortunately, however, the brave new world cannot allow Savage that right, nor, if it would, is he fully capable of exercising it. His designation as "savage" is both ironical and true. He is civilized compared to the dehumanized infantilism of most brave new worlders, but he is also still the primitive, as Huxley himself admitted. Shakespeare alone is not enough to equip him for the complexities of life. His upbringing among the precivilized natives, who practice a religion that is a form of fertility cult, has left him without the real emotional and religious resources needed to face a brave new world on his own. Denied a chance to escape, the Savage tries to separate himself from its influence, but it follows him and exploits him as a quaint curiosity. Frustrated and guilt-ridden, he scourges himself and is horrified to discover that the brave new worlders can incorporate even his self-abasement into their system. Caught between the insanity of Utopia and the lunacy of the primitive village, John reacts violently—first outwardly, by assaulting Lenina and then inwardly, by killing himself.

It therefore remains for the other "rebellious" characters in the book to establish alternatives to the brave new world and here, perhaps, is where the book is artistically inferior to Huxley's previous works. One of the most impressive qualities in the novels that immediately preceded *Brave New World* is the way in which the author pursued and developed the qualities that he had given to his major characters. Unfortunately, in *Brave New World*, he does not fully develop the possibilities latent in his primary figures.

One of the sharpest ironies in *Brave New World* lies in the way Huxley carefully demonstrates that, in spite of mechanistic reproduction and incessant conditioning, individualistic traits and inclinations persist in the brave new world. As a result of alcohol in his prenatal blood surrogate, Bernard Marx shows elements of nonconformity. Because of an overdeveloped I.Q., Helmholtz Watson is dissatisfied with his situation and longs to write a book, although he cannot imagine what he wants to say. Even Lenina Crowne has dangerous tendencies toward emotional involvement; but Huxley largely fails to develop the potential of these deviations. After repeatedly showing Marx's erratic attempts to conform to a society in which he feels essentially alienated, Huxley abandons him once the Savage enters the narrative. On the other hand, Helmholtz Watson's character is hardly explored at all; and after her failure to seduce John, Lenina is almost completely forgotten except for her fleeting reappearance at the book's conclusion. Unlike the Savage, Marx and Watson are allowed a chance to travel to an isolated community and experiment with individualism, but the reader never sees the results of their austere freedom.

Although the "positive" side of *Brave New World* is never developed and all of the artistic possibilities are not fully exploited, the novel remains a powerful, perceptive, and bitterly funny vision of modern society; but let readers fervently hope, along with the author, that the final importance of *Brave New World* does not come from its prophetic accuracy.

THE BRIDE OF LAMMERMOOR
A Legend of Montrose

Type of work: Novel
Author: Sir Walter Scott (1771–1832)
Type of plot: Historical romance
Time of plot: Late seventeenth century
Locale: Scotland
First published: 1819

Principal characters:
EDGAR, the Master of Ravenswood
SIR WILLIAM ASHTON, Lord Keeper of Scotland
LUCY ASHTON, his daughter
LADY ASHTON, his wife
CALEB BALDERSTONE, Ravenswood's old servant
FRANK HAYSTON OF BUCKLAW, a young nobleman
THE MARQUIS OF A——, Ravenswood's powerful kinsman
ALICE, a blind old tenant on the Ravenswood estate

The Story:

Sir William Ashton, the new master of the Ravenswood estate, was delighted to hear of the disturbances at the late Lord Ravenswood's funeral. He hoped that the brave stand of Edgar, the young Master of Ravenswood, which made it possible for the previously prohibited Episcopal service to take place in Scotland, would put him in disfavor with the Privy Council and prevent his attempt to reclaim his family's property; however, when the Lord Keeper and his daughter Lucy visited old Alice, a tenant on the estate, they were warned about the fierce Ravenswood blood and the family motto, "I bide my time."

The Ashtons' first encounter with Edgar seemed fortunate; he shot a bull as it charged Sir William and Lucy, saving them from serious injury. The sheltered, romantic girl was fascinated by her proud rescuer, who left abruptly after he identified himself. Her more practical father gratefully softened his report of the disturbances at Lord Ravenswood's funeral and asked several friends to help Edgar.

On the evening of the rescue, Edgar joined Bucklaw, the heir to a large fortune, and the adventurer-soldier Captain Craigengelt at a tavern where he told them that he would not go with them to France. As he started home, Bucklaw, who thought himself insulted, challenged him to a duel. Edgar won, gave his opponent his life, and invited him to Wolf's Crag, the lonely, sea-beaten tower that was the only property left to the last of the once powerful Ravenswoods.

Old Caleb Balderstone did his best to welcome his master and his companion to Wolf's Crag in the style befitting the Ravenswood family, making ingenious excuses for the absence of whatever he was not able to procure from one of his many sources. The old man provided almost the only amusement for the two men, and Edgar thought often of the girl whom he had rescued. Deciding not to leave Scotland immediately, he wrote to his kinsman, the Marquis of A——, for advice. The marquis told him to remain at Wolf's Crag and hinted at political intrigue, but he offered no material assistance to supplement Caleb's meager findings.

One morning, Bucklaw persuaded Edgar to join a hunting party that was passing by the castle. An ardent sportsman, Bucklaw brought down the deer, while his friend watched from a hillside. Edgar offered Wolf's Crag as shelter against an approaching storm for an elderly gentleman and a young girl who had come to talk to him.

Poor Caleb's resourcefulness was taxed to its limit with guests to feed. When Bucklaw thoughtlessly brought the hunting party to the castle, he closed the gate, saying that he never admitted anyone while a Ravenswood dined. The old gentleman's servant sent them to the village, where Bucklaw met Captain Craigengelt again.

At Wolf's Crag, Edgar soon realized that his guests were Sir William and Lucy; Sir William had planned the hunt with the hope of securing an interview with Edgar. Lucy's fright at the storm and Caleb's comical excuses for the lack of food and elegant furnishings made relations between the two men less tense. When Edgar accompanied Sir William to his room after a feast of capon cleverly stolen by Caleb, the older man offered his friendship and promised to try to settle in Edgar's favor certain unresolved questions about the estate.

An astute politician, Sir William had heeded a warning that the Marquis of A—— was likely to rise in power, raising his young kinsman with him, and he feared the loss of his newly acquired estate. He felt that Edgar's goodwill might be valuable, and his ambitious wife's absence allowed him to follow his inclination to be friendly. A staunch Whig, Lady Ashton was in London, where she was trying to give support to the falling fortunes of her party.

Although Edgar's pride and bitterness against the enemy of his father kept him from trusting Sir William completely, the Lord Keeper had an unexpected advantage in the growing love between Edgar and Lucy. Anxious to assist the romance, he invited Edgar to accompany them to the castle where the young man had grown up.

Edgar and Lucy went together to see old Alice, who prophesied that tragedy would be the result of this unnatural alliance of Ravenswood and Ashton. Edgar resolved to tell Lucy good-bye, but at the Mermaiden Fountain, he asked her to marry him. They broke a gold coin in token of their engagement but decided to keep their love secret until Lucy's much-feared mother arrived home.

Sir William correctly interpreted the confusion of the pair when they returned, but he overlooked it to tell them of the approaching visit of the Marquis of A—— to Ravenswood. He urged Edgar to stay to meet his kinsman.

Sir William's elaborate preparations for his distinguished guest left Edgar and Lucy alone together much of the time, to the great disgust of Bucklaw, who had inherited the adjoining property. He unfairly resented Edgar, thinking that he had ordered Caleb to dismiss him summarily from Wolf's Crag. Bucklaw confided to his companion, Captain Craigengelt, that a cousin of his had become intimate with Lady Ashton and had made a match between himself and Lucy. He sent the captain to tell Lady Ashton of Edgar's presence and of the marquis of A——'s impending visit. Bucklaw hoped that she would return and intervene on his behalf.

Lady Ashton was so upset by the news that she left for home immediately, arriving simultaneously with the marquis and striking fear into the hearts of her husband and daughter. She immediately sent Edgar a note ordering him to leave, thereby incurring the displeasure of his kinsman. She became still more furious when Lucy told her of her engagement.

As Edgar passed the Mermaiden Fountain, traditionally a fateful spot for his family, he saw a white figure which he recognized as old Alice or her ghost. When he went to her cottage and found her dead, he realized that her appearance had been her final warning to him.

The marquis joined his young cousin, who had been helping with the funeral preparations, and reported that all his entreaties had failed to make Lady Ashton tolerate the engagement. He asked Edgar to let him spend the night at Wolf's Crag, insisting over the young man's protests about the lack of comfort there. When the two approached the old castle, however, they saw the tower windows aglow with flames. Later, after the people of Wolf's Hope had provided a bountiful feast for the marquis and his retinue, Caleb confessed to Edgar that he had set a few fires around the tower to preserve the honor of the family. Henceforth he could explain the absence of any number of luxuries by saying that they had been lost in the great conflagration.

Edgar went to Edinburgh with his kinsmen, who quickly acquired their expected power when the Tories took over Queen Anne's government for a short time. In prospect of better fortunes, Edgar wrote to Sir William and Lady Ashton asking permission to marry Lucy. Both answered negatively— the lady with insults and the gentleman in careful phrases, hopefully designed to win favor with the marquis. A brief note from Lucy warned her lover not to try to correspond with her; however, she promised fidelity. Edgar, unable to do anything else, went to France for a year on a secret mission for the government.

Bucklaw, whose suit was approved by the Ashtons, requested an interview with Lucy and learned from Lady Ashton, who insisted upon being present, that the girl had agreed to marry him only on the condition that Edgar would release her from her engagement. Lucy had written to ask him to do so in a letter dictated by her mother, but Lady Ashton had intercepted it, hoping that her daughter would give in if she received no answer. Lucy confessed, however, that she had sent a duplicate letter with the help of the minister and that she expected an answer before long.

She was little like the girl with whom Edgar had fallen in love, for she had been held almost a prisoner by her mother for weeks. Unable to stand the constant persecution, she had grown gloomy and ill. Lady Ashton hired an old woman as nurse for her, and at the mother's instigation, she filled the girl's wavering mind with mysterious tales and frightening legends about the Ravenswood family. Sir William, suspecting the reason for his daughter's increasing melancholy, dismissed the crone, but the damage had already been done.

Edgar, who had finally received Lucy's request that their engagement be ended, came to Ravenswood Castle to determine whether she had written the letter of her own free will; he arrived just as she was signing her betrothal agreement with Bucklaw. Unable to speak, the girl indicated that she could not stand against her parents' wishes, and she returned Edgar's half of the gold coin.

Lucy remained in a stupor after this encounter. Meanwhile, her mother continued making plans for the wedding. Old women outside the church on the marriage day prophesied that a funeral would soon follow this ceremony. Lucy's younger brother was horrified at the cold clamminess of the girl's hand. Later, she disappeared during the bridal ball, and Lady Ashton sent the bridegroom after her. Horrible cries brought the whole party to the girl's apartment, where they found Bucklaw lying stabbed on the floor. After a search, Lucy was discovered sitting in the chimney, gibbering insanely. She died the next evening, reaching vainly for the broken coin that had hung around her neck.

Bucklaw recovered, but Edgar, who appeared silently at Lucy's funeral, perished in quicksand near Wolf's Crag as he went to fight a duel with Lucy's brother, who blamed him for her death. Lady Ashton lived on, apparently without remorse for the horrors her pride had caused.

Critical Evaluation:

This novel of seventeenth century Scotland has a driving psychological as well as political, religious, and social determinism. The conflict between Presbyterian (Lord Ashton and family) and Episcopalian (Master of Ravenswood) is influential in motivating plot. So, to a lesser degree, is the politico-social turmoil that involves disintegration of old order Tory values before the energetic ambitions of the Whigs. Popular superstition thus thrives upon the inevitable confusion, disorder, and decay resulting from these changes. This power of the supernatural—manifest in omens, dreams, hidden fears, prophecy, visions, specters, and other phenomena—directs the thoughts and actions of both major and minor characters.

Sir Walter Scott, however, does not impose such superstitious paraphernalia upon the story; he employs them more subtly so that they seem the result of psychological conflict within character. The Master of Ravenswood, deprived of his castle and hereditary rights, can only, by submerging his proud loyalty, ally himself with the Ashtons, who have usurped all he holds significant in life. In his own eyes, his sudden, almost unconscious love for Lucy Ashton, although a solace and partial fulfillment of loss, still demeans him. He knows he cannot betray the values of the past, yet he has within him youth and ardor, which force him into an engagement with Lucy. All the characters in the novel, and the reader as well, know that such an alliance will lead to doom. Old Alice tells him this; Caleb Balderstone, Ravenswood's faithful, ingenious manservant, warns him against the marriage. The apparition at Mermaiden's Fountain confirms Ravenswood's fears; even Lucy's passive affection and terror of her mother all underline the Master's own perception, but he remains psychologically divided, unable to free himself emotionally from what he realizes intellectually is a disastrous union.

The schism within young Ravenswood, a truly Byronic hero, finds its dark expression in the ugly prophecies of the village hags, the superstitious talk of the sexton, the mutterings of the peasants, and Henry Ashton's shooting of the raven near the betrothed couple at the Well; but step-by-step, Ravenswood almost seeks his fate, driven relentlessly by factors deep within his personality.

Lucy is equally torn. She loves Ravenswood but is paralyzed before the dominating force of her mother. She submits to marriage with Bucklaw, but her divisive emotions drive her to murder, insanity, and death. Lord Ashton also has commendable motives in spite of his political chicanery, but he, like Lucy, is rendered ineffective by his wife's mastery.

To keep the novel from sinking into grotesque morbidity and Gothic excess, Scott provided comic relief through specific character action: Balderstone in his bizarre methods of replenishing the bare tables of Wolf's Crag and the rallying of all in the village to provide adequately for the marquis during his visit, furnish this needed humor. Scott's sense of timing and ability to tie supernatural elements to psychological divisions within personality manage to hold the novel together and make of it a controlled and well-structured work.

BRIDESHEAD REVISITED
The Sacred and Profane Memories of
Captain Charles Ryder

Type of work: Novel
Author: Evelyn Waugh (1903–1966)
Type of plot: Social criticism
Time of plot: Twentieth century
Locale: England
First published: 1945

Principal characters:

CHARLES RYDER, an architectural painter and the narrator
LORD MARCHMAIN, the owner of Brideshead
LADY MARCHMAIN, his wife
BRIDESHEAD (BRIDEY),
SEBASTIAN,
JULIA, and
CORDELIA, their children
CELIA, Charles Ryder's wife
ANTHONY BLANCHE and
BOY MULCASTER, Oxford friends of Charles and Sebastian
REX MOTTRAM, Julia's husband
CARA, Lord Marchmain's mistress

The Story:

Captain Charles Ryder of the British Army and his company were moved to a new billet in the neighborhood of Brideshead, an old estate he had often visited during his student days at Oxford. Brideshead was the home of the Marchmains, an old Catholic family. Following World War I, the Marquis of Marchmain went to live in Italy. There he met Cara, who became his mistress for life. Lady Marchmain, an ardent Catholic, and her four children, Brideshead, Sebastian, Julia, and Cordelia, remained in England. They lived either at Brideshead or at Marchmain House in London.

When Charles Ryder met Sebastian at Oxford, they soon became close friends. Among Sebastian's circle of friends were Boy Mulcaster and Anthony Blanche. With Charles's entrance into that group, his tastes became more expensive so that he ended his year with an overdrawn account of five hundred and fifty pounds.

Just after returning home from school for vacation, Charles received a telegram announcing that Sebastian had been injured. He rushed off to

Brideshead, where he found Sebastian with a cracked bone in his ankle. While at Brideshead, Charles met some of Sebastian's family. Julia had met him at the station and later Bridey, the eldest of the Marchmains, and Cordelia, the youngest, arrived. After a month, his ankle having healed, Sebastian took Charles to Venice. There they spent the rest of their vacation with Lord Marchmain and Cara.

Early in the following school year, Charles met Lady Marchmain when she visited Sebastian at Oxford. Her famous charm immediately won Charles, and he promised to spend his Christmas vacation at Brideshead. During the first term, Sebastian, Charles, and Boy Mulcaster were invited to a London charity ball by Rex Mottram, a friend of Julia's. Bored, they left early and were later arrested for drunkenness and disorderly conduct. Rex obtained their release.

As a consequence of the escapade, Charles, Sebastian, and Boy were sent back to Oxford, and Mr. Samgrass, who was doing some literary work for Lady Marchmain, kept close watch on them for the rest of the term. Christmas at Brideshead was spoiled for almost everyone by the presence of Samgrass. Back at Oxford, Charles began to realize that Sebastian drank to escape and that he was trying to escape his family. During the Easter vacation at Brideshead, Sebastian became quite drunk. Later, Lady Marchmain went to Oxford to see Sebastian. During her visit, he again became hopelessly drunk. Shortly afterward, he left Oxford. After a visit with his father in Venice, he was induced to travel in Europe under the guidance of Samgrass.

The next Christmas, Charles was invited to Brideshead to see Sebastian, who had returned from his tour. Sebastian told Charles that during their travels Samgrass had completely controlled their expense money in order that Sebastian might not get any for drink. Before coming down to Brideshead, however, Sebastian had managed to evade Samgrass by pawning his own valuables and by borrowing. He had enjoyed what he called a happy Christmas; he remembered practically nothing of it. Lady Marchmain tried to stop his drinking by having all the liquor locked up, but her efforts proved useless. Instead of going on a scheduled hunt, Sebastian borrowed two pounds from Charles and got drunk. Charles left Brideshead in disgrace and went to Paris. Samgrass was also dismissed when the whole story of the tour was revealed. Rex Mottram was given permission to take Sebastian to a doctor in Zurich, but Sebastian slipped away from him in Paris.

Rex Mottram, a wealthy man with a big name in political and financial circles, wanted Julia not only for herself but also for the prestige and social position of the Marchmains. Julia became engaged to him despite her mother's protests but agreed to keep the engagement secret for a year. Lord Marchmain gave his complete approval. Rex, wanting a large church wedding, agreed to become a Catholic. Shortly before the wedding, however, Bridey informed Julia that Rex had been married once before and had been divorced for six years. They were married in a Protestant ceremony.

When Charles returned to England several years later, Julia told him that Lady Marchmain was dying. At her request, Charles traveled to Fez to find Sebastian. When he arrived, Kurt, Sebastian's roommate, told him that Sebastian was in a hospital. Charles stayed in Fez until Sebastian had recovered. Meanwhile, word had arrived that Lady Marchmain had died. Charles returned to London. There, Bridey gave Charles his first commission; he was to paint the Marchmain town house before it was torn down.

Charles spent the next ten years developing his art. He married Celia, Boy Mulcaster's sister, and they had two children, Johnjohn and Caroline, the daughter born while Charles was exploring Central American ruins. After two years of trekking about in the jungles, he went to New York, where his wife met him. On their way back to London, they met Julia Mottram, and she and Charles fell in love. In London and at Brideshead, they continued the affair they had begun on shipboard.

Two years later, Bridey announced that he planned to marry Beryl Muspratt, a widow with three children. When Julia suggested inviting Beryl down to meet the family, Bridey informed her that Beryl would not come, because Charles and Julia were living there in sin. Julia became hysterical. She told Charles that she wanted to marry him, and they both made arrangements to obtain divorces.

Cordelia, who had been working with an ambulance corps in Spain, returned at the end of the fighting there and told them of her visit with Sebastian. Kurt had been seized by the Germans and taken back to Germany, where Sebastian followed him. After Kurt had hanged himself in a concentration camp, Sebastian returned to Morocco and gradually drifted along the coast until he arrived at Carthage. He tried to enter a monastery there but was refused. Following one of his drinking bouts, the monks found him lying unconscious outside the gate and took him in. He planned to stay there as an underporter for the rest of his life.

While Bridey was making arrangements to settle at Brideshead after his marriage, Lord Marchmain announced that he was returning to the estate to spend his remaining days. He did not arrive until after he had seen Bridey and Beryl, honeymooning in Rome. Having taken a dislike to Beryl, Lord Marchmain decided that he would leave Brideshead to Julia and Charles. Before long, Lord Marchmain's health began to fail. His children and Cara, thinking that he should be taken back into the Church, brought Father Mackay to visit him, but he would not see the priest. When he was dying, Julia again brought Father Mackay to his bedside, and Lord Marchmain made the sign of the cross.

That day Julia told Charles what he had known all along—that she could not marry him because to do so would be living in sin and without God.

These were some of Captain Charles Ryder's memories when he saw Brideshead again after many years.

Critical Evaluation:

Most of Evelyn Waugh's books are satires on some phase or precept of human life. *Brideshead Revisited* is no exception, but beneath the surface buffoonery and satire is a serious dedication of faith. Members of the Marchmain family attempt, each in a different way, to escape the promptings of their faith, but each is drawn back, sooner or later, into the enduring values of the Church. Even the droll, mocking hero is converted. In Waugh's mordantly comic world, man can no longer find his way without faith. The witty yet serious theme of the novel is suggested in its subtitle, "The Sacred and Profane Memories of Captain Charles Ryder."

Waugh's most "Catholic" novel, *Brideshead Revisited* has received the least approbation from his critics. Disappointed by the absence of the acerbic wit that characterized his earlier novels, unconvinced by Lord Marchmain's deathbed conversion, and discomfited by the author's stubborn Tory politics and the condemnation of human love unsanctified by the Church, readers have relegated the novel to a minor position in his canon.

Waugh was never an easy novelist for his audience to accommodate. Even in his works predating those in which he advances a conservative theology, he called into question the sanguine social assumptions of the twentieth century. Unconvinced by facile progressivism and humanitarianism, he brutally satirized a culture without a sense of history, limit, and sin. Beginning with *Brideshead Revisited* and continuing with his greatest work, the war trilogy, including *Men at Arms*, *Officers and Gentlemen*, and *The End of the Battle*, he dramatized the spiritual vacuity of secular man.

Charles Ryder is just that man; and, therefore, even though he is obsessed by the Marchmains, they remain a continuing enigma to him. He sees his values and happiness solely in terms of the world, whereas the Brideshead family, even the old reprobate Lord Marchmain, finally conceives of existence as having a supernatural dimension, a complexity beyond Ryder's imagination; therefore, Sebastian's entrance into a monastery and Julia's refusal to marry him—both choices of God over the world—confound and dismay Ryder.

The very structure of the novel succinctly undercuts the validity of Ryder's moral stance. Told as a flashback, the story takes place between the end of one war and the beginning of another—both worldwide conflagrations. The civilization that Ryder holds to so tenaciously is clearly dying. Like the Brideshead house itself, then, the novel has a late medieval atmosphere, an ascetic medievalism that is half in love with death.

THE BRUSHWOOD BOY

Type of work: Novelette
Author: Rudyard Kipling (1865–1936)
Type of plot: Fantasy
Time of plot: Nineteenth century
Locale: England and India
First published: 1895

Principal characters:
GEORGIE COTTAR, the brushwood boy
MIRIAM LACY, the girl in his dreams

The Story:

When he was three years old, Georgie Cottar was frightened by a dream about a policeman and screamed out in terror; but by the time he was six years old, his dreams fused into the stories he told himself while he was going to sleep. These dreams always started the same way. Near a beach was a pile of brushwood. Around this heap of brushwood, Georgie ran and played with other boys and girls. Strange and beautiful things happened in his dream story. Iron railings turned soft and could be walked on; houses filled with grown-up people were pushed over by the children. These wonderful things happened, however, only so long as Georgie knew he was dreaming. As soon as he thought them real, his dream left him sitting on a doorstep doing multiplication tables.

The princess of his dreams and his favorite, he called by the two names he thought the most beautiful in the world, Anna and Louise. These he ran together and pronounced Annieanlouise. She applauded his slaying of dragons and buffaloes and all the other brave deeds he performed in the country of dreams.

At age seven, Georgie moved with his family to "Oxford-on-a-visit." While there, he was taken to a magic show, where he sat next to a little girl who in a lisping voice admired the cut in Georgie's finger. The cut was the work of Georgie's first knife, and he was intensely proud of it. He hoped it might give him lockjaw. His conversation with the little girl was cut short by his nurse, who told him he must not talk to strangers. Georgie knew his friend was not a stranger, but he could not explain the fact to a grown-up. That night he had a new dream, and the girl of the theater waited for him at the brushwood pile, and the two played wonderful games around the brushwood.

Georgie spent the next ten years at an English public school. Those busy years did not leave much time for dreaming. In each form, he became a leader, excelling in athletics and dealing with the boys' personal quarrels. In his last year at school, he was the acknowledged leader of the students and a friend of the headmaster himself. From public school he went to Sandhurst, where he again started at the bottom of the Lower Third Form and worked his way up to a position of leadership. After Sandhurst, he received a commission as a subaltern in one of Her Majesty's regiments.

His training for leadership during his school years served him well in his new position of minor authority in the Indian service. His natural way with men made him a good leader; the poorest soldiers became men under his training. He knew his own men as few officers did, and they would follow him through any danger or through the boredom of garrison duty. He passed off heroic deeds as no more than duty. Although ladies of the garrison sought his favor, he was oblivious to their attentions.

In India, his dreams started again. They began like his dreams of old: by a brushwood pile. A sea lay beyond the brushwood pile, and on it he would travel far. Somewhere there was a lamppost, at which any wonderful thing could happen. Sometimes he raced for that lamppost in his dreams, for he knew it was a place of safety. Once a policeman waited there for him and filled him with terror, just as the policeman had terrified him in his babyhood dream. Sometimes his dreams were filled with pleasure. He sailed in a clockwork steamer, stopping by lilies labeled Hong Kong or Java. He knew that he had reached the world's end. Then a person unknown and unseen would lead him back to the brushwood pile and safety. He took a pony on a Thirty-Mile Ride, trying to reach the town with the lamppost on it. Then "They" could not harm him, whoever "They" were. So his dreams went, formless and weird.

Georgie was promoted, and under his leadership, his men won an important battle. As a reward, he was given a year's leave in England. His dreams continued throughout his furlough. Now a girl with black hair, combed in a widow's peak, was his companion in most of his dreams. She was the companion who helped him back to the lamppost and the brushwood pile. Although she had become a woman, Georgie still recognized her as his dreamland friend.

At home, Georgie was pampered and catered to by his father and mother and the servants. Mothers brought their daughters to parade before the eligible Georgie, but he was immune to them. Then Miriam Lacy was brought for a visit by her mother. Before he saw Miriam, he heard her singing a song about the policeman and the city of sleep, all from the land of his dreams. His heart stood still; he knew that here was the girl of the brushwood pile. When he met her, he saw the black hair and the widow's peak, and she spoke with a concealed lisp.

On a ride that evening, Georgie spoke to Miriam of the Thirty-Mile Ride and the lamppost. At first, she pretended ignorance, but her song had given her away. Then the two young people broke all barriers and shared in real life the dreams they had shared so long. Miriam, too, had seen all the wonderful things Georgie had seen. The companion of his dreams through all the years, she was his Annieanlouise. Now they would marry and be together in real life. In the darkness, each of them wondered what the other would look like in the light.

Critical Evaluation:

This novelette, so suggestive in its theme, appears to be at variance with other works by Rudyard Kipling. In his celebration of the troops and administrative staff of the British Empire and in his adventure stories, the author seems at first glance an unlikely candidate for the authorship of *The Brushwood Boy*.

The tale does, however, contain some of Kipling's special interests: the qualities of military leadership, the adventures of youth, and the commitment to the British way of life during the days of the Empire.

Essentially, *The Brushwood Boy* is an intense, childlike fantasy based on the ambiguous device of a shared dream. It is never clear whether the children had shared experiences and fantasies in their young lives or only imagined they had. (This ambiguity at the end preserves Kipling from the merely supernatural.) Kipling's device, however, is less interesting as "story" than as psychological examination.

In recent years, Kipling has come to be viewed more importantly as a thinker, or rather as the literary representative of a certain type of thought, than as a serious writer of fiction or verse. Although he wrote some memorable lines and phrases and created new rhythms in his poetry and although some of his books are still of great interest to children, Kipling's heavy-handed treatments and moralizing have reduced his popularity.

The Brushwood Boy is interesting, then, more for the psychological portrait of a military leader it offers, perhaps unintentionally, than for its plot or characterization. Georgie is an ideal leader of men, the type most admired by Kipling. A young man of the highest moral character yet able to relate to the most hard-bitten of his subordinates, he quickly rises in the military apparatus established by the British in India. He is loved and respected by his family, his commanders, and most of all, by his men.

What forms the central interest of *The Brushwood Boy*, however, is Georgie's continuing fantasies. These fantasies center around a pile of brushwood, which is a sort of imaginary touchstone; they consist of adventurous travels beyond the bounds of the known world and beyond the bounds of rules and regulations into a world of danger and irresponsible, malignant authority. (One of the recurring aspects of the dreams is a confrontation with an unfriendly policeman.) All these dream experiences contrast sharply with the external demeanor of such an exemplary soldier. In fact, *The Brushwood Boy* appears to offer a sort of underground vision of the British imperial mentality or the mentality of its administrative stalwarts. Beneath the "stiff upper lip," there is a residual, childlike world of wishes existing independently of the honor of Empire.

Kipling's manner of narration, simple and full of wonder, is entirely appropriate for his subject. Though *The Brushwood Boy* is not one of his better known works, its psychological insight into the functioning of a British "hero" of a bygone era remains interesting.

BULLIVANT AND THE LAMBS

Type of work: Novel
Author: Ivy Compton-Burnett (1884–1969)
Type of plot: Social satire
Time of plot: Indefinitely between 1900 and 1914
Locale: An English mansion occupied by Horace Lamb, his relatives, children, and servants
First published: 1947

Principal characters:
HORACE LAMB, the middle-aged master of his household
MORTIMER LAMB, Horace's cousin and his wife's lover
BULLIVANT, the butler who is content to know and understand all
GEORGE, his almost "criminal" helper
MRS. SELDEN, the cook
CHARLOTTE LAMB, the wife Horace married for her money
EMILIA LAMB, Horace's and Mortimer's aunt
SARAH LAMB,
MARCUS LAMB,
JASPER LAMB,
TAMASIN LAMB, and
AVERY LAMB, the children of Horace and Charlotte
GIDEON DOUBLEDAY, their tutor
GERTRUDE DOUBLEDAY, his mother
MAGDALEN DOUBLEDAY, Gertrude's daughter
MISS BUCHANAN, the storekeeper in the village

The eleventh of Ivy Compton-Burnett's novels shows her remarkable ability to dramatize fully the complicated relationships that arise in a family where master, servants, children, and relatives know nearly everything about one another and their accepted interconnections. *Bullivant and the Lambs*, published in England as *Manservant and Maidservant*, is at the same time the novel that represents best Compton-Burnett's ability to create children, servants, and their masters involved melodramatically in a meaningful interpretation of life's inevitable strange turnings and the novel that shows first her modification of her earlier view that human nature rarely changes for the better. One cannot say, of course, that Compton-Burnett ever denied man's ability to alter as well as edit himself. Still, it is true that the novels preceding *Bullivant and the Lambs* are most frequently an exploration in depth of the quantity of evil men can bear equably in themselves and others. All of them, from *Pastors and Masters*, published in 1925, through *Elders and Betters*, which appeared in 1944, show characters in apparently self-satisfied, self-centered action in which they may conceal but not change their "good" or "bad" natures. As one of the characters in *A Family and a Fortune*, published in 1939, says, it is impossible to choose the pattern we follow and so, if we are wise, we must, like the author—and for a very unbiblical reason—judge not lest we be judged. Most of us have committed or wished to commit major sins; indeed, as *Elders and Betters* made evident with particular vividness, those who are without sin are condemned to a virtue that is too pallid to be admirable and too unavoidable to be admired.

Perhaps it was the extremity of her portrayal of "evil" in *Elders and Betters* that impelled Compton-Burnett to show the possibility of change for an apparent better in *Bullivant and the Lambs*. Certainly, in her preoccupation with cold fact, she had not turned to it in her novels. Nevertheless, it is difficult to see how she could have gone further in the portrayal of the depths of unenlightened selfishness than she did in *Elders and Betters*. There, Anna Donne, from the first to the last page, is an unswerving egomaniac portrayed with devastating vividness. She treats the servants like members of the family and the members of the family like servants. She never forgets that Nature is ruthless in tooth and claw or feels that anyone but herself will serve her own interest. Anna's one accidental act of kindness to dying Aunt Sukey does not prevent her from destroying her will that would keep Anna from an inheritance. With ruthless believability, she drives Sukey's sister to suicide, marries her son, and even wins Aunt Sukey's rings as a token of her esteem without a faint sign of remorse. No one who has read *Elders and Betters* can be surprised by dictators or overcome the terrifying knowledge that they are a fact of nature.

In the beginning of *Bullivant and the Lambs*, Horace Lamb seems quite as horrifying as Anna. He tyrannizes through parsimony. An extra cutlet on the dinner table, a coal more than is needful for minimum comfort on the fire, and he is full of righteous indignation that encompasses his five children, his wife, his mother, and his servants. Only Bullivant, his butler, can accept his awfulness calmly, because he is a factualist like Compton-Burnett. He accepts even what he cannot account for and judges no one because he does not believe he or anyone else could bear to be judged. Horace Lamb does not love his children, who nevertheless maintain a precocious capacity to be witty in desperation, nor does he allow them a chance he can prevent to adjust to life normally (although somehow they do, like some citizens of totalitarian states).

Because of his ubiquitous awfulness, his wife intends to run away with his cousin so that both she and the children can escape a situation that never shows any indication it will grow less unbearable. No one can blame her. When Horace learns that his wife is to leave him and understands why, he nevertheless changes; these actions are both believable and praiseworthy. The children get new clothes and are urged to eat what they will. The house is kept warm, and there are no complaints about the coal it requires. Horace shows his affection so demonstratively that his children (always as delightfully candid and witty as any of Compton-Burnett's characters here and elsewhere) become amusedly uncomfortable. He even forgives George, Bullivant's helper, for an unsuccessful plot on his life. That both characters and the reader come to love him almost—especially if they can see with Mr. Bullivant and Cook the pathetic phoniness his character imposes upon him while he is a tyrant and when he changes to a benevolent dictator—is one of the finest triumphs of Compton-Burnett's art. It also marks the beginning of a new phase in her work, for, from *Bullivant and the Lambs* on through *A God and His Gifts*, published in 1963, Compton-Burnett's vivid factualism presents plentifully the sensational capacity for "evil" that inheres in all of her characters that matter, an ability to bear themselves without totally editing their true selves out of consciousness.

A BURNT-OUT CASE

Type of work: Novel
Author: Graham Greene (1904–   )
Type of plot: Psychological melodrama
Time of plot: Mid-twentieth century
Locale: The Belgian Congo
First published: 1961

> *Principal characters:*
> QUERRY, a spiritually maimed man of arid heart
> DR. COLIN, an atheist doctor serving at a leprosarium in the Belgian Congo
> MONTAGU PARKINSON, a news correspondent
> ANDRÉ RYCKER, the manager of a palm-oil factory
> MARIE RYCKER, his wife
> THE SUPERIOR, the head of the White Fathers mission and the leprosarium
> FATHER THOMAS, a credulous monk
> DEO GRATIAS, Querry's native servant and a burnt-out leper case

The novels of Graham Greene suggest those landscapes of the spirit that one sees frequently in Impressionistic paintings. Sometimes the scene is a bleak wasteland over which a sad, cold wind blows, twisting a few withered leaves on the boughs of stunted, storm-wrenched trees. The ground is bare and ashy. Behind the stark outlines of the trees, the sky appears dark and menacing; before long, snow will begin to fall quietly on this place of blight and desolation. Again, the scene may be a jungle riotously choked with monstrous plants. Leaves hang motionless in the heavy, fetid air. Strange flowers bloom, their hot yellows and sultry reds set against the poisonous green of the vegetation. A snake hangs like a drooping vine from a tree limb. A beast peers through the cane stalks or stands motionless over a prostrate figure lying on the bank of a river flowing through this world of silence, rank growth, and decay.

Images of the jungle and the wasteland merge in *A Burnt-Out Case* to provide a contrast between the tangled emotionalism and moral corruption in a man's past and the sterile emptiness of spiritual death in his present. The scene of the novel is a mission hospital and leprosarium maintained by the White Fathers, a minor order of Catholic monks, on a remote river in the Belgian Congo.

This is Conrad country, but in this novel it is described without Conrad's poetic, brooding vision and intensity. Perhaps Greene was aware of the difference when he wrote in his dedication that his Congo is a region of the mind. There is another important difference as well. Conrad sent his Marlow on a voyage of discovery: Africa, with its heat, jungle, and tribal mysteries, becomes the symbol of the greater darkness in the heart of man where men are all secret sharers. Querry, the central character of Greene's novel, carries his own darkness of spirit with him. He is the Roman Catholic of arid heart. Having passed beyond all that the world calls good or evil, he asks for nothing, and he has nothing to share. When the riverboat reaches the mission landing, he disembarks. He has traveled as far as he can go; beyond, there is only the overgrown jungle. Dr. Colin, the doctor at the mission, asks him if he is stopping there. Querry makes the only answer when he answers that the boat goes no farther.

Querry—Greene is adroit in his use of symbols—is that phenomenon of modern society, the burnt-out case, a term used to describe a leper in whom the disease has been halted, but not before it has eaten away its victim piecemeal. In this mutilated condition, he no longer feels the excruciating pain of those who are taking the cure for their malady and whose bodies are still whole. Querry's mutilation is spiritual, not physical, but the results are the same. He has lost the capacity to feel.

Once the monks and Dr. Colin have decided that their strange guest has not come to the mission to satisfy a morbid interest concerning leprosy, they accept him with little curiosity. They learn that he is a lapsed Catholic, a matter of concern to some of the fathers, of complete indifference to the atheist doctor, but that is all. What they do not know is that Querry is world-famous, a distinguished church architect and a notorious womanizer; but the buildings he designed and his affairs with women had been little more than the expression of his own absorbing self-love. Now the creation of beauty and the beauty of women have become meaningless to him, and he is in flight from his past. No matter how isolated a man may feel, however, and regardless of the causes of his spiritual death, no man is an island. Before long, Querry is doing small tasks about the mission, often as the doctor's assistant in the infirmary. One night he has a glimpse of what he might be seeking. Deo Gratias, the crippled, burnt-out native who has been assigned to him as his servant, disappears unaccountably, and Querry goes looking for him in the jungle. During the night he spends with the exhausted native, he hears Deo Gratias mutter something about Pendelé, the place of innocence, simple pleasures, and joy. Querry transforms his servant's words about Pendelé into terms of his own past.

The world then intrudes upon his refuge, first in the person of André Rycker, a *colon* who manages a palm-oil plantation, and then in the curious prying of Montagu Parkinson, a vulgar journalist to whom Rycker has communicated the fact that the guest at the mission is *the* Querry. (Rycker had recognized him after reading a magazine cover story about the famous architect.) With the help of Rycker and information gained from a sentimental priest who places the wrong interpretation of the shepherd and his lost sheep on Querry's night search for his servant, Parkinson proceeds to write several sensational stories in an attempt to make Querry look like another Albert Schweitzer, possibly a St. Francis, or at least a saint manqué. The fact that Querry is designing a new hospital for the mission seems to substantiate his report. This presentation of Querry as a sainted, whole man provides a titillating accompaniment to a morbid rehash of all the scandals in Querry's life, including the suicide of one of his mistresses. Parkinson is as horrible as his journalistic style and as false as the principle by which he operates, the belief that anything is true if it is believed.

Having come to Africa to report on the native riots, he is going ahead with his plans to exploit Querry after the political disturbance has died down. He is on the scene when Querry innocently spends a night in the same hotel with Rycker's wife. He says that his version of the story is as likely to be believed as Querry's version. He also tells Querry that he intended to build him up, but now it may make a better story if he tears him down.

Melodrama, common in Greene's fiction, sets the scene for the final tragedy. Marie Rycker, trying childishly to be revenged on the husband she despises, allows him to believe that Querry is the real father of her child. Rycker follows Querry to the mission and shoots him. Parkinson, who could have told the truth about the dead man's innocence but failed to do so, writes an article headed "Death of a Hermit. The Saint Who Failed." He also sends a wreath as a decoration for Querry's grave; the wreath, supposedly from the readers of his magazine, bears an inscription credited to Browning: "Nature I loved and next to Nature Art." Parkinson's quotations from the anthology poets are as mistaken as the facts in his lurid news stories.

In his dedication, Greene speaks of this novel as an effort to express different types of belief, half belief, and nonbelief. This announcement suggests at the outset that Greene intends to pigeonhole his characters and show them as limited and recognizable types. The effect of the novel, however, is quite different. His people spill over as they would in life. They are innocent and guilty, wise and foolish, skeptical and devout. Marie Rycker is in many ways an innocent child, for example, but she is the cause of Querry's death. A priest, Father Thomas, believes what he wants to believe when he sees Querry as a man destined for sainthood. Rycker, the failed priest, seeks an object of veneration outside himself and thinks that Querry is the man to revere; the murder he commits is more the sign of his own weakness than the act of an outraged husband. Only Dr. Colin, the humane atheist, and Parkinson, a monster of abstraction and a builder of the big lie, are completely themselves in their uncomplicated and thoroughgoing traits.

The quality of ambiguity exhibited in presenting his view of man's morality and faith is the secret of the appeal Greene holds for many readers. He raises questions; he clarifies; he withholds answers. He suggests by indirection the nature and mystery of man's relation to God. His bitter, disillusioned, and argumentative concerns make *A Burnt-Out Case* a serious novel, a religious parable on the possibility of redemption. William Faulkner once wrote that the world's solution lies in the suffering of man. This is Greene's theme as well.

CAKES AND ALE
Or, The Skeleton in the Cupboard

Type of work: Novel
Author: W. Somerset Maugham (1874–1965)
Type of plot: Literary satire
Time of plot: Early twentieth century
Locale: London and Kent
First published: 1930

Principal characters:
ASHENDEN, a writer
ALROY KEAR, a popular novelist
EDWARD DRIFFIELD, a great Victorian
ROSIE, Driffield's first wife
AMY, Driffield's second wife
GEORGE KEMP, Rosie's lover

The Story:

Alroy Kear, the most popular novelist of the day, arranged to have lunch with his friend Ashenden, another writer. Ashenden was fond of Kear, but he suspected that his invitation had been extended for a purpose. He was right. Kear wanted to talk about the late Edward Driffield, a famous English author of the past century. Kear had nothing but praise for the old man's books, but Ashenden said that he had never thought Driffield exceptional. Kear enthusiastically told how well he had known Driffield in his last years and said that he was still a friend of Driffield's widow, his second wife. Luncheon ended without a request for a favor. Ashenden was puzzled.

Returning to his room, Ashenden fell into a reverie. He recalled his first meeting with Driffield. Ashenden was then a boy, home for the holidays at Blackstable, a Kentish seacoast town, where he lived with his uncle, the local vicar. Ashenden met Driffield in the company of his uncle's curate; but the boy thought the writer a rather common person. He learned from his uncle that Driffield had married a local barmaid after spending a wild youth away from home.

Two or three days after Ashenden had lunched with Kear, he received a note from Driffield's widow. She wished him to visit her in Blackstable. Puzzled, Ashenden telephoned to Kear, who said that he would come to see him and explain the invitation.

Ashenden had seen Mrs. Driffield only once. He had gone to her house with some other literary people several years before, while Driffield was still alive. Driffield had married his second wife late in life, and she had been his nurse. In the course of the visit, Ashenden had been surprised to see old Driffield wink at him several times as if there were some joke between them.

After that visit, Ashenden recalled how Driffield had taught him to bicycle many years before. Driffield and his first wife, Rosie, had taught him to ride and had taken him with them on many excursions. He liked the Driffields, but he was shocked to find how outspoken they were with those below and above them in social station.

One evening, Ashenden found Rosie visiting his uncle's cook, her childhood friend. After Rosie left, he saw her meet George Kemp, a local coal merchant. The couple walked out of town toward the open fields. Ashenden could not imagine how Rosie could be unfaithful to her husband.

Ashenden went back to school. During the Christmas holiday, he often joined the Driffields for tea. Kemp was always there, but he and Rosie did not act like lovers. Driffield sang drinking songs, played the piano, and seldom talked about literature. When Ashenden returned to Blackstable the next summer, he heard that the Driffields had fled, leaving behind many unpaid bills. He was ashamed that he had ever been friendly with them.

Kear arrived at Ashenden's rooms and explained that he was planning to write Driffield's official biography. He wanted Ashenden to contribute what he knew about the author's younger days. What Ashenden told him was not satisfactory, for the biography should contain nothing to embarrass the widow. Kear insisted that Ashenden write down what he remembered of Driffield and go to Blackstable to visit Mrs. Driffield. Ashenden agreed.

Ashenden remembered how he had met the Driffields again in London when he was a young medical student. By chance, he saw Rosie on the street; he was surprised that she was not ashamed to meet someone from Blackstable, and he promised to come to one of the Driffields' Saturday afternoon gatherings. Soon he became a regular visitor in their rooms. Since Driffield worked at night, Rosie often went out with her friends. Ashenden began to take her to shows. She was pleasant company, and he began to see that she was beautiful. One evening, he invited her to his room. She offered herself to him and remained for the night; after that night, Rosie visited his room regularly.

One day, Mrs. Barton Trafford, a literary woman who had taken Driffield under her care, invited Ashenden to tea. He learned from her that Rosie had run away with Kemp, her old lover from Blackstable. Ashenden was chagrined to learn that Rosie cared for another man more than she did for him.

Ashenden then lost touch with Driffield. He learned that the author had

divorced Rosie, who had gone to New York with Kemp. Mrs. Barton
Trafford continued to care for Driffield as his fame grew. Then he caught
pneumonia. He went to the country to convalesce and there married his
nurse, the present Mrs. Driffield, whom Mrs. Trafford had hired to look
after him.

Ashenden went down to Blackstable with Kear. They talked with Mrs.
Driffield of her husband's early life. She and Kear described Rosie as
promiscuous. Ashenden said that she was nothing of the sort. Good and
generous, she could not deny love to anyone, that was all. Ashenden knew
this to be the truth, now that he could look down the perspective of years
at his own past experience. The others disagreed and dismissed the subject
by saying that, after all, she was dead.

Rosie, however, was not dead. When Ashenden had last been to New
York, she had written him and asked him to call on her. He found her now
a wealthy widow; Kemp had died several years before. She was an old
woman who retained her love for living. They talked of old times, and
Ashenden discovered that Driffield, too, had understood her—even when
she was being unfaithful to him.

Rosie said that she was too old to marry again; she had had her fling at
life. Ashenden asked her if Kemp had not been the only man she really
loved; she said that it was true. Then Ashenden's eyes strayed to a photograph of Kemp on the wall. It showed him with a waxed mustache; he was
dressed in flashy clothes, carried a cane, and flourished a cigar in one
hand. Ashenden turned to Rosie and asked why she had preferred Kemp
to her other lovers. Her reply was simple. He had always been the perfect
gentleman.

Critical Evaluation:
Somerset Maugham is one of the master craftsmen of the English novel.
Although his talents have been underrated by some critics who scoff at the
apparent simplicity of his novels, others more astutely point out Maugham's
considerable storytelling skills. Through his fiction, Maugham sought the
general truth in all things. His expression was direct, plain, and concise,
easily capturing the rhythms and colloquialisms of informal conversation.
His themes were usually not explicit, since he preferred to let his characters
form the bases of philosophies. Evidence suggests, however, that Maugham
was intensely interested in religion, ethics, and the psychology of artistic
creativity. He rarely dealt with political history, because people were more
important than world events to him. These interests resulted in a large out-
put of novels, which have enjoyed great popular success.

Maugham's emphasis on the human element is reflected in his technique
of characterization: most often, characters are paired in a thesis-antithesis
relationship. In *Cakes and Ale*, Ashenden, the narrator, is depicted as the

writer with integrity and Kear as the venal hack; Kemp is recalled as the dashing lover and Driffield as the rather indifferent husband; Rosie is portrayed as a kind, loving person and Amy, the second Mrs. Driffield, as a hypocritical prude. These pairings should not, however, be construed as oversimplifications of characterization, because the complexities of each character are gradually revealed over the course of the entire novel. Consequently, Kear, Driffield, and Amy are not irredeemably bad any more than Ashenden, Kemp, and Rosie are flawlessly good. Rather, all of them are human beings with strengths and weaknesses that Maugham skillfully discloses through his thesis-antithesis technique of characterization.

When *Cakes and Ale* was first published, it was a *succès de scandale*, since the character of Driffield was widely believed to be a caricature of the English novelist Thomas Hardy. Maugham denied any connection between his novel and Hardy's biography, and when the furor subsided, readers were left with an incisive satire of the English literary world, including such well-known types as the celebrity, the neophyte, the genuine artist, and the commercial scribbler. The barbed parodies of pretentious drawing-room conversations about literature echo—even in the title of the novel—Proust's "tea and cakes"; similarly, they call to mind T. S. Eliot's stinging rebukes of pseudosophisticated discussions about art in "The Love Song of J. Alfred Prufrock." Maugham once admitted that he preferred *Cakes and Ale* over his two more popular novels, *Of Human Bondage* and *The Moon and Sixpence*. To read *Cakes and Ale* is to know why.

CALEB WILLIAMS

Type of work: Novel
Author: William Godwin (1756–1836)
Type of plot: Mystery romance
Time of plot: Eighteenth century
Locale: England
First published: 1794

Principal characters:
CALEB WILLIAMS
FERDINANDO FALKLAND, Caleb's employer
COLLINS, Falkland's servant
BARNABAS TYRREL, Falkland's enemy
GINES, Caleb's enemy
EMILY MELVILE, Tyrrel's cousin

The Story:

Caleb Williams was engaged as secretary by Mr. Ferdinando Falkland, the wealthiest and most respected squire in the country. Falkland, although a considerate employer, was subject to fits of distemper that bewildered Caleb. Because these black moods were so contrary to his employer's usual gentle nature, Caleb soon questioned Collins, a trusted servant of the household, and learned from him the story of Falkland's early life.

Studious and romantic in his youth, Falkland lived many years abroad before he returned to England to live on his ancestral estate. One of his neighbors was Barnabas Tyrrel, a man of proud, combative nature. When Falkland returned to his family estate, Tyrrel was the leading gentleman in the neighborhood. Because of his graceful manners and warm intelligence, Falkland soon began to win the admiration of his neighbors. Tyrrel was jealous and showed his feelings by speech and actions. Falkland tried to make peace, but the ill-tempered Tyrrel refused his proffered friendship.

Miss Emily Melvile, Tyrrel's cousin, occupied the position of a servant in his household. One night, she was trapped in a burning building, and Falkland saved her from burning. Afterward, Emily could do nothing but praise her benefactor. Her gratitude annoyed her cousin, who planned to revenge himself on Emily for her admiration of Falkland. He found one of his tenants, Grimes, a clumsy ill-bred lout, who consented to marry Emily. When Emily refused to marry a man whom she could never love, Tyrrel confined her to her room. As part of the plot, Grimes helped Emily to escape and then attempted to seduce her. She was rescued from her plight by Falkland, who for the second time proved to be her savior. Further cruelties inflicted on her by Tyrrel finally killed her, and Tyrrel became an object of disgrace in the community.

One evening, Tyrrel attacked Falkland in a public meeting, and Falkland was deeply humiliated. That night, Tyrrel was found dead in the streets. Since the quarrel had been witnessed by so many people just before the murder of Tyrrel, Falkland was called before a jury to explain his whereabouts during that fatal night. No one really believed Falkland guilty, but he was hurt by what he considered the disgrace of his inquisition. Although a former tenant was afterward arrested and hanged for the crime, Falkland never recovered his injured pride. He retired to his estate where he became a moody and disconsolate recluse.

For a long time after learning these details, Caleb pondered over the apparent unhappiness of his employer. Attempting to understand his morose personality, he began to wonder whether Falkland suffered from the unearned infamy that accompanied suspicion of murder or from a guilty conscience. Determined to solve the mystery, Caleb proceeded to talk to his master in an insinuating tone, to draw him out in matters concerning murder and justice. Caleb also began to look for evidence that would prove Falkland guilty or innocent. Finally, the morose man became aware of his secretary's intent. Swearing Caleb to secrecy, Falkland confessed to the murder of Barnabas Tyrrel and threatened Caleb with irreparable harm if he should ever betray his employer.

Falkland's mansion became a prison for Caleb, and he resolved to run away no matter what the consequences might be. When he had escaped to an inn, he received a letter ordering him to return to defend himself against a charge of theft. When Falkland produced some missing jewels and bank notes from Caleb's baggage, Caleb was sent to prison in disgrace. His only chance to prove his innocence was to disclose Falkland's motive, a thing no one would believe.

Caleb spent many months in jail, confined in a dreary, filthy dungeon and bound with chains. Thomas, a servant of Falkland and a former neighbor of Caleb's father, visited Caleb in his cell. Perceiving Caleb in his miserable condition, Thomas could only wonder at English law that kept a man so imprisoned while he waited many months for trial. Compassion forced Thomas to bring Caleb tools with which he could escape from his dungeon. At liberty once more, Caleb found himself in a hostile world with no resources.

At first, he became an associate of thieves, but he left the gang after he had made an enemy of a man named Gines. When he went to London, hoping to hide there, Gines followed him, and soon Caleb was again caught and arrested. Falkland visited him and explained that he knew every move Caleb had made since he had escaped from prison. Falkland told Caleb that although he would no longer prosecute him for theft, he would continue to make Caleb's life intolerable. Wherever Caleb went, Gines followed and exposed Caleb's story to the community. Caleb tried to escape to Holland, but just as he was to land in that free country, Gines appeared and stopped him.

Caleb returned to England and charged Falkland with murder, asking the magistrate to call Falkland before the court. At first, the magistrate refused to summon Falkland to reply to the charge; but Caleb insisted upon his rights, and Falkland appeared. The squire had now grown terrible to behold; his haggard and ghostlike appearance showed that he had not long to live.

Caleb pressed his charges in an attempt to save himself from a life of persecution and misery. So well did Caleb describe his miserable state and his desperate situation that the dying man was deeply touched. Demonstrating the kindness of character and the honesty for which Caleb had first admired him, Falkland admitted his wrongdoings and cleared Caleb's reputation.

In a few days the sick man died. Although remorseful, Caleb was determined to make a fresh start in life.

Critical Evaluation:

William Godwin titled his novel, *Things As They Are: Or, The Adventures of Caleb Williams*; it survives under the name of its hero. It is a novel of divided interests, as it was written both to criticize society and to tell an adventure story. All the elements which contribute to Caleb's misery are the result of weaknesses in eighteenth century English laws, which permitted the wealthy landowners to hold power over poorer citizens.

Historians of the novel have always encountered great difficulty in categorizing Godwin's *Caleb Williams*. It has been called a great tragic novel, the first pursuit novel, a crime or mystery novel, a chase-and-capture adventure, a political thesis fiction, a Gothic Romance, a terror or sensation novel, even a sentimental tale. To some extent, it is all of these—and none of them. The novel has, like most enduring works of art, taken on many shapes and meanings as new readers interpret the narrative in terms of their own personal, cultural, and historical experiences.

Godwin had no doubts about his book's meaning or about the effect he hoped to achieve with it: "I will write a tale that shall constitute an epoch in the mind of the reader, that no one, after he has read it, shall ever be exactly the same man that he was before." Having achieved fame in 1793 with his powerful, influential, and controversial political treatise *Enquiry Concerning the Principles of Political Justice*, he sought a form in which to dramatize his ideas. At the most obvious level, then, *Caleb Williams* can be seen as a fictional gloss on Godwin's previous political masterpiece.

Caleb Williams, however, is no simple political tract. Godwin knew that he must first develop a narrative, in his words, "distinguished by a very powerful interest," if he expected readers to absorb and seriously consider his philosophical and social ideas; so he took the most exciting situation he could conceive, creating, as he said, "a series of adventures of flight and pursuit; the fugitive in perpetual apprehension of being overwhelmed with the worst calamities, and the pursuer, by his ingenuity and resources, keeping his victim in a state of the most fearful alarm." Having first decided on the outcome of his adventure, Godwin then worked backwards, like a modern mystery story writer, to develop a sequence of events leading up to his climax. The result is a well-constructed narrative in which each of the three volumes are tightly connected, both structurally and thematically, the action developing logically and directly with ever-mounting tension to a powerful, even tragic, dénouement.

In Godwin's words, Ferdinando Falkland has the ability to "alarm and harass his victim with an inextinguishable resolution never to allow him the least interval of peace and security," because of an unjust and fundamentally corrupt society. The worst villain is a legal system that gives absolute power to the rich and victimizes the poor, all in the name of "justice." Falkland fears Caleb's knowledge, because Falkland has committed the only crime that an aristocrat can commit in eighteenth century England—a crime against a social equal. Had Tyrrel been poor, the issue would never have been raised. Caleb's alleged crime—stealing from his master and accusing the master of conspiracy against him—arouses such extreme repugnance because it challenges the social hierarchy and the assumptions that support it.

The problem, however, is not one of simple, conscious tyranny. Both rich and poor are unaware of the injustice and cruelty that their social institutions foster. They have been conditioned by their environment to accept the system as necessary, proper, and even benevolent. It is not the willful malevolence of a few but "society" itself that distorts and dissipates the best qualities of men, regardless of their social class, although the poor suffer the most obvious physical oppressions. Falkland is not an example of deliberate evil; he is a good man who, because of his social role, has accepted a body of attitudes and moral values that are destructive. His passion to conceal his crime and his persecution of Caleb are the result not of any fear of legal punishment but of his obsessive concern for his aristocratic "honor." "Though I be the blackest of villains," he tells Caleb, "I will leave behind me a spotless and illustrious name. There is no crime so malignant, no scene of blood so horrible in which that object cannot engage me."

There are no human villains in this novel; social institutions are Godwin's targets. This explains the novel's strange ending, which seems to reverse all of the book's previous assumptions. Having finally succeeded in turning the law against his tormentor, Caleb realizes, as he faces a broken Falkland, that he, Caleb, is the real enemy. Falkland, for his part, admits his guilt and embraces Caleb; but, to Godwin, neither man is guilty. Both have been caught up in a series of causal circumstances created by their environment and resulting in their inevitable mutual destruction. Only when the environment can be altered to allow men's natural capacities to emerge, undistorted and unfettered by artificial, malevolent environmental conditioning, can such self-destruction be avoided and human potential realized.

CAPTAIN HORATIO HORNBLOWER

Type of work: Novel
Author: C. S. Forester (1899–1966)
Type of plot: Historical romance
Time of plot: Early nineteenth century
Locale: The Pacific Ocean, South America, the Mediterranean, Spain,
    France, England, and the Atlantic Ocean
First published: 1937, 1938, 1939

> *Principal characters:*
> CAPTAIN HORATIO HORNBLOWER, the captain of H.M.S. *Lydia*
>   and H.M.S. *Sutherland*
> BUSH, the first lieutenant
> BROWN, the captain's coxswain
> DON JULIAN ALVARADO (EL SUPREMO), a rich plantation
>   owner in Central America
> MARIA, Hornblower's wife
> LADY BARBARA WELLESLEY, the Duke of Wellington's sister
> ADMIRAL LEIGHTON, Hornblower's immediate commander
>   and Lady Barbara's husband

The Story:

Captain Horatio Hornblower, commander of H.M.S. *Lydia*, a thirty-six-gun frigate, was sailing under sealed orders from England around the Horn to the Gulf of Fonseca on the western shores of Spanish America. He had been ordered to form an alliance with Don Julian Alvarado, a large landowner, to assist in raising a rebellion against Spain. The *Lydia* carried the necessary munitions with which to start the revolution. In addition, Hornblower had fifty thousand guineas in gold, which he was to give for the support of the rebellion only if the revolt threatened to fail without English gold to back it. To do otherwise would result in a court-martial. His orders also casually mentioned the presence in Pacific waters of a fifty-gun Spanish ship called the *Natividad*. It was his duty to take, sink, burn, or destroy this ship at the first opportunity.

After the ship had been anchored in the Gulf of Fonseca, a small boat appeared containing emissaries from Don Alvarado, who now called himself El Supremo. They told Hornblower that El Supremo required the captain's attendance.

Hornblower was not pleased with evidences of El Supremo's tyranny. What he observed made him only the more cautious. He refused to hand over to El Supremo the arms and ammunition that he had until his ship had taken on food and water. The ship was loaded with stores as rapidly as possible, and the operation was going forward when a lookout on the mountain announced the approach of the *Natividad*.

Deciding to try to capture her in the bay, Hornblower hid the *Lydia* behind an island as the *Natividad* approached. At the moment which gave him the greatest advantage, Hornblower ordered the *Lydia* to sail alongside the *Natividad* and rake her decks with grapeshot. The British sailors lashed the two ships together and boarded the *Natividad*. El Supremo demanded the captured ship as his own. Hornblower hesitated to turn over his prize to El Supremo, but he dared not antagonize the dictator if he were to fulfill the requirements of his orders.

Hornblower sailed away and shortly afterward learned that England was now an ally of Spain because of Napoleon's deposition of King Ferdinand. He also received further orders, one from his Admiral and one from an English lady in Panama. The Englishwoman was Lady Barbara Wellesley, sister of the Duke of Wellington, who requested transportation to England. During this period, the *Lydia* met and defeated the *Natividad*, now under El Supremo. A long period of association between Lady Barbara and Hornblower ended in deep mutual love; but Hornblower could not bring himself to make love to her because of his wife Maria at home and because of his own chivalry. Lady Barbara was carried safely to England.

Captain Horatio Hornblower was next ordered to command H.M.S. *Sutherland*, a seventy-four-gun battleship. He sailed with the *Pluto* and the *Caligula* to protect a convoy of merchant ships as far as the latitude of North Africa. They then met French privateers and beat them off. Before parting company with the merchantmen, Hornblower impressed sailors from the convoy.

Sailing along the coast, he captured the *Amelie*, attacked the battery at Llanza, burned and destroyed supply vessels, and shelled two divisions of cavalry on a highway passing near the seashore.

Admiral Leighton, now Lady Barbara's husband, ordered Hornblower to join and take charge of Spanish forces at the siege of French-held Rosas, but the operation failed because the Spaniards did not cooperate. After his retreat, Hornblower met the *Cassandra*, a British frigate, and he learned that four French ships were bearing down upon them. Hornblower decided to fight, even though the odds were four to one, and sent the *Cassandra* to seek the *Pluto* and the *Caligula*. The *Cassandra* came back and relayed a message to Hornblower to engage the enemy. That order indicated the presence of the admiral's flagship. Hornblower engaged the French ships one at a time. The fourth French ship, however, came upon him as he was fighting a two-decker and forced him to surrender.

After his surrender, Hornblower and Bush were imprisoned at Rosas.

Admiral Leighton sailed into the bay with the *Pluto* and the *Caligula* and completed the destruction of the French squadron. Hornblower watched the battle from the walls and saw the *Sutherland*, which had been beached, take fire as a raiding party of British seamen burned her to prevent her use by the French. He learned from a seaman that Admiral Leighton had been injured by a flying splinter.

Colonel Caillard, Napoleon's aide, came to Rosas to take Hornblower and the wounded Bush to Paris. Bush was seriously ill as a result of losing a foot in the battle; therefore, Hornblower requested a servant to attend Bush on the long journey. He selected Brown, the coxswain, because of his strength, his common sense, and his ability to adapt himself to every situation. In France, their stagecoach was halted by a snowstorm near Nevers. Hornblower had noticed a small boat moored to the bank of a river and, as he and Brown assisted the French in trying to move the coach, he laid his plans for escape. He himself attacked Colonel Caillard, and Brown tied up the Frenchman and threw him into the bottom of the coach. They lifted Bush out of the coach and carried him to the boat. The whole operation required only six minutes.

In the dead of night, the fugitives made their way down the river with Hornblower rowing while Brown bailed the icy water from the boat. When the boat crashed against a rock, Hornblower, thinking he had lost Bush and Brown, swam ashore in the darkness. Brown, however, brought Bush safely to shore. Shivering with cold, the three men made their way to a farmhouse nearby, where they announced themselves as prisoners of war and were admitted.

Throughout the winter, they remained as guests of its owner, Comte de Gracay, and his daughter-in-law. Brown made an artificial foot for Bush and, when Bush was able to get around well, he and Brown built a boat in which to travel down the Loire. In early summer, Hornblower disguised himself as a Dutch customs inspector. To complete his disguise, the comte gave him the ribbon of the Legion of Honor that had been his son's. That decoration aided Hornblower in his escape.

When Hornblower and his two men arrived in the harbor at Nantes, Hornblower cleverly took possession of the *Witch of Endor*, taking with him a group of prisoners to man the ship. They made their way to England. Upon his arrival, Hornblower was praised for his exploits, knighted, and whitewashed at a court-martial. His sickly wife had died during his absence, and Lady Barbara had become guardian of his young son. Hornblower went to the home of Lady Barbara to see his son—and Barbara. Admiral Leighton had died of wounds at Gibraltar; Barbara was now a widow. Hornblower realized from the quiet warmth of her welcome that she was already his. He felt that life had given him fame and fortune—in Barbara, good fortune indeed.

Critical Evaluation:

Composed of three short novels—*Beat to Quarters* (1937), *A Ship of the Line* (1938), and *Flying Colours* (1939)—*Captain Horatio Hornblower* is the middle section of a series that begins with the intrepid officer's sea apprenticeship (the *Young Hornblower* trilogy) and concludes with *Commodore Hornblower*, *Lord Hornblower*, and *Admiral Hornblower in the West Indies*. For its broad scope and sustained vigor, the whole series has appropriately been described as a modern saga. Although C. S. Forester's Hornblower romances do not quite belong among the highest rank of sea fiction—that by Joseph Conrad, Richard Henry Dana, or Herman Melville—because they lack a philosophical and moral dimension, they certainly are the equal of sea-adventure novels by Captain Frederick Marryat or James Fenimore Cooper. Forester's novels combine meticulous historical reconstruction with a flair for storytelling. In 1932, he began writing screenplays for Hollywood. Unlike many other distinguished novelists who were either failures or were only moderately successful in adapting their skills to this medium, Forester excelled as a scriptwriter and, in turn, learned how to use certain cinematic techniques in his fiction. Lively, fast-paced, with each scene building to a climax, his Hornblower stories are easy to visualize. At the same time, they are packed with authentic historical pieces of information. Not only are his celebrated battle scenes bristling with sharp, concrete details that capture the excitement of the moment, but in his description of English manners, customs, and topical interests during the early nineteenth century, the robust age comes alive.

As a Realist, Forester does not gloss over the unpleasant truths about warfare at sea or the rigors of nautical life. Early in *Captain Horatio Hornblower*, readers learn that Hankey, the previous surgeon attached to H.M.S. *Lydia*, has died of the complications of drink and syphilis. Hornblower must perform several grisly operations on his wounded men. After one battle in *Beat to Quarters*, he cuts out a great splinter of wood lodged in a seaman's chest. Using no anesthetic (except whiskey), he performs the operation crudely, and Forester does not spare his readers the terrible details. Similarly, in *Flying Colours*, Hornblower must relieve the gangrenous pressure on the stump of his friend Bush's amputated leg. Applying cold vinegar to the stump to reduce the inflammation, he opens, cleans, and then sews up the victim's wound. Other scenes of grim realism impart a sense of truth to the romance. In *Beat to Quarters*, Hornblower sees a man horribly tortured by the cruel El Supremo for no reason at all, simply because the man has been judged "one of the unenlightened." Hornblower also witnesses the aftermath of battle: "dirty bodies with blood and pus and vomit." Forester creates realistic touches not only in the stark scenes of battle but also in the smallest details. He describes how ships are loaded with provisions, how the officers and crew function in a hierarchy of responsibilities, and how the ships operate in calm or storm. At one point, Hornblower's friend Gailbraith describes a poem that he admires, "The Lay of the Last Minstrel," whose author is "an Edinburgh lawyer." Instead of identifying the author as Sir Walter Scott, Forester thus creates a sense of historical realism; for at the time of the action, Scott, not yet famous, might have been known only as a lawyer who dabbled in poetry.

Moreover, in his characterization of Horatio Hornblower, Forester provides sharp, realistic details that make his hero seem human. Although he is high-minded, courageous, and capable, Hornblower is not without frailties. He is vain, sometimes squeamish, and—strange to say—naturally indolent. Near the beginning of *Beat to Quarters*, Hornblower views himself critically in a mirror, noting all of his physical liabilities as well as his strengths. He does not like his "rounded belly" and fears that he is growing bald. Several times in the book he reflects unhappily upon his receding hairline. For a hero, he has a weak stomach for scenes of squalor or bloodshed. He must be shamed by Lady Barbara Wellesley before he allows her to dress the wounds of the injured. Furthermore he is, by his own admission, lazy. After a battle involving the *Lydia*, Hornblower retires to his hammock to sleep. Although he feels "a prick of shame" that the other officers and men have to clean up the bodies and wreckage, he confesses to his physical limitations. Again, in *Flying Colours*, he wishes "to be idle and lazy." When his gentle wife Maria dies, he is plunged into grief; when he holds his child in his arms, he feels paternal elation; and when he courts Lady Barbara, he is an ardent yet awkward lover. Forester humanizes Hornblower, making him a man as well as a hero. Such a hero is worthy of his victories.

CAPTAIN SINGLETON

Type of work: Novel
Author: Daniel Defoe (1660–1731)
Type of plot: Adventure romance
Time of plot: Eighteenth century
Locale: The navigable world
First published: 1720

> *Principal characters:*
> CAPTAIN BOB SINGLETON, a sailor, explorer, and pirate
> WILLIAM WALTERS, a Quaker surgeon

The Story:

Captain Bob Singleton was stolen as a child and reared by the gypsy who bought him. His first voyages, which began when he was age twelve, were to Newfoundland. On one of these voyages, the ship was captured by Turks. The Turkish vessel was subsequently captured by a Portuguese ship. After many months on shore, Singleton sailed as a cabin boy from Portugal on a voyage to Goa on the Malabar coast. At this time, Singleton began to learn the arts of navigation, and he also became an accomplished thief.

On the return voyage, a storm drove the ship to the shore of Madagascar. There Singleton enthusiastically joined a group of malcontents who plotted the harsh captain's death, and he barely escaped hanging. However, he and twenty-six companions, with guns, tools, and provisions, were abandoned on shore. The natives were friendly and traded food with the sailors in exchange for metal charms cut out of beaten coins, as they had no knowledge of the value of currency. After exploring the island and the shore, the party was able to build a frigate and sail for the mainland.

Landing at Mozambique, they decided to trek across the entire unknown continent to the Atlantic. They began the journey with buffaloes loaded with their provisions and with some sixty captured natives as guides and bearers. Singleton was by this time their appointed leader. At first, they marched only when travel by river was impossible. By hunting and foraging, they survived well enough until they came to the first desert. After nine days on the desert, they reached a lake, fished, and renewed their water supply. In sixteen days, they completed the desert crossing and entered another fertile region where travel was easy until they came to an impassable river—possibly the Nile.

When the chief native prisoner found gold in a small stream flowing into the main river, they panned as much as they could and agreed to share it equally. After a time, they built a garrisoned camp to avoid traveling in the rainy season. Protected by palisades from wild animals that roamed the region, the travelers remained there through the rainy season. On the subsequent march, they almost perished while crossing a further stretch of arid land. Beyond this desert, they obtained meat from a native village and soon moved into a mountainous region. While proceeding along the main valley, they were astonished to meet an Englishman who had been captured and robbed by the French. Having managed to escape inland, he had stayed in the country of friendly natives. He joined the travelers and told them where to find more gold. After two profitable years, they continued on to the Gold Coast. There the party disbanded, and Singleton sailed to England.

During the next two years in England, Singleton spent lavishly and was often cheated. When his money was gone, he sailed for Cádiz. Off the coast of Spain, he broke his journey at the instigation of a friend and went aboard a vessel whose crew had mutinied and taken possession of the ship; thus began Singleton's career as a pirate.

Having obtained provisions in Cádiz, the pirate ship sailed for the Canary Islands and then on to the West Indies. After the capture of a Spanish sloop, Singleton sailed aboard her and arranged to meet the other ship in Tobago. He found that the crew of a captured ship was often willing to join him. One man who did so was a Quaker surgeon named William Walters. William and Singleton became friends, and the Quaker often saved him from wasteful maneuvers and bloodshed. After a meeting in Tobago, the pirates arranged to cruise separately again and later to join forces in Madagascar.

In a successful engagement off Brazil, Singleton captured and took command of a forty-six-gun Portuguese man-of-war. They acquired many slaves from the next captured ship. William persuaded Singleton and the crew not to kill these men. Instead, he sold them on the Rio Grande for gold and a fine French sloop. Continuing the voyage, they rounded the Cape of Good Hope to land on Madagascar for provisions.

During the night that followed the sighting of a wrecked European ship on the African shore, William and the coxswain both dreamed that if they landed, they would find gold. They discovered a group of their former companions who, shipwrecked on Tabago, had been taken aboard another ship and subsequently had captured several ships of their own and thereby gained much gold. The whole pirate fleet, including ships under Captain Wilmot and Captain Avery, gathered at Mangahelly. Some stayed in a camp on shore. Eventually, William and Singleton sailed for Ceylon in the man-of-war.

Off Ceylon, they captured a ship from the Mogul's court. The vessel yielded so much gold that the sailors wished to return at once to Madagascar. Together, William and Singleton persuaded them to continue the voyage.

Singleton's ambition was to capture ships from the Dutch Spice Islands.

After sailing north of the Philippines, they finally overtook a vessel laden with nutmegs. Unfortunately, they grounded the man-of-war on a group of rocks and were forced to beach and repair her. Soon after they resailed, they were hit by a violent storm that shook the ship and momentarily so terrified Singleton that he believed the lightning to be the punishment from Divine Providence for his crimes. However, nobody was hurt, and they continued on as before with the ship only slightly damaged.

North of Manila three Japanese ships yielded cinnamon, nutmeg, cloves, and some gold. From there, they sailed two months until they reached Formosa. By this time, everybody was agreed that they were rich enough. Off the Chinese coast they made contact with merchants with whom William traded spices and cloth for gold. Then they began the long journey southward and westward home.

The vessel sailed to Java for provisions and then to Ceylon, where they had great trouble with natives who nearly ignited the ship with fire-arrows. Finally, after tricking the native leaders through a Dutch interpreter who was a prisoner there, they managed to take him on board and to sail away unharmed.

William continued to trade; when he had satisfactorily disposed of most of the booty, he talked earnestly to Singleton about his crimes. Together, they agreed to abandon piracy. Furthermore, Singleton said that from then on he would be under William's command. William made two more trading trips. On the second trip, Singleton and another surgeon accompanied him in the sloop with their accumulated treasure. William sent a letter to the man-of-war saying that they had been captured and that they must sail away to save their own lives. The men quickly obeyed.

William and Singleton disguised themselves as Persian merchants. During this time, Singleton became profoundly troubled by his conscience. William dissuaded him from suicide by suggesting that they might be able to put their illegal fortunes to some good use. They traveled in caravan to Alexandria and then sailed to Venice.

In time, William wrote to his widowed sister in England. He and Singleton both sent her money to buy a house for her children and themselves. Finally, still disguised as merchants, they returned home. Singleton, whose repentance was complete, married William's sister and lived with her in great contentment and quiet.

Critical Evaluation:

Fascinated as they were by tales about remote nations of the world, Daniel Defoe's readers thrilled to such fictions as *Robinson Crusoe* (1719), *Colonel Jack* (1722), and *Captain Singleton.* Nor, of course, was Defoe the only writer of such literature. One thinks immediately of Jonathan Swift's *Gulliver's Travels* (1726), which, if it is not altogether typical of the genre, clearly attests to its popularity.

Defoe can justly be called the first English novelist. The three outstanding works of prose fiction before Defoe wrote were Lyly's *Euphues*, a courtly and philosophical work; Sidney's *Arcadia*, a chivalrous romance, and John Bunyan's religious and symbolic allegory, *The Pilgrim's Progress*. Realistic characters and the commonsense point of view were Defoe's contributions to prose fiction. In *The Life, Adventures, and Piracies of the Famous Captain Singleton*, unlike Robinson Crusoe to which it is undoubtedly inferior, character is subordinated to action. In both books, Defoe relied heavily on Dampier's accounts of voyages, travelers' tales, and available maps and geographies. The novel also contains a wealth of clearly imagined detail in its objective narrative, and two contrasted characters: the courageous, egocentric Singleton and the shrewd pacifist, William. Here and in the rest of Defoe's fiction is the germ of the English novel.

Captain Singleton not only fulfills the requirements for travel literature of the period but does so to a fault. The emphasis of the novel is on action—at the expense of character—and colorful, incidental detail. Nearly the entire first half of the book treats Singleton's wearisome trek from the east coast of Madagascar to the west coast of Africa; the second half, something of a *non sequitur*, embarks on quite a different course—Singleton's adventures as a pirate. The novel, therefore, betrays Defoe's tendency to indulge a tasteless reading public. It is diffuse, void of effective characterization, overly reportorial, and disconnected in its two major movements. It succeeds best in its fertile inventiveness and easy style. Only Defoe could build a lengthy episode around the idea of laying siege to a tree or cultivate such stylistic touches as: "to think of Death, is to dye; and to be always thinking of it, is to be all one's Life-long a dying."

This is a novel that also embraces much Puritan theology, as a reader would expect from the author of *Robinson Crusoe*. Singleton is "homeless" in two distinct senses of the word: he has neither a physical nor a spiritual domicile, since he has been stolen away both from his earthly parents and his divine Father; therefore he is tractable and indifferent to the decisions that others make for him. After all, he has no "Pilot" to direct his life. Like Crusoe, he eschews a safe, comfortable life in order to indulge his wanderlust (in *Robinson Crusoe* an evident sin against the "Father") with the result that God tries him with many perils. This theological undertow in the novel is not nearly so pronounced as it is in other Defoe novels (*Captain Singleton* is scarcely an allegory), but it is nonetheless present. In the end, Bob Singleton repents of his roguish life, but predictably keeps his ill-gotten gains in order to do good with them.

There are a number of minor points in the novel that are of interest, among them Defoe's intense dislike of the Portuguese (this surfaces in his other works) and his familiarity with eighteenth century geography. Readers today will also appreciate his attitudes toward slavery and toward so-called "natural law." Defoe seems to have condemned strongly the idea of enslavement (though his heroes practice it) even as he believed the black race to be unenlightened. He viewed natural law in the manner of Thomas Hobbes: what exists is the principal law governing human actions.

CAPTAINS COURAGEOUS

Type of work: Novel
Author: Rudyard Kipling (1865–1936)
Type of plot: Adventure romance
Time of plot: 1890's
Locale: Grand Banks of Newfoundland
First published: 1897

Principal characters:
HARVEY CHEYNE, a spoiled young rich boy
DISKO TROOP, the owner and captain of the *We're Here*
DAN TROOP, his son
MR. CHEYNE, Harvey's father

The Story:

Harvey Cheyne was a rich, spoiled fifteen-year-old boy, bound for Europe aboard a swift ocean liner. He was also such a seasick young man that he hardly realized what was happening to him when a huge wave washed him over the rail of the ship into the sea. Luckily, he was picked up by a fisherman in a dory and put aboard the fishing schooner *We're Here*. The owner and captain of the boat, Disko Troop, was not pleased to have the boy aboard but told him that he would pay him ten dollars a month and board until the schooner docked in Gloucester the following September. It was then the middle of May. Harvey, however, insisted upon being taken to New York immediately, asserting that his father would gladly pay for the trip. The captain, doubting that Harvey's father was a millionaire, refused to change his plans and hazard the profits of the fishing season. Harvey became insulting. Disko Troop promptly punched him in the nose to teach him manners.

The captain's son, Dan, soon became a friend of the castaway. He was glad to have someone his own age aboard the fishing boat, and Harvey's stories about mansions, private cars, and dinner parties fascinated him. Since Dan was a boy as well, he recognized the sincerity of the rich lad and knew that he could not possibly have made up all the details of a wealthy man's life.

As Harvey began to fit into the life aboard the schooner, all the fishermen took an interest in his nautical education. Long Jack, one of the crew, escorted him about the boat to teach him the names of the ropes and the various pieces of equipment. Harvey learned quickly for two reasons. First,

CAPTAINS COURAGEOUS by Rudyard Kipling. By permission of Mrs. George Bambridge and the publishers, Doubleday & Co., Inc. Copyright, 1896, 1897, by Rudyard Kipling. Renewed, 1923, by Rudyard Kipling.

he was a bright young lad, and, second, the sailor whipped him roughly with the end of a rope when he gave the wrong answers. He also learned how to swing the dories aboard when they were brought alongside with the day's catch, to help clean the cod and salt them away below the decks, and to stand watch at the wheel of the schooner as they went from one fishing ground to another on the Grand Banks. Even Disko Troop began to admit that the boy would be a good hand before they reached Gloucester in the fall.

Gradually, Harvey became used to the sea. There were times of pleasure as well as work. He enjoyed listening while the other eight members of the crew talked and told sea yarns in the evenings or on the days when it was too rough to lower the dories and go after cod. He discovered that the crew came from all over the world. Disko Troop and his son were from Gloucester, Long Jack was from Ireland, Manuel was a Portuguese, Salters was a farmer, Pennsylvania was a former preacher who had lost his family in the Johnstown flood, and the cook was a black who had been brought up in Nova Scotia and swore in Gaelic. All these men fascinated Harvey, for they were different from anyone he had ever known. What pleased the boy most was that they accepted him on his own merits as a workman and a member of the crew and not as an heir to millions. Of all the crew, only Dan and the black cook believed Harvey's story.

One day, a French brig hailed the *We're Here*. Both vessels shortened sail, while Harvey and Long Jack were sent from the schooner to the brig to buy tobacco. Much to Harvey's chagrin, he discovered that the sailors on the French boat could hardly understand his schoolboy French but that they understood Long Jack's sign language perfectly.

The French brig figured in another of Harvey's adventures. He and Dan went aboard the ship at a later time to buy a knife that had belonged to a deceased sailor. Dan bought the knife and gave it to Harvey, thinking it had added value because the Frenchman had killed a man with it. While fishing from a dory several days later, Harvey felt a weight on his line and pulled in the Frenchman's corpse. The boys cut the line and threw the knife into the sea; it seemed to them that the Frenchman had returned to claim his knife.

Although they were the same age, Harvey was not nearly as handy on the schooner or in the dory as was Dan, who had grown up around fishing boats and fishermen; but Harvey surpassed Dan in the use of a sextant. His acquaintance with mathematics and his ability to use his knowledge seemed enormous to the simple sailors. So impressed was Disko Troop that he began to teach Harvey what he knew about navigation.

Early in September, the *We're Here* joined the rest of the fishing fleet at a submerged rock where the cod fishing was at its best, and the fishermen worked around the clock to finish loading the holds with cod and halibut.

The vessel that first filled its holds was not only honored by the rest of the fleet, but it also got the highest price for the first cargo into port. For the past four years, the *We're Here* had finished first, and it won honors again the year Harvey was aboard. All canvas was set, the flag was hoisted, and the schooner made the triumphant round of the fleet, picking up letters to be taken home. The homeward-bound men were the envy of all the other fishermen.

As soon as the *We're Here* had docked at Gloucester, Harvey sent a telegram to his father informing him that he had not been drowned but was well and healthy. Mr. Cheyne wired back that he would take his private car and travel to Gloucester as quickly as he could leave California. Disko Troop and the rest of the crew, except Dan and the black cook, were greatly surprised to discover that Harvey's claims were true.

Mr. Cheyne and Harvey's mother were overjoyed to see their son, and their happiness was further increased when they observed how much good the work aboard the fishing schooner had done him. It had changed Harvey from a snobbish adolescent into a self-reliant young man who knew how to make a living with his hands and who valued people for what they were rather than for the money they had. Mr. Cheyne, who had built up a fortune after a childhood of poverty, was particularly glad to see the change in his son.

Disko Troop and the crew of the *We're Here* refused to accept any reward for themselves. Dan was given the chance to become an officer on a fleet of fast freighters that Mr. Cheyne owned. The cook left the sea to become a bodyguard for Harvey. In later years, when Harvey had control of the Cheyne interests, the black got a great deal of satisfaction out of reminding Dan, who was by then a mate on one of Harvey's ships, that he had told the two boys years before that some day Harvey would be Dan's master.

Critical Evaluation:

Captains Courageous was written in 1896 while Rudyard Kipling was dwelling in Vermont's forests. Why did Great Britain's poet laureate—who wrote during Britain's imperial heyday when "the sun never set" on an empire stretching "from palm to pine"—have an "American period" in which he wrote a noted sea story in the North American woods? This scarcely known phase of Kipling's career was a happy one but has a key explanation that is often curiously overlooked today.

Kipling loved Vermont's forests, especially during the colorful autumn, but he also praised the deep, vital kinship between America and its British motherland. He equated the "Captains Courageous" of the Grand Banks, such as Disko Troop and the pioneers who journeyed into the American-Canadian West (not only Daniel Boone, George Vancouver, and Kit Carson but also railroad magnates like King Cheyne), with bold Elizabethan adventurers such as Sir Francis Drake, Sir John Hawkins, Sir Martin Frobisher, Sir Walter Raleigh, and Sir Philip Sidney. He felt that the Elizabethan spirit of adventure and accomplishment was not dead, and the modern fishing captains and railroad magnates were blood brothers of the earlier Anglo-Saxon adventurers, displaying the same spirit of freedom, free enterprise, and bravery against odds.

Kipling, however, had long lived among Asian masses. Because Anglo-Saxons could not reproduce their own kind in Asia in a natural "living-space" and thus could never be more than a dissolving white drop in a colored ocean, Kipling felt a shuddering relief to plunge into Vermont's woods where his own race was prospering and having large families. Despite this typical nineteenth century racism, however, it must be conceded that a certain Kiplingesque respect for all sturdy breeds is revealed in *Captains Courageous*. In this sea novel, the British poet implies that men and the civilizations they create need challenges, not security, and must maintain healthy folk instincts while rearing each generation of their own kind in hardiness. In *Captains Courageous*, the representatives of European, expansionist, seafaring races—British, French, German, Portuguese—have braved the Grand Banks for centuries and are thus favorably presented. The black cook is favorably portrayed as well; for, despite his nineteenth century belief in a White Man's Burden, Kipling sometimes praised sturdy blacks such as the tough Sudanese.

Within this context, the novel stresses traditional virtues like those of Horatio Alger. Harvey Cheyne learns practical skills and escapes emasculating luxury. He also learns the salutary value of hard work, sweat, and plain living, and he returns to nature and healthy simplicity by recapturing his self-reliance amidst the sheer beauty of the high seas. The physical environment of sea and shore is thus a character in the story, and it has been pointed out that *Captains Courageous*, therefore, differs from most novels since it concerns the environment more than it does the protagonist. Even the theme of conversion stems from environment, but it is linked as well to individual will and hereditary character stemming from Harvey's Anglo-Saxon father, King Cheyne. The driving ambition of King Cheyne is paralleled in Kipling's eulogy of the redoubtable fishermen who brave cold storms and fogs off the Grand Banks to fish for cod in their small dories. A millionaire's son thus becomes a man through his hardships on a fishing boat and through sharing the lot of toiling fishermen from Massachusetts, Canada, Germany, and Portugal.

The very pith of Kipling's story can be found, therefore, in King Cheyne's conversation with the redeemed young Harvey. King Cheyne relates the story of his life—how he had to toil for everything he had earned; how he fought Indians and border ruffians before the West was tamed;

how he encountered deadly struggles against odds; and how he built his railroad empire. He stresses the progress that railroads represented, enabling families to cross the immense and mountainous continent without suffering for months in covered wagons, sometimes burying their tiny children along the way, as they had been forced to do before Cheyne built his railroads. Infused with pride at his heritage, young Harvey returns to Gloucester, borrows money from his father, and invests it in fishing boats, hiring some of the friends that he had made on his first fishing expedition; thus, Harvey starts his own fishing empire in the true Anglo-American tradition of creative enterprise.

Kipling's unexpected familiarity with the sea is evident. His descriptions of life on a fishing vessel, of how fish are caught and processed, and of the abrupt tragedies that sometimes overtake the "captains courageous" are not superficial. He evidently familiarized himself with the Gloucester accents and the idiom as well, for they are reproduced with the idiomatic skill for which Kipling has long been noted. Like so many Kipling works, *Captains Courageous* is easy for children to read, enjoy, and understand, but its meanings are subtle and its literary virtues considerable.

Having experienced personal troubles and an unfortunate lawsuit, Kipling left Vermont. It is interesting to note that shortly after this military poet wrote one of the better novels of North Atlantic sea literature, he composed his famous *Recessional* honoring Queen Victoria's Diamond Jubilee in London in 1897. Rather than vaunting Great Britain's military might on this august occasion, however, Kipling shocked Empire enthusiasts by worrying over how England's regiments were shedding their blood over the entire earth and how Royal Navy ships were sinking on distant headland and dune. Fearing "lest we be one with Nineveh and Tyre," Kipling wrote "Lord God of hosts, be with us yet, be with us yet," thereby shedding light on his geopolitical reasons for having written *Captains Courageous* at an earlier time.

Kipling died in 1936 as World War II loomed. His views on the North American landmass as the future center of Britannic racial strength—which is the inner message of *Captains Courageous*—might well have influenced Nazi racialist geopoliticians such as Karl Haushofer and Alfred Rosenberg, not to mention Hitler himself. *Captains Courageous* meanwhile continues to be a favorite among all ages of readers in many landlocked as well as seafaring nations.

THE CASTLE OF OTRANTO

Type of work: Novel
Author: Horace Walpole (1717–1797)
Type of plot: Gothic romance
Time of plot: Twelfth century
Locale: Italy
First published: 1764

Principal characters:

> MANFRED, Prince of Otranto
> MATILDA, Manfred's daughter
> CONRAD, Manfred's son
> ISABELLA, Conrad's fiancée
> FATHER JEROME, a priest
> THEODORE, a young peasant and the true heir to Otranto

The Story:

Manfred, the Prince of Otranto, planned to marry his fifteen-year-old son, Conrad, to Isabella, daughter of the Marquis of Vicenza. On the day of the wedding, however, a strange thing happened. A servant ran into the hall and informed the assembled company that a huge helmet had appeared mysteriously in the courtyard of the castle.

When Count Manfred and his guests rushed into the courtyard, they found Conrad crushed to death beneath a gigantic helmet adorned with waving black plumes. Theodore, a young peasant, declared the helmet was like that on a statue of Prince Alfonso the Good, which stood in the chapel. Another spectator shouted that the helmet was missing from the statue. Prince Manfred imprisoned the young peasant as a magician and charged him with the murder of the heir to Otranto.

That evening, Manfred sent for Isabella. He informed her that he intended to divorce his wife so that he himself might marry Isabella and have another male heir. Frightened, Isabella ran away and lost herself in the passages beneath the castle. There she encountered Theodore, who helped her to escape through an underground passage into a nearby church. Manfred, searching for the girl, accused the young man of aiding her. As he was threatening Theodore, servants rushed up to tell the prince of a giant who was sleeping in the great hall of the castle. When Manfred returned to the hall, the giant had disappeared.

The following morning, Father Jerome came to inform Manfred and his wife that Isabella had taken sanctuary at the altar of his church. Sending his wife away, Manfred called upon the priest to aid him in divorcing his wife and marrying Isabella. Father Jerome refused, warning Manfred that heaven would have revenge on him for harboring such thoughts. The priest unthinkingly suggested Isabella might be in love with the handsome young peasant who had aided in her escape.

Manfred, enraged at the possibility, confronted Theodore. Although the young man did not deny having aided the princess, he claimed never to have seen her before. The frustrated Manfred ordered him to the courtyard to be executed, and Father Jerome was called to give absolution to the condemned man; but when the collar of the lad was loosened, the priest discovered a birthmark which proved the young peasant was Father Jerome's son, born before the priest had entered the Church. Manfred offered to stay the execution if the priest would deliver Isabella to him. At that moment, a trumpet sounded at the gates of the castle.

The trumpet signaled the arrival of a herald from the Knight of the Gigantic Sabre, champion of Isabella's father, the rightful heir to Otranto. Greeting Manfred as a usurper, the herald demanded either the immediate release of Isabella and the abdication of Manfred or the satisfaction of mortal combat. Manfred invited the Knight of the Gigantic Sabre to the castle, hoping to get permission from him to marry Isabella and keep the throne. The knight entered the castle with five hundred men at arms and a hundred more carrying one gigantic sword.

During a feast, the strange knight kept silence and raised his visor only to pass food into his mouth. Manfred later broached the question of marrying Isabella, telling the knight he wished to marry again to insure himself an heir. Before he had finished, Father Jerome arrived with the news of Isabella's disappearance from the church. After everyone had gone to find Isabella, Matilda assisted Theodore to escape from the castle.

In the forest, Theodore met Isabella and promised to protect her. Shortly thereafter, they met the Knight of the Gigantic Sabre. Fearing the knight meant harm to Isabella, the young man overcame him in combat. Thinking himself about to die, the knight revealed to Isabella that he was her father in disguise.

They all returned to the castle. There Isabella's father confided to her that he had discovered the gigantic sword in the Holy Land. It was a miraculous weapon; on the blade it was written that only the blood of Manfred could atone for the wrongs committed on the family of the true ruler of Otranto. Manfred returned to the castle where he found Theodore dressed in armor. It seemed to Manfred that the young man resembled the Prince whose throne Manfred had usurped.

Manfred still hoped to wed Isabella, and he craftily won her father's consent by betrothing that nobleman to Matilda. At that point, a nearby statue dripped blood from its nose, an omen that disaster would follow the proposed marriages.

Manfred saw only two courses open to him. One was to surrender all claims to Otranto; the other was to proceed with his plan to marry Isabella. In either case, it appeared that fate was against his success. Nor did a second appearance of the giant in the castle ease the anxiety he felt. When news of the giant came to Isabella's father, he decided not to court disaster for himself by marrying Matilda or by permitting Manfred to marry his daughter. His resolution was increased when a skeleton in the rags of a hermit called upon him to renounce Matilda.

Hours later, Manfred was told that Theodore was in the chapel with a woman. Jealous, he went to the chapel and stabbed the woman, who was his own daughter Matilda. Over the body of Matilda, Theodore announced that he was the true ruler of Otranto. Suddenly, the giant form of the dead Prince Alfonso appeared, proclaiming Theodore to be the true heir. Then he ascended to heaven where he was received by St. Nicholas.

The truth was now made known. Theodore was the son of Father Jerome, then Prince of Falconara, and Alfonso's daughter. Manfred confessed his usurpation, and he and his wife entered neighboring convents. Theodore married Isabella and ruled as the new Prince of Otranto.

Critical Evaluation:

Horace Walpole's *The Castle of Otranto* is among the best-known, best-loved, and best-crafted novels of the Gothic genre in English. It is also one of the first. Gothic fiction was representative of the late eighteenth century rejection of the rational, realistic creed of Neoclassicism, which asserted the superiority of things familiar and contemporary for literary purposes. This reaction was but a phase of the revival of interest in the recondite past, an interest that focused on medieval life and manifested itself in pseudoscholarly antiquarianism, imitation Gothic castles, artificial ruins, balladry, and contrived narratives.

These narratives, permeated with fashionable melancholy, attempted to portray human conduct and sentiment with psychological realism while setting the action in remote and mysterious places and times. The emotional thrills of adventure provided the reader with an escape from humdrum existence; hence, the villain was characteristically somber and restless, and the heroine was beautiful, innocent, young, and sensitively perceptive; she waited dutifully to be rescued by a brave and courageous lover. The obligatory setting was a haunted castle, a cloister, or a ruined abbey, fortuitously furnished with underground passages, secret doors, and locked and unused rooms, and surrounded by wild and desolate landscape. The action inevitably included strange and deliberate crimes (often accompanied by rattling chains and other inexplicable phenomena), incidents of physical violence, and emotional anguish orchestrated with supernatural manifestations. A strong erotic element usually underscored the plot, and any comic relief, following Shakespeare's model, was confined to servants. In a bogus historical setting, chronologically and geographically remote, novels of mystery and passionate emotion depicted the trials and misfortunes of sentimental love with an overlay of ghosts, prescience, and preternatural forces together with the titillating horror of violence and crime.

In the very forefront of this Gothic revival was *The Castle of Otranto*, whose author personally seemed ideally suited to his book (rather than the more usual obverse). Walpole was a nobleman, respected for his antiquarian scholarship; he was also a fussy bachelor in precarious health, unable to join his peers in hunting, tippling, and wenching. He escaped the demands of this world by psychologically and physically retreating into the past. He built himself a pseudo-Gothic retreat at Strawberry Hill where he displayed his collection of antiques and led an active fantasy life, imagining himself at one time a feudal lord and at another time a learned monk. One evening he reportedly climbed his narrow Gothic staircase with his dog to his Gothic library so that he could dream—possibly with the aid of opium—of the romantic past.

The Castle of Otranto was spawned out of such dreams, illustrating two major themes in the Gothic novel. The story united a Baroque view of architecture and sentiment in a repudiation of Neoclassical ideals of proportion, balance, harmony, and ultimately narrow limitations. The physical appearance of the Castle of Otranto, therefore, was an exaggeration of genuine Gothic style, carrying the visual image to such excessive lengths that the structure bore hardly any resemblance to authentic examples of medieval Gothic architecture; yet the effectiveness of the description is undeniable in the context of the novel. Likewise, the emotional overreaction of the characters—in defiance of all Neoclassical canons of moderation—served a similar purpose: to transcend the mundane realities of common life on the wings of fancy. In the very uncommon life of this story, Walpole sought to liberate imagination and allow it to rove freely in what he characterized as "the boundless realms of invention . . . [thence] creating more interesting situations." Simultaneously (and without any sense of contradiction), Walpole claimed to strive for naturalness and probability in his character development, yet fanciful setting and untrammeled emotion were the hallmarks of his as well as many other Gothic novels.

Walpole, nevertheless, employed supernatural devices—decidedly not natural or probable—to create the so-called interesting situations that he avowedly wanted to create. The totally immersed reader can become so wrapped up in the plot that inconsistencies escape notice; thus, the plot itself is plausible even today, but the events surrounding it and somewhat precipitating it are more than a little suspect. The story opens with the ambiguous prophecy that "the castle and lordship of Otranto should pass from the present family, whenever the real owner should be grown too large to inhabit it." Intrigue thickens with Conrad's peculiar death and Manfred's frantic attempts to sire another heir. In due course, other supernatural manifestations intervene: two menservants see a strange apparition, which also appears to Bianca, Matilda's maid. Manfred's reasonable objections notwithstanding, these events very nearly unseat his reason; but even as Manfred argues with Hippolita to annul their marriage so that he can marry Isabella and produce an heir, three drops of blood fall from the nose of the statue of Alfonso, the original Prince of Otranto who won the principality through fraud and deceit. Manfred is thus given supernatural warning to desist from his wicked plan, but he is still undeterred. His intended new father-in-law, however, also sees an apparition when he goes to the chapel to pray for guidance. In the end, after many such scenes of terror, violence, and bewilderment, the true heir of Otranto is unexpectedly discovered amid a thunderclap, a rattling of armor, and a disembodied pronouncement about legitimate succession.

While in retrospect these contrivances may strain the credulity of today's reader, the chain of events is so enveloping that the act of reading suspends one's normal skepticism to such an extent that customary doubt and ordinary questions are effectively held in abeyance. It is only after the fact that the reader begins to examine the logic and question the veracity of Walpole's highly convincing tale, and therein lies the art of the story.

CASTLE RACKRENT
An Hibernian Tale

Type of work: Novel
Author: Maria Edgeworth (1767–1849)
Type of plot: Social criticism
Time of plot: Eighteenth century
Locale: Ireland
First published: 1800

> *Principal characters:*
> HONEST THADY QUIRK, the narrator
> SIR KIT RACKRENT, the owner of Castle Rackrent
> SIR CONDY RACKRENT, Sir Kit's heir
> ISABELLA, Condy's wife
> JUDY QUIRK, Thady's niece
> JASON, Thady's son

The Story:

After the death of Sir Patrick O'Shaughlin, his fine and generous master, Honest Thady Quirk found himself working at Castle Rackrent for the heir, Sir Murtagh, a penny-pinching owner with a vicious temper. Lady Murtagh was also more interested in money than in the happiness of her tenants. After Sir Murtagh died in a fit of temper, she stripped Castle Rackrent of its treasures and went to live in London. The estate passed to her husband's younger brother, Sir Kit Rackrent, a wild, carefree man. Finding the estate in debt and heavily mortgaged, Sir Kit went to England to marry a rich wife who would repair the estate and bring a dowry for his support.

At last, he came back with a wealthy wife, a Jewess he had married while staying in Bath. It was soon apparent to Honest Thady that there was no love between the honeymooners. One serious difficulty arose over the presence of pig meat on the dinner table. Lady Kit had insisted that no such meat be served, but Sir Kit defied her orders. When the meat appeared on the table, Lady Kit retired to her room, and her husband locked her in. She remained a prisoner for seven years. When she became very ill and appeared to be dying, Sir Kit tried to influence her to leave her jewels to him, but she refused. It was assumed she would die shortly, and all eligible ladies in the neighborhood were endeavoring to become the next wife of Kit Rackrent. So much controversy arose over his possible choice that Sir Kit was finally challenged and killed in a duel. Miraculously recovering from her illness, Lady Kit went to London. The next heir was Sir Condy Rackrent, a distant cousin of Sir Kit.

Sir Condy Rackrent was a spendthrift but a good-natured master.

Although the estate was more deeply in debt than ever, the new master made no attempt to relieve the impoverished condition of his holdings. Sir Condy soon began a steadfast friendship with the family who lived on the neighboring estate. The youngest daughter, Isabella, took a fancy to Sir Condy, but her father would not hear of a match between his family and the owner of Castle Rackrent. Sir Condy really loved Judy, the grandniece of Honest Thady. One day in Thady's presence, Sir Condy tossed a coin to determine which girl he would marry. Judy lost, and in a short while, Sir Condy eloped with Isabella.

It had been expected that Isabella could bring some money to the estate; but when she married Sir Condy, she was disinherited by her father. While the newlyweds lived in careless luxury, the house and grounds fell into neglect, and the servants and the tenants wrung their hands in distress. Learning of a vacancy in the coming elections, Sir Condy at last decided to stand for Parliament. He won the election, but too late to save himself from his creditors.

Honest Thady's son, Jason, a legal administrator, helped a neighbor to buy up all Sir Condy's debts. With so much power in his hands, Jason even scorned his own father. When Lady Condy learned that her husband's debtors were closing in on him, she complied with the demands of her family and returned to her father's house. True to his good-natured generosity, Sir Condy wrote a will for his wife in which he willed her his land and five hundred pounds a year after his death. When Jason demanded payment for the Rackrent debts, Sir Condy said he had no way of paying, explaining that he had given an income of five hundred a year to Lady Condy. Jason insisted Sir Condy sell Castle Rackrent and all the estates to satisfy his creditors. With no other recourse, Sir Condy agreed. The five hundred a year was still guaranteed for Isabella. Thady was grief-stricken that his son had maneuvered this piece of villainy against Sir Condy. Now Jason would have nothing to do with Honest Thady.

On her way back to her father's house, Lady Condy's carriage was upset, and she was nearly killed. Assuming she would surely die, Jason hurried to Sir Condy with a proposal that Sir Condy sell him Lady Condy's yearly income. Sir Condy, needing the cash, complied with Jason's proposal.

Judy Quirk had been married, and her husband had died. She paid a call on Sir Condy, who was staying at Thady's lodge. The old servant felt certain that now Judy would become Lady Rackrent, but Judy told her uncle that there was no point in becoming a lady without a castle to accompany the title. She also hinted that she might do better to marry Jason, who at least held the lands. Thady tried to dissuade her from such a thought, but Judy was bent on fortune hunting.

Sir Condy had been indulging in such excesses of food and drink that he suffered from gout. One night at a drinking party he drank a large draught too quickly and died a few days later. After Sir Condy's death, Jason and the now-recovered Lady Condy went to court over the title of the estate. Some said Jason would get the land, and others said Lady Condy would win. Thady could only guess the results of the suit.

Critical Evaluation:

Maria Edgeworth was famous in her day as the author of seven novels and as a writer concerned with the education of children, an interest shared with her father, Richard Lovell Edgeworth. An Irish landowner, Edgeworth settled his family in Ireland in 1782 when Maria was at the impressionable age of fifteen. He was an intellectual, a believer in social and political reform, father of a large family, and mentor to his illustrious daughter. Throughout his life, Maria Edgeworth deferred to his tastes, seeking not only his guidance but also his collaboration in much of her writing.

Castle Rackrent is the author's first novel, written sometime between 1797 and 1799 and published in 1800. It is a distinguished piece of work in several ways. A successful first novel, generally regarded as her best, it is also one of the few works in which her father had no part. The author herself declared that "it went to the press just as it was written."

In addition, *Castle Rackrent* holds a distinction in the history of the English novel as the first regional novel, a significance noted by Sir Walter Scott in the preface to his first historical novel, *Waverley* (1814), when he stated his purpose of creating a Scottish milieu with the same degree of authenticity as "that which Miss Edgeworth so fortunately achieved for Ireland." In her own preface, Edgeworth takes pains to indicate the realistically Irish quality of the novel. Her first-person narrator, Thady Quirk, is a character based upon her father's steward; he speaks in Irish idiom because "the authenticity of his story would have been more exposed to doubt if it were not told in his own characteristic manner." Moreover, the subject is peculiarly Irish: "Those who were acquainted with the manners of a certain class of the gentry of Ireland some years ago, will want no evidence of the truth of honest Thady's narrative."

In the use of certain devices, she anticipates the historical novel later developed by Scott—for example, in the historicity suggested by the subtitle: "An Hibernian Tale Taken from Facts, and from the Manners of Irish Squires, Before the Year 1782." More explicitly, Maria Edgeworth assures her readers that "these are 'tales of other times'; . . . the manners depicted . . . are not those of the present age: the race of the Rackrents has long been extinct in Ireland." Similar to the kind of documentation Scott was to employ is her anecdotal glossary of Irish "terms and idiomatic phrases." The convention of the "true story," of course, is an eighteenth century legacy; and, like many eighteenth century novels, *Castle Rackrent* purports to be an original memoir for which the author is merely the editor.

The theme of *Castle Rackrent* adumbrates Scott's characteristic theme, the conflict between a dying culture and a culture coming into being; the resemblance, however, stops there. Lacking historical events and personages, the Rackrent story is not too remote in time from the date of composition. Although the Rackrents indulge in gloriously absurd deeds— for example, the sham wake staged by Sir Condy in order to spy upon his own mourners—there are no heroic deeds in their bygone age. The name "Rackrent," referring to the exorbitant rents exacted by landlords from their tenants, reveals their main traits.

The novel, therefore, is a satire on the Irish ruling class. With the sustained irony of Thady's blind "partiality to *the family* in which he was bred and born," the author presents their reprehensible history. Except for Sir Murtagh, who wastes his fortune in lawsuits, all the Rackrents ruin themselves and their estates through extravagance and dissipation. Whether they are squires in residence or absentee landlords dealing through agents "who grind the face of the poor," they increase the misery of the common Irishman. Concealed behind Thady's comical anecdotes is the judgment that the Rackrents represent the destructive arrogance and stupidity of irresponsible landowners who answer to no one except, eventually, moneylenders such as Thady's ruthless son Jason, who finally takes possession of the Rackrent estates.

The novel is centered upon Thady himself, however, despite the title of the novel and Thady's unwavering focus on the Rackrents, even despite some unforgettable comic episodes of Rackrent peccadilloes. His voice speaks in self-importance:

Having out of friendship for the family, upon whose estate, praised be Heaven! I and mine have lived rent free time out of mind, voluntarily undertaken to publish the Memoirs of the Rackrent Family, I think it my duty to say a few words, in the first place, concerning myself.

His self-importance is based upon his illusions of the family grandeur and the reflected glory he enjoys. If he lives by his professed loyalty, he acts upon the example of his masters. He exploits his privileges as they do, blind to the inevitable outcome. For example, throughout the novel, Thady boasts of various strategies to push forward "my son Jason," who acquires his first lease on Rackrent land because "I spoke a good word for my son, and gave out in the county that nobody need bid against us"—and, comments the opportunistic Thady, "Why shouldn't he as well as another?" Yet he complains bitterly of Jason grown rich: ". . . he is a high gentleman, and never minds what poor Thady says, and having better than 1500 a-year, landed estate, looks down upon honest Thady, but I wash my hands of his doings, and as I have lived so will I die, true and loyal to the family."

Thady's praise of the Rackrents is often coupled with his appreciation of wealth. When a new heir neglects Thady, the old man is hostile; however, the first casual attention produces a characteristic response, in which money is amusingly mingled with family: "I loved him from that day to this, his voice was so like the family—and he threw me a guinea out of his waistcoat pocket." Another trait incompatible with honest devotion is Thady's evasive habit of silence at crucial moments, a silence very much at odds with his characteristic garrulity. There is a self-serving tone in the recurring motif, "I said nothing for fear of gaining myself ill will."

On the other hand, Thady's talkativeness, urged by vanity, contributes to the downfall of his favorite, Sir Condy, the last of the Rackrents. Although it is Thady's son who seizes the property, it is Thady who makes the youthful Condy his "white-headed boy," feeding his imagination with the disastrous "stories of the family and the blood from which he was sprung." He proudly takes credit for the adult Condy's unfortunate gambling instincts, boasting that "I well remember teaching him to toss up for bog berries on my knee." The ultimate irony is that his teachings indirectly bring about Sir Condy's death; for the family legend of Sir Patrick's prodigious whiskey-drinking feat, which the last Rackrent fatally duplicates, is "the story that he learned from me when a child."

Torn between his son and his master and called by his niece an "unnatural fader," he confesses, "I could not upon my conscience tell which was wrong from the right." He is unaware, even as he explains it, that Rackrent rights derive from money, even as Jason's pretensions do. Even the designation "ancient" is not appropriate for the Rackrents, since the estate had come into "*the* family" in Thady's great-grandfather's time when Sir Patrick, by act of Parliament, took the surname in order to receive the property. Thady's dilemma is treated comically, but there is also pathos in the position in which he finds himself in the end: "I'm tired wishing for any thing in this world, after all I've seen it—but I'll say nothing; it would be a folly to be getting myself ill will in my old age."

Thady Quirk is a masterful characterization, requiring none of the apologies which Edgeworth as fictitious editor appends to his memoirs. However, the appended remarks serve the purpose, not so much of the author of fiction, but of the daughter of Richard Lovell Edgeworth, as she offers her thoughts concerning a political resolution as her last word on the moral dilemma so convincingly portrayed in this short novel: "It is a problem of difficult solution to determine whether an Union will hasten or retard the amelioration of this country." Sir Walter Scott later praised her fictional Irishmen, England's "gay and kind-hearted neighbours," as having "done more towards completing the Union" than any subsequent legislation. Fortunately, Thady Quirk lives on as a fictional character, independent of the long-standing tumultuous relations between England and Ireland.

CASUALS OF THE SEA

Type of work: Novel
Author: William McFee (1881–1966)
Type of plot: Domestic realism
Time of plot: Early twentieth century
Locale: England
First published: 1916

> *Principal characters:*
> BERT GOODERICH, a machinist
> MARY, his wife
> YOUNG BERT, his son
> HANNIBAL, another son
> MINNIE, Mary's daughter
> BRISCOE, a ship's captain
> NELLIE, Hannibal's wife

The Story:

Mary fell in love with the baker's boy. When he deserted her, she went home, with country-bred fortitude, to bear her child. After Minnie was born, Mary received a proposal from Bert Gooderich, a stolid machinist. Bert offered nothing in the way of romance, but Mary accepted him thankfully. They settled in suburban London. In time Bert Junior was born, and later Hannibal.

Young Bert early showed a talent for fighting. He was big and strong and led the graders against the boarder pupils and the parochial boys. Noting his carefully planned skirmishes, the school inspector, an old army man, resolved to keep the boy in mind. His resolution was strengthened when Bert blurted out in school that he hoped to be a soldier. A few years later, the inspector encouraged the boy to enlist. Young Bert's career in the army, however, was short. He was killed at Pretoria.

Minnie was difficult. She was thin and reserved, and her mother, feeling powerless to mold her, finally let her go her own way. Minnie became engaged to a coal clerk but broke the engagement publicly when her fiancé asked her if she smoked.

Minnie worked at a shop where she retouched photographs. One day an American firm took over the place and introduced machines. Let out for a time, she refused to go back on the usual terms. Mary begged her to take back the coal clerk, but Minnie was adamant.

Next to the Gooderich family lived an American woman, Mrs. Gaynor,

---

and her small son Hiram. Mrs. Gaynor wrote an odd letter of reference
for Minnie, which stated that the girl was proud, stubborn, and conceited.
She sent the girl with the letter to Mrs. Wilfley, who was having a party
when Minnie arrived at the door. Despite her assurance, the girl was afraid
to go in, but middle-aged Anthony Gilfillan helped her to overcome her
shyness. Minnie attended the party, listened to Spanish music, and ate cu-
cumber sandwiches. She kept close to Anthony.

After the company had left, Mrs. Wilfley engaged Minnie as her secretary. When Bert Gooderich fell off a bridge one night and was drowned,
Mrs. Wilfley promptly arranged a benefit for the family, a musicale which
grossed seventy-four pounds. Mrs. Wilfley's fee was sixty-seven pounds; the
bereaved family got only seven, and Minnie was bitter on the subject.

One day Anthony Gilfillan sent a telegram to Minnie and asked her to
meet him at his office. He offered her a way to escape from the life she
hated. They went away to the Continent.

Five years later Minnie, now known as Mabel, was staying in a little hotel in Rouen. The mistress of Captain Briscoe, she was respected and even
envied by the world of occasional light ladies in Rouen. Minnie was nonetheless apprehensive; the ship captain had been gone three weeks, and he
had promised to be back in one. When Captain Briscoe finally did return,
he came only to say good-bye, explaining that he no longer dared to keep
her because his first mate was from his hometown. They parted without a
scene. Minnie went into the dressmaking profession in London. Soon, however, her smitten captain sought her out and offered to marry her. A little
amused at the idea, she consented.

Eighteen-year-old Hannibal had grown into a big lout. He was trouble-
some to his mother, who often had to get him out of foolish scrapes, and
he had lost his factory job. One day Hiram, in his merchant marine uniform, and Mrs. Gaynor came to call. Hannibal, inarticulate and bungling,
was attracted by the idea of going to sea and even went so far as to visit
Hiram's ship. Later he heard that the S.S. *Caryatid* needed a mess boy,
and so he signed on.

On shore, meanwhile, Minnie had asked her mother to come and live
with her during Captain Briscoe's long absences. Satisfied with this
arrangement, Briscoe joined his ship at Swansea, the S.S. *Caryatid*.

In port, Hannibal was spreading his wings. Quite by chance he met Nellie, a plump, merry girl who had come to town to work for her uncle, a
tavern keeper. Never understanding quite how it happened, Hannibal
became an engaged man before his ship sailed. He adapted himself easily
to life at sea. In time, he grew tired of his job in the mess room, and at
Panama he became a trimmer. Wheeling coal was hard work, but after a
while, Hannibal felt proud of his physical prowess.

In Japan, he met Hiram, and they went ashore together. Soon after the ship pulled out on the long trip home, Hannibal was stricken with fever.

Captain Briscoe wanted to look after his young brother-in-law, but he had other matters to worry him. He had picked up an English paper in port and had learned that Minnie was in jail, arrested for taking part in a suffragette demonstration. To add to his confusion, Minnie's letters were short and disappointing. The ship then piled up on a coral reef near the Dutch East Indies and was refloated only after long delay. The ship barely reached England in time for Christmas.

Captain Briscoe met Hannibal on the dock and persuaded him to go to the hotel where Minnie was waiting. Reluctant to go because of Nellie, Hannibal found both his mother and Minnie at the hotel. During her husband's absence, Minnie had earned fat fees by writing advertisements for a cough syrup. She and her mother urged Hannibal to stay with them, but he refused.

At Swansea he learned that Nellie, now the licensee of the tavern, still wished to marry him. Hannibal settled down in the pub, secure and well-loved by a capable wife.

His cough kept bothering him. Finally, after trying a patent cough syrup to no avail, Nellie called the doctor. Hannibal had lobar pneumonia. The coal dust had settled in his lungs and the cough syrup, which Nellie had bought after seeing an ad written by Minnie, had nearly killed him. Hannibal rallied a little, but he died within a few days. Death seemed as casual as life had always been.

Critical Evaluation:

William McFee's *Casuals of the Sea* is an example of one of the hundreds of novels that come out each year, receive good but not spectacular reviews, and then fall into obscurity after a year or so. The reason for the disappearance of such novels is not necessarily that they were not good pieces of literature, but that another set of novels were written to take their place on the reading tables of the general public.

Casuals of the Sea could not be considered a modern classic in the sense of *The Grapes of Wrath* or *Of Human Bondage*, because it is not being continually read and criticized; but still it has merits, which rank it as a fine novel. One of the elements which made it a success and which continues to make it pleasant reading today is its treatment of the sea scenes. McFee had spent considerable time at sea and, in fact, had written much of the novel aboard ship, although it was completed while he was living in the United States. His experience with the common seaman made his characters and their adventures at sea seem quite real to the landlocked reader. The characterizations of ordinary seamen and the English common man gave substance to a story whose plot alone might not have held the reader's interest.

An interesting sidelight of the book is McFee's treatment of the advertising world when Minnie takes to writing slogans for cough medicine. It amuses the modern reader, familiar as he is with anti-Madison Avenue literature, to find that advertising could have produced ill effects apparent enough to make the field a source of scorn in a work written in the early part of the twentieth century.

CECILIA
Or, Memoirs of an Heiress

Type of work: Novel
Author: Fanny Burney (Madame d'Arblay, 1752–1840)
Type of plot: Sentimental novel of manners
Time of plot: Eighteenth century
Locale: England
First published: 1782

Principal characters:
CECILIA BEVERLEY, a beautiful and virtuous heiress
MR. HARREL, her profligate guardian
MR. BRIGGS, her miserly guardian
MR. DELVILE, a proud aristocrat and also a guardian
MRS. DELVILE, his wife
MORTIMER DELVILE, their son
MR. MONCKTON, Cecilia's unscrupulous counselor
MR. BELFIELD, a pleasing but unstable young man
HENRIETTA BELFIELD, his modest sister

The Story:

Cecilia Beverley, just short of her majority, was left ten thousand pounds by her father and an annual income of three thousand pounds by her uncle, the latter inheritance being restricted by the condition that her husband take her name. Until her coming of age, she was expected to live with one of her guardians, the fashionable spendthrift Mr. Harrel, husband of a girlhood friend. One who warned her against the evils of London was Mr. Monckton, her clever and unscrupulous counselor. His secret intention was to marry Cecilia; at present, however, he was prevented by the existence of an old and ill-tempered wife, whom he had married for money.

The constant round of parties in London and the dissipation of the Harrels were repugnant to Cecilia. Kind but unimpressive Mr. Arnott, Mrs. Harrel's brother, fell hopelessly in love with the girl, but Harrel obviously intended her for his friend, insolent Sir Robert Floyer, whom Cecilia detested. After vainly begging Harrel to pay a bill, which Arnott finally paid, Cecilia became so disgusted with the Harrels' way of life that she decided to leave their household; but she found the abode of her miserly guardian, Mr. Briggs, so comfortless, and was so repulsed by the pride and condescension of her third guardian, Mr. Delvile, that she decided to remain with the Harrels.

At a masquerade party, she was pursued by a man disguised as the devil. He was Monckton in disguise, attempting to keep others away from her. She was rescued first by a Don Quixote and later by a domino whose conversation pleased her greatly. At first, she believed the domino was Mr. Belfield, a young man she had met before. Later, she was surprised to learn that Don Quixote was Belfield.

Angered at Cecilia's courtesy to Belfield, Sir Robert insulted him at the opera; a duel resulted, and Belfield was wounded. A young man, courteously attentive to Cecilia, proved to be the domino and Mortimer Delvile, the only son of her guardian and the pride and hope of his family, whose fortune he was to recoup by marriage. Cecilia visited his mother and was charmed by her graciousness and wit. She was disturbed, however, by the knowledge that she was universally believed to be betrothed to either Sir Robert or Belfield. Monckton, feeling that the Delviles were the only threat to him, attempted to destroy her friendship for them.

Cecilia met and immediately liked Henrietta Belfield. When she visited her new friend, she found Henrietta nursing her wounded brother, whom Mortimer wished to aid. Seeing Cecilia there, Mortimer believed that she was in love with Belfield. Having been educated above his station, Belfield had grown to feel contempt for business. He was clever and pleasant but unable to settle down to anything.

Although Cecilia had refused Sir Robert's proposal, she saw that Harrel was still bent on the marriage. Monckton's constant warnings against the Delviles disturbed her, for she was now in love with Mortimer. Knowing his father's pride, however, she determined to conquer her feelings.

Cecilia, who had previously discharged some debts for Harrel, was now so alarmed by his threats of suicide that she pledged herself to a total of seven thousand additional pounds. Since Briggs would not advance the money, she was forced to borrow from a usurer.

Mortimer, learning that Cecilia loved neither Sir Robert nor Belfield, betrayed his own love for her—and then avoided her. Cecilia discovered that Henrietta had also fallen in love with Mortimer. Mrs. Belfield, believing that Cecilia loved her son, constantly urged him to propose to her.

Cecilia lent another thousand pounds to Harrel, who was to escape his creditors by leaving the country. Meanwhile, his wife was to live with her brother until Cecilia's house was ready. Harrel shot himself, however, leaving a note for Cecilia in which he revealed that her marriage to Sir Robert was to have canceled a gambling debt.

Monckton discharged Cecilia's debt with the usurer; she was to repay him on coming of age. Against his wishes, she went with the Delviles to their castle. Only Mrs. Delvile was agreeable there. The family was too proud to encourage visitors, and Mortimer still avoided Cecilia. Much later, during a thunderstorm in which he contracted a fever, he betrayed his true emotions. Cecilia was puzzled and hurt; her emotions intensified when Mrs. Delvile, who had guessed the feelings of both Mortimer and Cecilia, let Cecilia know that they were not for each other. Mortimer, before going away for his health, told Cecilia that his family would never accept the change-of-name clause in the will.

Cecilia then went to live with an old friend. There she was surprised to see Mortimer's dog, sent, she discovered later, as a joke, unknown to the Delviles. She spoke aloud of her love for its master and turned to discover Mortimer beside her. She agreed to a secret wedding, but Monckton, chosen as their confidant, persuaded her of the wrongness of the act.

Cecilia went on to London with the intention of breaking off the match; but discovery made her feel she was compromised, and she agreed to go through with the wedding. She could not continue, however, after a disguised woman interrupted the ceremony. Later, Mrs. Delvile, whose family pride exceeded her love for Cecilia, made her promise to give up Mortimer. She renounced him in a passionate scene during which Mrs. Delvile burst a blood vessel. Cecilia consoled her misery by acts of charity which Monckton, feeling that she was squandering his money, tried in vain to prevent.

Finally of age, Cecilia went to London with the Moncktons. There she discharged her debt to Monckton. Abused by Mr. Delvile, she was sure that someone had slandered her. When Cecilia went to visit Henrietta, Mr. Delvile saw her there. Having just heard Mrs. Belfield say that Cecilia loved her son, his suspicions of Cecilia's impurity were confirmed.

Mrs. Harrel and Henrietta moved with Cecilia into her new home. Mortimer came to tell her that both his parents had agreed to a plan. If she would renounce her uncle's fortune, he would marry her, although she would have only the ten thousand pounds inherited from her father. Mr. Delvile knew, however, that she had already lost her father's money. Enraged at his father's treachery, Mortimer was determined to marry Cecilia, even though she was portionless. She agreed, but only if his mother would consent. Again, a secret wedding was planned, this time with Mrs. Delvile's approbation. They were married; Cecilia returned to her house, and Mortimer went to inform his father.

A woman Cecilia had befriended identified Mrs. Monckton's companion as the person who had stopped the first wedding. Mortimer was prevented from telling his father of the marriage by the scandals with which Delvile charged Cecilia. Upon learning that the slanderer was Monckton, Mortimer fought and wounded him and was forced to flee.

The man who was to inherit Cecilia's fortune, since her husband had not taken her name, demanded his rights. Cecilia determined to join her husband. Mrs. Harrel took Henrietta with her to Arnott's house. Cecilia hoped that Henrietta, as miserable in her hopeless love for Mortimer as Arnott was in his for Cecilia, would comfort and be comforted by him.

In London, Cecilia consulted Belfield about her trip. Mrs. Belfield, hoping to get her son married to Cecilia, had left them alone when Mortimer entered. The meeting seemed to confirm his father's accusations, and he sent her to wait for him at his father's house. Mr. Delvile refused to admit her. Wild with fear that Mortimer would fight a duel with Belfield, she began a distracted search for her husband. Fevered, delirious, and alone, she was locked up by strangers. When Mortimer found her, convinced of her purity by Belfield, she was too sick to know him.

After many days of uncertainty, Cecilia eventually recovered. Monckton also was out of danger and grudgingly admitted that he had deliberately lied to Mr. Delvile about Cecilia's moral character. Mr. Delvile then accepted her as his daughter. Mrs. Delvile recovered her health, and Mrs. Harrel married again and resumed her life of careless frivolity. Arnott and Henrietta married. With Mortimer's help, Belfield finally settled down to an army career. Monckton lived on in bitterness and misery. Impressed by Cecilia's unselfishness and sweetness, Mortimer's aunt willed her a fortune. Cecilia was then able to continue her charities, though never extravagantly. She did occasionally regret the loss of her own fortune but wisely recognized that life cannot be absolutely perfect.

Critical Evaluation:

Cecilia: Or, Memoirs of an Heiress is a blend of wit, sentiment, and morality. If, as has been charged, Fanny Burney's writing is marred by caricature and priggishness, it cannot be denied that she had a real gift for maintaining the interest of her readers. Seen in historical perspective, Burney merits credit for being one of the writers who made the novel respectable. She also has a special literary significance in having influenced Jane Austen, whose *Pride and Prejudice* (1813) got its title from a sentence in *Cecilia*.

Following the artistic achievement of *Evelina*, Burney's second novel, *Cecilia*, is in many ways a disappointment; it suffers from weaknesses of plotting, characterization, and narrative method. In spite of its flaws, however, the novel drew appreciative praise from writers such as Samuel Johnson and Edmund Burke; and even modern readers, who are distracted by Burney's sentimentality and didacticism, still find enjoyment in the amusing caricatures and the lively reproduction of eighteenth century manners.

The plot of *Cecilia* is divided into two halves, the first dealing with the heroine's financial problems during her minority when part of her inheritance is controlled by her guardians and part is held in suspension awaiting her marriage; and the second relating the course of her romantic attachment to Mortimer Delvile. The action in both portions of the story is packed with highly improbable, unbelievable events and with sensational or melodramatic incidents. Coincidences such as Cecilia's chance meeting with Belfield's sister and mother, Mrs. Delvile's sudden stroke brought on by a broken blood vessel, and Mortimer's handy proximity when Cecilia reveals her inmost feelings to his dog, tax the reader's credulity. The plot is also replete with all the accoutrements of melodrama, including a duel, an elopement, the temporary insanity and near-fatal illness of the heroine, and the macabre suicide of her profligate guardian. In addition to its overburdened plot, *Cecilia* is cluttered with too many characters who are never explored in any detail; the major figures tend to be wooden, static, and one-dimensional, while the minor ones are often caricatures who fail to amuse because they are overdrawn or belabored.

Most of these shortcomings in *Cecilia* can be traced to Burney's decision to abandon the more limited but highly successful epistolary form which she had used in *Evelina*, in favor of the omniscient author technique. Her use of this point of view leads Burney into several pitfalls: she describes her characters rather than allowing them dramatically to reveal their personalities through action and dialogue; she replaces her natural sparkling prose with a more stilted and formal style; she adopts a serious, somewhat heavy tone in place of her characteristic ironic but tolerant comic voice; in Cecilia Beverley, she creates a young woman too aloof and thoroughly virtuous with which to be easily identified; and she frequently interrupts the narrative to moralize and comment in her own voice. Regardless of these flaws, however, *Cecilia* has its artistic merits. The masquerade party and the opera are excellent examples of vivid scene painting in the best novel-of-manners tradition; a few of the minor characters, such as Mrs. Belfield and Honoria, are unforgettable comic portraits; and despite its improbability, the plot still has qualities of suspense and vitality.

CHARLES O'MALLEY
The Irish Dragoon

Type of work: Novel
Author: Charles Lever (1806–1872)
Type of plot: Picaresque romance
Time of plot: 1808–1812
Locale: Ireland and Europe
First published: 1841

Principal characters:

CHARLES O'MALLEY, an Irish dragoon
GODFREY O'MALLEY, his uncle
WILLIAM CONSIDINE, a family friend
CAPTAIN HAMMERSLEY, O'Malley's rival
GENERAL DASHWOOD
LUCY DASHWOOD, his daughter

The Story:

At age seventeen, Charles O'Malley was tall and broad-shouldered, deadly with a gun and sure in the saddle. He possessed in abundance the qualities of generosity and honor expected of Godfrey O'Malley's nephew. Godfrey, of O'Malley Castle, Galway, was still a good man on a horse and quick to pass the bottle. In his ruined old castle hard by the River Shannon, he held the staunch affections of his tenants.

Old Godfrey was standing for election to the Irish Parliament. Unable to leave home during the election campaign, he sent Charles to the home of a distant cousin named Blake to ask his support in the coming election. Blake, however, belonged to the opposition, and although Charles did his best to win help for his uncle, he hardly knew how to handle the situation.

Part of the trouble was Lucy Dashwood. She and her father were visiting Blake while the General tried to buy some good Galway property. Charles was jealous of the General's aide, Captain Hammersley, who was attentive to Lucy. At a fox hunt, Charles led the way at first, but Hammersley kept up with him. Charles's horse fell backward in jumping a wall. With cool daring, Charles kept on and took a ditch bordered by a stone rampart. Hammersley, not to be outdone, took the ditch too but fell heavily. Charles was first at the kill, but both he and Hammersley had to spend several days in bed.

One night at dinner, one of the guests spoke insultingly of Godfrey O'Malley, and Charles threw a wineglass in his face. Billy Considine, who had been in more duels than any other Irishman in Galway, arranged the affair as Charles's second. The duel came out in Charles's favor, and he left his man for dead on the field. Luckily the man recovered, and Charles escaped serious consequences for his rashness.

Charles went to Dublin to study law. Chance led him to share a room there with Frank Webber. For Charles, college life became a series of dinners, brawls, and escapades, all under the leadership of Frank.

While in Dublin, Charles saw Lucy again, but she was distant to him. Hammersley was now a favored suitor. Since he seemed so unfitted for study, Charles became increasingly attracted to military life. Perhaps Lucy would approve his suit if he became a dashing dragoon. Godfrey arranged for a commission through General Dashwood, and Charles became an ensign.

His first duty was in Portugal. Napoleon had invaded the peninsula, and England was sending aid to her Portuguese and Spanish allies. In Lisbon, Charles's superb horsemanship saved Donna Inez from injury. His friendship with Donna Inez was progressing satisfactorily when he learned that Inez was a close acquaintance of Lucy Dashwood.

At his own request, Charles was sent to the front. There he soon distinguished himself by bravery in battle and was promoted to a lieutenancy.

Lucy had given him letters for Hammersley. When Charles delivered them, Hammersley turned pale and insulted him. Only the good offices of Captain Powers prevented a duel.

Charles saw action at Talavera and Ciudad Roderigo. In one engagement, he sneaked under cover of darkness to the French trenches, and by moving the engineers' measuring tape, he caused the French to dig their trenches right under the British guns. Wherever Charles went, his man Michael Free looked out for his master, polished his buttons, stole food for him, and made love to all the girls.

After Charles received his captaincy, news came from home that the O'Malley estates were in serious trouble. The rents were falling off, mortgages were coming due, and Godfrey's gout had crippled him. Charles went home on leave, arriving in Galway shortly after his uncle's death. There was little money for the many debts, and the estate would require close management. Because a last letter from his uncle had asked him to stay in Galway, Charles decided to sell his commission and retire to civil life.

Billy Considine, who acted as his adviser, told him a distressing story. General Dashwood had sent an agent to Galway to buy property. Thinking of Dashwood as an English interloper, Godfrey had written him a harsh letter of warning to stay out of Ireland. In spite of his gout, Godfrey had offered to go to England to do battle with the general. Billy himself had sent a direct challenge to Dashwood. The general had answered in a mild tone, and the two hotheaded Irishmen felt their honor had been vindicated. Charles, however, heard the story with a heavy heart. Lucy seemed lost to him forever. For two years, Charles led a secluded life, scarcely quitting his farm.

Charles and Michael, his servant, were in Dublin on the day news came of Napoleon's return from Elba, and Charles decided to go back into the army. He and Michael went to London. There he was appointed to his old rank on the general staff.

Charles arrived in Brussels just before Waterloo. The Belgian city was crowded. General Dashwood and Lucy were there, as well as Donna Inez and her father. Charles was safe in one quarter, however, for Captain Powers and Inez were to be married. One day in a park, Lucy sat down alone to await her father. Hammersley came to her and asked hoarsely if he could ever hope for her hand. Although not meaning to eavesdrop, Charles heard Lucy dismiss Hammersley. Charles saw Lucy again at the ball, but she seemed as distant and cool as ever.

Charles became a special courier. In the discharge of his duties, he was captured by the French and thrown into prison. To his amazement, his cell mate was General Dashwood, condemned to die for having used spies against the French. St. Croix, a French officer whom Charles had befriended in Spain, offered to help him escape. Unselfishly, Charles let General Dashwood go in his place. Napoleon himself summoned Charles to an audience, and throughout the battle of Waterloo, he saw the action from the French lines. He was watching his chances, however, and when the French troops were scattered, he made his way back to the English lines.

After Charles's heroic action in saving her father from execution, Lucy could no longer refuse him. Charles and Lucy went back to Galway to stay, and the Irish tenantry bared their heads in welcome to the new mistress of O'Malley Castle.

Critical Evaluation:

Charles O'Malley portrays a world that existed for very few people, if, indeed, it existed at all. It is a romantic and adventurous world shown in the novel, one in which honor rises above all other considerations: honor in the hunt, in battle, in politics, and in love. If necessary, duels will be fought to preserve this honor. The code can never be broken without losing caste, and the "fair sex" must be worshiped and, at all times, protected. The characters in the novel have a multitude of eccentricities of personality and behavior but hold conventional values and are redeemed by conventional virtues. Only in such a romantic never-never land could the protagonist's life be determined by the casual word of a girl (when Lucy remarks that any man worth noticing should be a dragoon).

The narrative contains numerous anecdotes; many have little to do directly with the plot but are often amusing. Much of the humor relies on exaggerated personality quirks or on outlandish behavior, but the customs and habits of the Irish come in for a good share of humorous play, particularly the subjects of death, wakes, and drinking. The accounts of Irish electioneering at the beginning of the nineteenth century are interesting and often possess a more unforced and natural humor than many of the other tales. However, Charles Lever is not a satirist at heart. He ridicules rather than satirizes people and positions, as with Sir Harry Boyle, the "well-known member of the Irish House of Commons" who has so got into the "habit of making bulls that I can't write sense when I want it."

This thousand-page novel is the kind of book that once was read aloud by the fire to pass away long evenings. Today, readers would be less patient with its rambling and not always witty digressions. Many nuggets of rich and genuine humor and innocent gaiety, nevertheless, are buried in the book. Charles is a naïve hero, and, in many respects, an Irish cousin of Tom Jones; he is infectiously likable, whatever his mistakes. It is no surprise to the reader that he seems to spend a great part of his time rescuing the beautiful Lucy, or that, in the end, they are married. Anything can happen in such a romantic world, even a personal summons from Napoleon and permission to watch the battle of Waterloo from the French side.

CHILDREN OF THE GHETTO
A Study of a Peculiar People

Type of work: Novel
Author: Israel Zangwill (1864–1926)
Type of plot: Ethnocentric realism
Time of plot: Nineteenth century
Locale: London
First published: 1892

Principal characters:
MOSES ANSELL, a pious Jew
ESTHER, his daughter
HANNAH JACOBS, a beautiful young Jewess
REB SHEMUEL JACOBS, her father and a rabbi
DAVID BRANDON, Hannah's beloved
MELCHITSEKEK PINCHAS, a poor poet and scholar
MRS. HENRY GOLDSMITH, Esther Ansell's benefactress
RAPHAEL LEON, a young journalist
RABBI JOSEPH STRELITSKI, the minister of a fashionable
synagogue
DEBBY, a seamstress

The Story:
Moses Ansell accepted poverty as the natural condition of the chosen people. A pious man, he observed all the rituals of his religion; but even his meek wife, before she died, realized that he should have spent less time in prayer and more time working. His family consisted of Esther, a serious young girl, two smaller sons, a little daughter, and their complaining grandmother. The Ansells lived in one room in the ghetto. When the mother died, Benjamin, an older son, had been put in an orphanage.

One night, Esther returned from the soup kitchen with a pitcher of soup and two loaves of bread. She fell at the doorway of their room, and the soup spilled. The hungry family snatched at the bread. Becky Belcovitch came to complain that the soup had leaked through the ceiling of her room on the floor below. When the Belcovitches heard what had happened, they sent up their own rations to the Ansells.

Malka Birnbaum was the cousin of Moses' dead wife. Occasionally, when the Ansells grew too hungry, she would give Moses a few shillings and berate him for his pious ineptitude. Malka had two daughters, Milly and Leah, by her first husband. Milly was married, and Leah had become engaged to Sam Levine, a commercial traveler.

At the feast of redemption for Milly's infant son, Sam pretended that he had forgotten to give Leah a present. He took an expensive ring from his pocket and held it up for all to admire. Playfully, he slipped it on the finger of Hannah Jacobs, the beautiful daughter of Reb Shemuel, while he repeated the words he had memorized for his marriage to Leah. The horrified company realized at once what Sam was too secular to understand; he and Hannah were married according to the law. Hannah and Sam arranged for the ritualistic formality of a divorce after his next trip.

As compensation, Sam and Leah took Hannah to the Purim ball. There Hannah was greatly taken with David Brandon, a young South African immigrant who no longer observed orthodox practices. Hannah already had an earnest suitor, an impoverished poet and scholar named Pinchas. Although Reb Shemuel listened favorably to his bid for Hannah's hand, the indulgent rabbi refused to force his daughter to marry anyone she did not love.

Sugarman, the marriage broker, had a daughter, Bessie, who was in love with Daniel Hyams; but there was no talk of marriage because Daniel supported his aged parents. When the father saw that Daniel remained unmarried because he could not keep up two households, the old man pretended to receive word from a brother in America. With borrowed money, the two old people took steerage passage for New York.

Sugarman, seeing that Becky Belcovitch was of an age to marry, thought he could arrange a match with Shosshi Shmendrik, a street hawker. Bear Belcovitch, her father, gave his consent. Becky, having other ideas, tried never to be at home when Shosshi came courting. One day, Shosshi stationed his barrow in front of Widow Finkelstein's store. Because he started to leave without paying his sixpence rent, the determined widow harangued him in the street and continued the argument at his house. When she admitted to owning two hundred and seventeen golden sovereigns as well as her shop, Shosshi fell in love with her. Their marriage was a great success.

The disconsolate Pinchas met Wolf, a Jewish labor leader. When starving sweatshop workers struck for higher wages, Pinchas persuaded Wolf to let him address the strikers. In a speech filled with Messianic delusions, he asked them to support his candidacy for Parliament. The workers threw him out in disgust.

Occasionally, Benjamin Ansell came to see his family, but he did not get along well with them. Only Esther, who had dared to look into a New Testament, sympathized with him. Word came from his school that the boy had pneumonia. In his dying delirium, Benjamin spoke only Yiddish, and Moses, sitting by his bedside, rejoiced that his son died a real Jew.

When Hannah and David planned to marry, Reb Shemuel was apprehensive of her suitor's orthodoxy. David assured the rabbi that his family was orthodox and that he himself was a *cohen*, a priest. But Reb Shemuel declared they could never marry. Hannah had been divorced, and the law forbade a *cohen* to take a divorced woman. Hannah and David planned to run away to America, but after she had accompanied her father to the *Seder* services, Hannah realized the old traditions were too strong for her to break. Heartbroken, she renounced David forever.

Ten years later, wealthy Mrs. Henry Goldsmith entertained at a Hanukkah dinner. Most of the guests were artists and intellectuals who had drifted away from the strict practices of Old Jewry. Among them was Raphael Leon, a young journalist. One topic of conversation was *Mordecai Josephs*, a new novel scandalous to West End Judaism, written by an unknown author named Edward Armitage. Sidney Graham, a young dilettante, praised the novel but criticized the crudity and immaturity of the writer. Raphael noticed that a shy, dark girl followed the conversation closely but said nothing.

The girl was Esther Ansell. After packing old Moses and the rest of his brood off to America, Mrs. Goldsmith had adopted Esther and educated her. A graduate of London University, Esther was trying to decide upon a career. Unknown to all, she was Edward Armitage, the author of *Mordecai Josephs*.

Raphael's interest in her continued after he became editor of a Jewish paper, *The Flag of Judah*, financed by Mr. Goldsmith. Pinchas, the neglected poet, aspired to become a contributor. Raphael, unwilling to compromise between his principles and the wishes of his sponsor, was unhappy in his work.

At the theater, Esther encountered Leonard James, the snobbish, vulgar brother of Hannah Jacobs. A short time later, Leonard went to see Esther. They quarreled, and he reminded her that her family had always been schnorrers, beggars. Esther, feeling that he might be right, decided to abuse the generosity of the Goldsmiths no longer. When Raphael called, she told him her decision and announced that she was Edward Armitage.

Dissatisfied with himself, Raphael had an interview with the Reverend Joseph Strelitski, a fashionable minister who was, like Esther, of humble origins. Regarding himself as a hypocrite, a slave to wealth and outmoded ritual, Strelitski intended to resign his pastorate and go to America. Encouraged by his and Esther's examples, Raphael felt relieved when Mr. Goldsmith fired him and made Pinchas editor of the paper.

Meanwhile, Esther had returned to the ghetto to stay with Debby, a seamstress she had known years before. Surrounded by friends of her childhood, she felt herself drawn by family ties; she would go to America. She was glad when her publisher told her that her novel promised to be a success, for she would not go to her family empty-handed. She and Strelitski sailed for America on a ship loaded with Jewish emigrants; but there was no deep sadness in parting when Esther said good-bye to Raphael. He would come to her later.

Critical Evaluation:
Children of the Ghetto is divided into two books. The first and more interesting part is titled "Children of the Ghetto"; the second part, "Grandchildren of the Ghetto," deals mainly with the issue of assimilated Jews in England. Book 1 is basically a survey of the life of the ghetto; appearing in a loosely connected narrative, a number of characters struggle to survive in the hostile environment of the slum. In book 2, the central characters are Anglicized Jews who have lost the core of their beliefs. Israel Zangwill has no sympathy for them and exposes their hypocrisy and fears.

The ghetto, as here presented, was a separate community continually struggling with the influx of destitute Poles, and the fierce, surging life within—a life both comic and tragic—was regulated by the canons of strict orthodoxy. In one sense, this work is not a novel. There is no central plot, only a series of loosely grouped episodes, and the numerous characters are only vaguely connected in many instances. Although Zangwill wrote from a parochial point of view, the book is valuable for its descriptions of seething life, its study of racial strivings and discontents, and its warm, sympathetic character sketches.

The central theme of *Children of the Ghetto* is the conflict over the survival of the Jewish religion. In book 1, it is possible to see the beginnings of the end. The younger generation is no longer willing to carry on the traditions of the past in the same manner as older generations. Social and economic pressures are moving them away from the strict observances of their ancestors.

Zangwill's manner of presentation is uneven. At times, he appears to be merely cataloging various aspects of ghetto life: he presents Jewish folklore, songs, sayings, and jokes at great length; Yiddish words abound in the text. At the same time, Zangwill attempts to portray typical ghetto scenes, including dinners, religious ceremonies, a charity kitchen, and sweatshops. Along with these scenes are characters who, although sometimes touching, are often stereotyped and sentimentalized.

An early work in the career of its author, this novel is nevertheless an informative and for the most part realistic account of the life of the ghetto. As such, it clearly falls into the tradition of European realism. Its attempt to apply the techniques of realism to the ghetto—a hidden, forgotten community—is unique. One aspect of Zangwill's realism is a certain doubleness in approach. On the one hand, the author clearly identifies with the people of the ghetto and their life; on the other, he often adopts an ironic and occasionally patronizing tone toward the people he depicts in order to establish the distance necessary to be objective. Later in his career, perhaps trying to resolve this contradiction, he stopped writing fiction and became a polemicist and dramatist and an early advocate of Zion-

206
Masterplots

ism. His name is often linked to that of Theodor Herzl. It is because of his later career that Zangwill's reputation is more established in the history of thought than in the history of English literature.

A CHRISTMAS CAROL

Type of work: Novel
Author: Charles Dickens (1812–1870)
Type of plot: Sentimental romance
Time of plot: Nineteenth century
Locale: London, England
First published: 1843

> *Principal characters:*
> EBENEZER SCROOGE, a miser
> JACOB MARLEY'S GHOST
> BOB CRATCHIT, Scrooge's clerk
> TINY TIM, Cratchit's son
> SCROOGE'S NEPHEW

The Story:

Ebenezer Scrooge was a miser. Owner of a successful countinghouse, he would have in his bleak office only the smallest fire in the most bitter weather. For his clerk, Bob Cratchit, he allowed an even smaller fire. The weather seldom mattered to Scrooge, who was always cold within, never warm—even on Christmas Eve.

As the time approached for closing the office on Christmas Eve, Scrooge's nephew stopped in to wish him a merry Christmas. Scrooge only sneered, for he abhorred sentiment and thought only of one thing—money. To him, Christmas was a time when people spent more money than they should and found themselves a year older and no richer.

Grudgingly, Scrooge allowed Cratchit to have Christmas Day off; that was the one concession to the holiday that he made, but he warned Cratchit to be at work earlier the day after Christmas. Scrooge left his office and went home to his rooms in a building in which he was the only tenant. They had been the rooms of Scrooge's partner, Jacob Marley, dead for seven years. As he approached his door, he saw Marley's face in the knocker. It was a horrible sight. Marley was looking at Scrooge with his eyes motionless, his ghostly spectacles on his ghostly forehead. As Scrooge watched, the knocker resumed its usual form. Shaken by this vision, Scrooge entered the hall and lighted a candle; then he looked behind the door, half expecting to see Marley's pigtail sticking out into the hall. Satisfied, he double-locked the door. He prepared for bed and sat for a time before the dying fire. Suddenly an unused bell hanging in the room began to ring, as did every bell in the house.

Then from below came the sound of heavy chains clanking. The cellar door flew open, and someone mounted the stairs. Marley's ghost walked through Scrooge's door—Marley, dressed as always, but with a heavy chain of cash boxes, keys, padlocks, ledgers, deeds, and heavy purses around his middle.

Marley's ghost sat down to talk to the frightened and bewildered Scrooge. Forcing Scrooge to admit that he believed in him, Marley explained that in life he had never done any good for mankind and so in death he was condemned to constant traveling with no rest and no relief from the torture of remorse. The ghost said that Scrooge still had a chance to save himself from Marley's fate. Scrooge would be visited by three spirits who would show him the way to change. The first spirit would appear the next day at the stroke of one. The next would arrive on the second night and the last on the third. Dragging his chain, the ghost disappeared.

After Marley's ghost had vanished, Scrooge went to bed, and in spite of his nervousness, he fell asleep instantly. When he awoke, it was still dark. The clock struck twelve. He waited for the stroke of one. As the sound of the bell died away, his bed curtains were pulled apart, and there stood a figure with a childlike face, but with long, white hair and a strong, well-formed body. The ghost introduced itself as the Ghost of Christmas Past, Scrooge's past. When the ghost invited Scrooge to go on a journey with him, Scrooge was unable to refuse.

They traveled like the wind and stopped first at Scrooge's birthplace. There Scrooge saw himself as a boy, neglected by his friends and left alone to find adventure in books. Next, he saw himself at school, where his sister had come to take him home for Christmas. Scrooge recalled his love for his sister, who had died young. The ghost reminded him that she had borne a son whom Scrooge neglected. Their next stop was the scene of Scrooge's apprenticeship, where everyone made merry on Christmas Eve. Traveling on, they saw a young girl weeping as she told young Scrooge that she realized he loved money more than he loved her. The ghost showed him the same girl, grown older but happy with her husband and children. Then the ghost returned Scrooge to his room, where he promptly fell asleep again.

When the Ghost of Christmas Present appeared, he led Scrooge through the city streets on Christmas morning. Their first stop was at the Cratchit home, where Bob Cratchit appeared with frail, crippled Tiny Tim on his shoulder. In the Cratchit home, a skimpy meal became a banquet. After dinner, Bob proposed a toast to Mr. Scrooge, even though it put a temporary damper on the holiday gaiety. Then the ghost and Scrooge crossed swiftly through the city where everyone paused to wish one another a merry Christmas. As they looked in on the home of Scrooge's nephew, gaiety prevailed, and Scrooge was tempted to join in the games. There, too, a toast was proposed to Scrooge's health. As the clock began to strike twelve o'clock, the ghost of Christmas Present faded away.

With the last stroke of twelve, Scrooge saw a black-shrouded phantom approaching him, the Ghost of Christmas Future. The phantom extended his hand and forced Scrooge to follow him until they came to a group of scavengers selling the belongings of the dead. One woman had entered a dead man's room; she had taken his bed curtains, bedding, and even the shirt in which he was to have been buried. Scrooge saw a dead man with his face covered, but he refused to lift the covering. Revisiting the Cratchits, he learned that Tiny Tim had died.

After seeing his old countinghouse and his own neglected grave, Scrooge realized that it was he who had lain on the bed in the cold, stripped room with no one to mourn his death. Scrooge begged the spirit that it should not be so, vowing that he would change, that he would forever honor Christmas in his heart. He made a desperate grasp for the phantom's hand and realized that the ghost had shriveled away and dwindled into a bedpost. Scrooge bounded out of bed and thanked Jacob Marley's ghost for his chance to make amends. Dashing into the street, he realized that it was Christmas Day. His first act was to order the largest turkey available to be sent anonymously to the Cratchits. The day before, Scrooge had ordered a man from his countinghouse for asking a contribution; now Scrooge gave him a large sum of money for the poor. Then he astounded his nephew by arriving at his house for Christmas dinner and making himself the life of the party.

Scrooge never reverted to his old ways. He raised Bob Cratchit's salary, improved conditions in his office, contributed generously to all charities, and became a second father to Tiny Tim. It was said of him thereafter that he truly knew how to keep Christmas well.

Critical Evaluation:

Literally a hymn to the spirit of Christmas, this universally loved story has fascinated all ages and peoples. It appeals to a basic human instinct: the need to overcome self-hate and live in benign self-esteem. Man is no good to himself or anyone else unless he can find within his own soul the seeds of that goodness he hopes to find in the world. Miser and misanthrope, Ebenezer Scrooge has given up on others; he expects nothing and gives nothing. It is ironically fitting that Charles Dickens makes him the master of a countinghouse; his "ledger" is perfectly balanced: nothing has gone out and therefore nothing comes in.

Dickens' skill with humor and character analysis are particularly evident. At the beginning of the story, readers are made to dislike Scrooge for his miserly ways but are in sympathy with him as he is subjected to the tortures of his ghostly journeys. Dickens provides a psychological explanation for Scrooge's bitterness and desire to live apart from the rest of the world. At the same time, he paves the way for Scrooge's reform, so that it comes as no surprise. It is entirely right that Scrooge should become an example of the meaning of Christmas among men.

Marley's ghost provides the terrifying example: this is all Scrooge has to look forward to if he continues to live without involving himself in mankind. The ghosts that follow reveal to the reader the psychological reasons for Scrooge's warped character, but they are also messengers from Scrooge's unconscious mind that force him to confront repressed disappointments and failures of kindness; he is rewarded for standing up to the pain of confrontation with the balm of self-pity. As the various ghosts of Christmas Past, Present, and Future enable Scrooge to confront the truth about his own life, a subtle transference takes place. Scrooge shifts from self-pity to compassion and concern for others. He is reborn in Love.

He rises in the morning as a man possessed with the possibilities of kindness and charity. Remade by his dream, he now awakes "to find it true," as Keats said of Milton's Adam when he awoke to find Eve at his side. It is a triumph of the moral imagination. The ecstasy of his rebirth is infectious. The Cratchits, Scrooge's nephew, and the charity collectors are not only the beneficiaries of Scrooge's largesse; they are also the heirs of his spiritual awakening. When Tiny Tim cries "God Bless Us, Every One," he is emblematic of the cripple who finds God in his own affliction as did Scrooge in his loneliness, only to walk in the higher regions opened by the bliss of human love.

CLARISSA
Or, The History of a Young Lady

Type of work: Novel
Author: Samuel Richardson (1689–1761)
Type of plot: Sentimental romance
Time of plot: Early eighteenth century
Locale: England
First published: 1747–1748

> *Principal characters:*
> CLARISSA HARLOWE, a young woman of family and fortune
> ROBERT LOVELACE, her seducer
> JOHN BELFORD, Lovelace's friend
> WILLIAM MORDEN, Clarissa's cousin
> ARABELLA, Clarissa's older sister
> JAMES, Clarissa's older brother

The Story:

Robert Lovelace, a young Englishman of a noble family, was introduced into the Harlowe household by Clarissa's uncle, who wished Lovelace to marry Clarissa's older sister Arabella. The young man, finding nothing admirable in the older girl, fell deeply in love with Clarissa, but he quickly learned that his suit was balked by Clarissa's brother and sister. James Harlowe had disliked Lovelace since they had been together at Oxford, and Arabella was offended because he had spurned her in favor of Clarissa. Both were jealous of Clarissa because she had been left a fortune by their grandfather and they had not.

Having convinced his mother and father that Lovelace was a profligate, James Harlowe proposed that Clarissa be married to Mr. Solmes, a rich, elderly man of little taste and no sensibility. When Solmes found no favor in the eyes of Clarissa, her family assumed she was in love with Lovelace, despite her protestations to the contrary.

Clarissa refused to allow Solmes to visit with her in the parlor or to sit next to her when the family was together. Her father, outraged by her conduct, ordered her to be more civil to the man he had chosen as her husband. When she refused, saying she would never marry a man against her will, not even Lovelace, her father confined her to her room.

Lovelace, smitten with the girl's beauty and character, resolved to seduce her away from her family, partly out of love for her and partly in vengeance for the insults heaped upon him by the Harlowe family.

He was greatly aided in his scheme by the domineering personalities of Mr. Harlowe and his son. They took away Clarissa's trusted maid and replaced her with a girl who was impertinent and insolent to the young woman. They refused to let her see any member of the family, even her mother. Clarissa's only trusted adviser was Miss Howe, a friend and correspondent who advised her to escape the house if she could, even if it meant accepting Lovelace's aid and his proposal of marriage.

One evening, Lovelace slipped into the garden where Clarissa was walking and entreated her to elope with him. Wishing only to escape her domineering father, she went with him after some protest. Lovelace told her she would be taken to the home of Lord M—, a kinsman of Lovelace, who would protect her until her cousin, Colonel Morden, could return to England and arrange for a reconciliation between Clarissa and her family. Lovelace was not as good as his word, however, for he took her to a house of ill repute, where he introduced her to a woman he called Mrs. Sinclair. Inventing reasons why he could not take her to Lord M—'s house, he persuaded the bewildered girl to temporarily pose as his wife. He told Mrs. Sinclair that Clarissa was his wife with whom he could not live until certain marriage settlements had been arranged. Clarissa permitted him to tell the lie, believing that it would prevent her father and her brother from discovering her whereabouts.

In Mrs. Sinclair's house, she was amost as much a prisoner as she had been in her father's home. Meanwhile, her family had disowned her and refused to send her either money or clothes. Her father further declared that she was no longer his daughter and that he hoped she would have a miserable existence in both this world and the next.

This state of affairs was distressing to Clarissa, who was now dependent upon Lovelace for her very existence. He took advantage of the circumstances to press his love upon her without mentioning his earlier promises of marriage. Clarissa tried to escape and got as far as Hampstead before Lovelace overtook her. There, he had two women impersonate his cousins to convince Clarissa that she should return to her lodgings with them. Upon her return to Mrs. Sinclair's house, they filled her with drugs, and later Lovelace raped her. A few days later, Clarissa received a letter from Miss Howe in which she learned that she was in a house in which no woman of her station would be seen. Again, Clarissa tried to escape by calling for aid from a window. Lovelace finally promised to leave her unmolested until she could get aid from her cousin or from Miss Howe.

Lovelace left London for a few days to visit Lord M—, who was ill. While he was gone, Clarissa contrived to steal the clothes of a serving girl and escape from the house; but within a day or two, Mrs. Sinclair discovered Clarissa's whereabouts and had her arrested and imprisoned for debt. When John Belford, a friend of Lovelace, heard of the girl's plight, he rescued her by proving the debt a fraud. He found shelter for Clarissa with a kindly glovemaker and his wife. Tired of her miserable existence, Clarissa began to go into physical decline, in spite of all that the apothecary and doctor secured by John Belford could do for her.

She spent her time writing letters in an effort to secure a reconciliation with her family and to acquaint her friends with the true story of her plight. She refused to have anything to do with Lovelace, who was by that time convinced that he loved her dearly. He wished to marry her, to make amends for the treatment she had suffered at his hands, but she refused his offer with gentle firmness.

As she declined in health, Clarissa's friends did what they could to reunite her with her family. When her father and brother refused to receive her, she went to an undertaking establishment and bought a coffin that she had fitted as she wished, including a plaque that gave the date of her birth as the day on which she left her father's house.

On his return to England, Colonel Morden tried to raise her spirits, but his efforts failed because he, too, was unable to effect any change in the attitude of the Harlowe family. He also had an interview with Lovelace and Lord M—. The nobleman and Lovelace assured him that their family thought very highly of Clarissa. They wished her to marry Lovelace, and Lovelace wished to marry her; but even her cousin was unable to persuade Clarissa to accept Lovelace as a husband.

Everyone, including the Harlowe family, saw that Clarissa was determined to die. Her father and brother lifted their ban upon her entrance into the Harlowe house; her sister was sorry she had been cruel to Clarissa; and the mother was convinced that she had failed in her duty toward her daughter. They all wrote to Clarissa, begging the girl's forgiveness and expressing their hope that she would recover quickly and be reunited with her family. Their letters, however, arrived too late, for Clarissa had died.

Clarissa was returned to her father's house for her funeral. She was interred in the family vault at the feet of the grandfather whose fortune had been one of the sources of her troubles. Lovelace, who was quite distressed at her death, was persuaded by Lord M— to go to the Continent.

There Clarissa was avenged. Lovelace met Colonel Morden in France, and early one winter morning, Clarissa's cousin fought a duel with her betrayer. Lovelace was mortally wounded by a thrust through his body. As he lay dying, he expressed the hope that his death would expiate his crimes.

Critical Evaluation:

Few men would have seemed less likely than Samuel Richardson to be influential in the history of the novel. A successful printer, he did not publish his first work until after he was fifty years old. Because of a reputation as an accomplished letter writer, he was encouraged to write a book of sample letters. Even before the publication of this volume, *Familiar Letters* (1741), he turned his epistolary talent to didactic purposes in fiction with the publication of *Pamela* (1740). Predictably, *Pamela* was greeted with popular approval and critical disdain. By 1744, he had prepared a summary of his epistolary masterpiece, *Clarissa*. The massive novel was published in three installments between December, 1747, and December, 1748, and was subsequently printed in eight volumes. Richardson was aware of length (about one million words) as a serious failing in his narrative and, indeed, *Clarissa* is now rarely read except in George Sherburn's abridgement. The length was probably less an impediment for the more leisurely reading class of the mid-eighteenth century.

Richardson's main literary contribution is his mastery of the epistolary style. The use of letters as a means of narration has obvious drawbacks. Certainly the flow of the narrative is repeatedly interrupted, and it takes all the strength of the reader's will to suspend disbelief concerning the writing of thoughtful and informative letters by characters during periods of extraordinary stress. Conventions aside, it is difficult to sustain a continuous and progressive narrative in this form. The method frustrated Samuel Johnson, a friend of Richardson, who concluded that the work should be read for its sentiment. Richardson himself worried that his narrative technique had let his characters do too much in too short a period of time.

Richardson did, however, capitalize on the correlative advantages of the epistolary method. The immediacy of "writing to the moment" is a prime means of developing concerned attention in the reader. In addition, Richardson's talent for dialogue transforms many of the lengthier letters into poignant scenes, and the text of each letter is most decorously cast in a style appropriate to the correspondent. Moreover, there is the advantage, especially for a didactic novel, of the multiple points of view that add complexity and sympathy to the interpretation of the action. As Alan McKillop says, letters are not simply presented but "copied, sent, received, shown about, discussed, answered, even perhaps hidden, intercepted, stolen, altered or forged." The whole process of correspondence comes alive as Richardson blends theater, moral discourse, courtesy book, and romance into a compellingly tense analysis of contemporary morals and manners.

As the use of the epistolary style would suggest, action is less important to Richardson's fiction than reflection on the moral significance of actions. It may be that the author was familiar with the life of the gentry only through the theater. Nevertheless, despite an apparent ignorance of the frequent occupations of a rich country family, the focus is so much on the tenseness of the situations and the meaning of actions that little is lost by the absence of sociological verisimilitude. Although Richardson occasionally presents dramatically vivid details, he usually is less interested in setting than in what Sherburn calls, in the contemporary eighteenth century terminology, a "distress."

The main theme of the novel, as described by Richardson on the title page, is "the distresses that may attend the misconduct both of parents and children in relation to marriage." There is no doubt that the motives of the Harlowes are crassly materialistic—to improve the already comfortable family fortune by forcing Clarissa to marry the suitable, but elderly, Solmes. There is a lack of tenderness and family feeling toward Clarissa, which softens only after it is too late and she is well along in her final decline. Clarissa, for her part, is also strong-willed. As Richardson explains about his fiction, "The principal of the two young Ladies is proposed as an exemplar of her Sex. Nor is it any objection to her being so, that she is not in all respects a perfect character." This statement is made by Richardson, although he is especially fond of the companionship and adulation of ladies.

At first, Clarissa is attracted by the roguish but fascinating Lovelace. In fact, he occasionally seems not all a bad fellow. At least he is the most vivid character in the novel; yet his egocentrism and his attraction to intrigue, however appealing, are inconsiderate of others and are not recanted until his sentimental dying breaths. His assaults on Clarissa seem almost an aggression on her sex. Still, after the deed is done, practicality seems to demand that Clarissa turn virtue into its own reward, as Pamela had done by marrying her seducer. *Clarissa*, however, is a more complex novel than *Pamela*, and Clarissa and Lovelace have already shown a moral incompatibility that makes acquiescence by Clarissa impossible (despite the impassioned pleadings of Richardson's sentimental readers before the last third of the novel appeared).

At the heart of the incompatibility is Clarissa's admirable but rigid idealism. Although a gentle person, she is unreserved in her commitment to virtue and, as Sherburn puts it, to decorous behavior. She is not so much a puritan as a devotee of what is morally fit, and she carries her commitment to the grave. When her friend Miss Howe suggests that she take the expedient way out by marrying the ostensibly repentant Lovelace, Clarissa cannot give in. First, she would prefer reconciliation with her intransigent family, but second, and more important, her sense of propriety would not allow such moral and personal compromise. Nevertheless, it must be admitted that she is less interesting for her idealism than for the distressing situations and dilemmas her idealism occasions.

Despite its narrative improbabilities and the moral obstinacy of its main character, *Clarissa* became a revered example not only of the epistolary novel but also of the refined novel of sentiment and, by the end of the century, it had been imitated and acclaimed both in England and on the Continent.

CLAUDIUS THE GOD AND HIS WIFE MESSALINA

Type of work: Novel
Author: Robert Graves (1895–   )
Type of plot: Historical chronicle
Time of plot: A.D. 41–54
Locale: Rome, Britain, and the Near East
First published: 1934

> *Principal characters:*
> TIBERIUS CLAUDIUS DRUSUS NERO GERMANICUS, Emperor of
>   Rome
> MESSALINA, his third wife
> CALPURNIA, his mistress
> AGRIPPINILLA, his fourth wife
> LUCIUS DOMITIUS, Agrippinilla's son and Claudius'
>   grandnephew, later called Nero
> HEROD AGRIPPA, Tetrarch of Bashan

The Story:

When the Emperor Claudius was considered the neglected scholar of the Claudian family before his accession to the throne, one of his friends and well-wishers was Herod Agrippa. The Emperor Tiberius had imprisoned Herod for treasonous sentiments, but when Caligula came to the throne, he made Herod Tetrarch of Bashan. When Caligula was murdered and Claudius proclaimed Emperor by the palace guards, Herod was back in Rome on official business.

As the result of popular opinion that he was a cripple, a stammerer, and an idiot, Claudius' position was a difficult one at first. The Roman Senate did not expect much of such a man and certainly not a capable handling of public affairs after Caligula's four years of misrule. Claudius, however, immediately began a program of reforms, among them a reorganization of the Senate, a stabilization of the state's finances, and the abolition of many of Caligula's cruel decrees. To carry out his widespread program, Claudius appointed many new ministers of state. He entrusted the office of the Director of Public Morals to his wife Messalina, as she had been most helpful in reorganizing the Senate list. To his loyal friend, Herod, Claudius gave the lands of Judea, Samaria, and Edom. Then in the open market-place before an immense crowd, Claudius and Herod made a solemn pact of friendship and loyalty.

Soon after Claudius' ascent to the throne, his son Brittanicus was born,

---

followed approximately eleven months later by a daughter named Octavia. After the birth of his second child, Messalina came to Claudius and requested his permission to move into an apartment in the new palace and thus live apart from him. Claudius ruefully agreed to her plan. Messalina's real desire to move to the new palace was greater freedom than she could enjoy under the eyes of Claudius, and her removal to her new quarters began a life of debauchery, licentiousness, political intrigue, bribery, cheating, and murder. Claudius was so busy with matters of state that seven years passed before he heard rumors of Messalina's depravities.

After beginning a public works program, sending an expedition into Germany to recover the eagle standard lost by Varus' army, and putting down a minor revolt at home, Claudius turned his attention to the conquest of Britain. The war was hastened by the detention of Roman trading ships by Togodumnus, who was joint ruler with his brother Caractacus, and also by the rapid spread of the Druid cult through Britain and France. Claudius sent Aulus Plautius to Britain with a large invasion force and the promise of additional legions if Roman losses exceeded a certain figure. Aulus managed to cross the Thames and capture London. Then he camped just outside London to await the arrival of Claudius and reinforcements. A decisive battle took place at Brentwood Hill, a ridge between London and Colchester. The Romans won it by means of Claudius' armchair strategy. At the age of fifty-three, Claudius fought his first battle, won it, and never fought again. In Britain, he was deified as a god, and upon his return to Rome, he received a full triumph.

He now had to turn his attentions to the East, where for some time he had been receiving disquieting reports regarding Herod Agrippa and his plot to establish a united Jewish empire. Herod had been making secret alliances with neighboring princes and potentates, and he hoped to obtain the support of the Jews by declaring himself the long-awaited Messiah. Claudius realized that affairs had progressed to the stage where there was little he could do to forestall Herod's plans. At the great festival at which he proposed to proclaim himself the Messiah, Herod permitted neighboring rulers to address him as God without bothering to correct their error. At that moment, an owl flew into the arena, and Herod remembered a prophecy: when next he saw an owl, his death would be near, and the number of days left to him would be the same as the number of hoots. The owl hooted five times; five days later, Herod was dead. His plot to set up a Jewish kingdom collapsed.

About eight years after they were married, Messalina came to Claudius with a strange tale. Barbillus the astrologer had predicted that her husband would die within thirty days, not later than the Ides of September. She proposed that Claudius' death might be averted if he permitted her to divorce him in order to remarry Silius, her former husband. Claudius finally gave in to her pleading. The whole story, however, was a ruse to rid herself of Claudius so that she might marry Silius; the two were plotting Claudius' murder and their own accession to the throne. Her marriage to Silius was announced for September 10, but on September 5, while Claudius was out of the city, she married Silius. Calpurnia, a former mistress of Claudius, finally told him the whole truth regarding Messalina and her behavior throughout their marriage. Claudius tried and executed over one hundred people; most of them were the men with whom Messalina had committed adultery. Messalina herself was killed by an officer of the palace guards.

Claudius then married his niece, Agrippinilla, the mother of Lucius Domitius who later became the Emperor Nero. He no longer took any interest in life but allowed the affairs of state to be handled by Agrippinilla and his ministers. Claudius adopted Lucius and made him joint heir with Brittanicus. Lucius became of age first, and Agrippinilla, who wished to see her son sole ruler of Rome, poisoned Claudius. His death was concealed from the people until the empire had been secured for Nero. Thus Claudius, Emperor of Rome and a Roman god, ended his troubled reign.

Critical Evaluation:

In this sequel to *I, Claudius*, Robert Graves continues the development of the historical novel that he had begun in his earlier work. Before Graves, this literary form was seldom other than a romance, contemporary to whatever age in which it was written and covered over with a thin veneer reminiscent of exotic climates and distant times and places. Graves, however, uses the form of the historical novel not to disguise the present but to explore and bring to light the past. In *I, Claudius* and *Claudius the God and His Wife Messalina*, Graves does successfully what Gore Vidal has done in *Julian* and more recently in *Burr*. Graves studies the original historical sources—Tacitus, Suetonius, Pliny, Varro, Josephus, and many others—and tells the story of the Emperor Claudius. It is a measure of Graves's talent and skill that he can make his evocation of the past seem real and vivid, even to those with a solid grounding in the history of the early Roman Empire.

The solid historical background of *Claudius the God and His Wife Messalina* is only one of the reasons why it is worth the reader's time and effort. Another is Graves's skill with language. Readers of this book are not only educated about Roman history and enlightened by the author's interpretation of it, but they are entertained as well.

The form Graves uses is that of a memoir; the book is supposedly written in Claudius' own words and from his point of view. Claudius is known to most students of Roman history as a rather dull person, stupid and silly in equal measure. Graves, however, takes some of the historical anomalies of Claudius' life and reign and explains them from the Roman's point of view; for example, he describes Claudius' relationship with Messalina as a case of a decent and trusting man whose very decency and honesty is exploited by his wife. History seldom happened as the historians wrote it, and the great historical characters were only human beings living their everyday lives. Graves makes this point very forcefully, and his tool to do so is the poet's way with words and knowledge of motivations. Graves illustrates the fact that either poets should write more history or historians should be more poetic.

THE CLAYHANGER TRILOGY

Type of work: Novel
Author: Arnold Bennett (1867–1931)
Type of plot: Domestic realism
Time of plot: 1870–1895
Locale: England
First published: Clayhanger, 1910; *Hilda Lessways,* 1911; *These Twain,* 1915
   Principal characters:
     EDWIN CLAYHANGER, a businessman
     HILDA LESSWAYS, his wife
     MAGGIE CLAYHANGER, Edwin's sister
     MR. INGPEN, Edwin's friend
     GEORGE CANNON, Hilda's first husband
     DARIUS CLAYHANGER, Edwin's father

The Story:

In 1872, sixteen-year-old Edwin Clayhanger left school to aid his father in the Clayhanger printing shop. His father had disregarded Edwin's request that he be allowed to go to school and study to be an architect. Old Darius Clayhanger was a self-made man who had risen from a boyhood experience in the workhouse to the position of affluence he held in the Midland community, and it was his desire that his work be carried on by his only son. Since he was a complete tyrant in the home, no one dared to cross him.

Several years later, Darius Clayhanger built a new house in a more pretentious part of town. Edwin became friendly with the Orgreave family, who lived next door. The elder Orgreave was an architect, with whom Edwin spent many hours discussing his own interest in that profession. Unknown to Edwin, the oldest Orgreave daughter, Janet, had fallen in love with him.

Edwin met Hilda Lessways at the Orgreave home. She was an orphan living in Brighton with the sister of a former employer, George Cannon, who wished to marry her. Although she was attracted to Edwin, she returned to Brighton and soon married Cannon. At the time of her marriage, she gave Cannon her small patrimony to invest for her.

A year later, Hilda returned to visit the Orgreaves. During that year, she had learned that her husband had been married earlier and that her marriage to him was void. On this second visit, she fell in love with Edwin and promised to marry him, for no one knew of her marriage at Brighton. Then, learning that she was to have a baby, she returned to Brighton. She wrote to Janet Orgreave, saying that she was married and asking Janet to inform Edwin. Deeply hurt, he devoted himself entirely to his father's business, for his father had become mentally ill.

Hilda, meanwhile, had borne her child and had named him George Edwin, after his father and Edwin Clayhanger. She managed a rooming house owned by her husband's sister. Cannon, discovered by his first wife, was sentenced to serve a two-year prison term for bigamy. After his release, he was again imprisoned for ten years for passing a forged check. The money he had imprudently invested for Hilda was lost when the hotel corporation, whose shares he had bought, collapsed. Hilda was no longer financially independent.

After his father's death, Edwin and his sister Maggie continued to live alone in the Clayhanger house. Both of them became old-maidish in their habits, although many young women, including Janet Orgreave, would have gladly married Edwin, whose printing business continued to prosper and grow.

Edwin became quite fond of Hilda's son, who was living temporarily with the Orgreaves. When George Edwin became ill with influenza, it was Edwin who sent for the doctor and notified Hilda.

Although neither spoke openly of their feelings, Hilda and Edwin renewed their affection for each other when they met at the sick child's bed. When he was well again, George Edwin and his mother went back to Brighton. Nine years had passed since Edwin and Hilda first had met. Hilda was still struggling along with the failing boardinghouse at Brighton.

Months later, Edwin went to see Hilda and found her penniless and about to be evicted. Edwin paid her bills, and Hilda told him all that had happened to her, explaining that her marriage was void and her child illegitimate. Edwin returned home but at last resolved to marry Hilda quietly. They met in London and were married. They then moved into the Clayhanger house, and Maggie went to live with a maiden aunt. Edwin also adopted Hilda's son and gave him his name.

Edwin, long having had his own way, was accustomed to a certain routine in his home and to making his own decisions; but Hilda was a person of equally strong personality, and Edwin felt that she was trying to make him conform too much to her own domestic views and habits. Worst of all, she attempted to influence Edwin in business affairs, a realm which he thought was solely his own.

A few months after the marriage, the aunt with whom Maggie Clayhanger was living became seriously ill. During her last days, Mr. Ingpen, Edwin's business friend, was injured in a factory accident. At Ingpen's request, Edwin went to his room to destroy some letters and pictures, so they would not be found if Ingpen died in the hospital. Edwin found a woman asleep there. She was Ingpen's mistress, a woman whose husband was incurably insane. Edwin was disturbed for his friend, but Ingpen laughed and said that the situation was best as it was because he did not want to be trapped in a marriage.

When Edwin's aunt died, her estate was left to the children of Edwin's younger sister, Clara. Edwin and Maggie were pleased, but Hilda thought that she and Edwin should have received part of the estate. Her selfishness irked Edwin. He felt that he was rich enough and that his nephews and nieces deserved the money. Seriously thinking that a divorce was the answer to his present situation, he recalled with nostalgia his bachelor days. The only bright ray in his life seemed to be George Edwin, his stepson, who was studying the elements of architecture with the aid of John Orgreave. Edwin hoped that his son might now have the chance to become an architect.

On a visit to a nearby city, Hilda and Edwin were taken to inspect a prison. There they saw George Cannon. He was released soon afterward when he was found to be innocent of the forgery charge. Cannon then went to Edwin without Hilda's knowledge, and Edwin gave him money to go to America. Edwin never expected to see the money again, but he wanted to get the man out of the country. He was also bothered by the fact that Hilda had been in correspondence with Cannon's other wife.

The climax of Edwin's unhappiness with Hilda came on Christmas day, when she took him to see a house in the country. She tried to force him into buying it by diplomatic moves and conversations with their friends and family, so that Edwin would appear foolish if he did not buy the house.

After a violent argument with his wife, whom he accused of being grasping, underhanded, and dishonest, Edwin left the house in a rage; but after a long walk in the cold winter night, he realized that his marriage and his wife meant a great deal to him. He realized that he had to make concessions for his wife and for the fact that they had been married so late in life with their habits already fixed. Finally he saw, in his mind, his friend Ingpen, who was unable to marry the woman he loved.

He went back to the house to reconcile himself with Hilda. His faith in human nature was completely reestablished when he found a check from America in the mail for the money he had lent to George Cannon.

Critical Evaluation:

Arnold Bennett completed *Clayhanger*, the first novel of a trilogy concerning the life apprenticeship of Edwin Clayhanger, on June 23, 1910, two years after the publication of *The Old Wives' Tale*. At the height of his creative powers as well as of his critical reputation, Bennett ventured to write his most nearly autobiographical novel in a format popular with

Edwardian readers. Compared to George Moore's *Confessions of a Young Man* (1888), Samuel Butler's *The Way of All Flesh* (1903), E. M. Forster's *The Longest Journey* (1907), and H. G. Wells's *Tono-Bungay* (1909), *Clayhanger* is a fairly typical "education novel." The representative hero of this genre is an inexperienced, often confused, but generally likeable young man who, after learning from a series of valuable adventures, develops a better understanding about himself and about life. Typically, the hero comes to terms with his weaknesses and strengths, discovers a proper vocation for his talents, and begins to understand the meaning and limitations of romantic love.

Unlike the typical *Erziehungsroman* hero, whose "education" is completed at the end of the book, Edwin Clayhanger undergoes an extended apprenticeship from youth to middle age, testing the dreams and values of his young manhood against the often harsher realities of life itself. Indeed, in the novels that follow *Clayhanger*, *Hilda Lessways* (1911) and *These Twain* (1915), Bennett alters some of the conventions familiar to the genre. With a relentlessly deterministic philosophy, he pursues the romantic follies of Edwin and teaches him, at the last, a bitter lesson about his restricted place in the world.

It was a lesson Bennett well understood, for his own early life resembled that of his protagonist. His father Enoch Bennett—the Darius Clayhanger of the novel—was a Victorian tyrant who demanded absolute respect from his dreamy, seemingly feckless son and usually failed to get it. One theme of the novel that appears also in later twentieth century fiction (Joyce's *Ulysses*, Wolfe's *Look Homeward, Angel*, and Kafka's "The Judgment," for example) is that of the quest of a son for his spiritual father. Edwin hates Darius and longs for the old man's death. Yet he saves his father from financial ruin when, with astonishing presence of mind, he secures a cable to hoist a collapsing printing press; and when Darius dies of natural causes (a scene as harrowing as any deathbed drama in literature), the son is moved not to thoughts of vengeance but of pity. Other characters and locations in the novel are modeled after real people and places that Bennett knew intimately: Auntie Bourne is Auntie Clara Hamps; Absolom Wood is Osmond Orgreave; Cobridge is Bleakridge; Waterloo Road is Trafalgar Road. Probably many characteristics of Marguerite Soulé, Bennett's French wife, appear in Hilda Lessways. Above all, the trilogy is carefully crafted to simulate reality. Detail upon detail, the trivia and circumstances of life are reproduced, and the reader has a sense both of place solidly rendered and of time remorselessly passing.

To be sure, time itself is a mysterious force, almost a metaphysical fate-element in the trilogy. Like other twentieth century writers such as Proust, Joyce, Mann, Woolf, and Eliot, Bennett is deeply concerned with both the nature and effects of time. His characters develop, change, mature to the slow rhythm of time, and ultimately are destroyed by their silent adversary. Whether with tantalizing deliberation (as time plays with old Mr. Shushion, its "obscene victim") or with sudden brutal finality (as time fells Darius), it is the sole absolute, the single truth around which all life appears to revolve as an illusion.

Counterpoised to time is the rhythm of life. In the wild sensual delight of Florence Simcox, the "clog-dancer" of the Midlands, Edwin first perceives the beauty of woman. At the "Dragon," where the Burseley Mutual Burial Club holds a "free-and-easy," he responds to the vital warmth of friendship; and with a single kiss from Hilda Lessways, a woman he both fears and loves, he is turned for the first time from a shy, fussy bachelor into a man of passion. For her part, Hilda has ignored Edwin until he exclaims, in a moment of compassion and despair, "I'm ashamed of seeing my father lose his temper." At this point, this moment of spiritual illumination, she begins to fall in love with him. She is touched by what she believes to be his confession of weakness. Brutalized throughout her life by cruel men like George Cannon, she senses that Edwin has the strength of his tenderness. Her judgment is flawed, however, because life has conditioned her to see Edwin not as he is but as she wants him to be. Nor can Edwin truly understand the "real" Hilda, who is not (as he believes) a woman of romantic mystery; yet the illusion of the moment becomes the pattern for life. For Bennett, the small rather than great moments of life have their deepest effects upon character. Magic is in the rhythm of life, and beauty also; but the magic is terribly brief.

The last two novels of the trilogy, considerably less autobiographical than *Clayhanger*, show a decline in Bennett's emotional powers but complete his architectonic design. *Hilda Lessways* is interesting from a technical point of view, because the novel describes the life of Hilda parallel to that of Edwin. For each lover, the romantic partner is a projection of a dream, not the real person. Edwin and Hilda meet too late in their lives; their habits have been formed, and they are incapable of change. Indeed, the very qualities that they perceive in each other—willpower and assertiveness—are inimicable to their happiness. In *These Twain*, Bennett details the inevitable results of their mismating. Hilda becomes a shrew. Edwin becomes his father—or a man very much like his father: intolerant, smug, materialistic. His decision, at the end of the trilogy, to make the best of a marriage that has lost its charm, is a triumph of practicality over romance. To Bennett, life at best is imperfect, and it is best endured without illusion.

THE CLOISTER AND THE HEARTH
A Tale of the Middle Ages

Type of work: Novel
Author: Charles Reade (1814–1884)
Type of plot: Historical romance
Time of plot: Fifteenth century
Locale: Holland, Germany, France, and Italy
First published: 1861

Principal characters:
GERARD ELIASON, a young artist
MARGARET BRANDT, his betrothed
DENYS, a Burgundian bowman
MARGARET VAN EYCK, the sister of Jan Van Eyck
GHYSBRECHT VAN SWIETEN, a burgomaster

The Story:

Gerard was the son of Elias, a Dutch cloth and leather merchant, and Katherine, his wife. His talent for penmanship and illuminating developed at an early age. At first, Gerard was aided by the monks of the local convent for which he was destined. When the monks could teach the young artist no more, he became the pupil of Margaret Van Eyck, sister of the famous painter, Jan Van Eyck. She and her servant, Reicht Heynes, encouraged the lad to enter a prize art competition sponsored by Philip the Good, Duke of Burgundy and Earl of Holland.

On his way to Rotterdam to an exhibit of the entries, Gerard met an old man, Peter Brandt, and his daughter, Margaret, who sat exhausted by the wayside. He went with them into the town. There he took a letter of introduction from Dame Van Eyck to the Princess Marie, daughter of Prince Philip. Impressed by the lad's talent, the princess promised him a benefice near his village of Tergou as soon as he had taken holy orders. He won a prize in the contest and returned to Tergou, wondering whether he would ever again see Margaret Brandt, with whom he had fallen in love.

Gerard accidentally learned from Ghysbrecht Van Swieten, Tergou's burgomaster, that the old man and his daughter lived in Sevenbergen, a nearby village. He began to frequent their cottage. Ghysbrecht disclosed to Katherine, Gerard's mother, that the young man was interested in Margaret Brandt. A quarrel ensued in the family, and Elias threatened to have Gerard imprisoned to prevent his marriage. Margaret Van Eyck gave Gerard money and valuable advice on art and recommended that he and the girl go to Italy, where Gerard's talents were sure to be appreciated. Gerard and Margaret Brandt became betrothed, but before they could be married, the burgomaster had Gerard seized and put in jail. He was rescued at night from the prison by Margaret, his sweetheart; Giles, his dwarf brother; and Kate, his crippled sister. In the rescue, Giles removed from a chest in the cell some parchments that the villainous Ghysbrecht had hidden there. At Sevenbergen, Gerard buried all the parchments except a deed, which concerned Margaret's father.

After an exciting pursuit, Gerard and Margaret escaped the vicinity of Tergou. They separated; Margaret was to return to Sevenbergen, and Gerard was to proceed to Rome. On the way, he was befriended by a Burgundian soldier named Denys, and the pair traveled toward the Rhine. They experienced a variety of adventures together.

Meanwhile, in Sevenbergen, Margaret Brandt fell sick and was befriended by Margaret Van Eyck. Martin, an old soldier friend of the young lovers, went to Rotterdam where he procured a pardon for Gerard from Prince Philip. Dame Van Eyck gave a letter to Hans Memling to deliver to Gerard in Italy, but Memling was waylaid by agents of the burgomaster, and the letter was taken from him.

Gerard and Denys came upon a company of Burgundian soldiers on their way to the wars, and Denys was ordered to ride with them to Flanders. Gerard was left to make his solitary way to Rome. Released because of wounds received in the duke's service, Denys later set out for Holland, where he hoped to find Gerard. Elias and Katherine welcomed him in Tergou when he told them that he had been Gerard's comrade. Meanwhile, old Brandt and Margaret disappeared from Sevenbergen, and Denys searched all Holland for the girl. They had gone to Rotterdam, but only the burgomaster knew their whereabouts. When Margaret practiced medicine illegally, she was arrested and sentenced to pay a large fine. In order to stay alive, she took in laundry. Denys discovered Margaret in Rotterdam, and the pair returned to Tergou, where Gerard's family had become reconciled to his attachment to the girl.

Gerard made his dangerous way through France and Germany to Venice. From there, he took a coastal vessel and continued to Rome. When the ship was wrecked in a storm, Gerard displayed bravery in saving the lives of a Roman matron and her child. He went on to Rome and took lodgings, but he found work all but impossible to obtain. He and another young artist, Pietro, decorated playing cards for a living. Finally, through the good graces of the woman whose life he had saved in the shipwreck, Gerard was hired to decorate manuscripts for Fra Colonna, a leading classical scholar.

Hans Memling brought a letter to Rome. Sent by Ghysbrecht, the letter gave Gerard the false news that Margaret had died. Gerard forsook the Church and in despair threw himself into the Tiber, but he was saved and carried to a monastery, where he recovered and eventually took monastic vows. He became Brother Clement of the Dominican Order. After a period of training, he was sent to teach at the University of Basle in Switzerland. Meanwhile, in Holland, Margaret gave birth to Gerard's son.

Brother Clement received orders to proceed to England. Preaching as he went, he began the journey down the Rhine.

In Rotterdam, Luke Peterson became Margaret's suitor. She told him he could prove his love for her by seeking out Gerard, but Luke's and Brother Clement's paths were fated not to cross. The priest went to Sevenbergen, where he was unable to find the grave of Margaret. He proceeded to Rotterdam, and there Margaret heard him preach without recognizing him as Gerard. He next went to Tergou to see Ghysbrecht. The burgomaster was dying; he confessed to Brother Clement that he had defrauded Margaret of the wealth that was rightfully hers. On his deathbed, Ghysbrecht made full restitution.

When Brother Clement left the burgomaster, he returned to Rotterdam and took refuge in a hermit's cave outside the city. There he mortified himself out of hatred for mankind.

Having learned his whereabouts through court gossip, Margaret went to him, but he repulsed her in the belief that she was a spirit sent by Satan. Margaret took her son to the cave in an attempt to win back his reason. Brother Clement's acquaintance with his son, also named Gerard, brought him to his senses. By shrewd argument, Margaret persuaded him to come with her to Gouda, where he would be parson by arrangement with church authorities. They lived in Gouda but remained apart; Gerard tended his flock, and Margaret assisted him in his many charitable works.

After ten years at Gouda, Margaret died of the plague. Gerard, no longer anxious to live after her death, died two weeks later. Their son, Gerard, grew up to be Erasmus, the world-famous sixteenth-century biblical scholar and man of letters.

Critical Evaluation:

The two outstanding features of this novel are its photographic details of fifteenth century European life, and the vivid character portrayal of Denys, the Burgundian crossbowman. Charles Reade did tremendous research in order to achieve his accurate descriptions of fifteenth century European life. His Denys is one of the most delightful characters in English literature. Among the variety of literary types found in *The Cloister and The Hearth* are the long letter, poetry, dramatic dialogue, the tale within the tale, and picaresque romance. The description of the Catholic Church and clergy in the late Middle Ages is illuminating.

Essentially a picaresque novel, *The Cloister and the Hearth* is rich with incident and vividly drawn characters, if not always profound or thoughtful. The accurate detail is never boring, and a good-natured humor pervades the narrative. Despite its great length, the novel moves briskly, maintaining the reader's interest constantly. The scenes at the Burgundian Inn, for example, describing the gory battle between Gerard and Denys and the gang of thieves, are among the most thrilling in English fiction and are worthy of the senior Dumas or Balzac.

The Cloister and the Hearth may have been in part an imitation of Scott's historical novels (many others, including George Eliot in *Romola*, were also copying Scott at this time), but it became much more than that. It stands by itself as a great novel. Much of the book is a quest, the story of a youth's education and pursuit of both a livelihood and a romantic goal. The pattern of the first half of the book is that of Gerard's learning process. He does not know what his destiny will be, but each step takes him closer to it. Only at the end, after his death, is the pattern finished and the meaning made clear. Gerard and his beloved Margaret are living not only for themselves but for their future son.

Denys, the Burgundian bowman and "Pilgrim of Friendship," bursts with vitality, and every page on which he strides and boasts is filled with life. Katherine, Gerard's mother, is another excellent characterization: lively, witty, and sensible. She begins as a type but soon transcends type to become a sympathetic, clever, and amusing individual. The reader suspects that Reade was, himself, fond of her. The spinster Margaret Van Eyck emerges as a vivid personality—an intelligent, liberated female in an age when women were required to be both married and docile.

Reade kept voluminous files of clippings and notebooks in which he recorded all manner of information that interested him; in writing his novels, he made use of this material. A novel, he believed, must be based on facts. His method of handling detail, setting, and episodes brought artistic truth to his books. He saturated himself in medieval history, art, and social customs and manners to write *The Cloister and the Hearth*. By absorbing himself in the literature and history of the period, Reade produced in this novel a picture of a remote era so faithfully and so finely etched and so vividly realistic that it never has been surpassed and rarely approached.

In *The Cloister and the Hearth*, Reade caught much of the tone of light and dark that dominated the end of the Middle Ages and the beginnings of the Renaissance; it was a brutal and turbulent time, stiff and heavy with death. The Dukes of Burgundy, with their ostentation, violence, and half-mad pride, were perhaps its representative rulers. The novel is crowded with wandering, lost individuals and at times becomes a *danse macabre*, a picture of rapidly growing cities, violence, wild superstition, crumbling religion, cynical realism, and ever-lusty humor. Reade's style is sometimes nervous and irritating, but it is always vigorous and compelling and never fake or gushing like that of so many of his contemporaries. His perspective on the period of the novel is acute and perceptive, and his panorama crowded and colorful, yet never confusing.

Born in 1814 in Oxfordshire, the son of a country squire, Reade received his B.A. at Magdalen College, Oxford, and became a fellow of the college. He kept his fellowship at Magdalen all of his life but spent the greater part of his time in London where he began his career as a dramatist. On the advice of the actress Laura Seymour, who later became his housekeeper and mistress, he transformed one of his plays into a novel. Several other novels followed in quick succession. The flaws of his fiction, a certain theatricality and occasional falseness of tone, can be attributed to the sensational theater pieces of the day and their influence upon him.

The Cloister and the Hearth was originally published serially as the long story "A Good Fight" in the magazine *Once a Week*; it was then expanded to more than five times its length before it was published in four volumes. The novel, published (at the author's expense) on commission, provided Reade with his first financial success at the age of forty-eight.

Returning from the fifteenth century to modern English life, Reade produced another well-received novel, *Hard Cash*, in which he directed attention to the abuses of private lunatic asylums. Three other novels "with a purpose" followed, in which he grappled with trade unions, the degrading conditions of village life, and other problems. The Reade of later years, who had earned the admiration of such different artists as Dickens and Swinburne, was accused of wasting his talents in pursuit of social reforms.

Reade's last and greatest success as a dramatist was *Drink*, an adaptation of Zola's *L'Assommoir*, produced in 1879. In that year, Laura Seymour died, and soon Reade's health failed. He died in 1884, leaving behind him a completed novel, *A Perilous Secret*, which showed no decline in his abilities to weave a complicated plot and to devise thrilling situations.

The epic theme of *The Cloister and the Hearth* is the misery caused by the vow of celibacy demanded of its priests by the Roman Church. Margaret, who loves and is beloved by Gerard, is the mother of his child and yet is denied the privilege of being his wife because he is a priest. This situation is described with excruciating pathos. Reade's own study of medicine led to the minor theme and indictment of the practice of bleeding patients that is so vividly presented in the novel. The growth of the arts during the first days of the Renaissance provides a continuing theme that reaches its peak of interest in the chapters in Italy.

The imaginative power of the narration is shown in many vivid scenes (for example, the frail wooden ship battling the storm off the Italian coast), yet the author's imagination seems to fail with the minor characters, who tend to be reduced to clichés of good and evil. This oversimplification of character is the one serious flaw in the novel, but it does not distract from the power and sweep of the story and the impact of the conclusion when the reader learns that from these two troubled lives (Gerard and Margaret) will come the greatest humanist and writer of the period.

COLD COMFORT FARM

Type of work: Novel
Author: Stella Gibbons (1902–   )
Type of plot: Satire
Time of plot: Before World War II
Locale: Cold Comfort Farm, Howling, Sussex; London
First published: 1932

> *Principal characters:*
> FLORA POSTE, a newly orphaned gentlewoman
> AUNT ADA DOOM, Flora's aunt and the mistress of Cold
>   Comfort
> JUDITH STARKADDER, Ada's daughter and Flora's cousin
> AMOS STARKADDER, Judith's husband, a "Quiverer"
> REUBEN STARKADDER, Judith's elder son
> SETH STARKADDER, Judith's younger son
> ELPHINE STARKADDER, Judith's daughter
> URK, a Starkadder relation and a farmhand
> BIG BUSINESS, Cold Comfort's stud bull
> ADAM LAMBSBREATH, the cowherd at Cold Comfort
> MRS. AGONY BEETLE, the cook-housekeeper at Cold Comfort
> MERIAM BEETLE, her daughter
> MRS. SMILING, Flora's London friend
> CHARLES FAIRFORD, Flora's cousin and fiancé
> MR. MYBUG (MEYERBURG), a writer

Cold Comfort Farm is the private jest of a young woman of high spirits and firmly sensible convictions. In form, it parodies the English "country" novel from Thomas Hardy to D. H. Lawrence, Constance Holmes, and Mary Webb, particularly the work of the two women writers who were popular in prewar England about the time Stella Gibbons composed her counterblast.

The guiding genius is that of Jane Austen who, like the heroine, Flora, did not approve of mess; "Let other pens dwell on guilt and misery" announces the epigraph in a quotation from *Mansfield Park*.

The novel contains a number of ripostes to fashionable fads that tend to confuse the issue, but the object of the parody has become so popular, especially in the works of Lawrence, that the novel's continued readership is practically guaranteed, making it a minor classic of its kind. Most of the fun is satirical and depends on an almost complete identification of author and heroine, young Flora Poste. In the course of the novel, Flora deals a great many objects a number of glancing blows, but she comes off un-scathed herself and apparently preserves her own virtues intact. Common sense is the greatest of these virtues.

There are three grades of satire: mild, as in the case of Mrs. Smiling and her rather odd band of "Pioneer-O" (English gentlemen who govern the Empire in Kenya and other out-of-the-way places); tasty, as in the country gentry; and sharp, as in the treatment reserved for the inhabitants of Cold Comfort. Behind these, however, stand two literary types that the novel as a whole satirizes: the drama of the earth and the romance of young love. Gibbons chooses the latter as her vehicle, so that the novel begins in murk and ends in romantic radiance.

The murk begins in chapter 3, which opens with a description of dawn creeping over Cold Comfort Farm. While Adam Lambsbreath milks the cows (Aimless, Feckless, Pointless, and Graceless), Seth, Judith's son, lounges home from his philandering with Moll of the mill, Violet of the Vicarage, or Ivy of the ironmongery. The breakfast porridge snarls in its "snood" over the open fire. Seth quarrels with his mother and goes off to mock Big Business, the stud bull; the porridge boils over; the fire goes out. Sussex promises to be an adequate challenge to Flora's common sense when she accepts the invitation of her Aunt Ada Doom to visit Cold Comfort Farm.

Since there are some thirteen men on the farm and at least five women, together with a number more in the village below, Flora's tidy mind has a great deal on which to work. She is defeated only by Adam Lambsbreath, who remains nonsensical to the end.

Flora's first commonsense triumph is to have her bedroom curtains washed by Meriam, the hired girl who has just fallen in labor the night before; Seth is the suspected father. Flora finds that this is an annual visitation and combines directions for washing the curtains with some clear and simple advice about contraception, thus putting a stop to Meriam's annual tribute to the animal atmosphere of the Farm. After pumping Mrs. Beetle and Adam and listening to each Starkadder accuse the others, she forms a comprehensive plan of campaign, chiefly directed at Aunt Ada Doom through Elphine, Amos, and Seth. Aunt Ada remains closeted in the upper regions of the farmhouse and controls the farm folk by insisting that she is mad and will get madder if any Starkadder leaves Cold Comfort; her chief weapon is to remind the Starkadders that her childhood was warped because she had seen some nasty sight in the woodshed.

The campaign of common sense has both strategy and tactics. The strategy depends on making the Starkadders line up to their literary prototype or stereotype. Although, on the surface, the farm appears to offer cold comfort to a sensible young manager, underneath it is a cauldron of primal appetites. Flora discovers the little weakness in Aunt Ada's hold on the Starkadders: the family members are all in secret revolt. Seth is passionately interested in motion pictures; Reuben and the others falsify the farm accounts they show to Aunt Ada; Amos longs to become a peripatetic evangelist; and most of the Starkadders hide their wives in the village of Howling. Flora's many-sided plan is to bring these revolts into the open, thus providing a hectic and shifting pattern of events that is highly comic but sometimes confusing.

Flora's tactics, therefore, are to isolate the members of the family one by one from Aunt Ada. Flora begins with Amos; she attends his Bethel of "Quiverers" and encourages his ambitions to spread the Word by tempting him with the vision of a Ford van, complete with loudspeakers, in which he can visit all the sinful fairs and markets in the country. She is eventually so successful that Amos departs for the United States, his genius having been recognized by a visiting American evangelist, and he leaves Cold Comfort farm to Reuben. The latter is thus brought around to support Flora's schemes for the rest of the family.

The main plot is the rescue of Elphine from her pixie preferences and from the earthy clutches of Urk. The latter's claim to Elphine has been blood-linked with the "water voles" by having her feeding bottle marked with their blood. The initiation of the main plot is symbolized in Flora's release of Big Business as she and Elphine leave for a day in London's dress shops, hairdressing establishments, and society restaurants. The transformation from pixie curls and nouveau art cape to shining bob and white satin gratifies Elphine; at a ball for the young local squire, the new beauty is first shown to the county with such romantic effect that the squire announces his engagement to Elphine.

This social success is achieved with the help of both Seth and Charles Fairford, Flora's cousin. It is also achieved in spite of the persistent attentions of Mr. Mybug, a visiting writer who plagues Flora with his insistent recognition of phallic symbols in country life, which is his response to the yeasty atmosphere of Cold Comfort, Big Business, and Seth and is directly contrary to Flora's commonsense plans.

The most earthy scene in the book occurs when Flora's party returns to Cold Comfort after the County Ball. They find the yeasty atmosphere heaving because the "sukebinde" has burst into flower, and its overpowering scent, heady but also smacking of the loins, affects everyone, notably Aunt Ada Doom, who has descended to the flagged kitchen to conduct an awesome ritual known as "The Counting." Amos defies Aunt Ada and departs, and the other Starkadders become distinctly restless; events follow thick and fast to make this the last "Counting" at Cold Comfort.

Urk is fobbed off with Meriam. Later, Mr. Mybug is accommodated with a spare sex-starved Starkadder female. The next day, an American film director calls on Flora and sweeps Seth off to Hollywood. (When Aunt Ada brings up the something nasty she had seen in the woodshed, the director asks whether it had been her.) Shortly after, Judith is handed over to an amiable psychiatrist who receives the full flood of her starved affections. Mrs. Agony Beetle, Adam Lambsbreath, and Big Business are all content in their various ways; only Aunt Ada remains to be dealt with.

The time of the novel is supposed to be "the near future" as conceived in the early 1930's, and much has happened since. This Utopian projection accounts for such things as TV phones and a restaurant over the Thames, constructed wholly of glass. Both leaps of the imagination pale beside the approaching reality; today, they serve to date the novel or at least emphasize the capriciousness of the author's fancy.

Similarly, a number of the witticisms, satire at the expense of London's literati of the 1930's, principally in the person of Mr. Mybug, sometimes escape the reader. This is most obvious in the author's mock "Foreword" to "Anthony Pookworthy," the private fun of which is likely to escape the reader today. On the other hand, the satire of academic idiocy in Mr. Mybug's (his name is really Meyerburg) defense of Branwell Brontë as the author of the novels believed written by sisters Anne, Charlotte, and Emily is still enjoyable. Cold Comfort Farm, Howling, near Beershorn, Sussex, is now part of the literary geography of the English language.

THE COLLEGIANS
Or, The Colleen Bawn, a Tale of Garryowen

Type of work: Novel
Author: Gerald Griffin (1803–1840)
Type of plot: Domestic tragedy
Time of plot: Late eighteenth century
Locale: Ireland
First published: 1829

Principal characters:

EILY O'CONNOR, a beautiful girl of the lower classes
HARDRESS CREGAN, a spirited young man of wealth
ANN CHUTE, a young woman of the upper classes and
  Cregan's beloved
KYRLE DALY, a college friend of Cregan and Ann Chute's
  beloved
DANNY MANN, Cregan's villainous servant
MRS. CREGAN, Hardress Cregan's mother

The Story:

Hardress Cregan and Kyrle Daly had been companions in their college days, in spite of the fact that Kyrle was of the middle classes and Hardress was the son of an Irish gentleman. Their respective ranks were close enough, however, so that they could respect each other and not be ashamed of their friendship. After leaving college, they maintained the same close relationship, for they lived not far from each other. In fact, Kyrle, who had begun the study of law, became a suitor for the hand of Hardress' cousin, Ann Chute, a suit in which Kyrle had the good will of his friend.

Hardress Cregan, a spirited young man, lived more for sports and good times; he was actually shy in the presence of women, although he was bold enough in the face of danger. He was also disdainful of people from the lower classes as his attitude toward them revealed. One morning, Kyrle's family watched from a window of their house as Hardress ran down some fishermen with his yacht, when such action could have been averted by a slight shift of the yacht's tiller.

That same day, Kyrle set out for Chute Castle to attend the races and to press his suit with Ann Chute. He did not know that on board Hardress' yacht was Eily O'Connor, a young woman of the lower classes and the daughter of a ropemaker. Hardress had secretly married Eily a month before. The young woman was beautiful, but Hardress was afraid to make his marriage public, for he knew that his mother expected him to marry a young woman of wealth and position. He had taken Eily on board his yacht

and was sailing with her up the coast, where he intended lodging her close
to his family's home in the cottage of his servant's sister. She had consented
to go with him and to stay away from her father's home only because
Hardress had promised to acknowledge her publicly as his bride within a
matter of days. Hardress knew that he was safe in settling her with the sister of his servant, Danny Mann, because Danny, a hunchback, was devot-
edly loyal to his headstrong master.

At Chute Castle that same afternoon, Kyrle's suit for the hand of Ann
was ended. The girl told Kyrle in definite terms that she could not marry
him, although she loved no one else. That night, Kyrle met Hardress at the
cottage where the latter had taken Eily. Kyrle was too distraught to notice
anything unusual in the fact that the girl was with his friend. Hardress
promised to do everything he could to assist Kyrle in marrying Ann.

Ann accepted the invitation to stay at the home of Hardress' parents. A
few days after her arrival, she confided to a sick old huntsman that she was
in love with Hardress. Just before the old man died, he told his master that
someone was in love with the young man. He did not, however, tell who
loved him, but Hardress' mother soon realized the love Ann had for her
son. Even though the young people were cousins, she approved of the
match and threw them together at every opportunity. When Hardress tried
to avoid Ann, his mother scolded him bitterly. Her attitude completely prevented the young man from revealing his marriage to Eily.

Eily, meanwhile, grew restive when her husband refused to acknowledge
her as his bride; even the people with whom she stayed did not know that
Hardress was her husband. As the weeks went by, she realized that she had
outworn her welcome among the peasants with whom she was quartered.
Above all, she found her husband acting very strangely when he visited her.
The girl asked him the reasons for his strangeness and for his reluctance to
admit to the world that she was his wife. When she did, he burst out in
anger, pointing out that he had married below his station and was very
sorry he had done so. It was then that he realized his love for Ann. Leaving the cottage in a rage, he met his confidential servant, the hunchbacked
Danny Mann. The servant was so devoted to his master that he promised
to do away with the girl if Hardress so wished. His shocking offer brought
Hardress to his senses, although he was still torn between his duty to his
unacknowledged wife and his love for Ann.

At home, Hardress became increasingly perplexed by the love that Ann
openly showed for him as well as his mother's wishes that he marry the
girl. Gradually, his desire to marry Ann overcame his sense of duty to his
secret bride.

In the meantime, Eily decided to let someone know of her marriage.
Leaving the cottage, she went to see an uncle, the parish priest in a village
not far from where she was staying. She told her uncle that she was mar-

ried, but obedience to her husband kept her from telling who the husband
was. Upon her return to the cottage, she met Danny Mann, who gave her
a letter from Hardress. Finally yielding to temptation and resolving to be
rid of Eily, he had commissioned Danny to spirit her out of Ireland and put
her on a boat bound for Canada. In the letter, he told his wife of his decision; Eily, still obedient to her husband, submitted to his wishes.

Danny, however, misinterpreted his master's commands and murdered
the girl. Hardress realized too late what had happened, but in spite of the
blood on his hands, he determined to marry Ann. His hope was that
Danny would disappear for good and that the crime would never be discovered. As plans were being made for the wedding, Hardress began to act
rather strangely. No one knew of the crime that was preying on his mind;
people attributed his strange actions to cowardice and illness.

Quite by chance, a short time before the date set for the marriage,
Eily's body was discovered. At the inquest, nothing was learned of the
girl's death. Although the coroner suspected foul play, it seemed as if
Hardress' plans were to work out successfully. Then, on the day before the
marriage, Danny returned and was captured by the authorities. For a time,
it seemed as if fate were with the criminals. Hardress was able to effect his
servant's escape, but Danny continued to linger in the neighborhood, much
to Hardress' dismay. Discovering the servant, he beat the hunchback un-
mercifully. In revenge, Danny went to the authorities, confessed his crimes,
and thus implicated his master. Hardress, a few hours before his wedding,
was taken from his home and sent into exile as a criminal. Danny Mann
was hanged.

A happy ending of the tragedy came when, some months later, Ann
married Kyrle Daly, who she found was really a better man and more worthy of her love than wealthier and more spirited Hardress Cregan.

Critical Evaluation:

Gerald Griffin was a dramatist and poet as well as a novelist, but his
chief claim to fame is *The Collegians*, which was extremely popular in the
years immediately after its publication. The story is more familiar to
Americans in drama form, having been dramatized by Dion Boucicault
under the title of *The Colleen Bawn*, a play that capitalized upon the melodramatic qualities of the novel. Griffin attempted to do for the Irish and
Ireland what Sir Walter Scott had done in portraying Scotland and the
Scottish people, and like Scott, Griffin was intensely interested in the folk
traditions, customs, and personalities of the people about whom he wrote.
The pages of *The Collegians* are filled with items of Irish folklore and
more than a little attention has been paid to capturing the language of the
peasants.

Padraic Colum has called *The Collegians* the best of the Irish Romantic novels. *The Collegians* possesses a unique charm and vitality. It is definitely a young author's book, and it is no surprise to learn that Griffin was only twenty-five years old when it was written. A novel of love and murder, it is also a book rich with native humor and filled with delightful characterizations of the Irish folk. The book treads dangerously close to preciousness but fortunately misses that fatal flaw.

The superstitions of the common people are used like embroidery to fill out the picture of Irish life. A wonderful example is when Lowry Looby meets the redhaired woman on his way to get his new job, turns back because it is unlucky to meet a redheaded woman on a journey, and thus loses the job. A certain morbid quality, however, is also discernible in many of the characters; shadings of light and dark in their personalities give them a unique vividness.

It seems that the higher an individual's station in life, the more serious and rational he or she is portrayed. The lower classes and servants tend to be filled with comic chatter and droll observations and to perform comic routines that hold up the narrative. Eily O'Connor and her ropemaker father are the exceptions to the rule that the poor folk must be humorous, and they are soon established as living below their proper station. This is particularly true of Eily, for her beauty and learning set her apart from the other village girls; this is the beginning of her tragedy. Eily is described repeatedly as too elegant for a peasant girl but too modest to claim the rank of gentlewoman. In this world, it is necessary that no individual challenge class distinctions; lose sight of one's proper place and one will have an unfortunate end.

By the same token, Hardress should have known better than to stoop to marry a peasant; by betraying his class, he could only bring disaster to all concerned. His arrogance, however, is such that he believes he can get away with anything and can force people to do what he desires. Eily and Hardress upset the social balance and must pay the consequences. The world in which they live is a hard one and allows for no escape from its rules.

CONINGSBY
Or, The New Generation

Type of work: Novel
Author: Benjamin Disraeli (1804–1881)
Type of plot: Political romance
Time of plot: 1832–1840
Locale: England and Paris
First published: 1844

Principal characters:
HARRY CONINGSBY, a young nobleman
MARQUIS OF MONMOUTH, his grandfather
SIDONIA, a wealthy young Jew and Coningsby's friend
EDITH MILLBANK, Coningsby's sweetheart
OSWALD MILLBANK, Edith's father
MR. RIGBY, a member of Parliament
LUCRETIA, a young Italian noblewoman and later Lord
Monmouth's wife
FLORA, a member of a troupe of actors

The Story:

Harry Coningsby was fourteen years old when he met his grandfather, the Marquis of Monmouth, for the first time. He had been placed in his grandfather's charge when he was still very young with the understanding that his widowed mother, a commoner, was never to see him again. He had been turned over, sight unseen, to the care of Mr. Rigby, a member of Parliament who sat for one of Lord Monmouth's ten boroughs.

Lord Monmouth, who preferred to live abroad, had returned to his native land in 1832 in order to help fight the Reform Bill. Hearing favorable reports of his grandson, he had ordered Mr. Rigby to bring the boy from Eton to Monmouth House. Unfortunately, young Coningsby was unable to put out of his mind thoughts of his mother, who had died when he was age nine, and he burst into tears at the sight of his grandfather. Lord Monmouth, disgusted by this sign of weakness, ordered him to be led away. He thought to himself that the sentimental boy's future probably lay with the church.

Fortunately, the boy became friendly with the marquis' guests, Princess Colonna and her stepdaughter, Lucretia. The princess passed on such glowing descriptions of Coningsby to his grandfather that they were on excellent terms by the time he returned to school.

At Eton, one of Coningsby's close friends was Oswald Millbank, a manufacturer's son. When Coningsby left Eton in 1835, he went to explore Manchester's factories before going to Coningsby Castle to join his grandfather. During his journey, he visited the Millbank mills. Oswald was abroad, but he was hospitably greeted by his friend's father. At the Millbank mansion, Coningsby met beautiful but shy young Edith Millbank and learned from her Whig father that he favored the rise of a new force in government—a natural aristocracy of able men, not one composed of hereditary peers.

Before departing for Coningsby Castle, young Coningsby was tempted to inquire about the striking portrait of a woman which graced the dining-room wall. His host, much upset by his question, made a brusque, evasive answer.

Lord Monmouth, backing Mr. Rigby for reelection to Parliament, had returned to his borough and scheduled an elaborate program of dances, receptions, and plays to gain a following for his Conservative candidate. Princess Colonna and Lucretia were again his grandfather's guests. Coningsby had no need, however, to confine his attentions to them; as Lord Monmouth's kinsman and possible heir, he found himself much sought after. He also found time to encourage Flora, a member of the troupe of actors entertaining the marquis' guests. The girl was shy and suffered from stage fright.

Here Coningsby met Sidonia, a fabulously wealthy young Jew. Coningsby found his new friend impartial in his political judgments, not only because his fortune allowed him to be just but also because his religion disqualified him as a voter. During their lengthy discussions, Sidonia taught him to look to the national character for England's salvation. He believed that the country's weakness lay in developing class conflicts.

Lucretia made a brief effort to attract Coningsby when she observed the favor in which his grandfather held him, but before long she found Sidonia, a polished man of the world, more intriguing. Sidonia, however, was not to be captured. He was attracted by others' intellects, and Lucretia could not meet him on his own level.

After his holiday, Coningsby went to Cambridge for his last years of study. During his first year there, King William IV died, and the Conservative cause fell in defeat. Mr. Rigby was, as he had been for many years, the candidate from his borough, and with the marquis to back him, his victory seemed certain until Mr. Millbank entered the field. The manufacturer and the marquis had been enemies for many years, and their feud reached a climax when Millbank not only bought Hellingsley, an adjoining estate which Lord Monmouth had long coveted, but also defeated his lordship's candidate.

Prepared for the worst, the defeated Mr. Rigby went to Monmouth House, where the marquis was in residence. He was pleasantly disappointed, however, for his employer's thoughts were not on him. Lord Monmouth was preparing to marry Lucretia, who was determined at least to obtain power and riches through marriage even if she could not have the man she desired.

A year after the wedding, Coningsby was invited to join his grandfather and his bride in Paris at Christmastime. Stopping at his banker's on his way through London, he was given a package of his mother's correspondence. In the packet was a locket with an exact copy of the portrait he had seen at Millbank. It was a picture of his mother.

While visiting an art gallery in Paris with Sidonia, Coningsby again met Edith Millbank, who was traveling with her relatives, Lord and Lady Wallinger. Coningsby, who fell in love with her immediately, was distressed to hear reports that Sidonia intended to marry her. Finding the couple conversing on familiar terms one evening, he regretfully decided to withdraw from the scene. He returned to England.

Disappointed in love, Coningsby devoted himself to his studies for the remainder of his stay at Cambridge. Then, learning that Edith had not married and that Sidonia was no more than an old family friend, he went to Coningsby Castle in order to be near the Millbanks.

Coningsby spent every possible moment with Edith and her family during the next few weeks. When her father discovered the lovers' feelings, he asked Coningsby to leave. He would not, he explained, submit his daughter to the same fate the young man's mother had suffered at Lord Monmouth's hands. In this manner, Coningsby learned that his mother had once been Mr. Millbank's fiancée.

Leaving Hellingsley, Coningsby went on a sea voyage from which he was called home by the marquis. Parliament faced another crisis, and Lord Monmouth had decided that Coningsby should stand as his candidate. Coningsby refused, for he was of the opinion that men should cut across party lines to establish recognition of the bond between property and labor.

The same day that Lord Monmouth faced his rebellious grandson, he separated from Lucretia, who had proved unfaithful.

The marquis died at Christmas of that year. He left most of his fortune to Flora, his natural daughter. Coningsby was cut off with the interest on ten thousand pounds. Deeply disappointed in his expectations, Coningsby gave up his clubs and most of his friends and began to study law. He had resigned himself to the prospect of years of drudgery when Mr. Millbank repented his decision. The manufacturer withdrew his candidacy in the 1840 election to back Coningsby as the Tory candidate. Mr. Rigby was his rival candidate, but he was easily defeated.

A few months later, Edith became Coningsby's bride and went with him to live at Hellingsley, their wedding present from Mr. Millbank. As a final blessing, though not an unmixed one, Flora, who had always been weak, died, leaving the fortune she had inherited to the man who had befriended her many years before at Coningsby Castle.

Critical Evaluation:

Coningsby occupies a special position in literature because of its varied aims. Not only is it the literary history of young Harry Coningsby's fortunes, but it is an important political treatise as well. In it, Benjamin Disraeli traced the decline of the Whig and Tory factions and the developments which led to the birth of the Conservative Party. The characters may be readily identified with real personages of the time.

The reader of *Coningsby* feels that he is in the company of a genuine insider, who can describe from firsthand experience the workings of the government, the life at court, even the mode of existence at Eton. (Actually, Disraeli wrote with the obsessive fascination of an outsider who had to struggle to get inside.) Life among the very rich and very powerful is meticulously detailed for the pleasure of the reader; and although this was not Disraeli's purpose in writing *Coningsby*, it made the novel popular and has contributed to its lasting interest. Disraeli's avowed intention was to give a picture of the growth of the Conservative Party and to illustrate the change facing the new generation in the 1840's. He also wanted to educate the public concerning the true history and influence of the Jews in Western Europe.

Throughout the novel, Disraeli stresses the importance of "character," that is, the moral and intellectual makeup of an individual. Some people possess weak characters, others strong, and the incidents of life reveal these characters for what they are. Some men rise to an occasion while others are incapable of coping with a situation; thus, Disraeli implies, history is made. Character reveals itself as early as in a youth's school days; at Eton, Coningsby and his compatriots show the traits that cling to them throughout their lives.

The subtitle (*The New Generation*) is important, because the novel immortalizes the group in the 1840's that was nicknamed "Young England." This group, which looked to Disraeli for their inspiration, was hostile to the traditional, humdrum middle-class Conservatism; they were romantic and aristocratic and looked to a golden past where the people and the nobility were united in an alliance supporting throne and Church. Disraeli's distrust of the growing industrial class is strongly evident in Coningsby and lends force and direction to much of the narrative.

THE CONSCIENCE OF THE RICH

Type of work: Novel
Author: C. P. Snow (1905–1980)
Type of plot: Social melodrama
Time of plot: 1927–1936
Locale: London and the nearby countryside
First published: 1958

Principal characters:

LEWIS ELIOT, a barrister and the narrator and protagonist of the *Strangers and Brothers* series

CHARLES MARCH, a member of a wealthy Anglo-Jewish banking family

LEONARD MARCH, his retired father, called "Mr. L."

SIR PHILIP MARCH, Leonard March's older brother and the head of the March family

KATHERINE MARCH GETLIFFE, Leonard March's daughter

FRANCIS GETLIFFE, her husband and a Cambridge physicist

ANN SIMON MARCH, Charles's wife and an active Communist

HERBERT GETLIFFE, Francis' much older half brother and a lawyer, involved in unethical transactions

RONALD PORSON, an embittered failure despite great gifts and Ann Simon's beloved

HUMPHREY SEYMOUR, the editor of *Note*, a Communist scandal sheet

Lewis Eliot, the narrator of C. P. Snow's *Strangers and Brothers* series, struggles throughout his early years up the ladders of power and influence; in *The Conscience of the Rich*, he comes into contact with the Marches, a family long at or near the pinnacle of prestige, and in them he observes the way in which changing conditions have altered the meaning of being rich and powerful in the years between World Wars I and II. Specifically, he observes the clash between two generations of Marches, an older generation to whom wealth and influence come naturally and a younger generation for whom being wealthy and benevolent is not enough but is, at times, something to be ashamed of.

The Marches are one of the great Anglo-Jewish banking families; the history of their rise and partial decline is part of the history of wealth and wealthiness in England. The years from 1880 to 1914 were a great time for the making and accumulation of wealth. The Marches had grown steadily in importance after their ancestors migrated to England from Holland and opened a bank in London. Those were also years of nearly full freedom for English Jews: the Marches took seats in Parliament, owned strings of racehorses, befriended the arts, voted Conservative, and went to Oxford and Cambridge; they remained, however, members of a tightly knit circle of English Jews, among whom they married and socialized.

Their power was considerable, measurable in society and politics in terms of money; but international finance was, even then, becoming a vastly complicated business, and the time had passed in which a private loan to a South American government was significant. The Marches, though richer than ever, were already becoming anachronistic in the 1890's when they had to choose between taking nonfamily members into the bank or selling it. They sold the bank.

The influence of the older generation of Marches, who were wealthy in the best years for men to be so, is beginning to wane. A major source of conflict is the fact that they do not recognize the changes of the post-World War I years and the new kinds of responsibilities inherited by their children. The background of the novel is a drastic change in the world; the focus is on those most affected by the change, a rich family; and, somewhat ironically, the story is chronicled by someone gaining the kinds of influence congruent with the changing world, kinds that do not rest primarily on wealth.

At the center of the March family in the 1920's are Sir Philip, a Cabinet Minister, and his younger brother Leonard, familiarly called "Mr. L." Both are about seventy years old, and both are vigorous men. The hopes for the next generation of Marches rest solely on Charles, Mr. L.'s son and a close friend of Lewis Eliot. Charles is headed toward an outstanding, perhaps brilliant career in law; much of the novel centers on the conflicts leading to and generated by Charles's decision to give up law and become a physician.

The reason for his decision and the gravity of its consequences are identical: to him, the bar represents the community of wealthy and influential Jews, and this is the community from which he is trying to escape.

Mr. March cannot accept Charles's refusal to be tagged as a bright, rich Jew; Charles cannot accept the tag. About the same time, Katherine, Charles's younger sister, falls in love with and eventually marries Francis Getliffe, a young Cambridge physicist and a Gentile. Although Mr. March finally accepts Katherine's defection, he cannot accept his son's more crucial one: Charles's decision is a blow to the heart of Mr. March's existence, to the strong family ties, the involvement in affairs, and the strongly patriarchal tradition of the great house. It is clear enough that Snow sees the conflict as inevitable, the result of those same historical forces that first brought the March family into prominence and opened a place for the Jews in English social and political life. The Marches thrived under conditions produced by forces ultimately destructive to valuable traditions; a generation later, the same forces are destroying the traditions established by the March family. Wealth per se and the old family customs have both come to mean less. Charles must adapt to these new conditions. Mr. March must cling to the old ways, especially because they are so archaic.

When Charles persists in his plan of becoming a doctor and further complicates matters by deciding to marry Ann Simon, who, though Jewish, is from a social class much lower than that of the Marches, Mr. March withdraws his commitment to make Charles independently wealthy.

Following the marriages of Charles and Katherine in 1929, there is a break of some seven years in the narration. In 1936, Philip March has the same Parliamentary secretaryship he had held briefly before, and a scandal that had threatened to break then is once again in the air. The scandal concerns an investment Sir Philip made in a company doing business with his ministry. Mr. March asks Lewis Eliot for help for several reasons: first, because Eliot has worked for Herbert Getliffe, a half brother of Katherine's husband, who was doing legal work for Sir Philip's ministry at the time of the stock sale, and second because Lewis, unlike Mr. March, still maintains contact with Charles. This relationship is in turn important because Charles's wife Ann, an active Communist, knows of the stock transaction and is being urged to use it to discredit the Conservative government in power at the time. It is clear, and Ann knows the truth, that Sir Philip is guilty of nothing and that the only shady dealings were those made by Herbert Getliffe. She is, however, considering releasing damaging information simply in hopes of discrediting the government.

Lewis is sent to dissuade her and partially appears to succeed. During an almost fatal illness, Ann gives him information; if Charles decides to release it, the scandal will not only stop, but her paper, the *Note*, will also be put out of business. Charles, however, decides not to use the knowledge he has gained. *Note* publishes the information, and Sir Philip, as a scapegoat, is asked to resign. Mr. March completely disinherits Charles, who, though he could have stopped Ann, has refused to do so because he was incapable of using his love as a lever.

For all intents and purposes, this is the end of the Marches as a great family; but Snow—and this fact explains much of his strategy in the novel—is interested in the Marches more as types than as individuals; he is more concerned with the ending of an era than in the personal downfall of his characters. Much of the novel, therefore, is devoted to sketching the family as an example of a class, one that is ceasing to exist. Much of the book is devoted to neither character delineation nor plot development but rather to evocation of the way of life of the March family: to the Friday night institution of a great dinner at their house on Bryanston Square, to the anecdotes of Leonard March, to Charles March's reflections on what it means to be rich and Jewish, and, more than anything else, to Mr. March himself, the exemplar of the spirit of family and tradition. Mr. March, in fact, is the liveliest character in the novel. In this novel as in several of his others, Snow is at his best when presenting a character whose individual qualities or eccentricities are shown by means bordering on caricature. Given the aim of the novel, this method is artistically justifiable.

This aim is consonant with the plan of the whole *Strangers and Brothers* sequence. Lewis Eliot is on the way up. He is far from a simple man; his feelings often take him off ambition's path; his road to the top is not at all straight. The centers of power, however, are still his chief interest, and getting near them is his main goal. The Marches are the symbol of what was once the top. Their story, as related in the novel, brings home the fact that there have been a great many changes in the terrain Eliot wants to conquer. The Marches are still rich and still a great family, but they are no longer truly powerful. Sentiment and the aura of wealth and tradition draw Lewis to the family, but he recognizes that his road to power will take him elsewhere.

THE COUNTRY HOUSE

Type of work: Novel
Author: John Galsworthy (1867–1933)
Type of plot: Social criticism
Time of plot: Early twentieth century
Locale: England
First published: 1907

Principal characters:
GEORGE PENDYCE, the heir to Worsted Skeynes
MRS. HELEN BELLEW, a young woman, who had separated
    from her husband
HORACE PENDYCE, George's father
MARGERY PENDYCE, his mother
THE REVEREND HUSSELL BARTER, the rector at Worsted
    Skeynes
GREGORY VIGIL, Mrs. Bellew's guardian
CAPTAIN BELLEW, her husband
MR. PARAMOR, the family lawyer

The Story:

In the fall of 1891, Horace Pendyce invited several people to Worsted Skeynes, his country estate, for a hunt. Little had been changed at Worsted Skeynes since the time of Mr. Pendyce's great-great-great-grandfather. Mr. Pendyce, as head of the house, naturally took a conservative political stand and expected each member of his family to follow suit.

Included in the party for the hunt was George Pendyce, the oldest son of Horace and Margery Pendyce, who now spent most of his time in London and who had recently become interested enough in racing to buy his own horse and have him trained for that sport. There was also Mrs. Helen Bellew, a very attractive young woman who had separated from her husband simply because they had grown tired of each other and who, it was being rumored, now encouraged the attentions of George. In the English country society of that time, separation of married couples was still frowned upon and for a lady in such a position to favor at all the attentions of a gentleman was for her to invite criticism. Unfortunately, the young couple were seen kissing passionately at a dance given by Mrs. Pendyce during the week of the hunt. The observer was the Reverend Hussell Barter, rector of the parish of Worsted Skeynes and another member of the party.

Soon after the week of the hunt, Gregory Vigil, cousin of Mrs. Pendyce and guardian of Mrs. Bellew, who was himself in love with his beautiful ward, decided that Helen's situation was intolerable and had gone on quite long enough. After consulting Mrs. Pendyce on the matter, he approached his lawyer, Mr. Paramor, on the subject of divorce. Paramor advised against it, however, on the grounds that there must be some very tangible reason for the lady's wanting a divorce and also because of the fact that such an act was always extremely public and painful, even for the one bringing the action. Helen Bellew was subject to certain charges, unknown to her guardian, because of her growing relationship with George Pendyce.

When Mr. Vigil decided to go on with the action, Mrs. Pendyce took up the matter with the rector without, however, suspecting in the least his strong feelings against both divorce and Mrs. Bellew. Mr. Barter objected, of course, because of what he considered an immoral act, which he himself had witnessed. In his mind, it was the husband, Captain Bellew, who had been wronged, and he felt it his Christian duty to make that gentleman aware of the action that was about to be taken against him. Consequently, Captain Bellew began proceedings before Gregory Vigil had time to do so on behalf of Mrs. Bellew.

In the meantime, George had fallen in love with Mrs. Bellew. He felt he could not live without her, and he was willing to allow his name and reputation to be dirtied in the divorce courts in order that he might then marry the woman. Besides, he had also fallen very heavily into debt through gambling on the horses. This combination of circumstances proved too much for the conservative Mr. Pendyce; no Pendyce had ever been a gambler, and certainly none had ever been involved in a divorce suit. George had finally lost all his money and was forced to sell his horse to pay his debts; papers also had been served naming him corespondent in the case of Bellew vs. Bellew. At this time, Mr. Pendyce resolved to take action. Rather than see the estate and heritage of the family fall into the hands of one so irresponsible, he decided to disinherit George unless his son would promise never to see the woman again. If George would agree to this plan, Mr. Pendyce had Captain Bellew's word that he would drop the divorce proceedings, but George refused.

Mrs. Pendyce, however, would not consent to her husband's action. Because of a very tender and somewhat sympathetic feeling for her first-born child, she threatened to leave Mr. Pendyce if he carried out his decision. She was as good as her word. Having a small income of her own, she felt that she could support herself and George with some measure of comfort if not with the luxury they had known at Worsted Skeynes. Her first steps were to go to London, find George, and attempt to get him to fulfill his father's demands. When this effort failed, she visited Helen Bellew to see if she would give up George. By this time, Mrs. Bellew was as tired of

George as she had been of her husband, and she was quite willing—in fact, she desired—never to see George again.

Meanwhile, Mr. Pendyce was highly upset by his wife's desertion; such an act was very much out of keeping with the tradition in which he lived. He was, therefore, quite relieved to see her when she returned to their home. Horace Pendyce, however, was far too proud a man to write to Captain Bellew and acknowledge that his son had been discarded in the same way that the captain himself had been; thus, the danger of divorce proceedings, with the subsequent harm to the family reputation, was as great as ever. Again it was Mrs. Pendyce, only an insignificant part of the social system as Mr. Pendyce thought of it, who was able to solve the problem. She took it upon herself to visit Captain Bellew and ask him to drop proceedings. Because he had instituted the whole action as a kind of self-defense and because he was greatly impressed by a real lady, he agreed to do so. The Pendyce name, the country house, and the whole system of society, therefore, were again preserved.

Critical Evaluation:

John Galsworthy is a novelist who grew in stature between the era of Victorian certainties and the era of post-World War I despair and doubts. Once conflicts in his personal life were resolved, he began to portray with increasing vigor in his fiction those segments of the British upper classes which he felt were most in need of constructive criticism. In the preface to *The Country House*, Galsworthy remarks that birth into the upper class or the aristocracy is no reason for complacency. At the same time, he discounts those who mistake his attitude for that of a revolutionary. In fact, he argues that by taking seriously the criticisms he offers, radical change can be rendered unnecessary.

Before the two world wars had shaken the institutions of the world to the breaking point, the English country house was symbolic of many of the strongest traditions of the aristocracy. In this novel, readers see what happens when one such house is threatened with disrepute and, perhaps, eventual destruction because of the careless attitude of one of its sons. Galsworthy also gives a vivid account of the prejudices and feelings of English society, including the pettiness of some of its members. Everything, however, remains indestructible and, through the deft handling of one of its more insignificant members, society comes away without even a blemish.

The Country House is a strong novel, especially in its detailed exposure of the pettiness and narrowness of the landed English gentry. Horace Pendyce, for example, is revealed both for what he is and for what he thinks he is. The latter, of course, is the more damaging; and this satirical ingredient, more than the plot, affords the central interest of *The Country House*.

The plot itself revolves around the elements of money (and inheritance), sexual attraction, family feelings, honor, and the force of outward respectability. Galsworthy successfully maintains action and interest, particularly of a social nature; but since he is so adept at creating a social milieu, a setting of aristocratic manners and mannerisms, the plot which unfolds in that setting carries with it more external interest than internal motive. For example, the characters (including George Pendyce and Mrs. Helen Bellew) are less believable as individuals than as types and are less believable as types than as mechanical figures designed to play a role in a prearranged drama; thus, the motivation of characters, largely external in origin, never seems entirely adequate to the weight of the action demanded of them. The more memorable characters thus tend to be the minor types who embody most strikingly the complacent aristocratic ethos that Galsworthy wishes to expose.

In short, Galsworthy's characters as individuals lack the depth that grows from interior conflict. The real conflict occurs on the level of the social criticism itself. On this level, Galsworthy's fundamental attachment to the values of British society as a whole and his desire to criticize and satirize come into conflict, and the conflict is resolved in favor of the established order. Thus, the tension which might have enlivened his characters is dissipated in the reestablishment of the fictional social order; and the old world persists, soon to be shattered in the trenches of a barbaric war.

CRANFORD

Type of work: Novel
Author: Elizabeth Gaskell (1810–1865)
Type of plot: Comedy of manners
Time of plot: Early nineteenth century
Locale: England
First published: 1853

> *Principal characters:*
> MARY SMITH, the narrator
> MISS DEBORAH JENKYNS, a genteel spinster
> MISS MATILDA JENKYNS (MATTY), her sister
> PETER JENKYNS, their long-lost brother
> MRS. JAMIESON, a leader of society
> LADY GLENMIRE, Mrs. Jamieson's sister-in-law
> MARTHA, Miss Matilda's faithful servant

The Story:

Cranford was a small English village inhabited mostly by ladies. Few gentlemen took up residence there, and most of those who did seemed to disappear on various and mysterious errands. The doctor, the shopkeepers, and a few male servants were all of their sex who crossed the ladies' vision with any regularity.

Most of the ladies lived in "elegant economy," and the spending of money was considered vulgar and showy. There was no mention of anyone's being poor unless in privacy with one's dearest friend. When semiretired Captain Brown moved to Cranford and talked openly about being poor, therefore, it was quite an affront to the ladies; but the captain was so kind and considerate to everyone, whether more or less fortunate than he, that the ladies could not long resent his vulgar behavior and talk. He had two daughters. The elder, dying of an incurable illness, had a tongue sharpened by pain, but the kind women joined her younger sister in trying to make her last days pleasant and comfortable. Many a cup of tea and small delicacy found their way from the ladies' already poor stores to the suffering girl.

The women experienced great sorrow when the kind Captain was killed while rescuing a small child from an oncoming train. When his elder daughter soon followed him, all of the ladies were hard pressed to make suitable arrangements for the younger daughter, left alone. One day, a former suitor appeared and took her for his wife. The village ladies rested happily in the knowledge that Captain Brown would be pleased with his daughter's security.

Until her death, Miss Deborah Jenkyns was one of the more dominant spinsters in the town. She made all decisions for her younger sister, Miss Matilda, age fifty-five. Miss Matilda, affectionately called Miss Matty by all but her sister, knew that Deborah had the better mind and did not resent her sister's dominance. After Miss Deborah's death, Miss Matty almost had to learn how to live again. Her particular friends were Miss Pole, Mrs. Forrester, and Mrs. Jamieson, who became the social leader of Cranford after Miss Deborah's death. Miss Mary Smith often visited Miss Matty and brought her the good advice of Mr. Smith, Mary's father and Miss Matty's financial adviser. Mary was surprised to learn that Miss Matty had long ago had a suitor whom she rejected in order to stay with her mother. Not long after Miss Deborah's death, the gentleman returned to Cranford for a visit. Mary was disappointed that he did not renew his courtship of Miss Matty. Miss Matty grieved too, in secret, for she would never have admitted openly such vulgar sentiments.

Mary also learned that Miss Deborah and Miss Matty had once had a brother who had disappeared many years before, after being severely punished by their father for playing a practical joke on Miss Deborah. Peter Jenkyns was believed dead, although Miss Matty had heard rumors that he was living in India.

The genteel ladies were suddenly thrown into a flurry of excitement when they heard that Mrs. Jamieson's sister-in-law, Lady Glenmire, was to settle in Cranford. Since she was the first noblewoman they had encountered, they spent long hours discussing how they should address her. Their worries were in vain, however, for Mrs. Jamieson subtly but firmly informed them that they would not be included in her guest list. At first, the ladies were greatly hurt. Later, Mrs. Jamieson was forced to relent and invite them to call, for most of the county gentility were away or otherwise occupied. Miss Matty, Miss Pole, and Mrs. Forrester first thought they would be engaged elsewhere for the fateful night, but their innate kindness, or perhaps their curiosity, prevailed, and they accepted the invitation. They found Lady Glenmire delightful and no more refined nor genteel than they themselves—a fact they, if not Mrs. Jamieson, considered not surprising.

Mrs. Jamieson departed Cranford for a time, leaving Lady Glenmire in charge of her home. In her absence, Lady Glenmire became engaged to the doctor of the town, a man not even recognized by the ladies except when his services were needed for bleeding. He was no higher socially than a shopkeeper. Even more exciting was the fact that the ladies at last knew someone who was to be married. They awaited Mrs. Jamieson's return with fear and anticipation, and they were not disappointed. Mrs. Jamieson, deciding to cut Lady Glenmire, stated that she had always known her to be of low taste.

The engaged couple were married before Mrs. Jamieson returned. By

that time, a great tragedy had befallen Miss Matty. The bank in which her
estate was deposited had to close its doors, and she was left with only thirteen pounds a year. She made no complaint; her biggest worry was whether
Mrs. Jamieson would allow the ladies to continue their friendship with her.
Mary Smith sent for her father to see what he could plan for Miss Matty.
Careful that she should not know of their gift, Miss Pole, Mrs. Forrester,
and another friend gave up some of their own small incomes so that they
could help their friend. Mary and Mr. Smith persuaded Miss Matty to sell
tea, but it took a good deal of convincing to assure her that this would be
a genteel way for a lady to supplement her income. Miss Matty's faithful
maid, Martha, forced her young man to marry her sooner than he had
anticipated so that they could rent Miss Matty's house and have her for a
lodger. In this way, Martha could continue to look after her old mistress
without injuring Miss Matty's pride. Everyone was happy when Mrs.
Jamieson returned and said that the ladies could continue to call on Miss
Matty because her father had been a rector and his daughter, who had
never married, was entitled to the position he had left her.

More good fortune followed. Mary Smith wrote to Miss Matty's brother
in India. When he received the letter, Peter Jenkyns sold his property and
returned to Cranford to keep his sister in comfort and in some prosperity.
Peter also brought about a reconciliation between Mrs. Jamieson and Lady
Glenmire, who now called herself a vulgar Mrs. instead of Lady. Once
more, there was peace in Cranford.

Critical Evaluation:
    For a whimsical and kind yet humorous account of the habits and cus-
toms of genteel spinsters of nineteenth century England, *Cranford* is
unsurpassed. Only a very warm and gentle woman could have portrayed
the little peculiarities of her sex with affection and sly humor, as did Elizabeth Gaskell. There is something of Charles Lamb in her finely drawn
characters, her humorous accounts of even the most trivial events. The
writer shows great understanding and sympathy for the everyday problems
of poor but genteel ladies. All in all, *Cranford* is a book to please even the
most sober realist.

    "In the first place, Cranford is in possession of the Amazons; all the
holders of houses, above a certain rent, are women." This first sentence of
the novel suggests an emphasis that the book as a whole does not
support—that the ladies of Cranford are indeed self-sufficient. True,
Cranford's society is largely made up of women alone, who often congratu-
late themselves that they do not have to endure the opposite sex. In times
of difficulty, though—in illness or in the burglary scare or when it comes
to matters of finances—the ladies admit to needing the help of a gentleman or two. The narrator, a younger participant-observer, wryly under-

stands the inconsistencies of Miss Matty, Miss Pole, and the others and ironically details these in her consistent tone. The epitome of the Cranford attitude is revealed when Miss Pole exclaims, "My father was a man, and I know the sex pretty well."

Cranford was already anachronistic in Gaskell's time. She surrounds the village and the society with an aura of nostalgia: that era had gone forever, but it had had certain advantages, despite its idiosyncrasies. The motif of older childless ladies symbolically reinforces the theme of the passing of Cranford, whose traditions will not be carried on by another generation.

The novel is episodic in form, and very little of consequence happens that is not resolved in the course of one or two chapters. Like many Victorian novels, this one was published serially in *Household Words*, a periodical edited and published by Dickens. The first two chapters appeared as a complete story in 1851, and Gaskell had not intended to write more, but Dickens persuaded her to continue *Cranford*. This explains why two strongly defined characters, the Captain and Miss Deborah Jenkyns, who seem so important in the beginning, die in the second chapter. From there on, Gaskell had to begin again, so to speak, and make Miss Matty the central figure.

THE CROCK OF GOLD

Type of work: Novel
Author: James Stephens (1882–1950)
Type of plot: Fantasy
Time of plot: Any time
Locale: Irish countryside
First published: 1912

Principal characters:
THE PHILOSOPHER
THE THIN WOMAN, his wife
SEUMAS AND BRIGID, two children
ANGUS OG, an early Irish god
CAITILIN, his mortal wife

The Story:

In the center of a very dark pinewood lived the two old Philosophers and their wives, the Grey Woman of Dun Gortin and the Thin Woman of Inis Magrath. One couple had a little boy named Seumas, the other a little girl named Brigid. Both were born on the same day.

When the children were ten years old, one of the old Philosophers decided that he had now learned all that he was capable of learning. This conclusion depressed him so much that he decided to die. It was unfortunate, as he pointed out, that at the time he was in the best of health; however, if the time had come for him to die, then die he must. He took off his shoes and spun around in the center of the room for fifteen minutes until he fell over dead. So grieved was the Grey Woman that she, too, killed herself, but since she was much tougher than her husband, she spun for forty-five minutes before she died. The Thin Woman calmly buried the two bodies under the hearthstone.

The people who lived on the edge of the pinewood often came to see the Thin Woman's husband when they needed advice. One day, Meehawl MacMurrachu came to the Philosopher to learn who had stolen his wife's scrubbing board. The Philosopher, after much questioning, finally decided that the fairies had taken it. He advised Meehawl to go to a certain spot and steal the Crock of Gold that the Leprechauns of Gort na Gloca Mora had buried there. For years, the Leprechauns had been filling their Crock of Gold by clipping the edges of gold coins that they found in men's houses at night. They needed the gold to ransom any of the little people caught by human beings.

Losing their gold to Meehawl made the Leprechauns angry, and they tried to make Meehawl bring it back by giving him and his wife all kinds of aches and pains. Next, they came stealthily and lured Brigid and Seumas down into a little house in the roots of a tree; but fear of the Thin Woman was on them, and they set the children free. Then they sent the Great God Pan, the god of the beast which is in every man, to lure away Caitilin, Meehawl's daughter, with the music of his pipes.

When Meehawl came with his tale of sorrow, the Philosopher sent Brigid and Seumas to tell Pan to release the girl. Pan, however, refused to answer their questions. When they told the Philosopher, he became so angry that he ordered his wife to bake him some cakes to eat on the way, and he started off by himself to visit Pan. None of the Philosopher's arguments, however, could persuade Pan to free Caitilin, and the Philosopher went off to get the help of Angus Og of the old gods.

Angus Og went to see Pan and the girl in their cave and forced the girl to choose between them. Caitilin, who had learned the true meaning of hunger and pain with Pan, did not know how to choose. Angus Og explained to her that he was Divine Inspiration, and that if she would come and live with him and be his wife, he would show her peace and happiness. He proved by several signs that he was the favorite of the gods of the earth and had more power than Pan. Caitilin sensed that true happiness, which she had never known, would be found with Angus Og, and that only hunger could be found with Pan; so she chose to leave Pan and go with Angus Og and was saved from the beast in man.

The Philosopher, on his way back home, delivered several messages from the god. He gave one message to a young boy, a promise from Angus Og that in time the old gods would return and that before they did, the boy would write a beautiful poem in their praise. Cheered by the news that the gods would soon come back, the Philosopher finally arrived home and greeted his wife with such affection that she decided always to be kind to him and never again to say a cross word.

Unknown to them, the Leprechauns had informed the police in the village that there were two bodies buried under the hearthstone in the Philosopher's house. One day, the police broke into the house, found the bodies, and accused the Philosopher of murder. Meanwhile, Brigid and Seumas were playing in the woods, and, quite by chance, they happened to dig a hole and find the Crock of Gold where Meehawl had buried it. They gave it back to the Leprechauns, but the return of the gold was not enough to set matters right. The police kept the Philosopher in jail. Then the Thin Woman baked some cakes and set out to find Angus Og, dragging the children behind her and saying the worst curses there were against the police. The first gods she met were the Three Absolutes, the Most Beautiful Man, the Strongest Man, and the Ugliest Man. By her wisdom, the Thin Woman was able to answer their questions and save herself and the children from their frightful powers. When they had passed these gods, they found the house of Angus Og. He was waiting for someone to come and ask him to aid the Philosopher, for it is impossible for the gods to help anyone unasked.

Calling all the old gods together, Angus Og and his wife led a great dance across the fields, and then they went down into the town with all the gods following. In the town, their merry laughter brought happiness to all who saw them except the most evil of men. The charges against the Philosopher were forgotten, and he was free to go back to his house in the pinewoods and dispense wisdom once more. Then the gods returned singing to their own country to await the birth of Caitilin's and Angus Og's child and the day when the old Irish gods could again leave their hidden caves and hollows and rule over the land with laughter and song.

Critical Evaluation:

This tale of adventure and philosophical discussions is a modern classic in its field. James Stephens is most successful in his attempt to bring old Irish legends to life in the pages of a delightful book. The philosophic discussions abound with a delightful humor, and the seriousness of some of the observations in no way lessens the magic quality of the story. The tale is a wandering one, containing many elements and telling many stories. All of them are entertaining to read, and most of them are perfect in execution.

Stephens was a minor member of the Irish literary Renaissance that began toward the end of the nineteenth century. Like such major figures as W. B. Yeats, John Synge, and Sean O'Casey, Stephens embodies the wit, imagination, and satiric vein that distinguishes the movement. Another of its identifying characteristics was its intense Irish patriotism, which discovered a focus in the rebellion against England and the campaign for home rule. This nationalism finds its way into the literature in the form of the celebration of ordinary people—the peasants and the urban proletariat— and their history, including the myths of the ancient Irish gods.

Like all fables, Stephens' *The Crock of Gold* can be read on a number of levels. Much like *Alice's Adventures in Wonderland*, it is a delightful story in itself and can be enjoyed for Seumas' and Brigid's humorous adventures among such mythical creatures as the Leprechauns and the Great gods, Pan and Angus Og. The reader would be amiss, however, if he overlooked Stephens' political and moral intention and his call for Irish unity.

At the beginning of the story, the Irish people are hostile to one another. When matters are brought to a boil with the theft of the crock of gold and the arrival of Pan, the Philosopher, who is responsible for the upheaval, is unable to bring order. Representing Ireland's intellectuals, he has lost touch with his own people. Realizing his impotence, however, he seeks out Angus Og. It is in this turning toward ancient wisdom that the gold as well as harmony are restored. At the end of the story, the people are promised that Caitilin's and Angus Og's child will come to return Ireland to its rightful rulers. Stephens suggests that Ireland will be able to arrive at its true Renaissance and gain its freedom from English tyranny by following the same path.

CROME YELLOW

Type of work: Novel
Author: Aldous Huxley (1894–1963)
Type of plot: Social satire
Time of plot: 1920's
Locale: England
First published: 1921

Principal characters:

HENRY WIMBUSH, the owner of Crome
ANNE WIMBUSH, his niece
DENIS STONE, a young poet
MR. SCROGAN, a man of reason
GOMBAULD, an artist
MARY BRACEGIRDLE, a victim of repressions
JENNY MULLION, a keen-eyed observer

The Story:

Denis Stone, a shy young poet, went to a house party at Crome, the country home of Henry Wimbush and his wife. He went because he was in love with Wimbush's niece, Anne. Anne looked down on Denis because he was four years younger than she and treated him with scorn when he attempted to speak of love.

Mr. Wimbush was interested in little except Crome and the histories of the people who had lived in the old house. Mrs. Wimbush was a woman with red hair, probably false, and an interest in astrology, especially since she had recently won a bet on a horse with her star-given information. Other guests at the party included Gombauld, an artist who had been invited to paint Anne's picture; the diabolically reasonable Mr. Scrogan; deaf Jenny Mullion; and Mary Bracegirdle, who was worried about her Freudian dreams. Denis and Anne quarreled, this time over their philosophies of life. Denis tried to carry all the cares of the world on his back, but Anne thought that things should be taken for granted as they came. The quarrel cost Denis his first opportunity to tell Anne that he loved her.

Mary Bracegirdle discussed her dreams and repressions with Anne. Having decided to secure either Gombauld or Denis for a husband, she chose the wrong times to talk with both men. Gombauld was busy painting when Mary came up to him. Denis was smarting with jealousy over the time Anne and Gombauld spent together.

Ivor Lombard arrived for the party. Ivor, a painter of ghosts and spirits, turned his attentions toward repressed Mary and secretly visited her one night in the tower. He went away without seeing her again.

At various times, Mr. Wimbush called the party together while he read stories of the early history of Crome. These stories were from a history at which Mr. Wimbush had worked for thirty years. Denis often wondered if he would ever get a chance to tell Anne that he loved her. Walking in the garden after a talk with Mr. Scrogan, whose cold-blooded ideas about a rationalized world annoyed him, he found a red notebook in which Jenny had been writing for the past week. The notebook contained a collection of sharply satirical cartoons of all the people at the house party. Jenny had drawn him in seven attitudes which illustrated his absurd jealousy, incompetence, and shyness. The cartoons deeply wounded his vanity and shattered his self-conception.

He was further discouraged by the fact that there was nothing for him to do at a charity fair held in the park outside Crome a few days later. Mr. Scrogan made a terrifying and successful fortune-teller; Jenny played the drums; Mr. Wimbush ran the various races; and Denis was left to walk aimlessly through the fair as an official with nothing to do. Gombauld made sketches of the people in the crowd, and Anne stayed by his side.

The night after the fair, Denis overheard part of a conversation between Gombauld and Anne. Denis was unaware that Anne had repulsed Gombauld, for she had made up her mind to accept Denis if he ever got around to asking her; consequently, he spent hours of torture thinking of the uselessness of his life. At last, he decided to commit suicide by jumping from the tower. There he found Mary grieving, because she had received only a brisk postcard from Ivor. She convinced Denis that both their lives were ruined and advised him to flee from Anne. Convinced, Denis arranged a fake telegram calling him back to London on urgent business. When it arrived, Denis realized with dismay that Anne was miserable to see him go. The telegram was the one decisive action of his life. Ironically, it separated him from Anne.

Critical Evaluation:

Aldous Huxley has written an amusing satire on the ill-fated love affair of a sensitive young poet. Using the plot as an excuse for bringing together all sorts of interesting and unusual facts and stories, he holds the reader's interest by an almost continual shift of emphasis. One learns of each of the guests at the house party, their faults, interests, and virtues. As in all of Huxley's novels, there is much philosophical discussion. No particular ideas are set forth as correct but a precise picture of the early 1920's as Huxley saw them is presented to the reader with wit and dexterity.

Even an early work like *Crome Yellow* shows traces of the novels that were to transform Huxley into one of the major voices of his generation.

The novel is autobiographical, taken almost entirely from his early life. Written around the theme of a sensitive young poet's unsuccessful love, it is more, however, than the exegesis of his own unrequited love. Huxley uses the plot to bring together a wide variety of characters. The most interesting feature for the reader familiar with Huxley's best-known novel, *Brave New World*, is the introduction of Scrogan, whose personality undergoes a metamorphosis in the course of the book. Originally a mere houseguest, though a malignant one, Scrogan gradually becomes the voice that Huxley adopts later in *Brave New World*. His function in the book is the voice of the devil, whose mad theories of the herd and the elite will blossom completely in Huxley's later social satire.

Given the idiocy and banality of those gathered at Crome, it is not difficult to imagine Scrogan's philosophy coming into existence. Like Mary Bracegirdle (a name of singular significance), all the houseguests are shut off from their own feelings and obsessed by their own worlds and themselves. Like Mr. Wimbush who subjects them to his reading of the ridiculous history of Crome—to which no one listens—they all speak *at* one another, never *to* anyone. The essence of the comedy, therefore, arises from their failure to understand and to communicate; the pathos of the situation emerges from missed connections and, finally, from missed opportunities of love. Because Denis Stone (again an apt and telling name) fails to confront Anne, he loses her love. Only Jenny Mullion sees accurately and truly; it is an absurd world that deserves the reader's ridicule if not his pity; and it certainly deserves Mr. Scrogan.

CROTCHET CASTLE

Type of work: Novel
Author: Thomas Love Peacock (1785–1866)
Type of plot: Comedy of manners
Time of plot: Nineteenth century
Locale: England
First published: 1831

> *Principal characters:*
> EBENEZER MAC CROTCHET, a country squire
> YOUNG CROTCHET, his son
> LEMMA CROTCHET, his daughter
> SUSANNAH TOUCHANDGO, the beloved of young Crotchet
> MR. CHAINMAIL, an antiquarian
> CAPTAIN FITZCHROME, a young army officer
> LADY CLARINDA BOSSNOWL, the beloved of Fitzchrome

The Story:

The squire of Crotchet Castle had descended from Scotch and Jewish ancestors, but he tried to hide this ancestry under the guise of an English country squire. His background had given him the ability to make money readily, and he used his wealth to buy a manor and a coat of arms. His wife was dead and his son in London, leaving the squire alone with a daughter. Young Crotchet, who had inherited his father's love for money, had taken his father's gift of a large sum and turned it into enormous profits. His business dealings were shady, and many people thought his day of reckoning would come. For the present, however, he was riding on a crest of success. He had been engaged to Miss Susannah Touchandgo, the daughter of a great banker, but when that gentleman had absconded with the bank's funds, leaving his daughter almost penniless, young Crotchet had deserted his love without a backward glance. Susannah had retreated into Wales, where in simple surroundings she taught a farmer's children for her livelihood.

Squire Crotchet's daughter Lemma had assumed some of the facial characteristics of her ancestors, a fact which was compensated for in the eyes of local swains by the size of her father's fortune. A suitor had not yet been selected for her, but there would be no problem in choosing one from the many who sought her hand and her purse.

Crotchet Castle was a gathering place for philosophers and dilettantes picked at random by Squire Crotchet. These would-be intellectuals engaged in long and tiresome disputes on all branches of philosophy and science. One of them, Mr. Chainmail, longed for a return to the customs and morals of the Middle Ages; he believed that the present was decidedly in-

ferior to the past. He was violently opposed by other members of the
group who worshipped mammon. No one of the philosophers ever changed
his views; each found much pleasure in expounding his own pet theory.

While strolling through the grounds one day, some of the gentlemen
came upon a young army officer, Captain Fitzchrome. Invited to join the
group, the captain accepted readily, for he was in love with one of the
guests, Lady Clarinda Bossnowl. Lady Clarinda obviously loved the captain, but she had been promised to young Crotchet. The match was purely
a business arrangement; he would exchange his money for her title. The
captain pleaded with her at every opportunity, but she silenced him and her
own heart by ridiculing his lack of funds. Lemma Crotchet, in the meantime, was pledged to Lady Clarinda's brother. The four young people spent
many hours together, much to Captain Fitzchrome's sorrow.

One day, the squire took his guests on a river voyage down the Thames.
They visited places of learning and culture but saw little of either except
the buildings supposed to house those virtues. During the trip, the captain
finally gave up his hopes of winning Lady Clarinda, and he left the party
without notifying anyone. He settled in a village inn, where he was later
joined by Chainmail, the antiquarian, who had left the party in order to
study a ruined castle in the neighborhood. Since the captain knew the way
to the castle, he offered to guide Chainmail, but he was called back to
London on business before they could undertake their expedition.
Chainmail went on alone.

During his researches, Chainmail caught a glimpse of a nymphlike creature who fascinated him so much that he could not rest until he had made
her acquaintance. After many false attempts, he met her and learned that
she was Susannah Touchandgo, the lady betrayed by young Crotchet.
Chainmail found her perfect in every way but one. He knew she would
share the simple, old-fashioned life he loved, but he had determined to
marry a lady of gentle birth. Susannah, ashamed of her father's theft,
would tell him nothing of her family background. In spite of her reluctance
in this respect, Chainmail loved her and spent many happy hours at the
farmhouse in which she lived.

Captain Fitzchrome returned. Learning of his friend's plight, he encouraged Chainmail to ask for the lady's hand, but the antiquarian could not
change his views on his need for a wife of gentle birth. The situation was
brought to a climax when they saw in the paper an announcement of the
approaching marriage of Lady Clarinda and young Crotchet. Susannah was
temporarily overwrought by the news, and in trying to comfort her,
Chainmail inadvertently proposed. Then Susannah told him of her father's
crime. Chainmail, however, could overlook that fact in his joy over the
discovery that Susannah was of good blood. In a few days, the two were
married.

The following Christmas, most of the friends gathered again at Crotchet Castle. Lemma Crotchet had married Lord Bossnowl, but Lady Clarinda Bossnowl had not yet married young Crotchet. The young man was a little dismayed at seeing Susannah married to Chainmail, for he still held her in affection. Lady Clarinda cast longing glances at the captain, even to the point of singing a song that was obviously intended for him. There was no sorrow in her heart, consequently, when young Crotchet disappeared. His firm had failed, and he was penniless. It was assumed that he had crossed the Atlantic to join forces with Susannah's father, who had set up business there; the two rogues would make good partners.

Lady Clarinda would not again be put up for sale. She gladly accepted Captain Fitzchrome and his smaller but more stable fortune.

Critical Evaluation:

Born and educated in the eighteenth century, Thomas Love Peacock carried the ideas and ideals of the Century of Reason into the nineteenth century and the age of Victoria. Although ostensibly set in the first half of the nineteenth century, the scenes of *Crotchet Castle* might more easily be from the comedies of Sheridan or Goldsmith. Artificiality reaches the point of absurdity. The scenes at the country villa might almost be out of paintings by Watteau or even Boucher. The influence of Voltaire and the rationalists and satirists of the previous century on Peacock is well known. At one moment, the exchanges of Captain Fitzchrome and Lady Clarinda are worthy of Shakespeare's Beatrice and Benedict; then the scene abruptly changes to pseudophilosophic discussions that might have been taken from *The Satyricon* of Petronius. Peacock's writing always makes the reader think of something else, because it is based on previous creations rather than upon nature and direct observation of humanity. Quotations and exclamations in Greek, Latin, French, and other languages stud the dialogue like spangles on a ball gown, glittering but at times affected and gaudy.

In *Crotchet Castle*, as in his other novels, Peacock ridicules the excesses and exaggerations in human behavior. His satire is never unkind; rather, it is the product of a mind that is tolerant of weaknesses but vexed by an overabundance of those weaknesses in an imperfect world. The plot is almost nonexistent, and the people are caricatures; but in spite of these apparent defects the book gives a fairly accurate picture of nineteenth century English country life.

The word "fashion" is the be-all and end-all of the characters' existence. Only money is more important than the pursuit of the fashionable; and, in fact, they often seem to be inextricably intertwined. Although Peacock satirizes snobbery, the reader feels that Peacock is nevertheless a genuine snob himself; his sharpest barbs are for the nouveau riche Jews trying to buy their way into the gentry. Peacock looked dubiously upon the changing

times, particularly upon the growth and development of science during the
first half of the nineteenth century. In novels such as *Crotchet Castle*, he
satirizes the coming industrial age and the newfound riches of certain
classes rising on the wave of change, and he glorified that leisurely age
when people had the time and inclination to sit around eating and drinking
and talking . . . especially talking.

THE CRUISE OF THE CACHALOT

Type of work: Pseudofactual account
Author: Frank T. Bullen (1857–1915)
Type of plot: Adventure romance
Time of plot: Late nineteenth century
Locale: At sea
First published: 1898

>>> *Principal characters:*
>>> FRANK T. BULLEN, the narrator
>>> MR. JONES, the fourth mate
>>> ABNER CUSHING, a sailor
>>> MR. COUNT, the first mate
>>> CAPTAIN SLOCUM, the captain of the *Cachalot*

The Story:

By a strange combination of circumstances, Frank Bullen found himself in New Bedford, Massachusetts, looking for a ship. He was only eighteen years old at the time, but already he had spent six years at sea.

He was strolling down a street in New Bedford, intent on a possible berth aboard any ship, for his pockets were empty, when he was hailed by a scraggy Yankee with the inevitable tobacco juice dribbling down his whiskers. Asked if he wanted to ship out, he accepted eagerly without knowing the type of craft or any of the conditions of employment. He accompanied the sharp-featured Yankee to a small, dirty hall where he joined a group of men all bound for the same ship. When he saw the motley crowd of greenhorns, he felt doubts about joining the ship, but there was little chance to back out. After hastily signing the ship's articles, he went with his mates to the docks.

All of the crew were carefully kept together until they were safe in the small boat. On the trip out into the harbor, Bullen saw with many misgivings the *Cachalot*, which would be his home for three years. He deeply regretted signing on; the *Cachalot* was a whaler, and whalers were notoriously the worst ships afloat. The *Cachalot* did not compare favorably with the trim English whalers with which he was more familiar. She was small, a three hundred and fifty tonner, dirty and unpainted, and quite dumpy looking because she had no raised bow or poop.

Once on board, Bullen's worst fears were realized. The officers were hard and mean; they carried lashes with them, and a clumsy or slow sailor often felt the sting of a lash on his back. The men needed a great deal of

---

THE CRUISE OF THE CACHALOT by Frank T. Bullen. By permission of the publishers, Appleton-Century-Crofts, Inc.

discipline, however, to do a somewhat decent job. Of the twelve white crew members, Bullen was the only one who had been to sea before. The hands were beaten and cursed, and they were not even allowed to rest while they were seasick.

Along with the white greenhorns, there were a score of Portuguese, all experienced whaling men. There were also four mates and Captain Slocum. The captain was a hard driver and a foul talker. The first mate, Mr. Count, was an older man, the only decent officer aboard. The fourth mate, Mr. Jones, was a giant black man.

Because of his past experience, Bullen escaped most of the abuse meted out to his fellows. After the ship had been scrubbed and polished and the men had been licked into shape, he became almost fond of the ship. This feeling was heightened when he learned that the *Cachalot* was seaworthy in spite of her lines.

To the delight of the Portuguese, the ship was heading toward Cape Verde. At last, the first whale was sighted. Bullen was put into the boat of the first mate and told to mind the sail. The boat came up almost on top of the whale before Louis, the harpooner, threw his great hook. When the whale sounded, the hands paid out over two hundred fathoms of line. Then the whale began to rush away at full speed, towing the boat in his wake. When he slowed down, the boat was brought close enough for the harpooner to use his lance. After a final flurry, the whale died and was towed alongside.

After some months at sea, Bullen had an unpleasant picture of ship's discipline. Abner Cushing, a Yankee sailor, tried to make some beer in the forecastle. Needing some potatoes for his brew, he stole a few from the officers' gallery. One of the Portuguese reported the theft to the captain and, as punishment, Abner was strung up by the thumbs and lashed vigorously by one of the harpooners until he fainted. When his punishment was over, he was not allowed to go below but was forced to return to the active work immediately.

The cruise was an ill-fated one for Abner. He was in a small boat when a whale unexpectedly turned and bore down on the frail craft. The line was hurriedly pulled in. Then the whale sounded, and as the line was paid out, Abner's neck caught in a loop. The weight of the descending whale neatly severed his head.

After the *Cachalot* had been at sea over a year, Mr. Jones became greatly depressed. He recalled a fortune-teller's prediction that he would die in a fight with a white man and finally decided that Captain Slocum was destined to cause his death. Deranged, he went on the bridge, wrapped his huge arms around the captain, and jumped with him into the sea. When Mr. Count assumed command, he promoted Bullen to Mr. Jones's vacant post.

Once Bullen nearly met his end when a harpooned cachalot suddenly turned sidewise and smashed a boat to bits with his mighty tail. His foot tangled in the wreckage, and Bullen went under. When he came up, nearly exhausted, he caught blindly at a rope and hauled himself along until he came to the inert whale. He clambered aboard and clung to the harpoon in the side of the dead whale; but the whale suddenly came to life. When the other boats came alongside after the whale had finally died, Bullen had a dislocated thigh and severe rope burns on each arm.

At last, after three years, the *Cachalot*'s barrels were full, and the ship headed home around Cape Horn. In good time, the lookout sighted Cape Navesink. With every flag flying, she came into New Bedford. The cruise of the *Cachalot* was ended.

Critical Evaluation:

Frank T. Bullen's childhood was cruel. Like Charles Dickens, he lacked schooling and was a homeless waif and child laborer in London. He was adopted briefly by a kindly aunt and began to read Milton's *Paradise Lost* at five years of age; but the aunt, his solitary childhood friend, died when Bullen was eight years old, and he was cast into the street. Alone in the world with "no-one caring a straw for me," he trusted God and was signed on an English vessel when he was twelve years old. Bullen spent the next six years at sea. He landed in New Bedford, Massachusetts, when he was eighteen years old and secured a berth on a sailor's nightmare, a whaler, in this case the "Cachalot," a venerable tub "as leaky as a basket."

The Cruise of the Cachalot is a combined autobiographical/fictional narration, which gives an account of a South Sea whaler from a seaman's standpoint. Bullen also described the methods employed, the dangers met, and the woes experienced by whalers, using a clear style in order not to weary the reader. He scorned padding, sought accuracy of detail, and penned a tersely thrilling story of a voyage around the world that lasted for years. Its many fascinating passages include a description of a cyclone off the remote Seychelles Islands, storms at sea, the vast face of the sea and the sky, a passage through the Sargasso Sea, labors, landings, harpoonings, beatings, and a brush with the Confederate raider "Alabama," among other adventures. All this was done while pursuing cachalots, or sperm whales, which yielded by-products such as spermaceti and ambergris, mentioned by Shakespeare and Milton. The book's minor inaccuracies are the inevitable ones produced by its fast pace and man-of-action approach.

Bullen was at first puzzled as to how to write *The Cruise of the Cachalot* but decided to write it as if he were simply spinning a yarn to a single friend. When this approach met with difficulties, he offered his rich materials to the famous Rudyard Kipling, assuming that the latter could do it literary justice. Kipling declined the material and encouraged Bullen to handle it by himself. After reading Bullen's manuscript, Kipling wrote a foreword to it that has since been carried in every edition of *The Cruise of the Cachalot*. Kipling's foreword describes the book as "immense" and unequaled in sea wonder and mystery. Praising the manner in which Bullen depicted whaling through fresh and realistic sea pictures, Kipling commented that Bullen must have discarded enough material to write five books.

A DANCE TO THE MUSIC OF TIME

Type of work: A *roman-fleuve* comprising twelve novels
Author: Anthony Powell (1905–   )
Type of plots: Satiric realism
Time of plots: 1914–1971
Locale: Primarily London; various other locales in Great Britain; and Venice, Italy
First published: A Question of Upbringing, 1951; *A Buyer's Market,* 1952; *The Acceptance World,* 1955; *At Lady Molly's,* 1957; *Casanova's Chinese Restaurant,* 1960; *The Kindly Ones,* 1962; *The Valley of Bones,* 1964; *The Soldier's Art,* 1966; *The Military Philosophers,* 1968; *Books Do Furnish a Room,* 1971; *Temporary Kings,* 1973; *Hearing Secret Harmonies,* 1975

Principal characters:

NICHOLAS JENKINS, the narrator and a novelist

KENNETH WIDMERPOOL, a school acquaintance of Jenkins who later attains power as a financier and Member of Parliament; the only character besides the narrator to figure in all twelve volumes of the cycle

PETER TEMPLER, a school friend of Jenkins

JEAN TEMPLER, Peter's younger sister and Jenkins' lover before his marriage

CHARLES STRINGHAM, another school friend

SILLERY, a manipulative don

J. G. QUIGGIN, a student at the university with Jenkins who later attains celebrity as a left-wing critic

MARK MEMBERS, another fellow student who achieves recognition as a poet

CAPTAIN GILES JENKINS (UNCLE GILES), Jenkins' raffish uncle

SIR MAGNUS DONNERS, an industrialist

EDGAR DEACON, a bad painter

RALPH BARNBY, another painter, superior to Deacon

MRS. MILLY ANDRIADIS, a socialite

MONA, Peter Templer's first wife and a former model

BOB DUPORT, Jean Templer's first husband and an entrepreneur

ST. JOHN CLARKE, an Edwardian novelist despised by Jenkins

MRS. MYRA ERDLEIGH, a friend of Uncle Giles and a clairvoyant

CHIPS LOVELL, a friend and fellow scriptwriter of Jenkins

LADY MOLLY JEAVONS, Chip Lovell's aunt by a former marriage

TED JEAVONS, her husband

LADY PRISCILLA TOLLAND, a debutante who is pursued and
  later married by Chips Lovell
LADY ISOBEL TOLLAND, Priscilla's older sister who becomes
  Jenkins' wife
ERRIDGE, Priscilla and Isobel's eldest brother, later Lord
  Warminster
GENERAL AYLMER CONYERS, an old family friend of the
  Jenkinses
HUGH MORELAND, a composer and one of Jenkins' closest
  friends
MATILDA WILSON, an actress whose second marriage is to
  Moreland
MACLINTICK, a music critic and admirer of Moreland
DR. TRELAWNEY, a cult leader and magus
CAPTAIN ROWLAND GWATKIN, Jenkins' company commander
  in the Welsh regiment in which he is commissioned at the
  outset of World War II
PAMELA FLITTON, Stringham's niece who becomes
  Widmerpool's wife
LINDSAY (BOOKS-DO-FURNISH-A-ROOM) BAGSHAW, a disrepu-
  table journalist
X. TRAPNEL, a novelist and short-story writer of the
  immediate postwar period
RUSSELL GWINNETT, an American professor who writes a
  biography of Trapnel
SCORPIO MURTLOCK, a cult leader in the late 1960's who claims
  to be a reincarnation of Dr. Trelawney
FIONA CUTTS, a niece of the Jenkinses and one of Murtlock's
  disciples

Anthony Powell's *A Dance to the Music of Time* is a *roman-fleuve*, a
long sequence of novels which together make up a single unified work.
Other examples of the *roman-fleuve* in English fiction include C. P. Snow's
Strangers and Brothers, comprising eleven individual novels, and Henry
Williamson's *A Chronicle of Ancient Sunlight*, comprising fifteen novels. In
French, examples of the *roman-fleuve* include Romain Rolland's *Jean
Christophe* (ten volumes), Jules Romains' *Men of Good Will* (twenty-seven
volumes), Roger Martin du Gard's *Les Thibaults* (eight volumes), and
Marcel Proust's *Remembrance of Things Past* (seven volumes).
   The length of the *roman-fleuve* allows the novelist to develop characters
over a long span of time, to convey something of the density and complexity of life itself. Powell memorably achieves these effects; at the same time,
he is virtually unique among practitioners of the *roman-fleuve* in that his

viewpoint is essentially comic.

A Dance to the Music of Time draws its title from a painting by Nicholas Poussin. At the beginning of the first volume of the cycle, *A Question of Upbringing*, Powell's first-person narrator, Nicholas Jenkins, watches some workmen gathered round a fire and is reminded of Poussin's painting,

> in which the Seasons, hand in hand and facing outward, tread in rhythm to the notes of the lyre that the winged and naked greybeard plays. The image of Time brought thoughts of mortality: of human beings, facing outward like the Seasons, moving hand in hand in intricate measure: stepping slowly, methodically, sometimes a trifle awkwardly, in evolutions that take recognisable shape....

This image of "the music of time," to the tune of which "partners disappear only to reappear again, once more giving pattern to the spectacle," governs the entire sequence.

The twelve novels of the cycle are grouped in four subsections or movements. The first movement, which includes *A Question of Upbringing*, *A Buyer's Market*, and *The Acceptance World*, traces the progress of narrator Nicholas Jenkins from youth to experience. Powell's treatment of this passage is highly unsentimental; for Jenkins, youth is something to be endured and gotten over with, and the prevailing mood of the opening novels is one of waiting for life to begin in earnest. This mood is not Jenkins' alone; indeed, throughout the cycle, Jenkins himself is rarely the focus of attention. He is, rather, a participant-observer through whose experience the reader comes to know an extraordinary diversity of characters.

A Question of Upbringing begins in December, 1921. (Although Powell does not always supply exact dates for the action, they can usually be reconstructed with reasonable accuracy following the internal chronology of the cycle, and with reference to historical events mentioned throughout.) The location is an exclusive English public school; among Jenkins' schoolmates are three characters destined to play an important role in the cycle.

Of these, the most important is Kenneth Widmerpool. Widmerpool is the only character other than the narrator to figure in all twelve volumes of the sequence. A disagreeable youth and, ultimately, a despicable man, Widmerpool appears at intervals throughout Jenkins' life; their relationship embodies the metaphor of the dance, according to which one is bound to one's "partners" by an inscrutable design. More sympathetic characters are Jenkins' friends Charles Stringham and Peter Templer. Stringham is appealing yet self-destructive; Templer is smooth, confident, and mature beyond his years.

The first section of *A Question of Upbringing* introduces these characters in the school setting. In the summer following his graduation,

Jenkins visits the Templers and meets Peter's younger sister, Jean, then about sixteen or seventeen, to whom he is greatly attracted. In the fall of 1923, following a farcical interlude in France, Jenkins enters the university (unnamed, but presumably Oxford). A long comic scene set several months later in the rooms of a power-hungry don, Sillery, introduces two of Jenkins' fellow students who become recurring characters in the cycle: J. G. Quiggin, later to attain celebrity as a Marxist critic and all-around man of letters, although he leaves the university without a degree, and Mark Members, who makes his reputation as a poet and then, like Quiggin, branches out into the role of man of letters.

A Buyer's Market, the second novel in the sequence, opens in the summer of 1928 or 1929, four or five years after *A Question of Upbringing*, and concludes in October of the same year. Jenkins, having been graduated from the university, has found employment in London, where he works for a publisher that specializes in art books but issues other sorts of books as well. Stringham and Widmerpool, in a coincidence typical of the entire sequence, both find themselves working for Sir Magnus Donners, a prominent industrialist.

In structure, this volume follows the pattern established in the first volume. It consists of four chapters, each of which centers on a comic episode or set piece. With some variation, this is the method that Powell follows throughout.

A Buyer's Market introduces the first of many artists and artists manqué that populate the cycle: Edgar Deacon, a seedy, egotistical, untalented painter with a taste for young men (he dies in the course of the novel after a drunken fall), and Ralph Barnby, a far better painter than Deacon but one whose art is very much tied to the *Zeitgeist* of the 1920's; he is also a notorious womanizer.

The central scene of the novel is a party at the home of Mrs. Milly Andriadis, a socialite in her mid-thirties who has a brief affair with Stringham before his marriage, which takes place near the end of the volume. This party continues Jenkins' initiation into the world of experience: "I was...more than half aware," he reflects, "that such latitudes are entered by a door through which there is, in a sense, no return."

A second set piece features Sir Magnus Donners giving a tour of the dungeons at Stourwater Castle, his home, which occasions comment on his voyeuristic and otherwise perverse sexual proclivities. Among the party is the former Jean Templer, now Jean Duport; her loutish husband, Bob Duport, several years older than Jenkins and his contemporaries, is an aggressive entrepreneur who makes and loses great sums of money.

The Acceptance World (the title is British financial jargon for what is known in the United States as "trading in futures") completes Jenkins' initiation. In the course of this volume, which spans the period from

autumn 1931 to summer 1933, Jenkins publishes his first novel and carries
on an intense affair with Jean Duport, still going as the book ends but
showing signs of running down. Later, Jenkins learns that while their affair
was still going, Jean had already taken up with the man for whom she
eventually leaves him, Jimmy Brent, an odious character whose appeal to
Jean is incomprehensible to Jenkins.

An important figure in this volume is the novelist St. John Clarke, introduced briefly in *A Buyer's Market*. Clarke, an Edwardian writer who in his
time attains both popular and critical success, becomes a kind of litmus
test: Referred to in various ways by various characters throughout the
sequence, he represents for Jenkins all that is artistically cheap and
meretricious.

Also introduced here is the clairvoyant Mrs. Myra Erdleigh, whom
Jenkins meets in the hotel rooms of his Uncle Giles. This scene, the opening scene of *The Acceptance World*, is one of the most important in the
entire twelve volumes. Throughout the sequence there are many references
to occult phenomena, in addition to the often uncanny coincidences that
are the very texture of the action. Powell's attitude toward such phenomena
is neither credulous nor debunking. He clearly believes that some experiences of occult phenomena—second sight, telepathy (at least of a low-
grade variety), and so on—are valid. Their recurring presence in the cycle
(along with instances of obvious charlatanry) has a larger import as well,
for they point to the mystery of human existence—a mystery not confined
to realms designated "occult."

When Mrs. Erdleigh reads the cards and tells Jenkins his future, he is
immediately startled by her perspicacity, but he quickly discounts that
effect, observing that "such trivial comment, mixed with a few home truths
of a personal nature, provide, I had already learnt, the commonplaces of
fortune-telling." Yet Mrs. Erdleigh's insights into Jenkins' character are
genuinely perspicacious, and, as the reader gradually appreciates, her specific predictions concerning his future are all, in time, fulfilled—genuinely
fulfilled, not merely finding the loose "confirmation" of a fortune-cookie
oracle.

The first movement of the cycle, then, concludes with Jenkins and his
contemporaries firmly established in

> the Acceptance World...the world in which the essential element—happi-
> ness, for example—is drawn, as it were, from an engagement to meet a bill.
> Sometimes the goods are delivered, even a small profit made; sometimes the
> goods are not delivered, and disaster follows; sometimes the goods are deliv-
> ered, but the value of the currency is changed.

The second movement includes *At Lady Molly's*, *Casanova's Chinese
Restaurant*, and *The Kindly Ones*. It is 1934 as *At Lady Molly's* begins,

and Jenkins has moved from his publishing job to work as a scriptwriter for a British studio, having meanwhile published his second novel. A fellow scriptwriter, Chips Lovell, about five years younger than Jenkins (who is by this time twenty-eight or twenty-nine), is nephew by marriage to the Lady Molly of the title, Molly Jeavons, and early in the novel, he takes Jenkins to a party at the Jeavonses, where he hopes to meet Priscilla Tolland, a young woman whom he is pursuing. Later, at the country cottage of J. G. Quiggin (currently domiciled with Peter Templer's former wife, Mona, an ex-model), Jenkins meets Priscilla's older sister Isobel. (They are but two of the ten children of Lord Warminster; the eldest, Erridge, is Quiggin's landlord and patron, sharing his Marxist views.) In his understated way, Jenkins reports that he knew at first sight that Isobel would be his wife.

The novel begins by introducing, via Jenkins' reminiscences of long family friendship, the character of General Aylmer Conyers, one of the most delightful and most warmly portrayed figures in the entire sequence. Retired, nearing the age of eighty, General Conyers is still formidable: He trains dogs, plays the cello, and discusses the works of C. G. Jung, which he has recently discovered and absorbed with great interest. This volume also follows the fates of Widmerpool, whose fiancée breaks their engagement when he cannot perform as a lover, and Stringham, whose alcoholism and alienation are severe.

Casanova's Chinese Restaurant begins with a flashback to 1928 to 1929 that introduces Hugh Moreland, a composer who is one of Jenkins' closest friends and who becomes an important recurring character. The first section of this novel, discounting the flashback, is set in 1933 and 1934 and overlaps in time some of the action of *At Lady Molly's*. By this stage, the fifth novel in the sequence, the special effects of the *roman-fleuve* begin to come into play. The texture is more dense; much can be accomplished simply by mentioning the name of a familiar character in a new (and often surprising) context.

Much of *Casanova's Chinese Restaurant* is concerned with marriage and marriages. Jenkins marries Isobel; Moreland marries the actress Matilda Wilson (to whom Jenkins is introduced by Moreland after a performance in John Webster's *The Duchess of Malfi*), a former mistress of Sir Magnus Donners. There is also the bitterly—indeed, pathologically—unhappy marriage of the Maclinticks; Maclintick, a music critic who worships Moreland, in his own words, "with the proper respect of the poor interpretive hack for the true creative artist," ends by committing suicide after his wife Audrey leaves him. His suicide dissuades Moreland from pursuing his affair (as yet unconsummated) with Priscilla Tolland; a week later, her engagement to Chips Lovell is announced.

The movement concludes with *The Kindly Ones*, which begins with a long flashback to 1914. Jenkins recalls his governess' lesson, that the

Greeks so greatly feared the Furies that they renamed them the Eumenides—the Kindly Ones—hoping thus to placate them. The flashback evokes the mood of imminent disaster, the sense that the Furies are about to strike again, yet it does so only in an oblique fashion, for much of the action is broad comedy involving the Jenkinses' servants. Introduced in this section is the cult leader and magus Dr. Trelawney, a corrupt figure reminiscent of Aleister Crowley. After another brief flashback, to 1928 or 1929, and sections set in 1938 and 1939, the novel concludes in the fall of 1939, several weeks after the outbreak of World War II, with the brother of Ted Jeavons (Lady Molly's husband) promising Jenkins to expedite his call-up by the army.

The third movement, which includes *The Valley of Bones*, *The Soldier's Art*, and *The Military Philosophers*, spans the war years. As *The Valley of Bones* opens early in 1940, Jenkins has been commissioned as a second-lieutenant in a Welsh regiment, soon to be stationed at a school for chemical warfare quartered on a decaying estate in Northern Ireland. Much of the action of this volume centers on the tragicomic fate of Jenkins' immediate superior, Captain Rowland Gwatkin (in civilian life an employee of a small bank), whose romanticism proves his downfall. When, at the end of the volume, Jenkins is transferred and then told to report to the DAAG (Deputy-Assistant-Adjutant-General) at Divisional Headquarters in Northern Ireland, it is no surprise that the officer to whom he reports turns out to be Widmerpool.

Widmerpool's machinations and running battles with fellow officers figure prominently in the next volume, *The Soldier's Art*. Stringham makes an unexpected reappearance as a waiter in the Mess where Jenkins regularly eats; Widmerpool not only rejects Jenkins' suggestion that they help Stringham in some way but also arranges for his transfer to a Mobile Laundry Unit due to be sent to the Far East—an eventuality concerning which Stringham maintains indifference ("Awfully chic to be killed"). On leave in London, Jenkins meets Chips Lovell, currently estranged from Priscilla (who is carrying on an affair) but hopeful of getting her back. Later, after Chips has left the restaurant where he and Jenkins met, Jenkins sees Priscilla and her lover, Odo Stevens. That night, both Chips and Priscilla (and Lady Molly, at whose house Priscilla is staying) are killed in air raids at different locations.

In the final volume of the third movement, *The Military Philosophers*, Jenkins has a new posting, working in the War Office in Whitehall in Allied Liaison, with special responsibility for Polish forces. Widmerpool, who has been promoted, is also working in Whitehall, with access to policymakers at the highest levels. Early in the volume, Jenkins meets Peter Templer and is struck by his air of detachment and fatalism. Templer has recently had an affair with Stringham's niece, Pamela Flitton, a beautiful but malicious femme fatale who inexplicably turns her attention to Widmerpool, to whom she is soon engaged. Later in the volume, when Templer is sent to the Balkans on a secret mission and killed by Communist partisans, Pamela accuses Widmerpool of complicity in Templer's death. There is also word, confirmed by Widmerpool, that Stringham was captured by the Japanese at the fall of Singapore and died in a prisoner-of-war camp. Finally, this volume features the reappearance of Jean Duport, at first unrecognizable to Jenkins as the wife of a Latin American attaché, Colonel Flores, some years her junior.

The deaths of Templer and Stringham are symbolic of the end of a period and, indeed, a way of life. The postwar world presents a strange new landscape. Such is the mood of the final movement, comprising *Books Do Furnish a Room*, *Temporary Kings*, and *Hearing Secret Harmonies*.

In *Books Do Furnish a Room*, which begins in the winter of 1945–1946 and concludes in the fall of 1947, Jenkins, who was unable to write during the war and finds that he is still not ready to attempt a novel, undertakes a study of Robert Burton, entitled *Borage and Hellebore*. Much of this volume is concerned with the postwar literary scene, especially with antics of J. G. Quiggin and the crowd associated with his magazine *Fission*, edited by the disreputable journalist Lindsay "Books-do-furnish-a-room" Bagshaw ("Books" for short). Also introduced in this context is one of the most interesting characters in the cycle, X. Trapnel (based on Powell's acquaintance with the writer Julian Maclaren-Ross). Trapnel is a novelist and short-story writer of enormous gifts and idiosyncratic manner whose immediate postwar success is not followed up; his decline to a premature death is hastened by an affair with Pamela Widmerpool.

Between the time of *Books Do Furnish a Room* and that of *Temporary Kings*, there is an interval of more than ten years—the first such substantial gap in the sequence. *Temporary Kings* begins in the summer of 1958 at an international writer's conference in Venice. The arrival of an American professor, Russell Gwinnett, who is at work on a biography of X. Trapnel, prompts memories of Trapnel's death. After a leisurely and blackly comic account of the conference and its attendant intrigues, the scene shifts back to England, where Widmerpool is about to be charged with espionage on behalf of the Soviets. (Later, the case is dropped, presumably in exchange for information from Widmerpool.) Pamela pursues Gwinnett and dies in bed with him in a hotel, having taken an overdose of drugs; there are rumors of necrophlilia, consistent with Gwinnett's past. Hugh Moreland, long in ill health and living in reduced circumstances with Maclintick's widow, Audrey, dies at the end of this volume.

There is another ten-year interval between the conclusion of *Temporary Kings* and the opening of the final volume of the sequence, *Hearing Secret Harmonies*, in the spring of 1968. Several new characters are introduced in this volume, including the cult leader Scorpio Murtlock (who claims to be a reincarnation of Dr. Trelawney) and the Jenkinses' niece, Fiona Cutts, who is one of Murtlock's disciples. (The time of the action is the same as that of the Manson Family and similar phenomena of the 1960's.) Familiar figures appear as well: Widmerpool, after a stint in California, has returned to England in a new guise, as a champion of the counterculture, while Gwinnett's book on X. Trapnel, *Death's-Head Swordsman*, thought to have been abandoned, not only is published but also wins the Magnus Donners Memorial Prize. New and old characters come together when Widmerpool joins Murtlock's cult (which he tries to take over) and Gwinnett, in England to receive the Donners Prize and pursue research for his new book, *The Gothic Symbolism of Mortality in the Texture of Jacobean Stagecraft*, attends the cult's rites and witnesses Murtlock's assertion of supremacy over Widmerpool. A year or so later, Widmerpool dies on a dawn run with fellow cultists; meanwhile, Gwinnett has married Fiona.

The final volume concludes with Jenkins lighting an autumn bonfire, the smoke of which reminds him of the workmen's fire that he contemplated at the beginning of the first volume. In turn, the memory brings to mind a long passage from Robert Burton's *The Anatomy of Melancholy*, asserting with a kind of biblical eloquence the cyclical order of human life ("one purchaseth, another breaketh; he thrives, his neighbor turns bankrupt; now plenty, then again dearth and famine...").

A Dance to the Music of Time is a remarkable achievement for many reasons, but above all it is distinguished by its richly varied cast of characters. Powell's great work is sometimes compared to Proust's *Remembrance of Things Past*, but in fact it has little in common with that masterpiece of introspection; rarely does Powell's narrative turn inward. At the same time, it is a mistake to claim, as some critics have, that Powell has documented the British experience in the middle decades of the twentieth century. Certainly, his novels give the flavor of the period as it was experienced by a certain class, but his interest is always in his characters as individuals, not as types.

Indeed, insofar as it is possible to summarize the message of a twelve-volume sequence of novels, that message may be found in Powell's approach to his characters. Powell himself has observed that if one writes about people as they are, one will inevitably write comedy. His characters are unpredictable, frequently contradictory in their twists and turns, yet for that very reason they are extremely lifelike. *A Dance to the Music of Time* suggests that at the heart of human experience, as of every individual life, there is an irreducible mystery.

DANIEL DERONDA

Type of work: Novel
Author: George Eliot (Mary Ann Evans, 1819–1880)
Type of plot: Social realism
Time of plot: Mid-nineteenth century
Locale: Rural England, London, and the Continent
First published: 1876

> *Principal characters:*
> DANIEL DERONDA
> MIRAH LAPIDOTH, a girl he saves from drowning
> SIR HUGO MALLINGER, Daniel's guardian
> LADY MALLINGER, his wife
> GWENDOLEN HARLETH, a beautiful young lady
> MRS. DAVILOW, her mother
> MRS. GASCOIGNE, Mrs. Davilow's sister
> MR. GASCOIGNE, her husband
> REX GASCOIGNE, their son
> ANNA GASCOIGNE, their daughter
> MALLINGER GRANDCOURT, Gwendolen's husband and Sir
>   Hugo's heir
> LUSH, his follower
> HERR KLESMER, a musician
> CATHERINE ARROWPOINT, his wife and an heiress
> HANS MEYRICK, one of Deronda's friends
> MRS. MEYRICK, his mother
> EZRA COHEN, a shopkeeper in the East End
> MORDECAI, a boarder with the Cohens and Mirah's brother
> MRS. LYDIA GLASHER, Grandcourt's former mistress

The Story:

Gwendolen Harleth, a strikingly beautiful young woman, was gambling at Leubronn. Playing with a cold, emotionless style, she had been winning consistently. Her attention was suddenly caught by the stare of a dark, handsome gentleman whom she did not know and who seemed to be reproving her. When her luck changed and she lost all her money, she returned to her room to find a letter from her mother requesting her immediate return to England. Before she left, Gwendolen decided that she would have one more fling at the gaming tables. She sold her turquoise necklace for the money to play roulette, but before she could get to the tables, the necklace was repurchased and returned to her with an anonymous note. Certain that the unknown man was her benefactor, she felt that she could not very well return to the roulette table. She went back to England as soon as she could. Her mother had recalled her because the family had lost all their money through unwise business speculations.

A high-spirited, willful, accomplished, and intelligent girl, Gwendolen was Mrs. Davilow's only child by her first marriage, and her favorite. By her second marriage—Mr. Davilow was also dead—she had four colorless, spiritless daughters. About a year before, she had moved to Offendene to be near her sister and brother-in-law, the prosperous, socially acceptable Gascoignes. She also wished to arrange a profitable marriage for her oldest daughter. Gwendolen's beauty and manner had impressed all the surrounding gentry, but her first victim was her cousin, affable Rex Gascoigne. Although he had been willing to give up his career at Oxford for Gwendolen, his family refused to sanction so unwise a move. Rex, broken in spirit, was sent away temporarily, but Gwendolen remained unmoved by the whole affair.

Soon afterward, the county became excited over the visit of Mallinger Grandcourt, the somewhat aloof, unmarried heir to Diplow and several other large properties owned by Sir Hugo Mallinger. All the young ladies were eager to get Grandcourt to notice them, but it was Gwendolen, apparently indifferent and coy in conversation with the well-mannered but monosyllabic Grandcourt, who had most success. For several weeks, Grandcourt courted Gwendolen, yet neither forced to any crisis the issue of possible marriage. Gwendolen's mother, uncle, and aunt urged her to try to capture Grandcourt. Just when it seemed that Grandcourt would propose and Gwendolen would accept, Mrs. Lydia Glasher appeared. She had been brought to the scene by the scheming of Grandcourt's companion, Lush, to tell Gwendolen that she was the mother of four of Grandcourt's illegitimate children and that she had left her husband to live with Grandcourt. She begged Gwendolen not to accept Grandcourt so that she might have the chance to secure him as the rightful father of her children. Gwendolen, promising not to stand in Mrs. Glasher's way, had gone immediately to join friends at Leubronn.

Before he came to Leubronn, Daniel Deronda, the man whom Gwendolen had encountered in the gambling casino, had been Sir Hugo Mallinger's ward. He did not know his parents, but Sir Hugo had always treated him well. Sir Hugo, who had married late in life, had only daughters. Although he lavished a great deal of expense and affection on Deronda, his property was to go to his nephew, Mallinger Grandcourt. At Cambridge, Deronda had been extremely popular. There, too, he had earned the undying gratitude of a poor student named Hans Meyrick, whom Deronda helped to win a scholarship at the expense of his own studies. One day after leaving Cambridge while in a boat on the river, Deronda saved a pale and frightened young woman, Mirah Lapidoth, from committing suicide. She told him that she was a Jewess who had returned after years of wandering with a brutal and blasphemous father to look for her lost and fondly remembered mother and brother in London. Deronda took her to Mrs. Meyrick's home. There Mrs. Meyrick and her daughters nursed the penniless Mirah back to health.

When Gwendolen returned to Offendene, she learned that her family would be forced to move to a small cottage and that she would have to become a governess. The idea oppressed her so strongly that when she saw Grandcourt, who had been pursuing her on the Continent, she agreed at once to marry him in spite of her promise to Mrs. Glasher. Her mother, aunt, and uncle knew nothing of Mrs. Glasher; Grandcourt knew only that she had spoken to Gwendolen, knowledge that he kept to himself.

After their marriage, Grandcourt soon turned out to be a mean, domineering, and demanding man. He had set out to break Gwendolen's spirit, and he did. In the meantime, at several house parties, Gwendolen had met Daniel Deronda and found herself much attracted to him. At a New Year's party at Sir Hugo Mallinger's, Gwendolen, despite her husband's disapproval and biting reprisals, had spoken to Deronda frequently. When she told Deronda her whole story and confessed her guilt in breaking her promise to Mrs. Glasher, Deronda suggested that she show her repentance by living a less selfish life, caring for and helping others less fortunate than she. Gwendolen, realizing the folly of her marriage to Grandcourt and wishing to find some measure of happiness and peace, decided to follow the course Deronda had proposed.

Meanwhile, Deronda was attempting to secure Mirah's future and, if possible, to find her family. Mirah had been an actress and had some talent for singing. Deronda arranged an interview for her with Herr Klesmer, a German-Jewish musician with many connections, who could get Mirah started on a career. Herr Klesmer was very much impressed with Mirah's singing. He had known Gwendolen at Offendene and, in his honesty, had refused to help her when she also asked for singing engagements; he had thought her without sufficient talent and had given her ego its first blow. Herr Klesmer had also married Miss Arrowpoint, the most talented and attractive girl, save Gwendolen, in the vicinity of Offendene.

Still trying to find Mirah's family, Deronda went wandering in the London East End. There he became friendly with the family of Ezra Cohen, a shopkeeper of craft and generosity. On the basis of some slight evidence, for a time Deronda believed that the man might be Mirah's brother. There also, through Ezra's family, he met Mordecai, a feeble and learned man who immediately felt a great kinship with Deronda. Mordecai took Deronda to a meeting of his club, a group of men who discussed scholarly, political, and theological topics far removed from the commercial interests of Ezra.

Deronda was delighted when he finally learned that Mordecai was really

Mirah's brother. This discovery helped Deronda to acknowledge and accept his own spiritual and literal kinship with the Jews. The boy of unknown origin, able to move successfully in the high society of England, had found his real home in London's East End.

Critical Evaluation:

Daniel Deronda shifts from a novel depicting the difficulties and romances of a group of English people to a treatment of anti-Semitism in Victorian England. The character Daniel Deronda, the ward of Sir Hugo Mallinger, provides a bridge between the two portions of the book. With all its heavy evidence against the evil of anti-Semitism, the novel does not become an essay, for, throughout the work, George Eliot maintains sharp observation of the follies and delusions of Victorian life, as well as a keen sense of moral discrimination between her characters. Like *Middlemarch*, this novel is distinguished by realistic appraisals of people in all levels of society from the august and benevolent Sir Hugo Mallinger to Ezra Cohen, the crafty yet generous shopkeeper in the East End. If the novel does not show the consistency of theme or careful construction of Eliot at her best, it still propagandizes skillfully for worthy causes and creates a vivid, clear, and varied scheme of life.

Eliot's last novel, it is still a powerful and in some ways inspired work. It is as fascinating in its defects as in its successes, since both reflect not only the author's established strengths as a novelist but also her inventiveness and willingness to explore new areas and strive for greater depth and breadth in her fiction. *Daniel Deronda*, therefore, shares with its predecessors a penetrating insight into human relationships, a sensitive portrayal of individual moral and emotional growth, an astute and critical analysis of Victorian values, and a unifying moral vision of life. At the same time, many of the novel's shortcomings result from Eliot's ambitious experimentation with new methods, issues, and emphases; *Daniel Deronda* contains several new departures. A love story like the earlier works, this novel presents a love story with entirely new angles: Gwendolen marries for power, only to be later attracted to a man (Daniel) whose loyalties are divided between her and another woman; the sexual aspect of love relationships is explored with uncommon openness; certain feelings and emotions are treated that were almost universally ignored by Eliot's contemporaries; and the typical happy ending is denied the heroine, who instead grows in emotional and moral maturity as a result of her sufferings.

The two major weaknesses in the novel lie in the presentation of the Jewish problem and in the characterization of Daniel Deronda. Eliot tends to paint too consistently glowing a picture of the Jewish characters. The portrayal of Mirah's father Lapidoth is splendid but is the exception; in general, Mirah, Mordecai, Daniel, and the others suffer from idealization and from their language, which is often sentimental, stylized, or oversimplified. The author's almost uniform approval of the Jewish characters is further accentuated by contrast to her portrayal of the English figures, who are without exception (although to varying degrees) treated critically or satirically. The Wessex gentry are exposed for their shallowness, hypocrisy, and greed; Grandcourt represents a particular type of English gentleman in his cruelty, oppressiveness, contemptuous superiority, and narrow-mindedness; and the numerous minor characters serve as indictments of such Victorian faults as snobbishness, dullness, pretentiousness, and complacency. The second quite noticeable flaw in the novel is in the delineation of Daniel's character. Eliot endowed him with all the qualities requisite to make an interesting and complex personality—his excessive altruism, his ambivalence toward lower-class Jews, his jealousy of Hans Meyrick—and yet he comes across as a static, somewhat wooden, and rather unengaging figure; his actions are all predictable, and his personality is transparent. This problem is a result of Eliot's failure to develop Daniel's complexity through varied and shifting point of view as she does for all the other characters.

In spite of its weaknesses, however, *Daniel Deronda* exhibits Eliot's novelistic genius in numerous ways. The portrayal of Gwendolen Harleth is splendid; Eliot's masterful use of flashback and retrospection in the first half is highly effective; and the novel's conclusion is of rare force and realism. If Eliot's performance in *Daniel Deronda* falls short of her demanding and ambitious intent, the "experiment in life" that she has left the reader is nevertheless a great work of literature.

DAVID COPPERFIELD

Type of work: Novel
Author: Charles Dickens (1812–1870)
Type of plot: Sentimental romance
Time of plot: Early nineteenth century
Locale: England
First published: 1849–1850

>   *Principal characters:*
>   DAVID COPPERFIELD, the narrator
>   CLARA COPPERFIELD, his mother
>   MISS BETSEY TROTWOOD, David's grandaunt
>   CLARA PEGGOTTY, a nurse
>   MR. DANIEL PEGGOTTY, her brother
>   LITTLE EM'LY, his orphan niece
>   HAM, his orphan nephew
>   MR. MURDSTONE, David's stepfather
>   MISS JANE MURDSTONE, his sister
>   MR. CREAKLE, the master of Salem House
>   JAMES STEERFORTH, David's schoolmate
>   TOMMY TRADDLES, a student at Salem House
>   MR. WILKINS MICAWBER, a man of pecuniary difficulties
>   MR. WICKFIELD, Miss Trotwood's solicitor
>   AGNES WICKFIELD, his daughter
>   URIAH HEEP, a clerk
>   MR. SPENLOW, the man under whom David studied law
>   DORA SPENLOW, his daughter and later David's wife
>   MR. DICK, Miss Betsey's protégé

The Story:

David Copperfield was born at Blunderstone, in Suffolk, six months after his father's death. Miss Betsey Trotwood, an eccentric grandaunt, was present on the night of his birth, but she left the house abruptly and indignantly when she learned that the child was a boy who could never bear her name. David spent his early years with his pretty young mother, Clara Copperfield, and a devoted servant named Peggotty. Peggotty was plain and plump; when she bustled about the house, her buttons popped off her dress.

The youthful widow was soon courted by Mr. Murdstone, who proved to be stingy and cruel after marriage. When his mother married a second time, David was packed off with Peggotty to visit her relatives at Yarmouth. There her brother had converted an old boat into a seaside cottage, where he lived with his niece, Little Em'ly, and his sturdy young nephew, Ham. Little Em'ly and Ham were David's first real playmates, and his visit to Yarmouth remained a happy memory of his lonely and unhappy childhood. After Miss Jane Murdstone arrived to take charge of her brother's household, David and his mother were never to feel free again from the dark atmosphere of suspicion and gloom the Murdstones brought with them.

One day in a fit of childish terror, David bit his stepfather on the hand. He was immediately sent off to Salem House, a wretched school near London. There his life was more miserable than ever under a brutal headmaster named Creakle; but in spite of the harsh system of the school and the bullyings of Mr. Creakle, his life was endurable because of his friendship with two boys whom he was to meet again under much different circumstances in later life—lovable Tommy Traddles and handsome, lordly James Steerforth.

His school days ended suddenly with the death of his mother and her infant child. When he returned home, he discovered that Mr. Murdstone had dismissed Peggotty. Barkis, the stage driver, whose courtship had been meager but earnest, had taken Peggotty away to become Mrs. Barkis, and David was left friendless in the home of his cruel stepfather.

David was put to work in an export warehouse in which Murdstone had an interest. As a ten-year-old worker in the dilapidated establishment of the wine merchants Murdstone and Grinby, David was overworked and half-starved. He loathed his job and associates such as young Mick Walker and Mealy Potatoes. The youngster, however, met still another person with whom he was to associate in later life: Wilkins Micawber, a pompous ne'er-do-well in whose house David lodged. The impecunious Mr. Micawber found himself in debtor's prison shortly afterward. On his release, he decided to move with his brood to Plymouth. Having lost these good friends, David decided to run away from the environment he detested.

When David decided to leave Murdstone and Grinby, he knew he could not return to his stepfather. The only other relative he could think of was his father's aunt, Miss Betsey Trotwood, who had flounced indignantly out of the house on the night of David's birth. Hopefully, he set out for Dover where Miss Betsey lived, but not before he had been robbed of all his possessions. Consequently, he arrived at Miss Betsey's home physically and mentally wretched.

At first, David's reception was not cordial. Miss Betsey had never forgotten the injustice done her when David was born instead of a girl; however, upon the advice of Mr. Dick, a feebleminded distant kinsman who was staying with her, she decided to take David in, at least until he had been washed thoroughly. While she was deliberating further about what to do with her bedraggled nephew, she wrote to Mr. Murdstone, who came with his sister to Dover to claim his stepson. Miss Betsey decided she disliked both Murdstones intensely. Mr. Dick solved her problem by suggesting that she keep David.

Much to David's joy and satisfaction, Miss Betsey planned to let the boy continue his education and almost immediately sent him to a school in Canterbury, run by a Mr. Strong, a headmaster quite different from Mr. Creakle. During his stay at school, David lodged with Miss Betsey's lawyer, Mr. Wickfield. David became very fond of Agnes, Wickfield's daughter. At Wickfield's he also met Uriah Heep, Mr. Wickfield's cringing clerk, whose hypocritical humility and clammy handclasp filled David with disgust.

David finished school when he was seventeen years old. Miss Betsey suggested that he travel for a time before deciding on a profession. On his way to visit his old nurse Peggotty, David met James Steerforth and went home with his former schoolmate. There he met Steerforth's mother and Rosa Dartle, a girl passionately in love with Steerforth. Years before, the quick-tempered Steerforth had struck Rosa, who carried a scar as a reminder of Steerforth's brutality.

After a brief visit, David persuaded Steerforth to go with him to see Peggotty and her family. At Yarmouth, Steerforth met Little Em'ly. In spite of the fact that she was engaged to Ham, she and Steerforth were immediately attracted to each other.

At length, David told his grandaunt that he wished to study law. Accordingly, he was articled to the law firm of Spenlow and Jorkins. At this time, David saw Agnes Wickfield, who told him she feared Steerforth and asked David to stay away from him. Agnes also expressed a fear of Uriah Heep, who was on the point of entering into partnership with her senile father. Shortly after these revelations by Agnes, David encountered Uriah himself, who confessed that he wanted to marry Agnes. David was properly disgusted.

On a visit to the Spenlow home, David met and instantly fell in love with Dora Spenlow, his employer's pretty but childish daughter. Soon they became secretly engaged. Before this happy event, however, David heard some startling news—Steerforth had run away with Little Em'ly.

This elopement was not the only blow to David's happiness. Shortly after his engagement to Dora, David learned from his grandaunt that she had lost all her money; and Agnes informed him that Uriah Heep had become Mr. Wickfield's partner. David tried unsuccessfully to be released from his contract with Spenlow and Jorkins. Determined to show his grandaunt he could repay her, even in a small way, for her past sacrifices, he took a part-time job as secretary to Mr. Strong, his former headmaster.

The job with Mr. Strong, however, paid very little; therefore, David undertook to study for a position as a reporter of parliamentary debates. Even poor, simple Mr. Dick came to Miss Betsey's rescue, for Traddles, now a lawyer, gave him a job as a clerk.

The sudden death of Mr. Spenlow dissolved the partnership of Spenlow and Jorkins, and David learned to his dismay that his former employer had died almost penniless. With much study on his part, David became a reporter. At the age of twenty-one, he married Dora, who, however, never seemed capable of growing up. During these events, David had kept in touch with Mr. Micawber, now Uriah Heep's confidential secretary. Though something had finally turned up for Mr. Micawber, his relations with David and even with his own family were mysteriously strange, as though he were hiding something.

David soon learned the nature of the trouble; Mr. Micawber's conscience got the better of him. At a meeting arranged by him at Mr. Wickfield's, he revealed in Uriah's presence and to an assembled company including Agnes, Miss Betsey, David, and Traddles, the criminal perfidy of Uriah Heep, who for years had robbed and cheated Mr. Wickfield. Miss Betsey discovered that Uriah was also responsible for her own financial losses. With the exposure of the villainous Uriah, partial restitution both for her and for Mr. Wickfield was not long in coming.

Mr. Micawber's conscience was cleared by his exposure of Uriah Heep's villainy, and he proposed to take his family to Australia. There, he was sure something would again turn up. Mr. Peggotty and Little Em'ly also went to Australia; Little Em'ly had turned to her uncle in sorrow and shame after Steerforth had deserted her. David watched as their ship put out to sea. It seemed to him that the sunset was a bright promise for them as they sailed away to a new life in the new land. The darkness fell about him as he watched.

The great cloud now in David's life was his wife's delicate health. Day after day she failed, and in spite of his tenderest care, he was forced to see her grow more feeble and wan. Agnes Wickfield, like the true friend she had always been, was with him on the night of Dora's death. As in his earlier troubles, he turned to Agnes in the days that followed and found comfort in her sympathy and understanding.

Upon her advice, he decided to go abroad for a while. First, however, he went to Yarmouth to put a last letter from Little Em'ly into Ham's hands. There he witnessed the final act of her betrayal. During a storm, the heavy seas battered a ship in distress off the coast. Ham went to his death in a stouthearted attempt to rescue a survivor clinging to a broken mast. The bodies washed ashore by the rolling waves were those of loyal Ham and the false Steerforth.

David lived in Europe for three years. On his return, he discovered again his need for Agnes Wickfield's quiet friendship. One day, Miss Betsey Trotwood slyly suggested that Agnes might soon be married. Heavy in heart, David went off to offer her his good wishes. When she burst into tears, he realized that what he had hoped was true—her heart was already his. To the great delight of matchmaking Miss Betsey, Agnes and David were married, and David settled down to begin his career as a successful novelist.

Critical Evaluation:

"But, like many fond parents, I have in my heart of hearts a favorite child. And his name is David Copperfield."

This is Charles Dickens' final, affectionate judgment of the work that stands exactly in the middle of his novelistic career with seven novels before and seven after (excluding the unfinished *The Mystery of Edwin Drood*). When he began the novel, he was in his mid-thirties, secure in continuing success that had begun with *Sketches by Boz* (1836) and *Pickwick Papers* (1836–1837). It was a good time to take stock of his life and to make use of the autobiographical manuscript he had put by earlier; nor did he try to conceal the personal element from his public, which eagerly awaited each of the nineteen numbers of *David Copperfield*. The novel was issued serially from May, 1849, through November, 1850. Charles Dickens, writer, is readily identified with David Copperfield, writer, viewing his life through the "long Copperfieldian perspective," as Dickens called it.

Although much in the life of the first-person narrator corresponds to Dickens' own life, details are significantly altered. Unlike David, Dickens was not a genteel orphan but the eldest son of living and improvident parents; his own father served as the model for Micawber. Dickens' childhood stint in a shoeblacking factory seems to have been somewhat shorter than David's drudgery in the warehouse of the wine distributors Murdstone and Grinby, but the shame and suffering were identical. Young Dickens failed in his romance with a pretty young girl, but the author Dickens permits David to win his Dora. Dickens, however, inflicts upon Dora as Mrs. Copperfield the faults of his own Kate, who, unlike Dora, lived on as his wife until their separation in 1858.

However fascinating the autobiographical details, *David Copperfield* stands primarily on its merits as a novel endowed with the bustling life of Dickens' earlier works but controlled by his maturing sense of design. The novel in its entirety answers affirmatively the question posed by David himself in the opening sentence: "Whether I shall turn out to be the hero of my own life."

In addition to the compelling characterization of the protagonist, the novel abounds with memorable portrayals. The square face and black beard of Mr. Murdstone, always viewed in conjunction with that "metallic lady," Miss Murdstone, evoke the horror of dehumanized humanity. Uriah Heep's writhing body, clammy skin, and peculiarly lidless eyes suggest a subhuman form that is more terrifying than the revolting nature of his "umbleness." Above all the figures that crowd the lonely world of the orphan rises the bald head of Wilkins Micawber, flourishing the English language and his quizzing glass with equal impressiveness, confidently prepared in case some opportunity turns up.

David Copperfield, nevertheless, is very definitely the hero of his own story. This is a novel of initiation, organized around the two major cycles of the hero's development—first in childhood, then in early manhood. It focuses steadily upon the testing that will qualify him for full manhood. He makes his own choices, but each important stage of his moral progress is marked by the intervention of Aunt Betsey Trotwood.

Initially, David is weak simply because he is a child, the hapless victim of adult exploitation; but he is also heir to the moral weakness of his childish mother and his dead father, who was an inept, impractical man. Portentously, David's birth is the occasion of a conflict between his mother's Copperfieldian softness and Aunt Betsey's firmness, displayed in her rigidity of figure and countenance.

From a state of childish freedom, David falls into the Murdstone world. The clanking chains of Miss Murdstone's steel purse symbolize the metaphorical prison that replaces his innocently happy home. Indeed, for David, the world becomes a prison. After his five days of solitary confinement at Blunderstone, he enters the jail-like Salem House School. After his mother's death, he is placed in the grim warehouse, apparently for life; nor is his involvement with the Micawbers any real escape, for he is burdened with their problems and retains his place in the family even after their incarceration in the King's Bench Prison.

Although David repudiates the tyrannical firmness of which he is a victim, he does not actively rebel except for the one occasion when he bites Mr. Murdstone. Instead, like his mother, he indulges his weakness; he submits, fearfully to the Murdstones and Creakle, worshipfully to the arrogant Steerforth. In addition, he escapes into the illusory freedom of fantasy— through books and stories and through the lives of others, which he invests with an enchantment that conceals from him whatever is potentially tragic or sordid.

David's pliant nature, nevertheless, shares something of the resolute spirit of Aunt Betsey, despite her disappearance on the night of his birth. Looking back upon his wretched boyhood, David recalls that he kept his own counsel and did his work. From having suffered in secret, he moves to the decision to escape by his own act. The heroic flight is rewarded when Aunt Betsey relents and takes him in. Appropriately, she trusses up the small boy in adult clothes and announces her own goal of making him a "fine fellow, with a will of your own," with a "strength of character that is not to be influenced, except on good reason, by anybody, or by anything." The first cycle of testing is complete.

The conventionally happy years in Dover and Canterbury mark an interlude before the second major cycle of the novel, which commences with David's reentry into the world as a young man. Significantly, he at first resumes the docile patterns of childhood. Reunited with Steerforth, he once again takes pride in his friend's overbearing attitude. He allows himself to be bullied by various inferiors. He evades the obligation to choose his own career by entering into a profession that affects him like an opiate. In Dora's childlike charms, he recaptures the girlish image of his mother. At this point, however, the firm Aunt Betsey, having cut short his childhood trials, deliberately sets into motion his adult testing with her apparent bankruptcy.

In response to his new challenges, David is forced back upon his childhood resources. At first, he unconsciously imitates Murdstone in trying to mold Dora; but he again rejects tyranny, choosing instead resignation, understanding that she can be no more than his "child-wife." He responds with full sympathy to the tragedy of Little Em'ly's affair with Steerforth, but he is finally disenchanted with the splendid willfulness that had captivated his boyish heart. Most important, he recovers the saving virtue of his childhood, his ability to suffer in secrecy, to keep his own counsel, and to do his work. As his trials pile up—poverty, overwork, disappointment in marriage, his wife's death, and the tribulations of the friends to whom his tender heart is wholly committed—he conquers his own undisciplined heart.

The mature man who emerges from his trials profits from his experiences and heritage. His capacity for secret suffering is, for him as for Aunt Betsey, a source of strength; but his, unlike hers, is joined to the tenderheartedness inherited from his parents. Her distrust of mankind has made her an eccentric. His trusting disposition, though rendering him vulnerable, binds him to mankind.

Although Aunt Betsey sets a goal of maturity before David, Agnes Wickfield is the symbol of the hard-won self-discipline which he finally achieves. She is from the beginning his "better angel." Like him, she is tenderhearted and compliant; yet, though a passive character, she is not submissive, and she is always in control of herself in even the most difficult human relationships. Moreover, her firmness of character is never distorted by fundamental distrust of mankind; thus hers is the only influence that David should accept, "on good reason," in his pursuit of the moral goal that Aunt Betsey sets before him.

By the time David has recognized his love for Agnes, he has also attained a strength of character like hers. The appropriate conclusion to his quest for maturity is his union with Agnes—who is from the beginning a model of the self-disciplined person in whom gentleness and strength are perfectly balanced. Furthermore, the home he builds with her is the proper journey's end for the orphaned child who has grasped at many versions of father, mother, family, and home: "Long miles of road then opened out before my mind, and toiling on, I saw a ragged way-worn boy forsaken and neglected, who should come to call even the heart now beating against him, his own." He has outgrown the child-mother, the child-wife, the childhood idols, even the childhood terrors, and he is a mature man ready to accept love "founded on a rock."

In the context of a successful completed quest, the novel ends with a glimpse of the complete man, who writes far into the night to erase the shadows of his past but whose control of the realities is sufficient in the presence of the woman who is always, symbolically, "near me, pointing upward!"

DEATH OF A HERO

Type of work: Novel
Author: Richard Aldington (1892–1962)
Type of plot: Social criticism
Time of plot: World War I
Locale: England
First published: 1929

        Principal characters:
            GEORGE WINTERBOURNE, a man killed in the war
            MR. GEORGE WINTERBOURNE, his father
            MRS. GEORGE WINTERBOURNE, his mother
            ELIZABETH, his wife
            FANNY WELFORD, his mistress

The Story:

When word was received that George Winterbourne had been killed in the war, his friend tried to reconstruct the life of the dead man in order to see what forces had caused his death. The friend had served with George at various times during the war, and it was his belief that George had deliberately exposed himself to German fire because he no longer wanted to live.

George Winterbourne's father had been a sentimental fool and his mother a depraved wanton. The elder Winterbourne had married primarily to spite his dominating mother, and his bride had married him under the mistaken notion that he was rich. They gave themselves up to mutual hatred, and the mother showered her thwarted love on young George. She imagined herself young and desirable and was proud of her twenty-two lovers. Her husband conveniently went to a hotel when she was entertaining, but he prayed for her soul. All in all, they were the most depressing parents to whom a child could be exposed, and undoubtedly, they caused young George to hate them both. Soon after receiving word of their son's death, the elder Winterbourne was killed in an accident. After thoroughly enjoying her role as a bereft mother and widow, Mrs. Winterbourne married her twenty-second lover and moved to Australia.

When he reached young manhood, George mingled with all sorts of queer people. He dabbled in writing and painting—the modern variety. Sexual freedom was his goal, even though he had experienced little of it. At an affair given by his pseudointellectual friends, he first met Elizabeth. They were immediately compatible; both hated their parents, and both sought freedom. At first, Elizabeth was shocked by George's attacks on Christianity, morals, the class system, and all other established institutions, but she soon recognized him as a truly "free" man. In fact, it was not long before she adopted his ideas and went him one better. Free love was the only thing she could talk or think about. Thinking themselves extremely sensible, they saw no reason to marry in order to experience love as long as they were careful not to have a baby. Babies complicated matters, for the ignorant middle classes still frowned on such children. Unknowingly, George and Elizabeth were about as middle class as it was possible to be.

The two lovers planned carefully to have no sordidness cloud their affair. They did not talk of love, only sex. They were to take all the other lovers they pleased. That was freedom in an intelligent way. Elizabeth was even more insistent than George upon such freedom.

Finally, Elizabeth mistakenly thought that she was pregnant. Gone were the new freedoms, the enlightened woman; George must marry her at once, for female honor was at stake. All the old clichés were dragged out for poor old George. They were married, much to the horror of their families. When the mistake was discovered, supplemented by the doctor's statement that Elizabeth could not possibly have a child without an operation, back came freedom, stronger than ever. She became an evangelist for sex, even though she detested the word. Marriage made no difference in their lives. They continued to live separately, meeting as lovers.

When Elizabeth had to make a trip home, George became the lover of her best friend, Fanny Welford, another enlightened woman. He was sure that Elizabeth would not mind, for she had become the mistress of Fanny's lover; thus, he was quite stunned when Elizabeth created a scene over Fanny. The girls, however, remained surface friends, each one too free to admit horror at the other's duplicity.

While these friends had been practicing their enlightened living, war had been approaching fast. George was drafted and sent quickly to France. The war poisoned George. Killing horrified him, and he began to imagine his own death. He was brave, but not from any desire to be a hero; it was just that the monotony of his existence seemed to demand that he keep going even though he was ready to drop from fatigue. The knowledge of the ill-concealed dislike between Fanny and Elizabeth began to prey on his mind. There seemed to be only two solutions: to drift along and accept whatever happened or to get himself killed in the war. It seemed to make little difference to him or anyone else which course he chose. His letters to his two women depressed each of them. Had he known their feelings, he could have been spared his worry about them. Each took other lovers and gave little thought to George.

His own depression increased. He felt that he was degenerating mentally as well as physically and that he was wasting what should have been his best years. He knew that he would be terribly handicapped if he did live through the war, that those not serving would have passed him by.

George was made an officer and sent back to England for training. There he lived again with Elizabeth, but she left him frequently to go out with other men. Fanny, too, seemed to care little whether she saw him or not. Talk of the war and his experiences obviously bored them, and they made only a small pretense of interest. He spent his last night in England with Fanny while Elizabeth was off with someone else. Fanny did not bother to get up with him the morning he left. In fact, she awoke lazily and then went to sleep again before he even left the flat.

Back at the front, George found that he was ill-suited to command a company. Although he did his best, he was constantly censured by his colonel, who blamed George for all the faults of his untrained and cowardly troops. George could think of little but death. During a particularly heavy German shelling, he simply stood upright and let the bullets smash into his chest. No one knows whether his death was an act of heroism or one of complete and utter futility.

Critical Evaluation:

Richard Aldington records the incredible innocence and disillusionment of the first generation of the modern world—if one takes that world to have begun in 1914. Like Robert Graves's memoir *Goodbye to All That*, Ford Madox Ford's *Parade's End*, and the poetry of Rupert Brooke, Charles Sorley, and Siegfried Sasson, *Death of a Hero* dramatizes the impact of the "Great War" upon the children of the late Victorians. Raised in the twilight of that age to believe that their culture rested on granite, they discovered that it, as well as their own lives, had no more foundation than a bed of quicksand.

The accomplishment of Aldington's novel consists in his perception that the seeds of war lay not only in the greed and stupidity of the politicians but also—and more importantly—in the anarchy of personal relationships. The first generation of the twentieth century was unprepared for war as well as unfit to carry on their own love lives. The repression and hypocrisy of their Victorian parents destroyed any chance that young George Winterbourne, Elizabeth, and Fanny have of forming adult relationships. Their sexual lives are those of children let out of school who are unable to handle their newfound freedom; ignorance combined with license must always end in violence.

The title of the novel is, of course, ironic. The traditional idea of the hero—especially the military one—is of the great man who sacrifices himself for the good of society. George Winterbourne's end comes with a whimper, not a bang; his death is at last an admission that he no longer has the will to continue. Insofar as he represents his generation, his suicide suggests its inability to understand and unwillingness to deal with a world that it has not made.

With cynicism that is almost morbid in its brutality, Aldington here tells the story of a soldier killed in World War I. It was the author's belief that the hero deliberately allowed himself to be killed, so confused and miserable was the life which he had attempted to divide between his wife and mistress. The author, attempting to show that the shabby childhood through which the hero lived was responsible for his troubles, purports to tell only the truth; but the truth as he sees it is so bitter that in the telling, Aldington condemns not only a generation but also a whole society.

THE DEATH OF THE HEART

Type of work: Novel
Author: Elizabeth Bowen (1899–1973)
Type of plot: Psychological realism
Time of plot: After World War I
Locale: London and Seale, England
First published: 1938

> *Principal characters:*
> THOMAS QUAYNE, the owner of Quayne and Merrett, an
> advertising agency
> ANNA QUAYNE, his wife
> PORTIA QUAYNE, his sixteen-year-old half sister
> ST. QUENTIN MILLER, an author and a friend of the Quaynes
> EDDIE, an employee of Quayne and Merrett
> MAJOR BRUTT, a retired officer
> MRS. HECCOMB, Anna's former governess

The Story:

Anna Quayne's pique demanded an outlet—she could no longer contain it all within herself; therefore, while St. Quentin Miller shivered with cold, she marched him around the frozen park, delivering herself of her discontent. The trouble, of course, had started with Portia, for the Quayne household had not been the same since the arrival of Tom's sixteen-year-old half sister. Not that Portia was all to blame; the business had begun with a deathbed wish. Who could expect dying old Mr. Quayne to ask Tom to take a half sister he hardly knew, keep her for at least a year, and give her a graceful start in life? As she explained to St. Quentin, Anna herself hardly knew how to cope with the arrangement, although she had tried to accept it with outward tranquillity. Now she had stumbled across the girl's diary, glimpsed her own name, and had been tempted to read. It was obvious that Portia was less than happy and that she was scanning the atmosphere of her brother's house with an unflattering eye.

While Anna was thus unburdening herself, the subject of her discussion returned home quietly from Miss Paullie's lessons. She was vaguely disturbed to learn from Matchett, the housekeeper, that Anna had commented upon the clutter in Portia's bedroom. Later, she shared tea with Anna and St. Quentin when they came in tingling with cold; but the atmosphere seemed a bit stiff, and Portia readily acquiesced in Anna's suggestion that she join her brother in his study. Portia felt more at ease with Tom, even though he obviously found conversation with her awkward.

By now, Portia knew that there was no one in whom she could readily confide. At 2 Windsor Terrace, Matchett offered a certain possessive friendship; at school, only the inquisitive Lilian took notice of her. Major Brutt was better than either of these; in her presence, his eyes showed a fatherly gleam, and she liked the picture puzzle he had sent. Anna tolerated the Major—he was her only link with an old friend, Pidgeon—but Major Brutt seldom ventured to call, and Portia saw him mostly in the company of others.

Another of Anna's friends whom Portia sometimes saw was Eddie. Eddie, however, was Anna's property and seemingly beyond the range of Portia's clumsy probing for companionship. He was twenty-three years old and brightly self-assured as well. Anna found it amusing to have him around, although she often rebuked his conceit and presumption; she went so far as to find him a job with Quayne and Merrett. One day, Portia handed Eddie his hat as he took leave of Anna; the next day he wrote to her. Before long, they were meeting regularly and secretly.

Having no wish to alienate Anna, Eddie cautioned Portia not to mention him in her diary, but he reveled in Portia's uncritical adoration. They went to the zoo, to tea, and ultimately to his apartment. Matchett, who found Eddie's letter under Portia's pillow, soon became coldly jealous of his influence. Even Anna and Tom became slightly restive as they began to realize the situation. Meanwhile, Portia was falling deeper and deeper in love. When Eddie lightly declared that it was a pity they were too young to marry, Portia innocently took his remarks as a tentative proposal. Although he carefully refrained from real lovemaking, Portia felt sure he returned her love.

With the approach of spring, Anna and Tom revealed their intention of spending a few weeks in Capri. Since Matchett would houseclean while they were gone, they decided to send Portia to Mrs. Heccomb, Anna's old governess, who lived in a seaside house at Seale. Portia, dismayed by the prospect of separation from Eddie, was only partially consoled by his promise to write.

Eddie did write promptly; so did Major Brutt, with the promise of another picture puzzle; and Seale, happily, turned out better than expected. Having none of Anna's remoteness, Mrs. Heccomb deluged her guest with carefree chatter. Her two grown-up stepchildren reacted somewhat more cautiously, since they were prepared to find Portia a highbrow. Finding her only shy, they quickly relaxed; the radio blared while they vigorously shouted over it about roller skating, hockey games, and Saturday night parties. Portia gradually withdrew from her shell of loneliness. Within a few days, she felt enough at home to ask Daphne Heccomb if Eddie might spend a weekend at Seale. Daphne consented to relay the request to her mother, and Mrs. Heccomb affably approved.

Eddie's visit was not a success. His efforts to be the life of the party soon had Mrs. Heccomb wondering about the wisdom of her invitation. At the cinema, his good fellowship extended to holding hands enthusiastically with Daphne. When distressed Portia uttered mild reproaches, he intimated that she was a naïve child. Walking together in the woods on their final afternoon, Portia learned that Eddie had no use for her love unless it could remain uncritical and undemanding. Her vision of an idyllic reunion shattered into bits as she began to see his instability. Two weeks later, her stay at Seale ended. Back in London, Matchett triumphantly informed her that Eddie had left word that he would be out of town a few days.

Walking home from school not long afterward, Portia encountered St. Quentin, who inadvertently revealed Anna's perusal of the diary. Upset, she sought comfort from Eddie once more. No longer gratified by her devotion, he made her feel even more unwanted; and the sight of a letter from Anna, lying on Eddie's table, convinced her that they were allied against her. As she left his apartment, it seemed unthinkable that she could ever return to Windsor Terrace; her only possible refuge now was Major Brutt. She went, therefore, to the Karachi Hotel, surprising the worthy Major as he finished his dinner. Surprise changed to alarm as she pleaded her case: Would he take her away, would he marry her? She could relieve his loneliness, she could care for him, she could polish his shoes. With as much serenity as he could muster, the Major affirmed that polishing shoes was a job women had little success with; with a little time and patience, her position would soon appear less desperate. He wished very much to call the Quaynes, for it was getting late and they would be worried. Portia felt that she had been defeated, but she could still choose ground on which to make a final stand. Very well, she finally agreed, he might call them, but he was not to tell them she was coming. That would depend, she finished enigmatically but firmly, on whether they chose to do the right thing.

The Major had been right; the Quaynes were worried. After the telephone rang, their momentary relief was succeeded by real confusion. What, after all, would Portia consider the right thing for them to do? It would have to be simple, without fuss or feathers. With help from St. Quentin, they finally decided, and Matchett was sent in a taxi to fetch her.

Critical Evaluation:

Maturity's gain in awareness, Elizabeth Bowen implies in *The Death of the Heart,* is offset by childhood's loss in idealism and simplicity; adulthood involves compromises with one's heart and thoughts which the young find intolerable, at least at first. Thus, the arrival of Portia, with her innocent longings and candid curiosity, provides a catalyst for an upper middle-class English household where compromise and boredom have long held sway.

Portia's loneliness and her search for love and understanding are characteristic of her age, sex, and particular situation; but Bowen never allows the
individual to be submerged in the typical. Although the ending of the story
is no more conclusive than life itself, it crystallizes some truths that are often elusive.

Sixteen-year-old Portia Quayne may seem to be the protagonist of *The
Death of the Heart*, but her role actually serves to illustrate the shallowness
of the world of Thomas and Anna. Portia's progressive disillusionment with
the "real" world of adult life is detailed in the three sections of the novel—
"The World," "The Flesh," and "The Devil." Her disenchantment, sensi-
tively portrayed by a sympathetic narrator, is in every case contrasted to
Anna's passionless existence. Life at 2 Windsor Terrace, so idealized by
Portia's dead father, is "the world" of the first stage of her disillusionment.
Eddie—with his fickle attention and passes at Daphne—constitutes the
temptation and disillusionment of "the flesh." "The devil" is the novelist
St. Quentin Miller, who with "no loyalty" reveals to Portia that Anna has
been reading her diary and laughing with others about it. The structure of
the novel is carefully worked out, so that Anna's opening revelation to
St. Quentin of having read Portia's diary becomes the catalyst for the crisis
of the end. The body of the novel gives the details of the contrast between
Portia's romantic illusions and the Quaynes' disillusioning boredom. Significantly, the section titles of the novel refer to the baptismal rite in the Book
of Common Prayer.

In the end, Portia's demand for "the right thing" forces Anna and
Thomas to understand the sterility of their lives and of the "preposterous
world," devoid of value. Anna finally empathizes with Portia as she muses
that Portia must have a "frantic desire to be handled with feeling" as well
as a wish "to be let alone." Matchett, the only adult interested in tradition
or value, ends the novel with her interior monologue in the taxi. As she
enters the hotel to meet Portia, the strident sounds of a piano come
together in a harmonious chord. This resolution suggests, at least, a new
beginning for Portia and Anna, each having learned from the other: Portia
that the heart dies a little, and Anna that the heart does not completely die.

Elizabeth Bowen's greatest talent lies in detailing the inner life of a
young person and the subtleties of the tensions between generations.

DECLINE AND FALL
An Illustrated Novelette

Type of work: Novel
Author: Evelyn Waugh (1903–1966)
Type of plot: Social satire
Time of plot: Twentieth century
Locale: England and Wales
First published: 1928

Principal characters:

PAUL PENNYFEATHER, a serious-minded young Oxonian
SIR ALASTAIR DIGBY-VAINE-TRUMPINGTON, a young aristocrat
ARTHUR POTTS, a noble-minded young man
DR. AUGUSTUS FAGAN, the head of Llanabba Castle School
FLOSSIE and
DIANA, his daughters
MR. PRENDERGAST, a former clergyman
CAPTAIN GRIMES, a public-school man
PETER BESTE-CHETWYNDE, one of Paul's pupils
MARGOT BESTE-CHETWYNDE, his mother
SOLOMON PHILBRICK, a confidence man
SIR HUMPHREY MALTRAVERS, later Lord Metroland and a
  British politician

The Story:

At Scone College in Oxford, the annual dinner of the Bollinger Club ended with the breaking of glass. Reeling out of Sir Alastair Digby-Vaine-Trumpington's rooms, the drunken aristocrats ran to earth the inoffensive divinity student, Paul Pennyfeather, and forcibly left him trouserless before they went roaring off into the night.

Bollinger members could be fined, but the college authorities felt that Paul deserved more severe punishment for running across the quadrangle in his shorts, and he was sent down for indecent behavior. After informing him that under his father's will his legacy could be withheld for unsatisfactory behavior, his unsympathetic guardian virtuously announced his intention to cut off Paul's allowance.

Through a shoddy firm of scholastic agents, Paul became a junior assistant master at Llanabba Castle, Wales. Llanabba was not a good school. Its head was Dr. Augustus Fagan, whose lectures on service were intended to cover up the inadequacies of his institution. He had two daughters—

Flossie, a vulgar young woman of matrimonial ambitions, and Diana, who economized on sugar and soap. One of the masters was Mr. Prendergast, a former clergyman who suffered from doubts. The other was Captain Grimes, who wore a false leg and was, as he frankly admitted, periodically in the soup. A bounder and a scoundrel, he put his faith in the public-school system, which may kick a man out but never lets him down. Grimes thought he had been put on his feet more often than any public-school man alive. His reluctant engagement to Flossie was his protection against the next time he found himself in trouble.

Paul was in charge of the fifth form. When he met his class for the first time, most of the boys claimed that their name was Tangent. An uproar arose between the would-be Tangents and a few non-Tangents; Paul announced that the writer of the longest essay would receive half a crown. Mr. Prendergast wondered why Paul's classes were always so quiet. His own students behaved outrageously and made fun of his wig. Paul found young Peter Beste-Chetwynde the most interesting of his pupils.

Arthur Potts was one of the few men Paul had known at Scone; he wrote that Alastair Trumpington had regretted Paul's dismissal and wanted to send him twenty pounds. Hearing of the offer, Grimes wired for the money in Paul's name.

Some parents planned to visit Llanabba Castle. Dr. Fagan decided to honor their visit with the annual field sports meet. Philbrick, the butler, objected to his extra duties. He confided to Paul that he was a crook who had taken the post in order to kidnap little Lord Tangent but that he had reformed after falling in love with Diana. He told Mr. Prendergast that he was really Sir Solomon Philbrick, a millionaire shipowner, and he left Grimes under the impression that he was a novelist collecting material for a book.

The sports meet was not a gala occasion. Lady Circumference, Lord Tangent's mother, was rude to everyone in distributing the prizes. The Llanabba Silver Band played. Margot Beste-Chetwynde created a social flurry when she arrived with a black man. Mr. Prendergast, the starter, accidentally shot Lord Tangent in the heel. Later, he became abusively drunk. Paul, without intending to, fell in love at first sight with Peter Beste-Chetwynde's beautiful widowed mother.

The term dragged to a close. Lord Tangent's foot became infected, and he died. Grimes, landing in the soup once more, announced his engagement to Flossie, but the marriage turned out as badly as he had expected. Detectives arrived to arrest Philbrick on charges of false pretense, but their man had already flown. A few days later, Grimes's clothing and a suicide note were discovered on the beach.

Engaged to tutor Peter during the vacation, Peter went to Margot's country house, King's Thursday. When she bought the place from her impoverished bachelor brother-in-law, Lord Pastmaster, it had been the finest example of Tudor domestic architecture in England. Bored with it, however, she had commissioned Otto Silenus, an eccentric designer, to build a modernistic house in its place. Silenus built a structure of concrete, glass, and aluminum, a house for dynamos, not people; but people went there anyway for endless house parties.

When Paul finally found enough courage to propose to Margot, she accepted him because Peter thought the young Oxonian would make a better stepfather than rival suitor, Sir Humphrey Maltravers, Minister of Transport. During preparations for the wedding, Paul learned that Margot still carried on her father's business, a syndicate vaguely connected with amusement enterprises in South America. Grimes turned up mysteriously in her employ. Potts, now working for the League of Nations, also took an unexplained interest in Margot's business affairs.

A few days before the wedding, Margot asked Paul to fly to Marseilles and arrange for the passage of several cabaret entertainers to Rio de Janeiro. He did so without realizing that he was bribing the officials he interviewed. On his wedding morning, Paul was having a final drink with Alastair Trumpington when a Scotland yard inspector appeared and arrested him on charges of engaging in an international white-slave traffic.

Margot fled to her villa at Corfu and did not appear at the trial. Potts, a special investigator for the League of Nations, was the chief witness for the prosecution. Convicted of Margot's crimes, Paul was sentenced to seven years' penal servitude. He served the first part of his sentence at Blackstone Gaol, where he found Philbrick a trusty and Mr. Prendergast the chaplain. Shortly after, Prendergast was killed by a crazed inmate, and Paul was removed to Egdon Health Penal Settlement. Grimes was one of his fellow prisoners, but not for long. One day while serving on a work gang, he walked off into the fog. Everyone assumed that he perished later in a swamp, but Paul believed otherwise. Grimes, whose roguery was timeless, could never die. Margot came to visit Paul. She announced her intention to marry Maltravers, now Lord Metroland and the Home Secretary.

Paul's escape from Egdon Heath was carefully contrived. On orders from the Home Secretary, he was removed for an appendicitis operation in a nursing home owned by Dr. Fagan, who had forsaken education for medicine. After a drunken doctor had signed a death certificate stating that Paul had died under the anesthetic, Alastair Trumpington, who had become Margot's young man, put him on a yacht that carried him to Margot's villa at Corfu. Officially dead, Paul enjoyed the rest he thought he deserved. Wearing a heavy mustache, he returned to Scone some months later to continue his reading for the church. When the chaplain mentioned another Pennyfeather, a wild undergraduate sent down for misconduct, Paul said that the young man was a distant cousin.

At Scone, the annual dinner of the Bollinger Club ended with the breaking of glass. Paul was reading in his room when Peter Beste-Chetwynde, Lord Pastmaster since his uncle's death, came in; he was very drunk. Paul's great mistake, Peter said, was that he had become involved with people like Margot and himself. After his departure, Paul settled down to read another chapter in a book on early church heresies.

Critical Evaluation:

Decline and Fall mingles farce with grim tragedy. Episodic in form, with many of its scenes no more than a page or so in length, it is a penetrating yet hilarious study of disordered English society in the period between wars. Evelyn Waugh insists that his books are not intended as satires, since the satirical spirit presupposes a stable and homogeneous society against which to project its critical exposure of folly and vice. For all that, the writer demonstrates in this novel a tremendous talent for comic satire. Paul Pennyfeather's misadventures reflect one phase of the contemporary mood of disillusionment. On the other hand, Grimes, a bounder and a cad, is timeless, a figure who would have been as much at home in the days of the Caesars as he was in the reign of King George V. Waugh's distortions and exaggerations have also the quality of fantasy, for in his pages the impossible and the believable exist on the same plane at the same time.

Decline and Fall is the first and possibly the best work of Waugh, a luminary of the brave company of English satirists. The novel is notable for its economy of time and space. The action extends over a year, and the protagonist's circumstances at the beginning and end are virtually identical, lending a neat roundness to the story. Another feature is the spareness of the prose and the unlabored epigrams, as, for example, Paul Pennyfeather's quip that the English public school is a perfect conditioner for life in prison. Waugh lays low individuals and whole classes of society with a flick of a proper name: Digby-Vaine-Trumpington for a vain, trumpeting young aristocrat; Maltravers for a Secretary of Transportation; Prendergast for a clergyman aghast at his apprehension of divine indifference; Grimes for an earthy rascal; Pennyfeather for an impecunious, half-fledged scholar.

The tone is persistently cheerful. No amazement is expressed, even by the innocent and beleaguered protagonist, at anything that befalls him. Tragedies occur offstage. The death of Prendergast, for example, is revealed in a hymn. Lord Tangent's demise is recorded as follows: in chapter 8, he is shown crying because he has been wounded in the foot by a bullet from the starter's pistol; in chapter 12, Beste-Chetwynde reports in an aside that Tangent's foot is gangrened; in chapter 13 the news comes that the foot is being amputated; and finally in chapter 19, it is reported in an offhand way that he has died. The list of groups and institutions that

excite the author's scorn is extensive; his opprobrium falls on the aristocracy, the newly rich, the universities, the public schools, old-school penology, newfangled penology, the House of Lords, the House of Commons,
the Church of England, historical landmarks, modern architecture, and the
League of Nations, to name a few. Although the novel manages to be
hilarious at the expense of practically everybody, it has a serious side, or
rather a serious center; namely, the schoolboy virtue of Pennyfeather contrasted with the cheery rascality of Grimes.

It is evident from the start that Paul Pennyfeather is a right thinker and
a square shooter. He owes his educational opportunities as much to his
own industry, intelligence, and moderation as to the legacy left by his parents. He is earnest, diffident, and idealistic; in short, he is the very model
of a middle-class English divinity student. The incredible things that happen to him seem at first reading to represent repeated assaults of a corrupt
society on a genuinely decent character. Captain Grimes, on the other
hand, shows up as a bounder of the very worst kind, a poseur who relies
on public-school connections to rescue him from his frequent immersions in
"the soup." He milks the fellowship of honor and duty for all it is worth
and does not hesitate to abandon ship at the first sign of bad weather—
women, children, and gentlemanly behavior notwithstanding.

For all his roguery, however, Grimes is not a villain. He is instead the
most sympathetic character in the novel. The chief element of his personality is common sense; it is he, and not Pennyfeather, who is the author's
persona, who embodies the impulses of sanity as opposed to the precepts
of class and culture. During the war, for example, when faced with court-
martial or honorable suicide, he relies on drink and old school ties to see
him through alive, and they do. Trapped into marriage, he simply bolts,
once into the public schools, once into the sea. Imprisoned, he makes his
escape by sinking into a quicksand from which, Paul and the reader are
confident, he will rise to drink his pint in new guise but with the old
elemental verve. He is self-indulgent, brave, resourceful, and not to be
humbugged.

Although self-disciplined, Paul is meek, credulous, and fundamentally
passive by contrast. Everything that happens to him, good or bad, simply
happens. His rather mild passion for Margot Beste-Chetwynde strikes him
like lightning; his actual proposal of marriage is all Margot's doing. He ac-
quiesces alike to expulsion from college and rescue from prison with the
same spongy plasticity cloaked in a sort of ethical good-sportism. In fact, it
may be argued that believers in this schoolboy code of ethics suffer from a
profound moral laziness and invite the outrages perpetrated on them in its
name by those who do not believe in it. Paul's explanation of why he does
not outface Potts and take money from Trumpington is illustrative. He
defines a gentleman as someone who declines to accept benefits that are

not his by right or to profit from windfall advantage. Implicit in this stance are a kind of flabby ethical neutrality disguised as self-respect and a certain pride in taking no action. Grimes's judgment is sounder and more vigorous, for he recognizes Potts as a stinker in prosecuting Paul for a crime he committed inadvertently.

The author remarks at one stage that Paul does not have the makings of a hero. No more has he the makings of a villain, for villainy requires a certain enterprise as exemplified by Margot. It is not Paul's decline and fall that are recorded here but the degeneration of a society in which custom and privilege combine to nurture all manner of waste and wickedness. Paul is merely part of the problem. Grimes, the voice of blackguardism and good sense, is part of the solution. Paul toasts the stability of ideals, Grimes the passing moment.

Despite Grimes, however, *Decline and Fall* ends on a rather grim note, with Peter Beste-Chetwynde a wastrel and Paul embracing a pinched orthodoxy. The underlying sense is of honorable old forms giving way to a new and nastier regime, a theme that Waugh pursued in later works. Indeed, he espoused it in his own life to the extent of rejecting the new order altogether, and as a result, he was virtually a hermit at the time of his death.

DEIRDRE

Type of work: Novel
Author: James Stephens (1882–1950)
Type of plot: Legendary romance
Time of plot: The Heroic Age
Locale: Ireland
First published: 1923

> Principal characters:
> CONACHÚR MAC NESSA, King of Ulster
> CLOTHRU, his first wife
> MAEVE, his second wife
> CATHFA, his father and a magician
> LAVARCHAM, his conversation-woman
> FERGUS MAC ROY, his stepfather
> NESSA, his mother
> FELIMID MAC DALL, his storyteller
> DEIRDRE, Felimid's daughter and the ward of Conachúr
> UISNEAC, Conachúr's brother-in-law
> NAOISE,
> AINNLE, and
> ARDAN, Uisneac's sons

The Story:

The King of Ulster had a daughter who was called Assa, the Gentle. She loved knowledge and had many tutors. One day, returning from a visit to her father and finding her tutors killed, she buckled on her armor and set out to find the murderer. Henceforth her name was Nessa, the Ungentle. While she was bathing in the forest, Cathfa, the magician, saw and loved her. He offered to spare her life only if she would marry him. Their son was Conachúr mac Nessa. After a while, Nessa left Cathfa, taking her son with her.

When Conachúr was sixteen years old, Nessa was still the most beautiful woman in the land. Fergus mac Roy, the new King of Ulster, was only eighteen years old, but he fell in love with Nessa as soon as he saw her. She promised to marry him only if Conachúr could be king for a year while she and Fergus lived away from court. Fergus agreed; but after the year was up, Conachúr kept the throne, and Fergus became one of his most trusted followers.

Nessa arranged a marriage between Conachúr and Clothru, daughter of

---

the High King of Connacht. On a visit to her father, Clothru was killed by
her sister Maeve. Conachúr's first son was born just before she died.

Bent on vengeance, Conachúr went to Connacht. There he saw Maeve
and, changing his mind, he married her against her wishes. When she went
to Ulster with him, she took along great riches and also a guard of one
thousand men.

During one of his journeys at a time when Maeve had refused to accompany him, he stopped at the house of Felimid mac Dall, his storyteller.
That night, Conachúr sent a servant to say that Felimid's wife should sleep
with him. The servant returned to say that Felimid's wife could not accommodate him as she was then expecting a child. Soon the men heard the
wail of the newborn infant. Conachúr asked his father to interpret the wail
and other evil omens that men had seen recently. Cathfa prophesied that
the child then born, a girl, would be called The Troubler and that she
would bring evil and destruction in Ulster. When one of his followers suggested that Conachúr have the child killed immediately, he sent for the infant; but he decided it did not become a prince to evade fate, and he let
the child live. Deirdre was her name.

Conachúr had Deirdre brought up at Emania by Lavarcham, his conversation woman, who let the girl see no one but women servants and a
guard of the oldest and ugliest swordsmen in Ulster. Lavarcham could
adapt herself to any situation or group of people; while acting as a spy for
Conachúr, she also learned everything that had to be taught to Deirdre to
prepare her for the place Lavarcham had decided she should have in the
kingdom.

Lavarcham reported regularly to Conachúr so that, while he never saw
Deirdre, the King knew how she progressed month by month. He refused
to believe Lavarcham's glowing reports; besides, at that time, he was well
satisfied with Maeve. On the other hand, Lavarcham reported at length to
Deirdre about Conachúr until the child knew all his whims, his boldness,
and his majesty.

Maeve, who had never forgiven Conachúr for marrying her against her
will, finally decided to leave him. She was so unforgiving that she refused
to leave behind one thread of her clothes or one bit of her riches. Since
some of the riches included great herds of cattle, flocks of sheep, heaps of
silver and jewelry, and pieces of furniture, she had to make careful plans to
get everything away when Conachúr was not looking. She trusted no one
entirely, but she had a spy, mac Roth, who was even more diligent than
Conachúr's Lavarcham. He discovered that Conachúr was to take a trip to
Leinster; he even followed Conachúr's company for two full days until he
felt the group was far enough away to be unable to get back in time; then
he returned to help Maeve in her flight. Only Lavarcham guessed that
something might happen, but her messengers did not reach Conachúr

before Maeve had fled.

Conachúr grieved for Maeve, but he was unable to bring her back to Ulster. In the meantime, Lavarcham began to brood about the matter. The whole kingdom wanted the King to remarry, and Deirdre was age sixteen. Lavarcham persuaded the King to come to see Deirdre.

Although Lavarcham had taught Deirdre all that she needed to know about Conachúr, she did not realize that the child thought of the King as an ancient and feared him a little. Nor did Lavarcham know that Deirdre, longing for people of her own age, had learned how to escape the guards around Emania.

Deirdre was first tempted to go beyond the walls by a campfire that she wanted to investigate. Around it she saw three boys: Naoise, who was nineteen; Ainnle, who was seventeen; and Ardan, who was fourteen. They were the sons of Uisneac, who had married Conachúr's sister. Deirdre startled them when she first appeared in the light of the fire, but they all laughed and told so many good stories that she knew she would have to go back again. The younger boys insisted that Naoise would soon be the champion of Ulster, and Deirdre did not doubt it.

When Conachúr went to see Deirdre, he found her the most beautiful girl in Ulster, and he intended to marry her immediately. Lavarcham, however, made him wait a week, after which he would have a three-month feast. In love with Naoise, Deirdre was horrified at the idea of marrying one so old and huge, but several nights passed before she could make her way to the campfire again. At her pleading, the brothers took her out of the country.

Six years later, Conachúr decided that Deirdre and the sons of Uisneac should be brought back from Scotland, their place of refuge, but the boys would not return except under the protection of one of Conachúr's trusted men. Fergus and his sons were sent to Scotland with assurances of safety. Deirdre had a dream and begged Naoise not to leave, but he declared that Fergus was honorable.

When the travelers reached the coast of Ulster, Fergus was detained by one of Conachúr's men, and Fergus' sons took Deirdre and the sons of Uisneac under their protection. Arriving at Conachúr's court at night, they were lodged in the fortress called the Red Branch. Then Deirdre knew there would be trouble, because Conachúr had not received them under his own roof.

Conachúr sent his men to batter down the doors and to bring Deirdre to him. The sons of Uisneac and Fergus made quick sallies, dashing out one door and in another, and killed so many of Conachúr's warriors that at last the King ordered the fortress set afire. As Deirdre and the boys fled, Conachúr asked Cathfa to stop them. Cathfa cast a spell that made the boys drop their arms, and they were captured. Conachúr had the sons of

Fergus and Uisneac killed. When Deirdre knelt over Naoise's dead body, she sipped his blood and fell lifeless.

Critical Evaluation:

One of the primary features of the Irish literary Renaissance was the discovery, regeneration, and translation of ancient Irish myths into modern forms. Among the great Celtic legends, perhaps the most popular was the tragic love story of Deirdre, The Troubler, and her lover, Naoise. Probably the greatest artistic representations of this fable of fate, love, betrayal, and death are the dramatic versions by William Butler Yeats (*Deirdre*, 1907) and John Millington Synge (*Deirdre of the Sorrows*, 1910). However, although James Stephens' prose interpretation of the myth may lack the austere poetic grandeur of Yeats's play or the tragic intensity of Synge's, it has a psychological penetration and lively narrative thrust that makes it not unworthy of mention alongside those great predecessors.

In many ways, Stephens' version is the most modern of the Deirdre legend. Although very different from each other, both Yeats and Synge sought to capture the atmosphere of the romantic Irish past of legend and folklore in their plays. Stephens, however, is more interested in a modern psychological analysis of the characters and their actions. At the same time, he did not ignore the flavor of archaic Celtic myth; in developing his story, he took great pains to present the medieval culture and background as authentically and thoroughly as he could. *Deirdre*, therefore, contains that mixture of the lyrical and the Realistic, the ancient and the modern, and the solemn and the irreverent that characterizes Stephens' best work in all genres.

Stephens was a brilliant Irish writer of poetry and prose, whose best work was grounded in the early literature of his own country. Just as he attempted to bring Irish folklore to life in *The Crock of Gold*, so he tried to revitalize ancient Gaelic legend in *Deirdre*. In this novel, he wrote of the beautiful and mystical Deirdre, of brave and handsome Naoise, and of strong and willful Conachúr, who was loved by all his people and who was almost great. It is not only the people in the story that are remembered afterward, but there are also memorable scenes. *Deirdre* is a novel of legend and fantasy with a core of Realism.

It has been claimed—with some justice—that Stephens' emphasis on detailed psychological analysis and explanation slows down the action in the first book and that he fails in the crucial scene—the flight of the lovers—by having it reported secondhand; but if the first book is uneven, the second is delightful and occasionally powerful. Their personalities and motivations having been carefully delineated in the first book, the characters, and their decisions and actions, are thoroughly believable in the second one. All of book 2 is excellent, and several moments—such as the suppressed tragedy evident in the gaiety of Naoise's younger brothers, Deirdre's realization of Conachúr's treachery, and especially Deirdre's death on the body of her freshly killed lover—approach greatness.

It was not Stephens' purpose to idolize the old Irish myths but to make them alive and familiar for his own times. In spite of a setting eight centuries in the past, readers of *Deirdre* have little difficulty in believing in and relating to a gallery of vivid, passionate characters: the gentle, aristocratic King Fergus, too casual and perhaps lazy to avert tragedy; Conachúr, brave yet insecure, whose sense of honor and duty cannot overcome his passionate nature; the sons of Uisneac, united yet individualized, apparently carefree yet serious and heroic; and finally, Deirdre herself, intense, intuitive, innocent yet wise, who passionately and courageously strives for a happiness that she knows from the beginning will never be granted to her.

DESCENT INTO HELL

Type of work: Novel
Author: Charles Williams (1886–1945)
Type of plot: Philosophical fantasy
Time of plot: June and July in the 1930's
Locale: Battle Hill, a residential area near London
First published: 1937

Principal characters:

PAULINE ANSTRUTHER, an orphaned girl in her twenties
MARGARET ANSTRUTHER, her grandmother
PETER STANHOPE, an eminent poet
LAWRENCE WENTWORTH, a military historian
ADELA HUNT, an aspiring actress
HUGH PRESCOTT, her suitor
MRS. LILY SAMMILE, a neighbor
MRS. PARRY, a civic leader engaged in directing a play

The events of this novel are on two planes which intersect at so many points that the ordinary barriers between the natural and supernatural worlds disappear. On the realistic plane of activities in the suburb of Battle Hill, the narrative concerns the production of a verse drama written by Peter Stanhope, an eminent poet and inhabitant of the Manor House, which had belonged to his family before the housing estate was built. Under the leadership of the capable Mrs. Parry, a group of his neighbors have the privilege of performing his new play in his garden, but only one of them, Pauline Anstruther, even remotely grasps the spiritual significance of his pastoral fantasy. Pauline's sensibility is so quickened by the nuances of his verse that she confides to him the terror that has haunted her for years: the recurrent appearance of her *Doppelgänger*.

Peter Stanhope explains to her the principle of substitution that was fundamental in Charles Williams' thought: one person through love can take over and bear the burden of another so that the sufferer is relieved. When Pauline is willing to accept his offer to bear her burden, she discovers that she is no longer tortured by her own problem; instead, she is given the opportunity to bear someone else's burden of fear. Her growth in grace is the principal subject of the novel.

As the rehearsals for the play proceed, Pauline's role as leader of the chorus is paralleled by her role in the supernatural drama that takes place concurrently in Battle Hill. The spiritual energy released through the play sets in motion a series of events that transcend ordinary time, affecting a number of other inhabitants of the suburb. The housing estate built in the 1920's had taken its name from the hill, which had been a scene of battle from the time of the ancient Britons to the period of the Tudors. While the estate was being built, the timeless "magnetism of death," still alive on the Hill, as the suburb was usually called, had touched a despairing unskilled laborer, who had hanged himself on the scaffolding of an unfinished house. His unresting spirit still inhabits the area, unrecognized by the occupier of the finished house, Lawrence Wentworth, a noted military historian and adviser to the producer of the play. As a middle-aged bachelor, Wentworth has developed a secret passion for pretty, conceited Adela Hunt, who is both the heroine in the play and the girlfriend in ordinary life of the leading man, Hugh Prescott. Wentworth's jealousy is so consuming that he is destroying himself as surely as the suicide did. Also dying is Pauline's grandmother, Margaret Anstruther, but her death is the natural fulfillment of a well-spent life. Shortly before she dies, she is visited by an unpleasantly ingratiating and vaguely sinister neighbor, Mrs. Lily Sammile, who appears unexpectedly at several crises in the novel. Each of these characters is involved in the action of which Pauline is the protagonist.

The plot is comprehensible only in terms of the theme: the triumph of love over death. Pauline's love for her grandmother has been dutiful but detached during the years since her parents' death when she has lived in Mrs. Anstruther's house as dependent and companion. It is not until Stanhope has relieved her of her fear that Pauline can talk to her grandmother about it and appreciate the depth of the old woman's love. Mrs. Anstruther initiates Pauline further into the doctrine of substituted love by explaining that she may be called upon to bear the pain of their ancestor, John Struther, whose martyrdom by fire is well-known as family history.

As the dying woman approaches the limits of mortality, she can see the face of the suicide as he looks into her window during his ceaseless wandering, and soon she tells Pauline that the girl must go out in the middle of the night because someone needs her near Mr. Wentworth's. The nurse thinks the patient's mind is wandering, but Pauline knows that she must go. She discovers she no longer fears the dark, and she sees the dead man in ordinary mortal form. He asks the way to London, gently refuses her offer to pay his fare, and sets off to walk to the city. As she watches him, his form is transmuted into the agonized body of her ancestor, and she is given the opportunity of bearing his burden by enduring the fire in a mystical experience of very real pain. All this happens during the night between the dress rehearsal and the performance of the play. Mrs. Anstruther dies five minutes after Pauline gets home, but the death does not keep her from acting in the play as the producer had feared: Love has given Pauline a new perspective on time and mortality.

As a counterpoint to Pauline's experience throughout the novel, Lawrence Wentworth's love operates negatively because it is focused on himself. His passion is for his idea of Adela Hunt rather than for the real person, and his jealousy of Hugh Prescott is so powerful that it creates a tangible image of the girl who, he imagines, visits him with increasing frequency and becomes his mistress. In the bedroom where the suicide hanged himself, Wentworth's reason is destroyed by his fantasies of false love. The crisis of his descent into hell is reached on the day of the dress rehearsal when Mrs. Parry consults him as a military historian on a detail in the costumes of the guards. Wentworth knows that they are wrong and that he could arrange for them to be altered; but he is so preoccupied with his erotic experience that he cannot be bothered and tells a lie instead of the truth. This sacrifice of the historian's integrity confirms the loss of his soul. The next day his seat at the play is empty.

On the afternoon of the performance, there is an unnatural stillness in the atmosphere, like the calm before a storm. Some of the cast complain of the heat, but the play proceeds successfully, and the only disturbance is Mrs. Sammile's fainting at the end. After that, a number of residents of the Hill feel unwell, but life proceeds normally. Margaret Anstruther is buried. Pauline makes plans to move into London and take a job.

A few days after the funeral, Adela and Hugh are walking and carrying on a mild argument that reveals the difference between them: Hugh's love for Adela is consistent with his habit of seeing life clearly, while Adela's love for him is an aspect of her desire to manipulate others. As their walk takes them near the cemetery, they meet Mrs. Sammile. While they are talking to her, they become transfixed by the sight of the graves opening. Mrs. Sammile shrieks and disappears into a small shed at the edge of the cemetery. Adela screams and starts running, pursued by Hugh shouting that the illusion was caused by the wind blowing up loose earth on the graves. His mind clears rapidly, and just as quickly his love fades, so that he gives up the pursuit.

Adela's wild flight leads her instinctively to the house of the man who she knows idolizes her, but when she looks through the window, she too sees the image of herself that his diseased imagination has created, and she collapses in terror. Found by a policeman and taken home, she awakens delirious with the impression that she has forgotten her part in the play, a key passage about perception and love. When Pauline calls to see her, Adela insists that Pauline must find Mrs. Sammile in the shed by the cemetery, to give her Adela's part and thus make her well. Pauline, sensing that Lily Sammile is in fact Lilith, the image of false love, tries to offer Adela her own help in recovering her part, but she finds that only by promising to look for the old woman can she ease the tortured spirit.

The climax of love's triumph over death in the novel comes when Pauline goes, as she went out into the night at the request of her dying grandmother, to confront Lily Sammile in the cemetery shed. Recognizing her as the illusion rather than the reality of love, Pauline rejects her promises of rewards with a laugh of such pure contented joy that Lilith and her murky retreat dissolve into the dust and rubble of an old unused shed that has collapsed from her strong push on the door. In attempting to bear Adela's burden, Pauline has thus found the completion of her own part in the drama of Battle Hill and is ready to leave for London. Seen off on the train by Stanhope, who says his own role is to comfort the many people in the community who are ill, she looks forward with joy to her new life in the city. Lawrence Wentworth travels on the same train but refuses her company and goes in a daze to a historian's dinner at which his lifelong historical rival is honored and he himself sinks into complete insensibility.

The surrealistic effect of supernatural events taking place in a natural setting is the keynote of Charles Williams' narrative treatment of spiritual experience. Ordinary life is revealed as an image of a deeper reality. The play in which all the characters are involved becomes an image of life itself in which each person must perfect his own role in harmony with others. The setting of Battle Hill suggests the hill of Golgotha, and Lily Sammile's lair is revealed to Pauline as an aspect of Gomorrah. For Wentworth, the journey into the city becomes the way to Gomorrah; but Pauline's destination is the Eternal City. She tells Stanhope that it seems funny to be discussing the times of trains to the new Jerusalem, but for the poet the interdependence of the temporal and the eternal is fully assimilated fact.

The characterization, like the plot, is determined by the theme. Only Pauline Anstruther and Lawrence Wentworth, who experience salvation and damnation respectively, are fully delineated. The other characters are sketched in with just enough detail to give them substance as examples of different aspects of love. Stanhope and Mrs. Anstruther are seen only in relation to Pauline, Adela Hunt primarily in contrast to Pauline, and Hugh Prescott in contrast to Wentworth. Williams never falls into the error often attributed to Milton and other authors of making his diabolical characters more attractive than the good ones. Mrs. Sammile is described with a few telling details that make her seem real, slightly pathetic, and obscurely repulsive. Peter Stanhope, in contrast, expresses his sanctity through an easy kindliness and sense of humor. The essence of goodness is seen as a quality of joy that permeates the lives of those who accept it in love. This joy is reflected not only in the characters but in the style, taking the form of wry humor in the descriptions of the play rehearsals and almost poetic rhapsody in the passages of mystical experience. The great variety in style and mood emphasizes Williams' conviction, exemplified in the plot, that reality in human life exists in multiple planes of time and space.

DESTINY BAY

Type of work: Short stories
Author: Donn Byrne (Brian Oswald Donn-Byrne, 1889–1928)
Type of plot: Regional romance
Time of plot: Early twentieth century
Locale: Ireland
First published: 1928

> *Principal characters:*
> SIR VALENTINE MACFARLANE, the lord of Destiny Bay
> JENEPHER, his blind sister
> KERRY, his nephew and heir
> JAMES CARABINE, his valet and friend
> JENICO HAMILTON, Kerry's cousin
> ANN-DOLLY, Jenico's wife
> PATRICK HERNE, Jenepher's husband
> COSIMO, Sir Valentine's brother
> ANSELO LOVERIDGE, Cosimo's friend

The Story:

Kerry's uncle, Sir Valentine MacFarlane, lord of Destiny Bay, with his great fan-shaped red beard that came to his waist, was the courtliest and most hospitable of men. In twenty minutes, he had persuaded the old Duke of la Mentera and his grandson that he could not allow Spanish royalty to stay at the Widow McGinty's village hotel when there was plenty of room at Destiny Bay. With the simplicity that comes with great age, the Duke said that his life had been full of many turnings; now he was on the last path, and he had come hoping to find a treasure chest, said to have been lost when one of his ancestors was killed off the Irish coast after Drake's defeat of the Armada. His grandson must be provided for; he had nowhere else to turn.

Aunt Jenepher, beautiful, blind, but seeming to see people better than anyone, said that the Duke and Don Anthony, his grandson, were noble and good, and she treated them with that kindness of hers that went straight to the heart.

A short time later, the Duke died, leaving his girlish-looking grandson to the MacFarlanes' several cares—the courtliness of Uncle Valentine, the trust of his valet, James Carabine, the kindness of Aunt Jenepher, and Kerry's companionship. That friendship was not always pleasing to Don Anthony, since he could not bear to see their prizefights or cockfights,

---

although he was beside himself with joy at their horse races; but it was Jenico for whom the boy conceived a hero worship.

Jenico was not a large man like Uncle Valentine, but he had the look of burnished strength that made women try to get his attention, and he was innately courteous, although his mind might be a thousand miles away. His home was near Destiny Bay and nearer Spanish Men's Rest, the spot where the Spaniards were buried after their ships had been wrecked. For a long time, the bees and birds had shunned the place, and it was a chill on the heart to go there; but when Jenico and Kerry took Don Anthony to Spanish Men's Rest, they heard the bees and birds again, and the place seemed sunnier.

Jenico, trying to get the boy's mind off the settlement of the grandfather's estate, finally asked him to take off with him on a trip to the Atlas Mountains. The boy was flattered and obviously wanted to go but begged off. Shortly after, as the three walked near the river, Jenico and Kerry decided to go swimming. Jenico went on ahead, and Kerry could see his head like that of a sleek seal in the waves. When Kerry started to strip, Don Anthony begged him not to take off his clothes. Jenico laughed and told Kerry to strip the boy and throw him in. Kerry headed for the boy. Don Anthony flashed a knife and then ducked away. As Kerry turned to follow him, Uncle Valentine appeared, roaring that there was once a time when a lady could be trusted among Irishmen.

With a change of clothes, Ann-Dolly, as she asked to be called, was one of the loveliest girls they had ever seen, and there was a new spirit in her. They made her companion to Aunt Jenepher so that she would feel free to stay. At that time, her relations with Jenico were strained, but whenever they were in a room together, she would look at him when he was not looking, and then he would look at her when she had turned away.

Jenico tried a foolish scheme of planting treasure for her to find, but he and Kerry had a fight about that and he never told her. Finally, she had enough of the MacFarlanes and ran away in the night. Jenico and James Carabine and Kerry used horses, bicycles, and even bloodhounds to follow her. At last, they found her huddled in an old ruin. She was deathly white and scared, and nothing they did could make her move. James Carabine plucked Kerry's sleeve, suggesting that they return the horses, the bicycles, and the dogs they had borrowed, but Kerry brushed him off. Finally, Carabine picked Kerry up like a feather and forcibly carried him out, to leave Jenico and Ann-Dolly together.

After Ann-Dolly became mistress of Jenico's house, the birds always sang, and the bees knew it was a fair and happy home.

One never knew what or whom Uncle Valentine might bring back from a trip. One of the kindest of men was Patrick Herne, a man who looked like a double for Digory Pascoe, who was to have married Aunt Jenepher

after he made his fortune. Digory had died in a fight, but Uncle Valentine
had kept him alive for twelve years by writing letters from him, until he
found Patrick Herne and brought him home as Digory. Aunt Jenepher
played along for a while until she had to ask who the man really was who
thought just as she did. Theirs was a happy wedding.

One time Uncle Valentine went off to America to find James Carabine,
who had once saved his life. James Carabine was the Irish champion in the
prize ring when he had an urge to sail to America to take care of a
drunken friend. Because the friend died at sea, he was lonesome in New
York and married a hard-faced and, as it turned out, two-faced singer
whose friends ran illegal fights in and around the city. When Uncle Valentine found him, he had taken to drink after losing a bad fight and his wife;
but he regained his self-respect and rewon his title before Uncle Valentine
took him home. There was no more devoted valet and friend in Ireland
than Uncle Valentine's James Carabine.

It was not only Uncle Valentine who traveled distances to help a friend.
Anselo Loveridge, the gypsy whom Uncle Valentine's brother Cosimo
saved from the hangman's noose, worried about Uncle Cosimo's heavy
drinking; Uncle Cosimo had told him that the drinking had been brought
on because of a Chinese girl he called the Fair Maid of Wu, whom he had
seen three times and never spoken to. Anselo disappeared for six years,
and when he came back, he brought the Chinese girl as a present to Uncle
Cosimo. Having lost his heart in those hard years, he would not wait to see
Uncle Cosimo but continued his wanderings. When he went to see what
Anselo had brought, Uncle Cosimo was happy, and his pocket was bulging
with his big flask. After one look, his head cleared, and he turned on his
heel and left the country. From that day, he worked to reclaim drunks in
the slums of London and became so straightlaced that he was made Bishop
of Borneo.

Critical Evaluation:

In the preface to one of his works, Donn Byrne made the rather
immodest claim that he was the last of the great Irish storytellers. Certainly
the statement was an exaggeration, but it nevertheless accurately identified
the author's two main appeals: his gift for engaging the reader's imagination through romantic and effectively told tales; and his ability to capture
in his prose the spirit of the Irish people and the beauty of the land where
he grew up. All of Byrne's fiction, whether novels or short stories, reflects
these two concerns and reveals the author's preoccupation with Irish
themes and love of his childhood home.

Destiny Bay was the first of a series of Byrne's works that were published posthumously. In form, it is a collection of nine short stories that are
unified by their common narrator, Kerry MacFarlane, who will inherit his

uncle's estate in Destiny Bay. The point of view of Kerry—a thinly disguised version of the author as a young man—gives consistency to the tales as does Byrne's use of the same cast of characters throughout the book with a different character coming into prominence in each new story. The characterizations in *Destiny Bay* are not deep, but they are colorful and memorable in their lovable eccentricities. Leading the cast is the protective, patriarchal figure of Uncle Valentine, with his red beard so huge that it covers his chest like a breastplate, and his blind sister Jenepher, who whistles birdcalls and "sees," with her wisdom and kindliness, much more clearly than anyone around her. The minor characters are equally romantic and eccentric: Uncle Cosimo, driven to alcohol over love of a Chinese girl he has seen but never met; his faithful gypsy friend Anselo, who travels six years to find Cosimo a replacement for the "Fair Maid of Wu"; James Carabine the prizefighter, who is taken in by a scheming New York singer and left heartbroken; the Spanish Duke's shy and elusive "grandson," who turns out to be Ann-Dolly; and her eventual husband, the courtly and sensitive dreamer Jenico.

The incidents that form the plots of Byrne's stories are as romantically improbable as his characters. Stories such as that of Ann-Dolly's disguise as Don Anthony, Cosimo's deliverance from drink and subsequent missionary work in London, and Uncle Valentine's twelve-year correspondence with Aunt Jenepher under the name of her dead lover Digory, abound in *Destiny Bay*, but what ties such scattered events as these together is the ever-present Irish background. The nostalgic mood and vivid setting is established early in the first tale, and this setting remains almost as tangible a presence as the characters themselves throughout the book. Although Destiny Bay is not on any map of Ireland, Byrne's stories make it a real place, with its thirty square miles of territory on the North Sea, unvisited by any trade save that of the gypsies; with its sometimes gentle, sometimes ruthless coast, and its brown bogland studded with flowers and inhabited only by snipes and moor hens; with its tall mountains purple with heather and its tiny, ten-house village of Ballyfale.

When Byrne died in 1928 in an automobile accident, he was only thirty-nine years old. When one reads his lyrical descriptions, rich with Gaelic imagery and vivid scenes of natural beauty, one feels that if his talent falls far short of excellence, he nevertheless died with a great deal of his potential yet unrealized.

DIANA OF THE CROSSWAYS

Type of work: Novel
Author: George Meredith (1828–1909)
Type of plot: Psychological realism
Time of plot: Nineteenth century
Locale: England
First published: 1885

> Principal characters:
> DIANA MERION WARWICK, a woman of beauty and charm
> AUGUSTUS WARWICK, her husband
> LADY EMMA DUNSTANE, Diana's friend
> THOMAS REDWORTH, Diana's friend and admirer
> LORD DANNISBURGH, another friend
> SIR PERCY DACIER, a young politician in love with Diana

The Story:

All fashionable London was amazed and shocked when Diana Warwick suddenly left her husband's house. Society, however, should not have been surprised at her action; the marriage had been ill-fated from the start. For Augustus Warwick, a calculating, ambitious politician, his marriage to the beautiful and charming Diana Merion had been largely one of convenience. Diana, in her turn, accepted his proposal as a refuge from unwelcome attentions to which her own position as an orphan had exposed her.

Diana Merion had first appeared in society at a state ball in Dublin, where her unspoiled charm and beauty attracted many admirers. Lady Emma Dunstane introduced Diana to Thomas Redworth, a friend of her husband, Sir Lukin Dunstane. Redworth's attentions so enraged Mr. Sullivan Smith, a hot-tempered Irishman, that he attempted to provoke the Englishman to a duel. Redworth pacified the Irishman, however, to avoid compromising Diana by a duel fought on her account.

Later, while visiting Lady Emma at Copsley, the Dunstane country home in England, Diana was forced to rebuff Sir Lukin when he attempted to make love to her. Leaving Copsley, she went to visit the Warwicks. Meanwhile, Thomas Redworth announced to Lady Emma that he loved Diana. His announcement came too late. Diana was already engaged to Augustus Warwick.

In London, the Warwicks lived in a large house and entertained lavishly. Among their intimates was Lord Dannisburgh, an elderly peer who became Diana's friend and adviser. While Warwick was away on a government mission, the two were often seen together, and Diana was so indiscreet as to let Lord Dannisburgh accompany her when she went to visit Lady Emma. Gossip began to circulate. On his return Warwick, who was incapable of understanding his wife's innocence and charm, served Diana with a process in suit. Accusing her of infidelity, he named Lord Dannisburgh as co-respondent. Diana disappeared from Warwick's house and from London. In a letter to Lady Emma, she had said that she intended to leave England. Her friend, realizing that flight would be tantamount to confession, felt sure that before she left the country, Diana would go to Crossways, her father's old home. Determined that Diana should remain and boldly defend the suit, Lady Emma sent Redworth to Crossways with instructions to detain Diana and persuade her to go to stay with the Dunstanes at Copsley.

Lady Emma had guessed correctly; Diana was at Crossways with her maid. At first, Diana was unwilling to see Lady Emma's point of view, for she thought of her flight as a disdainful stepping aside from Warwick's sordid accusations; but at last, she gave in to Redworth's arguments and returned with him to Copsley.

Although the court returned a verdict of not guilty to the charge Warwick had brought against her, Diana felt that her honor had been ruined and that in the eyes of the world she was still guilty. For a time, she was able to forget her own distress by nursing her friend, Lady Emma, who was seriously ill. Later, she left England to go on a Mediterranean cruise. Before her departure, she had written a book, *The Princess Egeria*.

In Egypt, she met Redworth, now a brilliant member of Parliament. He was accompanied by Sir Percy Dacier, Lord Dannisburgh's nephew and a rising young politician. Falling in love with Diana, Sir Percy followed her to the Continent. He was recalled to London by the illness of his uncle. Diana followed him a short time later and learned on her arrival in London that Redworth had been active in making her book a literary triumph. He had stirred up interest among the critics because he knew that Diana was in need of money.

Lord Dannisburgh died, with Diana at his bedside during his last illness. He had been her friend, and she paid him that last tribute of friendship and respect regardless of the storm of criticism it created. When Lord Dannisburgh's will was read, it was learned that he had left a sum of money to Diana.

In the meantime, Diana had made an enemy of the socially ambitious Mrs. Wathin, who thought it her social duty to tear Diana's reputation to shreds. Part of her dislike was motivated by jealousy that Diana should be accepted by people who would not tolerate her. Some of her actions were inspired by Warwick, Mrs. Wathin's friend, who, having lost his suit against Diana, was trying to force his wife to return to him.

Sir Percy's attentions were also distressing to Diana. Half in love with him, she was not free to marry again. She faced a crisis in her affairs when Mrs. Wathin called to announce that Warwick, now ill, wanted Diana to return and to act as his nurse. Diana refused. Warwick then threatened to exercise his legal rights as her husband. Sir Percy, who informed her of Warwick's intention, asked her to elope with him to Paris. She agreed. She was saved from that folly by the appearance of Redworth, who arrived to tell her that Lady Emma was ill and about to undergo a serious operation at Copsley. Diana went with him to be at her friend's side.

Lady Emma nearly died, and the gravity of her condition restored Diana's own sense of responsibility. She ordered Sir Percy to forget her; but in spite of her protests, he continued to follow her about. One day, he confided a tremendous political secret to her—the prime minister was about to call upon Parliament to pass some revolutionary reform measures. Having told her his secret, he attempted to resume his former courtship. Diana refused to listen to his pleadings. After he had gone, she felt broken and cheated. She felt that if she would not have Sir Percy as a lover, she could not keep him as a friend. In desperate need of money, Diana had been forced to sell Crossways to pay her debts, and her later novels had been failures. Feeling herself a complete adventuress, she went to the editor of a paper that opposed the government party and sold him the information Sir Percy had given to her.

When the paper appeared with a full disclosure of the prime minister's plan, Sir Percy accused her of betraying him and discontinued his friendship with her. A short time later, he proposed to a young lady of fortune. About the same time, Warwick was struck down by a cab in the street and killed. Diana had her freedom at last, but she was downcast in spirit. She knew that she was in public disgrace. Although she had burned the check in payment for the information she had disclosed, it was common knowledge that she had betrayed Sir Percy and that he had retaliated by his marriage to Constance Asper, an heiress. When Sullivan Smith proposed marriage, Diana refused him and sought refuge in the company of her old friend, Lady Emma. Her stay at Copsley freed her of her memories of Sir Percy, so much so that on her return to London she was able to greet him and his bride with dignity and charm. Her wit was as sharp as ever, and she took pleasure in revenging herself upon those who had attempted to destroy her reputation with their gossip and slander.

On another visit to Copsley, she again encountered Redworth, now a railroad promoter and still a distinguished member of Parliament. When he invited her and Lady Emma to visit Crossways, Diana learned that it was Redworth who had bought her old home and furnished it with her own London possessions, which she had been forced to sell in order to pay her debts. He bluntly told Diana that he had bought the house and furnished it for her because he expected her to become his wife. Not wishing to involve him in the scandals that had circulated about her, she at first pretended indifference to his abrupt wooing. Lady Emma, on the other hand, urged her to marry Redworth, who had loved her for many years, so that he could protect her from social malice. At last, aware that she brought no real disgrace to Redworth's name, she consented to become his wife.

Critical Evaluation:

Any novel by George Meredith requires attention not only to the book in question but also to the wider aspects of the technique of fiction, for Meredith, always an original, was a writer of deep concentration and mature force. His Diana is a character head and shoulders above most heroines in nineteenth century English novels. She offers the charm of femininity, perplexed by convention and yet aware of its force. Her predicament is at once an error in judgment and a glory to her. Her career compels the reader's belief that a life that will not let go its harvest of errors until they are thoroughly winnowed is a human drama of deepest interest, for that life extracts the wisdom experience can offer. Diana, beautiful, witty, skeptical of social convention and moral expediency, is the embodiment of Meredith's philosophy and art.

The novel is the most emphatically feminist of George Meredith's novels, but the woman too intelligent and spirited to accept willingly her "place," as defined by Victorian society, figures prominently in virtually all of his fiction. Some, such as Diana's friend Emma Dunstane or Lady Blandish of *The Ordeal of Richard Feverel*, manage to confine their protest to witty commentary while playing their assigned roles; others, like Diana, are forced by circumstances into active rebellion.

It is generally agreed that Meredith's chief model for his beautiful, brilliant, and hard-beset heroines was his own first wife. In the fine poem-sequence *Modern Love*, he traces in thin disguise the course of their marriage, from its happy and passionate beginnings, through the conflicts that led to his wife's running off with an artist, to her early death. Although bitter at first, Meredith learned much from the failure of his first love and came to accept major responsibility for it. His novels repeatedly depict a loving and loyal woman virtually driven into the arms of another man by the blind egotism of her husband or lover. Asked by Robert Louis Stevenson whether the protagonist of *The Egoist* was not a portrait of him, Meredith replied that his fatuous hero was drawn "from all of us but principally from myself."

Meredith saw his society as dominated by egotism, chiefly male, and both fearful and suspicious of the bright and beautiful because of the threat they posed to complacency. He shared the Victorian belief in progress, but he defined progress in terms of intelligence and sensibility. Choosing the comedy of wit as his preferred mode, he attacked the dull and smug and called for "brain, more brain." He recognized the tragedy of life but ascribed it to human failure. As he wrote in *Modern Love*, "no villain need be. We are betrayed by what is false within." The falseness may spring from self-deception or from unquestioning acceptance of what "the world" proclaims. What can save people is the ability to be honest with themselves and to see the world as it is, and the courage to act on their perceptions even in defiance of social norms.

Many of Meredith's contemporaries shared his belief in a continuing evolution of man's spiritual and intellectual capacities, but few besides Browning were as ardent in affirming also "the value and significance of flesh." For Meredith, the goal of life was to realize one's full potentialities in a vital balance: "The spirit must brand the flesh that it may live."

Meredith's Diana fully exemplifies his philosophy of life. The central metaphor of the novel is the "dog-world" in hot pursuit of its quarry, a beautiful woman too intelligent and sensitive to play the roles society demands of her, either "parasite" or "chalice." Diana, however, is no spotless, perfect victim of malign persecutors. In precept and practice, Meredith scorned sentimental melodrama. Young and inexperienced, Diana brings much of her trouble on herself. She marries for protection and position, a prudent move by worldly standards but disastrous in its consequences. Achieving a measure of independence, she soon endangers it by her extravagance, and she is finally almost destroyed by an impulsive act of desperation. Although elements of the "dog-world" are moved by envy and malice, most of Diana's adversaries act "honorably" in their own eyes; it is the conventions of honor, respectability, and—most importantly—of women's place in Victorian society that nearly overpowers her.

The resolution of the plot would seem a compromise if the novel were the feminist tract it has been called: Diana does not finally triumph as a fully independent person, accepted by society on her own terms and admired for her wit and nerve. Only rescued from despair by her friend Emma, she does prove herself capable of standing alone but chooses instead to marry again. As Meredith presents her choice, however, it is not compromise but fulfillment. Her marriage to Redworth, who truly understands and values her, represents the ideal wedding of flesh and spirit, achieved not by good luck but by striving, blundering, learning from mistakes, and finally seeing and accepting life as it is.

Diana of the Crossways was an immediate success upon publication, probably because its theme had been taken from a recent scandal involving a brilliant and beautiful Irishwoman, Mrs. Caroline Norton, who had been accused (as it proved, falsely) of selling an important government secret. Despite its wit, its vitality, and its vivid characterizations, the novel has not maintained its popularity. Critics generally rate it high among Meredith's works, often second only to his masterpiece *The Egoist*, and its themes are of perhaps even broader interest today than they were in 1885, yet it is apparently little read. The difficulty is probably with Meredith's famous style, the joy and the despair of his admirers.

From his first work of fiction, *The Shaving of Shagpat*, to his last, the prose of this admirable poet became progressively more poetic in its richness, its precision, its compactness, and its indirection. In the earlier novels, it is a beautiful addition to plot and characterization; in the later, it may detract from or even obscure them. Oscar Wilde may not have been entirely accurate in saying that as a novelist Meredith could do everything but tell a story; but in *Diana of the Crossways* and other later novels, he often seems fastidiously averse to saying anything directly. The texture of his prose places demands upon his readers that not all are willing to meet. The attentive reader is richly rewarded in beauty, wit, and subtlety of thought and expression. Let his attention waver, though, and he may find that he has missed a significant turn in the plot.

The very dazzle and density of Meredith's style, embodying as it does his vigorous and invigorating vision of life, will certainly continue to delight readers willing to submit to it; among less strenuous readers, however, Meredith may continue to be as he has been for decades, more honored than read.

DIGBY GRAND

Type of work: Novel
Author: George J. Whyte-Melville (1821–1878)
Type of plot: Picaresque romance
Time of plot: Early nineteenth century
Locale: England
First published: 1853

Principal characters:
DIGBY GRAND, a spirited young Englishman and an officer in the Guards
SIR PEREGRINE GRAND, Digby's father
SHADRACH, a moneylender
TOM SPENCER, Digby's friend
CAPTAIN LEVANTER, a fellow officer
COLONEL CARTOUCH, Digby's commanding officer
FLORA BELMONT, Digby's beloved

The Story:

Digby Grand's father, Sir Peregrine Grand of Haverley Hall, had one fond wish with respect to his son: he wanted Digby to be a man of fashion and to know his position in society. With that in mind, he decided that when Digby, then a youngster at Eton, should finish school, he would be commissioned in the British Army. Digby, taken with the idea, wished to have his appointment made at once.

As luck had it, Digby met General Sir Benjamin Burgonet, who was pleased with the young man. He made every effort to secure Digby's commission. Within a few weeks, Digby received a letter announcing his commission in the army as an ensign in a regiment of infantry.

Digby Grand reported to his regiment's headquarters in Scotland, where he rapidly adjusted to military life. Digby was an adventurous young man; he enjoyed sports and gambling and quickly became a sought-out addition to any party. He soon discovered, however, that the slim allowance provided to him by his father and his small pay as an ensign did not cover his large expenditures, and so he fell into the habit of gambling on horses, cards, and billiards to augment his income. Most of his fellow officers existed in much the same fashion.

While in Scotland, Digby had a narrow escape from marriage when an officer's daughter, a woman in her thirties, persuaded Digby to become engaged. His friends saw through the woman's plot, however, and rescued him from his predicament. He had the satisfaction of seeing her become instead the wife of Dubbs, the regimental drum major.

Shortly after that incident, Digby was sent to Canada for a tour of duty.

Memorable events of that short tour were the slaughter of a huge bull moose and a love affair with a French-Canadian girl named Zoë. Colonel Cartouch, Digby's commanding officer, befriended the high-spirited young man and prevented him from marrying the girl, because he felt that the teenage ensign was not yet ready for marriage.

Upon his return to England, Digby found himself with a new commission in Her Majesty's service; his father had purchased a lieutenancy in the Life Guards for him during his absence in Canada. Digby was now in the most honored and social brigade in the service, the Guards being the units that were stationed in London. Within a short time, Digby had once again won a place in fashionable London life. He was voted into several of the choicest gambling clubs, appeared in the best society, and became accepted by some well-known people. One of his friends was a youthful peer named St. Heliers; another was an officer named Levanter; a third was Mrs. Mantrap, a woman who basked in the attentions of young men.

To maintain his life of ease, including gambling for high stakes, maintaining good rooms, drinking only the best wines, and buying expensive horses, required all of Digby's resourcefulness. Because his resourcefulness was not sufficient at times, his friend Levanter introduced him to a moneylender named Shadrach, who was quite willing to lend Digby money at a high rate of interest, the principal to be repaid when Digby inherited the family estates. Not once but many times Digby borrowed from Shadrach.

One day, while in charge of a small group of military police at parade, Digby met Flora Belmont, who had attended the parade with her father, a retired colonel. Immediately Digby fell in love, in spite of the fact that the colonel had little or nothing to pass on to his daughter in the way of a fortune.

On his twenty-first birthday, spurred on by his own love and that which Flora Belmont had declared for him, Digby went home to Haverley Hall to request a definite and sizable income from his father so that he and Flora could be married. Instead of being happy, Sir Peregrine was furious that Digby would even think of marrying anyone but an heiress, for the Grand estate was in poor financial condition and Sir Peregrine had been counting on a brilliant marriage by his son to recoup the family fortunes.

Downhearted, Digby returned to duty in London. To while away the time, he continued his old life, living beyond his means and borrowing money to pay his expenses. He even borrowed from Shadrach when his boyhood chum, Tom Spencer, who was studying for holy orders at Oxford, had to sign the notes with him. For a time, Digby had an affair with Coralie de Rivolte, a famous dancer, but that romance ended, though only after Digby had made an enemy of a scar-faced Spaniard who seemed to be the dancer's relative.

Eventually, Digby got so deeply into debt that only a change of regiments could help him. As an officer in the Guards, he had too many social responsibilities, and he exchanged commissions with an officer in a dragoon regiment stationed in Kent, at some distance from London. Within a few weeks, he made still another move. Old General Sir Benjamin Burgonet, who had secured Digby's original commission, made him his aide, and Digby prepared to go with the General to India. He was somewhat aghast, however, to learn that the girl who had married the drum major was now Lady Burgonet.

In spite of his precautions, Digby was unable to leave England without falling into the hands of Shadrach and other creditors, who had him imprisoned for debt. To satisfy his creditors, Digby had to sell his commission and give up all he owned. At that black hour, word came that Sir Peregrine had died, leaving Digby with the title and the estate. When the will was settled, however, it became apparent that the estate was too heavily in debt to be of any use to the new heir. To salvage himself, Digby had to sell the land; he inherited only the title.

He was saved by a meeting with Tom Spencer, who had been prevented from finishing his degree at Oxford by an arrest made for a note he had signed on Digby's behalf. Spencer, far from being downcast, had become a successful wine merchant. He took Digby into the business with him, and the two built up a flourishing trade. By that time, Digby had acquired a great deal more discretion and a few gray hairs.

After some years, Digby ran across his old commanding officer, Colonel Cartouch. The Colonel was engaged in prosecuting a man who had forged checks on his name, and the two discovered that the man was married to Coralie de Rivolte, Digby's old love. That surprise was not the end, for the Colonel also discovered that Coralie was his own daughter by a Spanish woman who had run away from him after killing her sister, whom she believed in love with Cartouch.

The appearance of Coralie reminded Digby of Flora Belmont, the girl whom his father had forbidden him to marry because she lacked a fortune. Digby found her in mourning for her father, but she was still single. Digby learned through friends that she had remained faithful to him. In a short time, they had made plans for their approaching marriage. Digby Grand was ready to be tamed.

Critical Evaluation:

Because George J. Whyte-Melville's works have been cataloged as sporting fiction, they have never been given their rightful place in the history of English literature, and most scholars pass them by completely. Although Whyte-Melville wrote particularly for the sporting world, his novels, especially *Captain Digby Grand* (as it was originally titled), interested wider audiences in their time. His writings have an air of liveliness, a note of authenticity, and an ineffable freshness. *Digby Grand* was Whyte-Melville's first novel, and it was truly termed by the novelist an autobiography, for the author's own early career as an officer in a Highland regiment and the Guards is mirrored in the novel. Digby Grand is, in fact, partly young Whyte-Melville. Considered in his time an authority on fox hunting, the author refers to the sport frequently in *Digby Grand*, as in his other novels.

The values and traditions of Eton play a significant part in this rambling tale of "old boys." The horseman and huntsman (the two aspects of the "gentleman" considered most important, aside from perfect grooming and decorum) are the models that the motherless hero aspires to emulate. His interests are as narrow as those of the people around him; lacking intellectual drive, he is content with a physically active but superficial existence. The military is considered the only acceptable career for a gentleman or sportsman such as he early considers himself. Cigars, sherry, and horses are the main interests of the men in the book except for brief encounters with a tepid form of romance.

The preparations for a career in the Guards are detailed with humor and enthusiasm, and the six-week voyage of the young soldier across the Atlantic is exhaustively presented. The author tends to overwhelm readers with unselective details, but the enthusiasm of the telling carries readers over the dull spots; the unusual facts and novelty of some of the events are often interesting in themselves, although they contribute to no pattern or plot in the book. The novel, like a genuine "autobiography" (as the book is subtitled), simply recounts one event after another. The life of the Guards, on duty in Canada is described with as much indefatigable detail as everything else in the narrative. The narrator-protagonist devotes much space to describing the scenery he encounters in his travels, from Niagara and Lake Erie to the northwoods sites of hunting parties to the fields and streams of England. In England, America, or wherever the hero is, horses, horse racing, and hunting play the major part in both his thoughts and actions.

The book is not subtle in either its humor or its efforts for effect. The names of most of the characters suggest caricatures rather than efforts to create fully developed personalities: for example, the reader encounters Admiral Portfire, Mr. Stubble, Arabella Ramrod, Lawyer Sheepskin, and Mrs. Mantrap. The heroines are all conventional, pale maidens with little personality of their own; they are merely mannequins of ethereal beauty upon which Digby can shine his admiration and devotion.

The strengths of the novel lie in the density of the narrative and the variety and vividness of the boldly sketched characterizations. Some of the characters are overdrawn, but others are humorous, colorful, and often entertaining. The accounts of the activities of the class portrayed (gambling, hunting, racing) are described with authenticity. As a record of the mid-Victorian period and the attitudes and occupations of its people, the book presents an interesting, if limited, portrait. The book is greatly flawed by the highest, most objective standards, but it has a place in literary history as an example of a type of popular novel and in social history as a document of a bygone era.

THE DIVINE FIRE

Type of work: Novel
Author: May Sinclair (1870?–1946)
Type of plot: Psychological romance
Time of plot: The 1890's
Locale: England
First published: 1904

Principal characters:
SAVAGE KEITH RICKMAN, the genius
HORACE JEWDWINE, a literary editor
LUCIA HARDEN, Rickman's beloved
FLOSSIE WALKER, Rickman's fiancée
MR. PILKINGTON, a financier

The Story:

Horace Jewdwine, a literary editor, had a problem. He thought he had discovered a genius in Savage Keith Rickman, a young and unknown poet who earned his living by making catalogs for his father, a bookseller. Jewdwine, however, was afraid to say openly that Rickman was a genius; his reputation could be damaged if he called Rickman a genius publicly and then the young man proved otherwise. He encouraged Rickman privately but failed to give him the public recognition that would have meant so much to the young writer.

Rickman himself cared little for fame or money. He also knew that he was a genius—that is, part of him was a genius. He was also a student, a young man about town, a journalist, a seeker after simple home life, and sometimes a drunk. It was hard to have so many facets to one's nature. One part warred constantly with the others; but no matter in what form he found himself, honor never left him. Even when drunk, he continued to be honorable.

Rickman's intelligence and his ability to judge books were the foundations upon which the elder Rickman had built his financial success as a book dealer. The father and son could never understand each other. Money was the father's god; the muse was Rickman's. The father was backed by and supported by Mr. Pilkington, a financier of questionable ethics but great success. When Pilkington informed him that the Harden library might soon be on the market, the old man sent his son to evaluate it. At the same time, Miss Lucia Harden, daughter of the owner of the library, asked for someone to catalog it for her. Rickman was sent because his knowledge of old books was infallible.

Rickman was awed by Lucia. She was the daughter of a baronet, so far above him that he could never hope to have her return his affection; but from the first, he knew that she was destined to be his inspiration. Lucia was Jewdwine's cousin, and he was unhappy when he learned of her association with Rickman. He knew Rickman was beneath her, but he also knew that his cousin was moved by poetry. In addition, Jewdwine himself thought he would one day marry Lucia and inherit the library and the country estate, but he could not bring himself to ask for her hand; decisions were almost impossible for Jewdwine.

While working for Lucia, Rickman soon learned that his father and Pilkington were planning to pay a ridiculously low price for the Harden library. In order to help the girl, he wrote to Jewdwine and asked him to buy the library at a fair figure. Jewdwine failed to answer the letter. When Lucia's father died suddenly, leaving her indebted to Pilkington, Rickman went to his father and tried to persuade him to change the offer. The old man refused, and Rickman left the bookshop forever, refusing to compromise his honor in return for the partnership his father offered him if he would stay. Not wanting to hurt Lucia, he told her little of what had happened. He even tried to excuse Jewdwine's failure to buy the library and so salvage some of her father's estate.

Pilkington took the Harden house and furniture and Rickman's father the library. After Rickman left him, the old man's business began to fail, and he was forced to mortgage the library to Pilkington. The books were stored, pending redemption. Rickman left Lucia and returned to his rooming house; he did not see her again for five years.

Back in London, Rickman continued to write for various journals. Jewdwine gave him a junior editorship on the journal that he edited, and the job allowed Rickman to live fairly comfortably. He had put away his serious writing in a drawer. Although the product of his genius, it would bring no money. Meanwhile, he was trapped into a proposal by little Flossie Walker, a fellow boarder. Flossie was a girl who could never understand the ways of genius; her proper world was a house in the suburbs, decorated with hideous furniture. Rickman found himself with the house bought and the wedding date set.

Chance was to save him. After five years, Lucia visited a friend in Rickman's boardinghouse, and the two met again. No word of love was spoken, for Lucia, even without her fortune, was still above him, and Rickman had no desire to hurt Flossie, who had waited two years for him to make enough money for their marriage. He and Lucia, however, found inspiration and comfort in their renewed acquaintance. The real blow to Flossie's dreams came when Rickman's father died, leaving him a small inheritance. With it, Rickman could possibly redeem the mortgaged

Harden library from Pilkington and return it to Lucia. To do so would mean a wait of at least two more years for Flossie. This she could not understand. A legal debt was one thing, a debt of honor another. With great relief, Rickman learned that she refused to wait. She quickly married another boarder and found her house in the suburbs, complete with nursery.

Rickman lived through years of the most killing labor he would ever know. He worked all night, starved himself, and lived in an unheated attic in order to redeem the complete library. He got extensions from Pilkington, who enjoyed the sight of genius chasing an impossible goal. His friends lost track of him. He lost his job with Jewdwine because he would not compromise his honor even in his desperate need to help Lucia. At last, he seemed doomed to fail, for his lack of food and his feverish work made him desperately ill. Friends found him and took him, unconscious, to a hospital. Later, they found the work of his genius while going through his belongings. When it was published, Rickman's fame was assured. Poor Jewdwine! How he wished now that he had had the courage to claim Rickman in time. By that time, however, Jewdwine had sacrificed his own principles, and success was beyond hope for him.

Recovered, Rickman went to Lucia. He found her ill and unable to walk. When she learned that his illness had been caused by work for her, the gift was almost more than she could bear. With his aid, she arose from her bed. Cured of the malady that she knew now was only heartbreak, she saw Rickman whole, the genius and the man fused at last.

Critical Evaluation:

One of May Sinclair's numerous and varied novels, *The Divine Fire* deals with the frustrations of a young poet of exceptional talent whose valuable energies are wasted in the struggle to make a living and to fulfill an enormous self-imposed financial obligation. Despite the wide variety in her work, Sinclair uses techniques in *The Divine Fire* that are characteristic of her general style; the novel also contains many of the same attitudes and psychological concerns frequently found in her fiction.

Stylistically, Sinclair is somewhat of a Naturalist. Although *The Divine Fire* is relatively long and leisurely-paced compared to her other works, it shares with them an acute attention to detail and an objectivity of observation. Through her skillful and unobtrusive selection of which details are to be presented, Sinclair creates a powerful impression of Realism that carries its own meaning without need of comment by the author. Thematically, this novel—like her others—reveals a strain of Naturalism. Influenced by H. G. Wells, Sinclair was interested in exposing the mediocrity of middle-class values and their deadening effect on the spirit and in dramatizing how an individual life—whether an unusual one like Keith Rickman's or a quite ordinary one such as Harriet Frean's—is molded by external forces. Keith Rickman's career, therefore, illustrates to some extent the dictum found in an earlier novel, *Audrey Craven* (1897): "In our modern mythology, Custom, Circumstance, and Heredity are the three Fates that weave the web of human life." Sinclair, nevertheless, does not approach the pessimism of Hardy or Dreiser, and she is often unwilling to accept the Naturalist solution; Rickman, after all of his suffering, is finally recognized as a genius and united with Lucia.

Although Sinclair was not a Freudian, she was certainly aware of the important psychological assumptions beginning to be made in her generation and of their implications. The reader discovers in all of her work that same sensitivity and insight into emotions and motivations that inspires *The Divine Fire*. She is particularly aware of the various kinds of oppression that produce frustration; one type that appears frequently—and reminds readers of Sinclair's similarities to Henry James—is the oppressiveness of parents toward their children. Also reminiscent of James are her portraits of seemingly nice people who are in reality self-serving and unscrupulous—portraits that reflect not only her interest in the discrepancy between appearances and reality, but her desire to expose hypocrisy and false values.

DR. JEKYLL AND MR. HYDE

Type of work: Novelette
Author: Robert Louis Stevenson (1850–1894)
Type of plot: Fantasy
Time of plot: Nineteenth century
Locale: London
First published: 1886

Principal characters:

DR. HENRY JEKYLL, a London physician
MR. UTTERSON, the counselor for Dr. Jekyll
POOLE, Dr. Jekyll's manservant
DR. HASTIE LANYON, Dr. Jekyll's close friend

The Story:

Mr. Richard Enfield, and his cousin, Mr. Utterson, a lawyer, were strolling according to their usual Sunday custom when they came upon an empty building on a familiar street. Mr. Enfield told that some time previously he had seen an ill-tempered man trample down a small child at the doorway of the deserted building. He and other indignant bystanders had forced the stranger, who gave his name as Hyde, to pay over a sum of money for the child's welfare. Enfield remembered Hyde with deep loathing.

Utterson had reasons to be interested in Hyde. When he returned to his apartment, he reread the strange will of Dr. Henry Jekyll. The will stipulated that in the event of Dr. Jekyll's death all of his wealth should go to a man named Edward Hyde.

Utterson sought out Hyde, the man whom Enfield had described, to discover if he were the same person who had been named heir to Dr. Jekyll's fortune. Suspicious of Utterson's interest, Hyde became enraged and ran into his house. Questioned, Dr. Jekyll refused to discuss the matter but insisted that in the event of his death the lawyer should see to it that Mr. Hyde was not cheated out of his fortune. The lawyer believed that Hyde was an extortioner who was getting possession of Dr. Jekyll's money and who would eventually murder the doctor.

About a year later, Hyde was wanted for the wanton murder of a kindly old man, Sir Danvers Carew, but he escaped before he could be arrested. Dr. Jekyll presented the lawyer and the police with a letter signed by Hyde, in which the murderer declared his intention of making good his escape forever. He begged Dr. Jekyll's pardon for having ill-used his friendship.

About this time, Dr. Lanyon, who had been for years a great friend of Dr. Jekyll, became ill and died. A letter addressed to Utterson was found among his papers. Opening it, Utterson discovered an inner envelope also sealed and bearing the notice that it was not to be opened until after Dr. Jekyll's death. Utterson felt that it was somehow associated with the evil Hyde, but he could in no way fathom the mystery.

One Sunday, Enfield and Utterson were walking again in the street where Enfield had seen Hyde abusing the child. They now realized that the strange deserted building was a side entrance to the house of Dr. Jekyll, an additional wing used as a laboratory. Looking up at the window, they saw Dr. Jekyll sitting there. He looked disconsolate. Then his expression seemed to change, so that his face took on a grimace of horror or pain. Suddenly, he closed the window. Utterson and Enfield walked on, too overcome by what they had seen to talk further.

Not long afterward, Utterson was sitting by his fireside when Dr. Jekyll's manservant, Poole, sought entrance. He related that for a week something strange had been going on in Dr. Jekyll's laboratory. The doctor himself had not appeared. Instead, he had ordered his meals to be sent in and had written curious notes demanding that Poole go to all the chemical houses in London in search of a mysterious drug. Poole was convinced that his master had been slain and that the murderer, masquerading as Dr. Jekyll, was still hiding in the laboratory.

Utterson and Poole returned to Dr. Jekyll's house and broke into his laboratory with an ax. They entered and discovered that the man in the laboratory had killed himself by draining a vial of poison just as they broke the lock. The man was Edward Hyde.

They searched in vain for the doctor's body, certain it was somewhere about after they discovered a note of that date addressed to Utterson. In the note, Dr. Jekyll said he was planning to disappear, and he urged Utterson to read the note that Dr. Lanyon had left at the time of his death. An enclosure contained the confession of Henry Jekyll.

Utterson returned to his office to read the letters. The letter of Dr. Lanyon described how Dr. Jekyll had sent Poole to Dr. Lanyon with a request that Dr. Lanyon search for some drugs in Dr. Jekyll's laboratory. Hyde had appeared to claim the drugs. Then, in Dr. Lanyon's presence, Hyde had taken the drug and had been transformed into Dr. Jekyll. The shock of this transformation had caused Dr. Lanyon's death.

Dr. Jekyll's own account of the horrible affair was more detailed. He had begun early in life to live a double life. Publicly, he had been genteel and circumspect; privately, however, he had practiced strange vices without restraint. Becoming obsessed with the idea that people had two personalities, he reasoned that men were capable of having two physical beings as well. Finally, he had compounded a mixture that transformed his body into the physical representation of his evil self. He became Hyde. In his disguise, he was free to haunt the lonely, narrow corners of London and to perform the darkest acts without fear of recognition.

He tried in every way to protect Hyde. He cautioned his servants to let him in at any hour; he took an apartment for him, and he made out his will in Hyde's favor. His life proceeded safely enough until he awoke one morning in the shape of Edward Hyde and realized that his evil nature had gained the upper hand. Frightened, he determined to cast off the nature of Hyde. He sought out better companions and tried to occupy his mind with other things. He, however, was not strong enough to change his true nature. He finally permitted himself to assume the shape of Hyde again, and on that occasion Hyde, full of an overpowering lust to do evil, murdered Sir Danvers Carew.

Dr. Jekyll renewed his effort to abandon the nature of Hyde. Walking in the park one day, he suddenly changed into Hyde. On that occasion, he had sought out his friend Dr. Lanyon to go to his laboratory to obtain the drugs that would change him back to the personality of the doctor. Dr. Lanyon had watched the transformation with horror. Thereafter the nature of Hyde seemed to assert itself constantly. When his supply of chemicals had been exhausted and could not be replenished, Dr. Jekyll, as Hyde, shut himself up in his laboratory while he experimented with one drug after another. Finally, in despair, as Utterson now realized, he killed himself.

Critical Evaluation:

The Gothic Novel in England enjoyed its heyday in the eighteenth century. In this sense, Robert Louis Stevenson's *The Strange Case of Dr. Jekyll and Mr. Hyde* is but a late appendage to a popular trend. In terms of content and style, however, it is in the mainstream of that highly popular genre. The novel has predilections for the far and remote, the marvelous and abnormal. It is an escape from reality, emphasizing intuition over reason and impulse over rationality. Like most Romantic novels, it values impulsive, childlike, savage, or peasant behavior as uncorrupted by civilized ways. It is transcendental, grotesque, and bizarre while maintaining a sensitive approach to nature, beauty, and women. It is Rousseauistic and anti-intellectual in philosophy, but it is notable for being remote, simple, and democratic while focusing on the supernatural.

The central feature of *The Strange Case of Dr. Jekyll and Mr. Hyde* is its theme of duality. Two personalities—opposite and antagonistic—mesh within one body, a psychological insight which, in its time, was remarkably prescient. Dr. Jekyll, an essentially good man, was fascinated by the idea of evil. As a research scientist, he pursued the idea to the point of developing a drug that would alter his conscious state from an intrinsically good person to a fundamentally bad one. Taking the drug, he developed a dual personality, combining the extremes of good and evil. The evil self emerged as the violent Mr. Hyde. This schizophrenia persisted until the "bad" Mr.

Hyde overcame "good" Dr. Jekyll to become the dominant personality of the two—at which time it became apparent that Mr. Hyde would have to be annihilated—by then a solution both inevitable and desirable.

The process of transformation was alchemic and tainted with witchcraft. This touch of the occult—a distinct Gothic feature—rescued the novel from the banal and elevated it to the realm of genuine Gothic horror. Alchemy, witchcraft, and the occult were to earlier ages what technology— especially the computer—is to the present day: a threat to the status quo and comfortable assumptions. The occult and technology are usually treated in like manner: with awe and apprehension. *The Strange Case of Dr. Jekyll and Mr. Hyde* continues to fascinate readers—as well as motion-picture audiences—for just those qualities of verisimilitude, fear, and hostility. The novel ultimately succeeds by terrifying the reader, for who does not contain the potential for developing that split-personality of good and evil which the protagonist so vividly portrays. It is Stevenson's almost mystical capacity in language and characterization to evoke reader identification with his protagonist which accounts for the powerful impact of his novel.

DOCTOR THORNE

Type of work: Novel
Author: Anthony Trollope (1815-1882)
Type of plot: Domestic realism
Time of plot: Mid-nineteenth century
Locale: Barsetshire, England
First published: 1858

Principal characters:
DOCTOR THORNE, a country doctor
MARY THORNE, his niece
SQUIRE GRESHAM, the owner of Greshamsbury Park
LADY ARABELLA, his wife
FRANK GRESHAM, their son
ROGER SCATCHERD, a stonemason and later a baronet
LOUIS PHILIPPE, his son
MISS DUNSTABLE, an heiress

The Story:

Greshamsbury Park, in the county of Barsetshire, dominated the life of the surrounding countryside. Unfortunately, Greshamsbury's lord, Squire Gresham, was rapidly spending himself into poverty.

Most of his financial troubles resulted from the desire of his wife, Lady Arabella De Courcy Gresham, to get him into politics. The Squire had inherited his father's seat in Parliament. He had lost favor, however, because of his Whig leanings. Barsetshire was overwhelmingly Tory and did not approve of Gresham's Whig friends or the fact that his wife's aristocratic family, the De Courcy's, were aggressively Whig in sentiment. Having lost his seat in the Parliamentary elections, Gresham twice tried to regain it. These attempts were stimulated by his wife, who fancied being the wife of a member of Parliament. Gresham, however, was unsuccessful, and he lost a great deal of money in financing his campaigns.

Consequently, when his son Frank came of age, Squire Gresham had not much to offer him in the way of financial security. Lady Arabella saw as their only hope the possibility of Frank's marriage to a wealthy heiress. That he might do such a thing, however, seemed rather doubtful; much to the distress of his mother and her family, young Frank was highly enamored of Mary Thorne, niece of the local doctor. Frank and Mary had known each other all their lives, and Mary had been educated along with the young Greshams at Greshamsbury Park. Hers was an interesting history.

She had been brought to live with her uncle, Doctor Thorne, when she was a mere infant. The real circumstances of her birth—that she was the illegitimate child of Doctor Thorne's brother and Mary Scatcherd, a village girl—were known only to the doctor. Even Mary Scatcherd's brother Roger, who had killed his sister's betrayer, did not know that Doctor Thorne had adopted the child. Roger Scatcherd, a poor stonemason, had been sentenced to six months in prison for his crime. When his term was up, he was told that the child had died. Since the doctor stood in high favor with Squire Gresham and regularly cared for Lady Arabella, it was natural that his niece should visit the estate. Because she was an attractive child and near the age of the Gresham children, she soon took her lessons with them. By the time Frank was of age, Mary Thorne seemed part of the family. Lady Arabella, however, was determined that this was not to be the literal state of affairs; Mary had no money.

One of Squire Gresham's greatest misfortunes was the loss of a particularly choice part of his estate, land sold to pay off his numerous and most pressing debts. Doctor Thorne, acting as agent for the Squire, found a buyer in Sir Roger Scatcherd, a wealthy baronet. Sir Roger was the former stonemason who had prospered well after his jail term and was now the possessor of a title, a seat in Parliament, and a large fortune. Although he knew nothing of the existence of his sister's illegitimate child, Sir Roger was in close contact with Doctor Thorne. Sir Roger was a chronic alcoholic, and Doctor Thorne was often called on to attend to him during his drinking sprees.

The loss of this piece of property was indeed a tragedy to the Gresham family for the sale greatly diminished the estate Frank would someday inherit. Nervously, Lady Arabella began to plan for the future of her family. Fortunately, one of the daughters was engaged to marry money, a politician who wanted the Gresham and De Courcy position and family connections. Another daughter would marry the local vicar and so would be assured of a respectable position, although one without much money. Frank, however, was his mother's real hope. If he could make a wealthy marriage, their troubles would be over; but Frank, in love with Mary Thorne, had no lofty matrimonial ambitions. To save him from an unfortunate romance, Lady Arabella's family invited Frank to De Courcy Castle for a visit.

It was the Countess De Courcy's plan to make a match between Frank and Miss Dunstable, a family friend. Miss Dunstable was considered the wealthiest heiress in England, but she was wary and sharp-tongued. Mostly to humor his aunt, Frank pretended to woo the heiress, and to his surprise, he found her rather good company. Miss Dunstable, ten years his senior and much more worldly-wise, soon uncovered his plot. Thereafter, they became the best of friends, and she acted as an adviser to Frank in his affair with Mary Thorne.

Meanwhile, Sir Roger Scatcherd was in such poor health from excessive drinking that he decided to make his will, leaving everything to Louis

Philippe, his equally alcoholic son. When Dr. Thorne learned the terms of the will, he told Sir Roger that Mary Scatcherd's child was still living. Sir Roger made her his second heir in the event of his son's death.

Other matters were not going well for Mary. Lady Arabella, finding Frank's attachment for Mary unchanged, would not allow the girl to visit Greshamsbury. When Frank arrived home and became aware of the shabby treatment she had received, he was furious. The family, however, insisted that he had to marry wealth, particularly after his sister, who was to marry money, had been jilted.

Sir Roger was also in difficulties. Having discovered a fraud in his election, the committee unseated him, and the shock was too great for the old man. He went on one final drinking bout and died from the effects. Louis Philippe, having inherited the estate, also formed an attachment for Mary, but she remained true to Frank. Dr. Thorne's only hope for the happiness of Mary and Frank lay in the possible death of Louis Philippe. Meanwhile, the young man was well on his way to fulfilling the doctor's half-wish. Having paid a visit to the Squire for the purpose of foreclosing on some debts, Louis Philippe went on a drinking spree that rivaled any of his father's. Weak and very ill, he was finally sent home.

In a stormy interview soon afterward, Lady Arabella demanded that Mary end her engagement to Frank. Mary refused to break her promise, but she did ask the young man to release her because of the hopelessness of the situation in which they found themselves. Frank refused, insisting that they loved each other. Then Louis Philippe died. Doctor Thorne jubilantly told Mary the news of her inheritance, news which opened the way for her marriage to Frank. With Mary now an heiress in her own right, not even the proud De Courcys could object to so excellent a match. For the first time in years, an atmosphere of rejoicing hung over Greshamsbury Park.

Critical Evaluation:

The third novel in Anthony Trollope's Barsetshire series, *Doctor Thorne*, like its two predecessors, *The Warden* and *Barchester Towers*, describes with psychological insight the social realities of his mythical county. Unlike the first two works, which were concerned with the insular ecclesiastical world of a cathedral town, Trollope turns his attention in this novel to the landed wealth of Barsetshire. The gentry, represented by the Greshams, are in decline because of the political imprudence of the Squire who early in his married life aligned himself with his wife's family, the De Courcys, notoriously aristocratic and notoriously Whig. Having lost his Tory constituency and his money, Squire Gresham attempts to retrench to save the estate for his son.

It is at this point that Doctor Thorne, one of Trollope's ideal gentlemen, enters the story. The Squire's only confidant, he serves not only as the family physician but also as its moral and spiritual counselor. Rigorous in his ethics, proud of his social station, and in no way awed by the upper classes, Doctor Thorne joins the Squire in an attempt to restore the estate to its former vigor. An enemy of the snobbish and pretentious aristocrats like the De Courcys, who have no loyalty to the life of the land, he seeks to help his friend by advising various economies and by suggesting judicious loans.

If the moral strength that saves Greshamsbury Park comes from the doctor, it is the money of Sir Roger Scatcherd, however, which enables Gresham to recoup and permits young Frank and Mary to wed. Scatcherd, part of the new industrial wealth, unwittingly saves the agriculture of the area from the moneylenders of London. It is in this alignment that Trollope reveals his political sympathies with the English upper-middle class and his antagonism to the aristocracy and their morality.

DOMBEY AND SON

Type of work: Novel
Author: Charles Dickens (1812–1870)
Type of plot: Sentimental romance
Time of plot: Early nineteenth century
Locale: England
First published: 1846–1848

Principal characters:

MR. DOMBEY, a rich London merchant
PAUL, his son
FLORENCE, his daughter
EDITH GRANGER, his second wife
MR. CARKER, his trusted agent
WALTER GAY, Florence's beloved

The Story:

Mr. Dombey was a stiff and dignified man who rarely showed emotion, but the birth of an infant son, who was named Paul, was cause for rejoicing. Mr. Dombey had longed many years for a child who would fill the second part of the mercantile firm of Dombey and Son. Even the fact that Mrs. Dombey died shortly after the boy's birth did not particularly concern him; he was centered entirely on the little infant who he hoped would someday take over the business. Mr. Dombey also had a daughter, Florence, but she meant almost nothing to him, for she could not take a place in the firm.

Little Paul was first given over to a wet nurse, but the woman proved to be unreliable and was dismissed. After her dismissal, little Paul was cared for by Mr. Dombey's sister and one of her friends. Despite their vigilant care, however, little Paul's health was poor. He was listless and never cared to play. At last, Mr. Dombey arranged to have him sent to a home at Brighton, together with his sister, to gain the benefits of the sea air.

In spite of his father's dislike for little Florence, Paul loved his sister very much, and they were constant companions. Paul's love for Florence only made Mr. Dombey dislike the girl more, for the father felt that his daughter was coming between himself and his son.

One weekend while Mr. Dombey was visiting at Brighton, Walter Gay, a young clerk in the firm, came to the inn where Mr. Dombey and his children were dining. Some time before, the clerk had rescued Florence from an old female thief. Now his uncle was about to become a bankrupt, and Walter had come to ask for a loan to save his uncle's shop. Mr. Dombey let little Paul, who was then six years old, make the decision. Paul asked Florence what he should do; she told him to lend the money, and he did.

Shortly afterward, little Paul was placed in a private school at Brighton, where he was to be educated as quickly as possible. The pace of his studies proved too much for him, and before the year was out, his health broke down. Even after his father took him home to London, he never seemed to grow any better. Before many months had elapsed, little Paul died, mourned by his father and his sister, although for different reasons.

Mr. Dombey took his son's death as a personal blow of fate to his plans. His sister and her friend became so concerned about him that they planned to have him take a trip to Leamington with Major Bagstock, a retired officer. While they were there, they met Edith Granger, a young widow whose mother the Major had known. Mr. Dombey immediately began to court Mrs. Granger, seeing in her a beautiful, well-bred young woman who would grace his household. Mrs. Granger, coaxed by an aged mother who was concerned for her daughter's welfare, finally accepted Mr. Dombey, although she was not in love with him.

Florence Dombey had seen young Walter Gay several times since their meeting at Brighton. After her brother's death, she came to look upon young Walter as a substitute brother, despite his lowly station. Then their friendship was broken temporarily when Mr. Dombey sent Walter on a mission to the West Indies. Weeks passed, but no word was heard of the ship on which he had sailed. Everyone believed that it had sunk and that Walter had been drowned.

After Mrs. Granger had accepted Mr. Dombey's suit, they began to make plans for the wedding and for reopening the Dombey house in London. Edith Granger first met Florence at the house. The two immediately became fast friends, even though Mr. Dombey disliked his daughter and made it plain that he did not want his wife to become too fond of the girl.

Mr. Dombey's second marriage was unsuccessful from the start. Edith Granger was too proud to give in to Mr. Dombey's attempts to dictate to her and to his claim upon her as a piece of merchandise, and she resisted him in every way. Dombey, who was too dignified to argue with her, sent his business manager, Mr. Carker, to tell his wife that he was dissatisfied with her conduct. Carker warned Mrs. Dombey that, unless she obeyed Mr. Dombey, Florence would be the one to suffer. Edith Dombey then became outwardly cool to her stepdaughter, but she still resisted her husband. Mr. Carker was once more dispatched to tell her that Mr. Dombey meant to be obeyed in everything.

The wife then openly revolted. She felt that she could get complete revenge by running off with Carker, her husband's most trusted employee, who was also so far below Mr. Dombey socially that the blow would hurt even more. After she and the employee disappeared, Florence was only rebuffed in her attempts to comfort her father. When he struck her, she ran away from the house and went to the shop owned by Sol Gills, Walter

Gay's uncle. There she found that Gills had disappeared and that an old ship's captain named Cuttle was in charge. Captain Cuttle recognized Florence and took her in.

At last, Mr. Dombey learned the whereabouts of his wife and Carker from a young woman whom Carker had seduced and deserted. Mr. Dombey followed the pair to France but failed to locate them. Carker, meanwhile, returned to England. Mrs. Dombey had refused to have anything to do with him. She had her revenge, she said, in ruining him and her husband. Carker, trying to escape into the English countryside, met Mr. Dombey at a railway station. An accident occurred, and Carker was killed by a train.

Florence was staying with Captain Cuttle and hoped that Walter would return, even though everyone had given him up for dead. Her faith was at last rewarded. Walter had been picked up by a vessel bound for China and so had not had the opportunity to send back word of his safety. Shortly after his return, he revealed to Florence that he no longer felt as a brother toward her, since she had become a woman during his absence. Realizing that she, too, had fallen in love with him, she accepted his proposal. Walter had found work as a clerk on a ship, and after their marriage, they sailed on a ship bound for the Orient.

The failure of his marriage had broken Mr. Dombey's spirit, and he took little interest in his firm from that time on. His lack of interest was unfortunate, for the firm had been placed in a difficult position by some of Carker's dealings while he had been Dombey's trusted agent. As a result of Carker's mismanagement and Dombey's lack of interest, the firm went bankrupt. After the bankruptcy, Mr. Dombey stayed alone in his house, saw no one, and gradually drifted into despair.

On the very day that Mr. Dombey had decided to commit suicide, Florence returned to London from the Orient with her year-old son, who was named Paul, after his dead uncle. Florence and the baby cheered up Mr. Dombey, and he began to take a new interest in life. Reconciled to his daughter, he realized that she had always loved him even though he had been exceedingly cruel to her. Walter Gay succeeded in business, and all of them lived together happily; his misfortunes had made a changed man of the almost indomitable Mr. Dombey.

Critical Evaluation:

Dombey and Son, which appeared after *Martin Chuzzlewit,* was an effort by Charles Dickens to regain popularity he had lost with the publication of his previous novel. *Martin Chuzzlewit,* which had heavily satirized America and Americans, had caused Dickens to lose a great deal of favor, a loss that greatly irritated Dickens, who was by that time in something of a competition for the public's attention with another great Victorian novelist, William Makepeace Thackeray. *Dombey and Son* is also a milestone in Dickens' work in that he placed the story at a higher social level than he had done in his previous novels. For the first time, he indicated an interest and a sympathy in the upper-middle classes and the aristocracy. The story is a very serious one, involving the downfall of a dignified and pompous merchant and his learning of the power of love as compared to the lesser power of money. In typical Dickensian style, however, there is a whole catalog of characters to provide a humorous background.

In *Dombey and Son*, Dickens for the first time attempted to portray the full panorama of English society—from beggar to magnate, from baronet to housemaid. Although less successful than *Bleak House* in expressing the connection of each level of society to every other level, the novel is nonetheless prodigious in scope.

The theme of the work is the relationship between parents and children, chiefly Mr. Dombey's relationship with Paul and Florence and subordinately those of various parents and their offspring, ranging in social station from Mrs. Skewton and Edith down to Mrs. Brown and her Alice. Each family situation is thrown into relief by contrast with another, similar in social class yet utterly different in kind. Edith Granger, schooled almost from infancy to be "artful, designing, mercenary, laying snares for men," is shown in opposition to the son of Sir Barnet Skettles, whose parents willingly interrupt his studies at Dr. Blimber's academy in order to enjoy his company during their sojourn abroad. Mr. Dombey's crude attempt to mold his fragile son to a shape that does his father honor in the world's eyes contrasts with the honest and unpretentious course that Solomon Gills recommends to his nephew Walter: "Be diligent, try to like it, my dear boy, work for a steady independence, and be happy!" The miserable devices of greed that Mrs. Brown urges on her daughter as the only recourse of the poor is proven a lie by the love and warmth shown by Polly Toodle toward her erring son Rob.

The sad ends of Edith, little Paul, and Alice Marwood all result from two things, or perhaps two facets of one thing: the corruption of childhood by adult concerns, and the disregard of individuality in children that sees them as *things*, as counters in a game, or as a hedge against destitution or mortality. Mr. Dombey, for example, views Paul as an object, a little mirror of his own greatness. He expects his son to reflect himself—that is, to love him as he loves himself. In his stubborn individuality, Paul perceives the merit of Florence and turns to her; Mr. Dombey is amazed and outraged, because he sees Paul as an extension of himself and cannot conceive of the little boy's having a private opinion. A mirror, after all, cannot have a point of view. In Mr. Dombey's own mind, therefore, no blame accrues to himself; he decides that Florence must be the cause of the "distortion" of Paul's feelings. In this way, she too falls victim to her father's self-love and becomes the object of his hatred, almost a scapegoat for his repressed feelings of guilt about Paul's death; for in his view, she had spoiled Paul as a tool for advancing his father's self-approbation, the function for which his elaborate education was to prepare him.

In the same way, Edith Granger was formed in her youth to fulfill her mother's nasty ambitions; and the shining ideal that both Mrs. Skewton and Mr. Dombey urge on their children is a glossy standing in the eyes of the world, a value that is essentially an adult concern. In contrast, Walter's mentor in his own invincible childishness (he rebukes himself for being "old-fashioned") guides his charge in the path of honesty, the natural behavior of childhood. Young Paul is the chief exemplar of this virtue in the novel, and his resistance to corruption is likewise referrable to that curious quality of being "old-fashioned." Paul was "born old"; he possesses that wisdom of extreme age that constitutes a return to the innocence of childhood. He is fey and resists classification. His obdurate honesty shows itself in his concern for first principles. For example, he inquires of his father what money can do, and when his father proudly replies that money can do anything, he suggests two things that it cannot do: bring back his mother or give him health. Then he asks the question again, still more pointedly: "What's money, *after all*?" as if to direct his father's attention to the extreme paltriness of those things which money *can do*, to that vain show which nurtures his father's pride. His father, however, takes no notice; it is not for him to be lessoned by a child. Despised, neglected, and thought unfit to prepare for any great purpose, Florence has her brother's memory for a master and educates herself to his truth rather than to her father's ambition.

Dombey and Son is unique among Dickens' novels in its profusion of strongly drawn female characters. Indeed, the author seems intent on ringing the changes on female nature from best to worst. For the most part, these figures though vivid have but one dimension, but two evidence a greater depth of understanding than the author had heretofore achieved in his representation of women. One is the character of Florence, whose states of mind illustrate a classic psychological progression. Rejected by a loved parent, she reasons thus: "I am unloved, therefore unlovable." Her early conviction of unworthiness dictates not only her subsequent actions but indeed shapes the main plot of the novel.

Dickens marks Florence with the token of ideal womanhood, she even displays talents of a housewife, in Solomon Gills's parlor. Still, she is truly good without being saccharine, a major advance in Dickens' treatment of women characters. Miss Tox is even more an unusual creation; for heretofore Dickens had not produced a female character at once such an object of satire and so generally sympathetic. She comes in for her share of ridicule for her delusions about Mr. Dombey's intentions and for her genteel pretentions in general, but the author allows her the virtue of her consistency: " . . . poor excommunicated Miss Tox, who, if she were a fawner and a toad-eater, was at least an honest and a constant one. . . ." She is as unlikely a vessel of kindness and simple wisdom as the dandy Toots, or the exhausted aristocrat, Cousin Feenix; yet Dickens puts wisdom into their mouths as if to show that although corruption might seem to reign supreme everywhere, truth remains, and although hidden, it can flourish and even prevail.

DRACULA

Type of work: Novel
Author: Bram Stoker (1847–1912)
Type of plot: Horror romance
Time of plot: Nineteenth century
Locale: Transylvania and England
First published: 1897

> *Principal characters:*
> JONATHAN HARKER, an English solicitor
> MINA MURRAY, his fiancée
> COUNT DRACULA, a mysterious nobleman
> DR. SEWARD, the head of a mental hospital
> DR. VAN HELSING, a Dutch medical specialist
> LUCY WESTENRA, Mina's friend
> ARTHUR HOLMWOOD, Lucy's fiancé

The Story:

On his way to Castle Dracula in the province of Transylvania in Rumania, Jonathan Harker, an English solicitor, was apprehensive. His nervousness grew when he observed the curious, fearful attitude of the peasants and the coachman after they learned of his destination. He was on his way to transact business with Count Dracula, and his mission would necessitate remaining at the castle for several days.

Upon his arrival at the castle, Harker found comfortable accommodations awaiting him. Count Dracula was a charming host, although his peculiarly bloodless physical appearance was somewhat disagreeable to Harker's English eyes. Almost immediately, Harker was impressed with the strange life of the castle. He and the Count discussed their business at night, as the Count was never available during the daytime. Although the food was excellent, Harker never saw a servant about the place. While exploring the castle, he found that it was situated high at the top of a mountain with no accessible exit other than the main doorway, which was kept locked. He realized with a shock that he was a prisoner of Count Dracula.

Various harrowing experiences ensued. While Harker half dozed in the early morning hours, three phantom women materialized and attacked him, attempting to bite his throat. Then the Count appeared and drove them off, whispering fiercely that Harker belonged to him. Later, Harker thought he saw a huge bat descending the castle walls, but the creature turned out to be Count Dracula. In the morning Harker, trying frantically to escape, stumbled into an old chapel where a number of coffinlike boxes of earth were stored. Harker opened one, and beneath the cover lay the Count, apparently dead. In the evening, however, the Count appeared as usual, and Harker demanded that he be released. The Count obligingly opened the castle door. A pack of wolves surrounded the entrance. The Count, laughing hysterically, left poor Harker a prisoner in his room.

The next day Harker, weak and sick from a strange wound in his throat, saw a pack cart, loaded with the mysterious boxes, drive from the castle. Dracula was gone and Harker was alone, a prisoner with no visible means of escape.

Meanwhile, Harker's fiancée, Mina Murray, had gone to visit her beautiful and charming friend, Lucy Westenra in England. Lucy was planning to marry Arthur Holmwood, a young nobleman. One evening, early in Mina's visit, a storm blew up and a strange ship was driven aground. The only living creature aboard was a gray wolflike dog. The animal escaped into the countryside.

Soon afterward, Lucy's happiness began to fade because of a growing tendency to sleepwalk. One night, Mina followed her friend during one of her spells and discovered Lucy in a churchyard. A tall, thin man who was bending over Lucy disappeared at Mina's approach. Lucy could remember nothing of the experience when she awoke, but her physical condition seemed much weakened. Finally, she grew so ill that Mina was forced to call upon Dr. Seward, Lucy's former suitor. Lucy began to improve under his care, and when Mina received a report from Budapest that her missing fiancé had been found and needed care, she felt free to end her visit.

When Lucy's condition suddenly grew worse, Dr. Seward asked his old friend, Dr. Van Helsing, a specialist from Amsterdam, for his professional opinion. Examining Lucy thoroughly, Van Helsing paused over two tiny throat wounds that she was unable to explain. Van Helsing was concerned over Lucy's condition, which pointed to unusual loss of blood without signs of anemia or hemorrhage. She was given blood transfusions at intervals, and someone sat up with her at night. She improved but expressed fear of going to sleep at night because her dreams had grown so horrible.

One morning, Dr. Seward fell asleep outside her door. When he and Van Helsing entered her room, they found Lucy ashen white and in a worse condition than ever. Van Helsing quickly performed another transfusion; she rallied, but not as satisfactorily as before. Van Helsing then secured some garlic flowers and told Lucy to keep them around her neck at night. When the two doctors called the next morning, Lucy's mother had removed the flowers because she feared their odor might bother her daughter. Frantically, Van Helsing rushed to Lucy's room and found her in a coma. Again, he administered a transfusion, and her condition improved.

She said that with the garlic flowers close by she was not afraid of nightly flapping noises at her window. Van Helsing sat with her every night until he felt her well enough to leave. After cautioning her to sleep with the garlic flowers about her neck at all times, he returned to Amsterdam.

Lucy's mother continued to sleep with her daughter. One night, the two ladies were awakened by a huge wolf that crashed through the window. Mrs. Westenra fell dead of a heart attack, and Lucy fainted, the wreath of garlic flowers slipping from her neck. Seward and Van Helsing, who had returned to England, discovered her half dead in the morning. They knew she was dying and called Arthur. As Arthur attempted to kiss her, Lucy's teeth seemed about to fasten onto his throat. Van Helsing drew him away. When Lucy died, Van Helsing put a tiny gold crucifix over her mouth, but an attendant stole it from her body.

Soon after Lucy's death, several children of the neighborhood were discovered far from their homes, their throats marked by small wounds. Their only explanation was that they had followed a pretty lady. When Jonathan Harker returned to England, Van Helsing went to see him and Mina. After talking with Harker, Van Helsing revealed to Dr. Seward his belief that Lucy had fallen victim to a vampire, one of those strange creatures who can live for centuries on the blood of their victims and breed their kind by attacking the innocent and making them vampires in turn. According to Van Helsing, the only way to save Lucy's soul was to drive a stake through the heart of her corpse, cut off her head, and stuff her mouth with garlic flowers. Dr. Seward protested violently. The next midnight Arthur, Dr. Seward, and Van Helsing visited Lucy's tomb and found it empty. When daylight came, they did as Van Helsing had suggested with Lucy's corpse, which had returned to its tomb.

The men, with Mina, tried to track down Dracula in London in order to find him before he victimized anyone else. Their object was to remove the boxes of sterilized earth he had brought with him from Transylvania so that he would have no place to hide in the daytime. At last, the hunters trapped Dracula, but he escaped them. By putting Mina into a trance, Van Helsing was able to learn that Dracula was at sea, and it was necessary to follow him to his castle. Wolves gathered about them in that desolate country. Van Helsing drew a circle in the snow with a crucifix, and the travelers rested safely within the magic enclosure. The next morning, they overtook a cart carrying a black box. Van Helsing and the others overcame the drivers of the cart and pried open the lid of Dracula's coffin. As the sun began to set, they drove a stake through the heart of the corpse. The vampire was no more.

Critical Evaluation:
Legend is inextricably twined with Bram Stoker's novel *Dracula*, for the

novel is based on the legend. It is impossible to separate the two: the reader will inevitably supply legendary associations between the lines of the novel; but more often than not, readers tend to forget that both legend and novel were based on reality. This is not to say, of course, that vampires do or did roam Transylvania or elsewhere. However, the prototype for the Dracula legend was a verifiable historical figure, Prince Vlad Tepes, ruler of Transylvania and Walachia (now Rumania) in the mid-fifteenth century. Tepes, nicknamed "The Impaler," earned a bloody reputation by spearing his victims (some 100,000 of them in a six- to ten-year reign, so it is reported) on wooden sticks, a tactic that served to deter domestic criminals and potential outside invaders alike. He assumed the name Dracula, variously interpreted as "son of the dragon" and "son of the devil," as a further reminder of his vicious tendencies. The subjects of his small kingdom, however, were convinced that such blood lust could be found only in a human vampire; hence Vlad Tepes, self-proclaimed Dracula, was the basis for the legend that Stoker captured so well.

Vampirism has been traced by historians, studied by scholars, embellished by artists and writers, and feared by the superstitious. In Western culture, vampirism has been associated mainly with the Transylvania region of Eastern Europe; however, the vampire phenomenon in one form or another is attested in all parts of the world from ancient times onward. Outside of Europe, the vampire has appeared in the ancient cultures of the Middle East and the Mediterranean, in China as well as throughout Asia, in several African cultures, and in Aztec civilization and later in Mexico. Some references are in allegedly official reports and in religious works on demonology; others occur in folklore and in literature, drama, painting, and sculpture. Clearly, the vampire was no nineteenth century European invention, but the Romantic obsession with Gothic horror certainly stimulated a spate of vampiric literature among its other supernatural preoccupations. A short story, "The Vampyre," by John Polidori, was published in 1819. The melodrama *Les Vampires*, by Charles Nodier and Carmouche, was first produced in Paris in 1820. *Varney the Vampire, or The Feast of Blood* (authorship is disputed; either John Malcolm Rymer or Thomas Peckett Prest), a long novel, appeared in 1847. Joseph Sheridan Le Fanu's redoubtable "Carmilla" first saw print in 1871; but it was Stoker's *Dracula*, published in 1897, that surpassed them all and remains the paragon of vampire stories even today.

Drawing primarily upon European sources, Stoker produced a terrifyingly credible tale by eliminating the inconsistencies and the contradictions common to legendary matter. Wisely avoiding some of the more outlandish explanations of vampirism, for example, Stoker portrayed the trait as transmitted from vampire to victim, who in turn became a vampire, and so on. To evade straining credulity, Stoker required prolonged contact between vampire and victim before the victim was irrevocably enlisted in the ranks. Thus, Jonathan Harker, whose sustenance of Count Dracula was brief, recovered with no lasting ill effects; but Lucy Westenra was literally drained and consequently became a vampire herself. As a result—and given the perilous circumstances—Van Helsing was compelled to restrain forcibly Lucy's ertswhile fiancé Arthur from giving her a deathbed kiss on her frothing, fanged mouth. Stoker also conceded the vampire's power to exercise a species of demonic possession, without physical contact, as the affliction of Mina Murray Harker illustrates.

In like manner, Stoker employed only the most conventional techniques for repelling vampires: garlic and the crucifix. The requirements for vampire survival were equally simplified from the vast complexity of alternatives that accumulated in the legend. Stoker limited his vampires to nocturnal activity; mandated, of course, the periodic sucking of blood (allowing for moderate stretches of hibernation or abstinence); insisted upon daylight repose in a coffin filled with Transylvania soil; and claimed vampiric invulnerability to ordinary human weapons.

Finally, Stoker's methods for the total annihilation of vampires were similarly conventional without resort to esoteric impedimenta. He stipulated that a wooden stake be driven through the vampire's heart (although Dracula was dispatched with a bowie knife); that the vampire's head be cut off; and that the vampire's mouth be stuffed with garlic flowers. Again, the inconsistency of these remedies accounts for much of the impact of Stoker's horror story.

In fact, Stoker's recounting of the vampire legend has become the "standard version" in Western culture. Short stories and novels have spun off from the Stoker novel—all distinctly imitative and inferior; attempted sequels have been likewise unsatisfactory, never rising above the level of cheap journalism. A number of theatrical and film adaptations have been mounted, but the classic stage and screen performances of Bela Lugosi, based upon Stoker's *Dracula*, have never been equaled. Lugosi's 1932 portrayal of Dracula still spellbinds motion-picture audiences as no other production has been able to do; and in this atmosphere of at least semicredulity, reported sightings of vampiric activity—much like reported sightings of flying saucers or unidentified flying objects—continue to the present.

In the meanwhile, Vlad Tepes's castles in Walachia and the Carpathians have been refurbished by the Rumanian government as tourist attractions, and the historical Dracula is being hailed as a national hero who strove to upgrade the moral fiber of his subjects. In many ways, therefore, Stoker's Dracula lives on to influence the present as powerfully—albeit in a different manner—as he influenced the past.

EBONY AND IVORY

Type of work: Short stories
Author: Llewelyn Powys (1884–1939)
Time of plots: Early twentieth century
Locale: Africa and Europe
First published: 1923

Llewelyn Powys, the youngest of three brothers to achieve literary fame, was a rather gifted and remarkable British writer. He was educated at Cambridge, worked as a stock farmer in Kenya during World War I, and then moved to New York to work as a journalist for five more years. The stories in *Ebony and Ivory*, many of which were published in the best magazines of the time, were written during his stay in Kenya and New York. They present perhaps the best and most representative examples of his outlook and art.

Powys' outlook and art are very closely related. His vision of life informs every aspect of his art, while his art is an attempt to answer that vision. This tension between outlook and art, truth and style, content and form, provides Powys' stories with their intensity and force.

Powys' vision of life, the spirit that informs these stories, was grounded in pain and death, cruelty and mortality, vanity and doom, for Powys was obsessed with agony and fate, which for him were the sole absolutes of life. His stories dwell overwhelmingly on the tragic soul-destroying aspects of life and have much the same spirit as *Ecclesiastes*, the *Rubáiyát of Omar Khayyám*, and much of the fiction of Joseph Conrad. They show an intimate acquaintance with the terror, cruelties, and savagery that plague men. Powys knew the futility and mortality of humanity. This was the lesson he learned in Africa.

In this collection, there are the Ebony stories and sketches, which take place in British East Africa, and the Ivory tales, which take place in Europe. The title obviously contains an ironic play on skin color, on black and white, but beyond this fact and far more important is the reference to the Arab proverb: "On Ebony and Ivory the same dark doom is writ."

The Ebony stories provide the hard core of Powys' vision; their total effect is that of hopelessness and despair. These sketches show the soul-killing effect of Africa on the European and African alike. The unrelenting sun, the harshness of color and noise, the voraciousness of animal and human life all reduce men to their naked, cruel selves. The European is demoralized, and all of his illusions are destroyed. His rule is stripped of its benevolence in Africa and is shown to rest on brutality and cunning. In "Black Parasites," a hard-hearted, mediocre farmer sets fire to his brushland after tying up a native sheep thief in the middle of it. In "How

It Happens," a sensitive boy arrives in British East Africa from England, and in his harsh, new surroundings, he is demoralized by his mediocre associates, gets syphilis, and commits suicide. Given his outlook on life, Powys' theme, the loss of innocence, was almost inevitable. In "Black Gods," he declared that the bottom of the well of life contains no hope, that the surface was all, the depth hollow and empty.

When Powys' heroes undergo any change, it is in the direction of shedding illusions, of descending to the bottom of the well of life and facing life without hope. This does not mean that they necessarily give up; Powys' most memorable heroes face life's savagery with a hopeless defiance. In "Dead Matter in Africa," a zebra guards his dead mate against the vultures, against all hope and reason, and against the universe. Again, in his Ebony story, "The Stunner," a dumb brute of a man rises from his deathbed and staggers miles to his sweetheart solely on the strength of his love; but this kind of heroism, however admirable, is essentially futile—it means involving oneself in pain, in death, and in tragedy. Although Powys' stories are not Christian in outlook, the figure of the crucified Jesus runs through the majority of them, for Jesus is the epitome of this futile heroism, of this agonized defiance of fate.

As the Arab proverb suggests, Powys' Ivory tales elaborate the ideas and motifs of the Ebony section. In "Threnody," "Death," and "The Brown Satyr," Powys develops the same theme he used in "How It Happens," namely the loss of innocence and the problem of facing a world devoid of hope. In "Not Guilty," "Un Mufle," and "The Wryneck," Powys shows again the impossibility of love in a cursed and savage world devoid of meaning and full of doom.

The Ebony stories seem slightly superior in quality to the Ivory tales simply because Africa provided a more appropriate background for Powys' despairing vision; however, he does a fine job of conveying that vision in the Ivory section as well. For Powys, the world was cursed and damned, and it was damned no matter where one was, whether in the heart of Africa or in the heart of civilization. To him, it was as if some evil wizard had desolated the world and left it in agony and despair.

Such a vision of life could easily become intolerable to the person who possessed it unless he had some means of protecting himself against it, some means of converting it into something productive. Powys' method of achieving release was through writing, through art which gave a tangible form to that vision. Powys sought his salvation through his stories and through observation. If participation in the world meant pain and tragedy, observation was a way of protecting oneself from pain and tragedy, a way of keeping the world at a distance. Art, for Powys, was a way of reshaping life's pain and thereby controlling it. Passive observation and active artistic creation were his way of protecting himself against his vision.

As the reader might expect, Powys wrote about pain and tragedy in a detached style that was both cool and evocative. Powys possessed a happy feeling for the right word, the precise expression, which contributed greatly to the crisp, cold, clear quality of his writing. This detached mode of writing, which at times approached cruelty, considerably heightened the horror of his tales. If Powys had written with sympathy for his characters, the effect would have been reduced, and the full power of his vision would not have come through.

Powys was essentially an ironist. His irony was engendered by the conflict between his vision and his art. On the one hand, he saw the world as irrevocably damned; on the other, he tried to escape this damnation through art. Therefore, he wrote about cruelty, pain, and doom with detachment and reserve. Truth, for Powys, was only to be gained through passive observation. He hoped to gain a kind of salvation through truth, but the truth proved to be just as ironic as himself. What Powys did gain through passive observation was the ability to transform horror into beauty. His stories possess a cruel, evocative beauty, but his beauty, like his truth, was essentially ironic, frigid, and sterile in its revelation.

Powys' failings and virtues as a writer arise from his vision of life and his attempt to cope with that vision. He was a fine writer of short stories and sketches and had a remarkable ability to express himself with clarity, beauty, and force, but he paid for this ability in terms of agony and coldness. His stories are comparable with those of Poe, Bierce, and Hemingway in vividness, beauty, and power. The reader must be prepared to pay for these things.

THE EGOIST
A Comedy in Narrative

Type of work: Novel
Author: George Meredith (1828–1909)
Type of plot: Social satire
Time of plot: Nineteenth century
Locale: England
First published: 1879

Principal characters:
SIR WILLOUGHBY PATTERNE, the egoist
VERNON WHITFORD, his cousin
COLONEL DE CRAYE, his relative
LAETITIA DALE, a neighbor
CLARA MIDDLETON, Sir Willoughby's betrothed
DOCTOR MIDDLETON, her father
CROSSJAY PATTERNE, Sir Willoughby's distant kinsman

The Story:

On the day of his majority, Sir Willoughby Patterne announced his engagement to Miss Constantia Durham. Laetitia Dale, who lived with her old father in a cottage on Willoughby's estate, bore her love for him—she thought—secretly, but everyone, including Willoughby himself, knew about it. Ten days before the wedding day, Constantia astonished her betrothed by eloping with Harry Oxford, a military man. For a few weeks after the elopement, proud Willoughby courted Laetitia while the neighborhood gossiped about the poor girl's chances to become his wife. There was great disappointment when he suddenly decided to go abroad for three years. On his return to his estate, he brought with him his cousin, Vernon Whitford, as an adviser in the management of his properties, and a young distant kinsman named Crossjay Patterne.

Faithful Laetitia was overjoyed, at first, at Willoughby's return, but soon she saw that again she was to lose him, for he became engaged to Clara Middleton, the daughter of a learned doctor. Middleton and his daughter came to Willoughby's estate to visit for a few weeks. It might have been the controversy over Crossjay or even the existence of Laetitia that caused Clara to see Willoughby for what he really was. In spite of Willoughby's objections, Vernon wanted Crossjay to enter the Marines, and the young man was sent to Laetitia to be tutored for his examination. A literary man, Vernon wanted to go to London, but Willoughby overruled him. Noting Willoughby's self-centered attitude toward Crossjay, his complete and selfish concern with matters affecting himself, and his attempt to dominate her own mind, Clara began to feel trapped by her betrothal. She reflected that

Constantia had escaped by finding a gallant Harry Oxford to take her away, but she sadly realized that she had no one to rescue her.

When Clara attempted to break her engagement, she found Willoughby intractable and her father too engrossed in his studies to be disturbed. Meanwhile, Willoughby had picked Laetitia Dale as Vernon's wife. This was Willoughby's plan to keep near him both his cousin and the woman who fed his ego with her devotion. Vernon could retire to one of the cottages on the estate and write and study. Asked by Willoughby to aid him in his plan, Clara took the opportunity to ask Vernon's advice on her own problem. He assured her that she must move subtly and slowly.

In desperation, she persuaded Doctor Middleton to agree to take a trip to France with her for a few weeks. By taking the trip, she hoped never to return to Willoughby; but this wary lover then introduced Dr. Middleton to his favorite brand of claret. Two bottles of the wine put the doctor in such an amiable mood that when Clara asked him if he were ready to go to London with her, he told her that the thought was preposterous. Willoughby had won the first round.

Colonel De Craye arrived to be best man at the wedding. Little by little, he sensed that Clara was not happy at the prospect of her approaching marriage. In desperation, Clara resorted to other means of escape. She wrote to her friend, Lucy Darleton, in town and received from that young lady an invitation to visit her in London.

Clara gave Crossjay the privilege of accompanying her to the train station. A hue and cry was raised at her absence from the estate, and Vernon, accidentally discovering her destination, followed her to the station and urged her to come back. Only because she believed that her behavior might cause an injury to Crossjay's future did Clara return to her prison. If she were to leave now, Willoughby would have full control of the young boy, since Vernon was soon to go to London to follow his writing career.

Complications resulted from Clara's attempted escape. At the station, Vernon had her drink some brandy to overcome the effects of the rainy weather. The neighborhood began to gossip. Willoughby confronted Crossjay, who told him the truth about Clara's escape. Clara hoped that Willoughby would release her because of the gossip, but he refused. Doctor Middleton seemed ignorant of what was happening. He was determined that his daughter should fulfill her pledge to marry Sir Willoughby. Furthermore, he liked Willoughby's vintage wines and Willoughby's estate.

By this time, the egoist knew that his marriage to Clara would not take place. He decided upon a move that would soothe his wounded vanity—he asked Laetitia to become his wife. She refused, declaring she no longer loved him.

Colonel De Craye shrewdly surmised what had happened. He told Clara the hopeful news. Clara felt that her only remaining obstacle was her father's insistence that she must not break her promise to Willoughby. Now she could show that Willoughby had broken his promise first by proposing to Laetitia while he was still pledged to Clara.

Willoughby's world blew up in his face. Dr. Middleton announced firmly that Clara need not marry Willoughby. He had decided that he admired Vernon's scholarship more than he liked Willoughby's wines. The twice-jilted lover, however, had other plans for his own protection. He must even the score. If he could get Clara to consent to marry Vernon, he felt there would be some measure of recompense for himself, for such a marriage would have the ironic touch to satisfy Willoughby. Clara, however, told him it was already her intention to wed Vernon as soon as her engagement to Willoughby could be broken. The egoist's selfishness and arrogance had brought them together.

The egoist was defeated. He went straight to Laetitia, offering her his hand without love. He was willing for her to marry him only for his money. Laetitia accepted on the condition that Crossjay be permitted to enter the Marines. Clara and the doctor planned to leave for Europe. Vernon arranged to meet them in the Swiss Alps, where he and Clara would marry.

Critical Evaluation:

George Meredith expressed what he thought were the essential social conditions for successful comedy in his famous essay "On the Idea of Comedy and of the Uses of the Comic Spirit," first delivered as a lecture two years before the publication of *The Egoist*. In the essay, Meredith argues that the comic poet cannot function without the stimulus of a clever society, a society sensitive to ideas and witty in its perceptions. A merely fad-conscious period, giddy and emotional, is too primitive to inspire true comedy. Of major importance is at least some intellectual activity and a tolerance of women in society; feminine wit is essential to a healthy social climate, one that will permit a society to laugh at itself.

Meredith's curious antihero, Willoughby, is devoid of any ideas, totally wrapped up in a giddy love affair with himself, and singularly incapable of any objective perceptions. Clara tells him to his face that he is boring her to death. Immersed in his own ardor, he is so oblivious to insult that he calls her a "sleeping beauty" immediately after she has intimated that he is putting her to sleep. Therefore, Willoughby is the incarnation of everything that makes the Comic Spirit impossible; and yet, the irony of the novel is that he is at the same time the ideal subject for Comedy's ridiculing power.

Willoughby's selfishness and egotism are nowhere more clearly revealed than in his insistence on the servility of women to men. This is his primary violation of Meredith's "Social Law" of Comedy, and it is what finally brings about his comic punishment. By agreeing to marry him without love, Laetitia treats him as an object and caps his downfall by condemning him to the same treatment he extended to others: "I was once a foolish romantic girl; now I am a sickly woman, all illusions vanished. Privation has made me what an abounding fortune usually makes of others—I am an Egoist."

The novel creates a fantastic world where, in scenes of subtle comedy, the characters are treated realistically. The effect is one of drollery. Each character is a symbol of some virtue or vice rather than a living individual. All the characters speak alike, and they speak the language of Meredith. This novel stands apart from Meredith's other novels, distinguished as it is by its originality of technique and purpose. It is, to use Meredith's own term, "a comedy in narrative."

THE EMIGRANTS OF AHADARRA
A Tale of Irish Life

Type of work: Novel
Author: William Carleton (1794–1869)
Type of plot: Local color romance
Time of plot: 1840's
Locale: Ireland
First published: 1848

Principal characters:
BRYAN M'MAHON, an honest young farmer
KATHLEEN CAVANAGH, Bryan M'Mahon's beloved
HYCY (HYACINTH) BURKE, a well-to-do libertine and rascal
JEMMY BURKE, Hycy's father
NANNY PEETY, a beggar girl
KATE HOGAN, Nanny's aunt and a tinker's wife
PATRICK O'FINIGAN, the master of a hedge-school

The Story:

Hycy Burke was the son of a wealthy and respected peasant who had allowed his wife, a woman with social pretensions of her own, to spoil the young man. With his mother's approval, Hycy had become a dissolute young man. Because his father, Jemmy Burke, tried to curb him, Hycy entered into partnership with whiskey smugglers to supplement the diminished allowance from his father.

When one of the prettiest girls in the area, Kathleen Cavanagh, caught Hycy's eye, he determined to seduce her. Unfortunately for his plans, he misdirected two letters: one, intended for Kathleen, went to Bryan M'Mahon, who truly loved the girl; another, intended for young M'Mahon, went to Kathleen. Later, publicly snubbed on more than one occasion, Hycy resolved to have revenge on the girl and her true admirer. Any additional villainy could scarcely put him in greater danger; he had already been an accomplice to burglarizing his father's house, taking a large sum of money, as well as an active accomplice of smugglers. It was through his fellow smugglers that he planned to get his revenge. At the time, there was a law in Ireland that required the inhabitants of a township to pay fines for illegal distillation and smuggling of whiskey if the actual culprits were not known. Bryan M'Mahon's farm at Ahadarra covered an entire township; if he were required to pay such a fine by himself, he would be ruined. To carry out his plan, Hycy tried to get the help of the nephew of the local gauger. Hycy promised the exciseman's nephew the chance to lease a fine farm if the latter would press Hycy's suit for his sister's hand. The farm, of course, was Bryan M'Mahon's.

Bryan was not the only member of his family facing tragedy. Both his and his father's farm leases had run out, and death had prevented the absentee landlord from renewing them. The new landlord, a well-meaning but weak and inexperienced young man, was ruled by his agent, who wished to see the M'Mahons lose their farms, leased by the family for generations.

Hycy carefully made his plans. What he failed to realize, however, was that he had made enemies while Bryan had made friends; consequently, some persons who knew of his villainy were prepared to take measures to thwart him. In his father's house was Nanny Peety, a pretty, virtuous beggar girl who resented Hycy's attempts to seduce her. She knew something of his plans, and she had been a witness to the burglary that Hycy and his accomplice had committed. Nanny Peety's aunt, Kate Hogan, loved her niece and thought highly of Kathleen Cavanagh. She was willing and able to help them, because she was married to one of Hycy's smuggling associates. Patrick O'Finigan, the drunken master of the local hedge-school, was also friendly to Kathleen and Bryan.

The plot against Bryan was put into operation when Hycy's anonymous letter sent the gauger to discover the illicit still at Ahadarra, on Bryan's farm. Faced with financial ruin and his family's loss of their leases, the young peasant did not know what to do. Because his own honesty kept him from believing that Hycy was working against him in such a manner, Bryan even took advice from the man who was bent on ruining him. Before long, he found himself worse off by taking the advice. A parliamentary election was about to take place in which the M'Mahons' landlord was standing for a seat. The voting turned out to be a tie until Bryan, angry with his landlord and following Hycy's advice, voted for his landlord's opponent. By doing so, he made himself appear false in everyone's eyes, for his landlord was a liberal who favored the Irish peasantry and religious freedom, while the opponent was a conservative who worked against the peasants and the Roman Catholic Church.

When Hycy sent another letter enclosing a fifty-pound note, it looked as if Bryan had accepted a bribe for his vote. The evidence was so damning that even Kathleen, who loved Bryan sincerely, was forced to believe him guilty. Faced with calamity and disfavor in his community, Bryan and his family planned, like so many unfortunate Irish at the time, to emigrate to America in order to start a new and more successful life.

Bryan's friends, however, began to work for him. Displeased at Hycy's treatment of her niece and the troubles facing Kathleen when she lost her fiancé, Kate Hogan began investigating Hycy's activities. She, Patrick O'Finigan, Nanny Peety's father, and others gathered additional information and presented it to the magistrates with demands for a hearing. At the hearing, it was proved that Hycy had robbed his father, had been an accomplice of the whiskey smugglers, had placed the still at Ahadarra to incriminate Bryan, had plotted to make his victim appear to have taken a bribe, and had also become a counterfeiter. Confronted with these proofs, Jemmy Burke gave his son two hundred pounds to leave the country and stay away. Hycy's accomplices were arrested, convicted, and transported as criminals from Ireland, thus becoming the "emigrants" of Ahadarra. Cleared of all charges, Bryan resumed his rightful place in the community and in the affections of Kathleen.

Critical Evaluation:

By the time that he wrote *The Emigrants of Ahadarra* in 1848, William Carleton was considered the truest novelist of Ireland's "awfullest hours," and Yeats was to concede that the Irish novel began with him. *The Emigrants of Ahadarra* was avowedly written not to amuse but to reform and inform. Published while the Potato Famine was raging, it is informative and readable. Folkloric value is enhanced by Carleton's exuberance and hyperbole, which are similar to the imaginative flights that created the ancient Celtic wonder tales. The novel loftily defends virtue. Kathleen's simple dignity and virtue are not cloying but almost biblical and contrast with the paler virtues of other characters. Bridget M'Mahon is also convincingly admirable and uniquely graces the story, which expounds human ideals. Landlords are near-ogres, members of secret societies, and Orangemen (although to a less prominent degree than in other of Carleton's works), but many individuals are tenderly etched. The novel is Realistic; and in the Spain of the same day, it would have been classified as costumbrista, owing to its museumlike pictures of customs.

Modern critics sometimes flay *The Emigrants of Ahadarra* for allegedly sloppy construction, mushy sentiment, and—curiously enough—vagueness of purpose. Carleton is also accused of inserting excessive scenery and folklore for their own sake rather than to augment the novel's dramatic effect. Carleton did lack the benefit of proofreading by his publishers, but the novel accomplished its obvious objective of dramatizing the life of the Irish of over a hundred years ago. Even its supposedly overdone rhetoric does not bore the reader.

Herbert Kenney maintains that readers have an accurate picture of the famine-ravaged Irish peasants from Carleton alone. Carleton was an enigmatic novelist who hated landlordism and the Penal Laws and who was a convert to Protestantism in a very Catholic land; but he scarcely owed loyalty only to his own pen as has been accused. Furthermore, some critics concede that they did not really know Irish life until they read *The Emigrants of Ahadarra*.

Carleton's fiction is best known for its realistic pictures of Irish peasant life during the nineteenth century, and *The Emigrants of Ahadarra* is one of his best novels in this respect. The most noteworthy sections are the chapters describing such things as a "kemp" (a spinning contest among the peasant women), a country funeral, an election, and illegal distillation of whiskey. While his treatment of these matters is outstanding, the entire novel is filled with specific and colorful details of peasant life. The speech and character of the people, the homes they live in, the farm routine, landlord-peasant relations, whiskey smuggling, all are related with a view to giving the reader a true picture of rural Irish life a century ago.

EMMA

Type of work: Novel
Author: Jane Austen (1775–1817)
Type of plot: Social comedy
Time of plot: Early nineteenth century
Locale: Surrey, England
First published: 1816

Principal characters:
EMMA WOODHOUSE, the heiress of Hartfield
MR. WOODHOUSE, her father
HARRIET SMITH, Emma's protégée
MISS BATES, the village gossip
JANE FAIRFAX, Miss Bates's niece
MR. GEORGE KNIGHTLEY, a landowner of the neighborhood
MRS. WESTON, Emma's former governess
FRANK CHURCHILL, the stepson of Emma's former governess
MR. ELTON, a rector
ROBERT MARTIN, a yeoman

The Story:

A rich, clever, and beautiful young woman, Emma Woodhouse was no more spoiled and self-satisfied than one would expect under such circumstances. She had just seen her friend, companion, and former governess, Miss Taylor, married to a neighboring widower, Mr. Weston. While the match was suitable in every way, Emma could not help sighing over her loss, for now only she and her father were left at Hartfield, and Mr. Woodhouse was too old and too fond of worrying about trivialities to be a companion for his daughter.

The Woodhouses were the great family in the village of Highbury. In their small circle of friends, there were enough middle-aged ladies to make up card tables for Mr. Woodhouse, but there was no young lady to be a friend and confidante to Emma. Lonely for her beloved Miss Taylor, now Mrs. Weston, Emma took under her wing Harriet Smith, the parlor boarder at a nearby boarding school. Although not in the least brilliant, Harriet was a pretty seventeen-year-old girl with pleasing, unassuming manners and a gratifying habit of looking up to Emma as a paragon.

Harriet was the natural daughter of some mysterious person; Emma, believing that the girl might be of noble family, persuaded her that the society in which she had moved was not good enough for her. She encouraged her to give up her acquaintance with the Martin family, respectable farmers of some substance though of no fashion. Instead of thinking of Robert Martin as a husband for Harriet, Emma influenced the girl to aspire to Mr. Elton, the young rector.

Emma believed from Mr. Elton's manner that he was beginning to fall in love with Harriet, and she flattered herself upon her matchmaking schemes. The brother of a London lawyer married to Emma's older sister and one of the few people who could see Emma's faults, Mr. Knightley was concerned about her intimacy with Harriet. He warned her that no good could come of it for either Harriet or herself, and he was particularly upset when he learned that Emma had influenced Harriet to turn down Robert Martin's proposal of marriage. Emma herself suffered from no such qualms, for she was certain that Mr. Elton was as much in love with Harriet as Harriet—through Emma's instigation—was with him.

Emma suffered a rude awakening when Mr. Elton, finding her alone, asked her to marry him. She suddenly realized that what she had taken for gallantries to Harriet had been meant for herself; he had taken what Emma had intended as encouragement to his suit of her friend as encouragement to aspire for her hand. His presumption was bad enough, but the task of breaking the news to Harriet was much worse.

Another disappointment now occurred in Emma's circle. Frank Churchill, who had promised for months to come to see his father and new stepmother, again put off his visit. Churchill, Mr. Weston's son by a first marriage, had taken the name of his mother's family. Mr. Knightley believed that the young man now felt superior to his father. Emma argued with Mr. Knightley, but she found herself secretly agreeing with him.

Although the Hartfield circle was denied Churchill's company, it did acquire an addition in the person of Jane Fairfax, niece of the garrulous Miss Bates. Jane rivaled Emma in beauty and accomplishment; this was one reason why, as Mr. Knightley hinted, Emma had never been friendly with Jane. Emma blamed Jane's reserve for their somewhat cool relationship.

Soon after Jane's arrival, the Westons received a letter from Churchill setting another date for his visit. This time he actually appeared, and Emma found him a handsome, well-bred young man. He frequently called upon the Woodhouses and also upon the Bates family, because of prior acquaintance with Jane Fairfax. Emma rather than Jane was the recipient of his gallantries, however, and Emma could see that Mr. and Mrs. Weston were hoping that the romance would prosper.

About this time, Jane Fairfax received the handsome gift of a pianoforte, anonymously given. It was presumed to have come from some rich friends with whom Jane, an orphan, had lived, but Jane seemed embarrassed with the present and refused to discuss it. Emma wondered if it had come from Mr. Knightley, after Mrs. Weston pointed out to her his seeming preference and concern for Jane. Emma could not bear to think of Mr. Knightley's marrying Jane Fairfax; after observing them together, she concluded to her own satisfaction that he was motivated by friendship, not love.

It was now time for Frank Churchill to end his visit, and he departed with seeming reluctance. During his last call at Hartfield, he appeared desirous of telling Emma something of a serious nature; but she, believing him to be on the verge of a declaration of love, did not encourage him because in her daydreams she always saw herself refusing him and their love ending in quiet friendship.

Mr. Elton returned to the village with a hastily wooed and wedded bride, a lady of small fortune, extremely bad manners, and great pretensions to elegance. Harriet, who had been talked into love by Emma, could not be so easily talked out of it; but what Emma had failed to accomplish, Mr. Elton's marriage had, and Harriet at last began to recover. Her recovery was aided by Mr. Elton's rudeness to her at a ball. When he refused to dance with her, Mr. Knightley, who rarely danced, offered himself as a partner, and Harriet, without Emma's knowledge, began to think of him instead of Mr. Elton.

Emma began to think of Churchill as a husband for Harriet, but she resolved to do nothing to promote the match. Through a series of misinterpretations, Emma thought Harriet was praising Churchill when she was really referring to Mr. Knightley.

The matrimonial entanglement was further complicated because Mrs. Weston continued to believe that Mr. Knightley was becoming attached to Jane Fairfax. In his turn, Mr. Knightley saw signs of some secret agreement between Jane Fairfax and Frank Churchill. His suspicions were finally justified when Churchill confessed to Mr. and Mrs. Weston that he and Jane had been secretly engaged since October. The Westons' first thought was for Emma, for they feared that Churchill's attentions to her might have had their effect. Emma assured Mrs. Weston that she had at one time felt some slight attachment to Churchill, but that time was now safely past. Her chief concerns now were that she had said things about Jane to Churchill which she would not have said had she known of their engagement, and also that she had, as she believed, encouraged Harriet in another fruitless attachment.

When she went to break the news gently to Harriet, however, Emma found her quite unperturbed by it; after a few minutes of talking at cross-purposes, Emma learned that it was not Churchill but Mr. Knightley upon whom Harriet had now bestowed her affections. When she told Emma that she had reasons to believe that Mr. Knightley returned her sentiments, Emma suddenly realized the state of her own heart; she herself loved Mr. Knightley. She now wished she had never seen Harriet Smith. Aside from the fact that she wanted to marry Mr. Knightley herself, she knew a match between him and Harriet would be an unequal one, hardly likely to bring happiness.

Emma's worry over this state of affairs was soon ended when Mr. Knightley asked her to marry him. Her complete happiness was marred only by the fact that she knew her marriage would upset her father, who disliked change of any kind; she was also aware that she had unknowingly prepared Harriet for another disappointment. The first problem was solved when Emma and Mr. Knightley decided to reside at Hartfield with Mr. Woodhouse as long as he lived. Harriet's problem, however, still remained; but when Mr. Knightley was paying attention to her, he was really trying to determine the real state of her affections for his young farm tenant. Consequently, Mr. Knightley was able to announce one morning that Robert Martin had again offered himself to Harriet and had been accepted. Emma was overjoyed that Harriet's future was now assured. She could always reflect that all parties concerned had married according to their stations, a prerequisite for their true happiness.

Critical Evaluation:

Jane Austen had passed her fortieth year when her fourth published novel, *Emma*, appeared in 1816, the year before her death. Although *Pride and Prejudice* has always been her most popular novel, *Emma* is generally regarded as her greatest. In this work of her maturity, she deals once more with the milieu she preferred: 3 or 4 Families in a Country Village is the very thing to work on." The seventh of eight children of the learned village rector, she had grown to womanhood in her native Hampshire village of Steventon. She spent the remainder of her life, except for brief intervals in Bath and Southampton, in another Hampshire village, Chawton, and was thoroughly familiar with the world she depicted.

The action of *Emma* cannot be properly considered apart from the setting of Highbury, the populous village only sixteen miles from London. Its physical attributes are presented in such circumstantial detail that it becomes a real entity. London seems far away, not because of the difficulty of travel but because of the community's limited views. It is a village where a light drizzle keeps its citizens at home, where Frank Churchill's trip to London for the alleged purpose of getting a haircut is foppery and foolishness, where the "inconsiderable Crown Inn" and Ford's "woollen-draper, linen-draper, and haberdasher's shop united" dominate the main street. Emma's view of the busiest part of town, surveyed from the doorway of Ford's, sums up the life of the village:

> Mr. Perry walking hastily by, Mr. William Cox letting himself in at the office door, Mr. Cole's carriage horses returning from exercise . . . a stray letter boy on an obstinate mule . . . the butcher with his tray, a tidy old woman . . . two curs quarrelling over a dirty bone, and a string of dawdling children round the baker's little bow-window.

The novel concerns the interrelationship between such an inconsequential place and Emma Woodhouse, a pretty and clever young lady almost twenty-one years old, who is rich and has few problems to vex her. Ironically, however, her world is no bigger than the village of Highbury and a few surrounding estates, including her father's Hartfield; nevertheless, in that small world, the Woodhouse family is the most important. As the author states, the real dangers for Emma are "the power of having rather too much her own way, and a disposition to think a little too well of herself."

Moreover, these dangers are unperceived by Emma. Thus, in the blind exercise of her power over Highbury, she involves herself in a series of ridiculous errors, mistakenly judging that Mr. Elton cares for Harriet rather than for herself; Frank Churchill for herself rather than for Jane Fairfax; Harriet for Frank rather than for Mr. Knightley; and Mr. Knightley for Harriet rather than for herself. It is the triumph of Austen's art that however absurd or obvious Emma's miscalculations, they are convincingly a part of Emma's charming egotism. The reader finally agrees with Mr. Knightley that there is always "an anxiety, a curiosity in what one feels for Emma."

Emma's vulnerability to error can in part be attributed to inexperience, her life circumscribed by the boundaries of Highbury and its environs. Although Emma's only sister lives in London, no mention is made of visits there. She has never been to the seacoast, nor even to Box Hill, a famous scenic attraction nearby. She is further restricted by her valetudinarian father's gentle selfishness, which resists any kind of change and permits a social life limited to his own small circle, exclusive to the degree of admitting only four people as his closest acquaintances and only three to the second group.

Nevertheless, Emma's own snobbery binds her to the conclusion that she has no equals in Highbury. Mr. Knightley well understands the underlying assumption of superiority in Emma's friendship for Harriet Smith: "How can Emma imagine she has anything to learn herself, while Harriet is presenting such a delightful inferiority?" Emma fears superiority in others as a threat. Of the capable farmer Robert Martin, Harriet's wooer, she observes: "But a farmer can need none of my help, and is therefore in one sense as much above my notice as in every other way he is below it." Her resolution to like Jane Fairfax is repeatedly shattered by the praise everybody else gives Jane's superior attractions.

While Emma behaves in accordance with her theory that social rank is too important to be ignored, she fails to perceive that she is nearly alone in her exclusiveness. Indeed, the Eltons openly assume airs of superiority, and Jane Fairfax snubs Emma. Emma's increasing isolation from Highbury is epitomized in her resistance to the Cole family, good people of low rank who have nevertheless come to be regarded socially as second only to the

Woodhouse family. Snobbishly sure that the Coles will not dare to invite the best families to an affair, she finds only herself uninvited. Therefore, ironically, she imagines her power in Highbury to be flourishing even as it is already severely diminished.

Emma's task is to become undeceived and to break free of the limitations imposed by her pride, by her father's flattering tyranny, and by the limited views of Highbury. She must accomplish all this without abandoning her self-esteem and intelligence, her father, or society. The author prepares for the possibility of a resolution from the beginning, especially by establishing Mr. Knightley as the person who represents the standard of maturity that Emma must assume. Emma is always half aware of his significance, often putting her folly to the test of his judgment. There are brief, important occasions when the two, united by instinctive understanding, work together to create or restore social harmony; however, it is not until Harriet presumes to think of herself as worthy of his love that Emma is shocked into recognition that Mr. Knightley is superior to herself as well as to Harriet.

Highbury itself, which seems so confined, also serves to enlarge Emma's views simply by proving to be less fixed than it appears. As John Knightley observes: "Your neighbourhood is increasing, and you mix more with it." Without losing her desire for social success, Emma increasingly suffers from it. She is basically deficient in human sympathy, categorizing people as second or third rank in Highbury or analyzing them to display her own wit. She begins to develop in sensitivity, however, as she experiences her own humiliations. While still disliking Jane, she is capable of "entering into her feelings" and granting a moment of privacy. Her rudeness to Miss Bates is regretted, not only because Mr. Knightley is displeased but also because she perceives that she has been brutal, even cruel to Miss Bates.

Despite her love of small schemes, Emma shares an important trait with Mr. Knightley, one which he considers requisite for his wife—an "open temper," the one quality lacking in the admirable Jane. Emma's disposition is open, her responsiveness to life counteracting the conditions in herself and her circumstances, which tend to be constricting. Her reaction to news of Harriet's engagement to Robert Martin is characteristic: she is "in dancing, singing, exclaiming spirits; and till she had moved about, and talked to herself, and laughed and reflected, she could be fit for nothing rational." Too ready to laugh at others, she can as readily laugh at herself. Impulsive in her follies, she is quick to make amends. She represents herself truthfully as she says, in farewell to Jane, "Oh! if you knew how much I love every thing that is decided and open!"

A fully realized character who develops during the course of the action, Emma is never forced by the author to be other than herself, despite her new awareness. Once Harriet is safely bestowed upon Robert Martin, she complacently allows their friendship to diminish. The conniving to keep her father reasonably contented is a way of life. If he wishes to marry her, Mr. Knightley is required to move into Hartfield. Serious reflection upon her past follies is inevitably lightened by her ability to laugh at them—and herself. The novel is complete in every sense, yet Emma is so dynamic a characterization that one shares Mr. Knightley's pleasure in speculation: "I wonder what will become of her!"

EREWHON
Or, Over the Range

Type of work: Novel
Author: Samuel Butler (1835–1902)
Type of plot: Utopian satire
Time of plot: 1870's
Locale: Erewhon and England
First published: 1872

Principal characters:
HIGGS, a traveler in Erewhon
CHOWBOK, a native
NOSNIBOR, a citizen of Erewhon
AROWHENA, his daughter

The Story:

Higgs, a young man of twenty-two years, worked on a sheep farm. From the plains, he looked often at the seemingly impassable mountain range that formed the edge of the sheep country and wondered about the land beyond those towering peaks. He learned from an old native named Chowbok that the country was forbidden. Chowbok assumed a strange pose when questioned further and uttered unearthly cries. Curious, Higgs persuaded Chowbok to go on a trip with him into the mountains.

They were unable to find a pass through the mountains. One day, Higgs came upon a small valley and went up it alone. He found that it led through the mountains. When he went back to get Chowbok, he saw the old native fleeing toward the plains. He went on alone. After climbing down treacherous cliffs and crossing a river on a reed raft, he finally came to beautiful rolling plains. He passed by some strange manlike statues, which made terrifying noises as the wind circled about them. He recognized in them the reason for Chowbok's performance.

Higgs awoke next morning to see two girls herding a flock of goats about him. When the girls saw him, they ran and brought some men to look at him. All of them were physically handsome. Convinced at last that Higgs was a human being, they took him to a small town close by. There his clothing was searched, and a watch he had with him was confiscated. The men seemed to be especially interested in his health, and he was allowed to leave only after a strict medical examination. He wondered why there had been such confusion over his watch until he was shown a museum in which was kept old pieces of machinery. Finally, he was put in jail.

In jail, he learned the language and some of the strange customs of the country, which was called Erewhon. The oddest custom was to consider disease a crime; anyone who was sick was tried and put in jail. On the other hand, people who committed robbery or murder were treated sympathetically and given hospital care. Shortly afterward, the jailor informed Higgs that he had been summoned to appear before the king and queen and that he was to be the guest of a man named Nosnibor. Nosnibor had embezzled a large sum of money from a poor widow, but he was now recovering from his illness. The widow, Higgs learned, would be tried and sentenced for allowing herself to be imposed upon.

In the capital, Higgs stayed with Nosnibor and his family and paid several visits to the court. He was well received because he had blond hair, a rarity among the Erewhonians. He learned a great deal about the past history of the country. Twenty-five hundred years before, a prophet had preached that it was unlawful to eat meat, since man should not kill his fellow creatures. For several hundred years, the Erewhonians were vegetarians. Then another sage showed that animals were no more the fellow creatures of man than plants were; if man could not kill and eat animals, he should not kill and eat plants. The logic of his arguments overthrew the old philosophy. Two hundred years before, a great scientist had presented the idea that machines had minds and feelings and that, if man were not careful, the machine would finally become the ruling creature on earth. Consequently, all machines had been scrapped.

The economy of the country was unusual. There were two monetary systems—one worthless except for spiritual meaning, one used in trade. The more respected system was the valueless one, and its work was carried on in Musical Banks where people exchanged coins for music. The state religion was a worship of various qualities of godhead, such as love, fear, and wisdom, and the main goddess, Ydgrun, was at the same time an abstract concept and a silly, cruel woman. Higgs learned much of the religion from Arowhena, one of Nosnibor's daughters. She was a beautiful girl, and the two fell in love.

Because Nosnibor insisted that his older daughter, Zulora, be married first, Higgs and his host had an argument, and Higgs found lodgings elsewhere. Arowhena met him often at the Musical Banks. Higgs visited the University of Unreason, where the young Erewhonian boys were taught to do anything except that which was practical. They studied obsolete languages and hypothetical sciences. He saw a relationship between these schools and the mass-mind, which the educational system in England was producing. Higgs also learned that money was considered a symbol of duty; the more money a man had, the better man he was.

Nosnibor learned that Higgs was meeting Arowhena secretly. Then the king began to worry over the fact that Higgs had entered the country with a watch, and he feared that Higgs might try to bring machinery back into use. Planning an escape, Higgs proposed to the queen that he make a balloon trip to talk with the god of the air. The queen was delighted with the idea. The king hoped that Higgs would fall and kill himself.

Higgs smuggled Arowhena aboard the balloon with him. The couple soon found themselves high in the air and moving over the mountain range. When the balloon settled on the sea, Higgs and Arowhena were picked up by a passing ship. They were married in England, and Higgs tried to get up an expedition to go back to Erewhon. Only the missionaries listened to his story. Then Chowbok, Higgs's faithless native friend, showed up in England teaching religion, and his appearance convinced people that Erewhon actually did exist. Higgs hoped to return to the country soon to teach it Christianity.

Critical Evaluation:

Erewhon is Samuel Butler's attempt to work into novel form four philosophic papers written between 1860 and 1870; these appear as the chapters in the novel entitled "The Book of the Machines," "The World of the Unborn," "The Musical Banks," and "Some Erewhonian Trials." While apparently dissimilar, these pivotal chapters all treat the theme of free will, thus unifying the book.

Erewhon is an anagram of nowhere, but the institutions satirized in this story of an imaginary land are unmistakably British. Beginning as an adventure story, the book becomes an elaborate allegory. Some of Butler's satire grows out of the ideas of Darwin and Huxley. Principally, the book is original and often prophetic: The "straighteners" of Erewhon are psychologists, and the treatment of Erewhonian criminals is somewhat like that advocated by some modern liberal thinkers. The novel is humorous, but it is also serious.

In adapting to his environment, man constructs machines that threaten his survival. With prophetic insight, Butler examines this irony. He argues that the laws governing organic evolution also apply to machines and their development. Challenging the distinction between "organic" and "inorganic," Butler reduces all processes to their mechanical basis and shows how machines are evolving independently of human control. Like Marx, he sees man's nature as changing under the impact of a mechanized environment; but unlike Marx, he predicts man's ultimate enslavement by this environment.

Both comic and serious elements mingle in the Erewhonian myth of preexistence. Because the "unborn" *will* to become humans, they must bear the consequences of their choice. Thus, the Erewhonians make babies sign "birth formulae" that absolve parents from responsibility for the deprivations and deficiencies that go with living. The unborn also elect to share man's essential fate: to be "fettered" to free will while knowing that its proper exercise requires such accidental advantages as innate talent and high social position.

In "The Musical Banks," Butler satirizes the corruption of religion by commercialism; the Banks symbolize the existence of "a kingdom not of this world" whose laws measure and judge human laws. For Butler, there is a Divine Will which inhabits the subconscious and which all cultures tacitly acknowledge. In the trials of the unfortunate and sick, Butler uses absurdity to examine further the nature of freedom and responsibility. In Erewhon, crime is a disease and disease a crime; Butler accepts the first equation while mocking the second.

ESTHER WATERS

Type of work: Novel
Author: George Moore (1852–1933)
Type of plot: Naturalism
Time of plot: Late nineteenth century
Locale: England
First published: 1894

Principal characters:
ESTHER WATERS, a servant girl
WILLIAM LATCH, her betrayer
MRS. BARFIELD, her mistress
SARAH TUCKER, her enemy
JACKIE, her son
FRED PARSONS, her betrothed
MISS RICE, her employer

The Story:

The first person Esther Waters met when she arrived at Woodview was William Latch, the son of the cook under whose direction Esther was to work. William was the bane of his mother's life; like his dead father, he was a gambler. Mrs. Latch had hoped that William would become a delivery boy and leave Woodview, but William was determined to go into service for Mr. and Mrs. Barfield, the owners of Woodview, in order to observe their racing stable.

The position as kitchen maid at Woodview was a godsend to Esther, for her stepfather, claiming that he had too many mouths to feed, had forced her to leave home. The workhouse might have been her only refuge if she had not secured a position with the Barfields; but in spite of her efforts to do her work well, it was hard for her to get along with the other servants. Mrs. Latch seemed to go out of her way to make life unpleasant for Esther, and the maids teased her because she was religious. William was at first her only champion among the servants, and she was grateful to him. Then Esther found an unexpected friend in her mistress, Mrs. Barfield. She, too, was deeply religious, and she invited Esther to join the services she held in her room each Sunday morning. Learning that Esther could not read, Mrs. Barfield tried to teach her. To Esther, Mrs. Barfield seemed a friend as well as an employer.

Mrs. Barfield's interest made Esther's life easier for a time. William continued to pay her special attention, to the anguish of Sarah Tucker, another of the maids. After a servants' ball in celebration of the victory of one of the Woodview horses, William took Esther out to some wheatstacks and seduced her after telling her that they would be married as soon as he had enough money. By the following morning, Esther had convinced herself that she had been betrayed, and she refused to speak to William. He tried to reason with her, telling her that he loved her and they would be married soon, but she would not listen. Tiring at last of her sulking, he turned to Miss Peggy Barfield, a cousin of his master, and after a few weeks eloped with her.

Three months later, Esther realized that she was pregnant. Strangely, the servant girls who had been her former tormentors became kind and sympathetic, and their kindness made her feel even more ashamed of her wickedness. In spite of her sympathy, Mrs. Barfield had to send Esther away, for she had become a bad example for the other girls.

There was no place for her to go but to her home. There she found her mother also pregnant. Her stepfather was more cruel than ever, but he tolerated her as long as she paid her rent and gave him money to buy beer. At last, Esther knew that she would have to leave before all her savings were used up and there would be nothing left for her baby.

She took lodgings close to the hospital where she was to be confined. After her son Jackie was born, she was filled with a happiness she had never known before, but her joy was lessened when she learned that her mother had died in childbirth, just a few days after Esther's baby was born. Soon afterward, Esther's stepfather and the other children went to Australia; Esther now felt that she was really alone in the world.

The next few years were terrible ones for Esther. Sometimes she worked seventeen or eighteen hours a day. Once she had to go to the workhouse. Her greatest grief was the need to leave her child in someone's care while she worked, for Jackie was her whole life. When he was six years old, Esther found work with Miss Rice, a writer whose home was a haven to Esther. Miss Rice knew Esther's story and tried to make the girl's life easier for her.

One day, Esther met Fred Parsons, a colorless man, but honest, dependable, and religious. When Esther told him her story, he readily forgave her. She took Fred to see Jackie, and the man and the boy were fast friends from the first meeting. Esther and Fred planned to be married as soon as Miss Rice could get another servant, for Esther would not leave her mistress uncared-for. One evening while on an errand for Miss Rice, Esther unexpectedly met William Latch, who told her that Peggy had left him. When he learned that Esther had borne his child, he pleaded to come back to her and hinted that it was her Christian duty to Jackie to give the boy his rightful father. Esther knew that she would be better off with Fred, as would Jackie, for William had become a tavernkeeper and a bookie. Jackie, however, met his father and loved him instantly. For his sake, Esther and William were married.

At first, William made money. Jackie was put in a good school, and Esther had two servants to wait on her. Nevertheless, there were many days of anxious waiting to hear the results of a race. Often William had thousands of pounds to cover if the favorite won. After a time, he began to lose heavily. It was illegal to accept bets at the tavern, and William was in constant danger of being reported to the police. Fred Parsons came to warn Esther to leave William, to tell her that the tavern was to be raided, but she refused to desert her husband. Then Sarah Tucker came to her tavern to ask for help after she had stolen a silver plate from her employer. The police found her there. Later, when the tavern was raided, William's fine was heavy. Business began to dwindle, and Esther and William had lean times.

After William contracted tuberculosis, the dampness and fog of the racetracks only made him cough more, and at last he had to go to the hospital. There the doctors told him that he must go to Egypt for his health. He and Esther gambled all of their money on a single race and lost. Esther tried to be cheerful for William's sake, but when he died a few days later, she wished that she too had died. She had no money, no place to go. Her only blessing was that Jackie was big enough to take care of himself.

Esther went back to Woodview. Only Mrs. Barfield was left, and she was poor. Most of the land had gone to pay racing debts. Esther, however, would have stayed with Mrs. Barfield without wages, for she had never forgotten her old friend's kindness. Jackie enlisted in the army and went to Woodview to tell his mother good-bye. With pride, she introduced him to Mrs. Barfield. She knew that her sin had been redeemed and that she would never have to be ashamed again. She had given her country a fine soldier. Few women could do more.

Critical Evaluation:

English fiction in the nineteenth century maintained a delicate balance between Realism and Romanticism, with an often strong underlayer of sentimentality. At the end of the century, George Moore led British fiction toward Flaubert and Zola and modern French Realism; but he saw that the most carefully observed facts are insufficient unless they are seen through the glass of imagination and humanity. With a frankness previously unknown in the country, *Esther Waters* is the first English novel to reveal the pilgrimage through life of a human being as a physical creature. The novel caused a scandal almost as great as that caused by Hardy's *Jude the Obscure* and was banned from circulating libraries; it had a tremendous influence on younger writers, such as Somerset Maugham in his *Liza of Lambeth*.

Moore deliberately took a mundane subject and wrote about it with much circumstantial Realism and without melodrama; his simple prose style established place and setting with a surprisingly poetic impact. The heroine Esther is seen as a sensual young woman from her first entry into the story, when it is explained that she is fond of touching living creatures. Her physical desires, however, are in conflict with her strict Christian background and later with her duties as a mother. No scene in modern literature is more powerful than that of Esther confronting Mrs. Spires and the cradles of sickly babies and refusing Mrs. Spires's offer to murder her baby for five pounds, so that she can be free from responsibility. The horror that Esther feels is transmitted to the reader, who sees the social importance of the terrible situation.

The book presents a vivid picture of life downstairs in large country houses and in lower-middle-class homes. The life of a servant at the end of the nineteenth century was grim, and the only alternatives for a girl like Esther were prostitution or suicide. The realities of such an existence are shown without exaggeration but with great feeling. Always, Esther is absorbed by one central thought: how to save her child, raise him, and make him into a decent man. Her struggle is told in human terms, and she emerges as a heroine of majestic proportions, all the more magnificent because in her own eyes she is only a miserable creature doing the best she can with little hope and few expectations. Meanwhile, the narrowness and hypocrisy of the middle-class households through which Esther passes are exposed fully, illuminating the genuine goodness of Esther, Miss Rice, and a few other characters.

EUGENE ARAM

Type of work: Novel
Author: Edward George Earle Bulwer-Lytton (1803–1873)
Type of plot: Mystery romance
Time of plot: Mid-eighteenth century
Locale: England
First published: 1832

Principal characters:
ROWLAND LESTER, an English gentleman
MADELINE, his daughter
ELLINOR, another daughter
WALTER LESTER, a nephew
HOUSEMAN, a rogue
EUGENE ARAM, a scholar

The Story:

Geoffrey Lester, a roving and dissipated man, ran away from his wife and only son. His brother, Rowland Lester, took the forsaken family into his own home at Grassdale. Both brothers' wives soon died, and kindly old Rowland took over the responsibility of rearing not only his two daughters, Madeline and Ellinor, but also his young nephew Walter. As the children grew up, Walter fell in love with Madeline, but his love was not returned. It was Ellinor who idealized her cousin as a perfect young man.

One day, a stranger came to Grassdale, a crude, ugly man who was to affect all their lives. Startled by the man while they were out walking, Madeline and Ellinor fled to the house of Eugene Aram, a young recluse and scholar whom they knew slightly. Aram did his best to make the two sisters comfortable and went to secure a carriage to take them home. During his absence, the stranger came to the cottage and asked if Eugene Aram were in. He was sent away. That night, he appeared again at the cottage. Aram recognized him as a man named Houseman, whom he had known under dreadful circumstances years before.

In spite of his solitary preoccupation with science and philosophy, Aram began to visit the Lester family. Before long, it was obvious to Walter that Madeline and Aram were falling in love, and Walter begged Rowland to let him go away for a while. Rowland, sensing his nephew's feelings, allowed him to go. Before he left, Walter had a long talk with Madeline and warned her to carefully consider her fondness for Aram, who he felt would not make her happy. Madeline took his advice as an insult to her intelligence, and the anger she showed went far to dispel the love Walter had felt for her.

Walter and Bunting, a servant, set out for London. Old Rowland had given Walter several letters of introduction to his friends there and had advised the boy to learn what he could about the fortunes of his lost father. From an old friend of his uncle, Walter learned that Geoffrey Lester had been to India, had returned, and under the name of Clarke had gone to Yorkshire to collect a legacy left him by a friend he had known in India. Walter and Bunting started for Yorkshire to trace Geoffrey's whereabouts.

Meanwhile, Houseman reappeared in Grassdale and again bothered Aram. In past times, Houseman had been connected with Aram in a way that Aram did not wish to have announced to the world. Aram knew that Houseman was involved in robbery and worse, but he was not in a position to expose the man. Houseman promised to leave the country if Aram would settle a yearly allowance on Houseman's daughter, the only person in the world whom he loved or who loved him. Aram went to London, where he was able to raise the sum demanded by Houseman. When he returned to Grassdale, Aram thought that he was rid of Houseman forever.

In Yorkshire, Walter learned that his father had been seen last in the village of Knaresborough. On the way there, he and Bunting met Houseman, whom Walter recognized as a man who had robbed him on a previous occasion. Bunting recognized him as a man who had been in Grassdale. Having learned that his daughter was dying, Houseman was hastening to Knaresborough, where she lay on her deathbed. Because his horse had gone lame, Houseman begged Walter to lend him his, and Walter, despite Bunting's objections, was so moved by the man's story that he did so.

When they arrived at Knaresborough, the two travelers learned that Houseman had arrived in time to hold his daughter in his arms before she died. Walter also learned more of his father, who under the name of Clarke had come to the town years before. Walter was told that his father had also stolen some jewels and run up bills in all the shops of the town before he had mysteriously disappeared. An inquest had been held after Clarke's disappearance, and the last two men who had seen him had been tried but released for lack of evidence. With surprise and horror, Walter heard that these two men were Houseman and Eugene Aram.

Walter immediately went to see Houseman, whom he found almost mad over the death of his child. He was unable to answer Walter's questions. Then came word of the discovery of a body that had been buried about the time Clarke had disappeared. Walter forced Houseman to go with him to the newly opened grave and demanded to know if those were the bones of his father. Houseman said that the bones were not those of Clarke; Clarke had been killed and his body buried in a cave. He said that he and Aram had planned to rob Clarke, but that in the struggle, Aram had killed Clarke. The remains of Clarke were uncovered in the place Houseman had described. Walter prepared to return home with the news that Madeline's lover was a murderer.

Meanwhile, Rowland had given his permission to the marriage of Madeline and Aram; he had come to love his prospective son-in-law almost as much as he loved his daughter. Walter's arrival with the terrible news threw the household into despair. Aram was arrested for the crime but denied his guilt. Madeline wasted away with grief over the affair, and old Rowland could not understand the reasons why his nephew brought his charge against Aram.

As the day of the trial drew near, Madeline grew weaker and weaker. Walter realized that whether Aram was found guilty or not guilty, there was no place for him in England. If Aram was judged not guilty, Walter could never ask forgiveness, especially as he would always doubt the judgment. If Aram was found guilty, Walter could not face his family and Madeline again.

At last, the day of the trial arrived. Convinced of Aram's innocence, Madeline went dressed in the clothes she had hoped to wear at her wedding. Houseman was called as a witness by the prosecution. Aram defended himself by pointing out the lack of evidence and the contradiction between his own life and the life of a man who could commit such a crime. Houseman's testimony, he said, could not be counted, as Houseman was known as a thief and robber. Nevertheless, the jury, in accordance with the judge's statement that it was often possible for a man who had led an exemplary life to commit a crime, brought in a verdict of guilty.

As she returned home from the court, Madeline died, brokenhearted. In jail, Aram still maintained his innocence. Walter, in great mental turmoil over the decision of the court, was disturbed by fears that Aram might not be guilty and that he had caused both the death of his cousin and Aram without reason. Granted permission to visit Aram in jail, Walter pleaded with the prisoner to tell him the truth. Aram promised to leave a letter that Walter could read after the execution.

With anxiety, Walter awaited the day of the execution. When it was over, he opened the letter and read Aram's confession of guilt. Aram tried to justify his deed. He had robbed so that he would have money to continue scientific studies that he thought would be of great benefit to mankind. The murder had been the accidental killing of a worthless rogue who had run away from his family, a liar and a thief. Aram thought it only right that such a man should be robbed, even killed, if the money gained went to the betterment of mankind. He had not known that Clarke had really been Geoffrey Lester, uncle of the woman he later planned to marry. Walter was astonished at a mind, so brilliant in so many respects, which could draw such false conclusions.

Walter kept the letter a secret. Knowing the grief he had caused, he left the home of his uncle and cousin and lived for many years abroad. On his return, he went secretly to Grassdale. There Bunting recognized his old master, showed him old Rowland's grave, and gave him directions to the place where Ellinor lived. After a time, Walter and Ellinor married and lived a happy life that served to compensate for all the grief the family had known in the past.

Critical Evaluation:

Although best known for his historical romance, *The Last Days of Pompeii*, Edward Bulwer-Lytton achieved literary prominence in a variety of forms. His account of English manners, *England and the English* (1833), and his account of English dandyism, *Pelham* (1828), have gained an increasing number of appreciative readers. Bulwer-Lytton stressed sensationalism in his romances in order to win readers away from Walter Scott's historical novels, but his own historical objectivity and almost clinical fascination with all kinds of psychological aberrations acted as a corrective to the vulgarizing tendencies of his lurid plots and occult themes.

In writing *The Last Days of Pompeii*, Bulwer-Lytton carefully examined the ancient site and read closely in recent studies of antiquity as well as in the works of Pliny, the diarist; Vitruvius, the architect; and Strabo, the geographer. Similarly, when writing *Eugene Aram*, Bulwer-Lytton had access not only to the public records of the actual crime and trial but also could rely on his own family's association with the historical Aram. The Eugene Aram of real life had been engaged by Bulwer-Lytton's grandfather as an occasional tutor to his daughters. Bulwer-Lytton also established contact with Admiral Burney, who as a schoolboy had known Aram. The whole account of Aram's relations with the Lester family in the novel was taken "word for word, fact for fact," from Burney's notes.

Bulwer-Lytton was intrigued by the opportunity of telling a story about a highly abnormal personality (Eugene Aram, the idealist scholar who could rationalize the act of murder; an anticipation of Dostoevski's Raskolnikov in *Crime and Punishment*) based almost entirely on actual records. Bulwer-Lytton discovered the "dandy" as a literary type, and it is a short distance from social hedonism to a metaphysics of psychological superiority. Pelham and Eugene Aram, although such opposites in personality and character, provide a fascinating paradigm for the later theories of Oscar Wilde and Nietzsche on the superior or super man.

EUPHUES AND HIS ENGLAND

Type of work: Novel
Author: John Lyly (c. 1554–1606)
Type of plot: Didactic romance
Time of plot: 1579–1580
Locale: England
First published: 1580

Principal characters:

EUPHUES, a young gentleman of Athens

PHILAUTUS, a young gentleman of Naples and Euphues'
friend

CAMILLA, a young maiden of England

LADY FLAVIA, a lady of England

SURIUS, an English nobleman

FIDUS, an elderly Englishman

FRANCES, a young English girl and Lady Flavia's niece

The Story:

As they had previously planned, Euphues and Philautus embarked from
Athens for England. During the two-month voyage, Euphues offered
Philautus considerable counsel on how to behave while in the strange country and cautioned him especially about his penchant for falling too easily in
love. To illustrate his point, Euphues told the tale of young Callimachus,
who learned through bitter experience the perils of travel. Euphues closed
his discourse with a description of the island to which they sailed.

Upon their arrival, the two young men encountered Fidus, an old man
who kept bees. After telling them of the folly of discussing the queen about
whom they had asked, Fidus illustrated for them the principles of a sensible monarchy by describing his colony of bees with its queen, workers, and
drones. Upon the urging of Philautus, he also told them of his own
unhappy experience when he fell in love with a young maiden who loved
another man and who died of grief after her lover was killed in a distant
land. This experience had led Fidus to retire to beekeeping in a secluded
area near Dover.

Leaving the old gentleman with thanks for his hospitality and his story,
Euphues and Philautus proceeded toward London. The trip was largely
taken up with another warning by Euphues to Philautus about the dangers
of love, advice given in spite of the Italian's vehement denials of any such
weakness.

Soon the two strangers arrived in London, and they were welcomed
because of their wit and address. Admitted into court circles, they were
delighted with English virtue and charm. Philautus' eye soon fell upon Ca-

milla, a young maiden not of high birth but of great beauty and virtue. He fell immediately and hopelessly in love. After a heated debate with himself about his plight, Philautus was discovered by Euphues, who began praising English women for their beauty and virtue. Philautus stopped his friend and accused him of being in love. The two young men quarreled, and Euphues moved to new lodgings.

At a masque, Philautus revealed his affection to Camilla, who received his overtures coldly. After further rebuffs, he went to an Italian sorcerer in search of a charm to win his beloved. The sorcerer told Philautus that stories of such spells of love, about which he told many popular tales, were all false and that only God, who made the human heart, could govern its inclinations. He advised Philautus to write to his love of his devotion.

The young Italian did so several times, one letter being secretly transported to Camilla in the hollowed-out core of a pomegranate and her reply returned in a volume of Petrarch. Camilla still refused his love, however, and soon she refused to answer his letters. During his pursuit of Camilla, which took place mostly at the house of Lady Flavia, his hostess introduced Philautus to Frances, a girl who was almost as beautiful as Camilla and quite as witty and virtuous. She engaged in several debates with him about love and looked with considerably more favor upon the young Italian.

Camilla was also courted by Surius, a young English nobleman, and Philautus finally became convinced of the hopelessness of his love for her and began to feel strongly the loss of his friendship with Euphues. After an exchange of letters, in which Philautus begged his former friend's pardon, the two young men were reunited.

At a party given by Lady Flavia, Camilla and Surius, Frances and Philautus, and Lady Flavia and an old friend engaged in a three-sided debate that Euphues judged. Wisely taking the middle ground, he declared that virtue and honor must be part of love for both the man and the woman, and he praised the higher love that is above lust. At the party, Philautus discovered that he was very fond of Frances, and Camilla realized that she loved Surius.

While Philautus wooed Frances in the country, Euphues remained in London to study the court and English ways. Before long, however, he was called back to Athens by urgent business. From his home, Euphues wrote his *Euphues' Glass for Europe*, in which he praised at some length English life, the English court, and especially the English sovereign, whose beauty, chastity, and wisdom Euphues declared to be perfect.

In a letter from Philautus, Euphues learned of his friend's plan to marry Frances, of Camilla's marriage to Surius, and of the good wishes of his English friends. Euphues replied with a long letter containing counsel for his friend concerning the management of a marriage. Then the wise Athenian retired to a distant mountain for study and meditation.

Critical Evaluation:
  Euphues and His England is a sequel to the enormously popular *Euphues, the Anatomy of Wit* (1578). Both of these prose romances were widely acclaimed in the 1580's. Indeed, euphuism, the prose style named for the linguistic mannerisms of these works, was cultivated by contemporary ladies of the court. The style is excessive in its exaggerated use of certain rhetorical figures. It was attacked in its own time by Sir Philip Sidney for its violations of decorum, and its vogue was over before the end of Queen Elizabeth's reign.
  John Lyly's elaborate prose style did not appear out of nowhere. Lyly combined and concentrated elements that had appeared in Lord Berner's translation of Froissart's *Chronicles* (1523, 1525), Sir Thomas North's translation of Guevara's *The Dial of Princes* (1557), and, most important, George Pettie's *A Petite Palace of Pettie His Pleasure* (1576). To a great extent, the style seems to have been designed to attract female readers. Even if it was a short-lived phenomenon, the style does seem to reflect many characteristics and concerns of its age. In a period that was increasingly self-conscious about the potentialities of English as opposed to the classical languages for literary expression, it is a highly artful attempt to refine English prose.
  The refinements are primarily in the repeated and extended use of a few decorative rhetorical figures. Balance and, in particular, antithesis are so omnipresent that they frequently overpower the flow of the plot and the dialogue. Narrative sequence and logical consistency are less important than parallel structures. The parallelisms are further embellished with consonance, assonance, alliteration, and other figures of speech that develop self-conscious rhythms and harmonies. The result is like the most ornate poetry of Spenser turned into prose and gone wild. Nevertheless, it does share the Elizabethan preoccupation with linguistic decoration.
  The narrative is also adorned with proverbs and with allusions to classical antiquity and to the bizarre matter of Renaissance natural histories. The fondness for proverbial wisdom, which can be noticed even in Shakespeare's plays, is quite characteristic of the period; however, it should be added that in *Love's Labour's Lost*, Shakespeare did satirize Lyly's verbal excesses. The fanciful descriptions in the natural histories, some borrowed from Pliny and more fashioned out of the wild imaginations of the Naturalists, are bizarre but very much a part of the extravagant wit of the Elizabethan age. What is eccentric is the overwhelming repetition of the features. Like the figures of speech, the proverbs and allusions tend to smother the narrative and reduce the style to a clever curiosity. Paradoxically, the potential orderliness of the balanced style, with its frequent repetitions, is an apt medium for an age that saw an order in the cosmos and in the life of man, which it tried to recreate in the artful control of language. At its

best, as in the poetry of Spenser, the style is a leisurely, pleasing, and decorous elaboration of common themes. At its worst, in Lyly's prose, it becomes monstrous and sometimes even comic.

Euphues and His England is much less remembered as a narrative than as a stylistic fad. As a piece of fiction, it is a romance that gathers several essentially unrelated stories together and unites them only by means of a single central character and a few recurrent themes that punctuate the action. All characters in the work, including Euphues, are highly conventional. They do not come to any epiphanies or undergo moral evolutions; rather, they are stock figures who are put into standard situations and given the opportunity to expatiate at considerable length on a variety of time-honored themes. In speeches, dialogues, and letters, the characters deliver themselves of opinions on the prominent topics of the day—love, youthful excess, constancy, friendship, and education. Although the loose structure of the plot owes much to the contemporarily popular Italian romances, the themes are strikingly those of Elizabethan England, topics repeatedly addressed in the lyric poetry of the sonneteers and in the popular books on behavior, such as Ascham's *The Schoolmaster* and Hoby's translation of Castiglione's *The Courtier*.

The two most frequent preoccupations of the narrative are first, the combination of Platonism and Christian moralism that emanated from the writings of the Humanists of the later Renaissance and, second, self-congratulatory reveling in the imperial glories of Elizabethan England. Events provide a pretext for philosophical debate. Therefore, when Philautus becomes infatuated with Camilla and later when he falls in love with Frances, there is ample opportunity for extensive discussion of the levels of love and of the ultimate superiority of the divine over the human. Similarly, Fidus' advice on the principles of monarchy and Euphues' praise of English customs and governmental institutions are extensive presentations of the habitual themes of the courtesy books and of even so distinguished a work as *The Faerie Queene*.

Some critics have suggested that the Euphues romances are predecessors of the novel of manners and of the psychological novel; yet they seem to contain too little plot or character development to assign them this seminal role in the history of fiction. Rather they seem to look to the past—to the combination and elaboration of conventional themes in the episodic Medieval romance. If Lyly had any influence, it was more probably on the history of style. For all his absurdities, he did much to loosen the rigidity of the Latinate rhetoric, which had been superimposed on English. Certainly he influenced the earlier work of writers such as Robert Greene. Even as a stylist, however, he has barely survived his age except as an oddity. Indeed, in his concentration of the conventional ideas of Platonism, Protestantism, and courtesy, and in his sometimes maniacal overuse of ornamentation,

Lyly not only reflected his age but unconsciously parodied it, and himself.

This sequel deals less directly with morals and more openly with the psychology of love and is, in some ways, an improvement on the first book. Although there is the same dependency on classical sources, such as Pliny and Erasmus, for examples to illustrate truths and for the truths themselves, this work has a better, more coherent plot and depends less on the use of letters from one character to another as a narrative method. The style is, if anything, more graceful and delicate than that in the earlier narrative. Some passages might well please the more fastidious modern reader, and certainly most of the book pleased the Elizabethan reader. Perhaps the most pleased was Queen Elizabeth, since much of the book is taken up with praise of England, Englishmen, and the queen herself. Also of interest to Lyly's contemporaries, undoubtedly, were the extensive and often penetrating passages on the many facets of love. Much sound advice is freely given among the characters, and the events in the plot serve to support the wisdom embodied in action and character.

EUPHUES, THE ANATOMY OF WIT

Type of work: Novel
Author: John Lyly (c. 1554–1606)
Type of plot: Didactic romance
Time of plot: Sixteenth century
Locale: Naples and Athens
First published: 1578

Principal characters:

EUPHUES, a young gentleman of Athens
PHILAUTUS, a nobleman of Naples and his friend
DON FERARDO, a governor of Naples
LUCILLA, his daughter and Philautus' fiancée
LIVIA, her friend
EUBULUS, an old gentleman of Naples

The Story:

Euphues, a young gentleman of Athens, was graced by nature with great personal beauty and by fortune with a large patrimony, but he used his brilliant wit to enjoy the pleasures of wickedness rather than the honors of virtue. In his search for new experiences, the young man went to Naples, a city famed for loose living. There he found many people eager to encourage a waste of time and talent, but he was cautious, trusting no one and taking none for a friend. Thus, he escaped real harm from the company of idle youths with whom he associated.

One day, Eubulus, an elderly gentleman of Naples, approached Euphues and admonished the young man for his easy ways, warning him of the evil results that were sure to follow and urging him to be merry with modesty and reserve. In a witty reply, Euphues rebuffed the old man's counsel and told him that his pious urgings only resulted from his withered old age. In spite of the sage warning, Euphues remained in Naples, and after two months there he met a pleasing young man named Philautus, whom he determined to make his only and eternal friend. Impressed by the charm of Euphues, Philautus readily agreed to be his firm friend forever. Their friendship grew, and the two young men soon became inseparable.

Philautus had long before earned the affection and trust of Don Ferardo, a prominent official of Naples, and he had fallen in love with his beautiful daughter Lucilla. While Don Ferardo was on a trip to Naples, Philautus took his friend with him to visit Lucilla and a group of her friends. After dinner, Euphues was given the task of entertaining the company with an extemporaneous discourse on love. He declared that one should love another for his mind, not for his appearance. When the conversation turned to a discussion of constancy, Lucilla asserted that her sex was wholly fickle. Euphues began to dispute her, but, suddenly struck by Lucilla's beauty and confused by his feelings, he broke off his speech and quickly left.

Lucilla discovered that she was attracted to the young Athenian. After weighing the respective claims of Euphues and Philautus on her affections, she convinced herself that it would not be wrong to abandon Philautus for Euphues; however, she decided to pretend to each that he was her only love. Euphues, meanwhile, had persuaded himself that Lucilla must be his in spite of Philautus: friendship must give way before love. In order to deceive his friend, Euphues pretended to be in love with Livia, Lucilla's friend. Philautus was overjoyed and promised to help him win Livia.

The two young men went immediately to the house of Don Ferardo. While Philautus was attending the governor, who had finally completed arrangements for his daughter's marriage to the young man, Euphues and Lucilla engaged in a subtle debate about love and finally declared their passion for each other. When Don Ferardo told his daughter of his plans for her marriage to Philautus, she told him of her love for Euphues.

Philautus, betrayed at once by both his friend and his beloved, blamed first one and then the other. He wrote a scathing letter to Euphues, saying that they were friends no longer and that he hoped Euphues would soon be in his own unhappy situation; he warned that Lucilla, having proved untrue, might be faithless again. Euphues replied in a taunting letter that deception in love is natural. He expressed confidence that Lucilla would be faithful to him forever.

After what had happened, however, it was impossible for Euphues to visit Lucilla while her father was at home. During her lover's absence, she fell in love again, this time with Curio, a gentleman who possessed neither wealth nor wit. When Euphues at last went to apologize for being away so long, Lucilla replied curtly that she had hoped his absence would be longer. Admitting that her new lover was inferior to both Philautus and Euphues, she supposed God was punishing her for her fickleness. Although she realized that her life was likely to be unhappy, a fate she had earned, she did not hesitate to scorn Euphues. Don Ferardo argued that it was her filial duty to give up the worthless Curio. When she refused, her father died of grief shortly thereafter.

Having renewed his friendship with Philautus before departing from Naples, Euphues left with his friend a written discourse against the folly of love. It stated that love, although it started with pleasure, ended in destruction and grief, and he urged his friend to forget passion and to turn his attention toward more serious pursuits.

After returning to Athens where he engaged in long hours of study, Euphues wrote a treatise on the proper way to rear a child. His own upbringing had not steered him away from the shoals of sloth and wickedness. With this weakness of upbringing in mind, he urged that a young man should be legitimately born and reared under the influence of three major forces: nature, reason, and use. In this manner, the young man would be educated in the ways of virtue as well as in the customs of use.

Euphues wrote many other letters and treatises: in one, he urged the gentlemen scholars of Athens to study with the laws of God in mind; in another, he debated with an atheist and converted him to godliness; a letter to Philautus encouraged him to abandon his dissolute life in Naples; in a letter to Eubulus, Euphues thanked the old man for his good advice and told him of his return to righteousness; another letter to Philautus expressed regret at the death of Lucilla and at the irreligious character of her life; two letters to a pair of young men told them to accept their destiny and to live virtuously; in response to a letter in which Livia told of her intention to be virtuous, Euphues praised her and told her of Philautus' possible visit to Athens.

Critical Evaluation:

Although John Lyly wrote drama, poetry, and other prose, his major fame rests on his two prose romances, *Euphues, the Anatomy of Wit* and its sequel, *Euphues and His England* (1580). Both are more noted for their style than their substance. *Euphues, the Anatomy of Wit*, for example, combines the biblical parable of the Prodigal Son with a tale from Boccaccio's *Decameron* (Day 10, Story 8) creating the merest wisp of a story, which, in turn, serves mainly as a springboard for a series of moralistic treatises on such topics as love, friendship, women, and education.

Style, however, is the key to *Euphues, the Anatomy of Wit*. To be sure, Lyly did not invent the ornate style that came to be known as "euphuistic," but the fame of *Euphues* lent it an influence that appeared as imitation in numerous other works. Lyly's intent was to adapt poetic devices to a prose medium in order to create poetic prose. To this end, Lyly wedded poetry and rhetoric in a rococo explosion of verbal contrivances. He utilized the imagery, rhythm, and meter of poetry; he incorporated conventions of animal personification—the dull, stupid ass, the ravenous wolf, the timorous hare, the courageous, magnanimous lion—among dozens of others; he drew upon the balanced sentence structure, the rhetorical question, the classical and historical allusion, and similar devices associated with oratory. The results were more spectacular than substantial, but Lyly set an important precedent that gave impetus to such later and more successful writers as De Quincey, Ruskin, and Pater.

As always, Lyly's intention was to refine the manners of an era that realized its need for delicacy and sophistication. There is, in addition, a strong strain of moralistic didacticism in *Euphues*, which was also written to oppose Italian influences in the court of Queen Elizabeth. Athens is generally accepted to have been, in Lyly's mind, a symbol of Oxford University; and he addressed a brief epilogue to the "Gentlemen Scholars of Oxford." What little plot there is in *Euphues* is probably based on some of Lyly's own experiences during his college days, but the story is less important for its own sake than as a vehicle for ornately written digressions, so that its essential purpose, the development of a graceful and ornate prose style, is undeniably well achieved. That the Elizabethan age welcomed such a development is shown by the fact that the extreme popularity of *Euphues* gave the name that still clings to the kind of writing that Lyly perfected.

Especially in its own time, *Euphues* was praised, condemned, and widely copied. Robert Greene and Thomas Lodge admired the style of *Euphues* and adopted it in their own writing. Sir Philip Sidney deplored euphuism in his treatise *The Defence of Poesie*, yet his own prose romance, *Arcadia*, is very nearly as ornately contrived as *Euphues*. Shakespeare ridiculed the euphuistic style in several of his plays, and in one play (*Love's Labour's Lost*) employed both ridicule and imitation. The influence of and the controversy over *Euphues* did not disappear with the passing of the Elizabethan era. As late as the nineteenth century, Sir Walter Scott mocked euphuism in one of his novels, while Charles Kingsley defended it in one of his. To the modern reader, this dispute over the merits of euphuism may seem trivial, since Lyly's style, judged by today's standards, is preposterously affected. Nevertheless, *Euphues* stands as a warning to any literary age, illustrating that the chic, extreme fashion of one era may appear as comical and self-conscious contrivance to a later time.

EVAN HARRINGTON

Type of work: Novel
Author: George Meredith (1828–1909)
Type of plot: Social satire
Time of plot: Nineteenth century
Locale: England
First published: 1861

> *Principal characters:*
> EVAN HARRINGTON, a tailor's son
> HARRIET COGGLESBY,
> CAROLINE STRIKE, and
> LOUISA, THE COUNTESS DE SALDAR, Evan's sisters
> ROSE JOCELYN, an heiress
> FERDINAND LAXLEY, Evan's rival

The Story:

Melchisedec Harrington was a tailor with the bearing and manners of a great nobleman. When he died, his neighbors spoke fondly of him and wondered what his son, who was in Portugal, would do. His widow knew that the great Mel, as he was called, had left debts amounting to more than four thousand pounds, which Evan would want to repay. The boy was to go to Mr. Goren in London to learn the tailor's trade.

There had been three daughters in the tailor's household, each of whom had married so well that they had henceforth cut themselves apart from their father, a common tradesman. Harriet had married a brewer, Andrew Cogglesby; Caroline had married Major Strike, and Louisa had become the Countess de Saldar. The Countess decided that her brother Evan must also marry well, and she tried to ally him with Rose Jocelyn, who had money of her own.

When Mrs. Harrington told Evan about old Mel's debts, the son consented to go to London and learn his trade from Mr. Goren; not even the Countess' entreaties and assurances that Rose loved him could dissuade him from his course. Setting out for London on foot, he met Jack Raikes, an old school friend. They went to the Green Dragon Inn, where they joined a group of men at dinner. Old Tom Cogglesby, brother of Andrew, the brewer, presided. Among those present were Harry Jocelyn, Rose's brother, and Ferdinand Laxley, his friend. Evan and Jack got into a drunken brawl involving much name-calling and many threats. The gentlemen present scoffed at Evan's choice of trade. Laxley challenged Evan to a duel, but on learning that Evan was the son of a tailor, he haughtily declined to fight a common tradesman.

While watching a cricket match on the green on the day after the tavern brawl, Evan met Rose Jocelyn and her party, which included the Countess de Saldar. He was prevailed upon to visit the Jocelyns at Beckley Court before he went to London. As he rode along beside Rose, one of the men with whom he had quarreled the night before pointed him out as a tailor. At Beckley Court, the Countess was able to persuade Harry Jocelyn that Evan was not the tailor but that Jack Raikes was. Laxley still demanded that Evan deny his trade and fight the duel as a gentleman or else acknowledge it.

Laxley was one of Rose's suitors. Resenting Evan, he continually challenged him to admit he was not a real gentleman. Since claiming that he was a gentleman would mean a duel with Laxley, Evan resolved to leave Beckley Court.

The Countess, fearing to see all her plans ruined, prevailed upon Evan to seek the advice of his relatives. Harriet, Caroline, and Andrew were also visiting at Beckley Court; Evan's predicament concerned all of them. Andrew offered the young man a position in his brewery.

Glorying in her position, Rose encouraged her admirers to outrace each other in an amateur steeplechase; the prize would be her handkerchief. Evan won the prize but was injured when thrown from his horse.

There was a rumor in Lymport that at the age of sixteen the Countess de Saldar tried to run off with a certain George Uploft. Melchisedec allegedly had chased the pair down and ended the romance. When Uploft appeared at Beckley Court, the Countess brazenly defied him to recall her background. At dinner, the conversation swung to old Mel, and during the last anecdote, which involved Mel's oldest daughter, Caroline swooned and was taken from the room. Uploft, however, had already recognized her as Mel's daughter.

Although confined to bed because of his injury, Evan was still determined to leave Beckley Court. His masquerade of pretending to be one of the upper class when he was actually a tailor's son was too much for him. That evening, seeing Rose in the garden, he followed her to claim the handkerchief that he had won. When Evan revealed his love for Rose and she responded, he promised himself that he would disclose his base origin to her.

The next day, Evan told Rose the facts about himself. She admitted that she already knew his story and loved him in spite of it, and she promised to fight her family for the right to marry him. She also asked him to accept employment as her Uncle Melville's secretary.

Awaiting Evan's arrival in London, Mr. Goren learned from Jack Raikes that Evan was loitering at Beckley Court. Mr. Goren wrote a complaint to Mrs. Harrington, who proceeded at once to Beckley Court. Stopping overnight at the Green Dragon Inn, she met the obstreperous Tom Cogglesby and tamed him with her efficiency and good sense. Since both were going to Beckley Court, they traveled together the next day. Tom said that he was on his way to help a tailor marry a gentlewoman.

The social involvements at Beckley Court grew more tense. Laxley was blamed for an outrageous blunder in revealing the whereabouts of a runaway wife whom Lady Jocelyn had befriended, and he was sent away. The Countess de Saldar had a triumphant moment. Mrs. Harrington conducted herself with finesse in the midst of a difficult situation.

The Harringtons, however, had been publicly exposed as the family of the tailor Melchisedec. Evan, fearing that he had lost Rose, discovered that his sister, the Countess de Saldar, was responsible for the anonymous letter Laxley was supposed to have written. Failing in his entreaties to convince his sister to confess the truth to Lady Jocelyn, Evan decided to take the blame for Laxley's dismissal. After declaring his guilt to Lady Jocelyn, he also wrote to Laxley. Evan decided beforehand that if Laxley challenged him to a duel, he would refuse the challenge.

Juliana, Rose's cousin and a plain-looking crippled girl, was in love with Evan and had always been loyal to him. From the beginning, she had known the facts about his background. When the question of his infamous deception involving Laxley arose, Juliana refused to believe ill of Evan.

On the day of Evan's departure from Beckley Court, Rose came to him and asked him if he had been responsible for Laxley's Fumiliation. Feeling that if she truly loved him she would not need to ask, he refused to explain. Laxley arrived and took possession of Rose. A note from Juliana informed Evan that she believed in him.

Evan prepared to follow his trade in Mr. Goren's shop. The Cogglesbys, receiving Juliana as a guest in their home, set out to win Evan's heart for the invalid girl; but Evan still pined for Rose, who cut him cruelly when she met him on the street.

When Andrew's brewery went bankrupt and he lost all his property, the three sisters, who had been living in the Cogglesby house, were forced to go to their mother in Lymport. Juliana was in poor health, and at Evan's request, Lady Jocelyn had taken her back to Beckley Court.

Juliana inherited Beckley Court upon the death of her grandmother. Just before she died of an incurable malady, Juliana wrote to Rose and revealed Evan's innocence. She also wrote a will leaving her estate to Evan. Meanwhile Rose, engaged to Laxley, felt herself bound by promise to Evan and sent for him to release her before she could marry his rival. Evan did so with no show of self-sacrifice. Later Rose learned that Evan, rejecting Juliana's bequest, had returned Beckley Court to Lady Jocelyn.

Everyone had become indebted to Evan for his generosity; he had simply tried to make everyone happy. Lady Jocelyn and Rose went to Lymport to thank him. There Rose, speaking with Evan alone, asked him why he had blackened his name to her. No longer compelled to pretend anything about himself, Evan rose manfully to the occasion. When he declared his love, Rose accepted him. Old Tom Cogglesby was delighted and offered to give Evan an income.

The sisters went back to their former ways of life. Mrs. Harrington became Tom Cogglesby's housekeeper.

Critical Evaluation:

Evan Harrington displays George Meredith's keen irony and fine sense of distinctions, both social and human, while his sense of appropriate detail lends the book a density and richness of design. It is easy to see the influence of Meredith's friend and father-in-law Thomas Love Peacock in this early novel, especially in the witty dialogue. Epigrams stud the narrative— many of them truly witty, others too strained. For example, Meredith observes: "Most youths are like Pope's women; they have no character at all." The narrative, however, does not possess the extreme artificiality of Peacock; the story moves well, and many scenes are funny in themselves without the embroidery of added wit.

Meredith's genius for comedy is allowed full scope in *Evan Harrington's* almost farcical exposure of snobbery. What is a gentleman? The question is asked frequently in different forms throughout the book. The postillion thinks that he is a man with "a purse long and liberal," but the Countess holds that he is indefinable. Evan seeks to become a gentleman safely and permanently, yet he is not happy about denying his filial past. The deceptive nature of appearances also plays an important part in the story. Is a man what he appears? asks Meredith. How far do a fine figure and bearing and patrician features go toward making a person truly of the gentry? Are the qualities that make a gentleman hereditary, or can they be acquired? How far can they be stretched without appearing absurd? Meredith poses the questions and then lets the reader draw his own conclusions from the events in the story. *Evan Harrington* is one of George Meredith's most readable novels, filled with delightful characterizations, such as the Cogglesby brothers and Evan's trio of snobbish sisters. Its comedy makes some shrewd points but is no less fun for its serious intent.

EVELINA
Or, The History of a Young Lady's Entrance into the World

Type of work: Novel
Author: Fanny Burney (Madame d'Arblay, 1752–1840)
Type of plot: Sentimental romance
Time of plot: Eighteenth century
Locale: England
First published: 1778

Principal characters:
SIR JOHN BELMONT, an English nobleman
EVELINA, Sir John's unacknowledged daughter
THE REVEREND MR. VILLARS, Evelina's guardian
MADAME DUVAL, Evelina's grandmother
LORD ORVILLE, the man Evelina married
SIR CLEMENT WILLOUGHBY, a gentleman of fashion
MRS. MIRVAN, Evelina's patroness

The Story:

Abandoned by her father and her maternal grandmother upon the death of her mother, Evelina had been for many years the ward of the Reverend Mr. Arthur Villars, an English clergyman. At last, her grandmother, Madame Duval, wrote from France to say that she would take charge of the girl, providing proper proof of the child's relationship was forthcoming. Mr. Villars, however, refused to send Evelina to France. He also objected to the invitation of Mrs. Mirvan, who wanted Evelina to join her family in London. He felt that Evelina, having been brought up carefully at Berry Hill in Dorsetshire, should not be exposed to the unhappiness of London society life, particularly so since her own father, Sir John Belmont, would not admit his parentage and she was without enough income to permit her to live as the Mirvans did.

After some urging, he finally allowed Evelina to visit Lady Howard, Mrs. Mirvan's mother, at Howard Grove. A short time later, Mrs. Mirvan and her daughter, who were delighted with Evelina, secured permission to have her accompany them to London.

Almost at once, she was swept into fashionable London life. Having grown up in the provinces, the city was a constant joy to her. She soon met Lord Orville, and both were attracted to each other. On several occasions, her lack of London manners caused her embarrassment, and she expressed a desire to return to Dorsetshire. Sir Clement Willoughby was her chief tormentor.

By chance, she met her odious grandmother, the vulgar and presumptuous Madame Duval. On an outing, the Frenchwoman became the subject of ridicule when she was pitched into a mudhole. Evelina met some of her other relations and found them no better than her grandmother.

Madame Duval, attaching herself to the Mirvans, succeeded in making Evelina very unhappy. Evelina went reluctantly to the opera with her relatives and was made miserable by their crudeness. Hoping to escape them, she joined Sir Clement but was only further embarrassed when Sir Clement intentionally delayed his coach while escorting her to her lodging. Evelina was severely scolded by her guardian for the escapade. In a letter to her, he indicated that he lived in daily fears for her honor. He was relieved when he heard that the Mirvans were at last returning with her to Howard Grove.

Lady Howard, urged on by Madame Duval, put forth the plan of forcing Sir John Belmont to acknowledge Evelina as his daughter. Mr. Villars did not approve of this action; he had promised Evelina's mother that the girl would never know her cruel and unnatural father.

At Howard Grove, Evelina unknowingly participated in a cruel joke planned by Captain Mirvan and Sir Clement. Again made a laughingstock, Madame Duval took to her bed after she had been sent upon a fool's errand and had lost her false curls.

When Sir John Belmont refused to admit that Evelina was his daughter, Madame Duval planned to take Evelina to confront Sir John in person and to demand his recognition. Mr. Villars would not listen to her proposal. He did agree, however, to let Evelina spend a month with her grandmother in London. Evelina was unhappy under Madame Duval's chaperonage because her vulgar relations attempted to use her to ingratiate themselves with her fashionable friends. Sir Clement Willoughby visited Evelina while she was staying with her grandmother, but Madame Duval embarrassed everyone by her uncivil remarks to him. She remembered the joke played on her at Howard Grove.

In her London lodgings, Evelina was instrumental in preventing the suicide of Mr. Macartney, an impoverished Scottish poet. Out of pity for his plight, she relieved his need with money from her own purse.

At a fireworks display, Evelina was again chagrined, having been discovered by Lord Orville while she was in vulgar company.

Madame Duval announced that she hoped to marry Evelina to the boorish young son of Mr. Branghton, a silversmith. Mr. Branghton was Madame Duval's nephew. Evelina was much distressed, the more so when her grandmother's friends attached themselves to Lord Orville in a familiar manner. When Mr. Branghton asked his lordship's custom for any silver the nobleman might want to buy, Evelina felt ruined forever in Lord Orville's eyes.

In her distress, Evelina wrote to Mr. Villars, who ordered her to return immediately to Berry Hill. From there, she wrote about her London adventures to her friend, Miss Mirvan. A most painful surprise to her was a letter she had received from Lord Orville, to whom she had written to disclaim responsibility for her relatives' crudeness. His reply was so insulting that she became ill and had to be sent to a rest home at Bristol Hot Wells, where she went in the company of Mrs. Selwyn, a neighbor.

At the watering place, Evelina met many of her fashionable London friends, among them Lord Orville. He was so courteous that she had to forgive him for his impolite letter. As Evelina was beginning to feel at home once more among people of wealth and position, Mr. Macartney appeared and embarrassed her with his importunities.

A new arrival at the baths was Miss Belmont, an heiress reputed to be Sir John Belmont's daughter. Mrs. Selwyn, hearing of the girl's identity, decided to learn more about Miss Belmont. Mrs. Selwyn was convinced that Evelina was the true daughter of Sir John.

Mr. Macartney was trying to return the money Evelina had given him, but she did not want her friends to learn that she had ever known him. She feared that they would suspect her of having had an affair with him. Lord Orville, however, encouraged her to see the unfortunate young poet. From Mr. Macartney, Evelina learned that he believed himself to be an unacknowledged son of Sir John Belmont. Evelina, realizing that she herself must be the sister of Mr. Macartney, did not reveal her knowledge.

When Sir John Belmont returned to England, Mr. Villars was finally stirred to action against him; for by introducing to society the woman who posed as his daughter, Sir John was indicating that Evelina was an impostor. Determined that Evelina should have her rights, Mr. Villars prepared to force Sir John to acknowledge Evelina as his daughter.

Through the good offices of Mrs. Selwyn and others, the affair was at last untangled. The supposed daughter of Sir John proved to be the daughter of a penniless nurse, who had substituted her own child for Lady Belmont's infant. Evelina, delighted to learn that Sir John's attitude had been the result of error and not neglect, was happily reconciled with her father, who received her warmly. The impostor was treated with great kindness by all concerned as she herself was innocent of the design. She married Mr. Macartney, who was also acknowledged by Sir John. As Sir John's daughter, Evelina was sought after by Lord Orville, to whom she gladly gave her hand in marriage.

Critical Evaluation:

Evelina is Fanny Burney's first and most successful novel. When it was published in 1778, the book's appeal was attributed to its sentimental value, but it has held lasting interest because of the realistic portrayal of eighteenth century English life. In *Evelina*, Burney's attentiveness to the manners and pretentiousness of socialites enabled her to show not only the culture but its foibles. *Evelina* is particularly descriptive of the social position of women.

Sensitively reared by the Reverend Mr. Villars, the heroine, Evelina, has become a kind, compassionate young woman. As she steps into the social life of London, her unblemished perception of society affords both delight at its marvels and disdain for its unscrupulousness and frivolity. Her letters to Mr. Villars convey clear images of London high society.

Evelina first writes with some amazement that London life begins so late that people spend the morning in bed. She adjusts, however, to the nightlife and enjoys the opera, plays, and other events with which she and her company are entertained almost nightly. She is annoyed by audiences who are so talkative throughout the events that the artists cannot be heard, and she quickly realizes that the purpose of the events is more for socializing than for the merit of the performances themselves.

Burney places her heroine with various guardians in a variety of situations in both city and country. Evelina's first awkward fortnight in London with the kind Mirvan ladies abruptly contrasts with her second visit in London in the company of Madame Duval and her relatives, the Branghtons. Crude and ill-mannered, they cause Evelina embarrassment by her forced association with them. In her third venture away from her benefactor Mr. Villars, Evelina is again in cultured company under the guardianship of the aggressive Mrs. Selwyn.

In each group, regardless of its social position, Evelina finds individuals of sincerity and those who are masters of divisiveness and deception. Mrs. Mirvan and Maria are sincere and well-mannered. Although uncouth, cruel, and contemptuous, Captain Mirvan is, nevertheless, sincere. He is his own person, honest in his brutal way. Madame Duval shares with her tormentor, Captain Mirvan, the quality of being her own person, disagreeable as she, too, may be.

Evelina readily acknowledges the honorable qualities of Lord Orville and Mr. Macartney. She also quickly perceives the duplicity of Sir Clement, Mr. Lovel, Lord Merton, and the Branghtons, Lady Louisa, and Mr. Smith. In lady or silversmith, airs and presumptuousness repel Evelina. Evelina is shocked at the insincerity of those whose honor and good manners directly relate to dress, immediate company, and situation. Lord Merton ignores Evelina while Lady Louisa is present yet lavishes her with attention at Lady Louisa's absence. Sir Clement is a chameleon whose attention to Evelina is gained at any expense. Lady Louisa acts out roles constantly, purposely ignoring Evelina until she learns that Evelina is to become her brother's wife.

Evelina detects affectation and shows it as being ridiculous. She describes for Mr. Villars an episode from her first dance at which a young man approached her with comically stilted mannerisms and speech. "Allow me, Madam . . . the honour and happiness—if I am not so unhappy as to address you too late—to have the happiness and honour." She confesses that she had to turn away to conceal her laughter.

Evelina is bewildered by the social etiquette that she has had no opportunity to learn at Berry Hill, but her sense of propriety causes her to suffer for her ignorance. She is always aware of her dependent position and constantly relies on her protectors, benefactors, or guardians.

Burney did not intend for Evelina's dependence to be read negatively. On the contrary, Evelina was idyllic in her feminine compliance and sensibility. She was a model lady for the times. It is interesting to note, however, how vastly the roles and rights of men and women in the novel differ. Mr. Lovel says, "I have an insuperable aversion to strength, either in body or mind, in a female." Lord Merton echoes a similar view—"for a woman wants nothing to recommend her but beauty and good nature; in everything else she is either impertinent or unnatural."

Burney comments on women's sensibility through her characters. Lady Louisa, whose feigned delicate nature corresponds with her posturing, seems to be the extreme of insincere sensibility. Mrs. Selwyn represents another extreme. She is powerful and aggressive and is disliked by both men and women for her outspokenness. Evelina wishes that Mrs. Selwyn were more sensitive to her needs in awkward situations and finds her lacking in femininity. Evelina writes, "I have never been personally hurt by her want of gentleness, a virtue which nevertheless seems so essential a part of the female character." Lord Orville, the ideal male in the novel, is described by Evelina as "feminine," a compliment to his gentle character. Evelina's description of Mrs. Selwyn as "masculine," however, is definitely a negative criticism.

Because of the impropriety of acting independently, Evelina and all gentlewomen must rely upon others for advice. Unfortunately, those counselors are likely to take advantage of women's dependency. Fortunately, Evelina's good sense alerts her to unreliable protectors, but her situation clearly indicates the powerless situation of women who are perpetually rescued or victimized.

Perhaps Mr. Villar's response to Evelina's interference in the attempted suicide of Mr. Macartney best expresses Burney's attitude toward women. "Though gentleness and modesty are the peculiar attributes of your sex, yet fortitude and firmness, when occasion demands them, are virtues as noble and as becoming in women as in men."

Evelina was first published without the name of the author and was generally assumed to have been written by a man. Burney was indeed as dependent as her Evelina in getting the book into publication; a male secret agent smuggled the manuscript to the publisher.

THE FAIR MAID OF PERTH

Type of work: Novel
Author: Sir Walter Scott (1771–1832)
Type of plot: Historical romance
Time of plot: 1396
Locale: Scotland
First published: 1828

> *Principal characters:*
> HENRY GOW, the smith and armorer of Perth
> CATHARINE GLOVER, the Fair Maid of Perth and his
> sweetheart
> SIMON GLOVER, her father
> CONACHAR, Simon's apprentice and heir to the chief of Clan
> Quhele
> THE DUKE OF ROTHSAY, heir to Scottish throne
> SIR JOHN RAMORNY, his Master of Horse
> ROBERT III, King of Scotland
> THE DUKE OF ALBANY, his brother
> THE EARL OF DOUGLAS, the "Black Douglas"
> OLIVER PROUDFUTE, a Perth burgher, a bonnet-maker, and a
> friend of Henry Gow
> HENBANE DWINING, Ramorny's physician and a Perth
> apothecary
> SIR PATRICK CHARTERIS, the provost of Perth

The Story:

As Catharine Glover and her father Simon walked to Mass, an unidentified young nobleman, muffled in a cloak, joined them and asked the girl's permission to come to her window the next morning to take part in the traditional Valentine ritual. When she sensibly refused to make any alliance above her social standing, he left her in anger.

A welcome guest, Henry Gow, appeared at the Glovers' that evening; he had just returned from a trip on which he had sold armor throughout Scotland. Although Simon approved heartily of Henry's suit for Catharine's hand, she was disturbed by his propensity for quarreling. His fiery spirit led him to rise up vigorously that evening against Conachar, Simon's Highlander apprentice, who jealously poured a tankard of beer on the armorer and then tried to stab him.

Henry's martial bent was put to better use the next morning when, coming to present himself to Catharine as her Valentine, he discovered a party of men attempting to climb into her room. While fighting them off, he severed the hand of one assailant. Again, a mysterious nobleman was involved. When Simon heard his voice, he sent Henry into his house and freed the other. In gratitude for Henry's protection, Catharine agreed to be his Valentine, but she would not promise to marry him; although, she assured him that she was not in love with Conachar, who had just returned to his Highland home, or any other man.

King Robert was discussing the rising power of the Earl of Douglas with his confessor. The Earl then arrived at the castle just in time to see his son-in-law, the Duke of Rothsay, kiss a traveling gleemaiden. The "Black Douglas" was infuriated and threatened to kill both the prince and the innocent girl. The Duke of Albany, King Robert's brother James, and another nobleman calmed the two men, and Rothsay committed the girl to the care of Henry, who had just entered the courtyard engaged in a scuffle with some of Douglas' men. Although he was reluctant to accept such a charge, especially on the day he had become Catharine's Valentine, he took the girl home with him and sent her on to Dundee the next morning.

The council that followed Rothsay's foolish flirtation revealed the tensions surrounding the weak and easily influenced King. After King Robert had prevented a duel between the archrivals, the earls of March and Douglas, March stalked out to join the English. Albany and the prince, too, were obviously struggling for control over king and country.

As these personal conflicts smoldered, the men discussed the enmity between Clans Quhele and Chattan and decided to settle it by setting the bravest men from each group against one another in a combat to be fought before the King. After Douglas had gone, the King and Albany questioned the prince about the early morning disturbance at Simon's house, reported to them by Sir Patrick Charteris, provost of Perth. Confronted with a ring found at Simon's house, Rothsay confessed that he had been present; the ring belonged to Sir John Ramorny, his Master of Horse. Rothsay agreed to dismiss Ramorny, whom both older men regarded as an evil influence over the young prince.

Conachar came back to Perth briefly at Catharine's request that he give refuge to Father Clement, her confessor, who had been accused of heresy. The Highlander told her that he was the son of the chief of Clan Quhele and that his real name was Eachin (Hector) MacIan. As he promised protection for Father Clement, he hinted also at his love for Catharine.

Ramorny, the owner of the hand cut off in Perth, planned vengeance on his assailant with Henbane Dwining, an apothecary who was jealous of Henry's power and influence. Having gained only a mild revenge by spreading the tale of Henry's association with the gleemaiden, he was eager to help Ramorny plot Henry's assassination.

That night, as Shrovetide revelers milled about Perth, Oliver Proudfute, a well-meaning but tactless burgher, assured the still angry Simon that Henry was not hiding the gleemaiden; he had seen him send her to Dundee. Then, fearing that he had made matters worse, he escaped from a group of taunting masquers and went to Henry to apologize. Proudfute, who liked to think of himself as a hero but who was really a timid soul, avoided the subject of his visit as long as possible. His belated and sheepish confession served only to deepen Henry's depression over his relationship with Catharine; Henry ordered his friend out, after granting the burgher's request for his helmet and jacket to frighten away assailants. Ironically, these garments caused Proudfute's death, for as he walked down the street imitating Henry's swagger he was struck down from behind and killed.

Rothsay, who had been among the masquers, went to Ramorny's to rouse him to join the gaiety. He was horrified to learn of his missing hand, and he suspected him of attempting revenge when he noticed the surly murderer Bonthron in the room. Ramorny's suggestion that they "allow" Albany to die and force King Robert to abdicate shocked him further. The prince left immediately, vowing to see Ramorny no more and arousing the bitter hatred of his former friend.

The discovery of Proudfute's body the next morning set off a rumor that Henry was dead. Catharine flew disheveled through the streets to see whether he was safe. Henry's joy at this evidence of her affection was marred by the news of the murder and his realization that he must ignore Catharine's feelings and declare himself the champion of Proudfute's widow.

After a brief investigation, the provost suspected that Proudfute's death was the result of the enmity aroused during the Valentine encounter between Henry and Ramorny. The council decided to determine the identity of the murderer by an ancient test—the bier-right—based on the superstition that a body bleeds in the presence of its killer. Ramorny's household was later marched by Proudfute's body but with no result until Bonthron refused the test and chose the alternative, trial by combat. Henry defeated the murderer, who in his confession followed the instructions of Ramorny and Dwining and laid the principal blame on Rothsay. Albany immediately put the prince in the hands of the High Constable to protect him and keep him out of further trouble.

Sir Patrick Charteris came to tell Simon and Catharine that they were to be arrested for heresy. Simon planned to seek asylum with his old friend, Conachar's father, in the Highlands; however, knowing his former apprentice's feelings, he was relieved when the provost offered to take Catharine to Lady Marjory, Duchess of Rothsay.

When he reached his destination, Simon learned that his friend had died, but he was received courteously by the young chief. Conachar confessed to him that he feared the coming combat with Clan Chattan; a coward was not a fit leader for a brave clan. He begged Simon to let him marry Catharine, for he felt that her love would strengthen him. Simon refused, however, to break his word to Henry.

Meanwhile, Ramorny had enticed Rothsay to flee to the former residence of his duchess by telling him that Catharine was coming there. When the girl arrived, thinking Lady Marjory was still there, the prince at first tried to seduce her but later gave in to her appeal to his honor. He entrusted her to Louise, the gleemaiden, whom he had encountered again by chance.

Ramorny and Dwining starved the prince to death and at the same time spread a rumor that he was ill. Louise and Catharine discovered what was happening, and the gleemaiden escaped to bring Douglas to the rescue while Catharine tried to get food to Rothsay. Douglas arrived in time to force Ramorny's surrender and to save Catharine's life; Dwining poisoned himself to avoid his confederate's fate of death by hanging.

Douglas and Albany decided to keep Rothsay's death secret until after the clan combat on Palm Sunday. That morning, Henry volunteered to take the place of a missing Chattan warrior and fought valiantly in order to have a chance to meet Conachar, whom he believed a rival about to wed Catharine. Conachar's foster father sacrificed his eight sons and himself in an endeavor to protect Conachar, but their efforts were useless. When the young leader faced Henry at last, the Highlander fled across the river Tay. Late that day, he went to Catharine to tell her of his cowardice before he plunged to his death in the torrent.

Catharine and Henry were married a few months later. Although she was by that time reconciled to her husband's warring impulses, he vowed to take up arms again only in behalf of his country. Their first son had as godparents the Earl of Douglas, Lady Marjory, and Sir Patrick Charteris.

King Robert died soon afterward, brokenhearted by the death of one son and the capture by the English of the other, later James I of Scotland, whom he was sending away to protect him from Albany's power. Albany, acquitted by Parliament of the charge that he was responsible for Rothsay's death, nevertheless did penance for his guilt. His son, who inherited the regency, paid for his father's sins on the scaffold when James I came to the throne years later.

Critical Evaluation:

In this novel, Sir Walter Scott sets his finely drawn fictional and historical characters against the background of the rise to power of the Earl of Douglas, the Scottish leader who fought against Percy at the famous battle of Chevy Chase. The author is justly praised for his ability to create living beings. The characters of *The Fair Maid of Perth* do not stand out among Scott's greatest creations, but they are believable and interesting; good and bad exist among both the nobility and the citizenry and are present in each individual in varying degrees.

Over the years, as critical standards have changed, emphasizing polished writing and careful literary construction, the faults of Scott's writing have become only too obvious. *The Fair Maid of Perth*, for example, shows evidence of the same hurried composition, unnecessarily Latinate style, and excessive verbiage that his earlier novels exhibit; it also contains the characteristic idealization of women and improbable plot. Positive values, however, still remain in Scott's historical novels such as *The Fair Maid of Perth*. These values are most evident in the concrete historical life that Scott is able to evoke, in the themes that he chooses to treat, and in the historical insight he is able to bring to his fiction.

The life of fourteenth century Scotland—its houses, churches, streets, and businesses—is described in the most complete detail. Methods of warfare, trading, and lovemaking are presented. Furthermore, Scott is able to integrate this vast complex of late medieval detail into a single though loosely connected structure. Scott is expert at painting a great variety of social strata on the same canvas; in *The Fair Maid of Perth*, there are nobility, rising mercantilists, churchmen, peasants, and poor folk. Not only are all these groups given roles in the drama, but all of them are shown in dramatic relationship to one another. In this way, Scott succeeds in creating an organically developed society.

It is not, however, a society at rest. The story of *The Fair Maid of Perth*, recounting the victory of middle-class citizens over the schemings and violence of aristocratic forces, might stand as an emblem for the general historic trends of the era. Medieval institutional structures and morality were crumbling. A new system, based on men such as Henry Gow, was developing and coming into conflict with the old. The drama of this conflict as well as the thematic tension between pacifism and the need for arms (between Henry and Catharine) overshadow the plot as such; but the historical process and the themes Scott raises through his characters more than compensate for artificial plot lines and stylistic deficiencies.

FAR FROM THE MADDING CROWD

Type of work: Novel
Author: Thomas Hardy (1840–1928)
Type of plot: Psychological realism
Time of plot: 1869–1873
Locale: Wessex, England
First published: 1874

Principal characters:
GABRIEL OAK, a shepherd
BATHSHEBA EVERDENE, the mistress of Weatherbury Farm
SERGEANT TROY, her first husband
WILLIAM BOLDWOOD, her suitor and a farmer and neighbor
FANNY ROBIN, a woman betrayed by Troy

The Story:

Gabriel Oak was a small-scale farmer, but his honesty, integrity, and ability had won him the respect of all his neighbors. When he heard that a young girl named Bathsheba Everdene had moved into the neighborhood, he went out of his way to see her and fell immediately in love. Gabriel was the kind of man who had to look only once to know that he had found the right woman. After seeing her only a few times, he went to her aunt, for whom Bathsheba worked, and asked for the girl's hand in marriage. Although he was refused, he felt that it was the relative, not Bathsheba, who had denied him.

A short time later, Gabriel's sheepdog became excited and chased his flock of sheep over a cliff, killing them all. Ruined, Gabriel had to give up his farm and go elsewhere to find work. On his way across the country, he passed a burning barn and ran to aid the men fighting the flames. After the fire had been put out, the owner of Weatherbury Farm arrived, and it was suggested that Gabriel be hired as shepherd in return for the fine work he had done. To his surprise, the owner of the farm was Bathsheba Everdene, who had recently inherited the place from her uncle. Gabriel became her shepherd. He was struck by the change in their positions in such a short while. Now Bathsheba was landowner, and Gabriel was the servant.

On his way to his new quarters, Gabriel met a girl standing in the woods. She spoke to him and asked him not to say that he had seen her, and he promised to keep silent. The next morning while working at his new job, he heard that Fanny Robin, one of Bathsheba's maids, had disappeared, and he rightly guessed that Fanny was the girl he had met. It was suspected that she had gone off to meet a soldier who had been stationed in the area a short time before. This suspicion was correct. Fanny had gone to find Sergeant Troy at his new station, for he had promised to marry her if she came to him. A date was set for the wedding, but Fanny went to the wrong church. When she finally found Troy, he refused to make arrangements for a marriage a second time.

Bathsheba was a good manager, and Weatherbury Farm prospered; but she had her caprices. One of these was to send an anonymous valentine to William Boldwood, a conservative, serious man who was her neighbor. Boldwood was upset by the valentine, especially after he learned that Gabriel had recognized Bathsheba's handwriting. The more Boldwood saw of Bathsheba, however, the more deeply he fell in love with her. One day during the sheep washing, he asked her to marry him, but she refused his proposal. Nevertheless, Gabriel and the rest of the workers felt sure that she would eventually marry Boldwood.

About that time, Sergeant Troy returned to the neighborhood. Bathsheba was attracted to him at once. Gabriel knew enough of Troy's character to know that he was not the man for Bathsheba, and he told her so. Not knowing the story of Fanny Robin, Bathsheba was furious. She and Troy were married soon afterward, and the former Sergeant became the master of Weatherbury Farm.

With Troy running the farm, things did not go well. Gabriel was forced to do most of the work of overseeing, and often he was compelled to correct the mistakes Troy made. Troy gambled and drank and caused Bathsheba much unhappiness. Gabriel and Bathsheba were alternately friendly and unfriendly. One day Troy and Bathsheba, riding in a horsecart, passed a young girl walking down the road. Troy stopped the cart and went to talk to her. The woman was Fanny Robin, who was feeble and ill. Troy told her to go on to the next town and wait there for him to come and give her money. As soon as they arrived home, Troy asked Bathsheba for some money. She gave it to him after a quarrel.

Fanny went on to Casterbridge, but she was so weak and ill when she arrived there that she died shortly afterward. When news of her death reached Weatherbury Farm, Bathsheba, unaware that Troy had been the girl's lover, sent a cart to bring the body to the farm for burial. When the body arrived, Gabriel saw scrawled on the coffin lid a message that both Fanny and a child were inside. He erased the last words in his fear that the real relationship of Fanny and Troy might reach Bathsheba's ears; but Bathsheba, suspecting that the coffin concealed some secret, opened the casket late that night. At the same moment, Troy entered the room and learned of Fanny's death and the death of his child. Torn with grief, he told Bathsheba that she meant nothing to him and that Fanny had been the only woman he had ever loved. He had married Bathsheba only for her looks and her money. Bathsheba shut herself up in an attic room.

Troy had a beautiful tombstone put up over Fanny's grave, which he covered with roses and lilies. During a heavy storm that night, water poured from the church roof through the mouth of a gargoyle, splashed on the grave, and ruined all of his work. Troy disappeared from Casterbridge. News came shortly afterward that he had been caught in a dangerous current while swimming in the ocean and had been drowned.

Bathsheba did not believe that Troy was really dead; but Farmer Boldwood, convinced of Troy's death, did his best to get Bathsheba to promise to marry him if Troy did not reappear within seven years, at the end of which time he would be legally declared dead. At a party Boldwood gave for her one night, Bathsheba yielded to his protestations of love and said that after the time had passed, she would marry him. As she was leaving the party, Troy entered. He had been rescued at sea and had wandered slowly back to Casterbridge in the character of a strolling player.

At his entrance, Bathsheba fainted and fell to the floor. Everyone was so concerned for her and surprised by Troy's appearance that they did not see Boldwood when he took down a gun from the wall. Boldwood aimed at Troy and shot him in the chest. Troy died immediately.

Boldwood was tried for the murder, but because his mind had given way, he was committed to an institution. Gabriel, who had made every effort to save Boldwood from hanging, had become a leader in the neighborhood. As Bathsheba's bailiff, he managed her farm and that of Boldwood as well. Of her three lovers, he was the only one left.

One day, Gabriel went to Bathsheba and told her that he was planning to leave her service. Bathsheba listened quietly and agreed with all he had to say. Later that night, however, she went to his cottage and there told him, by gesture more than by word, that he was the only person left to her now and that she needed both his help and his love. The farmers of the district were all delighted when Bathsheba became Mrs. Oak, and Gabriel became the master of Weatherbury Farm.

Critical Evaluation:

As the title indicates, Thomas Hardy's first major novel has an isolated setting: rural, remote from the world, and mainly centered upon Upper Weatherbury Farm in "Wessex." Unlike that in *Under the Greenwood Tree*, however, this secluded environment at times gives way to the town: the busy corn exchange in Casterbridge, the King's Arms Hotel, the Casterbridge workhouse, the cities of Bath and Budmouth, and the lively Buck's Head Inn on the Casterbridge Road.

Nevertheless, the setting has a timeless quality, accentuated or perhaps engendered by the round of seasonal activities and the continuity of agricultural life. Major scenes in the novel focus around the sheep shearing, saving of hayricks in the storm, spring sheep washing, and the autumn sheep fair at Greenhill.

Nature here, however, is not merely background or a constant factor informing characters' actions and proclivities; it is more powerful, a force vast and indifferent to man's thoughts and actions. This is the Nature which in later novels will evolve into inexorable fate, before which man is helpless and in opposing which he comes to destruction. The main characters in this novel who survive are those who succeed in adjusting themselves to nature's laws and often hostile dominance: Gabriel Oak and Bathsheba Everdene.

Far from the Madding Crowd exhibits confident power throughout in its fully developed characters, the imperceptible movements in the various conflicts involving Bathsheba and her three lovers, and in the way these conflicts evolve from their varied personalities. The combination of the four personalities furnishes the most explosive potential for melodramatic situation: Bathsheba's capriciousness and attractiveness to men; Oak's stolid, patient, unswerving loyalty and love for her; Boldwood's composite character with its "enormous antagonistic forces" and "wild capabilities"; Sergeant Troy's impulsiveness, his living only for the present moment, dashing but totally irresponsible; and the simple nature of Fanny, unaffected and victimized. Interactions of these intimately associated characters, in an almost closed environment, engender passionate, at times almost unbelievable, conflicts.

Further complicating the clashes and intricate relationships among these four are the unforeseen, relentless accidents of nature: the initial loss of Oak's sheep, the heavy storm with water that ruins Troy's flowers on Fanny's grave and that precipitates his disappearance, the loss of Boldwood's hayricks in a second storm. The novel progresses in turns, driven headlong by Bathsheba's careless whim of sending Boldwood an anonymous valentine and again by Troy's determination to possess her in spite of all odds. Even Gabriel Oak and Fanny, the two who outwardly seem driven by the impulsive actions of others, unconsciously complicate the plot by their very quiet and uncomplaining natures. Fanny, betrayed by Sergeant Troy, goes down before forces she has no means to combat, although she has a macabre revenge in the scene where Bathsheba opens her coffin to find Troy's child dead with its mother.

Gabriel, of stronger stuff, endures—like the nature he is so close to and of which he seems an integral part. Although he feels Bathsheba rules his life and the reader may be swept into this illusion, it is the earth and all of its creatures to which he is bound. Only when Bathsheba comes full circle through her marriage to the dissolute, unstable Troy, her half acceptance of Boldwood's position and estate, back to an understanding of the land and its enduring qualities as embodied in Oak, can their marriage be possible. What Gabriel held to in Bathsheba and what she herself did not recognize was the same elemental belonging to the land and its eternal strength.

The very language of the novel is bound to the earth; the best example of this is the rural chorus, which is to figure in Hardy's later novels and which provides much of the humor. The habitués of Warren's Malthouse on the Casterbridge Road are intimately involved in the action and contribute to domestic scenes and rural atmosphere. They not only serve to comment on the various episodes but also reinforce the setting, for they, too, belong to the earth. In fact, they form part of the novel's foundation; it is of importance that Gabriel Oak is at home with them and shares their social outlook. When the Malthouse crowd appears at the end of the book to serenade the newly married Gabriel and Bathsheba with their "venerable worm-eaten instruments," Gabriel invites them: "Com in, souls, and have something to eat and drink wi' me and my wife."

In this novel, the reader finds the emerging role of nature, the typical romantic, dramatic situations that will even intensify in later novels, and devices such as the village chorus and rural activities to mark the continuity and coherence of man's existence. Also apparent are the chance encounters, series of coincidences, unforeseen accidents, overheard conversations, secretly observed actions—all of which make up the fabric of a typical Hardy narrative. His plots, because of these devices, share an improbability and sense of the miraculous found in folklore. The coffin scene where Bathsheba finds Fanny's and Troy's child is the stuff of which ballads are made. The sword exercise in its bold sexual symbolism also foreshadows such scenes as the fight between Henchard and Farfrae in *The Mayor of Casterbridge* and the entwined couples at the hay-trusser's dance in *Tess of the D'Urbervilles.*

Although not as carefully structured as his later novels, this work shows Hardy's ability to penetrate the minds of his characters, especially that of a complicated woman. He boldly draws his theatrical scenes, exploits his evocative rural settings, and for the first time dares give his work amplitude and passion.

Not yet, however, does the reader find here the intense sense of gloom over a vanishing way of life—a depression that marked much of Hardy's later writing; nor does the story embody man's defeat and tragedy that increasingly became Hardy's preoccupation.

FELIX HOLT, THE RADICAL

Type of work: Novel
Author: George Eliot (Mary Ann Evans, 1819–1880)
Type of plot: Political realism
Time of plot: 1832–1833
Locale: Rural England
First published: 1866

> *Principal characters:*
> FELIX HOLT, the radical
> HAROLD TRANSOME, the heir to Transome Court and a radical candidate for Parliament
> MRS. TRANSOME, his mother
> ESTHER LYON, a refined young woman
> RUFUS LYON, her father and a dissenting minister
> MATTHEW JERMYN, a lawyer
> MR. JOHNSON, another lawyer hired by Jermyn
> PHILIP DEBARRY, a Tory candidate for Parliament
> SIR MAXIMUS DEBARRY, his father and the owner of Treby Manor
> THE REVEREND AUGUSTUS DEBARRY, his brother
> THE REVEREND JOHN LINGON, Mrs. Transome's brother
> HENRY SCADDON (ALIAS MAURICE CHRISTIAN BYCLIFFE), a servant in the Debarry household

The Story:

Mrs. Transome, who had long held Transome Court together in spite of financial and legal difficulties and an incompetent husband, eagerly awaited the return of Harold, her younger son. Harold, who had been building up a fortune in Smyrna for the preceding fifteen years, had been called home to take his place as heir to Transome Court after the death of his weak older brother, Durfey. Harold, whose wife was dead, also brought with him a young son.

Mrs. Transome was soon disappointed in Harold. Although he was kind and promised to renovate the shabby mansion, he did not seem willing to fit into Mrs. Transome's pattern of genteel country life, particularly when he announced that he intended to run for Parliament as a Radical candidate. To his mother, he seemed to show a surprising knowledge and shrewdness about contemporary English life. In his campaign, he received the support of his family's lawyer, Matthew Jermyn, and his uncle, the Reverend John Lingon. Neither had thought of deserting the Tory colors before his arrival.

More understandably committed to the Radical cause was Rufus Lyon, the local dissenting minister. One day he received a visit from Mrs. Holt, one of his parishioners, who complained that her son had deliberately stopped the business in patent medicines that she and her late husband had painstakingly established. Her son, Felix, claimed that the business was fraudulent; Mrs. Holt, on the other hand, was convinced that God would not have allowed a fraudulent business to prosper. The minister later sent for young Felix, whom he found highly intelligent, energetic, honest, and independent. Although well educated, Felix was working as a watchmaker in order to feel close to the people. The two men soon became close friends. At the Lyons' home, Felix also met Rufus' daughter Esther, a slight, refined girl educated abroad, who was now teaching the daughters of the rich and reading Byron's poems. The energetic and socially conscious Felix railed at Esther's refinement and aestheticism; but as time passed, a strange attraction between the two began to grow. Esther, although she did not know it at the time, was not the daughter of Rufus Lyon. Her mother had been a Frenchwoman, alone and destitute, whom Rufus had found wandering the English streets. Her soldier husband had sent for her, but he had died before she could find him. With her child, she was befriended by Rufus Lyon, who gave up a successful post for her and later married her.

Harold, beginning his election campaign, left the organizing to his lawyer, Matthew Jermyn. Jermyn hired another lawyer, Mr. Johnson, to go to a workers' pub and stir the men into active support of the Radical candidate. Felix Holt was in the pub at the time. Although a Radical, he objected strongly to the rabble-rousing technique used by Johnson and carried his protest directly to Harold. Although sympathetic to Felix's point of view, Harold felt somewhat indebted to Jermyn, who had helped his mother retain her property through difficult years and an earlier lawsuit. While walking home through the woods, Felix found a purse belonging to Christian, one of the Debarry servants; as a practical joke, the purse had been stolen from his pocket and tossed away while Christian was asleep in the woods. Along with the purse were some papers belonging to Philip Debarry, the Conservative candidate for Parliament.

When Felix took the papers to Rufus Lyon, his friend was amazed to discover evidence that Christian was the first husband of Rufus' French wife and the father of Esther. Through Jermyn, however, Rufus learned that Christian was really a scoundrel named Henry Scaddon who, in order to save himself, had exchanged identities with Maurice Christian Bycliffe, Esther's real father, just before Bycliffe's death. Jermyn also knew that Bycliffe, and therefore Esther, was the real heiress of Transome Court should an old and senile bill-pasting Transome, who had moved to Treby, die. Although Jermyn kept his information for possible use against the Transome family, Rufus Lyon told his daughter of her origins. Meanwhile,

Harold Transome continued campaigning, and the friendship between Esther and Felix grew.

As Felix had feared, the workers rioted on the day of the election. Felix, hoping to quell the riot, led it for a time in a futile effort to lead the workers away from the town. Unsuccessful in his purpose, he was charged with killing a constable. The old bill-pasting Transome was also trampled in the riot. Esther was now legally the heiress of Transome Court.

Harold Transome, who had lost the election, now turned his attention to Transome Court. Discovering that Jermyn and Johnson, Jermyn's henchman, had been cheating the estate for years, he decided to get rid of Jermyn at once and sue him. Jermyn tried to avoid the suit by telling Harold that the estate really belonged to Esther and that the lawyer would remain silent if Harold dropped proceedings against him. Harold refused to accept the bribe. Later, he and his mother invited Esther to live with them at Transome Court. Both were charmed with Esther, and Harold fell in love with her.

Meanwhile, Felix's case was announced for trial. Rufus Lyon, Harold, and Esther testified to Felix's attempts to quell the riot, but he had killed a man, though inadvertently, and so he was sentenced to an imprisonment of four years. Esther's plea was so powerful that it moved even the arch-Tory, Sir Maximus Debarry, who helped petition Parliament to grant Felix a pardon. Felix was soon released.

In the meantime, Mrs. Transome had been unhappy that Harold had rejected Jermyn thoroughly and was attempting to sue him. Harold, claiming that Jermyn was a thief, intended to carry out the suit. In a final burst of fury, Jermyn told Harold the truth: He was Harold's father and, during his long affair with Mrs. Transome, had saved the estate during several difficult times. Harold was crushed, and only Esther was able to reconcile him to his unhappy mother.

Feeling his illegitimacy keenly, Harold told Esther that he could not, as he had intended, ask for her hand. This declaration saved Esther much embarrassment, for she had already acknowledged her love for Felix. To solve problems for all concerned, Esther signed over all of her rights to Transome Court to Harold, returned to her father's house, and soon married Felix.

Critical Evaluation:

Centered around a political election in a rural area of England at the time of the Reform Bill of 1832, *Felix Holt, the Radical* provides a vivid picture of the society of the times. As always in George Eliot's best work, all classes of the society are included in a thorough portrait of rural English life. The novel hinges on character, although it also uses such standard plot devices as an unknown ancestry and a strange will which settles important property in an unexpected way. The characters are skillfully presented: the energetic and unconventional young radical, Felix; the sharp and generous dissenting minister, Rufus Lyon; the competent, self-satisfied master of Transome Court, Harold Transome. In depth of insight and complexity of character, the novel looks forward to the later *Middlemarch*. Like *Middlemarch*, also, *Felix Holt, the Radical* ends in the affirmation of a transcendent love affair, the mating of two people, Felix and Esther, who see beyond the common and trivial experiences of men and share a kind of spiritual force. The romantic hero and heroine transcend the limitations, sympathetically depicted, of the earthbound characters around them.

In *Felix Holt, the Radical*, the complicated story line with the sudden twists and surprises means less to modern readers than the realistic treatment of characterization and the analysis of human motive at which Eliot excelled. The background of early Victorian society is skillfully painted, and the election riot, drawn from a recollection of one that Eliot saw as a child at Nuneaton, is a powerful piece of writing. Such figures as Mrs. Transome and Felix Holt and Esther Lyon and her father, however, give the book its greatness. The tragic character of Mrs. Transome is one of Eliot's triumphs; from the opening scene in which she waits for Harold's return to the manor through her disappointments and the subsequent revelations, her personality is subtly revealed with many delicate and moving touches. Mrs. Transome well knows that "half the sorrows of women would be averted if they could repress the speech they know to be useless—the speech they have resolved not to utter." Faced with her son's blind egotism, she sees what her life has amounted to and must silently accept the bitter fact.

Felix Holt is quite a different character, a man of ideals misunderstood by those around him. Rufus Lyon is portrayed with an especially authentic quality; Eliot's observations of the life of the poor clergyman are precise and vivid; such an existence easily could have spoiled a lesser man than Rufus Lyon.

The role of women is a prominent theme in *Felix Holt, the Radical*. Harold Transome sets the tone of the times when he states that women are incapable of changing their views, which they have inherited from their fathers; but Esther is too bright to accept such a dominated role. Felix is intelligent and sensitive enough not to demand that Esther pretend to be less than she is, and their love establishes them as equals.

THE FELLOWSHIP OF THE RING

Type of work: Novel
Author: J. R. R. Tolkien (1892–1973)
Type of plot: Epic romance
Time of plot: The Third Age in a remote legendary past
Locale: The Middle-Earth between the Northern Waste and Sutherland
First published: 1954

Principal characters:

BILBO BAGGINS, the finder of the One Ring and a famous hobbit of the Shire

FRODO BAGGINS, his young kinsman and heir and the chosen Ringbearer

MERIADOC BRANDYBUCK (MERRY), Frodo's cousin from Buckland

PEREGRIN TOOK (PIPPIN), another of Frodo's cousins

SAMWISE GAMGEE (SAM), Frodo's loyal servant and also a hobbit

GANDALF THE GREY (MITHRANDIR), a venerable wizard

ARAGORN (STRIDER), a ranger and the descendant of kings

BOROMIR, the son of Denethor of Gondor and a heroic warrior

GIMLI, the son of Glóin and a warlike dwarf

LEGOLAS, a wood elf and son of King Thranduil of Mirkwood

ELROND HALFELVEN, the ruler of Rivendell

GALADRIEL, the Elf Queen of Lothlórien

SAURON, the Dark Lord, maker of the One Ring, and the supreme agent of evil in the Middle-Earth

The Story:

Bilbo Baggins, most adventurous hobbit of the Shire, planned to celebrate his hundred-and-eleventh birthday. His old friend Gandalf the Grey, a wizard with special control over fire, tried to restrain him from using his magic ring to vanish at the end of the party. Gandalf was disturbed, for he suspected the ring of being the One Ring forged by Sauron, the Dark Lord, in the volcanic fires of Mount Doom. This Ring gave long life but corrupted its user. Even Bilbo, who had gained it without losing pity, had begun to show signs of its evil influence. On his departure, however, after his spectacular vanishing, he left his property, reluctantly including the Ring, to his nephew Frodo. Gandalf warned Frodo of its dangers and advised that he take it from the Shire.

Frodo left the Shire, accompanied by his loyal servant Sam Gamgee and two of his cousins, Merry and Pippin. Pursued by fearful Black Riders, they narrowly escaped destruction in the Old Forest, but they were rescued by jovial, earthy Tom Bombadil, who proved to be immune to the Ring's power. He sent them on their way refreshed.

At Bree, they met a mysterious ranger called Strider and found a letter from Gandalf urging them to go to Rivendell with Strider, whose real name was Aragorn. On their fourth night out of Bree, they were attacked by Black Riders. In terror, Frodo put on the Ring and became invisible to his friends but visible and vulnerable to the Riders, Sauron's Ringwraiths. Their leader stabbed Frodo with a weapon that broke off in the wound and melted. Aragorn drove them off with torches, and the company hastened toward Rivendell. Glorifindel, an elf, met them and put Frodo on his horse. At the Ford near Rivendell, the Riders tried to intercept him but were thwarted by a flood.

Frodo recovered consciousness to find Gandalf with him and to learn that Elrond of Rivendell had been treating his fearful wound for days. In Rivendell, Frodo found Bilbo and met Elrond, his daughter Arwen Evenstar, and others, including Glóin, an elderly dwarf who had formerly accompanied Bilbo. Elrond called a Council to discuss the Ring. At the Council, aside from Elrond's eleven subjects, were Legolas, a wood elf; Glóin and his son Gimli; Gandalf; the five hobbits; Aragorn and a noble gray-eyed warrior, Boromir of Gondor. Elrond recounted the history of the Rings of Power made by elvensmiths in the Second Age and of Sauron's secret forging of a Ring to rule and bind all the rest. In that age, Sauron had been overthrown by an alliance of men and elves, and Isildur had cut off the Dark Lord's finger and taken the Ring. Later, it had slipped from his finger and betrayed him to the orcs. Years later, it had been found in the river by Deagol, a hobbit whose kinsman Smeagol had murdered him for it and fled underground, becoming the repulsive Gollum. Bilbo had found it underground. Pitying the murderous Gollum, he had not killed him but had merely used the Ring to escape. Sauron, though defeated, had not been destroyed. He had gathered an evil host in Mordor and was seeking the Ring to make himself ruler of the world. Gandalf told of the treachery of Saruman the White, leader of the wizards, who had imprisoned him. Gandalf had escaped with the help of Gwaihir, King of the Eagles.

The Council decided to send the Ring to Mordor to unmake it in the fires of Mount Doom, the only heat that could destroy it. Frodo reluctantly volunteered to remain the Ringbearer. Eight others were chosen to complete the Fellowship of the Ring: Gandalf, Aragorn, Boromir, Gimli, Legolas, Sam, Merry, and Pippin. Aragorn's broken sword, Andúril, was reforged by the elves. Bilbo gave Frodo his elven sword Sting and a mail-coat of mithril, a precious light metal harder than steel. Frodo wore it under his weather-stained clothes.

The travelers passed through cold barren country and tried to cross over the Misty Mountains, but a blizzard drove them back, and they were attacked by wolves. Gandalf drove away the wolves with magic fire and led the company into the Caverns of Moria, the ancient dwarf kingdom. He told them of Durin, the dwarf King, and his people who delved so deeply for Mithril that they roused a terrible being that destroyed them. Bilbo's old companion Balin had led a company of dwarfs from the Lonely Mountains to retake Moria. The travelers found Balin's tomb and signs of a terrible battle and a bloodstained, tattered book from which Gandalf was able to reconstruct the fortunes of Balin's people to the beginning of their last battle.

A drum far below signaled an attack by orcs and trolls. The Fellowship repelled the first attack, but Frodo was struck down by a spear thrust. His mithril-coat saved him. When they were forced to retreat, Gandalf remained to hold a stone door. Something opposed his will fiercely, and the door shattered. They hastened to a narrow stone bridge across an abyss. A monstrous fire demon appeared. Gandalf opposed him and destroyed the bridge but was dragged into the cleft with the monster. Heavy-hearted, the others followed Aragorn to Lothlórien, home of high elves.

Lothlórien was a haven more wonderful than Rivendell. The ageless beauty of Queen Galadriel charmed them all, especially Gimli, in spite of ancient enmity between elves and dwarfs. Boromir alone was uneasy in her presence. On their departure, she gave them precious gifts, and the elves supplied them with boats and provisions to continue their journey by water down the Adnuin River. They soon learned they were being followed by Gollum, once owner of the Ring and now apparently Sauron's spy. They were again attacked by orcs, led by a Ringwraith on a flying mount like a pterodactyl. Legolas gained respite for them by killing the mount with an arrow. After this escape, the evil of the Ring corrupted Boromir, who attempted to take it from Frodo. In order to escape him, Frodo put on the Ring and vanished. Boromir returned sadly to the company in a penitent mood. They scattered to look for Frodo.

Alone and invisible, Frodo tried to decide on the right course of action. Suddenly he was aware of an evil Eye searching for him, and he was paralyzed with terror; then an inner voice commanded him to take off the Ring. He regained control of himself and removed it. A groping shadow seemed to pass over the mountain and to fade away. Frodo then decided to take an elven boat and continue his perilous journey alone; but Sam anticipated his decision, discovered him, and begged to be allowed to go along. Frodo accepted Sam's loyal company, and they set out together for Mordor. The Fellowship of the Ring was broken.

Critical Evaluation:

Samuel Johnson is credited with saying that "A book should teach us to enjoy life or to endure it." J. R. R. Tolkien's trilogy *The Lord of the Rings* teaches both. It also fits the dictum of another writer, Robert Louis Stevenson: "And this is the particular triumph of the artist—not to be true merely, but to be lovable; not simply to convince, but to enchant." Tolkien has been compared with Lodovico Ariosto and with Edmund Spenser. Indeed, he is in the mainstream of the writers of epic and romance from the days of Homer. His work is deeply rooted in the great literature of the past and seems likely itself to be a hardy survivor resistant to time. In *The Fellowship of the Ring*, the first volume of *The Lord of the Rings*, Celeborn the Elf King (no doubt speaking for his author) warns against despising the lore that has survived from distant years; for old wives' tales may be the repositories of needful wisdom.

Although *The Lord of the Rings* is advertised as a trilogy, with each volume bearing a different title, it is really a single, continuous romance. The author is in complete control of his copious material. He has created a consistent world with a sharply realized geography, even furnishing maps; he has worked out a many-centuried time scheme, summarizing the chronology in an appendix to the third volume, *The Return of the King*. (The second volume is *The Two Towers*.) With fertile inventiveness, Tolkien has poured out an amazing number of well-drawn characters and adventures; and his memory of the persons, places, and events of his creation is almost incredible. If there are any loose ends in the three volumes, they are so minor as to be negligible. The book has been pronounced an allegory; with equal positiveness it has been pronounced *not* an allegory. At any rate, it is a gigantic myth of the struggle between good and evil.

The author first presented his invented creatures, the hobbits or halflings, in an early book, *The Hobbit*, to which *The Lord of the Rings* is a sequel, but a sequel with significant differences. Hobbits are small, furry-footed humanoids with a delight in simple pleasures and a dislike of the uncomfortable responsibilities of heroism. They share the world with men, wizards, elves, dwarfs, trolls, orcs, and other creatures. Although many of these creatures are not the usual figures of the contemporary novel, the thoughtful reader can find applications to inhabitants and events of the current world, which has its share of traitors, malice-driven demidevils, and time-servers, and is not completely destitute of heroes and men of good will. Of the three volumes, *The Fellowship of the Ring* has the widest variation in tone: it begins with comedy and domestic comfort, then moves into high adventure, peril, and sorrow. Occasional verses appear in the pages, but the quality of Tolkien's poetry is in both his prose and his verse.

The Fellowship of the Ring introduces two tales that run side by side through the trilogy *The Lord of the Rings*. One is the high saga of the destruction of Sauron and the return of King Elessar to the throne of his fathers; the other is the story of the journey of the hobbits from jolly complacency to unexpected heights of self-knowledge and self-sacrifice. The former gives the work its quality of ancient romance, for the characters are larger than life and speak to one another in elevated language; natural descriptions and expressions of emotion tend to be more formal and ceremonious than realistic. The latter tale contains elements of realism; the most realistic, homey, and familiar characters are from Tolkien's invented race, the hobbits.

The major figure in Tolkien's high saga is Aragorn, later King Elessar. He is certainly the most heroic of the characters in the classical sense, but the very elevation of his character has led some critics to see him as inhuman, lifeless, or too good to be true. Actually, however, he is a character of considerable subtlety and complexity; he earns his credentials as a hero honestly. Initially, in his disguise as "Strider," Aragorn must use guile and indirection to win the confidence of the hobbits. On the one hand, they understand neither the implications of their situation nor their own personal danger. On the other hand, Aragorn realizes that he is as frightening to them as any of Sauron's agents. Therefore, he uses their apprehensions toward him to stimulate their sense of danger, and then he ingratiates himself to them by his wit and finally by Gandalf's letter of identification. When asked why he did not formally identify himself earlier, he replies that he wants to be accepted for *himself*. Once the quest begins, Aragorn proves his mettle and worthiness for kingship, not primarily by brute strength or heroic posturing but by his adroit handling of men and his subtle strategies. A special poignancy and humanity are further given to him by his prolonged and tender love affair with Lady Arwen. Readers may never feel close to Aragorn but can understand and feel for him as a human being, while still admiring him as a heroic figure.

Nevertheless, while Aragon leads the troops to victory in battle, the primary task of the epic falls not to the most heroic of the men but to the mildest of the hobbits, Frodo Baggins. The name of this little race suggests a hob, hobnobbing, a dobbin; it calls up visions of fireside comforts, companionship, patient steadfastness, and good sense. Descriptions of hobbits and hobbit life in the prologue outline the prototype: a steady, plain little person, none too clever.

This impression, however, is belied in the romance by the characters of Samwise and Frodo; in developing the character of Sam, Tolkien begins with a collection of those homely virtues that most nations of men arrogate to their own peasant class and then adds, without loss of credibility, a quirky intelligence that outstrips shrewdness and a fancy for elfish lore. In Frodo, he marries the homely world of the Shire with the high deeds of the Dunedain; in Frodo are combined the best things of both worlds: he is the wisest and most noble of the hobbits and the bravest of the heroes because he is the smallest and most afraid.

It is primarily because of Frodo's unpretentiousness that he is "chosen" for the crucial task of casting the ring into the fire of Mordor. All the "large" heroes of the book, Aragorn and Gandalf, refuse the task, not from fear of external dangers but from the knowledge that they would not be able to resist the ring's effect on them—they are too worldly and versed in the ways of power to be able to withstand the awful temptation to use it. Only Frodo is small enough and humble enough to withstand its corrupting influence right up to the edge of the fire—where even he weakens and the ring is finally destroyed by powers beyond his control.

THE FIFTH QUEEN

Type of work: Novel
Author: Ford Madox Ford (Ford Madox Hueffer, 1873–1939)
Type of plot: Historical romance
Time of plot: 1539–1542
Locale: England and France
First published: The Fifth Queen, 1906; *Privy Seal*, 1907; *The Fifth Queen Crowned*, 1908

> *Principal characters:*
> HENRY VIII, King of England
> PRINCESS MARY (later Mary I), his daughter
> ANNE OF CLEVES, his fourth wife
> KATHARINE HOWARD, his fifth wife
> THE DUKE OF NORFOLK, her uncle
> THOMAS CROMWELL, Lord Privy Seal
> THOMAS CULPEPPER, Katharine Howard's cousin
> STEPHEN GARDINER, Bishop of Winchester
> THROCKMORTON, one of Cromwell's spies
> NICHOLAS UDAL, the Latin tutor to the Princess Mary
> THOMAS CRANMER, Archbishop of Canterbury
> LASCALLES, Cranmer's spy

Written in the grand Victorian manner, *The Fifth Queen* is a full-bodied historical novel of the brief and tragic marriage of Katharine Howard to Henry VIII. Many readers will remember Henry's first wife, Katharine of Aragon, because of Shakespeare, and Anne Boleyn, his second, because she was the mother of Queen Elizabeth I; but the others—Jane Seymour, Anne of Cleves, Katharine Howard, and Katharine Parr—are only dim ghosts flickering through the twilight of history. Moreover, the reign of Henry VIII has not been a favorite topic with historical novelists, for it is overshadowed by the greater age of Elizabeth, which offers so much more to an imaginative writer. The period of Henry is also much more difficult for a modern reader to understand; it was not the high Renaissance of Elizabeth's time but, again, a twilight between the Middle Ages that were dying and the new age that was struggling to be born.

The story opens in the bitter winter of 1539 as the barges of the great officers of the Crown sweep up the river toward Greenwich in the wake of the king's barge. The new queen, Anne of Cleves, has landed in England, and already the rumor is that the King has said she resembles a pig studded with cloves and that her body stinks so vilely that no man can endure it. The inoffensive Jane Seymour had died two years before, having given Henry his long-desired son, the sickly Prince Edward; and the Cleves alliance was the next move in the complicated political chess game. It would present a strong Protestant front against France and the Empire. On the success of this alliance, the Protestant faction at Court had staked their political futures—and their heads; and now, the whole scheme was about to be wrecked upon the King's dislike for his new queen. It was no wonder that the Chancellor of the Augmentations, standing in the stern of Cromwell's barge, shivered with more than the winter wind.

To the court, as it lay in the palace at Greenwich, comes the heroine of the novel, Katharine Howard (in the charge of her cousin, Thomas Culpepper); she has come to seek the protection of her uncle, the Duke of Norfolk, Earl Marshal of England and the victor of Flodden Field. She is the daughter of poverty-stricken Lord Edmund Howard, a younger son of the ducal family, whose house, far in the north in Lincolnshire, had been burned in one of the all too frequent local uprisings. By chance, she is injured in a riot outside the palace between Lutherans and Catholics; again by chance, she meets the King and attracts his attention. She is appointed one of the ladies in waiting to Princess Mary, an appointment that will inevitably bring her into further contact with Henry. From that moment, her life becomes a part of English history, with the headsman's block on Tower Hill standing grimly only two short years away.

The Fifth Queen is in the tradition of Shakespeare's historical plays. In most novels of this type, the main characters are the author's inventions, while the figures from actual history appear in the background to give color and verisimilitude; but here, all the characters are real figures from history, even down to the Magister Nicholas Udal, author of the almost forgotten play, *Ralph Roister Doister.* So it is with Shakespeare's histories. Therefore, a reader familiar with the history of the period is aware of much dramatic irony as the story moves along: Bishop Latimer, for example, exhorting to repentance a friar who is to be burned for heresy. When the sinister figure of Cromwell appears, readers know that the axe is waiting even for him.

Thomas Cromwell, the Lord Privy Seal, dominates the larger part of the book as he had dominated Henry for years. Hated by the old nobility because of his low birth—he was the son of a brewer—and by the Catholics because of his destruction of the monasteries, he represents the "new men" whom the Tudors brought forward to do their work for them. The few noble families that had survived the Wars of the Roses could not be trusted; they looked back to a feudal past wherein their ancestors had set up and pulled down kings. Cromwell, however, had risen to power through his betrayal of Wolsey and now looked to the future: to an absolute monarchy in which the king's word would be supreme. With his treachery, his network of spies throughout England, he is a revolting figure; yet readers cannot help admiring his vision of a realm set free from a renewal of the anarchy of the Wars of the Roses. He favors the Protestant cause less from doctrinal than from political reasons; he is politically astute enough to sense that the new Protestantism will offer a firmer base for an absolute monarchy than the old Catholicism. He served Henry by treachery and cruelty, but he served him well; yet he is such a horrifying man that the reader rejoices in his downfall.

Among the characters of the second rank stands out the figure of Princess Mary—the future "Bloody Mary" of history books. Ford Madox Ford gives an unusually brilliant picture of her: a girl so bitten to the soul by her mother's divorce and her own subsequent proclamation as a bastard that she is now only a rigid figure of hate. To good Catholics, she is almost a saint; to her father, she is a frozen block against which even his imperious will is shattered; and to any reader who may be interested in her reign, little more than a decade in the future, this portrait gives an illuminating psychological insight into the causes that made her the ruler that she was to become.

Above all, however, there is the figure of Henry VIII, this giant of a man whose vast shadow stretches over the whole story. As depicted by Ford, he resembles nothing so much as a half-tamed wild animal—at one moment pathetically docile, and at the next, tearing into pieces those whom he had seemed to love. He is haunted by the fear of damnation for his persecution of the old faith, yet he cannot return to it. In the final dramatic scene between him and his fifth wife, she tells him what he is: a man who blows hot in the morning and cold at night, a straw tossed by every conflicting wind. For all of his absolute power and cruelty, he is a pathetic and tragic man.

Katharine has been called lewd, deceitful, grasping, and pitiable in her frailty. She had only a brief moment in history, and historians seem to agree that she was "probably" guilty of the crimes of unchastity charged against her. Ford gives the reader a very different interpretation. His Katharine Howard is a girl too honest and too deeply religious for the world in which she had to live. She sees men as only all white or all black; she sincerely believes that the old faith can be restored. Indeed, her brief reign did mark the return to power of the reactionary group, a momentary reversal of the triumphant march of Protestantism. Nevertheless, she is betrayed by everyone; even her uncle Norfolk, a hater of the new age, betrays her; and so Henry, who deeply loved her but who could never stay of one mind, sent her to the block on Tower Hill.

The real protagonists of this novel, however, are not Henry VIII and his queen; they are the old Catholicism of the Middle Ages and the new Protestantism of the Renaissance. The novel is set on one of those great dividing lines of history; and Henry himself has a foot, in its great square-toed shoe, on either side of it. He was half Catholic, half Protestant; he turned away from Latin because it reminded him of the old language of the Mass that he had destroyed, yet he wanted to be head of the English Church. The hands of the clock could be briefly stopped, but they could not be turned back. As Katharine is bluntly told, there is the inescapable fact that too many people in England have by now grown rich from the spoils of the Church and that these men will never give up the lands and goods that they have obtained. Even her uncle, the Duke of Norfolk and head of the Catholic party and of the old nobility, wears in his hat a jewel taken from a chalice in the Abbey of Risings. The new nobility, come up under the Tudors, is founded on wealth stolen from the Church. Here is a hard economic fact against which theology and even Katharine's faith will be shattered.

Katharine, "mazed," as she says, by the reading of old books, moves toward her tragic end because she expects men to be better than they can be. Her world is not peopled by heroic figures from classical antiquity. In the end, however, it is she who triumphs; and Henry, who sends her to execution, is defeated.

This long, elaborate historical novel has an immensely complicated plot—intrigue is piled upon intrigue, incident upon incident, and hardly a character in the story can be trusted. Each is utterly false, thinking only of himself, endlessly shifting sides, betraying and being betrayed; but at least these are full-blooded people, not the hollow men who flit, twittering like bats, through most contemporary novels—"these unfortunates," as Dante calls them, "who never were alive." The style fits the book. Readers are at one moment in the glare of torches and in the presence of the enormous scarlet king; at the next, plunged into the darkness of a corridor of one of the vast palaces. The warhorses, sheathed in iron, solemnly prance; the state barges slide up and down the Thames; Norfolk's tucket is blown in a triple convolution of sound. It was a magnificent and a terrible world, and Ford makes it live again in all of its terror and splendor.

THE FINN CYCLE

Type of work: Ballad cycle
Author: Unknown
Type of plot: Historical adventure
Time of plot: Third century
Locale: Ireland
First transcribed: Reputed eleventh century manuscript

Principal characters:

FINN, the leader of the Fianna Erinn
OISIN, Finn's son
OSCAR, Oisin's son
GOLL MAC MORNA,
DERMOT,
KEELTA, and
CONAN THE BALD, Finn's men
NIAM, Oisin's fairy mistress
GRANIA, King Cormac's daughter

The Story:

Long ago in Ireland, Cumhal was the leader of the Fianna Erinn, the king's warriors. A rival clan in this group grew envious of Cumhal, took up arms against him, and slew him at the battle of Castleknock. Cumhal's wife Murna gave birth to a boy shortly thereafter. Fearing for his life now that Goll Mac Morna was in power, she gave him to two wise women to rear.

Under these two women, the child grew to be a handsome lad. He learned to run faster than the rabbit, to kill deer without hounds, and to bring down birds with his sling. One day, while roaming in the fields, he found a group of boys playing. He joined them, and it was soon obvious that he was a match for all of them. In envy, the boys tried to kill him, but he overcame seven of them and chased the rest home. From that day, he was called Finn, meaning the fair. His two nurses, however, felt that since the warriors of the Morna clan would kill him if they found him, he must start off on his own.

Finn gathered a group of youths about him and began to seek adventure. His first exploit was to avenge a woman whose son had been killed by the Lord of Luachar. Finn and his companions stormed the ramparts of the chieftain's castle, recovered jewels Cumhal had lost in battle, and slew the Lord of Luachar and his men. Finn then returned the jewels to the old men who had fought with his dead father in battle.

Finn set out to learn wisdom and the art of poetry from the sage Finegas. While he was with the sage, he caught the salmon of wisdom and accidentally tasted it. Having learned wisdom and the art of poetry, Finn composed a song in praise of May and then set out to become the leader of the Fianna Erinn.

At that time, Conn was the ruler of Ireland. He held an annual banquet at which peace was declared among the various clans. When Finn entered the banquet hall unknown, Conn asked him who he was. The king accepted him immediately because he was the son of an old friend. Soon Finn inquired whether he would become captain of the Fianna Erinn if he rid the royal town of the goblin that now haunted it. The king said yes, and Finn set out with a magic spear to slay the goblin. The goblin appeared with his magic harp and enchanted Finn with the music, but with the aid of his spear, Finn slew the spirit and returned victorious. Conn kept his word, and Finn was made captain of the Fianna Erinn. Faced with the choice of serving his clan enemy or leaving Ireland, Goll Mac Morna chose to serve Finn, and the rest of his men followed him. .

Finn was a strong, generous, and wise captain who drew the best poets and warriors of Ireland around him. Oisin was his gallant son, one of the finest fighters and poets; Oscar, Oisin's son, was the fiercest fighter of the group; Goll Mac Morna was strong and loyal; Dermot of the Love Spot was the fair ladies' man of great endurance and agility; Keelta was another strong warrior and fine poet; Conan the Bald was full of trickery, gluttony, and sloth; and there was also Mac Luga, whom Finn instructed in the art of courtesy, and many another brave warrior. Finn was generous to all. It was necessary to pass extremely rigorous tests of strength, skill, poise, and poetic ability to enter the Fianna Erinn.

There was the time Finn and his companions gave chase to a doe. The doe far outstripped everyone but Finn and his two hounds. When Finn reached the doe, he found his two hounds playing with her, and he gave orders for no one to hurt her. That night, Finn awakened to find a beautiful woman standing by his bed. She informed him that she had been changed into a deer by the Dark Druid because she would not give him her love and that Finn had restored her to her original form. Finn took her to live with him as his wife. After a few months of happiness, Finn was called away to fight the Northmen. Returning victorious, he found his new wife gone; the Dark Druid had come for her in the shape of Finn, and unwittingly she had rushed to greet him and he took her away. For three days, Finn mourned before returning to his band. Seven years later, Finn found a brave young man fighting off a pack of hounds. On calling off the dogs and questioning the boy, Finn learned that this was the son he had had by his wife and that the Dark Druid had come again and taken her away forever. Finn took his son and trained him to be a great warrior-poet.

There was the time Finn and his men were hunting and the giantess Vivionn came seeking Finn's protection from her scorned lover. As she was talking, her lover appeared and thrust his spear into her breast. While Finn

and Goll stayed by the dying giantess, the rest of the company set out after
the giant. They chased him over hill and plain to the sea, where he escaped
after they had gained his sword and shield. Returning, they found the
giantess dead. They buried her and mourned her death.

There was the time Finn and his companions were hunting and saw an
ugly, clumsy giant coming toward them with an equally ugly old nag. In an
unmannerly way, the giant told Finn that he wanted to join his band, and
Finn reluctantly agreed. Finn's companions turned the giant's horse out to
pasture with the other horses, and it immediately began injuring them.
Finn told one of his men to ride the nag to death. When the animal refused to move, thirteen men got on its back in jest. Seeing that they were
making fun of him, the giant ran off in fury, and his nag followed with thirteen of Finn's men on its back. Finn and the rest of his men followed, but
they were soon outdistanced when the giant and his nag crossed the ocean.

Then Finn outfitted himself and his men with a ship, food, and gold and
set out across the sea in search of his missing men. At last, they came to a
huge, slippery cliff. Since Dermot was the ablest, he was sent to investigate
the land. Before long, Dermot came to a woodland pool where for three
days he fought an armed warrior. On the third night, he dived into the
pool with the warrior and found himself in a land of wonders. He was soon
beaten by the men of this land and left for dead. Presently, Dermot was
awakened by a man who led him into a friendlier kingdom. There he was
welcomed by the king, who himself had served in the Fianna Erinn under
Finn. In the meanwhile, Finn and his men had entered the underground
kingdom by another route, and he and his warriors were reunited. They
learned that they had been brought there to fight in the service of the
underground king against the King of the Well and his allies. In battle,
Finn and his men proved matchless. After winning the enemy king's daughter, Finn defeated the foe and restored peace to the land. Finn asked for
no reward from the king; but when Conan made a jest, the king transported the band back to the Irish hills in the space of a second. The whole
adventure seemed like a dream.

There was the time the old feud between Finn's clan and Goll's clan
reawakened over a dispute about booty. A battle started in the hall, and
blood was shed until Fergus, the minstrel, awoke and reminded them with
his music of the dangers they had shared. So peace was restored.

For many years, Finn and his men passed their lives in adventures, in
hunts, and in enchantments. There came a time, however, when the Fianna
Erinn began to disintegrate, when Finn's men became dishonest and un-
ruly, and when Finn lost his honor through treachery.

When Finn was an old man, he planned to marry Grania, daughter of
the King of Ireland. Grania fell in love with Dermot, the ladies' man, however, and begged him to run away with her. Dermot was extremely reluc-

tant to do so, but Grania bound him by the laws of Fian chivalry, and he was forced to abduct her on her wedding night. Finn jealously chased the pair over Ireland. At length, Dermot made peace with Finn. While Finn and Dermot were hunting one day, a boar fatally wounded Dermot. The only way to save Dermot was for Finn to bring him water. Remembering his hurt pride, Finn let the water fall, and Dermot died. The King of Ireland then ordered the Fianna Erinn to disband forever. The final blow to the company came at the battle of Gabhra in which Oscar, Finn's grandson, was killed and the Fenians were all but wiped out.

Niam, a fairy princess, then came to take Oisin to an enchanted land where all wishes came true. She sang a magic song to him, and he bade farewell to his companions forever. In this land, Oisin could love, hunt, and fight without growing old. The time came, however, when he longed to return to Ireland to see his old companions. Niam tearfully let him go but warned him not to set foot on the soil. On returning to Ireland, he found a degenerate race that was both smaller and weaker than the lowliest men of his time. Impetuously, Oisin dismounted from his horse to help the weaklings move a stone, and immediately he became an old man. He soon learned that his companions had been dead for three hundred years. Oisin was taken to Saint Patrick. At first, there was strong distrust between the two men, but gradually the saint grew to love Oisin's tales of the Fianna Erinn and recorded them. Oisin, on his part, was baptized into the Church.

Critical Evaluation:

The Finn Cycle, which is also known as the Fenian Cycle, is a series of ballad tales celebrating the deeds of Finn, a third century Irish hero, and his band of warriors. Their organization, known as the Fianna Erinn, fought and hunted under service to the king of Ireland. The warriors were quite respectable and enjoyed privilege and wealth. The tone of these ballad stories is romantic, and the stories show a delight in sensuous details, with deep feeling for the Irish countryside and glen. Finn himself stands out as a strong, courageous leader who inspired devotion in his men, but he is not without a touch of cunning and treachery. In many respects, he is like Robin Hood and King Arthur—a bold hero, a capable leader, a tender lover. Like them, he witnesses the passing of his strength, the dissolution of his band, and the waning of a heroic era.

The audience for whom *The Finn Cycle* was composed was naïve, socially young, and intellectually credulous, although it had a definite protocol and a certain dignified etiquette. This audience demanded stirring words from the storyteller; it also demanded that he have a stimulating imagination. Although these tales were very popular in the eleventh and twelfth centuries, the stories of Finn, Oisin, and the others had existed among the people for many centuries. A note of nostalgia for a past glory and a longing for a heroic period exist in the stories. There is perhaps a contrast between the old hierarchical society of the legends and the society telling them, a society facing a rapidly changing and hostile world. The old ballad system was breaking down by this time, and these tales were the beginnings of a new, popular literature in Ireland and Scotland. As the literature passed into the hands of the people, the ballads were easier, the meters drastically simplified, and the versification easier.

Most, although not all, of the ballads and prose of this period are concerned with the hero, Finn, and his war band, or fian (hence, the word "Fenian"). The original meaning of the word fian was "a driving, pursuing, hunting," although it came to apply to warfare. Eventually, it came to mean a band of warriors on the warpath. In a stricter sense, fian meant a band of roving warriors who had joined together for the purpose of making war on their own account. They were not, however, mere robbers or marauders. They were often men expelled from their clan, landless men, the sons of kings who had quarreled with their fathers, or men who seized this way of avenging some private wrong. They were the only professional soldiers in Ireland in the old times, apart from mercenaries, who often were foreigners. This was why the word fian was often used, especially in poetry, in a wider sense for any war band. The various fianna were held together by discipline and had their own organization and customs; as is shown in *The Finn Cycle*, men who wished to join the ranks had to pass a test of skill or bravery. The various fianna took their names from their leaders. From their roving life, adventures, and exploits, the various fianna and their chiefs naturally evolved into the early subjects of storytelling. Probably, many such stories and ballads have been lost.

In modern times, it has become usual to assume that the word fianna always refers to the war band headed by Finn, or Mac Cumhal, as he came to be called. The development of this legend overshadowed all the others, so that the ordinary meaning of the word fian or fianna was forgotten. Even as late as the tenth century, however, Finn and his fianna were only one among several well-known similar bands. In popular imagination, the figure of Finn overpowered other heroes and attracted to itself, from century to century, exploits originally attributed to others. *The Finn Cycle* absorbed much of the legendary lore of the older cycles, until all of Ireland held up Finn as the supreme heroic leader.

The popular imagination blended the tales and made them into the kind of legend the people needed and wanted. They were close to the earth and nature, and this is reflected in the tales of Finn. This was a time when the wild wood was giving way to pasture and tillage, and men no longer had reason to consider every wild cry of the night, to ponder each call of the birds and beasts. For Finn, the battles were only interruptions in the lifetime of hunting. The ballads speak of him delighting in the cackling of ducks, in the bellowing of the oxen, and in the whistle of the eagle. Many metaphors and allusions in the tales draw upon nature and animals. For example, when sorrow comes to the women, they feel sympathy for the wild birds and beasts which are like themselves.

Finn himself seems to transcend the world of which he is a part; certainly he is larger than time, than the moment in history. When the Fianna are broken up at last after hundreds of years of hunting and fighting, it hardly seems that he dies. More likely, he comes back repeatedly in different shapes, and his son, Oisin, is made king over a divine country. Finn is not an individual man in these ballads as much as a force of nature, a part of the universe like the clouds or the gods that shape and reshape the clouds. Seer and poet, king and Druid, Finn was a mortal who became immortal. He was a better fighter and hunter than any other man and was infinitely wiser than any other mortal. Quiet in peace, the ballads say, but angry in battle, Finn was always the perfect leader.

These men in the stories are warriors, men of action rather than thought. Their existence is devoted to love and companionship, and they can imagine no higher consideration. There is none of the philosophical worrying of Arthur and Merlin in these ballads. The men here do not speculate on eternity; they are sure of their simple values and fight to defend them. The brotherhood of the warrior is all. It is based on their hard and vigorous way of life and on their few necessary possessions; running through the ballads is a strong sense of material goods, of the things that men use to live. A feeling of the matter-of-factness of life colors the ballads and the attitudes of the characters.

The structure of *The Finn Cycle* is loose and rambling without the tightly woven pattern of the great epics. The many incidents that compose the cycle are a succession of detached episodes rather than a continuing story, such as the *Iliad* or King Arthur's legends. The people who imagined the cycle were unsophisticated and childlike and did not comprehend a large literary design. Their stories wander without aim, each adventure independent of the previous one and the one that will follow, but the ballads of the cycle tell vividly of the heroic life, of the strength necessary to survive in a young and hard world, and of the codes of honor and companionship that make survival worthwhile.

FINNEGANS WAKE

Type of work: Novel
Author: James Joyce (1882–1941)
Type of plot: Experimental
Time of plot: A cycle of history
Locale: Dublin
First published: 1939

Principal characters:

HUMPHREY CHIMPDEN EARWICKER (also HERE COMES EVERY-
BODY AND HAVETH CHILDER EVERYWHERE), a pub keeper

ANN, also ANNA LIVIA PLURABELLE, his wife

ISOBEL, their daughter

KEVIN, also SHAUN THE POSTMAN, CHUFF, JAUN, and YAWN,
and

JERRY, also SHEM THE PENMAN, DOLPH, and GLUGG, their twin
sons

From that wonderful passage of revelation and recall as Molly Bloom
hovers on the edge of sleep in the closing section of *Ulysses*, there was only
one short step to the conception of *Finnegans Wake* for James Joyce. *Ulysses*, centering on the events of a specific day and place, presented an exploration of the thoughts and myriad impressions of the waking mind.
Finnegans Wake, to which Joyce devoted seventeen years of concentrated
effort, attempts to create a complete world of nightmare fantasies and half-
conscious dream sensations experienced in the sleeping mind during an
interval that stretches out to enclose all space and time.

Like *Ulysses*, this novel has called into being an extensive literature of
criticism and explications, a process of exegesis needed if the majority of
readers are fully to understand Joyce's purpose and accomplishment. In the
stream-of-consciousness content of *Ulysses*, however, Joyce had kept the
edges of thought and imagery bright and sharp; here everything is blurred
and muffled by physical sleep sensuously recorded as well as by the
kaleidoscopic nature of Joyce's dream world and the shifting identities of
his people as the dreamer pursues erotic fancies or is oppressed by feelings
of guilt. Baldly stated, *Finnegans Wake* is the story of a man who in the
course of a single night dreams of everything that has ever happened in the
world. The dream shapes, and memories set free in sleep float up from the
subconscious in accordance with both Freud's and Jung's principles; in this
manner, the episodes of the novel and the bewildering array of cross-
references go beyond the experience of the individual to reflect a state of
being, which may be vaguely referred to as the collective consciousness of
the race.

Some facts about the dreamer are easily ascertainable. He is a man, apparently of Danish descent, named Humphrey Chimpden Earwicker, and he keeps a pub, the Bristol, somewhere between Phoenix Park and the River Liffey in Dublin. To Dubliners, his name has always been a matter for joking; in addition to its foreign sound, it suggests an insect, the earwig, and he is sometimes referred to as H. C. Earwigger. He has a wife, Ann, and three children—Isobel, a daughter now in her teens, and twin sons, Kevin and Jerry. At some time in the past, Earwicker had been involved in a scandal that is never really explained. Apparently, he had accosted some young women or exposed himself in Phoenix Park. The true circumstance is never made clear. Although the incident happened a long time ago, Earwicker still fears investigation by the authorities. Now his old feeling of guilt has been renewed by the fact that on a rowdy Saturday evening in the pub, Earwicker had drunk too much. There had also been some kind of altercation—possibly a drunk had been forcibly ejected—in which insults were exchanged and stones thrown; and this disturbance had reminded Earwicker of his earlier trouble.

Earwicker was still drunk when he went to bed, and the events of the day disturb his troubled sleep. Since he and his wife no longer feel the passion they once had for each other, his dream does not turn toward her but involves his children. His feeling of guilt is again aroused by the incestuous nature of his dream, but the incest taboo intervenes to transform Isobel into Iseult la Belle and Earwicker into Tristram, thus severing the father-daughter relationship. By much the same process, the other figures in the dream assume different personalities and meanings. Toward morning, his son Jerry calls out, and the mother goes into another room to comfort the child. Only half aware of her going, Earwicker resumes his sleep once more. As the book ends day is breaking, and Earwicker and his wife are about to awake.

To approach Joyce's novel in terms of narrative and character, however, is to do violence to his structure and style. *Finnegans Wake* is composed of many elements: an exile's memories of Dublin in his youth, theories of modern psychology, the substratum of myth and legend underlying the history of the race, and Joyce's marvelous command of the resources and texture of language. The book takes its structure from the *Principii d'una scienza nuova* by Giovanni Battista Vico, an early eighteenth century Italian philosopher. According to Vico's theory, human societies follow a progression of three distinct cycles, the ages of the gods, of great heroes, and of ordinary men. Vico also believed that each cycle created its appropriate institutions and forms of government; autocracy gives place to democracy, and democracy at last becomes anarchy before the cycle begins again. In the beginning, however, is Godhead, revealed in lightning and the crash of thunder, which leads man to restrain his brutish acts and appetites.

In the opening paragraphs of *Finnegans Wake*, such a polysyllabled thunderclap suggests the Viconian cycle, but it is also associated with the fall of Finnegan the hod carrier. His wake is a noisy affair satisfactorily ended, even though at one stage the corpse, reanimated by the Gaelic word for whiskey, threatens to rise and walk once more. The interment of Finnegan—the Finn MacCool of Irish legend—fades into the landscape of Howth Castle and Environs from which, bearing the same initials, Humphrey Chimpden Earwicker emerges. Like Finnegan, Earwicker is a figure of mythopoeic stature, and he takes on a more universal significance in the novel as indicated by his successive appearances as Here Comes Everybody and Haveth Childer Everywhere. His transformations on the universal and spiritual level are the essence of the novel. At the same time, he functions on a different level indicated by ambiguous family relationships—as Adam fallen from grace because of the incident in Phoenix Park; as Tristram who loved the two Iseults; as Swift, the Irish dean who loved Stella and Vanessa; and as the father of Shaun the Postman (Kevin) and Shem the Penman (Jerry).

Ann, the wife, also undergoes a transformation in the course of the novel. She becomes identified with the River Liffey, personified as Anna Livia Plurabelle, the stream of life eternally flowing toward the sea, the feminine principle into which all the women in the novel finally merge, just as in the end the river merges with the sea. The stream is time to Earwicker's history, and the Anna Livia Plurabelle sections are not only the finest in the novel but the particular triumph of Joyce's poetic prose.

Joined to these figures are others who function with only slightly less significance in the symbolic texture of the novel: the four old men who act as a kind of chorus but who may be identified at different times as the four apostles, the four points of the compass, the four ancient Irish kingdoms, the Four Masters of Irish legend, the four waves of myth; Shaun the Postman, who is Kevin and also Chuff, Jaun, and Yawn, the practical man who carries on tradition without knowing the nature of the message he bears any more than the postman knows the contents of the letter he delivers; Shem the Penman, also Jerry, Dolph, and Glugg, who is the writer, the maker of tradition. These figures are at all times surrounded by the history of past and present, shapes of legend and symbol in a dream vision that Joyce attempted to convey by a dream language to which he brought all the resources of his logopoeic faculty.

The style of *Finnegans Wake* represents a virtual re-creation of language. In this work, Joyce exhibits every variety of style in the range of literature. In order to achieve his multileveled effects, a battery of technical devices— the pun, the play on words, telescoped and portmanteau words, parodies, connotations, and many more are employed. Because so much of the understanding of the novel depends on linguistic techniques, its effects are auditory rather than visual. It is a book to be heard as well as to be read, for its structural devices within its cyclic outlines are more those of music than of narrative and drama.

Finnegans Wake is a bold experiment in form, meaning, and style. It is repetitious and irritating in its fragmented episodes and its efforts to push language to the limits of expression. Nevertheless, it is a tremendous if imperfect fable of the whole of mankind that carries man backward through the history of his moral and social habits to the mystery of his origin, tells the story of his fall, and affirms the promise of his rebirth. From the unfinished final sentence of the novel to its continuation in the first paragraph, with its images of the flowing river, Adam and Eve, and the circle of Howth Castle and its environs, the cycle runs its endless course of life, history, and time.

THE FOOL OF QUALITY
Or, The History of Henry, Earl of Moreland

Type of work: Novel
Author: Henry Brooke (1703?–1783)
Type of plot: Didactic romance
Time of plot: Eighteenth century
Locale: England
First published: 1765–1770

Principal characters:
HENRY CLINTON, Earl of Moreland
MR. FENTON, his foster father
NED, Henry's friend
FANNY GOODALL, Mr. Fenton's cousin
ABENAIDE, Princess of Morocco

The Story:
Put out to nurse when he was a baby, Henry Clinton, second son of the Earl of Moreland, saw little of his noble parents and their favorite older son. At the age of five and a half, young Harry, as he was called, made the acquaintance of Mr. Fenton, an old man of the neighborhood. The old gentleman was so impressed by the innate goodness of Harry's nature that he stole the boy away from his nurse, after leaving a note for the parents telling them that he would one day return their son. It was Mr. Fenton's purpose to train young Harry to become the most accomplished and perfect of men. The parents grieved for a short time but soon forgot the boy in favor of his older brother.

Mr. Fenton took Harry to a mansion at Hampstead. With them they took Ned, a beggar lad whom Harry had befriended. There, Harry's education began. Mr. Fenton, a very wealthy man, gave Harry large sums of money and hundreds of garments to distribute to the deserving poor. It was Harry's task to weed out the deserving from the rascals. At the same time, the boys were instructed in academic subjects, bodybuilding, and other suitable lessons. Ned had irrepressible spirits, and he constantly tormented his teachers. Sometimes Harry joined in the fun, but he was such a good boy that he immediately performed a favor for anyone who might have suffered because of Ned or himself.

Harry was so tenderhearted that he frequently brought whole families to live at the mansion and gave them money, clothing, and work. Mr. Fenton was highly pleased with the boy, who had purity of heart and a willingness to be instructed in all phases of life. The old gentleman taught him theology, principles of government, moral rules, and many other forms of philosophy.

Harry became the champion of all those who were tormented by bullies, even though the ruffian was often larger and stronger than he. He soundly thrashed many boys and men and then immediately helped them to their feet and became their friend. Once he trounced the son of a nobleman. The mother, not knowing Harry was also an earl's son, would have had him severely punished, but the father saw Harry's good character and defended the lad. Most of the people Harry thrashed became his devoted servants, seeing and loving the nobility of character he possessed.

One day, Mr. Fenton called on a lady who had issued several invitations to him. He was delighted to learn that the woman, now Lady Maitland, was his cousin Fanny Goodall. In their youth they had loved each other, but he was many years older than Fanny and there had been nothing but longing on the part of each of them. Recognizing Mr. Fenton, Fanny now called him Harry Clinton. He was the brother of young Harry's father, the Earl of Moreland; thus, he was Harry's uncle. Cast out with a small inheritance as was the custom with younger sons, he had made his fortune as a merchant, married a wealthy woman, and prospered still more; but his beloved wife, his children, and his dear father-in-law all died, leaving him bereft of any emotion but sorrow. Although he gained a great fortune on the death of his father-in-law, he considered himself the poorest of men. Fanny was also a widow, and the two friends comforted each other as they talked of their sad lives. Mr. Fenton saw that Fanny was almost overcome with grief and promised to tell her the rest of his story later, but the good lady was called away before she could hear more.

Harry's education continued. Mr. Fenton, as he was known to all but Fanny, sent him to the prisons to pay the debts of deserving persons and to secure their release. He continued to take unfortunates home with him, much to the joy of Mr. Fenton. Ned, too, was improving, although he still did not have the nobility of character that Harry possessed.

One day, Ned's parents were found. Harry had helped some people who had suffered an accident nearby, and these people became friends of the household. By a scar which his old nurse recognized, Ned was known to her and then to his parents. The boy had been stolen in infancy. It was with great joy that the parents greeted their son. Although Ned hated to leave Mr. Fenton and his beloved friend Harry, he went joyfully with his rightful parents.

Countless numbers of people became Harry's friends because of his concern for their well-being. Mr. Fenton sent him and his tutor, one of Harry's charities, to London to learn the ways of the city and the court. Even the king was impressed by the lad. Nevertheless, Harry retained his modesty through all the adulation he received, a fact which added to his popularity. The queen and other noble ladies sought his company, but he eluded them all, making them better, however, for having known him.

When Mr. Fenton learned of the death of Harry's mother and brother, he returned the boy to his father, the Earl of Moreland, who was overjoyed at finding his lost son. When he learned that the child's abductor had been his own brother, thought dead, the Earl was filled with remorse for having treated his brother so badly many years before. The brothers were united publicly, and everyone learned that Mr. Fenton was in reality the second son of the house of Moreland. The Earl was grateful to his brother for stealing the boy and making a perfect man of him.

Mr. Clinton, as Mr. Fenton was called from then on, told the rest of the story of his life. After the death of his loved ones, he lived in sorrow for many years. Then he married again after almost losing his life in his suit of the girl he loved, Louisa d'Aubigny. They had a lovely daughter named Eloisa. Sorrow, however, again haunted Mr. Clinton, for Louisa died from a fall and Eloisa was washed from a ship and seen no more. The bereaved man had lived in solitude and misery until he had met and abducted Harry.

Not long after learning his brother's story, Harry's father died, and the boy became the Earl of Moreland. He now had a huge fortune to spend for charity, and he spent wisely so that those who received would profit from the money in all ways.

Before long, Mr. Clinton learned from his dead wife's brother that he was coming to England, accompanied by Fanny Goodall. Fanny had married Louisa's brother and thus had become Mr. Clinton's sister-in-law. The old friends rejoiced at their reunion. Fanny was accompanied by a dark Moorish page to whom Harry was instantly attracted. The boy told Harry that he had a sister Abenaide, as fair as he himself was dark. She would soon accompany their father, the emperor, who was coming to England with his wife. The boy had been sent ahead as a page to be trained in genteel conduct. When the girl arrived, Mr. Clinton found her to be the daughter of his own supposedly dead Eloisa. Saved from the sea, Eloisa had married the Emperor of Morocco. To Harry's extreme surprise, the Moorish princess was the same page whom he had loved so dearly. She had been in disguise to escape an unwanted royal lover and had continued the deception in order to tease Harry.

The Princess Abenaide and Harry were married, their wedding being blessed with the prayers of the countless hundreds the perfect young man had befriended.

Critical Evaluation:

The Irish poet and playwright Henry Brooke used *The Fool of Quality* to expound the Rousseauean virtues of the "natural man." The dangers of civilized life (overpowering man's inborn virtues and strengths) are emphasized in this rambling story. The protagonist's older brother lives a dissolute life, a victim to the vices of civilization; conversely, the boy Henry strips off the fine new clothes that tie him to civilized society when he comes to believe that they will stifle his "natural" powers. Throughout the book, the "noble savage" concept is held up as the ideal to which man should aspire.

The long philosophical digressions in *The Fool of Quality*, for the most part, are dated and superficial; the narrator's profundities tend to be obvious and fashionable to the mid-eighteenth century mind. Nevertheless, these speculations and ramblings are set down with enough charm and style to be diverting and entertaining and of genuine historical interest. Although Brooke was not an original thinker or writer, he presents a good picture of the popular ideas and techniques of his day.

A friend of Swift, Pope, and other literary figures of the time, Brooke attempted to copy their success and methods in his own work. Different parts of *The Fool of Quality* owe their form and content to various writers of the period; the sentimental parts certainly may be linked with Laurence Sterne's *Sentimental Journey* and some passages of *Tristram Shandy*. Some of the humor and digressions may have been influenced by Fielding. The book oscillates between hectic activity and long-winded reflection, between sentimentality and genuine humor, but the novel is a very human and humane work. The protagonist, Henry Clinton, is supposedly reared by his foster father to be an ideal nobleman, but he possesses more than a little Don Quixote in his personality.

THE FORSYTE SAGA

Type of work: Novel
Author: John Galsworthy (1867–1933)
Type of plot: Social chronicle
Time of plot: 1886–1920
Locale: England
First published: 1922; *The Man of Property*, 1906; *In Chancery*, 1920; *To Let*, 1921

> *Principal characters:*
> SOAMES FORSYTE, a man of property
> IRENE, his wife
> OLD JOLYON FORSYTE, his uncle
> YOUNG JOLYON, Old Jolyon's son
> JUNE, Young Jolyon's daughter
> PHILIP BOSINNEY, an architect engaged to June
> ANNETTE, Soames's second wife
> FLEUR, their daughter
> JON, Irene's and Young Jolyon's son
> WINIFRED DARTIE, Soames's sister and Monty Dartie's wife

The Story:

In 1886, all the Forsytes gathered at Old Jolyon Forsyte's house to celebrate the engagement of his granddaughter, June, to Philip Bosinney, a young architect. Young Jolyon Forsyte, June's father, was estranged from his family because he had run away with a governess, whom he had married after June's mother died.

Old Jolyon complained that he saw little of June. Lonely, he called on Young Jolyon, whom he had not seen in many years. He found his son working as an underwriter for Lloyd's and painting watercolors. He had two children, Holly and Jolly, by his second wife.

The family knew that Soames had been having trouble with his lovely wife, Irene. She had a profound aversion for Soames and had recently reminded him of her premarital stipulation that she should have her freedom if the marriage were not a success. In his efforts to please her, Soames planned to build a large country place. Deciding that June's fiancé would be a good choice for an architect, he bought an estate at Robin Hill and hired Bosinney to build the house.

When Soames made suggestions about the plans, Bosinney appeared offended, and in the end, the plans were drawn as Bosinney wished. As the

---

work proceeded, both men argued over costs that exceeded the original estimate.

One day Swithin Forsyte, Soames's uncle, took Irene to see the house, and Bosinney met them there. While Swithin dozed, the architect talked to Irene alone. That day, Irene and Bosinney fell hopelessly in love with each other. Irene's already unbearable life with Soames became impossible. She asked for a separate room.

There were new troubles over the house. Bosinney had agreed to decorate it but only if he could have a free hand. Soames finally agreed. Irene and Bosinney began to meet secretly. As their affair progressed, June became more unhappy and self-centered. Finally, Old Jolyon took June away for a holiday. He wrote to Young Jolyon, asking him to see Bosinney and learn his intentions toward June. Young Jolyon talked to Bosinney, but the report he made to his father was vague.

When the house was completed, Soames sued Bosinney for exceeding his highest estimate, and Irene refused to move to Robin Hill. When the lawsuit over the house came to trial, Soames won his case without difficulty. That same night Bosinney, after spending the afternoon with Irene and learning that Soames had forced himself on her, was accidentally run over. Irene left her husband on the day of the trial, but that night she returned to his house because there was now no place else for her to go. June persuaded her grandfather to buy Robin Hill for Jolyon's family.

A short time after Bosinney's death, Irene left Soames permanently, settled in a small flat, and gave music lessons to support herself. Several years later, Irene visited Robin Hill secretly and there met Old Jolyon. She won him by her gentleness and charm, and during that summer, she made his days happy. Late in the summer, he died quietly while waiting for her.

After his separation from Irene, Soames devoted himself to making money. Then, still hoping to have an heir, he began to court a French girl, Annette Lamotte. At the same time, his sister Winifred was facing difficulties. Her husband, Monty Dartie, stole her pearls and ran away to South America with a Spanish dancer. When he decided to marry Annette, Soames went to Irene to see if she would provide grounds for his suit. He found that she had lived a model life. While visiting her, Soames realized that he still loved her and tried to persuade her to come back to him. When she refused, he hired a detective to get the evidence he needed.

Old Jolyon had willed a legacy to Irene; Young Jolyon, now a widower, had been appointed trustee. When Soames annoyed Irene, she appealed to Young Jolyon for protection. Irene went to Paris to avoid Soames; shortly afterward, Young Jolyon joined her. Her visit was cut short by Jolly, who announced that he had joined the yeomanry to fight in the Boer War. Holly had in the meantime fallen in love with Val Dartie, her cousin. When Val proposed to Holly, he was overheard by Jolly, who dared Val to

join the yeomanry with him. Val accepted. June then decided to become a
Red Cross nurse, and Holly went with her. Monty Dartie reappeared unexpectedly. To avoid further scandal, Winifred decided to take him back.

Soames went to Paris in a last effort to persuade Irene. Frightened,
Irene returned to Young Jolyon. Before they became lovers in deed, they
were presented with papers by Soames's lawyer. They decided to go abroad
together. Before their departure, Young Jolyon received word that Jolly
had died of enteric fever during the African campaign. Later, Soames
secured his divorce and married Annette. To the discomfiture of both
branches of the family, Val married Holly.

Irene presented Jolyon with a son, Jon. When Annette was about to
give birth to a child, Soames had to choose between saving the mother or
the child. Wishing an heir, Soames chose to save the child. Fortunately,
both Annette and the baby lived.

Little Jon grew up under the adoring eyes of his parents. Fleur grew up
spoiled by her doting father.

Years passed. Monty Dartie was dead. Val and Holly were training
racehorses. One day in a picture gallery, Soames impulsively invited a
young man, Michael Mont, to see his collection of pictures. That same
afternoon, he saw Irene and her son Jon for the first time in twenty years.
By chance, Fleur and Jon met. Having decided that he wanted to try farming, Jon went to stay with Val Dartie. Fleur also appeared to spend the
week with Holly. Jon and Fleur fell deeply in love.

They had only vague ideas regarding the cause of the feud between their
respective branches of the family. Later, Fleur learned all the details from
Prosper Profond, with whom Annette was having an affair, and from Winifred Dartie. She was still determined to marry Jon. Meanwhile, Michael
Mont had Soames's permission to court Fleur. When Soames heard of the
affair between Annette and Prosper, she did not deny it, but she promised
there would be no scandal.

Fleur tried to persuade Jon into a hasty marriage. She failed because
Young Jolyon reluctantly gave his son a letter revealing the story of Soames
and Irene. After reading the letter, Jon realized that he could never marry
Fleur. His decision became irrevocable when his father died. He left England at once and went to America, where Irene joined him. Fleur was disappointed and married Michael Mont.

Timothy was the last of the old Forsytes; when he died, Soames realized
that the Forsyte age had passed. Its way of life was like an empty house—
to let. He felt lonely and old.

Critical Evaluation:

The Forsyte Saga won the Nobel Prize in Literature for its author in
1932. After its initial popularity had subsided, it remained in a state of

semidormancy as far as the general reading public was concerned until the work was dramatized in twenty-six episodes on the BBC in 1969. The immense popularity of the series, which eventually reached the entire world, brought forth a burst of enthusiasm for the characters and the story that led to numerous reprintings of the original stories and a plethora of criticism on them.

The three novelettes that make up the trilogy, *A Man of Property*, *In Chancery*, and *To Let*, are actually sequences in the history of a well-to-do English family, the Forsytes. They are wealthy members of the middle class, conscious of their social position and eager to keep it intact. Their pettiness in matters of decorum was typical of the wealthy bourgeoisie of the times.

Comparing the early sections of the work with the later ones, the reader can see why differences arose among the various members of the Forsyte clan. The older members of the family, such as Uncle Swithin and Old Jolyon, were in different worlds from the youngest Forsytes, such as Fleur and Jolly, both chronologically and psychologically. In the middle stood people of both worlds such as Soames and Winifred. They were products of the tranquil Victorian period, but they had to live through changes in society that made them cling to the old familiar ways and fear acceptance of new ideas and new people. This transition from the old world into the new is one of the major strengths of the novel. John Galsworthy draws the reader into the lives of the Forsytes so that the reader feels that he is actually living through this time of change.

Perhaps the greatest merit of *The Forsyte Saga* is the fact that while its overall aim is one of social criticism, the characters are not sacrificed to this end but only further illuminate the comments. Though critics could claim that none of the characters is quite complete—sometimes the reader feels as if he were looking at the action through a screen—the mystery of the main characters, especially Irene and Bosinney, draws the reader deeper into their lives. At times, the novel can become so engrossing that one attempts to "read between the lines" of the story in an effort to discover what the various characters are thinking and feeling. It is particularly difficult at times to do this, however, because Galsworthy very often leaves the reader on the precipice of an insight and then abruptly changes the scene. The widespread appeal of the television series was owed in part to its ability to fill in these missing portions of the novel.

Although the novel is definitely a period piece, it can be appreciated by readers who are not historically or nostalgically minded. The situations of the story and the turns of fortune of the main characters could be appreciated if set in any age. There is a great deal of irony in the story that is timeless as well. The first episode of the story, the festive occasion of a party celebrating the engagement of young June to Philip Bosinney, is a case in point. The setting of a large family gathering intended to evaluate the worthiness of a prospective new member of the family is something that would appeal to anyone who had been at such a gathering. The conversation, at times, may have been uniquely Victorian, but the mood was quite ageless.

The romantic situation that arose among the characters of June, Bosinney, Irene, and Soames is another ironic one. While Irene hopes to help June obtain family acceptance for Bosinney, she falls in love with him herself. When Soames tries to gain Irene's love by having a beautiful house built for her, he only succeeds in forcing her to leave him because of her growing love for Bosinney and her disgust for her husband.

Further irony is found in the fact that Irene forces Soames into becoming even more of the distasteful "man of property" than he had been because of her rejection. This hardening of Soames's character is one of the things that makes him more of a tragic character than a bad one.

Of all the good points of the trilogy, the most lasting is, of course, the social criticism. Despite his episodic approach, Galsworthy has managed to capture the essence of the era that he is describing, even beyond the milieu of the upper middle-class English family of his concern. It was for this aspect of the novel that the author was awarded the Nobel Prize in Literature. Galsworthy has managed to show the reader the thought and actions of an age that was a transition from the staid and superficially tranquil Victorian age to the bustling, confused era of the early twentieth century. With a large family as a base, the various marriages and births enable the author to introduce a large variety of events and people.

The mixture of characters enables Galsworthy to present representatives of many personality types: Soames, the lonely businessman; Young Jolyon, the man who renounces his family to pursue a career as an artist; Fleur, the archetypal "flapper" of the post-World War I era. Not only are these and other characters important for their role in the progress of the story but their characterizations are representative of the times. It is for these characterizations and for the overall view of the period that this trilogy will retain its position in literature.

FORTITUDE
Being a True and Faithful Account of the Education of an Explorer

Type of work: Novel
Author: Hugh Walpole (1884–1941)
Type of plot: Sentimental romance
Time of plot: Late nineteenth century
Locale: England
First published: 1913

Principal characters:
PETER WESTCOTT, a young writer
STEPHEN BRANT, a friend
CLARE, Peter's wife
BOBBY GALLEON, a student at Dawson's School
JERRY CARDILLAC (CARDS), another student
MR. ZANTI, a bookseller
NORA MONOGUE, Peter's friend and adviser

The Story:

Peter Westcott lived with his harsh father and his invalid mother at Scaw House, near the town of Treliss in Cornwall. As he grew up, Peter made friends with Stephen Brant, a farmer who occasionally took the child to the Bending Mule Inn. One Christmas Eve at the inn, Peter watched Stephen fighting with another man over a girl. That night, he arrived home late from the Bending Mule, and his father gave him the most severe whipping he had yet received. On another day, Stephen took him to the curiosity shop operated by Zachary Tan. There Peter was introduced to jovial Mr. Emilio Zanti, from London, who treated the boy with special consideration. At supper that night, Peter's father told him that he was to go off to school in Devonshire.

The next phase of Peter's life revolved about Dawson's School, where his best friends were Bobby Galleon and Jerry Cardillac. Bobby was the son of a famous writer. Cardillac, called Cards, was Peter's idol; he was everything that Peter would have liked to have been but was not. After Cards left at the end of Peter's second year, affairs did not progress smoothly for Peter. One day, he found Jerrard, the best bowler in school, forcing whiskey down the throat of a small boy. It was the eve of a big game in which Jerrard's services were needed; nevertheless, Peter, in his capacity as a monitor, turned him in to the authorities. Jerrard was expelled, and Dawson's School lost the game. On the last day of the term, the whole school joined in hissing Peter when he called the roll. Bobby Galleon was the single exception.

He was spared the indignity of returning to Dawson's School when it was closed after the summer holidays because of a lack of funds. His father then sent Peter to read law in the office of Mr. Aitchinson in Treliss. Meanwhile, Peter became aware of his mother. For many years, she had been an invalid who never left her room, and Peter was not encouraged to visit her. One day when his father was away, Peter went to her room. He found that she was dying as the result of his father's cruel and harsh attitude toward her, and his visit hastened her death. A short time after her funeral, Peter again saw Mr. Zanti, who offered the lad a job in his bookshop in London. Finding life at Scaw House intolerable, Peter decided to leave home. On Good Friday, he met a little girl who gave her name as Clare Elizabeth Rossiter. According to his plans, Peter left home, but only after fighting with his father.

In London, Peter worked in Mr. Zanti's bookshop as an assistant to Gottfried Hanz. Mr. Zanti had found him lodgings with Mrs. Brockett, and there he met Nora Monogue, who encouraged Peter when he began to write. A strange aspect of the bookshop was the great number of people who visited it without buying any books, visitors who passed mysteriously into the back room of the shop. For seven years, Peter Westcott worked in Zanti's shop and wrote in his room at Brockett's. In November, 1895, he finished his first novel, *Reuben Hallard*, and began to look for a publisher. One day, he again met Clare Rossiter, who had come to visit Nora Monogue. Almost at once, Peter found himself falling in love with her. Meanwhile, strange things had been happening at the bookstore. When the Prince and Princess of Schloss visited London, one of the visitors to the shop threw a bomb at Queen Victoria as her procession passed. Shortly afterward, Stephen Brant appeared to take Peter away from the shop. They found lodgings in the slums of Bucket Lane.

Neither of the two was able to find steady employment. When Peter became ill from lack of food, Stephen notified Peter's friend from Dawson's School, Bobby Galleon, whom Peter had met in the city. Peter was relocated to his friend's house, where Bobby and his wife nursed him back to health. In a short time, *Reuben Hallard* was published. It was an immediate success, and Peter Westcott became known in literary circles. He then met Mrs. Launce, who was finally instrumental in bringing Peter and Clare together. After they were married, they moved into a house in Chelsea. There a child was born to Clare, a son named Stephen. The marriage, however, was not a success. Clare disapproved of Stephen and Mr. Zanti. Peter's second novel brought little money. Peter's old school friend,

Jerry Cardillac, came back to London and aroused Clare's interest.

The final blow to Peter's happiness came when little Stephen died. Peter blamed Clare for the child's death. A short time later, she left him to join Cardillac in France, after refusing Peter's constant offers to try to make her life as she wanted it. Then Peter's third novel proved a failure. He decided to leave London and return to Scaw House. In Treliss, he encountered Nora Monogue; she had been sent to Cornwall because she could live, at the most, only a few weeks. At Scaw House, he found his father sodden in drink and sharing the musty house with a slatternly housekeeper. Peter was slipping into the same useless life. Nora Monogue, however, felt that Peter, now thirty years old, could still be a successful writer, and she used the last of her rapidly failing strength to persuade him to go back to London. As a final resort, Nora admitted that she had always loved him, and her dying request was that he leave his father and return to London to start writing again. Therefore, Peter became a man, realizing for the first time that his attitude had been childish during his whole life. He learned fortitude from the dying Nora, and he became the master of his own destiny.

Critical Evaluation:

Hugh Walpole wrote the first page of *Fortitude* in Edinburgh on December 24, 1910. He came to regard this place and date as lucky, because the book enjoyed immense popularity when it was published in 1913. Thereafter, whenever possible, he had the habit of starting his other novels— thirteen of them—in the same city on Christmas Eve, even if he had to travel some distance for the occasion. The circumstance is worth remembering, for Walpole is best understood as an unabashed sentimentalist.

Although he counted as his close friends such masters of psychological Realism as Henry James, Joseph Conrad, Arnold Bennett, and W. Somerset Maugham among others, Walpole is curiously Victorian rather than modern in his approach to fiction. *Fortitude*, a sentimental romance that imitates the format of realistic "apprenticeship" (or "education") novels successful at the time—Forster's *The Longest Journey* (1907), Wells's *Tono-Bungay* (1908), Bennett's *Clayhanger* (1910), Compton Mackenzie's *Sinister Street* (1911), to mention a few examples—is different from representative books of this type. Subtitled "Being a True and Faithful Account of the Education of an Explorer," *Fortitude* is neither true (that is to say, mostly autobiographical) nor is it an authentic "education" novel. To be sure, the early part of the book recalls the author's own miserable childhood; Peter Westcott's public school resembled Walpole's unhappy experiences at Marlow; and two minor characters are based upon real people: Mrs. Launce upon Mrs. Belloc Lowndes and Henry Galleon upon Henry James. Nevertheless, the novel as a whole is not the story of Walpole's life. Moreover, the education theme is only fitfully developed. Peter, Walpole's protagonist, learns from life a single and rather simplistic lesson: courage and fortitude are necessary for success. Walpole states the theme, which is no more than a truism, in the opening sentences of the novel: "'Tisn't Life that matters! 'Tis the courage you bring to it." As the book progresses, Peter comes to understand the importance of this advice in his education to maturity.

From the standpoint of a modern reader, however, it is Peter's lack of maturity at all stages of his career that weakens the force of the novel. He is sentimental and naïve to the point of foolishness. He falls hopelessly in love with the self-indulgent Clare Rossiter when their fingers happen to touch. Clare proves to be a cool wife and careless mother; bored with her marriage, she finally runs off with a lover, one of Peter's former schoolboy chums. Shortly after this scene, Walpole melodramatically writes: "Peter Westcott was dead." The statement, however, must be taken as hyperbole. Peter is by no means dead; he is only wretched. Because of his obvious immaturity, he continues to be wretched throughout most of the novel. Structurally, the three major crises of the book concern Peter's misery on the occasions of the deaths of his mother, of his son, and of his true friend Nora Monogue. Only with the last tragedy is he able to evidence some maturity. Because life is difficult, he decides that one must face it with courage. If Nora (whom he had once described, with typical infelicity, as "the nicest ugly woman to look at I've ever seen") is able to die with dignity, Peter resolves that he can live with fortitude.

Five years after he published his novel, Walpole wrote in his diary: "*Fortitude* seems to me now an incredibly childish and naïve affair." Despite its obvious faults—sentimentality that approaches mawkishness, melodramatic exaggeration, feeble psychology—the novel nevertheless charmed readers in 1913 and continues to hold a dwindling but faithful audience. One reason for the survival of *Fortitude* is that the book is entirely sincere. Unlike other twentieth century sentimental romances that are written to produce calculated effects of pathos, Walpole's novel is obviously heartfelt. Peter's hatred of his father, his affection for Stephen Brandt (a friendship that is closer to love than is his supposed adoration for Clare), and his childhood terrors of punishment are episodes that are handled with fervor. Although Walpole is not a writer of Realism, he can simulate with realistic intensity the emotions that are close to his own feelings. Therefore, the reader, swept along by the author's emotionalism more than by his fiction, may finally be moved by Peter's trials as a child-man, vulnerable and alone, in a man's world.

THE FORTRESS

Type of work: Novel
Author: Hugh Walpole (1884–1941)
Type of plot: Historical chronicle
Time of plot: Nineteenth century
Locale: England
First published: 1932

> *Principal characters:*
> JUDITH PARIS, Rogue Herries' daughter
> WALTER HERRIES, Judith's cousin
> JENNIFER HERRIES, another cousin
> ADAM PARIS, Judith's son
> JOHN, Jennifer's son
> ELIZABETH, Walter's daughter
> UHLAND, Walter's son
> MARGARET, Adam's wife

The Story:

The quarrel between Walter Herries of Westaways and Jennifer Herries, his kinswoman at Fell House, went back many years. Christabel, Walter's weak mother, had been insulted by Jennifer over the breaking of a fan at a ball, and Walter never forgot the slight to his proud, snobbish family. He also resented the presence of Judith Paris and her illegitimate son, living brazenly, as he thought, at Fell House, so near Westaways, his own fine house. By one method or another, he had determined to drive out the whole household, and he might have succeeded had it not been for Judith.

Judith openly accused her cousin of having incited a riot in which Reuben Sunwood, another kinsman, had been killed. Admitting the charge, Walter Herries said there had been no way for him to foresee Reuben's death. He proposed that Jennifer and Judith should sell him Fell House at a fair price and move away. If they did not, Walter would persecute them until they would be glad to leave. When Judith refused, Walter bought Ireby, a high hill overlooking Fell House. He planned to build a huge mansion there to dwarf Jennifer's modest home, and he would be there always to spy on the people of Fell House and hurt them. He also reminded Judith of Francis, Jennifer's husband, who had committed suicide. Walter had exposed Jennifer's lover to him, and the coward had shot himself rather than the man who had defiled his home. Judith, however, defied Walter's angry boasts of his power and cunning.

She took complete charge at Fell House, and Jennifer thankfully let her assume management of the household. Since she was firm and headstrong, they did not give in to Walter even when he poisoned their cows.

Uhland and Elizabeth were Walter's children. The girl was beautiful and kind, but Uhland was his father's pride. The son was lame and pampered. At an early age, he shared his father's hatred of Judith and her close kin. One day as he walked in the woods, he saw his sister Elizabeth and John, Jennifer's son, together. He ordered his sister to see no more of John, but Elizabeth, who had a mind of her own, refused, knowing that her brother could never bring himself to tell his father. Uhland, lame and pale, was much attracted to robust Adam Paris, Judith's son.

As Adam Paris grew up into a strong, rebellious boy, he soon learned that he was illegitimate and that his aunt had taken a lover. The knowledge made him resentful of all restraint, and only by the grace of the family name was he allowed to remain at Rugby.

When Walter really began to build on Ireby Hill, the country folk named his great mansion The Fortress. Walter had carried out his threat to dwarf the house of Judith and to spy on her people. Jennifer was greatly disturbed. Her fear of Walter made her go every day to Ireby and survey the progress made. Finally, the strain was unbearable; Jennifer died quietly from sheer apprehension.

When Walter's family moved into the Fortress, they gave a big reception, but even the crowds and the huge fires could not warm the great stone house. Elizabeth was especially unhappy in the gloomy, rambling mansion. She and John had agreed not to see each other anymore, since marriage seemed an impossibility while their families were enemies. Consequently, when she was invited to visit her Herries cousins in London, she accepted gratefully; but once in fine society, she was troubled. She felt lonely and left out. Mr. Temple, a fat lawyer, pursued her vigorously.

Uhland followed his sister to London. When he saw that Elizabeth could marry the rich and eligible Mr. Temple, he fiercely urged the match. Elizabeth felt more than ever estranged from her family, and when her father wrote and commanded the marriage, Elizabeth promptly and vehemently refused Mr. Temple's awkward proposal. Enlisting the help of a friendly maid, she stole out of the Herries house and took a job as governess with a family named Golightly.

In her new position, Elizabeth had little to do. Her employers, however, were common, noisy people, and she soon began to detest her place with them. Then her ridiculous employer, old enough to be her father, declared his love for her and his resolution to leave his wife. Terrified, Elizabeth wrote an appeal to John. Forgetting their families' enmity, John and Elizabeth were quietly married.

At the age of twenty-two, Adam Paris decided to leave Fell House. He had been threatening to go away for five years, but his mother had put him off each time.

In London, Adam found only temporary employment; in a few weeks, he was hungry and penniless. Taken in by chance by the Kraft family, he soon joined the Chartist movement. In that struggle, Caesar Kraft became Adam's guide and Kraft's daughter, Margaret, offered Adam sympathy and finally love.

The 1840's were stirring times in England. Widespread unemployment, poverty, and child labor made reform necessary. Aided by Adam and many others, the Chartists planned their big procession to Parliament. Caesar Kraft was a moderate man, and at a Chartist meeting, he counseled patience. When the procession was broken up, the hotheads blamed him for their failure, and in the riot that followed, Kraft was clubbed to death.

Adam and Margaret were married shortly afterward. Adam's small skill at editing and hack writing kept them going in a tiny apartment. On their visits to Fell House, Margaret was very unhappy. She saw her husband engulfed by his mother's love and herself an outsider. When she broke down one night and wept, Adam began to understand her feelings and desires. From that time on, Judith took second place with him, even after they moved to Fell House to stay.

John Herries did well in London. As a parliamentary secretary, his future seemed bright. Uhland, however, was madly determined to make John pay for having the impertinence to marry his sister. Everywhere John went, he knew Uhland was dogging his path. John was not exactly afraid, but contact with Uhland left him powerless before that great hatred.

In a desperate attempt to shake off his incubus, John met Uhland in a deserted country house. There, he suddenly lost his terror of his tormentor and jumped up, daring Uhland to follow him anymore. In a mad rage, Uhland seized his gun, shot John, and then killed himself. Elizabeth was then left with Benjie, her small son. Walter's hate had borne its final, bitter fruit.

In the Fortress, Walter lived out his drunken old age with a gaudy housekeeper. Steadfastly, he refused to answer Elizabeth's letters or to let her call. Finally, when she was more than sixty years old, Elizabeth heard that her father was seriously ill. She stormed the Fortress, sent the blowzy housekeeper packing, and nursed the old drunkard back to health. She was so successful with the chastened old man that on Judith's hundredth birthday Elizabeth brought her father with her as a guest to Fell House.

Critical Evaluation:

The Fortress is the third part of the six-part Herries chronicle, which covers more than two hundred years of English social history. The present work portrays the later life of Judith Paris and her quarrel with Walter. The scope of the chronicle is vast, and *The Fortress* alone covers a space of more than fifty years and a host of people. Although at times *The Fortress* stalls among the multitude of characters and their gossip, it has considerable narrative power. Hugh Walpole must be considered a competent popular novelist.

The Fortress, while presenting important events in the story of the Herries family, is probably the weakest segment of the Herries chronicle. Although the action is intense in many spots, Walpole seems to feel the need to pad this novel with unnecessary descriptions of scenery and of social gatherings. Probably the strongest aspect of *The Fortress* is its predominant theme of the conflict between good and evil forces. This theme informs all the novels in the Herries chronicle; therefore, the present novel is, in spite of its weaknesses, an important link in the series.

The main impetus for the novel's action is the continuation of the "broken fan" feud begun in the preceding novel, *Judith Paris*. The feud itself is a rather tepid affair, but the events and consequences that spring from it comprise the most intense action. This feud and Walter Herries' egocentric greed for power and possessions lead to the death of Jennifer Herries, leaving Judith Paris to see the battle out to its conclusion, as well as providing the basis for the conflict between John and Uhland Herries, which ends in the tragic death of both. In the context of the events issuing from the feud, the thematic conflict of good versus evil is seen not so much in the senseless, petty indignation shown by one side of a family toward another, but, more important, in the abuse of wealth, power, and prestige when in the hands of one like Walter Herries. The Francis Herries side of the family and of the feud represents the moral, humane, positive elements in society. In the same fashion, the conflict between John and Uhland Herries does not merely involve the misfit's wrath toward the rest of the more normal world but demonstrates that jealousy can lead to tragic consequences like that of Uhland's, if allowed to be fed and to go unchecked—as Walter allowed it.

To complement and strengthen the thematic significance of the Herries feud, Walpole also presents a picture of the growing Chartist movement. By his involvement in the movement, we see Adam Paris as the vehicle by which it is made clear that the type of power and status that Walter seeks represents the same evil oppression of the innocent commoners by the upper classes throughout England. In terms of thematic content and continuity, therefore, *The Fortress*, like other novels in the chronicle, is largely a well-crafted work.

Although the action is intense at various times, the overall narrative pace is impeded by such digressions as "The Summer Fair" chapter and much of "Judith and Adam in London," both in part 1, as well as other instances throughout the novel. These indulgences in the description of scenery or social gatherings are somewhat enlightening as to the milieu of the novel, but otherwise they do little to advance thematic purpose. Furthermore, after the tragic murder-suicide scene in "Skiddaw Forest" (part 3), the novel loses a great deal of its force. The last two hundred pages do introduce Vanessa, the protagonist of the novel to follow, but the rest is largely trivial.

A further weakness in *The Fortress* is that it lacks a paramount character upon whom the author and reader can focus attention. Judith Paris is less a strong protagonist in the second novel than the "rogue" was in the first, but there is even less of a defined protagonist in this third novel. The characterization of Judith Paris is strong; but with reference to the novel bearing her name, she is little changed. The characterization of John, Adam, and Uhland are fairly complete but lack the thoroughness that would make any of them central figures. Walpole does go far enough with his major characters to be congratulated on making them memorable, but, as in the case of narrative pace, *The Fortress* suffers in the area of characterization as well.

The Fortress marks another stage in the momentous task that Walpole attempted in his Herries chronicle. In spite of the third novel's weaknesses, much of it is still very much a credit to Walpole's craftsmanship and an important link in the continuing story of the Herries family.

THE FORTUNES OF NIGEL

Type of work: Novel
Author: Sir Walter Scott (1771–1832)
Type of plot: Historical romance
Time of plot: Early seventeenth century
Locale: England
First published: 1822

Principal characters:
NIGEL OLIFAUNT, Lord of Glenvarloch
RICHARD MONIPLIES, his servant
GEORGE HERIOT, a goldsmith and friend of Nigel's father
MARGARET RAMSAY, Heriot's goddaughter
THE EARL OF HUNTINGLEN, an old nobleman
LORD DALGARNO, his son
LADY HERMIONE, a relative of Nigel
DAME SUDDLECHOP, a gossip
TRAPBOIS, a usurer
MARTHA TRAPBOIS, his daughter
JAMES I, King of England

The Story:

The threatened loss of his family estates in Scotland sent Nigel Olifaunt, Lord of Glenvarloch, and his servant, Richard Moniplies, to London. Their mission there was to petition King James I for the repayment of large loans made to the crown by Nigel's late father. After Richie Moniplies had made an unsuccessful attempt to deliver his master's petition, he was followed from the court by George Heriot, the royal goldsmith, who went to Nigel and offered to help him gain favor with the king. Heriot gave his friendship with Nigel's late father as his motive. He succeeded in presenting Nigel's petition to the king. King James, in royal good humor, ordered Heriot to provide Nigel with money needed to outfit himself properly for an appearance at court, so that he could speak in his own behalf. The King gave Heriot a small crown of jewels with instructions that the gems were to remain in Heriot's possession until the state repaid him for the money he would lend to Nigel. The state's finances were seriously depleted, and the King was forced to do business by warrant.

While dining at Heriot's house the next day, Nigel met Margaret Ramsay, Heriot's godchild and the daughter of David Ramsay, the royal clockmaker. Margaret promptly lost her heart to Nigel, but because he was a nobleman, she was too shy to talk with him. That same night, however, she commissioned Dame Suddlechop, a local gossip, to investigate Nigel and his business. The Dame already knew that Nigel had powerful enemies in court, who were interested in seeing that he was prevented from taking rightful possession of his estates. On the promise of more money in the future, the old gossip agreed to learn all she could about Nigel and his affairs.

Dressed in clothing bought by money advanced by Heriot, Nigel went to the King with his petition. At first, he had difficulty in gaining admittance, but at last, he managed to see the King. The King confessed that there were no funds available for the debt, but he made a notation on the petition to the Scottish Exchequer and told Nigel that perhaps he could borrow from moneylenders on the strength of the royal warrant. Nigel left the court with Heriot and the Earl of Huntinglen, who had also befriended him because of his father's name.

Anticipating a session with the moneylenders, the three decided to have a paper drawn up, a document that would allow Nigel ample time to redeem his estates by means of the king's warrant. Trusting Heriot and the old Earl to handle his business, Nigel devoted himself to becoming acquainted with the Earl's young son, Lord Dalgarno. Pretending friendship, Dalgarno in reality began a campaign to undermine Nigel's character and reputation and complete his financial ruin. Dalgarno himself hoped to gain possession of Nigel's estate.

Dalgarno took Nigel to gaming houses and other questionable places until Nigel's reputation began to suffer in the city and at court. At last, even faithful Richie asked for permission to leave his service and return to Scotland. Immediately after Richie's departure, Nigel received an anonymous note, telling him of Dalgarno's plot to ruin him. At first, Nigel refused to consider such a possibility; but at length, he decided to investigate the charges. When he confronted Dalgarno in the Park and accused him of knavery, Dalgarno was so contemptuous of him that Nigel drew his sword and struck Dalgarno. The young courtier was not injured. There was a severe penalty for drawing swords in the Park, however, and Nigel was forced to flee in order to avoid arrest. He was befriended by a young man he had met in a gaming house and was hidden in the house of an old usurer named Trapbois. His refuge was in Whitefriars, known as Alsatia, the haunt of bravos, bankrupts, bullyboys, and thieves.

Meanwhile, Margaret Ramsay was trying to help the young Scottish lord. A mysterious lady stayed apart in a secluded apartment in Heriot's house. She had seen Nigel once during his first visit at the house. This lady was Lady Hermione, who was in seclusion in Heriot's house following a tragic affair of the heart. Because she was extremely wealthy, Margaret begged her to help Nigel out of his difficulties. Lady Hermione revealed to Margaret that she was of the House of Glenvarloch and thus a distant relative of Nigel's. When Margaret told her of Dalgarno's plot to ruin Nigel, Lady Hermione gave her the money but warned her not to lose her heart to Nigel, for he was too highborn for a clockmaker's daughter.

Margaret arranged with an apprentice for Nigel's escape. The apprentice was willing to aid her because he was in love with Margaret and had been advised by old Dame Suddlechop that he might win the girl's heart by helping Nigel. In the meantime, Nigel killed one of two Russians who had murdered Trapbois. Nigel took Trapbois' daughter Martha with him when he escaped from Alsatia with the help of the apprentice sent by Margaret.

Nigel sent Martha to the house of a ship chandler with whom he had lodged for a time and then set out to find the King and present his own account of the quarrel with Dalgarno. Martha had difficulty in gaining admittance to the house where Nigel had sent her, for the ship chandler's wife had disappeared. She was discovered and protected by Richie Moniplies, who had returned to London to look for his master and try to help him. Nigel, in the meantime, tried to approach the King. James, believing that Nigel wanted to kill him, called out for help. His attendants seized Nigel and carried him off to the Tower. Dalgarno, one of the royal party, was only too glad to see Nigel imprisoned.

In his cell, Nigel was accused by Heriot of adultery with the ship chandler's wife and of duplicity in the disappearance of Martha Trapbois. Nigel denied his guilt in either of these affairs. Heriot, while refusing to believe him, nevertheless said that he would again try to help Nigel for his dead father's sake, and he asked Nigel for the royal warrant. His plan was to collect the money from the state and satisfy the moneylenders who were pressing for the repayment of Nigel's loan. Nigel was in despair when he discovered that the royal warrant had been taken from his baggage.

Through a noble friend, Nigel was cleared of the charge of treason— that is, his supposed attempt on the King's life in the Park. Nevertheless, he still had to stand trial for drawing his sword against Dalgarno. Richie went to Nigel in his cell and promised to help his master out of his troubles.

In the meantime, the King received a letter from the Lady Hermione, in which she charged that Dalgarno was the man who had betrayed her. In an attempt to amend the wrongdoing, the King forced Dalgarno to marry Lady Hermione; but after the ceremony, Dalgarno informed the King that he now possessed his wife's wealth and through her a claim upon the Glenvarloch estates. He announced that if the redemption money were not paid by noon of the following day, he would take possession of Nigel's property. Convinced at last that Nigel was the injured party in the affair with Dalgarno, the King informed Richie that this master would be restored to royal favor. Richie, armed with money given to him by Martha Trapbois, paid the mortgage on Nigel's estates. After trying to show that the redemption papers were gained unlawfully, Dalgarno proceeded on his way to Scotland to claim the property; but on the way, he was killed by the same ruffian he had hired to murder Trapbois some time before. His death restored to Lady Hermione the fortune that Dalgarno, as her husband, had claimed. She gave a large portion of her wealth to Margaret and the rest to Nigel, her kinsman. Nigel and Margaret declared their love for each other and were married. During the ceremony, Richie appeared with Martha Trapbois, whom he had married. Martha told Nigel that her father had stolen his royal warrant, and by returning the paper to him, she made his estates secure. In gratitude to Richie for his part in restoring honor in the court, the King made the faithful servant a knight of the land.

Critical Evaluation:

In *The Fortunes of Nigel*, Sir Walter Scott surpassed even his former efforts to introduce literally dozens of characters and plots into one novel. Although the multiplicity of people and events and the use of Scottish dialect may make this novel a difficult one for some readers, the reward in the end is worth the effort. This novel is an exciting tale of intrigue and mystery, one of the great adventure stories in the language. As is also common in stories by Scott, the novel takes much of its romantic atmosphere and dramatic vigor from the author's use of many characters drawn from the lower levels of society. To balance these creatures of his imagination, Scott also presents in the figure of James I, King of England and Scotland, his finest historical portrait.

Since most of Scott's important work was completed in the first twenty-five years of the nineteenth century, he is often considered part of the Romantic literary movement. Rebelling against the formalism of the eighteenth century, this literary impulse advocated the natural expression of feelings, the value of nature against artifice, and the possibilities of life beyond the strict confines of rationalism. The diverse intellectual and literary trends within the Romantic movement make the classification of most authors problematic; but there was a coherent movement, and it did stand for certain modes of expression and ideas.

Clearly, many of the features of Scott's novels and of *The Fortunes of Nigel* can be considered Romantic. Although he did not always succeed, he was interested in preserving and presenting the rhythms of the natural speech of his countrymen. His willingness to portray all the ranks of society, the loosely knit structure of the novel, the use of the past, the idealization of women, the intense sentiments—all these can be taken as Romantic features in Scott's work in general and in *The Fortunes of Nigel* in particular. At the same time, however, there are clearly principles of rationalism, Neoclassism, and literary Realism apparent in *The Fortunes of Nigel*. First, in the "Introductory Epistle" Scott attached to his novel, there is a defensive essay (written, significantly, in the form of a dialogue) that supports the didactic views of the literature of Neoclassism.

In fact, Scott's work stands at one of those junctures in the history of literature where various traditions meet, in mixtures of unpredictable and varying quality, only to separate again as historical and literary circumstances change; and it can be said that both historical Realists and historical Romantics claim him with justification. Alexandre Dumas and James Fenimore Cooper were profoundly influenced by him, but so were Honoré de Balzac and Leo Tolstoy. In short, whatever the value of Scott's novels (and there has been much disagreement on that score), Scott is a seminal figure in literary history. Therefore, *The Fortunes of Nigel* can be judged not only as a historical novel but as a work influential in the history of the novel.

Scott's literary production may be divided into four parts: the early poetry, the initial group of the Waverley series, the later group of historical novels, and the novels after his financial collapse in 1826. It was during the middle period of the Waverley novels and the years immediately following that Scott did his best work. *The Fortunes of Nigel* falls into the late Waverley period. *The Fortunes of Nigel*, like the early Waverley novels, was highly successful. Although the book was priced out of the reach of the ordinary reader, it nevertheless sold ten thousand copies in the first printing. Of these, Scott's publisher assured him that seven thousand had been sold before 10:30 in the morning of the day they were first issued.

In a manner characteristic of the Waverley series, *The Fortunes of Nigel* abounds in realistic detail. Often there is not the excess and little of the abstraction typical of the Romantic novel. In *The Fortunes of Nigel*, for example, an enormous variety of social strata are presented, the details of the characters' lives revealed, and their connections with other social groupings and classes dramatized. This sort of description is more exemplary of the historical Realist than of the historical Romantic. What separates *The Fortunes of Nigel* from the earlier Waverley group is the setting, which Scott chose to move from Scotland and the Scottish border to England. Although earlier readers and critics seem to have preferred the original setting, Scott's portrait of James I won him a much expanded audience south of the border.

Although the setting differs, the substance of the novel is similar to Scott's other work. *The Fortunes of Nigel* is about history—the social, personal, and political forces that comprise history; but in addition, the plot in *The Fortunes of Nigel* is less vivid than the scenes of life, of social contrasts and collisions, which appear throughout the book. Since Nigel is exceedingly passive and is more an observer of the action surrounding him than an active principal in it, he shares the plot's comparative weakness. The weakness of this character and the incidental nature of the plot led some contemporary critics of Scott, in reviewing *The Fortunes of Nigel*, to summarize its stereotyped features. In 1822, the *Quarterly Review* remarked:

"The poor passive hero is buffeted about in the usual manner, involved, as usual, in the chicaneries of civil process, and exposed to the dangers of a criminal execution, and rewarded by the hand of the heroine, such as she is, and the redemption of the mortgage on the family estate."

It is certainly true that Scott repeated himself from novel to novel. He wrote very rapidly, almost never reviewed or rewrote his own work, and was frequently guilty of poor and careless writing. At the same time, however, Scott was a master of describing social and historical clashes. Above all, he was concerned with the process of history—the confrontation between the old and the new. For example, in the opening pages of *The Fortunes of Nigel*, Scott draws a picture of the construction of a new palace by James I. As critics have remarked, the passage is designed to show the position of James I, a monarch poised between feudalism and mercantile capitalism, between Scotland and England, between the past and the present.

Scott was also highly sensitive in some cases to the English language and especially to the social and cultural contexts of dialect. In *The Fortunes of Nigel*, for example, Scott was able to switch fluently from Scots to English. Heriot, who uses formal English in his business transactions, finds himself speaking Scots when another character reminds him of home. The King himself uses an ornate, Latinized form in one social setting and then, for purposes of political image or personal satisfaction, returns to Scots or part Scots and part ornamented English.

Careful, polished writing, unhurried composition, and strong major characters have become bywords of modern literary criticism. As a result, the reputation of Sir Walter Scott has suffered an eclipse. Scott himself, in his introduction to *The Fortunes of Nigel*, shows an awareness of such questions—raised even in his own day—and tries to defend himself and his method of composition. Other critics, however, such as the Marxist George Lukàcs, argue that Scott was a great novelist. The introduction of history into the writing of novels, the vivid portrayal of social types, and the depiction of profound social and historical conflict, outweigh the stylistic and compositional faults of the novels for Lukàcs; and indeed, in addition to Lukàcs's comments, Scott's undeniable influence on writers such as Dumas, Cooper, Balzac, and Tolstoy only underscore his impact not only on his contemporaries but also on the history of fiction.

458

THE FORTUNES OF RICHARD MAHONY

Type of work: Novel
Author: Henry Handel Richardson (Ethel Richardson Robertson, 1870–1946)
Type of plot: Social chronicle
Time of plot: Nineteenth century
Locale: Australia
First published: 1930; *Australia Felix,* 1917; *The Way Home,* 1925; *Ultima Thule,* 1929

> *Principal characters:*
> RICHARD MAHONY, a doctor
> MARY, his wife
> PURDY SMITH, his friend
> JOHN TURNHAM, Mary's brother
> HENRY OCOCK, Richard's solicitor

The Story:

Richard Mahony was ill-suited to life in the Australian gold mines. A moderately successful doctor, he had left his practice in England and had gone to the colonies in hopes of a quick fortune. Having found the life of a digger unsuitable for him, he had taken what little money and goods he had left and set up a store; but he hated the raw country with bitter passion and longed for England and his native Ireland.

To that life, he brought his bride, Mary Turnham, whom he had met through an old schoolfriend, Purdy Smith. Purdy was as crude as Richard was fastidious. Mary wept at her new home, but she loved her husband, and she set about making the best of matters. The death of her baby matured and quieted her, but it did not kill her spirit.

When her sister-in-law died, Mary gladly cared for her children. Her other brothers and sisters, separated from their home in England, turned to her as they might a mother, and she comforted and encouraged them as she did her husband.

When Richard found his business declining, he decided to sell out and take Mary back to England. Mary, however, persuaded him instead to stay in Australia and set up a medical practice. With the help of Mary's brother, John Turnham, Richard borrowed enough money to buy a decent house and the necessary medical supplies. Henry Ocock, the son of a neighbor and a successful solicitor, arranged a loan and in other ways advised Richard.

Richard had a sudden stroke of luck. On Henry Ocock's advice, he had invested a small sum in some mining stock, Australia Felixes. The stock suddenly boomed, and Richard found himself a wealthy man overnight. As he prospered, so did his practice, until he had more than he could handle; but Richard began to assume an air that worried Mary. Thinking his old friends uncouth and crude, he wanted Mary to join more fashionable circles. She did so, but she quietly retained the old friendships as well.

After an exhausting illness brought on by overwork, Richard finally sold out his practice and prepared to return to England. He could return as he had always dreamed he would, rich and honored. They set sail—Richard with pride and Mary with sorrow.

In England and during their short visit in Ireland, Mary and Richard Mahony were welcomed and entertained. When Richard settled down to practice medicine again, however, he was twice scorned as a bushman from Australia, unfit to treat or to meet socially English snobs of the middle class. The snubs to Mary were the worst of all. Richard could not tolerate these, and so they returned to Australia. There Richard learned that his Australia Felix stocks had taken a new turn upward; he was wealthy beyond his wildest dreams. He bought a splendid house and called it Ultima Thule. To Mary's sorrow, he did not return to his practice. Feeling that he could retire and enjoy the quiet he had always desired, Richard turned to spiritualism and spent long hours in seances with charlatans and quacks, in spite of Mary's remonstrances and those of his friends. In the great house, he lived at times like a recluse with his books and fancies. Mary resumed her old ways with her friends and relatives. John remarried and had been widowed again; Mary once more had to care for John's children and soften his bitterness toward the world. John, successful in business and politics, was still dependent on Mary. Even after he married the third time, he could not find and hold the happiness that came naturally to his sister.

At last, Mary and Richard had the family they had hoped for. Mary gave birth to a son and, a year later, twin girls. Although they were getting on in years, Mary and Richard lavished all of their love and attention on the children; but Richard was withdrawing more and more from the world, and it was Mary who guided the children through their early days. Their happiness was marred when Mary's brother John died from cancer. Richard, although he no longer practiced medicine, had done everything possible to ease the sick man's pain. Then, because of Mary's grief after John's death, Richard decided to return to England. Ultima Thule was sold before the family left for the land Richard would always call home.

In England, Richard continued his preoccupation with spiritualism. He had for some time, even back in Australia, been bothered by weird dreams that became more frequent and confusing. Richard was convinced that he was actually communicating with the dead, but Mary could see that her husband was deteriorating in body and mind.

The worst blow of all came when he received news that the broker in charge of his financial affairs had absconded from Australia to America. Richard was completely ruined. Leaving Mary and the children to follow later, he left at once for Australia.

On his arrival in Australia, Richard learned that he had left only about three thousand pounds, and he was forced to resume his medical practice. When Mary and the children arrived, she found that in spite of his poverty he had lost none of his grand ideas. As they went from one miserable village to another, Richard's mental deterioration increased rapidly in the squalor in which they lived. His temper was short; he still scorned the old friends as louts to be avoided, and Mary had to meet them in secret. She herself suffered a shock that was almost too much for her to bear when Lallie, one of the twin girls, died a horrible, agonizing death. The tragedy, however, brought Mary and Richard close again, since Richard was her only comfort and strength. He insisted that Mary take the two remaining children for a vacation. Alone, Richard could no longer fight his strange dreams and illusions. His dead daughter appeared to him often, and the servant heard him talking to himself like a madman. In his depressed state of mind, he lost the pitifully few patients he had.

When Mary and the children returned, she found her husband seriously ill. After selling the house and her own few trinkets, she moved with Richard to an even more miserable town. There he grew steadily worse and once attempted suicide. Trying to manage, Mary put Richard in a private mental hospital and took a position as postmistress in a hovel far removed from any home they had ever known. When she had no more money to pay the hospital bills, she placed Richard, now mad, in a public asylum. When she tried to visit him and learned that he was being treated like a animal, she turned to her old friend, Henry Ocock, to help her get Richard out of the institution. At all costs, Richard should not die like a beast.

Richard went home at last. His sanity never returned, but on his deathbed, he looked at Mary and called her his dear wife. His words were all the reward Mary needed for her life of sacrifice for the husband buried in a strange land that could never claim his soul.

Critical Evaluation:

The publication of *Ultima Thule* in 1929 brought the first widespread popular success to Henry Handel Richardson, who had been known before that date to a small but dedicated group of admirers since her first novel, *Maurice Guest* (1908). In 1929, *Australia Felix* and *The Way Home*, by then out of print, were quickly revived, and the trilogy came out under the title of *The Chronicle of the Fortunes of Richard Mahony*.

Set in Australia in the period of the gold rush and based upon the experiences of her own parents, Richardson's trilogy is a brilliant and unsentimental treatment of the plight of a sensitive intellectual in the harsh environment of the Australian frontier. In contrast to many romanticized tales of adventure in the gold mines or the bush, Richardson wanted to deal with the problem of those who failed, who were unable to adapt to the strange hard world. Richard Mahony's tragedy is a personal, not a social one. There is no indictment of society as the cause of his decline. Those who possessed vigor, resourcefulness, and a large measure of common sense could survive and even prosper in the new land; but Mahony is doomed ultimately by his own nature, the inherent instability that keeps him always unsatisfied. As an educated Englishman and a doctor turned storekeeper, he is uncomfortable and inefficient. He turns to medical practice upon Mary's urging and succeeds as long as he relies upon her judgment; but restlessness seizes him, and he insists upon returning to England. Here the irony of the title *The Way Home* is revealed: the colonial becomes alienated from both the old and the new environments. Neither his native Ireland nor the England of his former life is now truly home for Mahony; both climate and people seem cramped and cold. Neither can Australia be a home for him as it becomes for Mary. On their return, his sense of alienation is exacerbated by their financial ruin, and his restlessness keeps them moving from place to place in a tragic attempt to find security. In *Ultima Thule*, the harrowing account of Mahony's deterioration into mental illness and of Mary's heroic devotion to him until his death forms a powerful conclusion to this superb trilogy.

FRAMLEY PARSONAGE

Type of work: Novel
Author: Anthony Trollope (1815–1882)
Type of plot: Domestic romance
Time of plot: 1850's
Locale: Barsetshire and London
First published: 1861

Principal characters:

MARK ROBARTS, the vicar of Framley in Barsetshire
FANNY, his wife
LUCY, his sister
LADY LUFTON, the mistress of Framley Court and Mark's
   benefactress
LORD LUFTON, her son and Mark's close friend
SOWERBY, the squire of Chaldicotes and an acquaintance of
   Lord Lufton and Mark
MISS DUNSTABLE, Sowerby's benefactress
DR. THORNE, the man she married

The Story:

Mark Robarts was the vicar of Framley, an appointment secured through Lady Lufton of Framley, who was very fond of him. He was ambitious, however, and he went to a house party at Chaldicotes, the estate of Mr. Sowerby, of whom Lady Lufton disapproved. Sowerby was notorious for living on other people's money, for he had long since run through his own fortune. While Mark was visiting him, Sowerby played on the vicar's sympathy to such an extent that Mark signed his name to a note for four hundred pounds. From Chaldicotes, Mark went to another house party at Gatherum Castle, home of the Duke of Omnium. The Duke of Omnium was also an enemy of Lady Lufton. Mark felt the contacts he would make at these parties would help him in climbing higher in his career.

When Mark returned home, he told Lord Lufton that he had signed a note for Sowerby. Young Lufton could hardly believe a man of Mark's position would do such a thing, for Mark could not afford to pay the note and certainly he would never recover the money from Sowerby. Before Mark told his wife, Fanny, about the debt he had incurred, his father died and his sister Lucy came to live at Framley parsonage. During the next three months, Lucy and Lord Lufton became very friendly. Lucy was a small girl without striking beauty; although inclined to be quiet, she found herself able to talk with great ease to Lord Lufton.

When Sowerby's note came due, he asked Mark to sign another note for five hundred pounds, a sum that would cover the first note and allow an additional hundred pounds for extras. Mark saw the treachery of Sowerby's scheme, but, unable to pay the note due, he was forced to sign.

Lady Lufton hinted to Fanny that she hoped to find a better match than Lucy for her son, but by this time, the two young people had fallen in love with each other. Also disturbed by Mark's attentions to the Chaldicotes set, Lady Lufton sent Mr. Crawley, a straitlaced clergyman from the nearby austere parish of Hogglestock, to remonstrate with Mark. After his visit, Mark resolved to act more in accordance with Lady Lufton's wishes.

One day, Lord Lufton declared his love for Lucy and asked her to marry him. Lucy, mindful of Lady Lufton's feelings, said she could not love him. Lufton was full of disappointment and grief.

Sowerby informed Mark that the new prime minister had it in his power to appoint the new precentor at Barchester Cathedral. Through Sowerby's influence, Mark received the appointment. He bought a racehorse from Sowerby to show his gratitude.

Sowerby, greatly in debt to the Duke of Omnium, was about to lose his estate. Sowerby's sister, Mrs. Harold Smith, was a close friend of Miss Dunstable, a middle-aged spinster whose father had left her a fortune made in patent medicine. Mrs. Smith suggested that Sowerby ask Miss Dunstable to marry him and to say frankly that he wanted her chiefly for her money, since Miss Dunstable herself was a forthright, outspoken woman. Sowerby sent his sister to propose for him. Although Miss Dunstable refused his proposal, she agreed to buy Chaldicotes and let Sowerby live in the house for the remainder of his life. She said she would marry only a man who was not interested in her money.

That man, she thought, was Dr. Thorne, a bachelor physician from Barsetshire. She had informed Dr. Thorne's niece of her admiration for him, and the niece had tried to show her uncle how wonderful life would be with Miss Dunstable. He was shocked at the idea of proposing. Although Miss Dunstable talked to him alone at a party she gave in London, Dr. Thorne said nothing at all about marriage. Back home, he decided that Miss Dunstable would, after all, make an admirable wife. He wrote her a letter of proposal and was accepted.

Lord Lufton went to Norway on a fishing trip. While he was away, Mrs. Crawley became ill of typhoid fever at Hogglestock, and Lucy went to nurse her through her sickness. The Crawley children were taken to Framley parsonage against Crawley's will, for he felt they might become accustomed to comforts he could not afford.

Sowerby's second note was coming due. Mark could consider no plan to get him out of his difficulty. If he had to go to jail, he would go. If he had to forfeit the furniture in his house, he would forfeit it; but under no circumstances would he ever put his name to another note.

Lord Lufton returned from Norway and learned from his mother that she thought Lucy insignificant. When he heard Lucy was at Hogglestock, he went there and again asked her to marry him. She replied that she did indeed love him, but she would not marry him unless his mother approved. At first, Lady Lufton refused to consider the match, but when she saw how determined her son was to have Lucy, she gave in and actually asked Lucy to become her daughter-in-law.

Meanwhile, the bailiffs had come to Framley parsonage to take inventory of the furniture, which was to be sold to pay Mark's obligations. When Lord Lufton discovered what was happening, he dismissed the bailiffs and persuaded Mark to accept a loan for payment of the note.

Sowerby lived at Chaldicotes for only a short time before he disappeared, and Mark was relieved of worry over his foolish debt. Miss Dunstable married Dr. Thorne and moved into the house at Chaldicotes after the departure of Sowerby. Lucy married Lord Lufton and became mistress, at least nominally, of Framley Court. Fate seemed to have for each some fair reward.

Critical Evaluation:

This novel, the fourth of the Barsetshire series, was brought out in the newly launched *Cornhill* magazine. Edited by William Makepeace Thackeray, it was an immensely popular success. Anthony Trollope's focus is on the social milieu and on the moral choices that confront his characters. Two clergymen are juxtaposed in the novel; both are good men, but one is too easily lured by worldly ambition, and the other is too proud to accept help. Mark Robarts learns painfully that he is essentially too naïve to cope with the accomplished chicanery of people like Sowerby and to engage in the political sophistries of the circle surrounding the Duke of Omnium. He ultimately retreats to the security of Lady Lufton's patronage and the knowledge that his brush with the vultures of the larger world enables him to appreciate the felicities of his position at Framley Court. It is Trollope's particular genius that this resolution is made to seem fulfilling rather than defeatist. In contrast, the Reverend Josiah Crawley is unworldly to the point of excess. His selfless dedication to the ministry represents a type of clergyman that Trollope sees as becoming regrettably obsolete in the increasingly materialistic society of the nineteenth century; nevertheless, Crawley's asceticism and his refusal to seek worldly advancement (or even to accept it when offered) brings needless suffering to his poverty-stricken family.

The women in the novel similarly confront moral choices. Lucy Robarts is no meek ingenue; a young lady of spirit, Lucy loves young Lord Lufton but is willing to give up both love and social position rather than be accused by his mother of social climbing. Griselda Grantly, however, has no such scruples. She coldly sets about using her great beauty and imposing manner to capture Lord Dumbello and succeeds despite the absence of real affection between them. Lady Lufton represents the kind of mixed character that is Trollope's special accomplishment: she is both domineering and kindhearted, both arrogant and willing at last to bend. She most nearly illustrates Trollope's thesis: that those are happiest who can adapt to social change.

FRANKENSTEIN
Or, The Modern Prometheus

Type of work: Novel
Author: Mary Wollstonecraft Shelley (1797–1851)
Type of plot: Gothic romance
Time of plot: Eighteenth century
Locale: Europe
First published: 1818

       Principal characters:
           ROBERT WALTON, an explorer
           VICTOR FRANKENSTEIN, an inventor
           ELIZABETH, his foster sister
           WILLIAM, his brother
           JUSTINE, the Frankensteins' servant
           CLERVAL, Victor's friend
           THE MONSTER

The Story:

Walton was an English explorer whose ship was held fast in polar ice. As the company looked out over the empty ice field, they were astonished to see a sledge drawn by dogs speeding northward. The sledge driver looked huge and misshapen. That night, an ice floe carried to the ship another sledge, one dog, and a man in weakened condition. When the newcomer learned that his was the second sledge sighted from the ship, he became agitated.

Walton was greatly attracted to the man during his convalescence, and as they continued fast in the ice, the men had leisure time to get acquainted. At last, after he had recovered somewhat from exposure and hunger, the man told Walton his story.

Victor Frankenstein was born of good family in Geneva. As a playmate for their son, the parents had adopted a lovely little girl of the same age. Victor and Elizabeth grew up as brother and sister. Much later another son, William, was born to the Frankensteins.

At an early age, Victor showed promise in the natural sciences. He devoured the works of Paracelsus and Albertus Magnus and thought in his ignorance that they were the real masters. When he grew older, his father decided to send Victor to the university at Ingolstadt. There he soon learned all that his masters could teach him in the field of natural science. Engaged in brilliant and terrible research, he stumbled by chance on the secret of creating life. Once he had gained this knowledge, he could not rest until he had employed it to create a living being. By haunting the butcher shops and dissecting rooms, he soon had the necessary raw materials. With great cunning, he fashioned an eight-foot monster and endowed him with life.

As soon as he had created his monster, however, he was subject to strange misgivings. During the night, the monster came to his bed. At the sight of the horrible face, he shrieked and frightened the monster away. The horror of his act prostrated him with a brain fever. His best friend, Henry Clerval, arrived from Geneva and helped to nurse him through his illness. He was unable to tell Clerval what he had done.

Terrible news came from Geneva. William, Victor's young brother, was dead by the hand of a murderer. He had been found strangled in a park, and a faithful family servant, Justine, had been charged with the crime. Victor hurried to Geneva.

At the trial, Justine told a convincing story. She had been looking for William in the countryside and, returning after the city gates had been closed, had spent the night in a deserted hut; but she could not explain how a miniature from William's neck came to be in her pocket. Victor and Elizabeth believed the girl's story, but despite all of their efforts, Justine was convicted and condemned.

Depressed by these tragic events, Victor went hiking over the mountainous countryside. Far ahead on the glacier, he saw a strange, agile figure that filled him with horrible suspicions. Unable to overtake the figure, he sat down to rest. Suddenly, the monster appeared before him. The creature demanded that Victor listen to his story.

When he left Victor's chambers in Ingolstadt, everyone he met screamed and ran away. Wandering confusedly, the monster finally found shelter in an abandoned hovel adjoining a cottage. By great stealth, he remained there during daylight and at night sought berries for food. Through observation, he began to learn the ways of man. Feeling an urge to friendship, he brought wood to the cottage every day; but when he attempted to make friends with the cottagers, he was repulsed with such fear and fury that his heart became bitter toward all men. When he saw William playing in the park, he strangled the boy and took the miniature from his neck. Then during the night, he came upon Justine in the hut and put the picture in her pocket.

Presently, the monster made a horrible demand. He insisted that Victor fashion a mate for him who would give him love and companionship. The monster threatened to ravage and kill at random if Victor refused the request; but if Victor agreed, the monster promised to take his mate to the wilds of South America where they would never again be seen by man. It was a hard choice, but Victor felt that he must accept.

Victor left for England with his friend Clerval. After parting from his friend, he went to the distant Orkneys and began his task. He was almost ready to animate the gross mass of flesh when his conscience stopped him.

He could not let the two monsters mate and spawn a race of monsters. He destroyed his work.

The monster was watching at a window. Angered to see his mate destroyed, he forced his way into the house and warned Victor that a terrible punishment would fall upon the young man on his wedding night. Then the monster escaped by sea. Later, to torment his maker, he fiendishly killed Clerval.

Victor was suspected of the crime. Released for lack of evidence, he went back to Geneva. He and Elizabeth were married there. Although Victor was armed and alert, the monster got into the nuptial chamber and strangled the bride. Victor shot at him, but he escaped again. Victor vowed eternal chase until the monster could be killed.

That was Victor's story. Weakened by exposure, he died there in the frozen North with Elizabeth, William, Justine, and Clerval unavenged. Then the monster came to the dead man's cabin, and Walton, stifling his fear, addressed the gigantic, hideous creature. Victor's was the greater crime, the monster said. He had created a man, a man without love or friend or soul. He deserved his punishment. After his speech, the monster vanished over the ice field.

Critical Evaluation:

Although Mary Wollstonecraft Shelley wrote other novels, such as *The Last Man* (1824) and *Lodore* (1835), she is remembered in literary history as the wife of Percy Bysshe Shelley and as the author of *Frankenstein*. The subject for her book arose in a discussion between her husband and Lord Byron. Although it is interesting to speculate whether Mary Shelley was influenced in writing her book by her relationship with either poet, the book itself does not reveal such facts. Nevertheless Shelley, like Victor Frankenstein, fancied himself an amateur scientist as well as a professional humanitarian; and both Shelleys suffered from the hatred of conventional people when they outraged the public sense of decency. At any rate, one theme of the novel is the unjust persecution of an outcast from society. The revenge of that outcast, the creature of Frankenstein, has become part of the popular imagination.

Frankenstein superficially resembles Ann Radcliffe's *The Mysteries of Udolpho* (1794), Matthew Gregory Lewis' *The Monk* (1796), and Charles Robert Maturin's *Melmoth the Wanderer* (1820). Like these Romances of suggested or actual physical horror, Shelley's novel is steeped in sentimental melancholy. Unlike most Gothic novels, however, *Frankenstein: Or, The Modern Prometheus* is at least partially philosophical and offers a scientific rather than supernatural explanation for the horror.

Indeed, for its serious ideas the novel more closely resembles *St. Leon* (1799) by Mary Shelley's father, William Godwin. As an illustration of the humanitarian philosophy of Jean Jacques Rousseau, *Frankenstein* shows the destructive results of undeveloped affection. The creature (who is at the time of his composition a "monster" only to the fearful and ignorant) craves but is denied ordinary human tenderness. Rejected as a man, he becomes a vengeful monster. Although he is given vital existence by science, he is never fully alive. Victor Frankenstein's science (or rather pseudoscience of vitalism, a belief in the "vital spark") is unable to produce a creature capable of attracting love. Instead, his scientific genius creates death—a theme that appears rarely in nineteenth century literature but is a major one in the twentieth century.

Readers familiar with the popular motion picture adaptations of *Frankenstein* during the 1930's—or, indeed, with the more accurate version produced by Christopher Isherwood and Don Bachardy for television in the 1970's—are likely to be surprised when they come upon Mary Shelley's novel. The book is considerably richer in details, fuller in its development of minor characters, and more complicated in plot structure than later adaptations and parodies; it also treats the creature from a significantly different point of view. Contrary to the popular stereotypes of the Frankenstein monster, he is articulate and, at least in the beginning, quite sympathetic. His revenge, although excessive, is motivated. From a modern reader's assessment, he is a monster too sentimental to be wholly frightening. Nevertheless, *Frankenstein*, for all of its appeal to modern readers, represents the culmination of a tradition of nineteenth century Gothic horror on the one hand and sentimentalism on the other. Given a different philosophical orientation, much of that horror is bound to be misunderstood. What is remarkable, to be sure, is that so much survives.

FRATERNITY

Type of work: Novel
Author: John Galsworthy (1867–1933)
Type of plot: Social criticism
Time of plot: Early twentieth century
Locale: London
First published: 1909

Principal characters:
HILARY DALLISON, a wealthy writer
BIANCA, his wife and an artist
STEPHEN, his brother
CECILIA, Stephen's wife and Bianca's sister
THYME, daughter of Stephen and Cecilia
MR. STONE, father of Bianca and Cecilia
IVY BARTON, a model
MRS. HUGHS, a seamstress
MR. HUGHS, her husband

The Story:

Bianca Dallison had begun the chain of events by asking her writer husband to find a model for her painting "The Shadow." Through a friendly artist, Hilary had located a girl from the country who suited his wife. The girl, Ivy Barton, was very attractive, and after she had finished posing for Bianca, the Dallisons tried to help her find work. They had also found her a place to live with the Dallisons' seamstress, Mrs. Hughs.

Ivy Barton, through no fault of her own, began to create trouble in the Hughs household when Mr. Hughs became enamored of her and Mrs. Hughs became extremely jealous. One day, Mrs. Hughs told Cecilia Dallison her troubles at home. Cecilia told Mrs. Hughs's story to the rest of the family. The Dallisons, all very much interested in social problems, wished to help the girl and the Hughs family; but the situation was a delicate one. Their interest was heightened by the comment of Mr. Stone that in the lower classes each of them had a counterpart, a shadow, and that everyone was bound together by the bonds of fraternity in the brotherhood of man. Mr. Stone was writing a book on that very subject.

Hilary Dallison found that the girl's work as a model was not regular and that she was finding it necessary to pose in the nude. He found her steady employment as a copyist for his father-in-law, Mr. Stone, who in his old age had embarked upon his strange philosophical work on the brother-hood of man. Bianca Dallison did not like the idea, for Mr. Stone lived with her and her husband. She began to be extremely jealous of the little model, although it had been years since she and her husband had lived as man and wife.

In spite of his wife's jealousy, it was Hilary who first investigated the trouble at the Hughs's home. He found only Mr. Hughs there. The visit only made the situation worse, for Hughs became convinced that Hilary was having an affair with Ivy. Hughs began to loiter about the Dallison house and to follow the model home when she finished her work with Mr. Stone. When Cecilia also learned that Hughs was beating his wife, the fam-ily decided that the situation was dangerous for the model and for Hilary. Cecilia tried to convince Hilary that the girl should be sent away and that he should stop trying to help Mr. and Mrs. Hughs. He only smiled at her suggestions.

Sometime later, Hilary followed Hughs when he saw him trailing Ivy home. Hilary was somewhat dismayed to discover that Hughs followed only to prevent the girl from meeting anyone else, including Hilary. Neverthe-less, Hilary met the girl in a park after she had shaken her follower. Ivy let Hilary notice that her clothing was very shabby; feeling sorry for her, he took her into a shop and purchased a complete outfit for her. His deed won her complete devotion; she was in love with Hilary Dallison.

After leaving Ivy at the store where they had purchased her outfit, Hilary went to spend the evening at his club; he knew that his wife would not mind his absence from her. When he got home, however, he found her in his room. They kissed and for a moment forgot they had agreed not to live as man and wife. Then the moment passed, and Bianca fled to her room. Needing someone to talk to, Hilary went down to Mr. Stone's room and had a cup of cocoa.

The daughter of Stephen and Cecilia Dallison, Thyme, also tried to help the Hughs family. Her interest was the Hughs's tiny baby. She also noted that Ivy had new clothes and guessed that her uncle had bought them for the girl. The word quickly ran through the family, and Stephen, trying to make Hilary see how the others looked at the situation, told him that Bianca was bound to be jealous, even though they did not live as man and wife. Hilary felt that the celibacy she imposed on him had taken away any grounds for jealousy she might have.

That same afternoon, Hughs went to the Dallison home and tried to tell Bianca about her husband's affair with Ivy. Although she refused to listen, the incident roused her emotions and suspicions. At least, her pride was hurt. That evening, Hilary and Bianca tried to talk over the matter, but all they succeeded in doing was hurting each other. Bianca refused to believe that her husband was innocent of any intentions toward the model and had simply bought the girl some clothing because he felt sorry for her.

With his sister-in-law's help, Hilary found another room for Ivy. Hoping to solve the problem of Bianca's jealousy, he also told her not to come to his house to copy for Mr. Stone. When Hughs returned home that night and learned that Ivy had left his house, he beat his wife and wounded her with a bayonet. As a result, he was put into prison for several weeks. During the time he was in prison, the Hughs's baby died; Mrs. Hughs had been too upset to nurse him.

At the same time, old Mr. Stone became very ill and unhappy. He missed the company of the model as well as the copying she had done for him. In an effort to help her father, Bianca sought out Ivy and had her return to be with the old man part of every day. Because of his child's death and the girl's return to work at Hilary's house, it seemed as if the problem would still be unsolved when Hughs returned from prison.

To avoid a repetition of the whole distasteful situation, Hilary resolved to go to Europe. Although Ivy was in love with him and wished to go along, he made up his mind that he would go alone. His wife, because of her conscience, resolved to help the girl in Hilary's absence. When she went to the girl's room, however, she found her belongings packed. It dawned on her that in spite of his resolve her husband was taking the model with him. Bianca left the house in a fury just as her husband arrived. Her jealousy and anger, however, were wasted; after she left, when Ivy kissed him, Hilary realized that he could never live for long with a girl from the lower classes. Flinging all the money he had with him on the bed, he left alone. He took a room in London and then sent a letter to Bianca through his brother Stephen. He told her of his decision to stop seeing Ivy and his further decision not to return to an unsatisfying marriage.

Critical Evaluation:

In both his novels and his plays, John Galsworthy reflected the social problems of his age. His conscience was bothered by the lack of understanding shown by the members of his own class, the intellectual and moneyed upper-middle class. In this novel, as in the others, his social satire is expressed by a delineation of the complacency of the upper classes rather than by an analysis of the lower classes and their situation. Here also, as in other works, his diagnosis is not profound, nor does he attempt to offer any remedy for the problems he shows. Some readers may feel that this volume shows how Galsworthy's efforts to understand his age and his indignation at what he finds lead to no satisfactory solution in the end. *Fraternity*, however, is generally regarded as one of Galsworthy's best works of fiction, aside from that series of upper-middle class novels upon which his fame rests, *The Forsyte Saga*.

Fraternity, the third of a four-volume series satirizing affluent society—

in the words of the author, "my long four volume image of England's upper crust"—deals with the subject of cultured aesthetic intellectuals of London. They are filled with idealism, but their self-consciousness and complacency prevent them from acting in any substantial manner.

The novel's earlier, rejected title, "Shadows," and the later title that became affixed to it are both appropriate, for Galsworthy presents two levels of society, the artistic intellectuals and the wretched slum dwellers, each of which are "shadows" of the other, as revealed throughout the novel by the shifting point of view. At the same time, the upper-class Dallison family is going through the superficial motions of conceptualizing a "fraternity" of all men, much like the supposed vision in Mr. Stone's apocalyptic "Book of Universal Brotherhood."

All the Dallisons' altruistic notions remain in the abstract, however, for the family represents "a section of society...who speculated on ideas,"and their self-consciousness and fidelity to convention paralyze them from taking any affirmative action. While most of the family flatter themselves by simply thinking about equality in society yet shrinking in fear from the thought that it might ever happen, three characters make a move forward but suffer for their transgression.

Hilary Dallison's attraction to and sympathy for Ivy Barton overtly manifests itself as a gesture to lift her out of her poor existence. Beyond this, however, Hilary is also paradoxically attracted by her sexuality while repulsed with fear at the risk to his own status in actually bringing about any union of the two levels of society. In response to this dilemma, he relies upon the expediency of a monetary gift to her and flees from the impending necessity to make a decision and commit himself to action. Fear motivates Hilary's behavior and defeats Thyme's attempt at unification with the lower strata of society. When she goes among them, she feels the strength and security of her station drain off and flow into them, and she fears the transformation that creates the "unreality of her intruding presence." As for the elder Mr. Stone, finally, fear was not his defeat as it was for the other two; rather, his overzealous commitment to the idea of a universal brotherhood and his agonized efforts to put into concrete terms the essence and elements of that concept drove him to defeat in madness, perhaps because readers are meant to feel that the consummation of his plan is an impossibility.

While *Fraternity* most clearly exposes the moral paralysis among the cultured upper classes, the slum dwellers are also paralyzed by their immersion in dreams, never to be fulfilled, and resignation to a poverty-stricken existence. Joshua Creed typifies the character of the slum dweller; while he ekes out a living selling newspapers in the slum, his thoughts are directed to the far-off, attractive Mayfair. His one expectation is death, and his only ambition is to be "respectable," both during and at the end of his life.

Galsworthy supplies no answers or solutions to the dilemma he has presented in *Fraternity*. Through the Dallisons' frustrations, complacency, sensitivity, and self-consciousness, his main purpose was to show how the intellectual segment of the country had been paralyzed by too many years of money and ease; they are unable to act in any decisive manner for the real benefit of anyone or even to resolve their own moral questions and dilemmas.

FREE FALL

Type of work: Novel
Author: William Golding (1911–   )
Type of plot: Symbolic fable
Time of plot: The 1920's to World War II
Locale: England and a German prison camp
First published: 1959

> *Principal characters:*
> SAMMY MOUNTJOY, the narrator and an artist
> BEATRICE IFOR, a young woman whom he seduced
> NICK SHALES, a science teacher
> MISS ROWENA PRINGLE, a Bible teacher
> JOHNNY SPRAGGE and
> PHILIP ARNOLD, Sammy's schoolfellows

V. S. Pritchett has called William Golding the most promising of English novelists. Frank Kermode considers him the most significant figure in the English novel since the 1920's. Philip Toynbee has announced that he is a writer to be examined with scrupulous interest and respect and one to be criticized only on the highest level. Golding himself has said that he sees little point at all in writing novels unless he can do something that he did not think he could do or that nobody else has tried before.

Under the circumstances, anything that this writer attempts is likely to be viewed with sharper attention than most reviewers give the average novel. This was the case in English literary circles in the autumn of 1959, when *Free Fall* was published. Few novels of recent years have received a better advance press or have been awaited with keener anticipation. Therefore, there was considerable disappointment and some surprise when the word out of England was that the novel did not live up to the expectations that the previous performances of Golding gave critics and readers every right to expect. The book's reception in this country early in 1960 turned out to be considerably less severe. Generally, American critics praised the writer for his vigor of imagination and expert technical control in a work of considerable moral implication and symbolic proportion.

The response to Golding's novel on this side of the Atlantic poses an interesting problem: Are Americans better conditioned to novels of existential themes, moral ambiguity, prophetic vision, philosophical weight, experimental structures, and a style richly textured by imagery and metaphor? This question is asked not to provoke a controversy but to suggest that Golding stands closer to William Faulkner or Robert Penn Warren or Saul Bellow, say, than to the tradition of the English novel. Like these writers, he is apocalyptic rather than social in his effects, and he exhibits in his fiction a central theme that he has been extending and elaborating from book to book until the whole pattern is beginning to take shape at last. His subject is immense: the fall and the bitter fruits of lost innocence. Each of his books has been, in effect, a point of reference where these great co-ordinates intersect with hairline precision on the graph of man's fate. Therefore, *Free Fall* cannot be discussed, as many critics tried to do, apart from Golding's larger design. The novel is a continuation—almost a cul-mination—of everything that he had written before.

William Golding had published three novels before *Free Fall* appeared. The best known is *Lord of the Flies*, a savagely ironic fable that reversed the subject matter and theme of R. M. Ballantyne's nineteenth century success, *The Coral Island*. In Ballantyne's romantic story, a group of young English castaways exhibit the most admirable traits of the public school tradition—courage, quickness of imagination, teamwork, pluck, and pas-sionate sympathy. Golding's account is exactly the opposite. His youngsters, survivors of a plane crash while being evacuated during an atomic war, quickly revert to the ruthless law of the jungle. The story is not only an account of the way in which man returns to his primitive state when the re-straints of civilization are removed; it is also an extended metaphor of the Garden and man's fall from his state of innocence and unsought grace. *The Inheritors* is another excursion into the primitive and a period removed in time. This novel deals with the last of "the people," a tribe of Neanderthal men, wiped out by "the others" who have invaded their hunting ground. These "others" are the human clan, already marked as Homo sapiens by their powers of reason; thus, they are conscious of their propensity for evil. In these novels, sin and guilt are shown as inherent in the nature of man.

The Two Deaths of Christopher Martin—its English title was *Pincher Martin*—is a story of fallen man brought to judgment. Christopher Martin is a naval officer engaged in a grim struggle for survival after his ship has been sunk by a submarine in the North Atlantic Ocean. His refuge is a solitary rock in the ocean waste. His struggle is twofold: between extinction and survival on the one hand, salvation on the other. In the course of his wretched life, Christopher (the Christ-bearer) has become Pincher, the liar, the thief, the impenitent. His experience on the rock shows that in his struggle to survive—metaphorically, to be saved—reason and intelligence are not enough.

These three novels examine the human condition under as many dif-ferent lights. The isolation of each case by space or by time is deliberate; Golding's chief concern in them is not the relationship of man to man but man to himself and to the presence of evil as inseparable from the human consciousness and will. *Lord of the Flies* deals with the absence of in-nocence, *The Inheritors* with man's relationship of guilt to the prehuman past, *The Two Deaths of Christopher Martin* with his relation to the life to come. In addition, each of these novels relies upon a "gimmick"—the term is Golding's—for its final effect. At the end of each novel, there is a surprising reversal of the point of view or the introduction of an unexpected metaphor in the light of which everything that has gone before must be reviewed and reinterpreted. In *Lord of the Flies*, the boys are rescued as the result of undergrowth set afire during a murderous manhunt, a situation which a British officer fails to understand in its true light, seeing it only as a childish game. *The Inheritors* ends with a switch from the point of view of "the people" to that of "the others," the guilty destroyers of innocence. In *The Two Deaths of Christopher Martin*, the gimmick is the discovery that the dead man is still wearing his sea boots when his body washes ashore: his struggle for survival has been only a fleeting series of images in a drowning man's mind.

The position of these three points on the graph point inevitably to the fourth, the theme of man's relationship to man developed in *Free Fall*. Rich in imagery, the opening paragraphs set the tone, images intended to reveal the contrast between the rationalistic world of "statistical probability" and the world of sin, remorse, and salvation suggested by the ecclesiastical purple and white, the shepherd's crook, the beam of divine light falling like fire, the pentecostal vision. These meanings may not be clear at the start, for their true significance cannot be interpreted until after the narrator has undergone a transforming experience in a Nazi prison camp and emerges into the light of day once more. In the light of Golding's conclusion, however, they give harmony and proportion to the novel as Sammy Mountjoy reviews the course of his life and tries to determine the point at which he fell, the occasion of that decision, freely made, which cost him his freedom.

The story is told in a series of brilliantly presented flashbacks, in which Sammy Mountjoy, a successful artist, traces his life from its beginning in an anarchic Kentish slum to his moment of revelation. Chronology is distorted but never arbitrarily or with self-indulgence; the events of Sammy's life are not important in the order in which they happened buy only as their meaning is disclosed. He never knew a father, and his mother was a drunken prostitute. A tainted priest rescued him from the sordid surroundings of his childhood after he had desecrated a church altar. His school-day friends were Johnny Spragge and Philip Arnold. (Johnny, he realizes years later, was a young tough protected by his own hard innocence, but Philip was evil because he acted out of reasoned cunning, not healthy instinct.) Like another youthful Samuel, Sammy mistook his vocation, found his spiritual parents in Nick Shales, a science teacher, and a Bible teacher, Miss Rowena Pringle (whom he rejected), studied art, seduced his first love, abandoned her and married another, was a member of the Communist Party for a time, went off to war and in a German prison camp came near betraying a plot to escape. At the end of each episode, he asks himself if this is the point at which he lost his freedom and fell from grace. The answer is always a flat no.

He finally realizes that the point of his fall was not in his childhood, for young Sammy Mountjoy had no choice; but by the time he seduced Beatrice, he had already given himself to guilt. The knowledge he seeks comes to him in a scene of shocking power after a Gestapo psychologist has threatened him with torture and ordered him locked in a dark cell to soften him up for betrayal. There he undergoes agonies of terror, because his imagination transforms a harmless object left on the floor into a dismembered sex organ—symbol of his own carnality—and he finds in his terror his own severance from the world of moral reality and responsibility. Released from the lightless cell, he goes out into the world of men, with the ironic apology of a Nazi official, the statement that the psychologist does not know about people, ringing in his ears.

He is then able to realize that the moment of his fall came when he decided to possess Beatrice Ifor, thus abandoning his concern for others and using them for his own selfish ends. Dante had found in the image of Beatrice an illuminative vision of the possible in man. Sammy Mountjoy had made Beatrice the object of his lust. A further revelation comes when Sammy visits the mental institution where Beatrice is a patient and learns that he can never know whether he caused her madness or whether, as the doctor suggests, he may have given her an extra period of sanity before her mind clouded over. All he knows is that the girl is both Beatrice, the spiritual vision he denied, and Miss Ifor, the creature shaped by his selfishness and pride. Given the chance to live by his vision, he had chosen a world of calculation and force. That was his moment of error, not the deed itself but the failure to recognize the relation of man to man—not to be viewed as an irrelevance but as the forge in which change and value are shaped to some good or evil design.

Golding makes no concessions to his readers. *Free Fall* is a powerful fable of the duality of man and is impressive despite the flaw to which criticism has already pointed. Sammy Mountjoy is both protagonist and commentator, and in his sin of despair, he denies what the novel itself affirms, the gift of mercy and grace to the undeserving. Although not perfectly achieved as a whole, *Free Fall* is nevertheless tremendously moving and meaningful in its parts. A partial failure by Golding can be more illuminating and instructive than many a writer's best.

THE GARDEN

Type of work: Novel
Author: L. A. G. Strong (1896–1958)
Type of plot: Impressionistic realism
Time of plot: Early twentieth century
Locale: Ireland
First published: 1931

Principal characters:
DERMOT GRAY, an Anglo-Irish boy who spends his holidays in
Ireland
MRS. GRAY, his mother
MR. GRAY, his father
EITHNE, his sister
GRANNY, his mother's mother
GRANDPAPA, his mother's father
BEN McMANUS, Dermot's uncle
AUNT PATRICIA, Ben's wife
CON, their son
EILEEN, their daughter
PADDY KENNEDY, a cripple

The Story:

The first time Dermot remembered coming into an Irish port he was so young that he had to keep reminding himself to look for his Granny. He, his younger sister Eithne, and his mother came to Dublin each year to spend the summer at Granny's house. Dermot remembered only that there had been a monkey and a cat there the summer before.

After the trip by boat across the Irish Sea, they rode in a carriage, a train, and then a tram before they reached Sandycove, where Grandpapa was leaning over the gate waiting to meet them. To Dermot and his mother, the cottage at Sandycove was really home, a place they loved as they could never love their home in England.

Besides such delights as Paddy-monkey and Pucker the cat, Dermot was glad to see once more the comfortable dining room with its loaded table. He loved the china, the little bone spoon with which he ate his egg, the different foods, and the corner where Grandpapa kept the well-worn books he taught Dermot to read.

Granny's garden was all mixed up in his mind with the Garden of Eden. That summer he spent most of his time there, playing with Paddy-monkey who was chained near the kitchen door, hunting for snails among the plants, investigating the farther reaches of the orchard that he had not known when he was smaller, and helping the gardener chase the half-wild cats that tore down the bushes.

There were two things he did not like about Sandycove. One was the walk far out on the pier in wild weather, while the nurse wheeled Eithne. The other was to be surrounded by Granny's gushing friends before and after church. He felt closer to his Grandpapa when the old gentleman stubbornly refused to stand in front of the church with the women but waited instead in a park across the way.

Often on Sunday afternoons, Dermot's cousins from Dalkey came to visit, sometimes accompanied by Uncle Ben, a boisterous retired mariner who was also, Dermot discovered, a strict puritan. Two of Uncle Ben's four children came often: Con, a strapping lad of twenty-one years, and Eileen, a lovely girl a few years younger. They were tremendously alive. Dermot, who had always been considered delicate, was exuberant when he was with his cousins.

The McManuses lived at Delgany on a cliff running down to the sea. Their house was full of all kinds of wonders, such as a telescope, the dried jaws of a whale, a painted wooden pig, and a bathroom with no taps. Ben and his family lived a carefree life that left Dermot breathless; it was so unlike the precise life he lived in England. Uncle Ben could answer Dermot's questions in more exact detail than anyone else, excepting perhaps Grandpapa; and even Grandpapa was likely to go on after the interesting part had been answered.

That year Uncle Ben, Con, and Eileen took Dermot in a boat to an island out from their home. There, while they were having a picnic, they looked up to see a ring of goats ranged on the rocks above them. It was a picture Dermot could not forget, and the trip was the first of countless excursions with the McManuses. That fall, as he sailed home to England, he looked back as long as he could see the Dalkey coast. Two years passed before he came back.

In England, before the plumbers laid a pipe in the Grays' yard, Dermot decorated a length of it by printing the plumber's name. Because he had used a chisel for the printing, he pierced the pipe. After it had been laid, the pipe leaked until the yard was a morass. Dermot confessed to his mother his fears that he had ruined the pipe but asked her not to tell his father. She had to tell Mr. Gray, of course, but he spoke kindly to Dermot when he asked the boy to be more careful the next time. A week later, Dermot was still amazed at his father's unusual patience. To please Mr. Gray, he decorated the halls with horses' heads in chalk. His father blasted him for defacing the house, and Dermot slunk away, cowed by the anger he had inadvertently brought on. He was afraid of his father, but when Mr.

Gray became very sick, Dermot was afraid for him as well.

After two years, the Grays again went to Ireland. They did so each summer until the year of World War I. As Dermot grew older, his Granny hired a crippled lad to teach the boy to fish and to watch over him. It was a grand day when Dermot caught his first conger. Paddy Kennedy and his pals, Long Mike Hogan and Peg-leg O'Shea, taught Dermot a great tolerance for the poor people that he could never have learned elsewhere, but they were careful not to allow any obscenity in his presence. He learned that in his public school.

Mr. Gray always arrived for his holiday just before the time came for the family to return to England. One year, he connived with the gardener to rid the place of the worst of the marauding cats that Grandpapa had refused to kill. To Dermot's surprise and delight, Mr. Gray allowed the boy to watch for Black Tom and Lord Spenser and let him, without the old gentleman's knowledge, shoot them.

As Eithne grew older, she was asked to accompany Dermot to Delgany. The children thrived at the house and adored their cousins; soon it became a ritual for them to spend a full week there each summer. Con, who had never really grown up, always made a special effort to entertain Dermot and his sister. If he could think of nothing else, he drove them around the country on his motorbike. Eileen also entered into their entertainment. For her, Dermot had a fondness verging on adoration.

The last year the Grays went to Ireland, Dermot was studying to enter Oxford. Riding the motorbike to take Eileen to a tennis match that summer, Dermot, Con, and Eileen all felt a strange lowering of their spirits at the same time. Soon afterward, another bike with two riders passed them and crashed into a post. Con and Eileen took care of the dead man and the injured one. Dermot, finally grown up, realized that he could face such a scene.

Although Eithne was only fourteen years old, Con asked Dermot if he thought his sister would marry him. Dermot recommended that Con wait. He knew, however, that Eithne adored her cousin.

Both Dermot and Con were killed only a day apart during the war. When Eithne went back to Ireland to visit Eileen and Aunt Patricia, the only ones left in the family, she told them that a letter from Con had arrived just after Dermot died, a letter written the day before Con himself was killed. Eithne had felt torn apart at losing the two who had meant most to her, but she felt better, after reading the letter, to think that Con and Dermot were together and surely happy.

Critical Evaluation:

The qualities that make this novel a book of rare and rich experience are the writer's exquisite, unspoiled perceptions of childhood and his memories of a lost world which delighted a small boy. Behind this tale of nostalgic reminiscence there is a subtle contrast of backgrounds and characters, and this blending of temperamental differences of race and culture gives a more tangible flavor and substance to L. A. G. Strong's biographical novel.

The Garden is a tender tale of Dermot's development from a boy into a young man. During most of his holidays, from a time he can barely remember to his last one in 1914, the English lad visits his grandparents and cousins in Ireland, "the dearest and loveliest place in the world," where one can see for "one hundred and ten miles." Eventually he grows up, and he and his cousin go off to die in a war. The story is beautifully told. Strong displays the narrative qualities of a gifted *raconteur*; his style is crisp and expressive, and his humor is gentle and without malice as he unfolds the life of Dermot. The author obviously has great empathy with his characters; he is sometimes sentimental, but the book is saved by the simplicity of its development. The novel is rich in dialogue, and most of Strong's characterizations are clear.

One of the most important decisions Dermot must make while growing up is whether to choose the matter-of-fact religion of his mother or the simple, demonstrative faith of his cousins. The latter faith makes life easier to live; it impresses him so much that he appreciates the sense of it, although his intellect tells him that it has not been fully explained. Dermot loves the ritual of his grandparents' church during his earlier childhood, and the stained glass window with Christ walking on the water is one of his delights. His favorite scripture, "Heaviness may endure for the night; but joy cometh in the morning," is his epitaph.

In the epilogue, after the deaths of Dermot and his cousin, Dermot's sister tells their cousin, Eileen, that she likes to think of them together, happy and laughing at her confusion about the faith of which her aunt said, "seems easy enough to me. It's the living of it that's hard."

THE GOOD COMPANIONS

Type of work: Novel
Author: J. B. Priestley (1894–1984)
Type of plot: Picaresque romance
Time of plot: The 1920's
Locale: England
First published: 1929

Principal characters:
MISS TRANT, a wealthy British woman
INIGO JOLLIFANT, a teacher at a boys' school
JESS OAKROYD, a workman
SUSIE DEAN, a comedienne
JERRY JERNINGHAM, a dancer

The Story:

Jess Oakroyd was a stolid, proper sort of Yorkshireman, but his wife's nagging, coupled with the sarcastic remarks of his son, finally forced him to pack a small basket of clothes and set off to travel about England. His adventures began immediately when he got a ride in a large van loaded with stolen goods. The driver of the van and the driver's helper left Jess at an inn in a small hamlet after having robbed him while he was asleep. Rudely awakened by the innkeeper, Jess had no money to buy his breakfast. Setting off afoot, he came upon another van, in which a man was attempting to repair a battered peddler's stall. In return for Jess's help, the owner gave him breakfast and a ride. Jess stayed for three days with the peddler, who sold fancy balloons.

After leaving the balloon trade, the Yorkshireman set out to walk the roads of England once again. Within the hour, he came upon a stalled car and helped the woman driver to start the motor. The woman was Miss Trant, who had inherited several hundred pounds from her father. Since all of her previous adventures had been in the realm of historical novels, Miss Trant had also decided to travel over England. At the age of thirty-five, she was already an old maid.

While they were getting the car started, rain began to fall; Jess and Miss Trant headed for a little tearoom nearby. There they met Inigo Jollifant and an odd-looking companion who was carrying a banjo. Inigo had begun his adventures on the previous Monday evening, as had Jess and Miss Trant.

An instructor at a boys' school, Inigo had been unhappy there because of the petty tyranny of the headmaster and his termagant wife. On Monday evening, he had been dismissed because he became drunk and played the piano in celebration of his twenty-sixth birthday. Inigo, too drunk to do the prudent thing, had packed a knapsack and set out on his travels immediately. In the railroad station of a small town, he had met his banjo-carrying companion, Morton Mitcham, a professional entertainer.

In the tearoom, the shrewish woman proprietress was berating a group of customers who were unable to pay their bill. The banjo player recognized them as members of a theatrical troupe stranded, as they explained, when their manager ran away with a young woman and their funds.

On impulse, Miss Trant decided to take over the stranded company. That night, they made plans for taking the show on the road once more. The new troupe took the name of The Good Companions. It was made up of an elderly comedian, a young and pretty comedienne named Susie Dean, Morton Mitcham, a dancer named Jerry Jerningham, a girl singer, and an older couple who sang duets. Miss Trant was the manager, Inigo the accompanist, and Jess, at Miss Trant's insistence, the handyman.

Their first appearance was in the little town where Miss Trant had found them. The show was not successful, but their second engagement, at a seaside hotel, met with obvious favor. The most appreciated actors were Jerry Jerningham and Susie Dean, who were aided by the merry songs that were written for their acts by Inigo Jollifant. For several weeks, the routine of the company was one of rehearsals and performances with train rides between two- or three-night engagements in each town.

As the weeks passed, Inigo Jollifant fell in love with Susie Dean; she laughed at him and said that she could not fall in love and marry until she had become a musical comedy star and had played in London. Miss Trant was having a delightful experience. All of her life had been spent in the sleepy village of Hitherton in southern England, where her father had settled upon his retirement from the army. Her theatrical associates were far more interesting than the small sedate group of her father's village friends.

Next, The Good Companions played in an almost deserted mill town in the Midlands. The mills had been shut down for some months, and the townspeople had little money or interest in a traveling vaudeville troupe. Since the audiences were small and unsympathetic, the troupe became dispirited and almost broke up. Jess Oakroyd, however, persuaded the troupe to stick with Miss Trant, since she would lose her money if they did not carry on with their engagements.

At last, the fortunes of the troupe had a turn for the better. Inigo Jollifant composed new tunes for the acts that met with great success. His love affair, however, did not fare as well. Susie Dean could not understand why he did not take his music as seriously as he did his writing for literary periodicals. She felt sure that he was making a mistake in trying to be a second-rate essayist when he could be a first-rate songwriter.

The Good Companions finally had a long engagement in a series of prosperous manufacturing towns. The large audiences they drew began to recoup the money Miss Trant had invested. They became bold enough to engage a large hall for a stand of several nights. In the meantime, Inigo went to London where a famous producer listened to his new songs. Inigo, determined to help Susie become a top-ranking musical comedy star, refused to let the producer use his songs unless the man went with him to hear Susie Dean.

The first night in the large auditorium was disastrous. The operator of the local motion picture houses hired toughs to start a riot and set fire to the hall during the performance. In the melee, the producer from London was punched in the nose and so refused to hear any more about either Inigo's music or Susie Dean. Miss Trant was injured during the riot.

Finally, when the future looked darkest, an elderly woman took a fancy to Jerry Jerningham. She married him and put her money and influence at his disposal. The result was that an even greater producer gave Susie Dean her chance at musical comedy in London and bought Inigo's music.

The troupe disbanded; but at Jerningham's request, the other performers found excellent places with the same producer. In the hospital, Miss Trant met a doctor with whom she had been in love for many years, and she prepared to marry him as soon as she was well. Jess Oakroyd did some detective work in connection with the riot. With the help of the balloon peddler, he discovered who had hired the men to start the rioting and set fire to the theater. Held responsible for the disturbance, these men had to take over Miss Trant's debts for the damages.

After solving the mystery of the riot, Jess went back to his home in Yorkshire; he had received a telegram from his son telling him that Mrs. Oakroyd was seriously ill. She died shortly thereafter, and Jess made preparations to continue his traveling. He had discovered that even a man as old and settled as he could become addicted to the pleasures of adventuring away from home, and he decided to visit his married daughter in Canada.

Critical Evaluation:

J. B. Priestley had his first success at the age of thirty-five with *The Good Companions*. Other novels, plays, and criticism followed, establishing him as one of the major literary figures of his time. Set in the 1920's, *The Good Companions* is a tale of a group of wandering English men and women from different classes and professions that reminds one of Chaucer. The novel possesses a scope that suggests the Victorian novelists, and the story moves briskly; both plot and characters maintain reader interest to the last page. If the coincidences of plot (Jimmy Nunn encounters his old wife at the train station, Miss Trant discovers her former lover, Dr. McFarlane, in the hospital, for example) strain credulity, the force of the narration, the freshness of the prose, and the richness of the characterizations prevent these coincidences from looming as too important.

In many ways, the novel is reminiscent of the work of Charles Dickens, both in characterization and in atmosphere. The descriptions of the English countryside and towns are particularly good. With such descriptions, the author effectively sets the locale of the various parts of the novel. The best character of the novel is the Yorkshire workman Jess Oakroyd. His northern dialect is a source of amusement both to the characters in the novel and to the reader, and he is the English parallel to the almost mythical American Yankee who says little, thinks much, and ends up by proving more astute than the sophisticated people about him.

The characters set this book above commonplace novels. The pages are crowded with fascinating figures; some soon disappear, while others stay and become old friends. All of them—from the little dressmaker, Miss Thong, who comes and goes with breathless speed, to the banjo-playing Morton Mitcham, who roars and tells his tall tales to the very end—are given the touch of life by Priestley's skill. Priestley portrays an amazingly broad spectrum of humanity, ranging from the aristocratic Miss Trant to the workman Jess Oakroyd to the small-time entertainers and the faculty at the third-rate boys' school. He often pokes gentle fun at people or attitudes, but the satire is never severe. Above all, Priestley succeeded in his comic purpose; *The Good Companions* is a comic masterpiece.

GOODBYE, MR. CHIPS

Type of work: Novelette
Author: James Hilton (1900–1954)
Type of plot: Sentimental romance
Time of plot: 1870–1933
Locale: An English boys' school
First published: 1934
> *Principal characters:*
> MR. CHIPS, an old schoolmaster
> MRS. WICKETT, his landlady
> BROOKFIELD BOYS

The Story:

Chips was eighty-five years old, but he thought himself far from ill. Dr. Merivale had told him he should not venture out on this cold November day, but he also added that Chips was fitter than the doctor himself. What Chips did not know was that the doctor had told the landlady, Mrs. Wickett, to look after him; Chips's chest clouded in bad weather.

Chips sank into his armchair by the fire, happy in the peace and warmth. The first thing about his remembered career set him laughing. He had come to teach at Brookfield in 1870, and in a kindly talk old Wetherby, the acting headmaster, advised him to watch his disciplinary measures. Mr. Wetherby had heard that discipline was not one of Chips's strong points. When one of the boys dropped his desktop too loudly on the first day of class, Chips assigned him a hundred lines and had no trouble after that. The boy's name was Colley—Chips seldom forgot a name or a face—and he remembered years later that he had taught Colley's son, and then his grandson, who, he said pleasantly, was the biggest young nitwit of them all. Chips was fond of making little jokes about the boys, who took his jibes well and grew to love him for his honesty and friendliness. Indeed, Chips's jokes were regarded as the funniest anywhere, and the boys had great sport telling of his latest.

Remembering these things, Chips thought growing old was a great joke, although a little sad; and when Mrs. Wickett came in with his tea, she could not tell whether Chips was laughing or crying. Tears were spilling down his withered cheeks.

Brookfield had known periods of both grandeur and decay. When Chips arrived there, the school was already a century old and regarded as a place for boys whose lineage was respectable but seldom distinguished. Chips's own background was not distinguished either, but it had been hard for him to realize that his mind was not the type to assume leadership. He had longed to work his way into the position of headmaster. After many failures, however, he knew that his role was one of teaching, and he gave up his administrative ambitions and grew to love his students. They would often come to chat with him over tea and crumpets. Sometimes they remarked, as they left, what a typical bachelor old Chips was.

It was painful to Chips that no one at Brookfield remembered his wife. When he was forty-eight years old, he had married Kathy Bridges, and even now he wondered how the miracle had taken place. He had seen a girl waving from the top of a rocky ledge one day when he was out walking, and thinking her in trouble, he set out to rescue her. On the way, he sprained his ankle, and Kathy had assisted him. It was a remarkable love, for she was years younger than he. Kathy, however, left an enduring mark upon Chips. He grew more lenient with the boys, more understanding of their problems, and more courageous in his teaching. Ironically, Kathy died on the first day of April in childbirth; that day, not realizing the tragedy that had befallen Chips, the boys played April Fool jokes on the stricken teacher.

Chips began to remember the war years. Names of boys whose faces he could still visualize were read out in chapel from the casualty lists. When the headmaster died and no one could be found to fill his place, Chips was asked to head Brookfield. Standing in his tattered gown, which was often considered disgraceful by newcomers, he read out the names as tears filled his eyes. Even now, sitting in front of the fire, he could recall that roll, and he read it over to himself, remembering the faces that had looked so hopefully at him in the classroom.

One day he was meeting a Latin class, while German bombs were crashing nearby. The boys squirmed in their seats as the explosions sounded nearer and nearer, but Chips quietly told them that they should never judge the importance of anything by the noise it made. Then, asking one of the more courageous lads to translate, Chips chose a passage from Caesar that was particularly apt because it dealt with German methods of fighting. Later, the boys told how Chips stood steady and calm, and they remarked that even though they might consider Latin a dead language, it was nevertheless valuable at times.

After the war, Chips gave up his headmastership and returned to his room at Mrs. Wickett's. Now, fifteen years later, he was always asked to greet visiting dignitaries who came to Brookfield. He was amused to find that many of the barons, Parliament members, and war heroes had been his former pupils, and he remembered their faces, although now, to his chagrin, he often forgot their names. He would make amusing, appropriate remarks, not always complimentary, and the visitors would shake with laughter. Sometimes during those postwar years, he was asked to make little speeches at school banquets, and because of his reputation for funny sayings, his audience would laugh uproariously, often before Chips reached the point of his jokes. Chips was privileged now; his eccentricities only made him more loved at Brookfield. Indeed, Chips was Brookfield.

Chips thought of the rich life he had led. There were so many memories that caused laughter and sorrow. Now, as he sat by the fire, he heard a timid knock at the door, and a youngster, much abashed, came in. He had been told that Chips had sent for him. The old man laughed, knowing that this was a prank the old boys often played on a newcomer, and he saved the boy from embarrassment by saying that he had sent for him. After conversation and tea, Chips dismissed the boy in his abrupt but kindly fashion. The boy waved as he went down the walk.

Later, the youth thought of Chips sadly and told his comrades that he had been the last to tell him good-bye; Mr. Chips died quietly in his sleep that cold November night.

Critical Evaluation:

It was not until the American publication of *Goodbye, Mr. Chips* in June, 1934, that James Hilton became a popular, successful, and critically admired author. Prior to that time he had written eight full-length novels along with a large body of topical commentary and literary criticism, but he was still relatively unknown and unappreciated. Even *Lost Horizon*, which was later to become one of the best-selling books of its time, was largely ignored when first issued in 1933. The spectacular success of *Goodbye, Mr. Chips* surprised all the critics, including the author, and even today it is difficult to account for the book's enormous and continuing popularity.

Since *Goodbye, Mr. Chips* is presented as the reminiscence of an old man, the dominant mood is that of sentimental, nostalgic reverie. Hilton adroitly maintains a fine balance between the gentle humor characteristic of Chips's everyday life and the pathos of a few sad incidents (the death of Chips's wife in childbirth, of his students in combat, and, finally, of the old man himself). Therefore, the book is neither overly cheerful nor maudlin, although it comes close, at times, to both.

Basing Chips on a synthesis of his own father and his favorite Latin teacher, Hilton created a character many readers recognized in their own experience. It is doubtful, however, that simple reader identification or the fact that Chips (Chipping, actually—Chips is a nickname) is a clearly defined, amiable, slightly eccentric, modestly humorous man is enough to account for the novel's enormous popularity. There must be something in this character of unexceptional ability, living an ordinary life, that struck a deeply responsive chord in the mid-1930's.

Chips's life covers the second half of the nineteenth century and the first third of the twentieth (1848–1933). The historically crucial events in the book, however, are World War I and, vaguely in the background, the Great Depression. Chips's appeal can be fully understood only by seeing his uneventful life in the context of the very eventful historical epoch in which it passed, with special emphasis on 1934, the time of publication.

Chips is, above all, a "common man." He admits to being an ordinary teacher at a good but essentially second-class preparatory school. He gives up his early headmaster ambitions, because he decides that he is not good enough for the job. When he courts and marries Kathy Bridges, he cannot understand what she sees in him.

Nevertheless, as an ordinary man, he demonstrates in moments of crisis an essential strength and resourcefulness, the outstanding example being the Latin lesson he conducts in the midst of an air raid. However frantic and chaotic the modern world becomes, Hilton assures readers that the common man can find the needed inner strength and will to survive with dignity.

Chips, however, is not just an ordinary man; he is also the embodiment of a tradition. Brookfield is not a great school, but it is a school rooted in the British tradition of greatness. As its exemplar, Chips stands for honor, dignity, continuity, and a strong organic connection to the past; and yet, primarily because of his marriage to Kathy, he has a sense of social movement and a compassion for the disadvantaged.

Therefore, Chips balances the best of the old and the new with emphasis on the old. He clashes with the modern headmaster over the issue, and it almost costs him his job. During World War I, he defies popular prejudice to publicly commemorate a former German teacher who died fighting for the enemy.

Accurately labeled "pre-war" by his students, Chips represents the traditional values and disciplined life-style that existed prior to World War I; and, through him, Hilton suggests that they remain valid and can survive even in the frenetic modern world.

GREAT EXPECTATIONS

Type of work: Novel
Author: Charles Dickens (1812–1870)
Type of plot: Mystery romance
Time of plot: Nineteenth century
Locale: England
First published: 1860–1861

Principal characters:
PIP, an orphan
JOE GARGERY, Pip's brother-in-law
MISS HAVISHAM, an eccentric recluse
ESTELLA, Miss Havisham's ward
HERBERT POCKET, Pip's roommate
MR. JAGGERS, a solicitor
ABEL MAGWITCH (MR. PROVIS), a convict
COMPEYSON, a villain

The Story:

Little Pip had been left an orphan when he was a small boy, and his sister, much older than he, had grudgingly reared him in her cottage. Pip's brother-in-law, Joe Gargery, on the other hand, was kind and loving to the boy. In the marsh country where he lived with his sister and Joe, Pip wandered alone. One day, he was accosted by a wild-looking stranger who demanded that Pip secretly bring him some food, a request which Pip feared to deny. The stranger, an escaped prisoner, asked Pip to bring him a file to cut the iron chain that bound his leg. When Pip returned to the man with a pork pie and file, he saw another mysterious figure in the marsh. After a desperate struggle with the escaped prisoner, the stranger escaped into the fog. The man Pip had aided was later apprehended. He promised Pip that he would somehow repay the boy for helping him.

Mrs. Joe sent Pip to the large mansion of strange Miss Havisham upon that lady's request. Miss Havisham lived in a gloomy, locked house where all clocks had been stopped on the day her bridegroom failed to appear for the wedding ceremony. She often dressed in her bridal robes; a wedding breakfast molded on the table in an unused room. Pip went there every day to visit the old lady and a beautiful young girl, named Estella, who delighted in tormenting the shy boy. Miss Havisham enjoyed watching the two children together, and she encouraged Estella in her haughty teasing of Pip.

Living in the grim atmosphere of Joe's blacksmith shop and the uneducated poverty of his sister's home, Pip was eager to learn. One day, a London solicitor named Jaggers presented him with the opportunity to go to London and become a gentleman. Both Pip and Joe accepted the proposal. Pip imagined that his kind backer was Miss Havisham herself. Perhaps she wanted to make a gentleman out of him so that he would be fit someday to marry Estella.

In London, Pip found a small apartment set up for him. Herbert Pocket, a young relative of Miss Havisham, was his living companion. When Pip needed money, he was instructed to go to Mr. Jaggers. Although Pip pleaded with the lawyer to disclose the name of his benefactor, Jaggers advised the eager young man not to make inquiries; when the proper time arrived, Pip's benefactor would make himself known.

Soon Pip became one of a small group of London dandies, among them a disagreeable chap named Bentley Drummle. Joe Gargery came to visit Pip, much to Pip's disturbance; by now, he had outgrown his rural background, and he was ashamed of Joe's manners. Herbert Pocket, however, cheerfully helped Pip to entertain the uncomfortable Joe in their apartment. Simple Joe loved Pip very much, and after he had gone, Pip felt ashamed of himself. Joe had brought word that Miss Havisham wanted to see the young man, and Pip returned with his brother-in-law. Miss Havisham and Estella noted the changes in Pip, and when Estella had left Pip alone with the old lady, she told him he must fall in love with the beautiful girl. She also said it was time for Estella to come to London, and she wished Pip to meet her adopted daughter when she arrived. This request made Pip feel more certain he had been sent to London by Miss Havisham to be groomed to marry Estella.

Estella had not been in London long before she had many suitors. Of all the men who courted her, she seemed to favor Bentley Drummle. Pip saw Estella frequently. Although she treated him kindly and with friendship, he knew she did not return his love.

On his twenty-first birthday, Pip received a caller, the man whom Pip had helped in the marsh many years before. Ugly and coarse, he told Pip it was he who had been financing Pip ever since he had come to London. At first, the boy was horrified to discover he owed so much to this crude former criminal, Abel Magwitch. He told Pip that he had been sent to the Colonies where he had grown rich. Now he had wanted Pip to enjoy all the privileges he had been denied in life, and he had returned to England to see the boy to whom he had tried to be a second father. He warned Pip that he was in danger should his presence be discovered, for it was death for a prisoner to return to England once he had been sent to a convict colony. Pip detested his plight. Now he realized Miss Havisham had had nothing to do with his great expectations in life, but he was too conscious of his debt to consider abandoning the man whose person he disliked. He determined to do all in his power to please his benefactor. Magwitch was using the name Provis to hide his identity. Furthermore, Provis told Pip that the man with whom Pip had seen him struggling long ago in the marsh was his enemy, Compeyson, who had vowed to destroy him. Herbert Pocket, a distant cousin of Miss Havisham, told Pip that the lover who had betrayed her on her wedding day was named Arthur Compeyson.

Pip went to see Miss Havisham to denounce her for having allowed him to believe she was helping him. On his arrival, he was informed that Estella was to marry Bentley Drummle. Since Miss Havisham had suffered at the hands of one faithless man, she had reared Estella to inflict as much hurt as possible upon the many men who loved her. Estella reminded Pip that she had warned him not to fall in love with her, since she had no compassion for any human being. Pip returned once more to visit Miss Havisham after Estella had married. An accident started a fire in the old, dust-filled mansion; although Pip tried to save the old woman, she died in the blaze that also badly damaged her gloomy house.

From Provis' story of his association with Compeyson and from other evidence, Pip had learned that Provis was Estella's father; but he did not reveal his discovery to anyone but Jaggers, whose housekeeper, evidently, was Estella's mother. Pip had also learned that Compeyson was in London and plotting to kill Provis. In order to protect the man who had become a foster father to him, Pip arranged to smuggle Provis across the channel to France with the help of Herbert Pocket. Pip intended to join the old man there. Elaborate and secretive as their plans were, Compeyson managed to overtake them as they were putting Provis on the boat. The two enemies fought one last battle in the water, and Provis killed his enemy. He was then taken to jail, where he died before he could be brought to trial.

When Pip fell ill shortly afterward, it was Joe Gargery who came to nurse him. Older and wiser from his many experiences, Pip realized that he no longer needed to be ashamed of the kind man who had given so much love to him when he was a boy. His sister, Mrs. Joe, had died and Joe had married again, this time very happily. Pip returned to the blacksmith's home to stay awhile, still desolate and unhappy because of his lost Estella. Later, Herbert Pocket and Pip set up business together in London.

Eleven years passed before Pip went to see Joe Gargery again. Curiosity led Pip to the site of Miss Havisham's former mansion. There he found Estella, now a widow, wandering over the grounds. During the years, she had lost her cool aloofness and had softened a great deal. She told Pip she had thought of him often. Pip was able to foresee that perhaps he and Estella would never have to part again. The childhood friends walked hand in hand from the place that had once played such an enormous part in both of their lives.

Critical Evaluation:

G. K. Chesterton once observed that all of Charles Dickens' novels could be titled "Great Expectations," for they are full of an unsubstantial yet ardent expectation of everything. Nevertheless, as Chesterton pointed out with irony, the only book to which Dickens gave the actual title was one in which most of the expectations were never realized. To the Victorians, the word *expectations* meant legacy as well as anticipations. In that closed society, one of the few means by which a person born of the lower or lower-middle class could rise dramatically to wealth and high status was through the inheritance of valuables. Consequently, a major theme of the Victorian social novel involved the hero's movement through the class structure, and often the vehicle for that movement was money, either bestowed before death or inherited. Unlike many nineteenth century novels that rely upon the stale plot device of a surprise legacy to enrich the fortunate protagonists, *Great Expectations* probes deeply into the ethical and psychological dangers of advancing through the class system by means of wealth acquired from the toil of others.

Although the story of Pip's expectations dominates the bulk of the novel, he is not the only person who waits to benefit from another's money. His beloved Estella, the ward of Miss Havisham, is wholly dependent upon the caprices of the unstable old woman. Moreover, other characters are the mysterious instrumentalities of legacies. The solicitor Jaggers, who acts as the legal agent for both Miss Havisham and Abel Magwitch, richly benefits from his services. Even his lackey Mr. Wemmick, a mild soul who changes his personality from lamb to wolf to please his employer, earns his living from the legal machinery of the courts. Just as the source of Pip's money is revealed at last to be socially corrupted, so the uses of tainted wealth inevitably bring about corruption.

In *Bleak House* (1852–1853), Dickens had already explored with great skill the ruthless precincts of the law courts. His next three novels—*Hard Times* (1854), *Little Dorrit* (1855–1857), and *A Tale of Two Cities* (1859)— were not so well sustained and, despite memorable scenes, were less popular with the critics and public alike. *Great Expectations* (1860–1861, first published serially in *All the Year Round*) recovered Dickens' supremacy with his vast reading audience. Serious, controlled, and nearly as complex structurally as *Bleak House*, the novel also reminded Victorian readers of *David Copperfield* (1849–1850). Both are apprenticeship novels that treat the life-education of a hero. *Great Expectations* is somewhat less autobiographical than *David Copperfield*, but it repeats the basic formula of the genre: that of an honest, rather ingenuous but surely likeable young man who, through a series of often painful experiences, learns important lessons about life and himself. These lessons are always designed to reveal the hero's limitations. As he casts off his own weaknesses and better understands the dangers of the world, he succeeds by advancing through the class system and ends up less brash, a chastened but wiser man.

   Great Expectations differs from *David Copperfield*, however, in the ways
that the hero matures to self-knowledge. In the beginning, both David and
Pip are young snobs (Pip more than David). Both suffer the traumas of a
shattered childhood and troubled adolescence; but David's childhood suffering is fully motivated on the basis of his separation from loved ones. An
innocent, he is the victim of evil that he does not cause. Pip, on the other
hand, suffers from a childhood nightmare that forms a pattern of his later
experience. An orphan like David, he lives with his brutal sister and her
husband, the gentle blacksmith Joe Gargery. For whatever abuse he endures from Mrs. Joe, he more than compensates in the brotherly affection
of this simple, generous man. He also wins the loving sympathy of Biddy,
another loyal friend. Nevertheless, he is not satisfied, and when he comes
upon the convicts in the fog and is terrified, he feels a sense of guilt—misplaced but psychologically necessary—as much for his crimes against his
protectors as for the theft of a pork pie. Thereafter, his motives, cloudy as
the scene of his childhood terror, are weighted with secret apprehension
and guilt. To regain his lost innocence, he must purge himself of the causes
of this guilt.
   Pip's life apprenticeship, therefore, involves his fullest understanding of
"crimes" against his loved ones and the ways to redeem himself. The
causes of his guilt are—from lesser to greater—his snobbish pride, his betrayal of friends and protectors, and finally his participation in the machinery of corruption.
   As a snob, he not only breaks the social mold into which he has been
cast but lords it over the underlings and unfortunates of the class system.
Because of his presumed great expectations, he believes himself to be superior to the humbler Joe and Biddy. He makes such a pompous fool of himself that Trabb's boy—that brilliant comic invention, at once naughty boy
and honest philosopher—parodies his absurd airs and pretensions. His
snobbery, however, costs him a dearer price than humiliation by an urchin.
He falls in love with Estella, like himself a pretender to high social class,
only to be rejected in place of a worthless cad, Bentley Drummle. Finally,
his fanciful dreams of social distinction are shattered forever when he
learns the bitter truth about his benefactor, who is not the highborn Miss
Havisham but the escaped convict Magwitch, the wretched stranger of his
terror in the fog.
   As Pip comes to understand the rotten foundations for his social position, he also learns terrible truths about his own weaknesses. Out of foolish
pride, he has betrayed his most loyal friends, Joe and Biddy. In a sense, he
has even betrayed Miss Havisham. He has mistaken her insanity for mere
eccentricity and allowed her to act out her fantasies of romantic revenge.
When he tries to confront her with the reality of her life, he is too late.
She expires in flames. He is almost too late, in fact, to come to the service

of his real benefactor, Magwitch. He is so disturbed with the realization of the convict's sacrifice that he nearly flees from the old man, now disguised as "Provis," when he is in danger. At best, he can return to Magwitch gratitude, not love, and his sense of guilt grows from his understanding that he cannot ever repay his debt to a man he secretly loathes.

Pip's final lesson is that, no matter how pure might be his motives, he has been one of the instruments of social corruption. In a sense, he is the counterpart to the malcontent Dolge Orlick. Like Orlick, as a youth he had been an apprentice at the forge; but whereas he was fortunate to move upward into society, Orlick, consumed by hatred, failed in every enterprise. In chapter 53, a climactic scene of the novel, Orlick confronts his enemy and blames Pip for all of his failures. He even accuses Pip of responsibility for the death of Mrs. Joe. The charge is paranoiac and false: Orlick is the murderer. In his almost hallucinatory terror, however, Pip can psychologically accept Orlick's reasoning. As a child, Pip had hated his sister. If he had not been the active instrument of her death, he nevertheless profited from it. Similarly, Pip profited from the hard-earned toil of Magwitch. Indeed, most of the success he had enjoyed, thanks to the astute protection of Mr. Jaggers, had come not as his due but for a price, the payment of corrupted money. Since he had been the ignorant recipient of the fruits of corruption, his psychological guilt is all the greater.

Nevertheless, Pip, though chastened, is not overwhelmed by guilt. During the course of his apprenticeship to life, he has learned something about himself, some valuable truths about his limitations. By the end of his career when his apprenticeship is over and he is a responsible, mature being, he has cast off petty pride, snobbery, and the vexations of corrupted wealth. Although he has lost his innocence forever, he can truly appreciate Herbert Pocket, Joe, and Biddy, who have retained their integrity. When he turns to Estella, also chastened by her wretched marriage to the sadistic Drummle, he has at least the hope of beginning a new life with her, one founded upon an accurate understanding of himself and the dangers of the world.

GREEN MANSIONS

Type of work: Novel
Author: W. H. Hudson (1841–1922)
Type of plot: Fantasy
Time of plot: Nineteenth century
Locale: South American jungles
First published: 1904

Principal characters:
MR. ABEL, an old man
RIMA, a creature of the forest
NUFLO, an old hunter

The Story:

No one in Georgetown could remember his full name, and so he was known only as Mr. Abel. He told a strange story one evening as he sat talking to a friend, a tale of his youth.

While he was living among the Indians in the jungle, a nearby savannah caught his fancy. The Indians claimed it was haunted and would not go near it. One day, he set out to explore the savannah for himself. For a long while he sat on a log trying to identify the calls of the birds. One particularly engaging sound seemed almost human, and it followed him as he returned to the Indian village. Soon he bribed one of the Indians to enter the haunted savannah. The Indian became frightened, however, and ran away, leaving Abel alone with the weird sound. The Indian had said that the daughter of the spirit Didi inhabited the forest. Abel felt sure that the nearly intelligible language of the birdlike sounds were associated with the one to whom the Indian referred.

Again and again, Abel returned to the forest in his search for the source of the warbling sound, but it always eluded him. Then one day he saw a girl playing with a bird. The girl disappeared among the trees, but not before Abel had decided that she must be connected in some way with the warbling sounds he had heard.

The Indians had been encouraging him to continue his quests into the area of mystery. He decided at last that they were hoping he would try to kill the creature who seemed to be haunting their forest. He was stricken with horror at the idea. One day, he came face to face with the elusive being. He had been menaced by a small venomous snake, and he was about to kill it with a rock when the girl appeared before him to protest vigorously in her odd birdlike warbling language. She was not like any human he had ever seen. Her coloring was her most striking characteristic; it was luminescent and changed with her every mood. As he stood looking at her, fascinated by her loveliness, the snake bit him on the leg.

He started back toward the village for help, but a blinding rainstorm overtook him on the way. After falling unconscious while running through the trees, he awakened in a hut with a bearded old man named Nuflo. The man expressed fear and hatred of the Indians who, he said, were afraid of his grandchild, Rima. It was she who had saved Abel from dying of the snake's venom, and it was she who had been following him in the forest. Abel could not believe that the listless, colorless girl standing in a corner of the hut was the lovely birdlike creature he had met. On closer examination, he could detect a likeness of figure and features, but her luminous radiance was missing. When Rima addressed him in Spanish, he questioned her about the musical language that she emitted in the trees. She gave no explanation and ran away.

In a few days, Abel learned that Rima would harm no living creature, not even for her own food. Abel grew to love the strange, beautiful, untamed girl of the green forest. When he questioned her, she spoke willingly, but her speech was strangely poetic and difficult to understand. She expressed deep, spiritual longings and made him understand that in the forest she communed with her mother, who had died long ago.

Rima began to sense that since Abel, the only person she had known except her grandfather, could not understand her language and did not understand her longings, she must be unlike other human beings in the world. In her desire to meet other people and to return to the place of her birth where her mother had died, Rima revealed to Abel the name of her birthplace, a mountain he knew well. Rima demanded that her grandfather guide her to Riolama Mountain. Old Nuflo consented and requested that Abel come also.

Before he took the long journey with Rima and Nuflo, Abel returned to the Indian village. There, greeted with quiet suspicion and awe because of where he had been, Abel was held a prisoner. After six days' absence, he returned to Rima's forest. Nuflo and Abel made preparations for their journey. When they started, Rima followed them, only showing herself when they needed directions.

Nuflo began Rima's story. He had been wandering about with a band of outlaws when a heavenly looking woman appeared among them. After she had fallen and broken her ankle, Nuflo, who thought she must be a saint, nursed her back to health. Observing that she was to have a baby, he took her to a native village. Rima was born soon after. The woman could learn neither Spanish nor the Indian tongue, and the soft melodious sounds that fell from her lips were unintelligible to everyone. Gradually the woman faded. As she lay dying, she made the rough hunter understand that Rima could not live unless she were taken to the dry, cool mountains.

Knowing their search for her mother's people to be in vain, Abel sought to dissuade Rima from the journey. He explained to her that they must have disappeared or have been wiped out by Indians. Rima believed him, but at the thought of her own continued loneliness, she fell fainting at his feet. When she had recovered, she spoke of being alone, of never finding anyone who could understand the sweet warbling language that she had learned from her mother. Abel promised to stay with her always in the forest. Rima insisted on making the journey back alone so that she could prepare herself for Abel's return.

The return to the savannah was not easy for Abel and the old man. They were nearly starving when they came to their own forest and saw, to their horror, that the hut was gone. Rima could not be found. As Abel ran through the forest searching for her, he came upon a lurking Indian. Then he realized that she must be gone, for the Indian would not have dared to enter the savannah if the daughter of Didi were still there. He went back to the Indian village for food and learned from them that Rima had returned to her forest. Finding her in a tree, the Indian chief, Runi, had ordered his men to burn the tree in order to destroy the daughter of Didi.

Half mad with sorrow, Abel fled to the village of an enemy tribe. There he made a pact with the savages for the slaughter of the tribe of Runi. He then went to the forest, where he found Nuflo dead. He also found Rima's bones lying among the ashes of the fire-consumed tree. He placed her remains in an urn that he carried with him back to civilization.

Living in Georgetown, Abel at last understood Rima's sorrowful loneliness. Having known and lost her, he was suffering the same longings she had felt when she was searching for her people.

Critical Evaluation:

The subject matter and the narrative structure of W. H. Hudson's *Green Mansions* became popular and familiar during the late nineteenth century: a story of an exotic, foreign land told by a retired and lonely traveler. It seemed to satisfy the civilized reader's desire for adventure and his curiosity in a primitive way of life. It also fulfilled a certain wish for escape. *Green Mansions'* popularity can also be traced to its loving, almost sacred treatment of nature; Hudson wrote of a new frontier, of particular interest to Americans who were gradually coming to the end of their own.

Hudson, however, did not imagine his frontier in a rough, masculine way, familiar to most Americans, but in both exotic and feminine terms. In the person of Rima, a rich and complex character, he presents his experience of the South American jungles. She embodies the playful, joyous spirit one sees in birds; she is also furtive, retiring, and vulnerable, speaking an inhuman language that seems to draw out man's hostility, superstition, and desire to destroy her. In one sense, she is a maternal figure protecting the creatures of the forest, such as the deadly snake that Mr. Abel is about to kill. After he is bitten, she also saves Abel's life. Rima is also a forest creature, living among them, shy and elusive. In another and more complicated sense, she assumes the significance of man's spirit, alone and lost, seeking its home. Rima's frustrated desire to find her mother's people in the mountains, a yearning that sickens her to death, is finally the sentiment with which the narrator can identify as he concludes his story, now that he is alone and old. It is also perhaps this spiritual theme that accounts for *Green Mansions'* popularity among its first as well as its contemporary readers.

The only legend of its kind that has become a modern classic, *Green Mansions* owes its popularity to the characteristics embodied in Rima. Loving nature and the wild life of the countries that he explored, Hudson was able to express his own deep feeling through the character of Rima, the strange girl who was one with the forest and whose sorrow of loneliness was so great that she would suffer no one to look into the depth of her soul. Perhaps, to Hudson, nature was like that; too lonely and sorrowful to import complete understanding and knowledge of herself to mankind.

GULLIVER'S TRAVELS

Type of work: Simulated record of travel
Author: Jonathan Swift (1667–1745)
Type of plot: Social satire
Time of plot: 1699–1713
Locale: England and various fictional lands
First published: 1726

Principal character:

LEMUEL GULLIVER, a surgeon, sea captain, and traveler

The Story:

Lemuel Gulliver, a physician, took the post of ship's doctor on the *Antelope*, which set sail from Bristol for the South Seas in May, 1699. When the ship was wrecked in a storm somewhere near Tasmania, Gulliver had to swim for his life. Wind and tide helped to carry him close to a low-lying shore where he fell, exhausted, into a deep sleep. Upon awakening, he found himself held to the ground by hundreds of small ropes. He soon discovered that he was the prisoner of humans six inches tall. Still tied, Gulliver was fed by his captors; then he was placed on a special wagon built for the purpose and drawn by fifteen hundred small horses. Carried in this manner to the capital city of the small humans, he was exhibited as a great curiosity to the people of Lilliput, as the land of the diminutive people was called. He was kept chained to a huge Lilliputian building into which he crawled at night to sleep.

Gulliver soon learned the Lilliputian language, and through his personal charm and natural curiosity, he came into good graces at the royal court. At length, he was given his freedom, contingent upon his obeying many rules devised by the emperor prescribing his deportment in Lilliput. Now free, Gulliver toured Mildendo, the capital city, and found it to be similar to European cities of the time.

Learning that Lilliput was in danger of an invasion by the forces of the neighboring empire, Blefuscu, he offered his services to the emperor of Lilliput. While the enemy fleet awaited favorable winds to carry their ships the eight hundred yards between Blefuscu and Lilliput, Gulliver took some Lilliputian cable, waded to Blefuscu, and brought back the entire fleet by means of hooks attached to the cables. He was greeted with great acclaim, and the emperor made him a nobleman. Soon, however, the emperor and Gulliver quarreled over differences concerning the fate of the now helpless Blefuscu. The emperor wanted to reduce the enemy to the status of slaves; Gulliver championed their liberty. The pro-Gulliver forces prevailed in the Lilliputian parliament; the peace settlement was favorable to Blefuscu. Gulliver, however, was now in disfavor at court.

He visited Blefuscu, where he was received graciously by the emperor and the people. One day, while exploring the empire, he found a ship's boat washed ashore from a wreck. With the help of thousands of Blefuscu artisans, he repaired the boat for his projected voyage back to his own civilization. Taking some cattle and sheep with him, he sailed away and was eventually picked up by an English vessel.

Back in England, Gulliver spent a short time with his family before he shipped aboard the *Adventure*, bound for India. The ship was blown off course by fierce winds. Somewhere on the coast of Great Tartary a landing party went ashore to forage for supplies. Gulliver, who had wandered away from the party, was left behind when a gigantic human figure pursued the sailors back to the ship. Gulliver was caught in a field by giants threshing grain that grew forty feet high. Becoming the pet of a farmer and his family, he amused them with his humanlike behavior. The farmer's nine-year-old daughter, who was not yet over forty feet high, took special charge of Gulliver.

The farmer displayed Gulliver first at a local market town. Then he took his little pet to the metropolis, where Gulliver was put on show to the great detriment of his health. The farmer, seeing that Gulliver was near death, sold him to the queen, who took a great fancy to the little curiosity. The court doctors and philosophers studied Gulliver as a quaint trick of nature. He subsequently had adventures with giant rats the size of lions, with a dwarf thirty feet high, with wasps as large as partridges, with apples the size of Bristol barrels, and with hailstones the size of tennis balls.

He and the king discussed the institutions of their respective countries, the king asking Gulliver many questions about Great Britain that Gulliver found impossible to answer truthfully without embarrassment.

After two years in Brobdingnag, the land of the giants, Gulliver miraculously escaped when a large bird carried his portable quarters out over the sea. The bird dropped the box containing Gulliver, and he was rescued by a ship that was on its way to England. Back home, it took Gulliver some time to accustom himself once more to a world of normal size.

Soon afterward, Gulliver went to sea again. Pirates from a Chinese port attacked the ship. Set adrift in a small sailboat, Gulliver was cast away upon a rocky island. One day, he saw a large floating mass descending from the sky. Taken aboard the flying island of Laputa, he soon found it to be inhabited by intellectuals who thought only in the realm of the abstract and the exceedingly impractical. The people of the island, including the king, were so absentminded that they had to have servants following them to remind them even of their trends of conversation. When the floating island arrived above the continent of Balnibari, Gulliver received permission to visit that realm. There he inspected the Grand Academy, where hundreds of highly impractical projects for the improvement of agriculture and building were under way.

Next, Gulliver journeyed by boat to Glubbdubdrib, the island of sorcerers. By means of magic, the governor of the island showed Gulliver such great historical figures as Alexander, Hannibal, Caesar, Pompey, and Sir Thomas More. Gulliver talked to the apparitions and learned from them that history books were inaccurate.

From Glubbdubdrib, Gulliver ventured to Luggnagg. There he was welcomed by the king, who showed him the Luggnaggian immortals, or Struldbrugs—beings who would never die.

Gulliver traveled on to Japan, where he took a ship back to England. He had been away for more than three years.

Gulliver became restless after a brief stay at his home, and he signed as captain of a ship that sailed from Portsmouth in August, 1710, destined for the South Seas. The crew mutinied, keeping Captain Gulliver prisoner in his cabin for months. At length, he was cast adrift in a longboat off a strange coast. Ashore, he came upon and was nearly overwhelmed by disgusting half-human, half-ape creatures who fled in terror at the approach of a horse. Gulliver soon discovered, to his amazement, that he was in a land where rational horses, the Houyhnhnms, were masters of irrational human creatures, the Yahoos. He stayed in the stable house of a Houyhnhnm family and learned to subsist on oaten cake and milk. The Houyhnhnms were horrified to learn from Gulliver that horses in England were used by Yahoolike creatures as beasts of burden. Gulliver described England to his host, much to the candid and straightforward Houyhnhnm's mystification. Such things as wars and courts of law were unknown to this race of intelligent horses. As he did in the other lands he visited, Gulliver attempted to explain the institutions of his native land, but the friendly and benevolent Houyhnhnms were appalled by many of the things Gulliver told them.

Gulliver lived in almost perfect contentment among the horses, until one day his host told him that the Houyhnhnm Grand Assembly had decreed Gulliver either be treated as an ordinary Yahoo or be released to swim back to the land from which he had come. Gulliver built a canoe and sailed away. At length, he was picked up by a Portuguese vessel. Remembering the Yahoos, he became a recluse on the ship and began to hate all mankind. Landing at Lisbon, he sailed from there to England; but on his arrival, the sight of his own family repulsed him. He fainted when his wife kissed him. His horses became his only friends on earth.

Critical Evaluation:

It has been said that Dean Jonathan Swift hated Man but loved individual men. His hatred is brought out in this caustic political and social satire aimed at the English people, representing mankind in general, and at the

Whigs in particular. By means of a disarming simplicity of style and of careful attention to detail in order to heighten the effect of the narrative, Swift produced one of the outstanding pieces of satire in world literature. Swift himself attempted to conceal his authorship of the book under its original title: *Travels into Several Remote Nations of the World, in Four Parts, by Lemuel Gulliver, First a Surgeon, and then a Captain of Several Ships.*

When Swift created the character of Lemuel Gulliver as his narrator for *Gulliver's Travels*, he developed a personality with many qualities admired by an eighteenth century audience and still admired by many readers. Gulliver is a decent sort of person: hopeful, simple, fairly direct, and full of good will. He is a scientist, a trained doctor; and, as any good scientist should, he loves detail. His literal-minded attitude makes him a keen observer of the world around him. Furthermore, he is, like another famous novel character of the eighteenth century—Robinson Crusoe—encouragingly resourceful in emergencies. Why is it, then, that such a seemingly admirable, even heroic character, should become, in the end, an embittered misanthrope, hating the world and turning against everyone, including people who show him kindness?

The answer lies in what Swift meant for his character to be, and Gulliver was certainly not intended to be heroic. Readers often confuse Gulliver the character and Swift the author, but to do so is to miss the point of *Gulliver's Travels*. The novel is a satire, and Gulliver is a mask for Swift the satirist. In fact, Swift does not share Gulliver's values: his rationalistic, scientific responses to the world and his belief in progress and the perfectibility of man. Swift, on the contrary, believed that such values were dangerous to mankind, and that to put such complete faith in the material world, as scientific Gulliver did, was folly. As Swift's creation, Gulliver is a product of his age, and he is designed as a character to demonstrate the great weakness underlying the values of the "Age of Enlightenment," the failure to recognize the power of that which is irrational in man.

Despite Gulliver's apparent congeniality in the opening chapters of the novel, Swift makes it clear that his character has serious shortcomings, including blind spots about human nature and his own nature. Book 3, the least readable section of *Gulliver's Travels*, is in some ways the most revealing part of the book. In it Gulliver complains, for example, that the wives of the scientists he is observing run away with the servants. The fact is that Gulliver—himself a scientist—gives little thought to the well-being of his own wife. In the eleven years covered in Gulliver's "travel book," Swift's narrator spends a total of seven months and ten days with his wife.

Therefore, Gulliver, too, is caught up in Swift's web of satire in *Gulliver's Travel*. Satire as a literary form tends to be ironic; the author says the opposite of what he means. Consequently, readers can assume that much of what Gulliver observes as good and much of what he thinks and does are the opposite of what Swift thinks.

As a type of the eighteenth century, Gulliver exhibits its major values: belief in rationality, in the perfectibility of man, in the idea of progress, and in the Lockean philosophy of the human mind as a *tabula rasa*, or blank slate, at the time of birth, controlled and developed entirely by the differing strokes and impressions made on it by the environment. Swift, in contrast to Gulliver, hated the abstraction that accompanied rational thinking; he abhorred the rejection of the past that resulted from a rationalistic faith in the new and improved; and he cast strong doubts on man's ability to gain knowledge through reason and logic.

The world Gulliver discovers during his travels is significant in Swift's satire. The Lilliputians, averaging not quite six inches in height, display the pettiness and the smallness Swift detects in much that motivates human institutions, such as church and state. It is petty religious problems that lead to continual war in Lilliput. The Brobdingnagians continue the satire in part 2 by exaggerating man's grossness through their enlarged size. (Swift divided human measurements by a twelfth for the Lilliputians and multiplied the same for the Brobdingnagians.)

The tiny people of part 1 and the giants of part 2 establish a pattern of contrasts that Swift follows in part 4 with the Houyhnhnms and the Yahoos. The Yahoos, "their heads and breasts covered with a thick hair, some frizzled and others lank," naked otherwise and scampering up trees like nimble squirrels, represent the animal aspect of man when it is viewed as separate from the rational. The Houyhnhnms, completing the other half of the split, know no lust, pain, or pleasure. Their rational temperaments totally rule their passions, if they have any at all. The land of the Houyhnhnms is a Utopia to Gulliver, and he tells the horse-people that his homeland is unfortunately governed by Yahoos.

But what is the land of the Houyhnhnms really like, how much a Utopia? Friendship, benevolence, and equality are the principal virtues there. Decency and civility guide every action. As a result, each pair of horses mates to have one colt of each sex; after that, they no longer stay together. The marriages are exacted to insure nice color combinations in the offspring. To the young, marriage is "one of the necessary actions of a reasonable being." After the function of the marriage has been fulfilled—after the race has been propagated—the two members of the couple are no closer to each other than to anybody else in the whole country. It is this kind of "equality" that Swift satirizes. As a product of the rational attitude, such a value strips life of its fullness, denies the power of emotion and instinct, subjugates all to logic, reason, the intellect, and makes all dull and uninteresting—as predictable as a scientific experiment.

By looking upon the Houyhnhnms as the perfect creatures, Gulliver makes his own life back in England intolerable:

> I...return to enjoy my own speculations in my little garden at Redriff; to
> apply those excellent lessons of virtue which I learned among the
> Houyhnhnms; to instruct the Yahoos of my own family as far as I shall find
> them docible animals; to behold my figure often in a glass, and thus if possi-
> ble habituate myself by time to tolerate the sight of a human creature.

When Gulliver holds up rational men as perfect man and when he cannot
find a rational man to meet his ideal, he concludes in disillusionment that
mankind is totally animalistic, like the ugly Yahoos. In addition to being a
satire and a parody of travel books, *Gulliver's Travels* is an initiation novel.
As Gulliver develops, he changes; but he fails to learn an important lesson
of life, or he learns it wrong. His naïve optimism about progress and rational man leads him to bitter disillusionment.

It is tragically ironic that Swift died at the age of seventy-eight after
three years of living without his reason, a victim of Ménière's disease, dying "like a rat in a hole." For many years, he had struggled against fits of
deafness and giddiness, symptoms of the disease. As a master of the language of satire, Swift remains unequaled, despite his suffering and ill
health. He gathered in *Gulliver's Travels*, written late in his life, all the
experience he had culled from both courts and streets. For Swift knew people, and, as individuals, he loved them; but when they changed into
groups, he hated them, satirized them, and stung them into realizing the
dangers of the herd. Gulliver never understood this.

GUY MANNERING
Or, The Astrologer

Type of work: Novel
Author: Sir Walter Scott (1771–1832)
Type of plot: Historical romance
Time of plot: Eighteenth century
Locale: Scotland
First published: 1815

Principal characters:
COLONEL GUY MANNERING, a retired army officer
JULIA MANNERING, his daughter
CAPTAIN BROWN, a soldier
LUCY BERTRAM, an orphan girl
CHARLES HAZLEWOOD, Lucy's suitor
SIR ROBERT HAZLEWOOD, his father
GILBERT GLOSSIN, the holder of the Bertram property
DIRK HATTERAICK, a smuggler
MEG MERRILIES, a gypsy
DOMINIE SAMPSON, the tutor to the Bertram children

The Story:

Guy Mannering, a young English gentleman traveling in Scotland, stopped at the home of Godfrey Bertram, Laird of Ellangowan, on the night the first Bertram child, a boy, was born. Mannering, a student of astrology, cast the horoscope of the newborn babe and was distressed to find that the child's fifth, tenth, and twenty-first years would be hazardous. The young Englishman puzzled over the fact that the boy's twenty-first year would correspond with the thirty-ninth year of the girl Mannering loved, which was the year the stars said would bring her death or imprisonment. An old gypsy, Meg Merrilies, also predicted danger for the new baby. Not wishing to worry the parents, Mannering wrote down his finds and presented them to Mr. Bertram, first cautioning him not to open the packet until the child had passed by one day his fifth birthday. Then he departed.

Young Harry Bertram grew steadily and well. He was tutored and supervised by Dominie Sampson, a teacher and preacher retained by his father; and at times, the child was also watched over by the gypsy Meg, who had great love for the boy. The child was four years old when the laird became a justice of the peace and promised to rid the countryside of gypsies and poachers. After he had ordered all gypsies to leave the district, old Meg put a curse on him, saying that his own house was in danger of being as empty as were now the homes of the gypsies. On Harry's fifth birthday, the prediction came true: the boy disappeared while on a ride with a revenue officer hunting smugglers. The man was killed and his body found, but there was no trace of the child. All search proving futile, he was at last given up for dead. In her grief, his mother, prematurely delivered of a daughter, died soon afterward.

Seventeen years passed. Old Mr. Bertram, cheated by his lawyer, Gilbert Glossin, was to have his estate sold to pay his debts. Glossin planned to buy the property without much outlay of money, for the law said that when an heir was missing a purchaser need not put up the full price, in case the heir should return and claim his inheritance. Before the sale, Guy Mannering returned and tried to buy the property to save it for the Bertram family, but a delay in the mail prevented his effort, and Glossin got possession of the estate. Old Mr. Bertram died before the transaction was completed, leaving his daughter Lucy homeless and penniless.

During these transactions, Mannering's past history came to light. Years before, he had gone as a soldier to India and married there. Through a misunderstanding, he had accused his wife of faithlessness with Captain Brown, who was in reality in love with Mannering's daughter, Julia. The two men fought a duel, and Brown was wounded. Later he was captured by bandits, and Mannering assumed that he was dead. When Mannering's wife died eight months later, the unhappy man, having learned she had not been unfaithful, resigned his commission and returned with his daughter to England.

When Mannering learned that he could not buy the Bertram estate and allow Lucy to remain there with the faithful Dominie Sampson, he leased a nearby house for them. He also brought his daughter Julia to the house after he learned from friends with whom she was staying that she had been secretly meeting an unknown young man. What Mannering did not know was that the man was Captain Brown, who had escaped from his bandit captors and followed Julia to England and later to Scotland. Both Julia and Lucy were unhappy in their love affairs. Lucy loved Charles Hazlewood, but since Lucy had no money, Charles's father would not permit their marriage.

Captain Brown, loitering near the house, met old Meg Merrilies, who took a great interest in him. Once she saved his life, and for his thanks, she made him promise to come to her whenever she sent for him. A short time later, Brown encountered Julia, Lucy, and Charles Hazlewood. Charles, thinking Brown a bandit, pulled a firearm from his clothing. In his attempt to disarm Charles, Brown accidentally discharged the weapon and wounded Charles. Brown fled.

Charles would have made little of the incident, but Glossin, desiring to gain favor with the gentry by whom he had been snubbed since he had bought the Bertram property, went to Sir Robert Hazlewood and offered to apprehend the man who had shot his son. Glossin, finding some papers marked with the name of Brown, used them in his search. He was momentarily deterred, however, when he was called to interview a prisoner named Dirk Hatteraick. Dirk, a Dutch smuggler, was the killer of the revenue officer found dead when the Bertram heir disappeared. Dirk told Glossin that the boy was alive and in Scotland. Because Glossin had planned the kidnaping many years before, it was to his advantage to have the young man disappear again. He was even more anxious to get rid of the Bertram heir forever when he learned from Dirk that the man was Captain Brown. Brown—or Harry Bertram—would claim his estate, and Glossin would lose the rich property he had acquired for almost nothing. Glossin finally captured Brown and had him imprisoned, after arranging with Dirk to storm the prison and carry Brown off to sea to be killed or lost.

Old Meg, learning of the plot in some mysterious way, foiled it when she had Harry Bertram rescued. She also secured Mannering's aid in behalf of the young man, whom she had loved from the day of his birth. Bertram was taken by his rescuers to Mannering's home. There his story was pieced together from what he remembered and from the memory of old Dominie Sampson. Bertram could hardly believe that he was the heir to Ellangowan and Lucy's brother. His sister was overjoyed at the reunion; but it would take more than the proof of circumstances to win back his inheritance from Glossin. Mannering, Sampson, and Sir Robert Hazlewood, who heard the story, tried to trace old papers to secure the needed proof.

In the meantime, old Meg sent Bertram a message reminding him of Brown's promise to come should she need him. She led him into a cave where Dirk was hiding out and there told him her story. She had kidnaped him for Dirk on the day the revenue officer was murdered. She had promised Dirk and Glossin, also one of the gang, not to reveal her secret until the boy was twenty-one years old. Now she felt released from her promise, since that period had passed. She told Bertram to capture Dirk for the hangman, but before the smuggler could be taken, he shot the old gypsy in the heart.

Dirk was taken to prison and would not verify the gypsy's story; his sullenness was taken as proof of Bertram's right to his inheritance. Glossin's part in the plot was also revealed, and he too was put into prison to await trial. When the two plotters fought in the cell, Dirk killed Glossin. Then Dirk wrote a full confession and cheated the hangman by killing himself. His confession, added to other evidence, proved Bertram's claim, and he was restored to his rightful position. Successful at last in his suit for Julia Mannering, he settled part of his estate on his sister Lucy and so paved the way for her marriage with Charles Hazlewood. The predictions had come true; Mannering's work was done.

Critical Evaluation:

Sir Walter Scott's gift for making the history and manners of people remote in time and place come alive has long been considered his most enduring contribution to fiction; his reputation as the father of the historical novel is common knowledge. Scott, however, was essentially a romancer and perhaps the greatest in English literature. He told marvelously exotic and heroic stories. They were rarely well plotted, indeed often contrived; and they were never afraid of sentimentality or exaggeration. Despite the originality and brilliance of the historical or social coloring, Scott's primary purpose in almost all of his works was to fascinate and entertain.

Guy Mannering, with its astrological beginnings, haunting descriptions of the desolate Cumberland landscape, and mysterious portrait of Meg Merrilies, is as exotic as anything Scott wrote. Meg recalls the witches in *Macbeth* when she curses Godfrey Bertram, Laird of Ellangowan, and yet despite her curses and prophesies, she is also the archetypal mother, protecting Harry Bertram and literally confirming his identity and title before she dies. This strange gypsy woman is more real, finally, than the more conventional characters of the novel. Her power comes largely from her asocial vitality and her mythic and choric function in the story; but it also has something to do with her importance to the plot. Unlike the interesting peasants in most of Scott's novels, Meg is not just part of the engaging background. She is integrally connected to the story. The same thing can be said for Dominie Sampson, the memorable tutor.

On the whole, the depiction of Scottish manners is more realistic than in *Waverley*, probably because the time pictured is closer to Scott's own. Nevertheless, at the thematic core of *Guy Mannering* is Scott's yearning for the richer tones of feudal life. The common people were still vessels of the older spirit, and Scott is characteristically at his best depicting their speech and action.

Certainly one of the greatest abilities of Scott was his flair for making people seem real, especially those drawn from the lower social ranks. No doubt his human touch was based on his own genuine love for people of all walks of life. In *Guy Mannering*, this familiarity with the ways and foibles of human nature is evident throughout. His peasants, tradesmen, and outcasts are not too ignorant or coarse to have fine sensibilities. Indeed, it was the loyalty of the old gypsy, Meg Merrilies, that was primarily responsible for the happy outcome of this novel. Through these people, Scott gave his readers an appreciation of the real values of life.

HAJJI BABA OF ISPAHAN

Type of work: Novel
Author: James Morier (1780–1849)
Type of plot: Picaresque romance
Time of plot: Early nineteenth century
Locale: Persia
First published: 1824

> Principal characters:
> HAJJI BABA, a rogue
> OSMAN AGHA, a Turkish merchant
> ZEENAB, a slave girl

The Story:

Hajji Baba was the son of a successful barber of Ispahan. By the time he was sixteen, he had learned the barber's trade as well as a store of bazaar tales and quotations from the Persian poets. With these, he entertained the customers who came to his father's shop, among them a wealthy Turkish merchant named Osman Agha, who was on his way to Meshed to buy goatskins of Bokhara. This merchant was so impressed with Hajji Baba that he begged the young man to accompany him on the journey. With his father's blessing and a case of razors, Hajji Baba set out with his new patron.

Before the caravan had been many days on its way, it was attacked by a band of Turcoman robbers. Osman Agha had prudently sewed fifty gold ducats in the skullcap under his turban, but when the caravan was captured, he was stripped of his finery, and the skullcap was tossed in a corner of the robber chief's tent. The robbers spared Hajji Baba's life when they learned he was a skilled barber, and he became a favorite of the wife of the chief. One day he persuaded the foolish woman to let him borrow Osman Agha's cap. He ripped the gold pieces from the lining and hid them, awaiting the time when he might escape from his captors. Osman Agha had been sold to some camel herders.

Hajji Baba traveled with the robbers on their raids throughout the region. One of these raids was on Ispahan itself, from which the robbers carried away a rich booty; but at the division of the spoils, Hajji Baba got only promises and praise.

One day the robbers encountered the armed escort of a Persian prince. When the others fled, Hajji Baba gladly allowed himself to be taken prisoner by the prince's men. They mistook him for a Turcoman, however, and cruelly mistreated him, stripping him of his clothes and his hidden gold. When he complained to the prince, the nobleman sent for the guilty ones, took the money from them, and then kept the gold himself.

Hajji Baba went with the prince and his train to Meshed, where he became a water vendor, carrying a leather bag filled with dirty water which he sold to pilgrims with assurances that it was holy water blessed by the prophet. With money so earned, he bought some tobacco which he blended with dung and then peddled through the streets of the holy city. His best customer, Dervish Sefer, introduced him to other dervishes. They applauded Hajji Baba's shrewdness and enterprise and invited him to become one of their number. One day, however, a complaint was lodged against him because of the bad tobacco he sold, and the authorities beat his bare feet until he lost consciousness. Having in the meantime saved a small amount of money, he decided to leave Meshed, which seemed to him an ill-omened city.

He set out on his way to Teheran. On the road, a courier overtook him and asked him to read some letters the messenger was carrying. One was a letter from a famous court poet, commending the bearer to officials high at court. Hajji Baba waited until the courier was fast asleep, took the messenger's horse, and rode away to deliver the courier's letters. Through these stolen credentials, he was able to obtain a position of confidence with the court physician.

Hajji Baba remained with the physician, even though his post brought him no pay. He soon found favor with Zeenab, the physician's slave, and sought her company whenever he could do so without danger of being caught. Then the shah himself visited the physician's establishment and received Zeenab as a gift. Hajji Baba was disconsolate, but he was soon made happy by a new appointment to the post of sublieutenant to the chief executioner of the shah. Again he received no pay, for he was supposed to get his money by extortion, as other members of the shah's entourage did. It was soon discovered that Zeenab was in a condition which could only be regarded as an insult to the shah's personal honor, and Hajji Baba was summoned to execute the girl. Soon afterward, suspicion fell on him for his own part in the affair, and he fled to the holy city of Koom.

In Koom, he pretended to be a priest. The shah made a pilgrimage to the city, and during his visit, the chief priest presented Hajji Baba's petition to the ruler. Hajji Baba explained that he had acted in all innocence, because he had no idea of the high honor to be conferred upon Zeenab. The shah reluctantly pardoned Hajji Baba and allowed him to return to Ispahan.

He arrived to discover that his father had died and that his fortune had disappeared. Hajji Baba sold his father's shop and used the money to establish himself as a learned scribe. Before long, he found service with Mollah Nadan, a celebrated priest, who planned to organize an illegal but profitable marriage market. Hajji Baba was supposed to find husbands for women the Mollah would provide. When Hajji Baba visited the three women for whom he was supposed to find husbands, he discovered them all to be ugly old hags, one the wife of his former master, the physician, who had recently died. Later, Hajji Baba discovered his first master, Osman Agha, who had finally escaped from the Turcomans and regained some of his fortune. Hajji Baba tricked Agha into marrying one of the three women.

Mollah Nadan undertook to gain favor by punishing some Armenians during a drought, but he incurred the shah's wrath, and he and Hajji Baba were driven from the city. Mollah Nadan's property was confiscated. Hajji Baba stole back into the city to see if any of the Mollah's property could be saved, but the house had been stripped. He went to visit the baths, and there he discovered Mollah Bashi, who had suffered a severe cramp and had drowned. Hajji Baba was afraid that he would be accused of murder, as Mollah Bashi had helped to bring about Mollah Nadan's ruin. The slave attendant, however, failed to recognize Hajji Baba in the darkness, and Hajji Baba escaped, dressed in the Mollah's robes. On the horse of the chief executioner, he set out to collect money owed to Mollah Bashi. In the Mollah's clothes and riding a fine horse, he presented a dashing figure until he met Mollah Nadan and was persuaded to change robes with him. Mollah Nadan was arrested and charged with the death of Mollah Bashi. Hajji Baba, who had kept the money he had collected, decided to become a merchant.

He encountered the caravan of the widow of Mollah Bashi. She was taking her husband's body to Kerbelai for holy burial. When the leader of the caravan revealed that Hajji Baba was suspected of the murder, he began to fear for his life; but about that time, a band of marauders attacked the caravan, and in the confusion, Hajji Baba escaped. In Bagdad, he reencountered his old master, Osman Agha, and with him proceeded to invest the money he had available. He bought pipe sticks and planned to sell them at a profit in Constantinople.

There a wealthy widow sought him out, and he decided to marry her, first, however, intimating that he was as wealthy as she. He married her and began to live on her income. His old bazaar friends, however, jealous of his good luck, betrayed him to his wife's relatives. Thrown out as an imposter, he was obliged to seek the help of the Persian ambassador. The ambassador advised him not to seek revenge upon his former wife's relatives, as they would surely murder him in his bed. Instead, he found use for Hajji Baba in an intrigue developing among representatives of England and France. Hajji Baba was employed as a spy to find out what the foreign emissaries sought in the shah's court.

Here, at last, Hajji Baba found favor. He discovered that his life among cutthroats and rogues had admirably fitted him for dealing diplomatically with the representatives of foreign countries, and he was finally made the shah's representative in his own city of Ispahan. He returned there with considerable wealth and vast dignity to lord it over those who had once thought his station in life far below their own.

Critical Evaluation:

James Morier's romance is both an Oriental tale and a picaresque narrative. With its treatment of exotic customs and manners, the novel resembles such eighteenth century romances as Samuel Johnson's *The History of Rasselas, Prince of Abyssinia* (1759) and William Beckford's less philosophical *Vathek, an Arabian Tale* (1786). As a picaresque narrative, *The Adventures of Hajji Baba of Ispahan* resembles the episodic novels of Defoe and Smollett. Like most novels concerning a rogue-hero, Morier's book satirizes the foibles not only of the characters in the story but also those of humankind. Hajji Baba is an amiable opportunist and schemer, experienced in the worldly arts of guile and deception, but not the sole rascal in the book. On the contrary, Hajji learns his impudent tricks from others, and although he is an apt pupil, he is simply more successful—not more wicked—than most people. As one of his teachers, the Dervish Sefer explains: "We look upon mankind as fair game—we live upon their weakness and credulity"; from such counsel, Hajji discovers how to expropriate riches from the weak and stupid for the sake of his own ease. In a world of scoundrels and fools, he is seen as amoral rather than immoral; the reader sympathizes with his desire, in the contest of life, to be the world's knave instead of its victim.

During the course of his roguish adventures, Hajji ranges through almost all the social levels and professions of Persian (and, indeed, Middle-Eastern) life. At various times he is a barber, a merchant, a robber, a slave, a "seller of smoke," a *saka* (water carrier), a *lûti* (privileged buffoon), a dervish, a physician's apprentice, a sublieutenant for the chief executioner, a scribe to a man of law, an ambassador to foreign powers, and finally, the shah's deputy. He travels throughout the Middle East, from Cairo to Aleppo and Damascus; from Mecca and Medina to Lahore and Cashmere. Mostly, however, he travels through the cities and villages of early nineteenth century Persia, learning to understand the passions and weaknesses of his fellowmen. In none of the ranks of society does he encounter true comradeship, civility, or altruism. At one point, after he escapes from the Turcoman robbers and throws himself at the mercy of his countryman, a Persian prince, he is robbed and threatened with further punishment by his protector. A simple muleteer chides Hajji for lamenting his losses. After all, what could he expect from a prince? "When once he or any man in power gets possession of a thing," the muleteer reasons, "do you think that he will ever restore it?"

In spite of Morier's broad-ranging satire, which sometimes approaches cynicism, his prevailing tone is comic rather than censorious. Hajji is, above all, an affable rogue, high-spirited and inventive, most resilient when he appears to be defeated. Through his resourceful imagination, he overcomes most of the obstacles in his way; yet he is never wholly successful and triumphant as are some other picaresque heroes in fiction. Morier is too much the Realist to allow his adventurer the fullest enjoyment of his romantic dreams. Hajji's true love, Zeenab, is kept from him, first by the crafty physician Mizra Ahmak, and later by the shah himself. Worse, as one of the royal executioners, poor Hajji is forced to witness her terrible death.

He suffers other misfortunes. When he is under the tutelage of the Turcoman bandits, he is forced to rob his own father; and years later, he arrives at his ancestral home just in time to watch the old man die. After his father's death, Hajji and his mother quarrel and part on unfriendly terms. His marriage to the rich widow Shekerleb is dissolved by her kinsmen when they discover that Hajji is not so rich as he had pretended to be. He is not only humiliated but beaten on several occasions, once by order of the *Mohtesib* (inspector), who has him thrashed on the soles of his feet until he loses consciousness from the pain. Morier, therefore, avoids the romantic stereotype of the swaggering outlaw—the corsair, the highwayman, the outcast—popularized by such authors as Scott, Byron, and Shelley. Instead, his rogue-hero is a fellow mortal, perhaps less scrupulous than most of us, but unquestionably human in his weaknesses. In *The Adventures of Hajji Baba of Ispahan in England* (1828), Morier continues the tale of Hajji's adventures, this time as an envoy from Persia to the barbarians of the West.

A HANDFUL OF DUST

Type of work: Novel
Author: Evelyn Waugh (1903–1966)
Type of plot: Social satire
Time of plot: Twentieth century
Locale: England
First published: 1934

Principal characters:
TONY LAST, the owner of Hetton Abbey
BRENDA LAST, his wife
JOHN, their son
MRS. BEAVER, an interior decorator
JOHN BEAVER, her son
JOCK GRANT-MENZIES, Tony's friend
DR. MESSINGER, an explorer
TODD, a half-caste trader who loved Dickens

The Story:

John Beaver lived in London with his mother, an interior decorator. Beaver was a worthless young man of twenty-five years who moved in the social circles of his mother's wealthy customers. He was not well liked, but he was often invited to parties and weekends to fill a space made vacant at the last moment.

One weekend, Beaver was invited to Hetton Abbey by its young owner, Tony Last. Tony lived in the old Gothic abbey with his wife, Brenda, and his young son, John. It was Tony's dream that someday he would restore his mansion to its former feudal glory. Brenda, however, was bored with her husband's attachment to the past; she found relief in her weekly trips to London.

Beaver's stay at Hetton Abbey was rather dull, but Brenda liked him and did her best to entertain him. On her next trip to London, she saw him again and asked him to take her to a party. At first, Beaver seemed reluctant; then he agreed to escort her.

Beaver and Brenda left the party early, creating some idle gossip. In a way, the gossipers were correct, for Brenda had definitely decided to have an affair with Beaver. She returned home to the unsuspecting Tony and told him that she was bored with life in the country. She said that she wanted to take some courses in economics at the university in London. Tony, feeling sorry for her, allowed her to rent a one-room flat in a building owned by Mrs. Beaver. Brenda moved to London and returned to Hetton Abbey only on weekends.

One day, when Tony went to London on impulse, he found that his wife already had engagements. He was forced to spend the evening getting drunk with his bachelor friend, Jock Grant-Menzies.

Tony's escapade bothered his conscience so much that when Brenda returned for the weekend she was able to persuade him to let Mrs. Beaver redecorate in modern style one of the rooms of the old house.

Brenda's conscience also bothered her. She tried to interest Tony in a girl she brought down for a weekend, but it was no use. He only wanted to have his wife back home. He still, however, trusted her and suspected nothing of her affair in London.

Things might have remained the same indefinitely if young John Last had not been killed by a horse while he was fox hunting. Tony sent Jock up to London to break the news to Brenda. At first, Brenda thought that Jock was speaking of John Beaver's death, for he was out of town. When she learned the truth, she was relieved, realizing for the first time how much she cared for Beaver.

With young John dead, she felt that nothing held her to Tony any longer. She wrote, telling him everything, and asked for a divorce. Stunned, Tony could not believe that Brenda had been unfaithful to him. At last, he consented to spend a weekend at Brighton with another woman to give her grounds for divorce.

Brenda's family was against the divorce and attempted to prevent it. Then, when they saw that the divorce was inevitable, they tried to force Tony to give Brenda more alimony than he had planned. He refused, for he could raise more money only by selling Hetton Abbey. The proposal angered him so much that he changed his mind about the divorce. He would not set Brenda free.

Wishing to get away from familiar faces, Tony accompanied an explorer, Dr. Messinger, on an expedition to find a lost city in the South American jungles. During the voyage across the Atlantic Ocean, Tony had a short affair with a young French girl from Trinidad; but when she learned that he was married, she would have nothing more to do with him.

Once the explorers had left civilization behind them, Tony found himself thinking of what was going on in London. He did not enjoy jungle life at all; insect bites, vermin, and vampire bats made sleep almost impossible.

When black boatmen had taken Tony and Dr. Messinger far up the Demarara River, they left the explorers in the hands of Indian guides. Then the expedition struck out into unmapped territory.

Meanwhile, back in London, Brenda no longer found Beaver to be an ardent lover. He had counted strongly on getting a considerably large amount of money when he married Brenda; now Brenda could get neither the money nor a divorce.

Brenda began to grow desperate for money. She asked Mrs. Beaver for a job, but Mrs. Beaver thought that it would not look well for her to employ Brenda. A short time later, Beaver decided to accompany his mother on a trip to California.

At last, Tony and Dr. Messinger came to a river they believed must flow into the Amazon, and they ordered the Indians to build canoes. The Indians obeyed, but they refused to venture down the river. There was nothing for the white men to do but to continue the journey without guides. Soon after they set out, Tony came down with fever. Dr. Messinger left him on shore and went on alone to find help, but the explorer drowned when his boat capsized. In his delirium, Tony struggled through the jungle and came by chance to the hut of a trader named Todd, who nursed him back to health but kept him a prisoner. Tony was forced to read the novels of Dickens aloud to his captor. When some Englishmen came in search of Tony, the trader made them believe his captive had died of fever. Tony faced lifelong captivity to be spent reading over and over Dickens' novels to the illiterate half-caste, for no white man could travel in the jungle without native help.

Beaver left for California. Brenda knew that their affair was over. No news came from Tony in South America. Without his permission, Brenda could not draw upon the family funds.

Then Tony was officially declared dead, and Hetton Abbey became the property of another branch of the Last family. The new owner of Hetton Abbey bred silver fox. Although he had even fewer servants than his predecessor and had shut off most of the house, he still dreamed that some day Hetton Abbey would again be as glorious as it was in the days of Cousin Tony.

He erected a memorial to Tony at Hetton Abbey, but Brenda was unable to attend its dedication. She was engaged elsewhere with her new husband, Jock Grant-Menzies.

Critical Evaluation:

Drawn from T. S. Eliot's *The Waste Land*, the title of Evelyn Waugh's novel suggests its theme and his attitude toward post-World War I civilization. In its last stages, English society is "dust," spiritually dead. Without belief or purpose, its members wander from one relationship to another, seeking energy and vitality. The atmosphere is of hectic but empty activity.

The only still point in this whirlwind is provided by Hetton Abbey. Associated with the Middle Ages, a time of Christian belief and social order, Tony Last's estate is a symbol of values that informs not only this novel but all of Waugh's satires. Indeed, if *A Handful of Dust* has a hero at all, it is the Gothic abbey. Despite the destructiveness of its owners and visitors, it alone survives—and, in fact, gives promise of growth at the end.

Tony Last is an unsuitable lord of this richly traditional home. If he is presented as sympathetic, he is also dramatized as morally effete, specifically in regard to his profligate wife, Brenda. He is also an anachronism, unable to adapt to the new age. Just as he cannot bring himself to renovate Hetton, he cannot live in the twentieth century. The absurd end that Waugh designs for him—reading Dickens aloud to a madman for the rest of his life—is an apt, if cruel justice.

Tony's successors at Hetton, the Richard Lasts, are of different mettle. Energetic, resourceful, and more important, a growing family, the Lasts seek to restore the abbey to economic independence. If in part Waugh derives his inspiration from Eliot's apocalyptic poem, the final chapter of the novel is one of hope, both in the revival of Hetton and also in the values it symbolizes: order, family, and continuity.

HANDLEY CROSS
Or, The Spa Hunt

Type of work: Novel
Author: Robert Smith Surtees (1803–1864)
Type of plot: Humorous satire
Time of plot: Nineteenth century
Locale: England
First published: 1843; enlarged, 1854

> ### Principal characters:
> JOHN JORROCKS, a wealthy grocer
> MRS. JORROCKS, his wife
> BELINDA, his niece
> PIGG, his huntsman
> CAPTAIN DOLEFUL, a master of ceremonies

The Story:

For years Michael Hardy had been the leader of the hunt in Sheepwash Vale. While he did not pay quite all the expenses of the sport, his personality and vigor kept fox hunting popular in the district. Michael was one of the old school; his hounds were unkenneled and boarded here and there, and the horses were mostly pickups. At his death, it seemed that fox hunting could no longer be accounted an attraction in the country.

There were some other difficulties. The village of Handley Cross was rapidly growing. Having discovered by chance the curative values of the local spring, a reprobate physician named Swizzle had established himself as a spa doctor, and in a few years, Handley Cross became a fashionable watering place. Swizzle was a perfect doctor for many people. He invariably prescribed game pie and rare beef for his patients and advised two quarts of port wine at dinner. He became a familiar sight in the village, as he buttonholed his patients on the street and inspected their coated tongues and gouty joints. With this new fame as a health resort, hotels and souvenir stands sprang up to bring life to the sleepy village.

There is, however, no good proposition without competition. Another shady practitioner, a sanctimonious doctor named Mello, moved in. He bought land with a small spring on it, poured epsom salts in the water every night, and set up a rival establishment. In no time the town was divided into Melloites and Swizzleites. The important change, however, was in the social life of Handley Cross.

Captain Doleful, a lean, hypocritical half-pay captain, appointed himself master of ceremonies for the town. With the help of Mrs. Barnington, the social arbiter of the fashionable set, balls and teas soon became popular, and social eminence became the goal of the visiting gentry.

In a resort so fashionable it was unthinkable not to have a hunt club. Captain Doleful and some other worthies attempted to carry on after Michael Hardy died, but their efforts were unsuccessful. First, the leaders of the hunt rode in gigs, conveyances unthinkable in Hardy's day. Second, the townspeople were too poor or too parsimonious to hire a whipper-in and a huntsman. Third, subscribers to the hunt were often slow in paying; soon there were not enough funds to pay for damage done to crops and fences.

The fashionables decided that the only solution was a real master of the hunt, one not too elegant for a small spa but rich enough to pay the difference between subscriptions and expenses. A committee headed by Captain Doleful and the secretary Fleeceall decided to invite John Jorrocks, whose fame had spread far, to become master of the hunt. Accordingly a letter was sent, and the negotiations were soon brought to a conclusion, for Jorrocks was an easy victim.

After a life devoted to selling tea and other groceries, Jorrocks was a wealthy man. He had turned to hunting as a hobby, and despite his Cockney accent and ample girth, he was soon accepted in the field. Although he had the bad habit of selling cases of groceries to his fellow huntsmen, Jorrocks soon became a fixture among the sporting set in Surrey. Now, he was to be master in his own right. Captain Doleful secured a lodge for him, and the date was set for his arrival in Handley Cross.

On the appointed day, the four-piece band turned out, and the whole town assembled at the station. Several of the villagers carried banners bearing the legend "Jorrocks Forever." When the train pulled in, Captain Doleful looked through the first-class section but found no Jorrocks. The second-class carriages produced no Jorrocks. Finally, on a flat car at the end of the train, he found Jorrocks and his family snugly sitting in their own coach with the horses already hitched. The cheers were loud as the new hunt master drove through the streets of Handley Cross.

Jorrocks was soon installed in his new lodging with Mrs. Jorrocks and Belinda, his pretty niece. Belinda added greatly to Jorrocks' popularity.

The new hunt master looked over his kennels and the few broken-down hacks in the stable. Besides building up both the pack and the stud, he had to have a real huntsman. He finally hired Pigg, chiefly because his skinny shanks and avowed delicate appetite outweighed his speech of such broad Scots that few could understand what he said. Jorrocks was quickly disillusioned with his new huntsman. When Pigg ate his first meal in the kitchen, there was a great uproar. Hurrying in, Jorrocks found Pigg greedily eating the whole supper joint and holding the other servants at bay; and Pigg could drink more ale and brandy than Jorrocks himself.

There were many fine hunts that winter. Because Pigg was skillful and Jorrocks persistent, the collection of brushes grew fast. One night, Jorrocks was far from home, separated from his trusty Pigg and the pack, and caught in a downpour of rain. He turned into the first gate he saw and knocked. An efficient groom took his horse, and two flunkies politely conducted the dripping Jorrocks to his room. On the bed were dry clothes, in the small tub was hot water, and on the table was a bottle of brandy. Jorrocks peeled off his clothes and settled into the tub. He had just started on his third glass of brandy when someone knocked. Jorrocks ignored the noise for a while, but the knocker was insistent.

At last, a determined voice from the hall demanded his clothes. Jorrocks quickly got out of the tub, put on the clothes that did not fit, and took a firm, possessive grip on the brandy bottle. Then he shouted forcefully that he would keep the clothes.

When Jorrocks came down to dinner, he was surprised to be told that he was in Ongar Castle. His unwilling host was the Earl of Bramber, whose servants had mistaken Jorrocks for an invited guest and by mistake had put him in the room of a captain. Jorrocks looked at the angry captain, who was wearing an outfit of his host. Only Jorrocks' Cockney impudence could have brazened out such a situation.

At last, the company sat down to dinner. As usual, Jorrocks drank too much, and while giving a rousing toast to fox hunting he fell fast asleep on the floor. He awoke immersed in water. Calling lustily for help, he struck out for the shore. When a flunky brought a candle, he saw that he had been put to bed in the bathhouse and that while walking in his sleep he had fallen into the small pool. Jorrocks, however, was irrepressible; in the morning, he parted from the Earl on good terms.

After a hard-riding winter, spring finally spoiled the hunting, and the Jorrocks family left for London. Pigg stayed in Handley Cross to dispose of the dogs and horses. Captain Doleful bought Jorrocks' own mount for twenty-five pounds. When the horse became sick and died soon afterward, parsimonious Doleful sued Jorrocks for the purchase price. The court decided in favor of Jorrocks, holding that no one can warrant a horse to stay sound in wind and limb.

Jorrocks' business associates looked on his hunting capers as a tinge of madness. That fall, Jorrocks was heard to exclaim in delight at the sight of a frostbitten dahlia; it would soon be fox hunting time. At last, however, Jorrocks was committed by a lunacy commission for falling victim to the fox hunting madness. In vain, Jorrocks sputtered and protested; his vehemence only added to the charge against him. Poor, fat Jorrocks spent some time in an asylum before an understanding chancellor freed him. Luckily, he regained his freedom before the hunting season was too far gone.

Critical Evaluation:
Handley Cross: Or, The Spa Hunt is a typical example of nineteenth

century English sporting tales. The novel contains little plot and little attempt at dramatic motivation, but to an enthusiastic fox hunter, *Handley Cross* is fascinating because of its gusty hunting tales and the single-minded devotion of its characters to the sport. Jorrocks, appearing in a number of Surtees' works, is dear to devotees of the hard-riding, hard-drinking sporting set.

For almost twenty years, Robert Smith Surtees regaled the huntsmen of Britain with his amusing tales of the grocer Jorrocks and his undying passion for all things having to do with the chase. Abused and ridiculed for his extreme love of the hunt, he is never totally absurd: there is too much intensity, sincerity, and humanity in the man's love of sport for him to be destroyed by his enemies and detractors. Although a cockney in manners and speech, a mere grocer by trade, Jorrocks achieves a lovable nobility all his own.

In his encouraging address to Benjamin, one of his huntsmen or glorified stable boys, Jorrocks reveals the high-minded values of character and true worldliness he associates with expertise in things of the hunt: There is no saying what "keenness combined with sagacity and cleanliness may accomplish." Benjamin is flattered into believing that he has all the "ingredients of a great man," and "hopportunity only is wantin' to dewelope them."

The hunt is everything to Jorrocks; it is the measure of all he holds dear. Everything else in life, including his grocery business and home, takes second place to the call of the hounds. Even when he is sorting his clothes, the primary consideration is what can be preserved for use in the hunt and what must be discarded because it no longer can be adapted to the hunt. He is so obsessed with his passion that he cannot, without some anxiety, entrust anything connected with hunting to others. When his celebrated horse is being auctioned, he constantly interrupts the auctioneer with praise of the animal's speed and leaping ability. Eventually, Jorrocks' passion becomes a form of madness, but Surtees insists, in a shower of good honor, on vindicating Jorrocks. As exaggerated as it is, his love of the hunt is too sincere and authentic to cause his downfall. He must be free to hunt again.

HANDY ANDY
A Tale of Irish Life

Type of work: Novel
Author: Samuel Lover (1797–1868)
Type of plot: Comic romance
Time of plot: Nineteenth century
Locale: Ireland
First published: 1842

Principal characters:
ANDY ROONEY, a young Irish boy
SQUIRE EDWARD EGAN, his employer
MURTOUGH MURPHY, an attorney
SQUIRE GUSTAVUS O'GRADY, a rival landlord
EDWARD O'CONNOR, a gentleman and poet

The Story:

From the day he was born, Andy Rooney was a mischievous trouble-maker. When he was old enough to work, his mother took him to Squire Egan of Merryvale Hall, who hired him as a stableboy. His literal mind and naïve ways frequently caused his superiors great agitation.

One day, Squire Egan sent Andy to the post office to get a letter. Thinking the postage unduly high, Andy stole two other letters in order to get his money's worth. The Squire's letter was from Murtough Murphy, an attorney, and it concerned a forthcoming election for a county seat held by Sir Timothy Trimmer, who was expected to die soon. Murphy warned Egan that although he could be certain of most of the votes in the election, Squire O'Grady of Neck-or-Nothing Hall was likely to support the Honorable Sackville Scatterbrain, another candidate. It happened that one of the purloined letters was addressed to Gustavus O'Grady. Peering through the envelope, Egan made out some unflattering words about himself. In anger, he threw the letter into the fire. To cover up his error, he also burned the other letter and then told Andy that he destroyed them to protect such a foolish gossoon from detection.

Andy could never get anything straight. When Squire Egan sent him on an errand to get a document from Murtough Murphy and Mrs. Egan sent him to the apothecary shop, Andy left Murphy's paper on the counter of the store and took up, instead, O'Grady's packet of medicine. The apothecary then unknowingly gave O'Grady the document from Murphy. On receiving O'Grady's medicine, Squire Egan was insulted and challenged Murphy to a duel. O'Grady, insulted at the contents of Murphy's legal document, challenged M'Garry, the apothecary. The matter was soon straightened out; Handy Andy fared the worst.

Edward O'Connor was a gallant cavalier. Well-educated and gifted as a poet, he was a favorite among the men of the community. He was in love with Fanny Dawson but had not declared himself as yet. A misunderstanding between Fanny's father and Edward had resulted in the young man's banishment from the Dawson house. After the quarrel, Major Dawson maintained an intense dislike for the poet. Although she brooded over the absence of her lover, Fanny was forced to obey her father's wishes.

While walking one night, Andy stumbled over a man stretched out in the middle of the road. He hailed a passing jaunting car. The driver, learning that the drunken man was his brother, stayed behind to care for him and asked Andy to drive his carriage. The passenger, Mr. Furlong, said he was on his way to visit the Squire. Assuming that he meant Squire Egan, Andy took Furlong to Merryvale Hall, but Furlong had wanted to see O'Grady on election business. Egan, continuing to deceive the visitor, sent for Murphy, and the two men contrived to pump as much information from Furlong as they could.

When the truth was revealed, Furlong set out for Neck-or-Nothing Hall. He met with more mischief there. O'Grady was in a terrible mood, for he had discovered that the letter announcing Furlong's arrival had gone astray. The climax came when O'Grady's daughter Augusta happened into Furlong's room while he was dressing. A moment later, O'Grady's knock at the door sent her hiding under the bed to avoid discovery. O'Grady caught her, however, and insisted that Furlong marry her.

The Honorable Sackville Scatterbrain arrived in time for the nomination speeches, a lively affair with a great deal of shouting and much merriment. On election day, Egan supporters succeeded in irritating O'Grady, who had no sense of humor and plenty of temper. O'Grady thought that the crowd was too boisterous and aroused the people by sending for the militia. When he ordered the militia to fire into the angry mob, Edward O'Connor rode into the crowd to disperse it and prevent the militia from firing. Impressed by his bravery, the militia captain refused to fire. O'Grady then challenged O'Connor to a duel. O'Connor wounded O'Grady. When the Honorable Sackville Scatterbrain won the election, Squire Egan began a suit to dispute its result.

Larry Hogan, one of O'Grady's employees, had learned about the purloining of O'Grady's letter, which Squire Egan had burned, and he hoped to put his knowledge to use by intimidating the Squire. One night, Andy happened to overhear Larry, who was very drunk, talking about his scheme. Confused, Andy went to Father Phil, his confessor, for advice. It so happened that the priest was attending to the nuptials of Matty Dwyer and James Casey. At the wedding feast, Casey failed to appear. Fearing that his daughter would be disgraced, Jack Dwyer asked if any of the guests present would marry Matty. Andy boldly offered himself, and the marriage was performed. After the couple had been left alone in their new cottage, James Casey arrived, accompanied by a hedge-priest who per- . formed a second ceremony. Andy, protesting, was dragged outside and tied to a tree.

O'Grady died from the ill effects of the wound O'Connor had given him. Because the dead man had been deep in debt and unpopular in the community, his body was in danger of being confiscated. To prevent such an action, the family made two coffins; one, the true coffin, was to be buried secretly at night. O'Connor, stumbling upon the scene of the clandestine burial, was struck with remorse at his own deed, but young Gustavus O'Grady forgave his father's slayer, who in return pledged himself to lifelong friendship with Gustavus.

When a beggar warned Mrs. Rooney that someone was plotting to carry off her niece Oonah, Andy disguised himself as the young girl. He was kidnaped and taken to Shan More's cave, where Andy's wild entreaties so aroused the pity of Shan More's sister Bridget that she took the distressed captive to bed with her. Discovering her error in the morning, Bridget lamented her lost honor, which Andy righted by marrying her. Andy discovered too late that he really loved Oonah and that he had married a woman of bad reputation.

It was discovered that Lord Scatterbrain, disguised as a servant named Rooney, had married Andy's mother, only to desert her before Andy's birth. After the death of the old nobleman—the Honorable Sackville Scatterbrain, his nephew, did not dispute the succession—Andy became his heir, with a seat in the House of Lords. He went off to London to learn fine manners and to enjoy his new estate. Shan More and Bridget followed to demand a settlement for the deserted wife. To escape the vulgar and persistent pair, Andy gladly gave Bridget some money.

Major Dawson met with an accident that resulted in his death. With the Major gone, all obstacles between Fanny Dawson and Edward O'Connor were removed, and O'Connor was finally able to enter the Dawson house and to marry Fanny.

Shan More made an attempt upon Andy's life. When the attempt failed, Andy went to Shan's den, where he found a wounded man, an escaped convict, who proved to be Bridget's true husband. Rid of his wife, Andy was free to marry Oonah.

Critical Evaluation:

Musician, painter, songwriter, novelist, playwright, and performer, Samuel Lover was above all an entertainer, and it is as entertainment that *Handy Andy* has endured for nearly a century and a half. Farcical, full of dialect humor and slapstick comedy, the book stops at nothing in its efforts to provoke good humor and laughter.

Written as a series of anecdotes published in twelve monthly installments, *Handy Andy* is not a cohesive novel insofar as plot is concerned. It
is, on the other hand, excellent in character portrayal and atmosphere. The
quality likely to hold the modern reader is its droll wit. Rich in Irish folk-
ways, peppered with clever Irish tales, and enhanced by Irish songs, *Handy
Andy* is more than a series of tales revolving around a political issue, a stupid lout of a boy, and a lovable hero. Accused of flattering his countrymen,
Lover replied that as an Irishman he was compelled to present his land as
he saw it.

One of the chief sources of amusement in the novel is Andy's ever-
present ignorance. A poor, uneducated lad, Andy means well but invariably
gets into trouble. To the unsophisticated readers of Lover's day, Andy's antics touched a familiar chord as well as being funny in a very basic way.
Above all, Lover possessed a horror of dullness, and perhaps this accounts
for the frenetic pace of *Handy Andy*. Certainly, the little tales are full of
action and nonsense. The humor is vigorous and rough-and-ready but never
malicious or cruel. Some of the humor directly attacks prejudices of and
toward the Irish; one of the most amusing sequences deals with the potato,
the Irish fondness for it and reliance upon it for nourishment and the English scorn toward it. A great deal of humor is made of the local elections,
the canvassing for votes, and the competition between the parties; but
whatever the issue involved, the characters tend to be portrayed in an
affectionate and kindly light, and any humor at their expense is gentle
rather than scornful or harsh. There is nothing satirical about this book.
Lover had no intention of reforming anything with his humorous sketches.

Lover seldom attempted subtle humor; the accounts of Sackville Scatterbrain on election day or of Andy's being kidnaped while disguised as a
young girl are as broad as they are lively. The plot, such as it is, dealing
with Andy's marriage, is contrived, and the surprise ending, revealing
Bridget's actual husband, is hardly plausible; yet none of this matters, for it
all is told with such humor that the reader willingly suspends disbelief.
Although the novel is weak, Handy Andy himself nearly ranks with Pickwick and Micawber as a comic hero.

HANGMAN'S HOUSE

Type of work: Novel
Author: Donn Byrne (Brian Oswald Donn-Byrne, 1889–1928)
Type of plot: Regional romance
Time of plot: Early twentieth century
Locale: Ireland
First published: 1926

Principal characters:
JAMES O'BRIEN, Lord Glenmalure, also called Jimmy the
    Hangman
CONNAUGHT, his daughter
DERMOT MCDERMOT, a neighbor
THE CITIZEN, Dinny Hogan, the Irreconcilable's son
JOHN D'ARCY, Dermot's cousin and Connaught's husband

The Story:

Dermot McDermot lived in the most pleasant homestead in the County of Dublin. He was a serious, slight man of twenty-five years, taking after his Quaker mother more than his Irish soldier father except in his intense love of Ireland and everything Irish.

Dermot's nearest neighbors were James O'Brien, Lord Glenmalure, and his daughter Connaught. They lived in a rather forbidding-looking house that the country people insisted on calling Jimmy the Hangman's House. James O'Brien had been a violent rebel in his youth, but he had found it to his advantage to make his peace with the English. Becoming Lord Chief Justice of Ireland, he was responsible for the hanging of many Fenians.

When Glenmalure was stricken on the bench, he was forced to retire. When his condition became worse, he called in doctors from Dublin and then England. One doctor told him that he would live a month, certainly no more than five weeks. Then he secretly sent off a letter to John D'Arcy, Dermot's cousin, son of an old friend called Tricky Mick. Dermot thought D'Arcy a twister; Connaught's father said he had merely made a youngster's mistake. Glenmalure knew John D'Arcy was devious but ambitious; he also knew that he might make his way in politics with Connaught's money and Hangman Jimmy's backing. In his remaining weeks, Glenmalure made contacts for D'Arcy and married him to Connaught. Glenmalure knew Dermot wanted to marry Connaught but would not leave his homestead; he thought Connaught, strong-willed as she was, could guide D'Arcy to a place in the world where she might even get a title.

Glenmalure had been a rebel of the old days, but there were still plenty of young men ready for a war for freedom if the word were given. Those who directed the movement decided there must be no war. They sent back to Ireland the Citizen, a commander of cavalry in the French army, but also the son of old Dinny Hogan the Irreconcilable, who had fled from Ireland and gone to live in France after the last uprising. The Citizen was to spend a year in Ireland, to make sure the young men would keep in line.

He had another reason for going to Ireland. John D'Arcy had married and then deserted his sister Maeve. Her shame caused her death and her son's, and their deaths brought on Dinny Hogan's. Dinny's son was out for revenge.

Glenmalure died the night of Connaught's wedding. She and D'Arcy returned from their honeymoon immediately.

Dermot saw them at the Tara Hunt, one of the best in the country. The Citizen also turned up at the hunt and approached D'Arcy to ask if he had been in Paris in '95. D'Arcy, after swearing that he had never been in Paris, went to the police to expose the Citizen. Connaught could not understand why D'Arcy had lied about being in Paris; she was furious when she heard that he had informed on a hunted man.

Dermot knew D'Arcy feared the Citizen but could not understand why. He also heard that things were not going well at Glenmalure and that Connaught kept a woman relative with her constantly, while D'Arcy spent his time gambling with people who would never have dared enter the house during Glenmalure's lifetime. D'Arcy's backers in politics had reneged after Glenmalure died, and D'Arcy was at loose ends.

On St. Stephen's Day, the first steeplechase of the year was held at the Hannastown races. Connaught's Bard of Armagh was entered. Dermot heard that long odds were being placed on him, although the horse should have been considered the best in the field. One of the bookmakers told him that D'Arcy had placed a large bet against the Bard but that there were many small bets on him that would spell disaster to the poor people if the Bard did not run. On the day of the race, Connaught's jockey did not show up. Dermot rode the Bard and won. He and Connaught found D'Arcy sobbing afterward because he had lost heavily. Then Dermot knew his cousin was a weakling. That night, D'Arcy killed the Bard.

Connaught left home, and even the gamblers refused to play with a man who had killed a horse. Connaught, meanwhile, was miserable in England. Dermot looked for D'Arcy to straighten him out and to offer him money to go away if that seemed best. D'Arcy told him that he had married Maeve. Thinking D'Arcy had been married to Maeve when he married Connaught, Dermot thrashed him and would probably have killed him if an innkeeper had not interfered. Dermot gave D'Arcy money and told him to leave the country.

Connaught came home a short time later to a house of bitterness and gloom. After she and Dermot finally admitted they loved each other, Dermot sought out the Citizen to see if they might not work out some way to keep the shame of D'Arcy's conduct from staining Connaught and yet dissolve that marriage so that he and Connaught could be married. The Citizen told Dermot that Maeve had actually died before D'Arcy married Connaught, although D'Arcy could not have known it at that time. Dermot's hands were tied.

Hearing that Maeve was dead, D'Arcy came back to Glenmalure, and Connaught sought refuge with Dermot and his mother. Finding her there, D'Arcy accused Connaught and Dermot of being lovers. When they admitted their feelings, he threatened to hale them into court, but Dermot's mother prevented him. Connaught went again to England.

Knowing that Connaught would do nothing to him, D'Arcy began to sell off all the possessions in the house. Dermot made arrangements in Dublin to be informed whenever these possessions came on the market, and he bought up all of them. One night, Dermot decided to pick some of Connaught's own roses and send them to her. As he went toward the house, Glenmalure looked empty and forbidding. At the gate, he met the Citizen, bent on killing D'Arcy. Dermot, not wishing the Citizen to be soiled with the murder of a twister like D'Arcy, tried to persuade him to go away. The Citizen, however, was determined. Dermot was afraid to let him go in alone.

Inside they found D'Arcy dressed for travel. The house had been stripped, and there was a smell of oil in it. Instead of killing D'Arcy outright, the Citizen allowed himself to be persuaded to a duel with pistols. D'Arcy shot before the signal had been given and wounded the Citizen. Then he smashed a lamp on the floor and dashed upstairs. The lamp started a sheet of fire that swept through the house as Dermot and the Citizen fought their way outside. D'Arcy caught his foot while jumping from a window and was dead when he hit the ground.

Dermot's mother went to Connaught for awhile. Dermot had the walls of Glenmalure torn down and a neat cottage built in its place. The Citizen, recovered from his wound, went back to his regiment. Then Connaught came home.

Critical Evaluation:

In *Hangman's House*, Donn Byrne intended to write an Irish novel for Irishmen, people for whom their own country was a passion. An intense love for Irish landscape, horse racing, coursing, Gaelic balladry, hunting, and the writer's freedom-loving countrymen is evident throughout the book. When the novel appeared, critics may have preferred his *Messer*

Marco Polo or *The Wind Bloweth*, but revised judgment is likely to put *Hangman's House* above the latter. The book was written in Dublin in 1922 and 1923, while the country was still being harried by the armed resistance of Republican irreconcilables. The state of Ireland at that time is presented in Byrne's characterization of the Citizen, a splendid man who had direct control over those who wanted to fight for freedom. The novel has been dramatized for the stage and for motion pictures.

Ireland and the strangely heroic Irish race are the subject of *Hangman's House*, perhaps Byrne's most noted novel. Certain medieval prophets had accurately predicted that Ireland would be tyrannized by England for "a week of centuries" (seven centuries); and that week ended during the 1920's, the decade in which Byrne's novel is set. The end of tyranny is the story's background theme. Despite the cluster of characters, ranging from the Citizen, to Lord Glenmalure, to Dermot McDermot, the dominant presence in the novel is Ireland's finally realized struggle for freedom. Therefore, the real protagonist of *Hangman's House* is Irish history with its centuries of oppression.

Nevertheless, Byrne is not hateful or propagandistic; the few British personalities in the novel are presented as decent men doing their duty, while Catholics are not painted as saints or Protestants as cohorts of the Antichrist. The one touch of overt Irish flag-waving occurs when a fairly amiable British officer seeks to bribe an Irish child into singing British rather than Irish ditties but is calmly rejected. Otherwise, the novel's characters move through their lives as their ancestors have done for centuries, living under an oppressive pall that never vanquishes them. The Citizen is the strongest symbolic personality of the story, and Connaught is a victim figure that is almost representative of Ireland itself. A curious void exists in the rather mild treatment of Lord Glenmalure, "The Hangman," who wreaks vengeance on many Fenians and who coerces Connaught into marriage with a spineless traitor for the most spurious of economic reasons. The selfishness and violence of Glenmalure—whose base actions are outwardly respectable and dignified—are treated more as a commentary on weak human beings than as a portrait of a willfully evil individual. The author's sensitivity for tints and color as well as his ability to use words musically are evident in the story.

HARD TIMES

Type of work: Novel
Author: Charles Dickens (1812–1870)
Type of plot: Social criticism
Time of plot: Mid-nineteenth century
Locale: England
First published: 1854

Principal characters:

THOMAS GRADGRIND, a schoolmaster and a believer in "facts"
LOUISA GRADGRIND, his oldest daughter
TOM GRADGRIND, Louisa's brother
MR. BOUNDERBY, Louisa's husband and a manufacturer and
  banker
SISSY JUPE, a waif befriended by the Gradgrinds
MRS. SPARSIT, Bounderby's housekeeper
STEPHEN BLACKPOOL, Bounderby's employee
JAMES HARTHOUSE, a political aspirant

The Story:

Thomas Gradgrind, proprietor of an experimental private school in
Coketown, insisted that the children under him learn facts and only facts.
He felt that the world had no place for fancy or imagination. His own five
children were models of a factual education. Never having been permitted
to learn anything of the humanities, they were ignorant of literature and
any conception of human beings as individuals. Even fairy tales and nursery rhymes had been excluded from their education.

One day as he walked from the school to his home, Gradgrind was immensely displeased and hurt to find his two oldest children, Louisa and
Tom, trying to peek through the canvas walls of a circus tent. Nor did it
ease his mind to discover that the two youngsters were not at all sorry for
acting against the principles under which they had been reared and educated. Later, Gradgrind and his industrialist friend, Mr. Josiah Bounderby,
discussed possible means by which the children might have been misled
from the study of facts. They concluded that another pupil, Sissy Jupe,
whose father was a clown in the circus, had influenced the young
Gradgrinds.

Having decided to remove Sissy Jupe from the school, Bounderby and
Gradgrind set out immediately to tell the girl's father. When they arrived at
the inn where the Jupes were staying, they found that the clown-father had
deserted his daughter. Moved by sentiment, Gradgrind decided to keep the
girl in his home and let her be educated at his school, all against the advice
of Bounderby, who thought Sissy Jupe would be only a bad influence on

the Gradgrind children.

Years passed, and Louisa and young Tom grew up. Gradgrind knew that Bounderby had long wished to marry Louisa. Educated away from sentiment, she agreed to marry Bounderby, who was thirty years her elder. Tom, an employee in Bounderby's bank, was very glad to have his sister marry Bounderby; he wanted a friend to help him if he got into trouble there. In fact, he advised his sister to marry Bounderby for that reason, and she, loving her brother, agreed to help him by marrying the wealthy banker.

Bounderby was very happy to have Louisa as his wife. After his marriage, he placed his elderly housekeeper in a room at the bank. Mrs. Sparsit disliked Louisa and was determined to keep an eye on her for her employer's sake. After the marriage, all seemed peaceful at the bank, at the Gradgrind home, and at the Bounderby residence.

In the meantime, Gradgrind had been elected to Parliament from his district. He sent out from London an aspiring young politician, James Harthouse, who was to gather facts about the industrial city of Coketown, facts which were to be used in a survey of economic and social life in Britain. In order to facilitate the young man's labors, Gradgrind had given him a letter of introduction to Bounderby, who immediately told Harthouse the story of his career from street ragamuffin to industrialist and banker. Harthouse thought Bounderby was a fool, but he was greatly interested in pretty Louisa.

Through his friendship with Bounderby, Harthouse met Tom Gradgrind, who lived with the Bounderbys. Harthouse took advantage of Tom's love for drink to learn more about Louisa. He had heard that she had been subjected to a dehumanizing education and felt that she would be easy prey for seduction because of her loveless marriage to the pompous Bounderby. For these reasons, Harthouse decided to test Louisa's virtue.

Before long, Harthouse gained favor in her eyes. Neither realized, however, that Mrs. Sparsit, jealous and resenting her removal from the comfortable Bounderby house, spied on them constantly.

Everyone was amazed to learn one day that the Bounderby bank had been robbed. Chief suspect was Stephen Blackpool, an employee whom Bounderby had mistreated. Blackpool, who had been seen loitering in front of the bank, had disappeared on the night of the robbery. Suspicion also fell on Mrs. Pegler, an old woman known to have been in Blackpool's company.

A search for Blackpool and Mrs. Pegler proved fruitless. Bounderby seemed content to wait; he said that the culprits would turn up sooner or later.

The affair between Louisa and Harthouse reached a climax when Louisa agreed to elope with the young man. Her better judgment, however,

caused her to return to her father instead of running away with her lover.
Gradgrind was horrified to see what his education had done to Louisa's
character, and he tried to make amends for her. The situation was complicated by Mrs. Sparsit. She had learned of the proposed elopement and had
told Bounderby. He angrily insisted that Louisa return to his home. Realizing that his daughter had never loved Bounderby, Gradgrind insisted that
she be allowed to make her own choice. Harthouse disappeared, giving up
all hope of winning Louisa.

Mrs. Sparsit returned to act as Bounderby's housekeeper during Louisa's
absence and tried to reinstate herself in Bounderby's confidence by tracing
down Mrs. Pegler. To her chagrin, Mrs. Pegler turned out to be
Bounderby's mother. Bounderby was furious, for his mother disproved his
boasts about being a self-made man. Meanwhile, Louisa and Sissy Jupe
accidentally found Blackpool, who had fallen into a mine shaft while
returning to Coketown to prove his innocence in the robbery. After his rescue, he told that Tom Gradgrind was the real culprit. When the young man
disappeared, his sister and father found him with the help of Sissy Jupe.
They placed him, disguised, in a circus until arrangements could be made
for spiriting him out of the country.

Before he could escape, however, Bounderby's agents found Tom and
arrested him. With the aid of the circus roustabouts, he was rescued and
put on a steamer that carried him away from the police and Bounderby's
vengeance.

Mrs. Sparsit, who had caused Bounderby great embarrassment by
producing Mrs. Pegler, was discharged from his patronage, much to her
chagrin. Bounderby himself died unhappily in a fit a few years later. The
Gradgrinds, all of them victims of an education of facts, continued to live
unhappily, unable to see the human side of life.

Critical Evaluation:

Charles Dickens began as an entertainer (*Pickwick Papers*) but gradually evolved into a moralist and social critic of major significance. In his
early works, there are heroes and villains; in his later works, victims and
victimizers. The distinction is important because it measures his development from a writer of fiction to an artist with a tragic vision.

This novel was Dicken's first story of outright social protest. Earlier
works had contained sections of social criticism, but this was the first motivated entirely by the writer's feelings about contemporary British culture.
The novel, appropriately dedicated to Thomas Carlyle, another critic of
nineteenth century British society, was based upon personal observations of
life in Manchester, one of England's great manufacturing towns and the
original for Dickens' Coketown. The story is loaded with the bitter sincerity of Dickens' dislike for the industrial conditions he found in his home-

land. Unfortunately for the value of the novel as a social document, Dickens overdrew his portraits of the industrialists responsible for conditions he abhorred; his industrialists became sheer grotesques and monsters.

Hard Times is a milestone in Dickens' art: caricature and allegorical names are used here in a form of Swiftian satire so bitter in its contempt and social rage that readers almost forget that the same devices are used to create lovable human beings in his other works. Mr. Gradgrind is offensive in a very serious way. His reduction of everything to "facts" constitutes a *gradual grinding* away of the humanity of his pupils and his own children. Louisa marries to obtain advantages for her brother—in itself a noble act; but her blind willingness to set aside personal feelings and needs only makes her more vulnerable to Harthouse's attempts at seduction. It is finally Louisa's responsibility, from the depths of her own denied feelings, to educate Gradgrind to his deficiencies as a father and teacher.

Although Dickens' satirical dismissal of rationalistic Utilitarianism (the doctrine that the greatest good for the greatest number must be the goal of a statistically rigorous and "fact" conscious social reform) is brilliantly effective in the classroom scenes, he does not entirely convince readers that Utilitarian education is directly responsible for the dehumanization of England. Dickens wanted to shock the middle-class reformers with the coldness of their ideas, but he himself was curiously limited in his own humanism. Although he was a humanitarian, he did not entirely respect the humanity of the very working classes he championed. The portrait of Slackbridge, the trade union organizer, reveals Dickens' contempt of labor as a political force.

Throughout his life, Dickens distrusted the people's ability to govern themselves; he always looked to the manufacturers and the aristocracy, the governing classes, to correct or avoid the evils of the society they held in trust. *Hard Times* is a blow at the ideas Dickens felt were preventing the leading classes from meeting their social responsibilities.

HEADLONG HALL

Type of work: Novel
Author: Thomas Love Peacock (1785–1866)
Type of plot: Comedy of manners
Time of plot: Early nineteenth century
Locale: Wales
First published: 1816

Principal characters:
SQUIRE HEADLONG, the host
MR. FOSTER, the optimist
MR. ESCOT, the pessimist
MR. JENKISON, a champion of the status quo

The Story:

Squire Harry Headlong differed from the usual Welsh squire in that he, by some means or other, had become interested in books, in addition to the common interests of hunting, racing, and drinking. He had journeyed to Oxford and then to London in order to find the philosophers and men of refined tastes introduced to him in the world of literature. Having rounded up a group of intellectuals, he invited them to Headlong Hall for the Christmas holidays.

Three of the men formed the nucleus of his house party. The first was Mr. Foster, an optimist. To him, everything was working toward a state of perfection, and each advancement in technology, in government, or in sociology was all for the good. He believed that man would ultimately achieve perfection as a result of his progress. Mr. Escot, on the other hand, saw nothing but deterioration in the world. The advances that Mr. Foster saw as improvement, Escot saw as evidences of corruption and evil that would soon reduce the whole human race to wretchedness and slavery. The third man of the trio was Mr. Jenkison, who took a position exactly in the middle. He believed that the amount of improvement and deterioration balanced each other perfectly and that good and evil would remain forever in status quo.

These philosophers, with a large company of other dilettantes, descended upon Headlong Hall. Among the lesser guests was a landscape gardener who made it his sole duty to persuade the Squire to have his estate changed from a wild tangle of tress and shrubs into a shaved and polished bed of green grass. Mr. Foster thought the grounds could be improved; Mr. Escot thought any change would be for the worse; and Mr. Jenkison thought the scenery perfect as it was.

There were ladies present, both young and old, but they did not join in the philosophical discussions. Many of the talks occurred after the ladies had left the dinner table and as the wine was being liberally poured, for Squire Headlong was aware that the mellowness produced by good burgundy was an incentive to conversation. The discussions took various turns, all of them dominated by the diametrically opposed views of Foster and Escot and soothed by the healing words of Jenkison. Escot harped constantly upon the happiness and moral virtue possessed by the savages of the past, virtue that lessened with each encroachment of civilization. As the savage began to build villages and cities and to develop luxuries, he also began to suffer disease, poverty, oppression, and loss of morality. Foster could not agree with this thesis. He pointed to the achievements of civilization in fields other than those of a materialistic nature. Shakespeare and Milton, for example, could not have achieved their genius in the primitive life Escot applauded. Escot, refusing to concede an inch, pointed to Milton's suffering, stating also that even if one man did profit from the so-called advancements, fifty men regressed because of them. Mr. Jenkison agreed that the subject left something to be said on either side.

Between these learned discussions, the gentlemen spent their time in attempts to fascinate the ladies. Escot had once been the suitor of one of the guests, but he had offended her father during an intellectual discussion and had fallen out of favor. He attempted now to regain his former place in her affection by humoring the father. During these periods of respite, the guests also entertained one another with singing and recitations, the selections being those they themselves had composed.

The Squire was planning a magnificent ball and had invited the whole neighborhood to be his guests. At the ball, the wine flowed freely, so that even Foster and Escot forgot some of their differences. Although he disapproved of any but aboriginal dances, Escot danced often with the lady of his choice. Foster, of course, thought the modern dance the utmost in refinement and an expression of the improved morality of man. Jenkison could see points both for and against the custom. During the evening, Squire Headlong was reminded by a maiden relative that should he not marry soon there would be no one to carry on the name that had been honored for many centuries. As his name implied, the Squire was not one to toy with an idea once it had entered his mind. Fixing on the lady of his choice in a matter of minutes, he proposed and was accepted. Then he arranged three other matches in an equally short time. Foster and Escot were aided in choosing brides and in getting permission from the father of Escot's beloved. Foster's bride was related to the Squire and presented no obstacle. Seizing on another man, the Squire told him of the plan and promptly chose a bride for the hapless individual.

Within a matter of days, the weddings took place. After promising to gather again in August, the guests then dispersed. Foster and Escot tried to the last to convince each other and the rest that only one philosophy was the true one, but Mr. Jenkison was not to fall into either of their traps. He would join them again in August, still convinced that there was merit in both of their arguments. Neither was right or wrong, but each balanced the other, leaving the world in its usual status quo.

Critical Evaluation:

Headlong Hall, Thomas Love Peacock's first novel, has been characterized as apprentice work because his later exercises in the genre are even more successful. Nevertheless, there is no awkwardness or hesitancy in this pioneer work; the later novels differ from it only in offering a richer variety of conversation and slightly more complex plots.

Plot is the least requisite element in a Peacock novel, and the author is inclined to mock even the minimal necessities of storytelling that he acknowledges. Chapter 14 of *Headlong Hall*, in which four marriages are clapped up in as many pages, is a reduction to absurdity of the propensity of popular novelists in his day to pair off their *dramatis personae* in the concluding chapters.

Characterization is not much more important to Peacock. What he provides instead is a group of quirky mouthpieces for different points of view, combined with caricatures, seldom malicious, of his associates. Aspects of his friend Shelley are caricatured in at least three of the novels (Foster is the Shelleyan figure in this one), and Shelley was highly amused by each portrayal. Although sharp, Peacock's wit is seldom wounding, and it touches virtually everywhere with a fine impartiality. He was delighted to learn of his readers' difficulty in ascertaining which, if any, of the opinions so entertainingly advanced in his novels he shared.

Opinions, or more precisely, the absurdity and pretentiousness with which people advance them and the gap between their propositions and their behavior are the real subject of all the novels. Literary historians, noting the customary setting for Peacock's gatherings of indefatigable talkers, have called him the father of the "country house novel." His progeny have been numerous and often brilliant, including such dazzling performances as Douglas' *South Wind* and Huxley's *Crome Yellow*, but none has surpassed its progenitor in wit and geniality.

HEART OF DARKNESS

Type of work: Novella
Author: Joseph Conrad (Józef Teodor Konrad Nalecz Korzeniowski,
 1857–1924)
Type of plot: Symbolic romance
Time of plot: Late nineteenth century
Locale: The Belgian Congo
First published: 1902

Principal characters:
MARLOW, the narrator
MR. KURTZ, the manager of the Inner Station, Belgian Congo
THE DISTRICT MANAGER
A RUSSIAN TRAVELER
KURTZ'S FIANCÉE

The Story:

A group of men were sitting on the deck of the cruising yawl, *The Nellie,* anchored one calm evening in the Thames estuary. One of the seamen, Marlow, began reflecting that the Thames area had been, at the time of the invading Romans, one of the dark and barbarous areas of the earth. Dwelling on this theme, he then began to tell a story of the blackest, most barbarous area of the earth that he had experienced.

Through his aunt's connections, Marlow had once secured a billet as commander of a river steamer for one of the trading companies with interests in the Belgian Congo. When he went to Belgium to learn more about the job, he found that few of the officials of the company expected him to return alive. In Brussels, he also heard of the distinguished Mr. Kurtz, the powerful and intelligent man who was educating the natives and at the same time sending back record shipments of ivory.

The mysterious figure of Mr. Kurtz fascinated Marlow. In spite of the ominous hints that he gathered from various company officials, he became more and more curious about what awaited him in the Congo. During his journey, as he passed along the African coast, he reflected that the wilderness and the unknown seemed to seep right out to the sea. Many of the trading posts and stations the ship passed were dilapidated and looked barbaric. Finally, Marlow arrived at the seat of the government at the mouth of the river. Again, he heard of the great distinction and power of Mr. Kurtz who had an enormous reputation because of his plans to enlighten the natives and his success in gaining their confidence. Marlow also saw natives working in the hot sun until they collapsed and died. Marlow had to wait impatiently for ten days at the government site because his work would not begin until he reached the district manager's station, two hundred miles up the river. At last, the expedition left for the district station.

Marlow arrived at the district station to find that the river steamer had sunk a few days earlier. He met the district manager, a man whose only ability seemed to be the ability to survive. The district manager, unconcerned with the fate of the natives, was interested only in getting out of the country; he felt that Mr. Kurtz's new methods were ruining the whole district. The district manager also reported that he had not heard from Kurtz for quite some time but had received disquieting rumors about his failing health.

Although he was handicapped by a lack of rivets, Marlow spent months supervising repairs to the antiquated river steamer. He also overheard a conversation which revealed that the district manager was Kurtz's implacable enemy, who hoped that the climate would do away with his rival.

The steamer was finally ready for use, and Marlow, along with the district manager, sailed to visit Kurtz at the inner station far up the river. The journey was difficult and perilous; the water was shallow; there were frequent fogs. Just as they arrived within a few miles of Kurtz's station, natives attacked the vessel with spears and arrows. Marlow's helmsman, a faithful native, was killed by a long spear when he leaned from his window to fire at the savages. Marlow finally blew the steamboat whistle, and the sound frightened the natives away. The district manager was sure that Kurtz had lost control over the blacks. When they docked, they met an enthusiastic Russian traveler who told them that Kurtz was gravely ill.

While the district manager visited Kurtz, the Russian told Marlow that the sick man had become corrupted by the very natives he had hoped to enlighten. He still had power over the natives, but instead of his changing them, they had debased him into an atavistic savage. Kurtz attended native rituals, had killed frequently in order to get ivory, and had hung heads as decorations outside his hut. Later Marlow met Kurtz and found that the man had, indeed, been corrupted by the evil at the center of experience. Marlow learned from the Russian that Kurtz had ordered the natives to attack the steamer, thinking that, if they did so, the white men would run away and leave Kurtz to die among his fellow savages in the wilderness. Talking to Marlow, Kurtz showed his awareness of how uncivilized he had become and how his plans to educate the natives had been reversed. He gave Marlow a packet of letters for his fiancée in Belgium and the manuscript of an article, written sometime earlier, in which he urged efforts to educate the natives.

The district manager and Marlow took Kurtz, now on a stretcher, to the river steamer to take him back home. The district manager contended that the area was now ruined for collecting ivory. Full of despair and the realization that devouring evil was at the heart of everything, Kurtz died while the steamer was temporarily stopped for repairs.

Marlow returned to civilization. About a year later, he went to Belgium to see Kurtz's fiancée. She still thought of Kurtz as the splendid and powerful man who had gone to Africa with a mission, and she still believed in his goodness and power. When she asked Marlow what Kurtz's last words had been, Marlow lied and told her that Kurtz had asked for her at the end. In reality, Kurtz, who had seen all experience, had in his final words testified to the horror of it all. This horror was not something, Marlow felt, that civilized ladies could, or should, understand.

Critical Evaluation:

In one sense, *Heart of Darkness* is a compelling adventure tale of a journey into the blackest heart of the Belgian Congo. The story presents attacks by the natives, descriptions of the jungle and the river, and characterizations of white men who, sometimes with ideals and sometimes simply for profit, invade the jungles to bring out ivory. The journey into the heart of the Congo, however, is also a symbolic journey into the blackness central to the heart and soul of man, a journey deep into primeval passion, superstition, and lust. Those who, like the district manager, undertake this journey simply to rob the natives of ivory, without any awareness of the importance of the central darkness, can survive. Similarly, Marlow, who is only an observer, never centrally involved, can survive to tell the tale; but those who, like Mr. Kurtz, are aware of the darkness, who hope with conscious intelligence and a humane concern for all mankind to bring light into the darkness, are doomed, are themselves swallowed up by the darkness and evil they had hoped to penetrate. Conrad manages to make his point, a realization of the evil at the center of human experience, without ever breaking the closely knit pattern of his narrative or losing the compelling atmospheric and psychological force of the tale. The wealth of natural symbols, the clear development of character, and the sheer fascination of the story make this a novella that has been frequently praised and frequently read ever since its publication in 1902. *Heart of Darkness* is, in both style and insight, a masterful short story.

Christened Jósef Teodor Konrad Nalecz Korzeniowski by his Polish parents, Joseph Conrad was able to write of the sea and sailing from firsthand knowledge. He left the cold climate of Poland early in his life to travel to the warmer regions of the Mediterranean where he became a sailor. He began reading extensively and chose the sea as a vehicle for the ideas that were forming in his psyche. He traveled a great deal: to the West Indies, Latin America, Africa. Eventually, he settled in England and perfected (through the elaborate process of translating from Polish into French into English) a remarkably subtle yet powerful literary style.

Criticism of Conrad's work in general and *Heart of Darkness* in particular has been both extensive and varied. Many critics concern themselves with Conrad's style; others focus on the biographical aspects of his fiction; some see the works as social commentaries; some are students of Conrad's explorations into human psychology; many are interested in the brooding, shadowy symbolism and philosophy that hovers over all the works. It is easy to see, therefore, that Conrad is a distinctively complex literary genius. E. M. Forster censured him as a vague and elusive writer who never quite clearly discloses the philosophy that lies behind his tales. Such a censure ignores Conrad's notion about the way some fiction can be handled. Partly as Conrad's mouthpiece, the narrator of *Heart of Darkness* states in the first few pages of the novel:

> The yarns of seamen have a direct simplicity, the whole meaning of which lies within the shell of a cracked nut. But Marlow was not typical (if his propensity to spin yarns be excepted), and to him the meaning of an episode was not inside like a kernel but outside, enveloping the tale which brought it out only as a glow brings out a haze, in the likeness of one of those misty halos that sometimes are made visible by the spectral illumination of moonshine.

The mention of the narrator brings up one of the most complex and intriguing features of *Heart of Darkness*: its carefully executed and elaborately conceived point of view. Readers can detect (if careful in their reading) that the novel is in truth two narratives, inexorably woven together by Conrad's masterful craftsmanship. The outer frame of the story—the immediate setting—involves the unnamed narrator who is apparently the only one on the *Nellie* who is profoundly affected by Marlow's tale, the inner story that is the bulk of the entire novella. Marlow narrates, and the others listen passively. The narrator's closing words show his feeling at the conclusion of Marlow's recounting of the events in the Congo:

> Marlow ceased, and sat apart, indistinct and silent, in the pose of a meditating Buddha. Nobody moved for a time. "We have lost the first of the ebb," said the Director suddenly. I raised my head. The offing was barred by a black bank of clouds, and the tranquil waterway leading to the uttermost ends of the earth flowed sombre under an overcast sky—seemed to lead into the heart of an immense darkness.

Since Marlow's narrative is a tale devoted primarily to a journey to the mysterious dark continent (the literal heart of darkness, Africa), a superficial view of the tale is simply that it is essentially an elaborate story involving confrontation with exotic natives, treacherous dangers of the jungle, brutal savagery, and even cannibalism. Such a view, however, ignores larger meanings with which the work is implicitly concerned: namely, social and cultural implications; psychological workings of the cultivated European left to the uncivilized wilderness; and the richly colored fabric of symbolism that emerges slowly but inevitably from beneath the surface.

Heart of Darkness can also be examined for its social and cultural commentaries. It is fairly obvious that a perverted version of the "White Man's Burden" was the philosophy adopted by the ivory hunters at the Inner Station. Kurtz's "Exterminate the brutes!" shows the way a white man can exploit the helpless savage. The futile shelling from the gunboat into the jungle is also vividly portrayed as a useless, brutal, and absurd act perpetrated against a weaker, more uncivilized culture than the one that nurtured Kurtz.

Here the psychological phenomena of Marlow's tale emerge. Kurtz, a man relieved of all social and civilized restraints, goes mad after committing himself to the total pursuit of evil and depravity. His observation "The horror! the horror!" suggests his final realization of the consequences of his life. Marlow also realizes this and is allowed (because he forces restraint upon himself) to draw back his foot from the precipice of madness. The experience leaves Marlow sober, disturbed, meditative, and obsessed with relating his story in much the same way Coleridge's Ancient Mariner must also relate his story.

On a symbolic level, the story is rich; a book could easily be written on this facet of the novel. An arbitrary mention of some of the major symbols must suffice here: the Congo River that reminded Marlow early in his youth of a snake as it uncoiled its length into the darkness of Africa and furnished him with an uncontrollable "fascination of the abomination"; the symbolic journey into man's own heart of darkness revealing blindingly the evil of man's own nature and his capacity for evil; the irony of the quest when the truth is revealed not in terms of light but in terms of darkness (the truth brings not light but rather total darkness). The entire symbolic character of the work is capsuled at the end of Marlow's tale when he is forced to lie to Kurtz's intended spouse in order to preserve her illusion; the truth appears to Marlow as an inescapable darkness, and the novel ends with the narrator's own observation of darkness.

Heart of Darkness is one of literature's most sombre fictions. It explores the fundamental questions about man's nature: his capacity for evil; the necessity for restraint; the effect of physical darkness and isolation on a civilized soul; and the necessity of relinquishing pride for one's own spiritual salvation. E. M. Forster's censure of Conrad may be correct in many ways, but it refuses to admit that through such philosophical ruminations Conrad has allowed generations of readers to ponder humanity's own heart of darkness.

THE HEART OF MIDLOTHIAN

Type of work: Novel
Author: Sir Walter Scott (1771–1832)
Type of plot: Historical romance
Time of plot: Early eighteenth century
Locale: Scotland
First published: 1818

Principal characters:
>DAVID DEANS, a dairyman
>JEANIE DEANS, his daughter
>EFFIE DEANS, another daughter
>REUBEN BUTLER, Jeanie's betrothed
>GEORDIE ROBERTSON, Effie's betrayer, in reality George
>Staunton
>MEG MURDOCKSON, an evil woman
>THE DUKE OF ARGYLE, Jeanie's benefactor

The Story:

The first knowledge Jeanie Deans had that her sister Effie was in trouble came just a few moments before officers of justice arrived at the cottage to arrest Effie for child murder. They told Jeanie and her father, David Deans, that Effie had borne a male child illegitimately and had killed him or caused him to be killed soon after he was born. Effie admitted the birth of the child but refused to name her seducer. She denied that she had killed her baby, saying that she had fallen into a stupor and had recovered to find that the midwife who attended her had disposed of the child in some unknown fashion. In the face of the evidence, however, she was convicted of child murder and sentenced to be hanged. Jeanie might have saved her sister, for it was the law that if a prospective mother had told anyone of her condition she would not be responsible for her baby's death. Jeanie, however, would not lie, even to save her sister's life. Since there was no one to whom Effie had told her terrible secret, there was no defense for her, and she was placed in the Tolbooth prison to await execution.

Another prisoner in the Tolbooth was Captain John Porteous, who was awaiting execution for firing into the crowd attending the hanging of Andrew Wilson, a smuggler. Wilson's accomplice, Geordie Robertson, had escaped, and the officers feared that Robertson might try to rescue Wilson. For that reason, Porteous and a company of soldiers had been sent to the scene of the execution to guard against a possible rescue. Because Porteous had fired into the crowd without provocation and had killed several people, he was to be hanged; but when his execution was stayed for a few weeks, a mob headed by Robertson, disguised as a woman, broke into the prison, seized Porteous, and hanged him. As a result of that deed, Robertson became a hunted man.

Meanwhile Jeanie Deans, who had refused to lie to save her sister, had not forsaken Effie. When she visited Effie in prison, she learned that Robertson was the father of her child. He had left her in the care of old Meg Murdockson, considered by many to be a witch, and it must have been Meg who had killed or sold the baby. Meg's daughter Madge had long before been seduced by Robertson and had lost her mind for love of him; Meg had sworn revenge on any other woman Robertson might love. It was impossible, however, to prove the old woman's guilt or Effie's innocence, for Robertson had disappeared, and Meg swore that she had seen Effie coming back from the river after drowning the baby.

Determined to save her sister, Jeanie decided to walk to London to seek a pardon from the king and queen. She told her plans to Reuben Butler, a minister to whom she had long been betrothed. Reuben had not been able to marry her, for he had no position other than that of an assistant schoolmaster and his salary was too small to support a wife. Although he objected to Jeanie's plan, he was able to aid her when he saw that she could not be swayed from her purpose. Reuben's grandfather had once aided an ancestor of the present Duke of Argyle, and Reuben gave Jeanie a letter asking the Duke's help in presenting Jeanie to the king and queen.

The journey to London was a long and dangerous one. Once Jeanie was captured by Meg Murdockson, who tried to kill her so that she could not save Effie. Jeanie, however, escaped from the old woman and sought refuge in the home of the Reverend Mr. Staunton. There she met the minister's son, George Staunton, and learned from him that he was Geordie Robertson, the betrayer of her sister. He admitted his responsibility to Effie, telling Jeanie that he had planned and executed the Porteous incident in order to rescue Effie from the prison; but she had refused to leave with him. He had tried many other schemes to save her, including an attempt to force a confession from Meg that she had taken the baby, but everything had failed. He told Jeanie that he had been on his way to give himself up in exchange for Effie's release when he fell from his horse and was injured. He told Jeanie to bargain with the Duke of Argyle, and as a last resort to offer to lead the authorities to Robertson in exchange for Effie's pardon. George promised not to leave his father's house until Effie was free.

Jeanie at last reached London and presented herself to the Duke of Argyle with Reuben's letter. The Duke, impressed with Jeanie's sincerity and simplicity, arranged for an audience with the queen. She too believed Jeanie's story of Effie's misfortune. Through her efforts, the king pardoned Effie with the stipulation that she leave Scotland for fourteen years. Jeanie secured the pardon without revealing George Staunton's secret.

The Duke was so moved by Jeanie's goodness and honesty that he made her father the master of an experimental farm on one of his estates in Scotland, and he made Reuben the minister of the church. Jeanie's heart was overflowing with joy until she learned that Effie had eloped with her lover just three nights after her release from prison. No one knew where they were, as the outlaw's life was in constant danger because of his part in the Porteous hanging.

Reuben and Jeanie were married and were blessed with three fine children. They prospered in their new life, and Jeanie's only sorrow was her sister's marriage to George Staunton. She kept Effie's secret, however, telling no one that George was actually Robertson. After several years, George and Effie returned to London. George had inherited a title from his uncle, and as Sir George and Lady Staunton, they were received in court society. Effie wrote secretly to Jeanie and sent her large sums of money, which Jeanie put away without telling her husband about them. She could not reveal Effie's secret, even to him.

By chance, Jeanie found a paper containing the last confession of Meg Murdockson, who had been hanged as a witch. In it, Meg confessed that she had stolen Effie's baby and had given him to an outlaw. Jeanie sent this information to Effie in London, and before long Effie, as Lady Staunton, paid Jeanie a visit. Effie had used a pretext of ill health to go to Scotland while her husband, acting on the information in Meg's letter, tried to trace the whereabouts of their son. Although it was dangerous for George to be in Scotland where he might be recognized as Geordie Robertson, he followed every clue given in Meg's confession. In Edinburgh, he met Reuben Butler, who was there on business, and secured an invitation to accompany Reuben back to the manse. Unaware of George's real identity, Reuben was happy to receive the Duke of Argyle's friend. Reuben did not know at the time that Effie was also a guest in his home.

As Reuben and George walked toward the manse, they passed through a thicket where they were attacked by outlaws. One, a young fellow, ran his sword through George and killed him. It was not until Reuben had heard the whole story of the Stauntons from Jeanie that he searched George's pockets and found information there that proved beyond doubt that the young outlaw who had killed George was his own son, stolen many years before. Because Effie was grief-stricken by George's death, Jeanie and Reuben thought it useless to add to her sorrow by revealing the identity of his assailant. Reuben later traced the boy to America, where the young man continued his life of crime until he was captured and probably killed by Indians.

Effie stayed with Reuben and Jeanie for more than a year. Then she went back to London and the brilliant society she had known there. No one but Jeanie and Reuben ever knew the secret of Effie and George.

After ten years, Effie retired to a convent on the continent, where she spent her remaining years grieving for her husband and the son she had never known.

Reuben and Jeanie Butler, who had been so unavoidably involved in sordidness and crime, lived out their lives happily and carried their secret with them to the grave.

Critical Evaluation:

Many critics have considered this novel Sir Walter Scott's best; but, although *The Heart of Midlothian* has received much praise, the reasons for its success are different from those of most of the Waverley series. The novel does not have the usual Gothic props of ruined abbeys, spectres, prophesizing old hags, or lonely windswept castles. Only one scene, where Jeanie Deans meets George Staunton at moonrise in Nicol Muschat's Cairn, is typical of wild, picturesque settings so frequent in Scott's fiction.

The plot is based upon authentic historical events; the Porteous Riot of 1736 in Edinburgh's famous Old Tolbooth prison, or as it was commonly called "the heart of Midlothian," sets the action on its course. The story, however, is not actually one of social history involving questions of justice. Nor is it a study of Scottish Presbyterianism. Long debates on both of these issues take up major portions of the work, but Scott comes to no clear conclusions. These issues do not provide the unifying force that holds the story together.

A strong moral theme is the binding element, for most of the main protagonists are caught in dilemmas of conscience. Jeanie Deans must decide between telling a lie to save her sister Effie's life or speaking the truth and thereby condemning her to execution. Effie herself has the choice of attempting to live virtuously as she was taught or being faithful to her dissipated, criminal lover. Their father, stern David Deans, must decide whether to adhere to his Presbyterian principles or to come to terms with the human condition and forgive Effie. George Staunton, alias Robertson, is forced either to follow his wild inclinations and stay with his desperate associates or to reform and assume responsibilities of position and inheritance. He must also confront his obligation to marry Effie, whom he has wronged. These varied dilemmas of conscience constitute the texture of the novel.

The heroine is the one strong character in the novel, but she differs strikingly from the usual Waverley heroine, who is tall, beautiful, exceedingly well bred, romantic and, of course, wealthy. Jeanie Deans is the unusual: a peasant heroine, plain in appearance, not trained in social deportment, and lacking a romantic, Gothic background to aid her. Perhaps the moral seriousness of *The Heart of Midlothian* in addition to the fact that Scott drew his heroine from the lower classes not only make the novel popular but also give it a coherence and unity unusual in his fiction.

In most of Scott's novels, minor characters are largely drawn from Scottish rural life and humble occupations and are more real than upper-class figures. When dealing with them, Scott has a more energetic and colorful style. Critics often remark that the strength of his work lies in such characters as Caleb Balderstone of *The Bride of Lammermoor*, Edie Ochiltree and Maggie Mucklebackit of *The Antiquary*, Callum Beg and Widow Flockhart of *Waverly*. Scott reproduces their speech faithfully and with obvious relish.

But in *The Heart of Midlothian*, although he still opposes the upper-class culture with that of the lower and exploits resulting tensions, he elevates a dairyman's daughter to the status of heroine. Furthermore, in spite of the unyielding virtue of her character and the contrived situation in which she becomes involved, he not only makes her believable but also enlists the somewhat skeptical, hesitant reader on her side. She has common sense, and the rough, matter-of-fact elements in her daily life leave no doubt that she will conquer all adverse forces to triumph in Effie's cause. The law of retribution is at work here as in Scott's other novels, but Providence has a fresh, indefatigable agent in Jeanie. It is interesting that she was Scott's own favorite heroine.

Believable, too, are several scenes in *The Heart of Midlothian*, particularly the Porteous Riot that opens the novel. Scott handles realistically the mob's capture of Tolbooth prison and the lynching of Captain Porteous. Another well-constructed scene and one which is moving, if sentimental, is that of Effie's trial. In such sections, Scott tightens his control of character interaction and effects economy of language.

The entire account of Jeanie's journey to London to obtain Effie's pardon from Queen Caroline, however, slows the novel down and fails to hold the reader's interest; and the last section of the work—almost an epilogue—although required by Scott's publisher, does not seem to be required by the story itself. Jeanie and Reuben with their children and old David Deans live out a mellowed existence in picturesque Roseneath; their rural domesticity is only enlivened by the reunion of Jeanie and her sister (now Lady Staunton) and George's murder by his and Effie's unrecognized son.

If some portions of the novel seem protracted and rather unexciting, the whole is still well-knit and more logical than much of Scott's fiction. Because Scott considered the function of the novel to furnish "solace from the toils of ordinary life by an excursion into the regions of imagination," he ordinarily was indifferent to technique; instead, he concentrated on subject matter. He stressed factual accuracy but felt that too much care in composition might destroy what he termed "abundant spontaneity." Following his own dicta, he wrote rapidly with disregard for planning and revision. He improvised with careless haste, and his novels often suffer from poor style and construction. Critics have repeatedly faulted his work for improper motivation and lack of organic unity.

Nevertheless, one does not get the impression from reading *The Heart of Midlothian* that the author wrote at his usual breakneck speed, casually assembling scenes and characters together without forethought. Motivation is more properly furnished, characterization consistent, and, as mentioned, the dilemmas of conscience are carried through logically. In this novel, Scott has dispensed with excess supernatural escapades and the often flamboyant trappings of decadent nobility. He concentrates on the sincerity and integrity of his lower-class protagonists to effect a democratic realism new in the historical English novel, a genre he himself had invented.

THE HEART OF THE MATTER

Type of work: Novel
Author: Graham Greene (1904–   )
Type of plot: Psychological realism
Time of plot: World War II
Locale: British West Africa
First published: 1948

     Principal characters:
         MAJOR SCOBIE, a police chief in one of the colony's districts
         MRS. SCOBIE, his wife
         MRS. ROLT, a shipwreck victim and Scobie's mistress
         WILSON, a counterintelligence agent
         YUSEF, a Syrian merchant

The Story:

Major Scobie was chief of police in a British West African district. For fifteen years, he had built up a reputation for honesty. Then he learned that in spite of his labors he was to be passed over for the district commissionership in favor of a younger man. Those fifteen long years now seemed to him to have been too long and filled with too much work. Worse than his own disappointment was the disappointment of his wife. Mrs. Scobie needed the encouragement that a rise in official position would have given her to compensate for the loss of her only child some years before and her unpopularity among the official family of the district.

A love for literature, especially poetry, had set Mrs. Scobie apart from the other officials and their wives. Once the difference was discerned, the other Britishers distrusted and disliked her. They even pitied the man whom she had married. Nor were the Scobies much happier than people imagined them to be. Mrs. Scobie hated the life she led, and her husband disliked having to make her face it realistically. Both drank. When she found he was not to be made district commissioner, she insisted that he send her to the Cape Colony for a holiday, even though German submarines were torpedoing many vessels at the time.

Scobie did not have the money to pay the expenses of the trip. For a previous excursion of hers from the colony, he had already given up part of his life insurance. After trying unsuccessfully to borrow the money from the banks, he went to Yusef, a Syrian merchant, who agreed to lend him the money at four percent interest. Scobie knew that any dealings he had with Yusef would place him under a cloud, for the official British family

---

knew only too well that many of the Syrian's doings were illegal, including the shipment of industrial diamonds to the Nazis. Pressed by his wife's apparent need to escape the boredom of the rainy season in the coast colony, Scobie finally took the chance that he could keep clear of Yusef's entanglements, even though he knew that the Syrian hated him for the reputation of integrity he had built up during the past fifteen years.

To add to Scobie's difficulties, he learned that Wilson, a man supposedly sent out on a clerkship with a trading company, was actually an undercover agent working for the government on the problem of diamond smuggling. First, Scobie had no official information about Wilson's true activities; second, Wilson had fallen in love with Scobie's wife; and, third, Mrs. Scobie had bloodied Wilson's nose for him and permitted her husband to see her admirer crying. Any one of the counts would have made Scobie uneasy; all three in combination made him painfully aware that Wilson could only hate him, as Wilson actually did.

Shortly after his wife's departure, a series of events began to break down Major Scobie's trust in his own honesty and the reputation he had built up for himself. When a Portuguese liner was searched on its arrival in port, Scobie found a suspicious letter in the captain's cabin. Instead of turning in the letter, he burned it—after the captain had assured him that the letter was only a personal message to his daughter in Germany. A few weeks later, Yusef began to be very friendly toward Scobie. Gossip reported that Scobie had met and talked with the Syrian on several occasions, in addition to having borrowed money from the suspected smuggler.

One day word came that the French had rescued the crew and passengers of a torpedoed British vessel. Scobie was with the party who met the rescued people at the border between the French and British colonies. Among the victims was a young bride of only a few months whose husband had been killed in the war. While she recuperated from her exposure in a lifeboat and then waited for a ship to return her to England, she and Scobie fell in love. For a time, they were extremely careful of their conduct, until one day Mrs. Rolt, the rescued woman, belittled Scobie because of his caution. To prove his daring as well as his love, Scobie sent her a letter that was intercepted by Yusef's agents. In payment for return of the letter, Scobie was forced to help Yusef smuggle some gems from the colony. Wilson, Scobie's enemy, suspected the smuggling done by Scobie, but he could prove nothing.

Mrs. Rolt pleaded with Scobie to show his love by divorcing his wife and marrying her. Scobie, a Roman Catholic, tried to convince her that his faith and his conscience could not permit his doing so. To complicate matters further, Mrs. Scobie cabled that she was already aboard ship on her way back home from Capetown. Scobie did not know which way to turn. On her return, Mrs. Scobie nagged him to take communion with her. Unable to receive absolution because he refused to promise to give up adultery, Scobie took the sacrament of communion anyway, rather than admit to his wife what had happened. He realized that according to his faith he was damning his soul.

The worry over his sins, his uneasiness about his job, the problem of Yusef, a murder that Yusef had had committed for him, and the nagging of both his wife and Mrs. Rolt—all these made Scobie's mind a turmoil. He did not know which way to turn; for the Church, haven for many, was forbidden to him because of his sins and his temperament.

In searching for a way out of his predicament, Scobie remembered what he had been told by a doctor shortly after an official investigation of a suicide. The doctor had told Scobie that the best way to commit suicide was to feign angina and then take an overdose of evipan, a drug prescribed for angina cases. Scobie carefully made plans to take his life in that way because he wanted his wife to have his insurance money for her support after she returned to England. After studying the symptoms of angina, Scobie went to a doctor, who diagnosed Scobie's trouble from the symptoms he related. Scobie knew that his pretended heart condition would soon be common knowledge in the colony.

Ironically, Scobie was told that he had been reconsidered for the commissionership of the colony but that he could not be given the post because of his illness. The news made little difference to Scobie, for he had already made up his mind to commit suicide.

To make his death appear convincing, he filled his diary with entries tracing the progress of his heart condition. One evening, he took his overdose of evipan, his only solution to difficulties that had become more than he could bear. He died, and only one or two people even suspected the truth. One of these was Mrs. Scobie, who complained to the priest after he had refused to give Scobie absolution. The priest, knowing of Scobie's virtues as well as his sins, cried out to her that no one could call Scobie wicked or damned, for no one knew God's mercy.

Critical Evaluation:

The fears and hopes, friendships and petty rivalries, loves and hates of Europeans immured in a colony on the African coast afforded Graham Greene, who actually worked in such a place during World War II, the material for this novel. The book continues the study of British people begun in earlier Greene work. Major Scobie, like Arthur Rowe in *The Ministry of Fear*, is a relatively friendless man—a type that seems to have fascination for the author. Like Rowe, in the earlier novel, Major Scobie is placed in a position where he can choose between life or death: The high point in both novels is that at which the choice is made. Beyond the immediate story, however, there are larger implications. *The Heart of the Matter*, written by one of the leading Catholic novelists of the day, is actually a religious story, a fable of the conflict between good and evil. It is a drama of the human soul in midpassage toward Heaven or Hell.

The Heart of the Matter is an intelligent, perceptive, and humane tour de force on the spiritual capacities and moral dilemmas of Henry Scobie, husband, chief of police, and Catholic. Each of these roles contributes something to the complications of Scobie's situation. It must be admitted, however, that the novel, for all of its sensitivity and insight, is not a work of fiction of the first rank—perhaps just because it is a tour de force. Greene, while accepting a stern Roman Catholic framework, challenges readers to find fault with a man who goes beyond dishonesty and infidelity to sacrilege and suicide. As Scobie degenerates, Greene dares readers, despite the evidence, to cast the first stone by involving their sympathies and appealing to a higher law of mercy that is beyond man's capacity to understand or forgive.

The hothouse setting in a British colony on the West African coast in the early 1940's is interesting in its own right. It affords opportunity for commentary on the uncertainties of the period and the limitations of the colonial mentality. Nevertheless, the setting is not the heart of the matter. Scobie's problems as a human being are always the central focus of the novel, and they spring from the confluence of his circumstances, his roles, and his character. Scobie is a perpetual outsider to the web of colonial life. Too self-contained, too reflective, too honest with himself and others, he is not able to assume the roles and act out the rituals that will bring him local success. Circumstances contribute to the evolution of the central conflict, but the maritime warfare and diamond smuggling are, for Scobie, rather occasions for sin than sin itself. They provide a context in which Scobie's character agonizes and falters as he takes on his major roles. In each of these roles, his character shines through, and it may be his ultimate transcendence that his strength of character maintains a stable core as its periphery comes into conflict with corrupting circumstances.

Scobie's first role is as husband to a wife who, to Scobie's credit, is far more irritating to readers than to him. It is through Scobie's patience and understanding that readers achieve any degree of sympathy for the human burden his wife bears. In the related role of father of a deceased daughter, readers see more of Scobie's, and his wife's, suffering. However, he understands her while she lacks the sensitivity, despite her love for poetry, to reciprocate. Paradoxically, Scobie's honesty about his own limitations and compassion for the plight of others leads to a kind of hubris, which manifests itself first in his attempts to make his wife happy. It is this same desire to fix up the world, to provide totally for another's security and happiness, that embroils him in his later relationship with the vulnerable Mrs. Rolt and occasions his infidelity.

In his role as chief of police, Scobie has the sort of reputation for impeccable honesty and fairness that, combined with a lack of ambition, is likely to stimulate the suspicion, gossip, and animosity of his small-minded peers. It is one of the novel's many fine ironies that Scobie's honesty is compromised by the compassion he feels for his wife's plight, for it is his perhaps excessive and blameworthy, even selfish, desire to free her that leads him to borrow money and put himself in the hands of Yusef. Indeed, it may ultimately be a desire to free himself, but it also lays him open to the less publicly dangerous but morally serious dishonesty with Mrs. Rolt. His desire, whether it is to please his wife or free himself, leads to a compromise of his office. His desire to provide insulation against suffering, whether it is compassionate or selfish, leads to a compromise of his marriage.

Scobie does not wish anything but to be at peace, and he hopes that if he can fix everything for his wife and thereby free himself of her, he can find peace. Subsequently, Scobie's compassion for Mrs. Rolt turns into a love that brings his desire to repair other lives to an impasse when he wins Mrs. Rolt and his wife decides to return. In the chain of consequences and of flawed moral decisions, his attempt to comfort Mrs. Rolt by a reckless declaration of love further leads to complicity in murder. Scobie's actions are, thus far, morally imperfect but entangled in mixed emotions and motives. It is in his role as Catholic that he commits the ultimate transgressions against God and the divine power of forgiveness.

Violation of public trust and infidelity can be pardoned or extenuated, but Scobie, as Catholic, proceeds to the institutionally "unforgivable" sins. His love for Mrs. Rolt makes valid confession impossible, because his selfishness and compassion make it impossible for him to promise to give her up. His concern for his wife forces him to receive Communion, without absolution, so that he will not betray himself to her and thus wound her. In so doing, he does violence to Christ in the Eucharist. Although well aware that Christ, for love of man, makes himself vulnerable to abuse by his availability in the sacrament, Scobie allows his human motives to lead him to desecrate that trust by receiving Christ while in a state of sin. Having sacrificed Christ to selfishness and human compassion, Scobie is left totally desolate; unable to live with these conflicts, he commits the sin that theoretically puts him beyond God's mercy—suicide.

Nevertheless, readers do not condemn Scobie. It is not that he is an automaton, a victim of circumstance. To excuse him on those grounds would trivialize the theology of the novel: "to understand all is to forgive all." Rather, readers clearly recognize his progressive sins but are led by Greene to participate in the mystery of divine mercy by extending compassion without selfishness. Raised to the divine level, the compassion that contributed to Scobie's corruption may also be his only hope of salvation.

THE HEAT OF THE DAY

Type of work: Novel
Author: Elizabeth Bowen (1899–1973)
Type of plot: Psychological realism
Time of plot: 1942–1944
Locale: London
First published: 1949

> *Principal characters:*
> STELLA RODNEY, an attractive widow
> RODERICK RODNEY, her son
> ROBERT KELWAY, her lover
> HARRISON, a British Intelligence agent
> LOUIE LEWIS, the wife of a British soldier

The Story:

The first Sunday afternoon of September, 1942, found Harrison sitting at a band concert in Regent Park. He was not listening to the music but was, in fact, merely killing time until he could see Stella Rodney at eight o'clock. Thinking of Stella and the awkward subject he must discuss with her, he kept thrusting the fist of his right hand into the palm of his left. This unconscious motion, as well as his obvious indifference to the music, aroused the curiosity of an adjacent listener. This neighbor, Louie Lewis, was a clumsy, cheaply clad young woman with an artless and somewhat bovine expression. Lonely without her soldier husband and entirely a creature of impulse, she offended Harrison by breaking into his reverie with naïve comments that were brusquely rebuffed. Unabashed, she trailed after him when he left the concert, giving up only when he abruptly left her to keep his engagement.

In her top-floor flat in Weymouth Street, Stella wondered rather idly why Harrison was late. Her attitude of waiting was more defiant than expectant, for she had no love for her visitor. She hardly knew how he had managed to insinuate himself into her life; first, he had turned up unaccountably at the funeral of Cousin Francis Morris, and since then, his attentions had shown a steady increase. There had been a subtle shade of menace in his demand that she see him that night, and a curious sense of apprehension had prompted her to consent. As she awaited his knock, her glance flickered impatiently about the charming flat, and she recalled the facts that gave shape to her existence: her young son, Roderick, now in the British army; her ex-husband, long divorced and dead; her own war work with Y.X.D.; and her lover, Robert Kelway, also in government service.

When Harrison arrived, he received a cool and perfunctory greeting. His first remarks were hesitant and enigmatic, but he soon launched into words that left Stella wide-eyed with shock and disbelief. He told her that her lover was a Nazi agent passing English secrets on to Germany. Harrison himself was connected with British Intelligence, and he had been assigned to cover Kelway's movements. There was just one way to save the traitor. Stella must give him up and switch her interest to Harrison. Then Kelway's fate might be averted or indefinitely postponed.

The blunt proposition unnerved Stella. She refused to believe in Kelway's guilt, for Harrison did not impress her as a man to trust. She played for time, winning a month's delay in which to make up her mind. Harrison sharply advised her not to warn Robert; the slightest change in his pattern of action would result in his immediate arrest. As the interview ended, the telephone rang. At the other end was Roderick, announcing his arrival for leave in London. Upon Harrison's departure, Stella pulled herself together and made quick preparation to receive her son.

Roderick's arrival helped a little; it temporarily deprived Stella of the time to worry. Roderick was young and vulnerable, and his father's early abdication had made Stella feel doubly responsible for her son. Roderick wanted to talk about his new interest in life, the run-down estate in Ireland recently bequeathed him by Cousin Francis Morris. The boy was determined to keep his new property; but until the war was over, the task of looking after it would be largely Stella's responsibility.

Roderick's leave expired. The next night, Robert Kelway came to Stella's flat. She gave no hint of her inward agitation, although she casually inquired if he knew Harrison. Gazing at her attractive, considerate lover, Stella silently marveled that he should be a suspect—he, a lamed veteran of Dunkirk! Considering, however, that she knew nothing about his family, she renewed her request that they visit his mother and sister in the country. A subsequent Saturday afternoon at Holme Dene revealed nothing strange about Robert's background. On the night of her return from Robert's home, she found Harrison waiting at her apartment; he confirmed his watchfulness by telling her where she had been and why.

Roderick's interests intervened by summoning Stella briefly to Ireland. Robert protested at losing her for even a few days, and they parted affectionately. In Ireland, Stella's distrust of Harrison received a jolt; he had been truthful, she learned, in telling her that he had been a friend of Cousin Francis Morris. She resolved that she would acquaint Robert with Harrison's accusation. When she returned to London, Robert met her at the station. Minutes later, in a taxi, she revealed what she had heard; and Robert, deeply hurt, made a complete denial. Later that night, he begged her to marry him, but Stella, both surprised and disturbed, succeeded in parrying the proposal.

A few nights later, Harrison had dinner with Stella in a popular restaurant. She stiffened with apprehension as he told her that she had disobeyed him by putting Robert on his guard. Before Stella could learn what Harrison intended to do, she was interrupted by the untimely intrusion of Louie Lewis, who crudely invited herself to their table after spotting Harrison in the crowd. Nevertheless, Stella managed to intimate that she would meet Harrison's terms if he would save Robert from arrest. Angry at Louie, Harrison made no response; roughly dismissing the two women, he stalked off, leaving them to find their way home through blacked-out London. Louie was fascinated by the superior charm and refinement of Stella and accompanied her to the doorway of her apartment.

Robert was at Holme Dene, so that not until the next night did Stella have a chance to warn him of his danger. In the early morning darkness of Stella's bedroom, they renewed their love and confidence with a sense that it was to be their last meeting. When Robert finally revealed that he was an ardent Nazi, prizing power above freedom, Stella found no way to reconcile their views. Faint footsteps, as of outside watchers, were heard as Robert dressed and prepared to leave. He climbed up the rope ladder to the skylight in the roof and then came back down again to kiss Stella once more. He told her to take care of herself as he hurriedly disappeared through the skylight. The next morning, Robert's body was found lying in the street where he had leaped or fallen from the steeply slanting roof.

More than a year passed before Stella saw Harrison again. There were Allied landings in Africa; there was the invasion of Italy; there was the ever-growing prospect of a Second Front. Finally, Harrison came back. Stella had had questions to ask him, questions about Robert, but now it seemed pointless to ask them. An air of constraint hung over their conversation, a feeling that Robert's death had removed any real link between their lives. Harrison made no romantic overtures; he even seemed faintly relieved when Stella told him that she was soon to be married.

Critical Evaluation:

The wartime setting of this book is no more than incidental, for the story treats of contrasting faiths and loyalties that are altogether timeless. Though the general atmosphere is electric with danger, the author muffles the sound of bombs and antiaircraft guns until they give only a tonal background for the drama of Stella Rodney, Robert Kelway, and the enigmatic Harrison. The problem of Stella Rodney is that of a woman asked to question her own judgment of the man she loves. Elizabeth Bowen is at her best in dealing with complex personal relationships, and here she inspects some barriers to emotional and intellectual harmony that are embodied in a conflict between patriotism and love. Like Henry James, she is interested in the collision of finely grained personalities; and the very nature of her subject matter demands a style that is sensitive and involved.

Bowen often expressed her concern for the disintegration of tradition and value in the twentieth century by depicting the discrepancy between modern woman's changing aspirations and her felt desire for the traditional roles. In *The House in Paris* (1936) and *The Death of the Heart* (1938), heroines are restless or dissatisfied in the roles of wife or mother, and in *The Heat of the Day*, Stella tests "free womanhood." *The Heat of the Day* combines the portrayal of modern woman's dilemma with two other representations of Bowen's concern—the neglected family estate and the events of World War II.

Stella Rodney is Bowen's "free woman." She is a professional working in military intelligence, a longtime divorcée, and the mother of a grown son. She has a lover whom she has known for two years, but she dates and knows other men. Still, the relationship with Robert is the most important. Stella is sensitive, strong, and articulate, not only about others but also about her own problems. She has let her son and others believe for years that she left her husband, that she was the femme fatale, the self-sufficient one. In fact, she was divorced by her husband, who left her for his nurse. Stella's son Roderick discovers this fact and confronts his mother, saying it puts "everything in a different light." She admits that it was a matter of saving face; when most people believed that she was the guilty party, she let the story go on. She says to Harrison that it is better to sound like "a monster than look a fool." That remark suggests the paradox in Stella's psyche: she craves to be identified as a free woman, *capable de tout*, but her inner self is not quite in concert with that image. Therefore, there is the divorce story, her relationship to Roderick (she takes pains to show that he is not tied to her, but she worries a great deal about him), and her attitude to Robert (their relationship is a stable one, but Stella refuses Robert's marriage proposal).

Stella is not alone in her ambivalence about how to react to changes in society. Cousin Nettie Morris is driven to insanity by the difficulties of woman's "place" at the family estate, Mount Morris. It seems she takes refuge in madness. One of the novel's most memorable scenes is the nonconversation between Roderick and Nettie at Wisteria Lodge, the asylum. Nettie is not so mad as others would like to think. Visiting Mount Morris in Ireland, Stella understands how the lack of real choices for the traditional woman can drive her insane.

Stella's dividedness is expressed in her attitude toward Mount Morris. She had sold her own house, stored her furniture, and rented a luxury furnished flat in London, thus making herself more independent. Nothing in the flat reflected her personality. Stella, however, finds herself again saddled with place, family, and tradition when Cousin Francis wills Mount

Morris to her son—whom he never met but who was conceived at Mount Morris where Stella and his father Victor honeymooned. Stella's ambivalence begins when she attends Cousin Francis' funeral; it grows as she revisits, after twenty-one years, Mount Morris, now knowing that Roderick will carry on the tradition she had rejected. (Bowen herself believed that the modern attitude against family estate was erroneous, that indeed it had contributed to the general disintegration of society. She became the first female Bowen to inherit Bowen's Court near Dublin since its construction in 1776; but in 1960, she was forced by financial exigency to sell the house, and in 1963 it was torn down.)

Stella is repeatedly characterized as being typical of her generation, and the generation is often described as having "muffed" the century. She became an adult just after World War I, and now there is World War II. The specific details of the war years in London give concrete reality to Stella's own trauma and are skillfully interwoven in her involvement with Robert. "The heat of the day" is Stella's middle-age, her "noon," and the agony of the decision to question Robert's loyalty. It is also, of course, the height of the war, a turning point in the century.

As Bowen's structure and symbols both clearly suggest, the generation that follows Stella's, that of Roderick and Louie Lewis, represents both a new integration and a rebirth. Stella's story—her "defeat" as a free woman—is framed and intersected by the story of the working-class Louie Lewis, whose vague desires for motherhood culminate in a triumphant pregnancy while her husband is fighting abroad. She is unaware of the identity of the child's father. The novel ends with the birth of her son just after D-Day and her return to the south coast of England where her parents had been killed by a bomb in the early days of the war. Roderick intends to reside at Mount Morris and has great plans about rejuvenating it with modern farming methods. Both members of the next generation, therefore, are able to resolve the dichotomies that so plagued their parents' generation—dichotomies about family, place, tradition, and role. The three white swans, a recurrent positive symbol in Bowen (they figure in *The Death of the Heart* as well) appear only at Mount Morris and at the end of the book as Louie wheels her new baby. Flying straight, the swans symbolize a positive rebirth and also suggest the resolution of the war in the "direction of the west." Bowen's symbols, however, are more suggestive than absolute. Louie's and Roderick's clear choices are more than enough direction for interpreting the novel. Stella's generation had "botched" it; the only hope is in the next.

HENRY ESMOND

Type of work: Novel
Author: William Makepeace Thackeray (1811-1863)
Type of plot: Historical romance
Time of plot: Late seventeenth and early eighteenth centuries
Locale: England and the Low Countries
First published: 1852

Principal characters:

HENRY ESMOND, a Castlewood ward
FRANCIS ESMOND, Viscount Castlewood
RACHEL ESMOND, his wife
BEATRIX, their daughter
FRANK, their son
LORD MOHUN, a London rake
FATHER HOLT, a Jacobite spy
JAMES STUART, the exiled pretender

The Story:

Henry Esmond grew up at Castlewood. He knew there was some mystery about his birth, and he dimly remembered that long ago he had lived with weavers who spoke a foreign tongue. Thomas Esmond, Viscount Castlewood, had brought him to England and turned him over to Father Holt, the chaplain, to be educated. That much he learned as he grew older.

All was not peace and quiet at Castlewood in those years; his lordship and Father Holt had been engaged in a plot for the restoration of the exiled Stuart king, James II. When James attempted to recover Ireland for the Stuarts, Thomas Esmond rode off to his death at the Battle of the Boyne. His widow fled to her dower house at Chelsea. Father Holt disappeared. Henry, a large-eyed, grave-faced twelve-year-old boy, was left alone with servants in the gloomy old house.

There his new guardians and distant cousins, Francis and Rachel Esmond, found him when they arrived to take possession of Castlewood. The new Viscount Castlewood, a bluff, loud-voiced man, greeted the boy kindly enough. His wife was like a girl herself—she was only eight years older than Henry—and Henry thought her the loveliest lady he had ever seen. With them were a little daughter, Beatrix, and a son, Frank, a baby in arms.

As Henry grew older, he became increasingly concerned over the rift he saw coming between Rachel and her husband, both of whom he loved because they had treated him as one of the immediate family in the household at Castlewood. It was plain that the hard-drinking, hard-gambling nobleman was wearying of his quiet country life. After Rachel's face was disfigured by smallpox, her altered beauty caused her husband to neglect her even more. Young Beatrix also felt that relations between her parents were strained.

When Henry was old enough, he was sent to Cambridge on money left to Rachel by a deceased relative. Later, when he returned to Castlewood on a vacation, he realized for the first time that Beatrix was exceptionally attractive. Apparently, he had never really noticed her before. Rachel, for her part, had great regard for her young kinsman. Before his arrival from Cambridge, according to Beatrix, Rachel went to Henry's room ten times to see that it was ready.

Relations between Rachel and the Viscount were all but severed when the notorious Lord Mohun visited Castlewood. Rachel knew her husband had been losing heavily to Mohun at cards, but when she spoke to the Viscount about the bad company he was keeping, he flew into a rage. He was by no means calmed when Beatrix innocently blurted out to her father, in the company of Mohun, that the gentleman was interested in Rachel. Jealous of another man's attentions to the wife he himself neglected, the Viscount determined to seek satisfaction in a duel.

The two men fought in London, where the Viscount had gone on the pretext of seeing a doctor. Henry suspected the real reason for the trip and went along, for he hoped to engage Mohun in a fight and thus save the life of his beloved guardian. The Viscount, however, was in no mood to be cheated out of an excuse to provoke a quarrel. He was heavily in debt to Mohun and thought a fight was the only honorable way out of his difficulties. Moreover, he knew Mohun had written letters to Rachel, although, as the villain explained, she had never answered them. They fought, and Mohun foully and fatally wounded the Viscount. On his deathbed, the Viscount confessed to his young kinsman that Henry was not an illegitimate child, but the son of Thomas, Lord Castlewood, by an early marriage, and the true heir to the Castlewood title. Henry Esmond generously burned the dying man's confession and resolved never to divulge the secret.

For his part in the duel, Henry Esmond was sent to prison. When Rachel visited Henry in prison, she was enraged because he had not stopped the duel and because he had allowed Mohun to go unpunished. She rebuked Henry and forbade him to return to Castlewood. When Henry left prison, he decided to join the army. For that purpose, he visited the old dowager Viscountess, his stepmother, who bought him a commission.

Henry's military ventures were highly successful and won for him his share of wounds and glory. He fought in the campaign of the Duke of Marlborough against Spain and France in 1702 and in the campaign of Blenheim in 1704. Between the two campaigns, he returned to Castlewood, where he was reconciled with Rachel. There he saw Frank, now Lord Castlewood, and Beatrix, who was cordial toward him. Rachel cautioned

Henry that Beatrix was selfish and temperamental and would make no man happy who loved her.

After the campaign of 1704, Henry returned to his cousins, who were living in London. To Henry, Beatrix was more beautiful than ever and even more the coquette; but he found himself unable to make up his mind whether he loved her or Rachel. Later, during the campaign of 1706, he learned from Frank that Beatrix was engaged to an earl. The news put Henry in low spirits because he now felt she would never marry a poor captain like himself.

Henry's affairs of the heart were put temporarily into the background when he came upon Father Holt in Brussels. The priest told Henry that while on an expedition in the Low Countries, Thomas Esmond, his father, had seduced the young woman who was Henry's mother. A few weeks before his child was born, Thomas Esmond was injured in a duel. Thinking he would die, he married the woman so that her child would be born with an untainted name. Thomas Esmond, however, did not die, and when he recovered from his wounds, he deserted his wife and married a distant kinswoman, the dowager Viscountess, Henry's stepmother.

When Henry returned to Castlewood, Rachel informed him that she had learned his secret from the old Viscountess and consequently knew that he, not Frank, was the true heir. For the second time, Henry refused to accept the title belonging to him.

Beatrix's interest in Henry grew after she became engaged to the Duke of Hamilton and learned that Henry was not illegitimate in birth but the bearer of a title her brother was using. Henry wanted to give Beatrix a diamond necklace for a wedding present, but the Duke would not permit his fiancée to receive a gift from one of illegitimate birth. Rachel came to the young man's defense and declared before the Duke, her daughter, and Henry the secret of his birth and title. Later, the Duke was killed in a duel with Lord Mohun, who also met his death at the same time. The killing of Rachel's husband was avenged.

The Duke of Hamilton's death gave Henry one more chance to win Beatrix's heart. He threw himself into a plot to put the young Stuart pretender on the throne when old Queen Anne died. To this end, he went to France and helped to smuggle into England the young chevalier whom the Jacobites called James III, the king over the water. The two came secretly to the Castlewood home in London, the prince passing as Frank, the young Viscount, and there the royal exile saw and fell in love with Beatrix.

Fearing the results of this infatuation, Lady Castlewood and Henry sent Beatrix to Castlewood against her will. When a report that the queen was dying swept through London, the prince was nowhere to be found. Henry and Frank made a night ride to Castlewood. Finding the pretender there in the room used by Father Holt in the old days, they renounced him and the

Jacobite cause. Henry realized his love for Beatrix was dead at last. He felt no regrets for her or for the prince as he rode back to London and heard the heralds proclaiming George I, the new king.

The prince made his way secretly back to France, where Beatrix joined him in his exile. At last, Henry felt free to declare himself to Rachel, who had grown very dear to him. Leaving Frank in possession of the title and the Castlewood estates, Henry and his wife went to America. In Virginia, he and Rachel built a new Castlewood, reared a family, and found happiness in their old age.

Critical Evaluation:

Critical reaction to *The History of Henry Esmond, Esq.: A Colonel in the Service of Her Majesty Q. Anne* is as varied as reader reaction to the characters themselves. What William Makepeace Thackeray attempted to do was to offset contemporary charges of his "diffusiveness" by providing a well-integrated novel, sacrificing profitable serial publication to do so. He concluded that *Henry Esmond* was "the very best" he could do. Many critics have agreed with him. Others, however, remain loyal to the panoramic social vision and ironic authorial commentary of the earlier *Vanity Fair*. What makes evaluation of *Henry Esmond* so variable?

Short of a full history of cycles and fashions in fiction, certain features may illustrate the problems. First is the narrative point of view. Thackeray cast *Henry Esmond* in the form of a reminiscential memoir—an old man recounts his earlier life, describing it from the vantage point of a later time and distancing it further with third-person narration. The occasional use of "I" suggests the involved narrator, either at emotional high points or moments of personal reflection. The distancing in time is increased by Esmond's daughter's preface, wherein Rachel Esmond Warrington not only "completes" certain details of the plot but also suggests the ambiguities in characterization of her own mother, Rachel, and of her stepsister, Beatrix. Readers of Henry James may react favorably to this early use of a central intelligence whose point of view, limited not omniscient, can suggest the disparities between appearance and reality. Readers may also welcome the shifting interpretations that can be formed of the narrator's "reliability." Is Esmond providing a framework within which to reveal only the exemplary, vindicating himself consciously, or is he recollecting as honestly as the self can permit, with the reader knowing more than he at many points?

Another point of contention involves the historical setting of the novel, which purports to be a historical romance. Thackeray casts the novel in the early eighteenth century and attempts to catch the flavor of the Augustan Age, its military conflicts, its waverings between Church of England and Catholicism, and the problems of its monarchs, William, Queen Anne, George II, and the Stuart Pretender. Most readers laud Thackeray's adept handling of the technical problem of suggesting the language and manners of that earlier time without sending readers to glossaries or lapsing into linguistic archness. The novel, therefore, is praised by many critics as a polished example of the historical romance and relished as many relish Scott or Stevenson—for its adventure and its depiction of society, at least those levels that Thackeray chooses to treat. In this novel as in *Vanity Fair*, he is less concerned with portrayal of the lackeys than of the masters, primarily the newly arrived and still aspiring scions of society. Their foibles were his special target.

For other readers, the novel's fascination lies in its domestic realism. Commentators find much to explore in the rendering of the marriage conventions. Lord and Lady Castlewood, new heirs to Castlewood, befriend the supposedly illegitimate Henry Esmond and gradually reveal the strained bonds that hold their marriage together. As narrator, Esmond takes sides with Rachel, seeing the husband as carousing, unfaithful, and not too intelligent. Despite the analysis of "domestic tyranny," readers, however, can also realize that Rachel's purity and coldness might lead the husband not only to drink but to other fleshly delights. Devoted Henry Esmond may lament the waste of such a fine woman, but the reader perceives in the dramatic scenes that Rachel, who began by worshiping her husband, is also quite capable of both restrictive possessiveness and emotional repression.

A historical romance and novel of domestic manners, *Henry Esmond* also illustrates a favorite nineteenth century form, the *Bildungsroman*, or novel of development and education, which is also represented in such popular contemporary examples as *David Copperfield* and *Great Expectations*. Henry Esmond remembers his childhood vaguely, a time spent with poor weavers. Brought to Castlewood, he is treated with favor by Lord Castlewood but kept in place as a page. It is only with the death of Lord Castlewood that Henry receives any emotional response, this from the new heirs—and most especially from Rachel, Lady Castlewood. Thackeray carefully distances Esmond to be eight years younger than Rachel and eight years older than her daughter Beatrix. Esmond's growth is the principal subject, but readers are also aware of the young son Frank and of Beatrix, both children who are alternately spoiled and then emotionally isolated from Rachel. The much sought after but "loveless" Beatrix reveals how isolated she was made to feel by the possessive nets her mother cast over the father and then over the seemingly favored brother. Momentarily consoling Esmond, Beatrix shows the motivation for her romantic conquests so that readers understand her complexity and ambivalence, though Esmond may choose not to do so.

As Esmond progresses through Cambridge, through imprisonment following a duel fatal to Lord Castlewood, through military campaigns, through the loss of one idol after another and on to a slow knowledge of the way of the world, the reader watches for his "present" age to come closer to his recollected past. The reader watches for his insight to develop, for memory and maturity to coincide. Whether or not Esmond achieves that wholeness is yet another point for critics and readers to ponder.

Esmond has virtuously denied himself his birthright as legitimate heir to Castlewood so that young Frank may assume the title and Rachel and Beatrix can stay ensconced in society, but some might think Henry revels in the self-sacrifice. He has also chosen to believe that Beatrix will admire him for military daring and political plotting. Therefore, when the Stuart Pretender misses a chance for the throne in order to secure an amorous chance with Beatrix, Esmond loses two idols at once. "Good" Henry Esmond is settled at the end of the novel on a Virginia plantation in the New World, and his marriage to the widowed Rachel is compressed into two pages. All ends happily, except for those strange overtones and even stranger suggestions in the preface by the daughter of this autumnal marriage. She reminds readers that Esmond was writing for a family audience, that his role had been carefully established, and that she, Rachel Esmond Warrington, like Beatrix, had also suffered from her mother's possessiveness and jealousy.

Ultimately, then, what the modern reader may enjoy most is the psychological penetration into love bonds that Thackeray provides through the "unreliable" narrator. Dramatic irony permits the reader more knowledge than Esmond permits himself. As readers circle back in their own memories to the daughter's preface, the whole range of interrelationships and the ambivalences of human affairs unfold. The characters, in short, remain fascinating puzzles long after the historical details fade. Emotional life, the subtleties of rejection and acceptance, time rendered both precisely and in psychological duration—these are the elements that continue to tantalize readers of *Henry Esmond.*

HEREWARD THE WAKE
Last of the English

Type of work: Novel
Author: Charles Kingsley (1819–1875)
Type of plot: Historical romance
Time of plot: Eleventh century
Locale: England, Scotland, and Flanders
First published: 1866

> *Principal characters:*
> HEREWARD THE WAKE, a Saxon thane and outlaw
> LADY GODIVA, his mother
> TORFRIDA, his wife
> ALFTRUDA, his second wife
> MARTIN LIGHTFOOT, a companion in his wanderings
> WILLIAM THE CONQUEROR, Duke of Normandy and King of
> England

The Story:

Hereward was the son of the powerful Lord of Bourne, a Saxon nobleman of a family close to the throne. A high-spirited, rebellious youth, he was a source of constant worry to his mother, Lady Godiva. Hereward lacked a proper respect for the Church and its priests and lived a boisterous life with boon companions who gave him their unquestioning loyalty.

One day, a friar came to Lady Godiva and revealed that Hereward and his friends had attacked him and robbed him of what the priest insisted was money belonging to the Church. Lady Godiva was angry and hurt. When Hereward came in and admitted his crime, she said that there was no alternative. She maintained that for his own good, he should be declared a wake, or outlaw. Upon his promise not to molest her messenger, for Hereward really did not mind being outlawed as he wished to see more of the world, Lady Godiva sent Martin Lightfoot, a servant, to carry the news of Hereward's deed to his father and to the king. Hereward was then declared an outlaw subject to imprisonment or death.

Before he left his father's house, however, he released his friends from their oath of allegiance. Martin Lightfoot begged to be allowed to follow him, not as his servant but as his companion. Then Hereward set out to live among the rude and barbarous Scottish tribes of the north.

His first adventure occurred when he killed a huge bear that threatened the life of Alftruda, ward of a knight named Gilbert of Ghent. He achieved much renown for his valorous deed. The knights of Gilbert's household, however, were jealous of Hereward's courage and his prowess, and they tried to kill him. Although he escaped the snares laid for him, he decided that it would be best for him to leave Scotland.

Accordingly, he went to Cornwall, where he was welcomed by the king. There the king's daughter was pledged in marriage to a prince of Waterford. A giant of the Cornish court, however, had become so powerful that he had forced the king's agreement to give his daughter in marriage to the ogre. With the help of the princess and a friar, Hereward slew the giant, whose death freed the princess to marry the prince whom she really loved.

After leaving Cornwall, Hereward and his companions were wrecked upon the Flemish coast. Hereward stayed there for a time in the service of Baldwin of Flanders and proved his valor by defeating the French in battle. There, too, Torfrida, a lady wrongly suspected of sorcery, schemed to win his love. They were wed after Hereward had fought in a successful campaign against the Hollanders, and a daughter was born of the marriage.

Meanwhile, King Edward had died, and Harold reigned in England. A messenger came to Hereward with the news that Duke William of Normandy had defeated the English at the battle of Hastings and that King Harold had been killed. Hereward then decided to return to Bourne, his old home. There, accompanied by Martin Lightfoot, he found the Norman raiders encamped. He found too that his family had been despoiled of all of its property and that his mother had been sent away. Without revealing their identity, he and Martin secretly went out and annihilated all the Normans in the area. Hereward swore that he would return with an army that would push the Norman invaders into the sea.

Hereward then went to his mother, who received him happily. Lady Godiva accused herself of having wronged her son and lamented the day she had proclaimed him an outlaw. He took her to a place of refuge in Croyland Abbey. Later, he went to the monastery where his aged, infirm uncle, Abbot Brand, was spending his last days on earth. There Hereward was knighted by the monks, after the English fashion. Hereward went secretly to Bourne and recruited a rebel army to fight against Duke William.

Although there were many men eager to fight the Normans, the English forces were disunited. Another king, an untried young man, had been proclaimed; but because of his youth, he did not have the support of all the English factions. Hereward had been promised help from Denmark, but the Danish king sent a poor leader through whose stupidity the Danes were inveigled into positions where they were easily defeated by the Normans at Dover and Norwich. Instead of coming to Hereward's aid, the Danes then fled. Hereward was forced to confess the failure of his allies to his men, but they renewed their pledge to him and promised to continue fighting. The situation seemed hopeless when Hereward and his men took refuge on the island of Ely. There, with Torfrida's wise advice, Hereward defeated Duke William's attack upon the beleaguered island. Hereward and his men retreated to another camp of refuge.

Shortly afterward, Torfrida learned of Hereward's infidelity with Alftruda, the ward of Gilbert of Ghent. She left Hereward and went to Croyland Abbey, where she proposed to spend the last of her days ministering to the poor and to Hereward's mother. Hereward went to Duke William and submitted to him. The conqueror declared that he had selected a husband for Hereward's daughter. In order to free herself from Hereward, Torfrida falsely confessed that she was a sorceress, and her marriage to Hereward was annulled by the Church. Hereward then married Alftruda and became Lord of Bourne under Duke William. His daughter, despite her entreaties, was married to a Norman knight.

Hereward, the last of the English, had many enemies among the French, who continually intrigued against him for the favor of Duke William. As a result, Hereward was imprisoned. The jailer was a good man who treated his noble prisoner as kindly as he could, although, for his own sake, he was forced to chain Hereward.

One day, while Hereward was being transported from one prison to another, he was rescued by his friends. Freed, he went back to Alftruda at Bourne, but his life was not a happy one. His enemies plotted to kill him. Taking advantage of a day when his retainers were escorting Alftruda on a journey, a group of Norman knights broke into Bourne castle. Although Hereward fought valiantly, he was outnumbered. He was killed, and his head was exhibited in victory over the door of his own hall.

When she heard of his death, Torfrida came from Croyland Abbey and demanded Hereward's body. All were so frightened, especially Alftruda, by Torfrida's wild appearance and her reputation as a witch that Hereward's first wife got her way and the body was delivered to her. She carried it away to Croyland for burial. Therefore, Hereward, the last of the English, died, and William of Normandy became William the Conqueror and King of England.

Critical Evaluation:

In his last novel, *Hereward the Wake: Last of the English*, Charles Kingsley treats a heroic figure whose character and adventures form the core of the *Gesta Hereward*. Based on the past, it is, however, more than an adaptation of existing legends. Kingsley makes the most of the rich material provided by this colorful period in history. He chooses to assign a new past to Hereward, making him the son of Lady Godiva, and he also gives much attention to the courtship and winning of Torfrida, a woman of exceptional virtue and talents, who is reputed to be a witch.

Hereward the Wake is one of the very few stories that deal realistically and credibly with the Anglo-Saxon period of English history. Although elements of the chivalric romance, in the more academic sense of that term, are present in this novel, Kingsley has re-created the age and its people in a believable and highly interesting manner. *Hereward the Wake* is both an interesting story and a valuable historical study.

Kingsley was undoubtedly attracted to the legend by the various elements that he himself felt were missing in his own time. An advocate of "muscular Christianity" as well as social benevolence to the poor and underprivileged, the Reverend Kingsley found in Hereward's life an opportunity to champion militant heroism blessed by the Church. After Hereward returns from an exile spent in reparation for his youthful rebellion, he goes to his uncle, Abbot Brand, and is knighted, literally annointed, as a soldier of the Church to battle the Normans. He displays all the virtues, even in his death, of the medieval soldier whose embassy is charity as well as bloodshed.

Hereward stands for the last "pure" English knight, moreover, because the foreigners, the Normans, are successfully installed as England's rulers after his death. It was also this racial purity that the Saxon represents that led Kingsley to the legend. The knight is unspoiled by any alien influence or blood; although finally defeated by the Normans, he is apotheosized and even in death his body is saved from his Norman wife by the mysterious Torfrida. It is these chauvinistic qualities that accounted for the success of the novel in England, a society that felt threatened by the Continental political revolutions of the nineteenth century.

A HERITAGE AND ITS HISTORY

Type of work: Novel
Author: Ivy Compton-Burnett (1892-1969)
Type of plot: Modernist
Time of plot: Late Victorian period
Locale: England
First published: 1959

> *Principal characters:*
>> SIR EDWIN CHALLONER, the lord of the mansion
>> HAMISH CHALLONER, his younger brother
>> JULIA CHALLONER, Hamish's wife
>> SIMON CHALLONER, their older son and Sir Edwin's heir
>> WALTER CHALLONER, Simon's younger brother
>> RHODA GRAHAM CHALLONER, Sir Edwin's wife and Simon's mistress
>> HAMISH, the son of Rhoda and Simon
>> FANNY GRAHAM CHALLONER, Simon's wife and Rhoda's sister
>> RALPH,
>> NAOMI,
>> GRAHAM,
>> CLAUDE, and
>> EMMA, the children of Simon and Fanny
>> MARCIA CHALLONER, the wife of young Hamish Challoner
>> DEAKIN, the butler who resembles a Greek chorus in his comments on the novel's events and on life generally

Encompassing more time than any other Ivy Compton-Burnett novel, *A Heritage and Its History* is, in a sense, the most representative of all her novels, although it is not quite her best. The heritage, as Compton-Burnett's readers and those who have studied their ancestors' lives will recognize, is the complex genetic and social inheritance of what man calls good and evil tendencies. It is the virtues and the sins of the fathers that are visited upon all generations; although the current generation lives in its own day, what it does has been done by all of its forebears, as Rhoda and Sir Edwin say and as parts of the Bible imply. In its encompassment of universalized and eternalized human activity in three generations, as in its inclusion of the wise butler and the excessively precocious children as commentators upon the sensational and usual events the dialogue of the novel advances, *A Heritage and Its History* is Compton-Burnett at her most representative. Because in presenting more characters and times than usual, she leaves even the alert reader occasionally baffled, the novel, though excellent, is inferior to its immediate predecessor, *A Father and His Fate*, and its two successors, *The Mighty and Their Fall* and *A God and His Gifts*.

It is not, as indeed it is not usually, of the utmost importance to give the intriguing complexity of the plot, which as one critic once said of another of her novels, combines complexities that might have arisen had Sardou and Sophocles collaborated. Of course, things are not what they seem. The apparently healthy Sir Edwin precedes in death his dying brother. The proper son of Hamish, Simon, has children by both the Graham sister he marries and the older one he does not, and he becomes, at the close of the novel, Sir Simon. The erratic son, Walter, who did not finish Oxford and who is a poet, leads a proper life. Behind the scenes, as in the Greek tragedies it resembles and, like them, interrupted by comic and satirical interludes, events of plausible sensationalism occur: sudden death, adultery, near incest, a conflict of parents and children, of brother and brother. The story is, therefore, the stuff of human nature told factually, palatably, wittily, and bearably, as it is in all but the first of Compton-Burnett's novels, the stuff of human nature in action.

Under its Victorian trappings, *A Heritage and Its History* retells the ancient dynastic story of the cuckolded king, the dispossessed heir, and usurper; but in this case the heir, Simon Challoner, brings about his own undoing. All the Challoners live in a large family house over which Sir Edwin Challoner, a bachelor, presides. For years, however, the job of running the estate has been entrusted to his younger brother Hamish. Julia, Hamish's wife, has been the mistress of the household ever since her marriage, and Simon, her older son, is Sir Edwin's heir. Because his uncle is more than sixty years old, Simon seems unlikely to have a long wait before he comes into his expectations. Walter, the younger son, is an impractical, frustrated poet. Then Hamish Challoner dies. Sir Edwin, lonely after his brother's death, marries Rhoda Graham, a young neighbor less than half his age. Because of his uncle's advanced years, there is no chance that Simon's prospects will be changed by this marriage. Then Simon, ironically, cuts himself off from his inheritance by fathering a child to Rhoda. To avoid scandal, Sir Edwin claims Hamish as his son and heir after swearing Simon and Walter to secrecy.

Forced to yield his place to his own son, Simon marries Fanny, Rhoda's sister, and Julia goes to live with them in the small house that had belonged to Rhoda and Fanny. Simon continues to help his uncle in administering the estate, but as the years pass and his family grows, he becomes more and more a disappointed, embittered man. By the time his sons and daughter are grown, he has driven them almost to distraction—certainly to the point of detesting him—by complaining gloomily that his family lives only one step away from the workhouse.

Guilt concealed, however, cannot remain hidden. The secret of Hamish's birth must be revealed to all when he falls in love with Simon's daughter Naomi and the young people tell their parents of their desire to marry. Simon accepts the burden of the story that must be told.

This family situation is further complicated when Hamish marries Marcia after Sir Edwin's death at the age of ninety-four. He dies childless, however, and the estate and title pass to Simon. At the end, his children are discussing his change of fortunes. Is he actually noble or merely deceiving himself and the others? A combination of both is the answer.

Counterpointing the Challoners in this grim comedy of possession and dispossession is the figure of Deakin, the butler. His true loyalty is not to the different masters and mistresses he serves but to the house itself, which is a symbol of history, of life in the stream of time. The others are like the creeping vine that grows outside the house, shadowing the rooms within; if they were to be exposed to the light, they would be startled.

The plot is not the main element but merely an unfolding of events that carries forward the revelation of life the characters enact or put in action. The characters are not the main element, either, in the individualized sense in which they would be in a novel by William Faulkner or Joyce Cary. Here, as in many of Compton-Burnett's novels, it would be possible to transpose some of the characters without causing the reader, unless he is constantly alert, to notice the difference. This statement does not mean that Compton-Burnett's characters are indistinguishable types any more than Hemingway's early characters, who were clarified almost exclusively by dialogue. It does mean that they represent all kinds of people in whom the likeness to ourselves and to the friends we know deeply is more marked than individuality.

Aesthetically speaking, the dialogue is the point at which, more in each novel it seems, Compton-Burnett's originality manifests itself most clearly. As in Congreve, Etherege, Hemingway, and Henry Green, to cite disparate aesthetic cousins, the dialogue is the thing wherein the consciousness of the human predicament and how it may be endured, sometimes with joy, sometimes with anguish, is forwarded and revealed. It is bared to the essential bone, increasingly without conventional props. The characters, never identified by more than a few sentences of description and their age, speak it condensedly and wittily. If the reader is not the cooperator in the aesthetic enterprise Compton-Burnett expects, alert as if it were poetry he is reading, the reader is likely to miss the plot, lost in a mesh of unidentified time and characters unknown. If the reader attends well, his reward is the aesthetic delight the most harrowing events, well-told, bring.

What occurs in *A Heritage and Its History* is united in tone by the controlled chorus of butler and children, all of whom keep readers aware, as Deakin the butler puts it, that life is not adapted to man and that it is up to man to conform as cheerfully as he can to its conditions if he is permitted to know them. To know all that the main characters and the commenting choruses say about themselves and others is to understand and forgive the facts of human nature as Compton-Burnett recognizes them.

This divine lack of reproof—even more apparent in *The Mighty and Their Fall* and *A God and His Fate*—has been increasing since Compton-Burnett published *Mr. Bullivant and His Lambs* in 1947. Evidently this development has burgeoned from both a growing reconciliation to the worst that may happen to all of mankind and a slight brightening of her worldview, so that it now approaches what may be called cheerful stoicism or uncritical, nearly omniscient, factualism. All of her novels deserve attention, the earliest for what they expose, the latest for what they show of how people may dispose themselves before what must be exposed. "If way to the Better there be," Thomas Hardy said, "it exacts a full look at the Worst." The early novels show the worst. The later suggest, with diffident hopefulness and no lack of clarity about the Worst one must face, how one may best aim toward the Better.

The kind, hard look the novels give on life and death and her unusual technique that requires a cooperative reader rather than one accustomed to the pap-feeding of popular fiction have kept Compton-Burnett from popularity in the United States. To a lesser extent, this has been true of the public even in England, where she has been honored by royalty, critics, and the awarders of prizes. Not to read Compton-Burnett is to deprive oneself of a depth of vision comparable with what one finds in Aeschylus, Shakespeare, Tolstoy, and other acclaimed writers. Not to read her is to deprive oneself of pleasure also, for Compton-Burnett's somewhat hopeful stoicism is always leavened by humor and wit. In her work and within the necessary human limit of fallibility, style and wisdom conjoin beautifully to delight.

HERSELF SURPRISED

Type of work: Novel
Author: Joyce Cary (1888–1957)
Type of plot: Social comedy
Time of plot: First quarter of the twentieth century
Locale: London and the English southern counties
First published: 1941

> *Principal characters:*
> SARA MONDAY, a cook
> MATTHEW (MATT) MONDAY, her husband
> GULLEY JIMSON, a painter
> NINA, his supposed wife
> MR. WILCHER, the owner of Tolbrook Manor
> BLANCHE WILCHER, his niece by marriage
> MISS CLARISSA HIPPER, her older sister
> MR. HICKSON, a friend of the Mondays

The Story:

In prison, Sara Monday realized that she was indeed guilty as charged. She hoped that other women would read her story and examine their characters before their thoughtless behavior brought them also to ruin.

Sara's first position was that of cook in a medium-sized country house. Matthew Monday, the middle-aged son of Sara's employer, had been dominated all of his life by his mother and sister. Then this rather pathetic man fell in love with Sara, who discouraged his attentions, both because she feared he would cause her to lose her job and because she found him slightly ridiculous. Nevertheless, and somewhat to her surprise, when he proposed marriage, she accepted him.

At a church bazaar a few months after her marriage, Sara met Mr. Hickson, a millionaire art collector with whom Matthew was associated in business. With Hickson's help, she was able to emancipate Matt from the influence of his family. Partly because she was grateful to him for his help, Sara did not rebuke Hickson when he tried to flirt with her. After Sara had been forced to spend a night at Hickson's country house because his car had broken down, Matt supported her against the gossip and disapproval the episode occasioned.

Except for the death of their son in infancy, Sara's life with Matt was a happy one during the first years of their marriage. They had four daughters, and Sara's time was filled with parties, clothes, her nursery, and work

---

on local committees.

Hickson brought an artist to stay with the Mondays. He was Gulley Jimson, who was to compete for the commission to paint a mural in the new town hall. Gulley settled in quickly, and soon his forbearing wife, Nina, joined him. After a quarrel over a portrait of Matt, the Jimsons left. Soon afterward, Sara visited them in their rooms at the local inn.

In jealousy, Hickson told Matt of these visits, and the infuriated man accused his wife of infidelity. After his outburst, Matt was very repentant and blamed himself for neglecting Sara. The incident, however, caused him to lose all the confidence his marriage had given him.

Sara did not see Gulley for years after this incident. One day during Matt's last illness, he reappeared. He looked shabby and wanted money to buy paints and clothes. After telling her that Nina was dead, he asked Sara to marry him after Matt's death. Although she was shocked, Sara did not stop seeing Gulley immediately. While Matt was dying, Gulley repeatedly proposed to her. Finally, she sent him away.

After Matt's death and the sale of her house, Sara went to Rose Cottage, where Gulley was staying with Miss Slaughter, one of the sponsors for the church hall in which he was painting a mural. Miss Slaughter encouraged Sara to marry Gulley; at the end of a week, they were engaged. Just before they were to be married, however, Gulley unhappily confessed that he had a wife and had never formally been married to Nina. Sara was furious and also bitterly disappointed, but in the end, she agreed to live with Gulley and to say they were married. After an intensely happy honeymoon, they lived with Miss Slaughter while Gulley worked on his mural. During that time, Sara tried to persuade Gulley to accept portrait commissions. Infuriated by her interference, Gulley struck Sara, who then left him. She was glad to return to Rose Cottage, however, when Miss Slaughter came for her.

Although Gulley's completed mural was considered unacceptable, he refused to change it. When Sara wanted him to repair some damage done to the painting, Gulley knocked her unconscious and left. Having exhausted her funds, Sara paid their outstanding bills with bad checks, and she was duly summoned by the police.

After Sara had thus lost her good character, the only position she could obtain was that of cook at Tolbrook Manor. The owner, Mr. Wilcher, had a bad reputation for molesting young girls and seducing his women servants. Sara, however, pitied him and liked him. Eventually, Mr. Wilcher moved Sara to his town house, having persuaded her to serve as housekeeper for both residences. She was glad for the extra money, because Gulley had been writing to her asking for loans.

For many years, Mr. Wilcher had a mistress whom he visited every Saturday. During one of many long talks by Sara's fireside, he told her that he was tired of visiting this woman. When he asked Sara to take her place, she was at first slightly hesitant and confused; in the end, however, she agreed. The arrangement worked well enough for several years.

Mr. Wilcher became worried with family and financial affairs, and Sara helped him by economizing on household expenses. At the same time, she managed to falsify her accounts and send extra money to Gulley. One day, a policeman came to the house with two girls who had complained of Mr. Wilcher's behavior. Mr. Wilcher disappeared, but Sara discovered him hours later hiding behind the chimney stacks on the roof. The family was appalled by this incident. After the impending summons had been quashed, Mr. Wilcher became even more unstable. Haunted by his past misdemeanors, he decided to confess them to the police. He also asked Sara to marry him after he had served his sentence. At this time, he had an attack of sciatica. While he was confined to his bed, Blanche Wilcher, his niece by marriage and a woman who had always been suspicious of Sara, dismissed her.

Returning from a visit to her daughter, Sara forgot that she was no longer employed and entered Mr. Wilcher's street. There she found that the house had burned down in the night. Mr. Wilcher had been taken to the house of his niece's sister Clarissa. After he had recovered from shock, he continued to see Sara and ignored Blanche. He rushed Sara to a registry office to give notice of their forthcoming marriage and then took a small new house for them to live in.

Sara had recently encountered Gulley once more and had gradually assumed financial responsibility for his new household. She maintained these payments for a time by selling oddments to an antique shop that Mr. Wilcher had told her to throw away.

The evening before her marriage, Sara arrived at the new house to find Blanche and a detective examining her possessions. She did not protest. After they had found receipts from the antique dealer and grocers' bills for supplies for Gulley, she was taken to the police station. She received an eighteen-month prison sentence and did not see Mr. Wilcher again.

A newspaper offered her money for her story. With this money, she paid Gulley's expenses and planned to become a cook again after she had served her sentence. She knew she could thus regain her "character," and she believed she could keep it now that she had discovered her weaknesses.

Critical Evaluation:

Herself Surprised is the first novel in a trilogy published in the early 1940's (the other titles are *To Be a Pilgrim* and *The Horse's Mouth*). Each novel may be read by itself with satisfaction, but for greatest enjoyment and understanding the trilogy should be experienced as a unit. In the trilogy, each novel is given over to a single character who tells his or her story with wonderful personal style and inflection. These novels establish Joyce Cary as one of the great mimics of literature. The basic scheme of the trilogy involves the conflict between the conservative attitude represented by the lawyer and landholder Tom Wilcher (*To Be a Pilgrim*), and the liberal attitude represented by the painter Gulley Jimson (*The Horse's Mouth*). Sara Monday, the heroine of *Herself Surprised*, has loved both of these men. She stands between them in a mediating position.

Sara is a warm, comfortable woman. She likes to make her men feel at ease. Her narrative is full of the imagery of the home and the kitchen. She has been Jimson's mistress and endured his rages as well as his ecstasies. He has painted some of his finest nude studies using her as a model. Basically, however, he rejects her because she threatens to domesticate him and dampen his creative fires. Her next companion is Tom Wilcher, a fussy old bachelor who is largely concerned with maintaining the traditions represented in the family estate of Tolbrook. Sara soothes and smooths Wilcher's thorny nature. He is a perfect object for her feminine arts.

In Cary's world, Sara Monday stands for the womanly virtues of love, acceptance, gratification, and nurturing. She may make her way in the world by employing these skills with some calculation, but it is a kind passage. Cary's prose style is simple, his language rich and colorful. Although critics have found it impossible to interpret his philosophy with any certainty, he is considered one of the foremost British novelists of his period.

THE HILL OF DREAMS

Type of work: Novel
Author: Arthur Machen (1863–1947)
Type of plot: Impressionistic romance
Time of plot: Late nineteenth century
Locale: England
First published: 1907

   Principal characters:
    LUCIAN TAYLOR, a would-be author
    THE REVEREND MR. TAYLOR, Lucian's father and a rural
     clergyman
    ANNIE MORGAN, Lucian's sweetheart

The Story:

 Lucian Taylor, son of an Anglican rector in a rural parish, was an extraordinary lad, even before he went to school. He was both studious and reflective, so much so that he was not accepted readily by the boys of the neighborhood. When Lucian went away to school, he did very well in his studies, but he formed an acute dislike for athletics and for social life with his fellow students. In his studies, he turned toward the less material and preferred to learn of the dim Celtic and Roman days of Britain, of medieval church history, and of works in magic.

 When he was fifteen years old, Lucian returned to his home during the August holidays and found it quite changed. His mother had died during the previous year, and his father's fortunes had sunk lower and lower. As a result, his father had become exceedingly moody, and Lucian spent much of his time away from the house. His habit was to wander through the rolling countryside by himself.

 One bright summer afternoon, he climbed up a steep hillside to the site of an old Roman fort. The site was at some distance from any human habitation, and Lucian felt quite alone. Because of the heat, he had an impulse to strip off his sweaty clothing and take a nap. He did, only to be awakened by someone kissing him. By the time he had fully regained his senses, the unknown person had disappeared. Lucian was not sure whether some supernatural being or Annie Morgan, daughter of a local farmer, had awakened him.

 Soon afterward, Lucian went back to school. At last, the rector told his son that he could no longer afford to send him to school and that matriculation at Oxford was out of the question. Lucian was disappointed, but he settled down to studying in his father's library or wandering about the countryside in solitary fashion as he had done during his vacations from school.

As the elder Taylor's fortunes had declined, his popularity in the parish had diminished. Lucian's own reputation had never been high, and his failure to take a job in some respectable business establishment turned the local gentry against him. Everyone felt that his studies and his attempts to write were foolish, since they brought in no money. Nor could the people understand Lucian's failure to maintain their standards of respectability in dress and deportment.

Lucian, however, felt that he could stand beyond such criticism of his habits, but his self-respect suffered a blow when he tried to sell some of his writings. Publishers refused to accept his work and pointed out to him that what they wanted was sentimental fiction of a stereotyped kind. Not wishing to cheapen himself or his literary efforts, Lucian refused to turn out popular fiction of the type desired. He felt that he had to express himself in a graver kind of literature.

Lucian's social and intellectual loneliness preyed upon him, plunging him at times into the deepest despair. One afternoon, while sunk in a mood of depression, he went out for a long walk. By dusk, he was far from home, or so he thought, and in the midst of a wood. Finally fighting his way clear of the dense brush, Lucian blundered onto a path and there met Annie Morgan. She sensed his mood and fell in with it. Both of them announced their love and pledged devotion. Lucian went home feeling better than he had in months.

As the days passed, Lucian fell into the habit of putting himself in a world apart, a world of the past, when Rome held Britain as a distant province. He dreamed that the modern town of Caermaen, near his father's rectory, was once again the Roman settlement it had been centuries before. Lucian called his land of make-believe Avallaunius and spent most of his time there, peopling it with men and women, buildings and customs, which he had learned of through his exhaustive studies of Roman times in Britain. He went wandering through the modern town, imagining that the people he met and the scenes before his eyes were those of ancient times. Even Annie Morgan's announcement that she was going away made little impression upon him, for he felt that she had accomplished her mission in his life by showing him how to escape into a better world.

People wondered at the strange behavior of the young man; even his father, not given to noticing anything, became worried because Lucian ate little and grew thin. People who knew him only by sight suspected him of being a drunkard because of his odd behavior and absentmindedness.

At last, however, Lucian escaped physically from Caermaen; he received notice that a distant cousin who had lived on the Isle of Wight had died and left him two thousand pounds. He immediately gave five hundred pounds to his father and invested the remainder for himself. With the assurance of a small, regular income, Lucian left Caermaen behind and went to London. There he felt he could escape from the moodiness that had held him prisoner in the country. He also hoped that the different mental atmosphere would prove helpful to him in his attempts at writing.

Upon his arrival in the city, Lucian found a single room in a private home. He soon settled down to a regular existence, writing late each night, sleeping late in the morning, reading over his work of the night before, and walking in the afternoons. His meals were sketchy, for he was forced to live on as little as fifteen shillings a week. The regular schedule, however, was not to hold for long. His inspiration was not a regular thing, and Lucian felt that he had to make his writings perfection itself. He threw away as much as he wrote. Disappointment over his efforts soon began to drive him into worse moods than he had known before.

Having been impressed as a boy by the work of De Quincey in *Confessions of an English Opium Eater*, Lucian turned to opium for solace and inspiration. After he began taking drugs, he knew little that was going on in the world about him. He spent much of his time lying quietly in his room and reliving the past in visions. Once he had a real inspiration to write; his story about an amber goddess was the product of true imagination. Publication of the story, however, did little to generate ambition and the will to create; he was too far gone in his addiction to opium.

A heavy snow and a severe wave of cold struck London and southern England, but the weather made little impression on him; he might just as well have been living in a ghost city. Then one night he took too much opium. His landlady, not hearing him stir for many hours, looked into his room and found him dead at his desk, his writings spread about him. Even she felt little sorrow for him, although he had made over his small fortune to her.

Critical Evaluation:
The Hill of Dreams is the depressing but haunting tale of an apparent failure. Lucian Taylor dreamed impractical dreams, failed to earn a respectable living, failed in his writings (which were plagiarized by unscrupulous publishers), and died unnecessarily, having ruined his own health. He was not liked by respectable people nor even by his landlady to whom he left money, and he had been the cause of strain to his father. Nevertheless, through the story of Lucian, Arthur Machen illustrates that many *apparent* failures at the time of their deaths, such as Jesus Christ or Lucian, are the *eternal* victors. Lucian's neighbors in his hometown and in West London could very well be the eternal failures, for they fail to see the proverbial beam in their own eyes, and they ignore the biblical injunction to "judge

not, that ye be not judged."

Lucian is the target of criticism and condemnation throughout the novel. Although this condemnation seems justified and crushingly final when he is found dead in his dismal rented room amid his illegible scribblings, *The Hill of Dreams* is not, ultimately, a novel of failure. It breathes of another life beyond the grave, a life that Lucian might have won, for he was loyal to his tortured dreams until the end. Lucian seemingly succumbed to satanic visions only under the unnatural influence of opium, when he had lost his reason. The real Lucian, however, is the youth of the early parts of the novel, who hates cruelty and mediocrity, who has not yet known opium, and who one afternoon walks up an old, neglected country lane when the air is still and breathless. He walks up his "hill of dreams" where wild, bare hills meet a still, gray sky. It is on such occasions, when his sensitive spirit vanquishes harsh reality and the ugly purgatory that enshrouds him in the "real" world, that the reader sees the victorious Lucian Taylor.

This novel—in part an autobiography—received little notice when it was published. During the 1920's, after Machen's books had won for him a reputation, this novel also came in for a share of attention and popularity. Machen himself said, in the introduction to a later edition of the book, that he had begun it as proof to the world and to himself that he was indeed a man of letters and that, even more important, he had thrown off the style of Robert Louis Stevenson, whom he had been accused of imitating, and had found a style of his own to express his ideas. He also related that the writing of the novel was imbedded in the work itself: that many of the trials and weird experiences which have been put into the life of the fictional Lucian Taylor were, in reality, the experiences of Machen himself as he wrote the novel. *The Hill of Dreams* is a somewhat difficult study of a highly introverted character, a man who, while searching for a way to express life, lost both himself and the power to understand humanity. Although such studies are too intense and yet too nebulous to appeal to a widely diversified body of readers, the book is likely to stand as a notable example of its type.

HILLINGDON HALL
Or, The Cockney Squire

Type of work: Novel
Author: Robert Smith Surtees (1803–1864)
Type of plot: Comic romance
Time of plot: Nineteenth century
Locale: England
First published: 1845

Principal characters:

JOHN JORROCKS, a wealthy cockney grocer and sportsman
MRS. JORROCKS, his shrewish wife
EMMA FLATHER, a country girl
MRS. FLATHER, her mother
THE DUKE OF DONKEYTON, Jorrocks' neighbor
THE MARQUIS OF BRAY, his son

The Story:

Hillingdon Hall was a charming example of the old-style manor house with its many haphazard additions and types of architecture. It was set in a pretty village, and the nearby river added to its attractions. Mr. Westbury, the former owner, had been an old-fashioned gentleman of talent and learning who spent his whole time in the country. Since he was a kind of patriarch for the district, the village wondered after his death who would be the new owner of the hall.

When the carriage drew up at the door, curious eyes were fastened on the new arrivals. The chaise was covered with dust. A package of apple trees lay on the roof, the coach boy clutched a huge geranium, and flowers and plants of all kinds were sticking out of the windows. A huge, fat man with roses in his back pocket got out, followed by his wife in stiff brocade. John Jorrocks, the new owner, had arrived.

Mrs. Flather announced the news to her blooming daughter Emma. The two ladies thought it would be only neighborly for them to call right away, especially since there might be a son in the family. At the time, Emma had an understanding with James Blake, who had been living at Hillingdon, but she was always on the alert for a better match. Mrs. Trotter, who was, if anything, quicker at gossip than Mrs. Flather, brought the news that Jorrocks was old and married and had no children.

Jorrocks tried hard to be a good gentleman farmer. He visited his tenants faithfully but found them a poor lot. They could scarcely understand his cockney accent, and they were full of complaints; besides, they knew much more than he did about farming. Mrs. Jorrocks got on better at first with her country folk. Traditionally, the lady of Hillingdon Hall was the patroness of the local school. When she visited the establishment, she was appalled at the drab uniforms worn by the girls. She immediately had an actress friend in London design new costumes in the Swiss mode. She forced these garments on the protesting girls. Unfortunately, when she had a new sign put up at the school, the spelling was bad; it announced to the world that the institution was "founder'd" by Julia Jorrocks.

One memorable day a magnificent coach drove up, and an impressive footman left a card from the Duke of Donkeyton. The Duke fancied himself as a politician. Thinking that Jorrocks might become a person of standing and feeling sure that he must be a Whig, the Duke wanted to make certain of his allegiance. The Jorrockses were still more astounded to receive an invitation to dine and stay the night at Donkeyton. Although much puzzled by the initials R.S.V.P., Jorrocks wrote a formal acceptance. Mrs. Flather and Emma were also invited, but characteristically they were thinking of the Duke's son, the Marquis of Bray, as a possible suitor for Emma.

On the way to Donkeyton, Jorrocks contrived to get in the same carriage with Mrs. Flather, squeezed the poor lady, and stole a kiss or two. He continued his boisterous tactics at the castle. The Duke was impressed by Jorrocks' appetite for food and drink. After dinner, he made the mistake of trying to keep up with Jorrocks in drinking toasts; consequently, he had to retire early and was unable to appear in time for breakfast.

The elegant and effeminate Marquis of Bray was quite impressed by Emma. He fell in with a scheme that Jorrocks and the Duke had for founding an agricultural society with Bray as president and Jorrocks as vice president. He readily agreed to come to an organizational meeting, since there he would see Emma again.

The meeting was a great success. Bray was horrified at the amount of food put away by Jorrocks and his farmers, but he did his best to keep up appearances. Jorrocks' speech sounded good, although some of the farmers did not follow him very well. He advocated the growing of pineapples and the making of drain tile with sugar as the principal ingredient. Bray topped off the occasion by a speech lauding the ancient Romans. Afterward, he was able to visit Emma and capture her willing heart.

Joshua Sneakington—Sneak for short—was a jack-of-all-trades. Sneak had served as Jorrocks' estate manager for some time. After he had arranged for fees and bribes to add to his income, Sneak thought himself well off. One morning, however, Jorrocks rose very early and decided to make a tour of inspection. In a secluded spot, he came upon Sneak netting pheasants. Furious at the trickery, he had Sneak sent to jail. His new manager was a doughty North Countryman, James Pigg, who had been with Jorrocks at Handley Cross.

The Duke showed favor to Jorrocks by giving him a prize bull, which

won a ribbon at a fair, and by appointing him magistrate. Bray came again
to visit, mostly to see Emma, but Jorrocks dragged him off to a rough
farmers' masquerade. Bray, who was a slender youth, made the mistake of
dressing as a woman. A loutish farmer who would not be put off tried to
kiss him. The boisterous treatment startled Bray so much that he wandered
off in the night and got lost. He came upon a sleeping household and, after
awaking the inhabitants, found he had blundered on the Flather's house.
After staying the night with the family, he had a chance to flirt with Emma
at breakfast.

After that adventure, Emma and her mother confidently expected an
offer from Donkeyton. When no word came, the desperate Mrs. Flather
went to the castle. The Duchess was amused at the idea of her son's marriage with a commoner, but the Duke was incensed; he knew that Bray had
conducted himself properly, for he had read Chesterfield. The son had no
voice in the matter at all. Later, Emma and her mother had to admit he
had never made an outright profession of love.

The member of Parliament from the district died. The Duke immediately sent out a bid for Bray to fill the vacancy, and no opposition was
expected. The Anti-Corn Law League wrote several times to Bray asking
his stand on repeal of the grain tariff, but Bray knew nothing of the matter
and did not reply. The League then put up its own candidate, Bill Bowker,
a grifting friend of Jorrocks. To avoid a campaign, the Duke bought off
Bowker for a thousand pounds and endorsed the proposals of the League.

It was a shocking action for the Duke to advocate removal of tariffs on
grain. When the farmers next tried to sell their produce at market, they
found that prices had tumbled. In their anger, they put forth the willing
Jorrocks as their candidate. The Duke was hurt that a man to whom he
had given a bull and whom he had elevated to a magistracy should run
against his son, but Jorrocks was obdurate. At the hustings, although the
Marquis of Bray won, Jorrocks' supporters demanded a poll.

The farmers all worked to get every eligible voter to vote. Pigg was a little tricky because he persuaded the Quakers to vote for Jorrocks on the
grounds that his candidate was a teetotaler. When the votes were counted,
Jorrocks won by a margin of two. Elated at beating a Marquis and glad to
go back to London, Jorrocks left Pigg in charge of Hillingdon Hall and
went on to bigger things.

Critical Evaluation:

The third of Robert Smith Surtees' novels treating the comic misadventures of "Cockney sportsman" John Jorrocks, *Hillingdon Hall* is somewhat
less episodic and more conventionally plotted than the picaresque *Jorrocks'
Jaunts and Jollities* (1838) or *Handley Cross* (1843). The author continues
the career of Jorrocks, now in his late middle age and fairly prosperous

from the success of his London grocery business, who determines to settle down with his wife and hounds at a country estate in order to enjoy the vigorous life of a sporting squire. By placing his parvenu hero among the landed gentry, Surtees is able to develop the amusing possibilities of an idea that he had proposed in his first novel: that if Jorrocks' lot had been "cast in the country instead of behind a counter, his keenness would have rendered him as conspicuous—if not as scientific—as the best of them."

The test of this proposition occurs at Hillingdon Hall. In spite of his urban background in vulgar commerce, Jorrocks is entirely at ease among both the aristocrats and simple country folk of the vicinity. Jorrocks is, after all, "frank, hearty, open, generous, and hospitable"—possessing virtues certain to prevail no matter where fortune leads him. There is no question that the onetime grocer is shrewder than his lordly neighbors, the effete Duke of Donkeyton and his blue-blooded but insipid son, the Marquis of Bray. Furthermore, Jorrocks is honest enough to recognize his own limitations in dealing with farm matters that he cannot comprehend and so allows the pragmatic James Pigg—another of Surtees' memorable creations—to manage the business part of the estate.

Thanks to his common sense (along with a measure of luck and the political acumen of Pigg), Jorrocks even wins a contested Parliamentary seat from his highborn rival Bray. Although the election issue at stake— the question of repealing the Corn Laws—is treated farcically, Surtees was in earnest about the matter in his personal life. A staunch conservative, he feared that a rising middle class would destroy the privileges of wealth and the stability of country life as he had known it. Jorrocks' Hillingdon Hall, to be sure, is a very modest estate compared to Surtees' own inherited properties: Milkwellburn, Byerside Hall, Espershields, and Hamsterley Hall in Durham.

Because of his experience in public life as well as his high social station, Surtees could view Jorrocks from two vantages: that of an aristocrat laughing at the common man's foibles, but also that of an adopted Londoner who appreciates the rugged strengths of the ambitious middle class. Consequently, he treats his hero both as bumpkin and solid citizen—or "cit." In the third novel of the Jorrocks series, the grocer is not so much a sportsman as he is a landholding squire. Much of the impetuous hilarity of the hunting scenes from the other two novels is missing; in its place, however, is a fuller portrait of the "cit" as a man of warmth and dignity. By the time Surtees takes his leave of Jorrocks, the master of Hillingdon Hall, he seems to resemble less Dickens' Sam Weller, the Cockney who similarly confuses his *v*'s and *w*'s, and more the greathearted gentleman Pickwick.

THE HISTORY OF COLONEL JACQUE

Type of work: Novel
Author: Daniel Defoe (1660–1731)
Type of plot: Picaresque adventure
Time of plot: Late seventeenth century
Locale: England, France, and Virginia
First published: 1722

Principal characters:
COLONEL JACQUE (JACK), a waif
CAPTAIN JACK, his foster brother
MAJOR JACK, another foster brother
WILL, a pickpocket
COLONEL JACQUE'S FOUR WIVES

The Story:

The illegitimate son of a gentleman and a lady, Colonel Jack, as he was later known, was early in his life given to his nurse to rear. There he was brought up with her own son, Captain Jack, and another unwanted child, Major Jack. She treated the boys well, but she had little money and so they were forced to fend for themselves. When Colonel Jack was ten years of age, the good woman died, leaving the three boys to beg for their food. Lodging did not bother them; they slept in ash piles and doorways in the winter and on the ground in summer. Captain Jack soon turned to picking pockets for a living and was so successful that he took Colonel Jack into partnership. The two young rogues preyed on wealthy men who were careless with their money. One of the boys would take the money, extracting only a small note from the whole; then the other would return the rest to its rightful owner and collect a reward for its return. One of the duped men was so grateful to honest-seeming Colonel Jack that upon the return of his wallet he agreed to keep the reward money for the boy and pay him interest on it. Since Colonel Jack had no place to keep the stolen goods safely, he had asked the gentleman to do him that service. Later, Colonel Jack took more stolen money to the same man for safekeeping and received his note for the whole amount, to be paid only to Colonel Jack himself. After the scamps had robbed a poor woman of all her savings, Colonel Jack was so ashamed that he later returned her money with interest.

Captain Jack, a real villain, was apprehended and taken to Newgate Prison. Colonel Jack then became a partner of a thief named Will, a vicious rogue who plundered, robbed, and at last killed. He also was caught and taken to Newgate to be hanged, a fate that Colonel Jack knew Will deserved but that made his heart sick and his conscience a heavy burden.

Captain Jack escaped from prison; Colonel Jack was also in danger because of his deeds. The two journeyed to Scotland. They were almost caught many times, but on each occasion, Captain Jack's foresight enabled them to elude capture. When they were ready to return to England, they took work on a ship bound for London, or so they thought. Since they were deserters from the army, which they had joined to save their skins, they could not afford to risk regular means of travel; but the two who had cheated so many were themselves duped. Instead of sailing for England, they found themselves on the high seas bound for America and servitude. Colonel Jack, knowing himself for a villain, accepted his fate calmly, but Captain Jack stormed against it. The defiant Captain Jack abused his master, escaped back to England, resumed his old ways, and some twenty years later was hanged.

In Virginia, Colonel Jack was the property of a good master who told him that after he had served five years he would be freed and given a small piece of land. Therefore, if he were industrious and honest, he might benefit from his ill fate. Jack respected his master and worked diligently for him. Soon he was made an overseer, and his kind heart and keen mind were responsible for changing the black slaves from rebellious fiends to loyal workers. His master was so fond of Jack that he bought him a small plantation nearby and lent him the money to supply it. He also arranged for Jack to secure his money left in keeping in London. The money was converted into goods for the plantation, goods that were lost at sea. The master offered Jack his freedom before the five years were up, but Jack was loyal and continued to serve until his master's death.

Jack's plantation prospered. The original two slaves given to him by his old master were increased by several more slaves and bonded white workers. Always a kind master, Jack won the loyalty of his workmen. He could neither read nor write and wanted to improve his education. He took one of his bonded men as a tutor and soon grew to admire him as he himself had been admired by his former master.

Resolving to return to England after an absence of almost twenty years, he tried to get his tutor to travel with him. When the man refused, Jack made him the overseer of his large plantations. It was some time before Jack arrived in his native land. He was first tossed about at sea, then captured by the French, and at last exchanged for a prisoner held by the English.

Soon Jack's heart was taken by a lady who lived nearby, and they were married; but she proved unfaithful to him, as well as being a gambler and a spendthrift, and shortly after the birth of their child, he left her. He first attacked her lover, however, and so had to flee for his life. He later learned that she was to have another child, and he divorced her and went to France. There he joined an Irish brigade and fought in France, Germany, and Italy. Captured, he was sent to Hungary and then to Italy, where he married the daughter of an innkeeper. Eventually, he was allowed to go to Paris with his wife. There he recruited volunteers to fight against the English. Tiring of war, he returned to Paris unexpectedly, only to find that his second wife had also taken a lover. After almost killing the man, he fled to London and then to Canterbury, where he lived as a Frenchman with the English and as an Englishman with the French.

Still desiring a happy home life, he married again. His wife, at first beautiful and virtuous, became a drunkard and finally killed herself. They had had three children. Wishing to provide for them, Jack married an older woman who had cared for them and whom they loved as a mother. After bearing him children, however, the good woman died from a fall, leaving him a widower once more. After smallpox took all but two of his children, he returned to Virginia. He left his daughter with her grandfather and took the remaining son with him.

In Virginia, he found his affairs in good order, the tutor having been a faithful overseer for twenty-four years. Several slaves and servants had been added to the plantations, and Jack found one of them to be his first wife. Since she had repented wholly of her sins, he married her again and lived happily with her for many years.

Nevertheless, he was not always to live in peace. Several captive servants who knew of his part in the rebellion, when he had served with the Irish brigade, were brought to neighboring plantations. His part in the rebellion became known, and he had to leave Virginia until he could secure a pardon from the king. He and his wife went to Antigua, from which she later returned to Virginia to await the news of her husband's pardon. Pardoned, he was on his way home when he was captured by the Spanish. After many long months as a hostage, he was released, having turned the experience into profit by trading with some of his captors. He continued the trade, which was illegal in the eyes of the Spanish government, and made thousands of pounds. He was often in danger during his voyages, even taken, but each time he turned the situation to his own advantage.

At last, he left danger behind, returned to England, and sent for his beloved wife. There they remained, leaving the Virginia plantations in the hands of the faithful tutor. In his old age, Colonel Jack spent many hours contemplating the goodness of the God he had formerly ignored. He believed that his story was one to make others repent of their sins and mend their broken ways.

Critical Evaluation:

Although Daniel Defoe is remembered chiefly for *Robinson Crusoe*, in its own time, *The History of Colonel Jacque* attained great popularity. Defoe declared that his twofold purpose was to show the ruination of youth through lack of proper training and to prove that a misspent life may be redeemed by repentance. The novel opens on a theme similar to that of *Oliver Twist* but follows a line of development modeled after *Gil Blas*. Although a rogue, Colonel Jack aspires to win back his good name, and in the end, he succeeds. Defoe, in the fashion of his day, gave the novel a grandiose title: *The History and Remarkable Life of the Truly Honourable Colonel Jacque, Vulgarly Called Col. Jack, Who Was Born a Gentleman, Put 'Prentice to a Pick-pocket, Was Six and Twenty Years as a Thief, and Then Kidnapped to Virginia; Came Back a Merchant, Was Five Times Married to Four Whores, Went into the Wars, Behaved Bravely, Got Preferment, Was Made Colonel of a Regiment, Came over and Fled with the Chevalier, Is Still Abroad Completing a Life of Wonders, and Resolves to Die a General.* The end of the novel does not fulfill, however, the promise of the title.

At its very commencement, the English novel indicated the direction of its subsequent development. In *The History of Colonel Jacque* as well as in his other novels, Defoe detailed the adventures of the rogue, society's outcast, in his attempt to find station, security, and identity in culture. Therefore, even at the beginning of the eighteenth century, the novel was a democratic, middle-class genre, growing out of the political and social rise of that class. It is middle class in its concern for wealth and station; it is democratic in its insistence that power, which lay in aristocratic hands, be dispersed and allowed to filter down to the parvenus.

Typically, Colonel Jack is an unwanted child who is excluded by his birth from the goods of society. Simply but accurately put, his aim during his adventures is to accumulate wealth, which, he soon discovers—and this is of course the edge of Defoe's moral satire—will give him power and place. It is also, however, a part of Defoe's wisdom, which is as well that of the middle class, that the pleasure goods afford gives man a fundamental nobility. It is a dignity achieved when he frees himself from poverty and gains substance in the eyes of society. Those goods, Defoe also tells the reader, make possible the pursuit of virtue; for if material security does not necessarily lead to virtue, the moral life is impossible without it.

Colonel Jack's conversion, therefore, like the more famous one of Moll Flanders, should not be seen as mere hypocrisy. It is a knowledge won at the expense of suffering and deprivation. If one condemns Jack's means to his end, one should be prepared to honor his middle-class sagacity that if man cannot live by bread alone, neither can he live without it.

THE HISTORY OF MR. POLLY

Type of work: Novel
Author: H. G. Wells (1866–1946)
Type of plot: Comic romance
Time of plot: Early twentieth century
Locale: England
First published: 1910

Principal characters:
MR. POLLY, a shopkeeper
MIRIAM, his wife
THE PLUMP WOMAN
UNCLE JIM, her nephew

The Story:

Mr. Polly sat on a stile and cursed. He cursed the world, his wife, and himself, for Mr. Polly was thirty-five years old and buried alive. He hated his slovenly wife, his fellow shopkeepers, and every other person in the world. He felt that his life had been nothing but one frustration after another, from babyhood into his middle thirties.

Mr. Polly had been the usual adored baby, kissed and petted by his parents. His mother had died when he was seven years old. After the routine sketchy schooling of his class, he was apprenticed by his father to the owner of a draper's shop.

Although Mr. Polly was ill-suited to work in that shop or in any other, he served out his apprenticeship and then began a progression from one shop to another, being unable to hold one position for very long. He hated the bleak life in dreary dormitories. He also hated being told to hustle when he wanted to dream beautiful dreams about adventure and romance. He spent most of his money and all of his spare time on books that took him away from the humdrum of socks and neckties. He did not know what it was that he really wanted, but to anyone who might have studied him, the answer would have been simple. He wanted companions.

When his father died, Mr. Polly found himself in possession of several useless bits of bric-a-brac and three hundred and ninety-five pounds. It seemed at first that a whole new world was open to him with this new wealth. Various relatives had sensible suggestions for him, most of them centering on his opening a little shop. He put them off, for he wanted to spend his time in taking a holiday.

At his father's funeral, which was a proper one, Mr. Polly had met aunts

---

and cousins he did not know existed. Three of his cousins, all female, began to show attention to their rich relative, and before he was sure of what had happened, Mr. Polly found himself in possession of a wife, his cousin Miriam, and a draper's shop. For the next fifteen years, Mr. Polly was a respectable though unhappy shopkeeper. He could get on with none of his neighbors, and he soon hated his slatternly wife as much as he hated the other shopkeepers.

For these reasons, Mr. Polly sat on the stile and cursed his luck. In addition to his other troubles, he found himself unable to meet the forthcoming rent for the first time in fifteen years. As well as he could figure, he was in debt sixty or seventy pounds. He knew how Miriam would greet this news; it was just too much for him.

At this point, a plan that had been forming in the back of his mind began to take shape. He would kill himself. Then the struggle would be over for him, and Miriam would be provided for by his insurance. He would set fire to the shop to obtain the fire insurance, and before he burned up, he would cut his throat. Craftily, he waited until a Sunday evening, when almost everyone was at church, and then carried out his plan. It worked so well that half the business area of the village was burned; but when Mr. Polly saw flames licking the leg of his trousers, he forgot all about cutting his throat and ran screaming down the street.

It was a beautiful fire; because of it, Mr. Polly was a hero for the first time in his life. He rescued a deaf old lady who lived on a top floor and for whose safety he felt responsible because he had started the fire. When the excitement was all over, it dawned on him that he had forgotten to cut his throat. He felt a little guilty. Nevertheless, that one night of fighting back against the world changed Mr. Polly forever. Taking only twenty-one pounds for himself and leaving the rest for Miriam, he simply disappeared. Wandering through the country, he enjoyed life for the first time. He discovered the world, the beauties of nature, and the casual friendship of passing acquaintances. It was wonderful.

After a month, Mr. Polly arrived at a little wayside inn run by a cheerful plump woman. They felt an instant closeness, and she offered him a job as handyman. His duties were endless and varied, but there was an unhurried peace about the plump woman and the inn that brought joy to Mr. Polly's soul. There was, however, a black spot on the peace. The plump woman had a nephew, Uncle Jim, who was a brute and a villain. He had run off all other males who had ever stopped there, and he beat his aunt and stole her money. She knew that he would return again when he was out of funds. Mr. Polly knew this was not his fight, but he had started fighting on the night of the fire and he would not stop now. Sometimes running when he should have been chasing, hiding when he should have been seeking his adversary, Mr. Polly nevertheless bested the scoundrel in two encounters.

Then Uncle Jim disappeared again, taking Mr. Polly's clothing and leaving in his place an unnecessary peace.

Uncle Jim did not appear again. After five years at the inn, Mr. Polly began to think of Miriam and her sadness at losing him. Conscience-stricken, he returned to the village and there found that Miriam and her sisters had opened a tearoom, untidy but successful enough to provide their living. They thought him dead, a body wearing his clothing having been fished out of the river. Miriam, recognizing him in terror, began at once to fret about having to pay back his insurance money. She could have spared herself the worry: Mr. Polly had no desire to reappear. He told her to keep her mouth shut, and no one would be the wiser.

Mr. Polly made his way back to the inn and the plump woman. With Uncle Jim gone for good, he knew at last a quiet, wonderful peace.

Critical Evaluation:

Alfred Polly, the English Walter Mitty, closely resembles some of the other protagonists of H. G. Wells. Polly is a more middle-class version of Artie Kipps and a less aggressive counterpart of the heroes of *Tono-Bungay* and *Love and Mr. Lewisham*. In *Mr. Polly*, the objects of Wells's attack are the same as in those earlier works: England's stultifying class system; the mind-numbing quality of lower-class education; the boredom of "a nation of shopkeepers"; the repression of sexual joy. The novel's humor and pathos derive from Polly's wonderfully confused ways of letting his romantic spirit find expression in such an unfavorable environment.

Like a Don Quixote on a bicycle, Polly seldom discovers a correspondence between his real and imaginary worlds. "The Three P's"—Polly and two fellow apprentices—do enjoy a robust picaresque fellowship. Polly summons up all of his malapropistic poetry in wooing his mysterious "lady" in the woods (while her hidden school chums stifle hysterical giggles). The world of commerce and convention, however, always interrupts such halcyon episodes, and bewildered Mr. Polly is dragged into matrimony by the heavy tides of custom. His courtship is hilariously painful. Terrified by the proposal he almost offered Minnie, he impulsively proposes to Miriam, only to discover that he would rather have had Minnie. During the wedding, Polly imagines far off "a sweet face in sunshine"; he then awakens to the drab little person next to him: "It was astounding. She was his wife!"

Never quite able to identify the source of his dissatisfaction, Polly still knows that a change must come. His suicide attempt is successful: killing the resigned, conformist, "practical" Polly. Connecting the liberated romantic of the end to the earlier spineless protagonist is the world of Potwell Inn, almost purely feudal. Mr. Polly, transformed into a latter-day Robin Hood, defends his damsel from Uncle Jim. The novel remains wonderfully comic as Wells toys with the reader's sense of psychological reality.

THE HORSE'S MOUTH

Type of work: Novel
Author: Joyce Cary (1888–1957)
Type of plot: Picaresque romance
Time of plot: The 1930's
Locale: London
First published: 1944

> *Principal characters:*
> GULLEY JIMSON, an unconventional artist
> SARA MONDAY, his onetime model
> COKER, a barmaid
> NOSY, an aspiring artist
> MR. HICKSON, an art collector
> PROFESSOR ALABASTER, a critic
> SIR WILLIAM BEEDER, Jimson's benefactor

The Story:

Just out of prison, Gulley Jimson looked up his old friend Coker, the ugly barmaid at the Eagle. Coker wanted him to press a lawsuit over some of his paintings; if Gulley collected, Coker would collect from him. At last, Gulley managed to get away from her and return to his studio in an old boat shed.

The shack roof leaked, and the walls sagged. His paints and brushes had either been stolen or ruined by rain and rats, but the Fall was there. The Fall, depicting Adam and Eve in their fall from grace, would be his masterpiece.

Gulley had a questionable reputation as an artist. Several years back, he had painted some nudes of Sara Monday, startling portraits of a lovely girl in her bath. Sara had lived with Gulley as his wife. When the breakup came, she had stolen the pictures and sold most of them to a collector named Hickson. She kept one or two for herself. Gulley, past sixty years old now, had done nothing since the Sara nudes to add to his reputation, but he still had faithful followers of tramps, beggars, and young Nosy. Nosy, wanting to be an artist, worshiped art and Gulley Jimson.

To complete the Fall, Gulley needed paints and brushes. In order to get Gulley to see Sara Monday and secure evidence for a lawsuit to compel Hickson to return the Sara nudes, Coker bought him some paints and brushes. He periodically worked on the Fall, driven sometimes by compulsion to paint, sometimes by desire for a beer or two.

When Coker pinned him down and took him to see Sara, Gulley was stunned to find her an old hag to whom he felt drawn even while he pitied and despised her. Sara willingly signed a statement that she had given the stolen pictures to Hickson; then she tried to renew her affair with Gulley. Sara had been badly treated by a succession of men, but, like Gulley, she had few complaints. Both felt that the short-lived prosperity and good times they had enjoyed were now being paid for.

Working intermittently on the Fall, Gulley frequently had to trick Coker into buying him paints. Once she forced him to go with her to Hickson to try to get the pictures or a settlement for them. When Hickson was ready to settle a small sum on Gulley, even though he had legitimately taken the pictures in return for a debt, Gulley slipped some valuable snuffboxes in his pocket and was caught by Hickson and the police. Although this bit of foolishness cost him six months in jail, he bore no malice toward Hickson.

In jail, Gulley received a letter from Professor Alabaster, who planned to write a life history of the painter of the Sara Monday pictures. Gulley thought the idea ridiculous, until he decided there might be money in it. He had had an idea for another masterpiece, and after his release, he hurried back to the boat shed to finish the Fall and get started on his new work. He found Coker pregnant and in possession of the shed. Betrayed by her latest lover and her job at the pub lost, she had moved to the shed with her mother. Gulley had to find some way to get the Fall out. Before he had made any plans, he met Professor Alabaster. Alabaster not only wanted to write Gulley's life history but also hoped to sell some of Gulley's work to Sir William Beeder, a collector who admired the paintings possessed by Hickson. Gulley tried to interest Alabaster and Sir William in one of the new masterpieces he was going to paint, but Sir William had a great desire for one of the Sara nudes or something similar.

Gulley still hoped to interest Sir William in the Fall; but when he went again to the boat shed, he found that Coker's mother had cut it up to mend the roof. Gulley decided there was no use in losing his temper and doing something foolish; then he would land back in jail before he could do another masterpiece or make a sale to Sir William. Besides, he suddenly realized that he was tired of the Fall.

In the meantime, if Sir William wanted a Sara nude, perhaps Gulley could persuade old Sara to give him one of the small ones she had kept; but Sara, still vain, loved to take out the portraits of her lovely youth and dream over them. Gulley tried every trick he could think of, without success.

When Sir William left London, Gulley wheedled Alabaster into giving him the key to Sir William's apartment. He pawned the furniture and art collections to buy canvas and paints and even grudgingly let a sculptor rent one end of the drawing room to chip away on a piece of marble. Gulley honestly kept the pawn tickets so that Sir William could redeem his posses-sions. He used one wall for a weird painting he was sure would please Sir William. When the owner returned unexpectedly, however, Gulley decided to talk to him from a distance and ducked out before his benefactor found him.

With faithful Nosy, Gulley went to the country for a time. There he devised a new scheme to obtain money, but another crook beat him up and sent him to the hospital. While recuperating, Gulley had another vision for a masterpiece and wrote Sir William about his idea. Alabaster replied for Sir William, who still insisted on a nude and thanked Gulley for caring for his furniture.

By the time Gulley got back to the boat shed, Coker had had her baby and was firmly installed there. Gulley moved into another empty building and set about preparing the wall for a painting of the Creation. He was aided by Nosy and several young art students he had shanghaied. He tried again to get a nude from old Sara. When Hickson died and gave the Sara pictures to the nation, Gulley was famous. Alabaster found a backer for the life history, and distinguished citizens called on Gulley to see about buying more pictures from him. In the meantime, Gulley copied one of his old pictures of Sara from the original in the Tate Gallery and had sold it on approval to Sir William for an advance payment of fifty pounds.

He made one last try to get a picture from Sara. When she refused, he pushed her down the cellar stairs and broke her back. Knowing the police would soon be after him, he raced back to the Creation and painted like a madman, trying to finish the picture before his arrest. He never completed the painting; his spiteful landlord tore the building down over his head. Thrown from his scaffold, he regained consciousness in a police ambulance and learned that he had suffered a stroke. He did not grieve. Rather, he laughed at all the jokes life had played on him and the jokes he had played on life.

Critical Evaluation:

The Horse's Mouth is the third novel in a trilogy published in the early 1940's (the other titles are *Herself Surprised* and *To Be a Pilgrim*). Each novel may be read by itself with satisfaction, but for greatest enjoyment and understanding, the trilogy should be experienced as a unit. In the tril-ogy, each novel is given over to a single character who tells his or her story. These novels establish Joyce Cary as a keen observer and a mimic. Gulley Jimson, the hero of *The Horse's Mouth*, stands in conflict with Tom Wilcher, the conservative lawyer and landholder in *To Be a Pilgrim*, with Sara Monday (*Herself Surprised*) mediating between them.

When Cary was a young man, newly graduated from the university, he went to Paris to study art and to perfect his skills as a painter. He continued to draw and paint all of his life. His treatment of Gulley Jimson as a painter was thus written from "inside." Many critics consider *The Horse's Mouth* to be the finest novel about painting and the painter's way of seeing.

In contrast to the traditionalist Wilcher, Jimson is constantly looking for new ways of expression. As an experimentalist, he is committed to rejecting the old forms. His early work may hang in the best museums and be worth a great amount of money to collectors such as Hickson, but it is meaningless to Jimson. He confronts the present like an innocent; no past solutions are of any use. His big work on the Creation, which seems so intractable and frustrating (partially because he is too poor to buy proper working materials), is an image of his own creative situation; it is full of the potential risks and problems incurred by any free, creative effort. Gulley Jimson is like the experimental, original writer and artist William Blake, whose poem "The Mental Traveller" is used as a kind of running commentary throughout the novel. In all Cary's fiction, Jimson is the hero who most meets the demands of Cary's free, creative world.